The Messianic Feast

Moving Beyond the Ritual

The Messianic Feast

Moving Beyond the Ritual

T. Alex Tennent

To Michael & Linda DeLorenzo, I pray you enjoy this,
T. Aly Te―

Copyright © 2014 by T. Alex Tennent

All rights reserved.
This book, or parts thereof, may not be reproduced in any form
without prior written permission of the author.

Messianic Publishing LLC.
Cover design by Harshika Rana and Mi Ae Lipe
Interior text design by Mi Ae Lipe, What Now Design

Printed and bound in the United States
by Mill City Press

For an electronically searchable version of this book,
an ebook is available.
To contact the author or order additional print copies or ebooks:
www.TheMessianicFeast.com

First Edition, January 2014
ISBN: 978-0-9897656-0-2
Library of Congress: 2013916296

About the cover:
The pillars of man-made religious traditions may crumble and fail;
yet God's love and His future promises beckon us further,
into His very presence.

To Laura (Jallie Crawford), who brought God's love into our home, and to my mom and dad, for putting up with me during all my growing-up years.

Abridged Table of Contents

Acknowledgments... xv
Introduction xvi
Note to Readers xxii

Part 1: Setting the Table & the Twelve Courses

Setting the Table for the Last Supper

Setting the Table 1: The Jewish Disconnect and the Fourteenthers.................. 3
Setting the Table 2: Words and Concepts Changed.. 22
Setting the Table 3: The Messiah Would Speak in Parables............................. 40
Setting the Table 4: The Jewish Idiom of Natural to Spiritual........................ 50

The Twelve Courses on the Last Supper

Course 1: Last Supper Ritual or Parable?
  The Messiah Held One *Leavened* Bread 71
Course 2: The Body of Christ Did Not Mean a Ritual 86
Course 3: The Jewish Idiom of Breaking Bread
  Among the Early Believers...104
Course 4: Breaking Bread Spiritually—the Progression 130
Course 5: Paul, 1 Corinthians, and the Last Supper 153
Course 6: The True Jewish Communion and the Messianic Feast...................183
Course 7: The Showbread: Who They Represent,
  Were They Unleavened, and Why It Matters 217
Course 8: God's Overall Plan and Pattern for Mankind 248
Course 9: God's Plan as Seen in the Showbread 275
Course 10: The Symbolic "Cup" and the Promised New Covenant................300
Course 11: Jacob, Moses, and the Fruit of the Vine 324
Course 12: The Messianic Feast, the Bride, and the Beast 344

Part 2: Proofs the Last Supper Was Not the Passover

The Template Challenge	365
The Three Major Greek Keys That Unlock the Gospels	397
50 Reasons the Last Supper Was Not the Passover	428
Between the Evenings—the Legal Time to Slay the Passover	451
The Ritual—Why Didn't the Jewish Disciples Teach It?	472

Appendix A: Proper Authority	497
Appendix B: Recommended Bible Study Tools	508
Glossary	512
Bibliography and Resources	542
Permissions	548
Index	549

Full Table of Contents

Acknowledgments xv
Introduction xvi
Note to Readers xxii

Part 1: Setting the Table & the Twelve Courses

Setting the Table for the Last Supper

Setting the Table 1: The Jewish Disconnect and the Fourteenthers 3

    The Beginnings of the Dispute 5
    The Fourteenthers Lay Out Their Case to Rome 7
    The Fourteenthers Knew the Crucifixion Day Was the Fourteenth 10
    Roman Emperor Constantine Imposes His Will on the Fourteenthers 14

Setting the Table 2: Words and Concepts Changed 22

    Did the Jews Before Paul Share in "Communion"
    or Partake in the "Eucharist"? 23
    Did the First-Century Jews Really Go to "Church"? 23
    Did the Early Jews Who Believed in the Messiah Become "Christians"? 27
    Was the Name of the Messiah Really "Jesus?" 29
    Will the Real "Lion of the Tribe of Judah" Please Stand Up? 31
    Were the Early Jewish Believers, Like Paul, Really Called "Saints"? 32
    What about the Word "Trinity"? 33
    What about the Word "Apostle"? 37

Setting the Table 3: The Messiah Would Speak in Parables 40

    Parables in the Jewish Tradition 41
    Parables at the Time of the Last Supper 43
    Bizarre Statements Point to Parables 44
    Why the Messiah Spoke in Parables at the Last Supper 46
    What Jesus Said or What He Meant 46

Setting the Table 4: The Jewish Idiom of Natural to Spiritual 50

    The Jewish Prophets 50
    Jesus Continues Using This Natural-to-Spiritual Idiom 51
    Spiritual Eating and Drinking 53
    List of Natural-to-Spiritual Examples 57

The Twelve Courses on the Last Supper

Course 1: Last Supper Ritual or Parable? The Messiah Held One *Leavened* Bread 71

- Uncontested Ritual 71
- Additional Punishment for Leaven at Passover 74
- Some Find It "Dangerous" to Even Question the Ritual 75
- Jesus Held One Bread, Not Multiple Breads 76
- The English Translations Can Cause Confusion 78
- Bread Is Bread? 80
- New Ritual or Spiritual Truth in Parables? 81
- Last Supper Prophecy, Betrayed with Bread 81

Course 2: The Body of Christ Did Not Mean a Ritual 86

- "This Is My Body," But What Is This? 87
- No, This Is Not the Flesh of the Messiah 88
- What the Apostles Taught about Us Being the Spiritual Body 90
- The Spiritual Body, the Spirit of God Dwells within Us 93
- "This Do," but Do What—a New Ritual? 96
- We Remember the Messiah and the Price That He Paid 97
- The Body of Christ as Anointed Tabernacle 100

Course 3: The Jewish Idiom of Breaking Bread Among the Early Believers 104

- Washing of the Hands before Eating Bread 106
- Twelve Sacred Breads Carried Forward in Jewish Daily Life 107
- Breaking Bread on Different Occasions 108
- Breaking Bread Spiritually 110
- Did "Breaking Bread" Mean Either Common Meals or a Ritual of Communion? 113
- They Weren't Just Sharing Common "Meals" 119
- They Weren't Partaking in a New Roman Catholic/ Christian/Protestant Ritual 125

Course 4: Breaking Bread Spiritually—the Progression 130

- An Overview of the Progression 131
  - Phase 1: Jesus Miraculously "Breaks Bread" Twice to Feed the Multitudes 131
  - Phase 2: Jesus "Breaks Bread" at the Last Supper in a Parable 132
  - Phase 3: Jesus Becomes Invisible Just as He "Breaks Bread" Right after His Resurrection 132

    Phase 4: Jesus Reappears and Is Recognized
        "in the Breaking of the Bread" 132
    Phase 5: The Disciples Go Forth in God's Spirit
        "Breaking Bread" Spiritually 132
    The Bread That *We* Break 133
    What, Regular Bread during the Festival? 141
    The First-Fruits Offering Before Eating the Bread in the Promised Land 143
    The Lost Tribes of the Diaspora 144
    The Promise of the Messiah Was to Recover Those Who Were Scattered 149

Course 5: Paul, 1 Corinthians, and the Last Supper 153

    1 Corinthians Chapter 10: Eating and Drinking Spiritually 154
    1 Corinthians Chapter 11: What Paul Received from the Lord 156
    1 Corinthians Chapter 12: *We* Are the Body of Christ 157
    Figurative Use of "Eating" and "Drinking" 159
    Paul's Intended Meaning in 1 Corinthians Chapter 11 162
    Spiritual Communion and Reciprocal Communal Meals 167
    Eating Unworthily 173
    Growing into the Perfected Bride 177

Course 6: The True Jewish Communion and the Messianic Feast 183

    The First Bread-and-Wine "Communal" Meal 183
    The Three Annual Festivals as Communal Meals 185
    Communal Meals and Communal Sacrifices 187
    Common Bond for the Communal Meals 189
    Natural Communion to Spiritual Communion 190
    Jewish Groups Emulate the Showbread 193
    The Last Supper and the Messianic Feast/Banquet 199
    The Bread and Wine of the High Priest Melchizedek 203
    Feasts of God's Love 207
    Was the Fruit of the Vine Partaken of with the Showbread? 209
    Wine and God's Love 215

Course 7: The Showbread: Who They Represent, Were They Unleavened, and Why It Matters 217

    The Twelve Breads in the Natural Sense 218
    The Twelve Breads Are Symbolic of the Twelve Tribes 220
    Why It Matters Whether These Twelve Breads Were Leavened or Not 223
    Pharisaic Tradition That the "Breads" Are to Be Unleavened 225
    God Commanded Certain Breads to Be Made with Leaven 230

God Also Clearly Commanded When Unleavened Was Required..................232
Twelve Breads Show Forth Aspects of God's Plan for His People..................233
If the Twelve Breads Were Unleavened …...236
Figurative Uses of Bread..237
"Bread of Affliction" Used Figuratively in Deuteronomy 16:3......................239
"Bread of God" Is Used Figuratively 241
Other Figurative Uses of Bread 243

COURSE 8: GOD'S OVERALL PLAN AND PATTERN FOR MANKIND 248

God's Plan from the Beginning..248
The Pattern Given to Noah in Type 250
The Pattern and Plan Shown to Moses for the Dwelling Place of God 253
The Plan and Pattern Given to David for the Dwelling Place of God............256
Stephen Gives the Progression of God's Plan in Acts,
    but His Message and Life Were Cut Short 260
The Logos of God Shows This Plan and Pattern..262
What the Logos Came to Mean in Rome..262
Logos to the First-Century Messianic Jews..263
God Speaks Through the Logos 270
The Logos Is the Plan, the Messiah Is the Expression and Pattern 271

COURSE 9: GOD'S PLAN AS SEEN IN THE SHOWBREAD 275

Names Used for These Breads Reveal Spiritual Truths 276
We Who Abide in God's Presence Are to Be Made
    into Spiritual Presence Breads..278
The Making of the Twelve Breads Shows God's Process
    to Make Us into His Image and Likeness..280
God's Part in the Process...281
    The rain from God must come for the wheat crops to grow.....................281
    The sunlight from God is needed to grow the crops.................................283
Man's Part in the Process...284
    The Israelite needed to till the ground..284
    The wise man planted the seed that came from God 284
    The Israelite needed to harvest and then winnow the wheat.....................285
    God also takes part in the spiritual winnowing 286
The Priest's Part in the Process 287
    The priest would then add water and mix it with the flour....................289
    The priests would oversee the baking of the Showbread 291
    The priests were to place the breads
        on the golden table in God's presence..292

    The priest from Aaron must partake of the breads 292
    Bread Is Instruction from God 293
    Reciprocal Giving and Receiving in the House of God 296
    Twelve Breads, Now One Spiritual Bread 298

Course 10: The Symbolic "Cup" and the Promised New Covenant 300

    Spiritual Truth and Not a New Ritual 302
    The Promised New Covenant 305
    God Showed That the Messiah Would Make
        a Firm Covenant, yet Be Cut Off 307
    God Said He Would Draw the Israelite People
        Back into a Relationship with Him 311
    The New Covenant Is Not Like the One under Moses 315
    Last Supper Parables Were Shocking in the Natural Sense
        so They Would Be Remembered, Discussed, and Understood Later 317
    The Messiah and the Ritual Purification 318
    The Apostles Grew in New Covenant Understandings
        After Receiving the Holy Spirit 322

Course 11: Jacob, Moses, and the Fruit of the Vine 324

    Israel's Historic Connection to the Grapevine 324
    John Gives the Spiritual Fulfillment of Jacob's Washing of Robes in Wine 326
    Whosoever Ingests Any Blood Is to Be Cut Off 327
    The Messiah and the Spiritual Lifeblood of the New Covenant 328
    The Blood of the Two Covenants Compared 329
    Old Covenant Blood Applied Without;
        New Covenant Blood Applied Spiritually Within 332
    God's Spirit to Indwell the Believer 333
    Christ Is the Grapevine—His Shed Blood Is the Spiritual Life Flow
        to the Branches 336
    Abide in Him and Stay Connected to the Spiritual Flow 338
    Our Fellowship Is with the Father, Christ, and One Another 340
    We Inherit the Lifeblood from Christ and Grow into His Likeness 341

Course 12: The Messianic Feast, the Bride, and the Beast 344

    The Soon-Coming Seventh Head of the Beast 346
    The Bride Keeps Her Focus on God's Leading 355
    The Lord Provides an Open Door 358

Part 2: Proofs the Last Supper Was Not the Passover

The Template Challenge 365
- The Challenge 365
- The Early Roman Catholic Option 367
- The Double Passover Option 369
- The Saturday Resurrection Option 373
- The True Scriptural Option 376
  - The 13th-Day Question 377
  - The 14th-Day True Passover 383
  - The 15th-Day Sabbath 389
  - Sunday the Third Day Since 394

The Three Major Greek Keys That Unlock the Gospels 397
- Key 1: The Subjunctive Mood 398
- Subjunctive Mood Used by Jesus in Reference to Eating the Passover 400
- Indicative Mood Used to "Perform" the Passover 402
- Double Negative Adds Extra Emphasis 403
- Key 2: The Dative of Reference 405
- How the Dative of Reference Unlocked the Door 407
- More Dative-of-Reference Examples 411
- What Were the Disciples Really Asking? 412
- The Gospels Do Not Contradict Each Other 413
- Key 3: The Aorist Tense 417
- The Aorist Tense in Luke 22:7 421
- One Additional Possibility for Luke 22:7 423
- More Greek Grammar and Hermeneutics as Applied to Luke 22:7 424

50 Reasons the Last Supper Was Not the Passover 428
- Bread Is Good, But Not During the Passover! 428
- Commentators Attempt to Shoehorn the Passover into the Last Supper 431
- Too Much Illegal Activity for This to Be the 15th-Day Sabbath 433
- Jesus Was Not to Be Arrested in or during the Seven-Day Feast—
  the Festival Called Passover 437
- The Hypothetical Last-Supper-Passover Story 440
- The 15th-Day Great Sabbath Was the Day after the Crucifixion 441
- The Gospels All Agree 443
- The Third Day Since 446
- Additional Scriptural Proofs 447
- Extra-Credit Reasons 449

Between the Evenings—the Legal Time to Slay the Passover 451
- What the Talmud Says 454
- What Other Jewish Sources Say 460
- The New Testament Agrees 463
- What Does John Mean by the Sixth Hour? 468

The Ritual—Why Didn't the Jewish Disciples Teach It? 472
- Setting the Stage 472
- The "Great Commission" 473
- The Apostles: Did They Teach or Even Mention a Ritual? 475
  - Did John the Beloved Teach This Doctrine? 475
  - Surely Peter the Apostle Taught This Ritual? 475
  - Let's Check James—Surely He Will Follow the Lord's Commandment, as He Also Writes to the Scattered Jews 477
  - What about the Other Gospels? 477
  - Surely Matthew Obeyed the Lord's Injunction and Taught This Ritual? 477
  - How about Mark—Will He Teach It? 478
  - What about Paul's Letter to the Romans and Others? 478
  - Have We Missed Anyone? 479
- "Do This," but Do What? 479
- The Azymites Shed Light on the Protestant Ritual 482
- Why Make This Late Change to Unleavened Bread? 485
- A Few More Points from the First-Century Jewish Idioms 486
- Since the Ritual Was Not Taught, How Then Did It Begin and Gain Its Foothold? 487
- Early Picture of the Roman Ritual Coming In 489
- Not All Quotes Are What They Appear on the Surface 490
- The True Communion Is Spiritual 494

Appendix A: Proper Authority 497
Appendix B: Recommended Bible Study Tools 508
Glossary 512
Bibliography and Resources 542
Permissions 548
Index 549

Acknowledgments

Many thanks to my editors who helped me shape 20 years of research into a highly readable and edifying format. Special thanks to editors Helen Townsend, Mi Ae Lipe, and Laurel Robinson, and for the additional assistance from author Debra Rae; without their help, this work would not have taken the shape it has today. Additional thanks to my wife Patricia, to Dr. Robert and Sandy Goodkin, and to the many other reviewers who offered their helpful input.

Introduction

"My, this really turns the whole thing on its head," exclaimed my editor after reading the first several chapters of this manuscript. I knew exactly what she meant. On the other hand I prefer to think of it as setting some things back down on their feet where they belong—on the feet of the first-century Jewish idioms in which the Messiah's statements at the Last Supper were meant to be understood.

The Messianic Feast

The issue of whether the Last Supper was a Passover or not has been hotly debated throughout history, but today for the most part it is given little thought. As a result, scripture intended to lead to true spiritual communion with God has instead been lost to man-made rituals that, for many, represent cornerstone beliefs.

Handing down information, beliefs, and customs from one generation to the next—whether by word of mouth or by example—ensures cultural continuity in social attitudes, customs, and institutions. Nevertheless, grievous error results when ceremonial or sacramental traditions involve stringently enforced, human-dictated ritual that ignores God's direction, empowerment, and revelation. Accordingly, differentiating between "traditions of men" and "commandments of God" is integral to both Jewish and Christian belief.

Religious teachings, rituals, and decrees that were based on neither the true teachings of the Messiah, nor on those of the Jewish apostles, remain in the Church even to this day.

Enter the Disconnect

The original Messianic Jews (later called Christians) understood New Covenant truth as God intended—that is, through the clarifying lens of Jewish practice and idiom. However, once Roman Emperor Constantine established Christianity as dominant within the Roman Empire, he personally convened the first ecumenical council to align doctrine and customs with Roman religious practices. Consequently, Rome commandeered what had begun as a strictly Jewish phenomenon—namely, that the Messiah had come to redeem Israel and reconcile all believers to God. This eventually caused a complete disconnect from the doctrines and understandings of the original Messianic believers.

Voiding Scripture

By rightly connecting scripture to first-century Jewish idioms and practice, it becomes clear that neither Jesus nor Paul taught the "traditions of men" that entered the Church through Rome. What original Messianic believers understood to be true—that Jesus was crucified on the 14th day, the legal time for sacrificing the Passover—was rejected by Rome. What this history shows is that the Jewish believers understood that since the Crucifixion took place the day after the Last Supper, the Messiah's final meal was not the Passover. To the contrary, the Roman-controlled church passed down the tradition that the Last Supper was the Passover, and a certain ritual, observed to this day, has been based on this belief.

Thus, the Roman ritual has done what the Messiah warned against, and has "nicely set aside" Bible truth to keep a tradition:

> NAS Mark 7:8 "Neglecting the commandment of God, **you hold to the tradition of men.**"

> NAS Mark 7:9 "He was also saying to them, '**You nicely set aside the commandment** of God in order to **keep your tradition.**'"

In doing so the Roman-controlled church masked, and thus invalidated, Bible truth. The feast prepared by God for New Covenant believers, which was foreshadowed in Jewish communal meals and often called the "Messianic Banquet" in Jewish writings, was turned into a ritual.

> NAS Mark 7:13 "***Thus* invalidating the word of God by your tradition** which you have handed down; and you do many things such as that."

We have been taught that the Last Supper was the Passover, yet many of us have never considered the conundrum that has been handed down since the time of Rome. For if the Last Supper was the Passover, how could the Messiah slay the Passover one day—at the legally acceptable day and time for the Passover sacrifice—and then be crucified the following day and still be, as Paul said, "Christ our Passover"?

In other words, how could Jesus have sacrificed and roasted the Passover one day (the day God commanded), eaten it that night with his apostles at the Last Supper, and then on the next day be slain as the fulfillment of the Passover? How can both days be the required 14th day in which God commanded for the Passover to be slain? Wouldn't that result in the Messiah dying as our "day-late" Passover?

Is it possible that the Christian belief that Jesus ate the Passover at the Last Supper was a "tradition of men" that originated in Rome, and not what the original Jewish believers taught or understood?

Is it possible that the resulting Communion ritual based on this belief and handed down through the centuries was not really what the Messiah wanted or what the apostles taught?

Lining these questions up to the plumb line of the Messiah speaking in parables, joined with the idioms and understandings of Jerusalem in his day, yield surprising results that are sure to spiritually bless all who want more of God and His love.

This Scriptural Journey

This scriptural adventure began for me after I graduated from Bible college, when as yet I had never considered the contradiction of Christ supposedly eating the Passover at the Last Supper, and then he himself being slain as the Passover the day following.

After I was accepted into the theology master's program in 1985, we graduate students were given an assignment to study and debate the long-held controversy of whether the Last Supper was the Passover or not. For this particular study, we charted the Jewish template for the seven-day Feast of Unleavened Bread and tried to place the Last Supper, the Crucifixion, and other time-specific events into this template (see "The Template Challenge" in Part 2). Our professor encouraged us to explore arguments on both sides of the controversy, and I remember that only one person was willing to take the side that Jesus did **not** eat the Passover at the Last Supper—a fiery Italian named Tony. The rest of the class, myself included, took the safer route and argued that it *was* the Passover. Tony focused on a few crucial points, especially the Greek double negative in which Jesus says he will *not* eat this Passover (Luke 22:15–16). But the rest of us were not buying it, for the scriptures (or more accurately the English *translations* of the Greek scriptures) seemed to make it too clear that it **was** the Passover.

At that point we were not particularly well versed in the Jewish idioms, and many in the group did not yet have a working knowledge of Greek, so some subtle but important nuances remained hidden from our view. We came away essentially agreeing that the scriptures (specifically the English translations) *seemed* to be clear that Jesus had indeed eaten the Passover at his Last Supper.

Yet enough questions remained unanswered that when the semester was over, several of us continued to meet in my home to discuss them. But even then we were unable to reconcile many seeming contradictions, and eventually we went our own ways. Over the next 17 years, every now and then—such as when I saw a new scriptural point, or I understood a Jewish idiom I had not comprehended before—I would pull out my files, spread them all over the floor, and try to find a way to make everything fit. But then in frustration, unable to harmonize the apparent contradictions, I would always put the files back and let them sit again.

However, the things I was discovering in both the scriptures and first-century Jewish idioms were causing me to believe more and more that the Last Supper was ***not*** the Passover, but rather that Jesus was crucified on the legal and proper day God commanded for the Passover: the 14th of Nisan.

Up until this time, I knew that the original Greek scriptures were the inspired word of God, and that Matthew, Mark, and Luke would not contradict John (as many commentators have believed) on such a major event in their Jewish idiom. Yet I could not find a way to make all the scriptures harmonize. Nor had I ever seen it done. It was not until around 2004 when I found the key that unlocked the whole riddle: a certain nuance that Greek words can contain, called the "dative of reference." This verified for me that the Last Supper was not the Passover, as it caused all of the controversial scriptures we had studied to fall perfectly into place. (These English translations that seem to so clearly have Jesus eating the Passover at the Last Supper will be explained in the chapter "Three Major Greek Keys That Unlock the Gospels.")

However, this was only the beginning, for after those first few scriptural dominoes fell into place, other truths came to light—truths that were far more important and that would even shock me at first. As a believer, I had been taught for many years that Communion was an important ritual commanded by the Lord. Therefore, these truths I was finding—the ones that shed negative light on this ritual—were troubling for me to initially consider.

But after years of thorough study proved to me that the Last Supper could not be the Passover in spite of the English translations that so clearly *seem to say* that it was, I came to realize that the ritual of Communion we all kept with unleavened bread was not what the Messiah taught or wanted. Because this supper was not the Passover, Jesus was eating regular *leavened* bread, as the Greek scriptures do show. My first reaction was, "Oh my, we are keeping the ritual wrong," since we used *unleavened* bread in the ritual. Almost immediately I felt a check in my spirit, a sick feeling that you get when you know you've been tricked; I had a real sense that the ritual had deceived us. I felt strongly that if I further investigated the scriptures that supposedly teach this rite of Communion, I would find that they actually meant something very different.

After I delved first into the Last Supper scriptures (as seen in Course 1 and 2) and then into what Paul wrote in 1 Corinthians 11 (covered in Course 5), I did indeed find that the Messiah and Paul taught something very different. They were teaching important truths for the soon-coming outpouring of God's love and showing how the last-day assembly will fulfill the scriptures by making herself ready as the Lord's spiritual bride. When these scriptures are understood correctly, they point out the important pathways to follow that will lead us to this desired place and to fulfill God's plan.

I do not expect everyone to accept my conclusions outright, for long-held beliefs are often difficult to change. However, any student of God's word will certainly be encouraged to examine the scriptural facts as I have laid them out in this book. Additionally, this presents an opportunity to see the scriptures from the light of the first-century Jewish idioms that the Messiah used.

The Way Forward—the Spiritual Bride Being Made Ready

Once the parables Jesus taught at the Last Supper are seen in the proper light (with the realization that this meal was not the Passover), they open the door to understanding how we can share in the true spiritual communion that God seeks with His people. God referred to Israel as His bride, and these truths show what is needed for all of us, from all nations, to make it to that calling that God desires for all who love Him.

When one takes into account the original Jewish idioms, the scriptures show that the Jewish communal meals in the first covenant pointed to a Messianic Feast, which is called the "Messianic Banquet" in many Jewish writings. These communal meals prefigured the partaking of His love, and the subsequent giving and receiving of it among the believers. This sharing of His love is what will ultimately help perfect believers into a bride without spot or wrinkle.

As communal meals, the three annual Jewish festivals pointed to spiritual feasting in the New Covenant and to a spiritual banquet where we all partake of God's love in purity, along with the word of God. This is the Messianic Feast that God has prepared for all of His people, and His desire is that we enter in now.

The scriptures clearly state that, in these last days, God is drawing the Jewish people back into covenant relationship with Him. When I enrolled in Bible college in the late 1970s, I had never heard of a Messianic Jewish fellowship, but today many have formed in most major cities across the United States and in other nations. This shows that the prophecies are coming to pass, and God is forming His assembly into a spiritual bride, made up of all those who love Him, whether Jew, Gentile, Protestant, Catholic, and all others who are willing to move into this high calling. As God said, "my house will be called a house of prayer for all nations" (Isaiah 56:7), and these things are now coming about in our day.

To align with His plan to bring the Jewish people into the New Covenant that was promised to them (see Course 10), I will do my part in this book by using certain words and portraying truths in a way that the Jewish people may more easily relate to. At the same time it should be understood that these New Covenant truths apply to any person who opens up to them and receives all that God provides. They apply to all people equally; no one is excluded. Of course, my hope is that all believers see these truths as self-evident and that they are then spiritually edified by what the Messiah truly meant in his teachings.

Note to Readers

This book has several typographical conventions that deserve clarification. In quoted material (from scripture or other sources), I have sometimes added **boldface** for emphasis. In quoted scripture, *italicized* text is part of that particular translation of the Bible, usually indicating that a particular word or phrase was not in the original Greek or Hebrew text but has been added to the English edition by the translators. The italicized words are part of the translation and have not been added or altered by me.

In this book, I have sometimes quoted only fragments of scriptures and other material and not entire sentences for the sake of brevity and context. Sometimes these scriptures end with a comma, semicolon, or no ending punctuation at all. I have chosen to keep the punctuation (or lack of it) as it was in the original source, especially in the case of scripture, so as not to jeopardize nuances in meaning or introduce distraction. While these may look like errors at times when scriptures end with a comma or semicolon, my intent was to preserve the exact translation in each scripture. With longer quotations, I have indicated omissions with the ellipses (…) at the beginning or end of the paragraph where appropriate.

While I have made every effort to avoid errors, I apologize in advance for any that may remain.

Part 1

Setting the Table for the Last Supper

Setting the Table for the Last Supper

In "setting the table" for the Last Supper, we demonstrate that a great Jewish disconnect took place in Rome, which led to the later misunderstanding of many spiritual idioms and expressions used by the Messiah and the mostly Messianic Jewish scripture writers. Because Rome reigned as the world power at the time of Christ, certain leaders cultivated this great disconnect with all things Jewish, and the Roman Church ridiculed and eventually outright rejected the Messianic believers and their beliefs. For us to properly understand the Messiah's words at the Last Supper, the ramifications of this Jewish disconnect must be understood.

SETTING THE TABLE I

The Jewish Disconnect and the Fourteenthers

This chapter will clarify a major segment of Jewish history that has not been accurately told before—not by Christian sources, by Jewish encyclopedias, or Dimont's Jewish histories. Specifically, it discusses the complete disconnect with all things Jewish that occurred when the early assemblies—with their many Messianic Jewish believers—were taken over by Rome.[1]

To the Jews, these believers in Christ became "Christians" who were therefore no longer acknowledged as truly Jewish. To the Roman Christians, these people were "Judaizers"[2] who continued to keep their Jewish customs while refusing to go along with the new Roman teachings. Therefore neither side has told this story accurately, as both sides rejected these early Messianic believers. We will cover at least some of the story of these early Messianic Jews and the rejection and persecution they suffered, for this sets the stage for the complete disconnect.

Early Messianic Jews were derisively called "Quartodecimans," a Latin term with a heretical sound to it; anyone with that strange name must have been a heretic, or so we have been told. However, once we translate this simple term meaning "Fourteenthers" into English, it becomes evident who Rome thought the heretics were—those Jewish believers who observed the 14th day of Nisan,[3] as their families had done since the time of Moses. Nisan was the Israelite month in which the Passover was to be celebrated each year—on the 14th day.

> NIV Numbers 28:16 "On the fourteenth day of the first month the LORD's Passover is to be held."

---

1   Emperor Constantine gave the Roman Church the power to impose unanimity of doctrine to unite the empire.
2   "Judaizer" is a term for one who seeks to bring the New Covenant believer back into Old Covenant laws.
3   In the Hebrew calendar, Nisan is the first month of the Ecclesiastical year (seventh month in the civil year). The Passover was to be sacrificed each year in this month, in the afternoon of the 14th day.

Throughout this discussion, I will use the English translation of "Fourteenthers," as it more accurately describes who these people were. Just as the Protestants would later be called heretics and be punished by Roman authorities, so it was with the original Messianic Jews.

Before delving deeper into this part of Jewish history, though, it is important to realize that many Jewish people were scattered from Israel to the region between the Black Sea and the Mediterranean, then known as Asia. Paul spent much of his time preaching and teaching among these "Asiatics," as they were called. Peter also wrote to these Jews of "the dispersion" (*diaspora* in Greek):

> NAB 1 Peter 1:1   Peter, an apostle of Jesus Christ, **to the chosen sojourners of the dispersion** in Pontus, Galatia, Cappadocia, **Asia**, and Bithynia,

Although the Asiatic assemblies were to a large degree Jewish, they also contained many Gentile believers. But from this history, we can see that Jewish concepts and customs were more prevalent among them than the traditions that would develop later in Rome.

In the book of Revelation, the Messiah directed John to write to the seven assemblies that were spread across Asia:

> DBY Revelation 1:4–5   John to the seven assemblies **which *are* in Asia**: Grace to you and peace from *him* who is, and who was, and who is to come; and from the seven Spirits which *are* before his throne; and from Jesus Christ, the faithful witness, the firstborn from the dead, and the prince of the kings of the earth....

> DBY Revelation 1:11   saying, What thou seest write in a book, and **send to the seven assemblies**: to Ephesus, and to Smyrna, and to Pergamos, and to Thyatira, and to Sardis, and to Philadelphia, and to Laodicea.

Jesus understood that these believers in Asia were already facing persecution and difficulties, so he specifically directed John to write words of comfort and teaching to them. It's worth emphasizing this point, because Rome painted these Asiatics as a fringe group of heretics, and mocked them as "Quartodecimans" for refusing to observe the rituals that had developed in Rome.

Proud Rome had taken over Israel and destroyed the Temple, so it definitely was not going to take instructions on religion from its vanquished foe. As history played out, this was how the complete Jewish disconnect occurred.

The Beginnings of the Dispute

What had begun as a strictly Jewish phenomenon—the understanding that the Messiah had come and redeemed Israel and all believers back to God—was eventually taken over by Rome and turned into something from which Jews were rejected. Rome introduced new religious dogmas, rituals, and decrees that were based on neither the true teachings of the Messiah nor on those of the Jewish apostles.

For example, whereas many of the believing Jews continued to observe the 14th-day Passover in some form, Rome instead held an Easter Sunday celebration. This led to disputes as Asiatics continued to celebrate the 14th day instead of obeying Roman decrees to celebrate Easter. This following quote from McClintock and Strong's *Cyclopedia* shows the Asiatics' refusal to convert to the new Roman decrees:

> The Asiatics remained unconverted and unconvinced, and continued to observe the **14th of Nisan** as a day of mixed character, fasting till the ninth hour, and then rejoicing for the achieved work of man's redemption.[4]

Jewish Messianic believers fasted until the ninth hour (about 3 PM) on this 14th day, and the following scriptures reveal why this time was important to them:

> NAS Matthew 27:46 And about **the ninth hour** Jesus cried out with a loud voice, saying, "Eli, Eli, lama sabachthani?" that is, "My God, My God, why hast Thou forsaken Me?"

> NAS John 19:30 When Jesus therefore had received the sour wine, He said, "**It is finished!**" And He bowed His head, and gave up His spirit.

The Fourteenthers fasted until the time that Jesus said, "It is finished," indicating that he had finished the work (that God had called him to) by paying the penalty for sin. Although historically Jews had never fasted during the 14th-day Passover, McClintock and Strong explain that the Messianic Jews *added* this partial-day fast as a tradition to honor the fact that Jesus was on the cross during this time. They ended their fast at the ninth hour, the time that his death fulfilled the Passover:

> The Western and more Catholic rule was to observe the **Friday** preceding the Easter-Sunday **as a rigid fast**, the Church identifying the apostles' sorrowing with their own, and the fast was not resolved till

---

[4] McClintock and Strong, *Cyclopedia*, vol. 7, p. 722, s.v. "Paschal Controversy."

Easter-morn; while the Asiatic Quartodecimani party regarded the **14th of Nisan** from a doctrinal point of view as the commemoration-day of man's redemption; and at the hour in which our Lord said "It is finished," i.e. at three o'clock in the afternoon, the fast was brought to an end (Eusebius Hist. Eccl. 5:23), and the day closed with the collective Agape and celebration of the Lord's Supper.[5]

This difference of opinion as to keeping the 14th day special first became evident around AD 150 when Polycarp, a prominent Fourteenther and leader in the Asiatic Assembly of Smyrna, was sojourning in Rome and met with the Roman bishop Anicetus.

In his *History of the Christian Church*, 19th-century church historian Philip Schaff discusses the early history of this dispute. This major point of contention would eventually lead to the rejection of all things Jewish, as well as to the introduction of many Roman rituals. Below, Schaff shows that Rome did not observe the 14th day (and instead had an Easter/Astarte Sun-day celebration), but that Polycarp and the Asiatics *did* keep the 14th day special:

> We have a brief, but interesting account of this dispute by Irenaeus, a pupil of Polycarp, which is as follows:
>
> "When the blessed Polycarp sojourned at Rome in the days of Anicetus, and they had some little difference of opinion likewise with regard to other points, they forthwith came to a peaceable understanding on this head [the observance of Easter], having no love for mutual disputes. For neither could Anicetus persuade Polycarp not to observe inasmuch **as he [Polycarp] had always *observed* with John, the disciple of our Lord, and the other apostles**, with whom he had associated; nor did Polycarp persuade Anicetus to *observe* Gr. (τήρειν) who said that **he was bound to maintain the custom** of the presbyters (= bishops) before him. These things being so, they communed together; and in the church Anicetus yielded to Polycarp, out of respect no doubt, the celebration of the eucharist,[6] and they separated from each other in peace, all the church being at peace, both those that observed and those that did not observe [the fourteenth of Nisan], maintaining peace."

---

5 McClintock and Strong, *Cyclopedia*, vol. 7, p. 721, s.v. "Paschal Controversy."
6 *Eucharist* is a Greek word meaning "thanksgiving."

> This letter proves that the Christians of the days of Polycarp knew how to keep the unity of the Spirit without uniformity of rites and ceremonies. "The very difference in our fasting," says Irenaeus in the same letter, "establishes the unanimity in our faith."[7]

So we see that Romans did not keep the 14th day special, which was fine since under the New Covenant they were no longer bound to keep the Sabbaths and the Feasts. However, Rome did begin to disapprove of the Asiatic Fourteenthers who continued to celebrate the 14th-day Passover as a "commemoration-day of man's redemption," as previously noted.

In the quote above, Irenaeus also mentioned a difference in the Roman fasting, which at one point lasted a full week as opposed to the Asiatic custom of fasting only until the ninth hour on the fourteenth day, the time in which the Messiah said "it is finished."

As an aside, *The Jewish Encyclopedia* also shows that Jewish scholars of long ago believed that man's redemption as brought by the Messiah would take place at the Passover, just as had happened with the original Passover under Moses:

> What Moses, the first redeemer, did is typical of what the Messiah as the last redeemer of Israel will do (Eccl. R. i. 9). The redemption will be in the same month of Nisan and in the same night (Mek., Bo, 14);[8]

The Fourteenthers Lay Out Their Case to Rome

The dispute grew more intense in the period between AD 190 and 194, when Victor was bishop of Rome. At this time Rome dramatically escalated pressure on the Fourteenthers to drop their 14th-day Passover commemoration and to adopt Easter and other Roman rituals and doctrines instead.

Schaff, in his *History of the Christian Church*, sums it up:

> The Roman bishop Victor, a very different man from his predecessor Anicetus, required the Asiatics, in an imperious tone, to abandon their Quartadecimanian practice.
>
> Against this Polycrates, bishop of Ephesus, solemnly protested in the name of a synod held by him, and **appealed to an imposing**

---

[7] Schaff, *History of the Christian Church*, vol. 2, pp. 213–214.
[8] *The Jewish Encyclopedia*, vol. 5, p. 214, s.v. "Eschatology."

array of authorities for their primitive custom. Eusebius has preserved his letter, which is quite characteristic.[9]

The Roman historian Eusebius (AD 263–339), mentioned above, brings this out in his own *Church History*. Eusebius makes it clear that this whole dispute and anger from Rome arose because Jewish believers continued to celebrate the 14th day rather than fasting and mourning as Rome had prescribed. The Asiatic bishops were led by Polycrates, who wrote the following letter of protest to the Roman bishop Victor, as Eusebius recorded below:

> We **observe the genuine day**; neither adding thereto nor taking there from. For in **Asia** great lights have fallen asleep, which shall rise again in the day of the Lord's appearing, in which he will come with glory from heaven, and will raise up all the saints: **Philip, one of the twelve apostles**, who sleeps in Hierapolis... moreover, **John, who rested upon the bosom of our Lord**, who was also a priest, and bore the sacerdotal plate, both a **martyr** and teacher; he is buried in Ephesus. Also **Polycarp** of Smyrna, both bishop and **martyr**, and Thraseas, both bishop and **martyr** of Eumenia, who sleeps in Smyrna. Why should I mention Sagaris, bishop and **martyr**, who sleeps in Laodicea; moreover, the blessed Papirius, and Melito, the eunuch [celibate]... who now rests in Sardis.... **All these observed the fourteenth day** of the Passover according to the gospel, deviating in no respect, but following the rule of faith.
>
> Moreover, I, Polycrates, who am the least of you, according to the tradition of my relatives, some of whom I have followed.... **my relatives always observed the day when the people of the Jews**[10] **threw away the leaven**. I, therefore, brethren, am now sixty-five years in the Lord... and having studied the whole of the Sacred Scriptures, **am not at all alarmed at those things with which I am threatened, to intimidate me**. For they who are greater than I have said, "we ought to obey God rather than men."... I could also mention the bishops that were present, whom you requested me to summon, and whom I did call; **whose names would present a great number**, but who seeing my slender body consented to my

---

9 Schaff, *History of the Christian Church*, vol. 2, p. 216.

10 The words "of the Jews" were added by Schaff and not present in the original text. These added words could imply that Polycrates himself was not Jewish when he almost certainly was, as indicated by his words "my relatives always observed the day."

epistle, well knowing that I did not wear my gray hairs for nought, but that I did at all times regulate my life in the Lord Jesus.[11]

Schaff explains further that "Victor turned a deaf ear to this remonstrance, **branded the Asiatics as heretics**, and threatened to excommunicate them."

Notice above how many of the Fourteenthers mentioned by Polycrates were killed (martyred), and yet Polycrates is not at all alarmed at those things with which "I am threatened, to intimidate me." Clearly Polycrates's Christ-like spirit is in marked contrast to Roman bishop Victor's disagreeable demeanor. What was so horrible that Rome needed to excommunicate these mostly Messianic Jews for simply keeping the 14th day in a way that they felt honored the Lord?

Victor ordered synods to be held and that "**the more Catholic rule** was everywhere pronounced **to be binding**."[12] In spite of this decree, many Asiatic believers did not yield to Roman threats but continued to keep the 14th day in accordance with their long Jewish history and custom.

These escalating Roman threats led Irenaeus, a Fourteenther and disciple of Polycarp, to see the writing on the wall, and he sought to avert a potential bloodbath by appealing for peace. He wrote to his fellow Fourteenthers who were ignoring Rome's decrees and reproved them for risking their lives to keep a day that was no longer required to be kept in the New Covenant:

> The apostles have ordered that we should "judge no one in meat or in drink, or in respect to a feast-day or a new moon or a sabbath day" (Col. 2:16). Whence then these wars? Whence these schisms? We keep the feasts, but in the leaven of malice by tearing the church of God and observing what is outward, in order to reject what is better, faith and charity.[13] That such feasts and fasts are displeasing to the Lord, we have heard from the Prophets.[14]

Messianic Jews had every right to keep the 14th day special, and yet as the danger escalated to the point where more people were losing their lives, Irenaeus appealed for peace and common ground. But other Messianic Jews wanted to draw the line in the sand with Rome and continued to honor this ancient feast and the Messiah's fulfillment of the Passover in the way they felt was proper. They did not want Rome dictating doctrine to them, and justifiably so.

---

11   Schaff, *History of the Christian Church*, vol. 2, pp. 216–217.
12   McClintock and Strong, *Cyclopedia*, vol. 7, p. 722, s.v. "Paschal Controversy."
13   "Charity" is a poor English translation of the Greek word *agape*, which means "love."
14   Schaff, *History of the Christian Church*, vol. 2, pp. 217–218.

The Fourteenthers Knew the Crucifixion Day Was the Fourteenth

When one studies this history in depth, it becomes evident that the earliest Jewish and Gentile believers understood that Jesus was crucified on the 14th of Nisan and therefore could not have eaten the Jewish Passover at the Last Supper. Greek scholar and commentator Brooke Foss Westcott pointed this out many years ago:

> Now, as far as it appears, early tradition is **nearly unanimous** in fixing the **Crucifixion on the 14th**, and in **distinguishing the Last Supper from the legal Passover**. This distinction is expressly made by Apollinaris, Clement of Alexandria, Hippolytus, Tertullian, Irenaeus, who represent very different sections of the early Church.[15]

Contrary to what almost all commentators believe today, these early Messianic followers knew Jesus *did not* eat a Passover at the Last Supper, but rather was *crucified* on the *14th day* of Nisan and thus fulfilled the Passover.

The Catholic Encyclopedia is honest in admitting that the historical evidence from writers of the first two centuries does not positively support their early point of view—that of Jesus eating the 14th-day Passover at the Last Supper—and that this early history connects the 14th-day Passover to the day of the Crucifixion:

> Again, there is the problem, much debated by modern scholars, whether the Pasch which the early Christians desired to commemorate was primarily the passion or the Resurrection of Christ. Upon this point **our data also do not admit of a very positive answer**. It has been very strongly urged that the writers of the first two centuries who speak of the Pasch have always in view the Pasch $\pi\acute{\alpha}\sigma\chi\alpha$ $\sigma\tau\alpha\upsilon\rho\acute{\omega}\sigma\iota\mu\text{o}\nu$, the Crucifixion day, when Jesus Christ himself was offered as a victim, the antitype of the Jewish Paschal lamb.[16]

Westcott also adds:

> …but Photius expressly notices that two writers who differed widely on other points of the Paschal controversy **agreed on fixing the Passion on the 14th, contrary to the later opinion of the Church**, and therefore reserves the question for examination.[17]

---

15 Westcott, *Introduction to the Study of the Gospels*, p. 347.
16 Herbermann et al, *The Catholic Encyclopedia*, vol. 5, p. 229, s.v. "Easter."
17 Westcott, *Introduction to the Study of the Gospels*, p. 347.

It must be understood that this conviction held by the Fourteenthers—that Jesus was crucified on the 14th day—was "**contrary to the later opinion of the Church.**" As the Church in Rome grew stronger and eventually evolved into the Roman Catholic Church, the Catholic tradition of Christ eating the Passover at the Last Supper became fixed as doctrine. Uniformity of doctrine was commanded by Roman religious leaders, and all were to believe that Jesus was crucified on "Good Friday" (the 15th of Nisan) after having eaten the Passover on the 14th. This Roman doctrine of celebrating Easter Sunday became *law* at the Council of Nicaea in AD 325.

So powerful did this Roman Church become that it saw itself as having the authority to excommunicate, punish, and even kill those who did not believe in its doctrines. Not surprisingly, having the backing of the mighty Roman military at its disposal heavily aided the spread of its doctrine.

One Fourteenther who knew this doctrine to be false was Hippolytus, whom Westcott mentions, and below we see that he also placed the Crucifixion on the 14th day. In his book *Against all Heresies*, Hippolytus wrote the following, correcting another writer who had fallen into error by believing that Christ ate the Passover at the Last Supper and was then crucified the day after the Passover, on the 15th day:

> I perceive, then, that the matter is one of **contention**. For he speaks thus: Christ kept the supper, then, on that day, and then suffered; whence it is needful that I, too, should keep it in the same manner as the Lord did. **But he has fallen into error** by not perceiving that at the time when Christ suffered **He did not eat** the passover **of the law.** For **He was the passover** that had been of old proclaimed, and **that was fulfilled on that determinate day**.

Hippolytus continues:

> ...Now that neither in the first nor in the last there was anything false is evident; for he who said of old, "I will not any more eat the passover," probably partook of **supper** before the passover. **But the passover He did not eat**, but He suffered; **for it was not the time for Him to eat**.[18]

Hippolytus agreed with the scriptures that the Passover was not to be two days in a row; this would be contrary to God's law. He states that at the Last Supper, "the

---

18 Roberts and Donaldson, *Ante-Nicene Fathers*, vol. 5, p. 240.

Passover he did not eat" for "it was not the time for him to eat." Furthermore, he wrote that Jesus was the Passover "that was fulfilled on that determinate day," which Acts 2:23 bears out as the determinate day **by God's foreknowledge** and the reason that He commanded the 14th-day Passover to Moses:

> NAS Acts 2:23 this *Man*, delivered up by the **predetermined plan** and **foreknowledge of God**, you nailed to a cross by the hands of godless men and put *Him* to death.

Westcott also included Clement of Alexandria as an early church writer who believed the Crucifixion was on the 14th day. Below we see Clement's extremely telling words quoted in the *Paschal Chronicle*:

> Accordingly, **in the years gone by**, Jesus went to eat the passover sacrificed by the Jews, keeping the feast. But when he had preached **He who was the Passover**, the Lamb of God, led as a sheep to the slaughter, presently taught His disciples the mystery of the type **on the thirteenth day, on which also they inquired**, "Where wilt Thou that we prepare for Thee to eat the passover?" It was on this day, then, that both the consecration of the unleavened bread and the preparation for the feast took place. Whence John naturally describes the disciples as already previously prepared to have their feet washed by the Lord. And on the **following day our Saviour suffered, He who was the Passover**, propitiously sacrificed by the Jews.[19]

Clement of Alexandria continues:

> Suitably, therefore, **to the fourteenth day, on which He also suffered**, in the morning, the chief priests and the scribes, who brought Him to Pilate, did not enter the Praetorium, that they might not be defiled, but might freely **eat the passover** in the evening. With this precise determination of the days both the whole Scriptures agree, and **the Gospels harmonize**. The **resurrection also attests it**. He certainly rose on the third day, which fell on the first day of the weeks of harvest, on which the law prescribed that the priest should offer up the sheaf.[20]

---

19   Roberts and Donaldson, *Ante-Nicene Fathers*, vol. 2, p. 581.
20   Roberts and Donaldson, *Ante-Nicene Fathers*, vol. 2, p. 581.

Notice that Clement states that the disciples asked their question on the **thirteenth** day, when they are concerned with preparing and making ready a location for the soon-coming 14th-day Passover Feast; since Christ was crucified the following day, we see that the Fourteenthers were correct in understanding that he died on the Passover.

Westcott also mentions Claudius Apollinaris—bishop of Hierapolis—as one of those who understood the 14th-day Crucifixion. Consider what Apollinaris wrote around AD 150 concerning those who "err" by believing that Jesus was crucified on the 15th day:

> **They err**, who affirm that our Lord **ate** the Passover on the 14th of Nisan with his disciples, and that he died on the great day of unleavened bread (i.e. the fifteenth). **They maintain that Matthew records the event as they have imagined it**; but **their notion agrees not with the law**; and **thereby the Gospels are made to wear a contradictory appearance**[21]

The Fourteenthers understood Jewish law and knew that Jewish authorities would not allow crucifixions in Israel on this holy 15th-day Sabbath, nor could Jesus have sacrificed a Passover the day before the 14th when he was crucified. Apollinaris pointed out how this "notion" that Jesus ate the Passover and then was crucified on the 15th-day Sabbath "agrees not with the law." Even today commentators argue that the Gospels show "a contradictory appearance," with John portraying Christ as having been crucified as the 14th-day Passover while the Synoptic Gospels (Matthew, Mark, and Luke) portray him actually eating the 14th-day Passover.

Later in this book, the chapter "The Three Major Greek Keys That Unlock the Gospels" shows that the Gospels—when interpreted correctly— all harmonize perfectly, which is what we should expect.[22]

Schaff includes an important additional part of this quote from Apollinaris that McClintock and Strong (above) left out:

> ***The Fourteenth is the true Passover of the Lord***, the great sacrifice, the **Son of God in the place of the lamb** ... who was lifted up upon the horns of the unicorn[23] ... and **who was buried on the day of the Passover**, the stone having been placed upon his tomb.[24]

---

21 McClintock and Strong, *Cyclopedia*, vol. 7, p. 722, s.v. "Paschal Controversy."
22 The Three Keys chapter also examines those English translations that *seem* to clearly show Jesus eating the Passover at the Last Supper.
23 The "horns of the unicorn" is a metaphor for the cross.
24 Schaff, *History of the Christian Church*, vol. 2, p. 215.

As seen when the two parts of the quote appear together, Apollinaris plainly wrote that in misinterpreting Matthew, "they err" who believe that Jesus ate the 14th-day Passover at the Last Supper, then suffered on the 15th day; thus he clearly agrees with the Fourteenthers that the 14th was the true day that the Messiah suffered and was buried.

Roman Emperor Constantine Imposes His Will on the Fourteenthers

The Fourteenthers knew that the 14th day was the Crucifixion, which is a major part of why they venerated it. However, as we've seen, Rome did not care for the Jewish details. As Schaff points out below, Roman custom was *not* based on doctrinal facts but was more ritualistic in observance:

> The **Roman custom** represented the principle of **freedom and discretionary change**, and the **independence of the Christian festival system**. Dogmatically stated, the difference would be, that in the **former case the chief stress was laid on the Lord's death**; in the latter, on his resurrection. But the leading interest of the question for the early Church was not the astronomical, nor the dogmatical, but the **ritualistic**. The main object was to secure uniformity of observance, and to assert the originality of the Christian festival cycle, and its independence of Judaism: for both reasons the Roman usage at last triumphed even in the East.[25]

The apostles never said anything about a ritualistic "Christian festival system." They knew that the festivals pointed to a spiritual fulfillment, as we will see throughout this book. What Schaff calls the "Christian festival cycle" was, in reality, a creation of Rome as it began linking pagan celebrations to Christian concepts.

As mentioned earlier, part of the Roman Church's bitterness arose because it had prescribed a weeklong fast for its Easter celebration. Yet the Messianic Fourteenthers fasted for only part of one day—until the ninth hour (about 3 PM) on the 14th day, marking the time Christ the Messiah said, "It is finished."

Then, because of differences between the Jewish and Roman calendars, the more Jewish-leaning assemblies were sometimes rejoicing in the Feast (Deuteronomy 16:14) and the finished work of the Messiah while the Roman Church was still fasting and mourning.

Schaff addressed Rome's bitterness over this:

---

25   Schaff, *History of the Christian Church*, vol. 2, pp. 212–213.

> This Roman practice created an entire holy week of solemn fasting and commemoration of the Lord's passion, while the Asiatic practice ended the fast on the 14th of Nisan, which may fall sometimes several days before Sunday. **Hence a spectacle shocking to the catholic sense of ritualistic propriety and uniformity** was frequently presented to the world, that one part of Christendom was fasting and mourning over the death of our Saviour, while the other part rejoiced in the glory of the resurrection.[26]

Jewish believers, of course, were not at all interested in the weeklong Roman fasting and mourning, or in the Easter (Astarte) celebrations. Eventually this Roman fast developed into a 40-day one, which, as Alexander Hyslop shows in his *The Two Babylons*,[27] originated from a different fast of the same length. This fast marked weeping and mourning for the false deity Tammuz, who was the consort of Ishtar, the springtime goddess of fertility. (Ishtar is the same as Ashtoreth, or Astarte in Greek, which evolved into *Easter* in English.) Even some Israelites observed this ritual weeping and mourning for Tammuz (Ezekiel 8:14).

In the Catholic Church, this lengthy fast (a giving up certain foods or activities) later became Lent, which starts a little more than 40 days before Easter on Ash Wednesday. During Lent, some adherents rub ashes on their foreheads in the sign of a cross to show mourning. What had begun as a true moving of God's spirit among Roman believers[28] was eventually taken over; thus, these spring deities were incorporated into what had previously been the Messianic celebration of Passover and the Resurrection (which also occurred during spring) to become Easter.

Jewish scriptures clearly indicated a duty to rejoice at the festivals (Deuteronomy 16:14, 15; Nehemiah 8:9–10), so Messianic Jews would not have been interested in Roman Catholic mourning. When the 15th day arrived, Messianic Jews believed they were fulfilling what God's commands through Moses *pointed to* by rejoicing in the spring Passover Festival as they always had done, only now with the Messianic understanding of the New Covenant. Since many of them had grown up with this Festival and it was deeply connected to their heritage, they wanted to continue celebrating it in some form.

---

26 Schaff, *History of the Christian Church*, vol. 2, p. 212.
27 Hyslop, *The Two Babylons*, pp. 103–113.
28 See Paul's letter to the Romans in the New Testament.

The fourth-century Roman Emperor Constantine was less interested in doctrine and more set on imposing standardized religious practices over the entire Roman Empire. This meant joining some Christian ideas with various pagan ones. At some point, Jesus, for example, was deliberately given the birthday of December 25, because this was understood by pagans as the day the Sun God was reborn after having died at the winter solstice. Every year on December 21 or 22, at the winter *solstice*—which means "sun standing still" in Latin— the sun completed its circuit and was in the farthest end of its cycle, where it seemed to stand still (die) for three days. Then, as the sun appeared to move again on December 25, it became "reborn."

Many other examples exist of Rome joining pagan beliefs to what had previously been Christianity, such as seen in an ancient tile picture of Christ as *Sol Invictus* ("invincible sun") that was found at St. Peter's Basilica.

But certain items needed resolution at the famous Catholic Council of Nicaea in AD 325, presided over by Emperor Constantine. The first item on the docket was standardizing the Roman doctrine of the Trinity to become the "Nicene Creed," which we will look at briefly in "Setting the Table 2: Words and Concepts Changed."

The second item to resolve at this Council was the Paschal/Easter controversy and the Jewish Messianic Fourteenthers refusing to observe the prescribed Roman Easter Sunday celebration. In his letter to the churches after the Council of Nicaea, Emperor Constantine addressed this point, stating emphatically that Rome's celebration should have "nothing in common with the perjury of the Jews":

> Let your pious sagacity reflect how evil and improper it is, that **days devoted by some to fasting**, should be spent by others in **convivial feasting**; and that after the paschal feast, some are rejoicing in festivals and relaxations, while others give themselves up to the **appointed fasts**. That this impropriety should be rectified, and that all these diversities of commemoration should be resolved into one form, is the will of divine Providence, **as I am convinced you will all perceive**. Therefore, this irregularity must be corrected, in order that we may no more have any thing in common with those parricides and the murderers of our Lord.[29]

You can feel Constantine's almost palpable anger at the Messianic Jews for refusing to observe the Roman "appointed fasts." Under the guise of opposition to Judaism, he connected these Messianic believers (and all Jews) to the leaders in Israel who had pushed for Christ's death, thus lumping them all together as heretics—and worse—for not following Rome. It was decreed that no one was to keep the 14th day special,

---

[29] Schaff and Wace, *Nicene and Post-Nicene Fathers*, vol. 3, p. 48.

because this was connected to Jewish history and therefore was to be rejected. He continued:

> An orderly and excellent form of commemoration is observed in all the churches of the western, of the southern, and of the northern parts of the world, and by some of the eastern; this form being universally commended, **I engaged that you would be ready to adopt it likewise, and thus gladly accept the rule** unanimously adopted in the city of Rome, throughout Italy, in all Africa, in Egypt, the Spains, the Gauls, the Britains, Libya, Greece, in the dioceses of Asia, and of Pontus, and in Cilicia, taking into your consideration not only that the churches of the places above-mentioned are greater in point of number, **but also that it is most pious that all should unanimously agree** in that course which accurate reasoning seems to demand, and which **has no single point in common** with the perjury of the Jews.[30]

The Roman emperor closed his letter to the churches by letting them know that **whatever** Rome decreed **was** the "Divine will," and all had better submit to it:

> Briefly to summarize the whole of the preceding, the judgment of all is, that the holy Paschal feast should be held on one and the same day; for, in so holy a matter, it is not becoming that any difference of custom should exist, and it is better to follow the opinion which has not the least association with error and sin. This being the case, receive with gladness the heavenly gift **and the plainly divine command**; for all that is transacted in the holy councils of the bishops is to be referred to **the Divine will**. Therefore, when you have made known to all our beloved brethren the subject of this epistle, **regard yourselves as bound to accept** what has gone before....[31]

In the following, Constantine set the tenor for the Roman-controlled Church. It was now "our holy religion" that would have nothing in common with the Jews, who were to be rejected as "parricides" (quoted earlier) and as "our adversaries":

> By rejecting their custom, we establish and hand down to succeeding ages one which is more reasonable, and which has been observed

---

30   Schaff and Wace, *Nicene and Post-Nicene Fathers*, vol. 3, p. 48.
31   Schaff and Wace, *Nicene and Post-Nicene Fathers*, vol. 3, p. 48.

ever since the day of our Lord's sufferings. Let us, then, have nothing in common with the Jews, **who are our adversaries**. For we have received from our Saviour another way. A better and more lawful line of conduct is inculcated **by our holy religion**. Let us with one accord walk therein, my much-honoured brethren, studiously avoiding all contact with that evil way.[32]

A short time after the Council of Nicaea, these Messianic Jewish Fourteenthers were

> "…universally regarded as heretics **and were punished as such**: The Synod of Antioch, 341, excommunicated them."[33]

From then on, all Messianic Jews who kept their customs and disobeyed the Roman practice of weeklong fasting and mourning at Easter were considered to be heretics and Judaizers. Sadly, the truth of this history is still not understood even today, as Fourteenthers (Quartodecimans) are still written off by most commentators as a fringe group of heretics. However, if that were really the case, the Roman emperor presumably would not have felt the need to hold the Council of Nicaea and write letters to all the churches merely to address a minor aberrant group.

McClintock and Strong mention that the Fourteenthers were being taunted by Rome for honoring the 14th day:

> The Asiatics commemorated the Lord's death on the 14th of Nisan, being guided by the day of the Jewish month, as the more general practice followed the day of the week on which Christ died. **They were taunted for the Judaizing practice, though the Church of Rome in its ritual and liturgy had more perhaps in common with the synagogue than the churches of Asia.**[34]

A few years later at the Council of Laodicea (AD 364), the Jewish people were again lumped together as heretics by the Catholic Church, as evidenced by the following Council canons:

> 29. Christians must not judaize by resting on the Sabbath, but **must work** on that day, rather honouring the Lord's Day; and, if they can,

---

32 Schaff and Wace, *Nicene and Post-Nicene Fathers*, vol. 3, p. 47.
33 Schaff, *History of the Christian Church*, vol. 2, p. 218.
34 McClintock and Strong, *Cyclopedia*, vol. 7, p. 721, s.v. "Paschal Controversy."

resting then as Christians. But if any shall be found to be judaizers, let them be anathema[35] from Christ.[36]

One of the following canons from the same Council deals with phylacteries, which were small leather boxes containing a few Bible verses. Many Jews wore a phylactery, believing that the words of Moses (i.e., in Deuteronomy 6:8; 11:18; Exodus 13:9, 16) were to be taken literally. Jesus wore tassels on his garments, as did many Jews (Numbers 15:38, 39), and "tassel" is usually translated into English as "hem" or "fringe" (Matthew 9:20; 14:36). So it is possible that Jesus would have also been thrown out of the new Roman Church for his Jewish ways:

> 36. Forbids the clergy dealing in magic, and directs that **all who wear phylacteries** be **cast out of the Church.**
>
> 37. **Forbids fasting with Jews** or heretics.
>
> 38. **Forbids receiving unleavened bread from Jews**.[37]

The Messiah's heart for his people was diametrically opposed to these Council rules—such as throwing out those who wore a phylactery:

> [NAS] John 6:37 "All that the Father gives Me shall come to Me, and the one who comes to Me **I will certainly not cast out.**"

So although the Messiah told the apostles to gather the lost sheep of the house of Israel, Rome decided to do the opposite of what the Messiah wanted. Rome rejected as adversaries all Jews (including those Fourteenthers who believed in the Messiah) who did not follow Roman decrees. Because of this and many other factors, the Messiah became falsely portrayed as someone who had rejected and forsaken the Jews and all things Jewish.

As an aside, these historical facts are in no way meant to impugn Catholic believers today; I know many honorable Catholic people and my goal is not to create animosity or contention toward them. These facts of history are considered only so we can

---

35 "Anathema" means "accursed."
36 Schaff and Wace, *Nicene and Post-Nicene Fathers*, second series, vol. 14, p. 148.
37 McClintock and Strong, *Cyclopedia*, vol. 5, p. 237, s.v. "Laodicea, Council of."

determine what the Messiah's true intentions were and see how they became confused in Rome. Only by doing this can we see how the various churches came to believe in the doctrines they hold today, and what changes are needed to do God's will.

The Roman Catholic Church has always referred to these Fourteenthers as heretics for continuing their own Jewish heritage and not following Rome's Easter celebrations. Catholics and even other Christian commentators have continued this error, either purposely or accidentally, as seen here in this passage from *The Catholic Encyclopedia*:

> In the early days of Christianity there existed a difference of opinion between the Eastern and Western Churches as to the day on which Easter ought to be kept, the former keeping it on the fourteenth day and the latter on the Sunday following. To secure uniformity of practice, the Council of Nicaea (325) decreed that the Western method of keeping Easter on the Sunday after the fourteenth day of the moon should be adopted throughout the Church, believing no doubt that this mode fitted in better with the historical facts and wishing to give a lasting proof that the Jewish Passover was not, as the **Quartodeciman heretics** believed, an ordinance of Christianity.[38]

The Catholic Encyclopedia's statement that these "Quartodeciman heretics believed" that keeping the 14th day special was an "ordinance of Christianity" is totally false, as is much of the historical disinformation about these believers. The Messianic Jews kept this 14th day special as their *custom* (not by ordinance) because they knew it was the day Jesus finished the work that God had called him to and that it therefore fulfilled the Passover, which was a deep part of their Jewish heritage and which they honored as such. No evidence exists that mainstream Fourteenthers believed everyone should follow this as an ordinance, and they certainly were not celebrating Easter on this 14th day.

Protestant commentators, too, have accepted the Catholic view that these Fourteenthers were heretics or just a fringe group of Judaizers, when in reality they were the main body of the original Messianic Jews. When we read these histories, we must understand that Roman Catholics were mainly concerned that all should celebrate Easter on Sunday in a unified manner—they did not like the confusion caused by these Fourteenthers not observing the Easter celebration.

The following quote from Schaff makes this clear:

> The council of Arles in 314 had already decreed, in its first canon, that the Christian Passover be celebrated "**uno die et uno tempore**

---

[38] Herbermann et al, *The Catholic Encyclopedia*, vol. 5, p. 480, s.v. "Epact."

> **per omnem orbem,"**[39] **and that the bishops of Rome should fix the time**. But as this **order was not universally obeyed**, the fathers of Nicaea proposed to settle the matter, and this was the second main object of the first ecumenical council in 325. The result of the transactions on this point, the particulars of which are not known to us, does not appear in the canons (probably out of consideration for the numerous Quartodecimanians), but is doubtless preserved in the two circular letters of the council itself and the emperor Constantine. The feast of the resurrection was thenceforth **required to be celebrated everywhere** on a Sunday, and **never on the day of the Jewish passover**, but always **after** the fourteenth of Nisan, on the Sunday after the first vernal full moon. The **leading motive** for this regulation was opposition to Judaism, which had dishonored the Passover by the crucifixion of the Lord.[40]

As we see in the quote above, Rome wanted all Jewish influence removed so that the new Roman religion could bring in its own doctrines and rituals unchallenged, and this was done under the guise of opposition to Judaism.

To summarize, the history covered here explains how what began as *a strictly Jewish phenomenon* in Israel—with a Jewish Messiah and Jewish disciples—could become something from which the *Jews were seen to be unwelcome*. This evolution completed the Jewish disconnect and was the devil's plan to exclude Jews from their own promised New Covenant (see Course 10).

This clear history of the Messiah's Crucifixion on the 14th day is crucial for properly understanding the parables he taught the previous night at the Last Supper, and how these figurative teachings were later misunderstood to be a new ritual, as we will soon see.

We have now laid the groundwork for understanding how such a complete Jewish disconnect could occur, and how the powerful Roman Church assumed a very different stance from what the Messiah wanted or taught. As we've already started to see, this sheds light on how doctrines were changed and new rituals were created that were not based on the original foundation of the Jewish Messiah and his Jewish disciples.

In the next chapter, we will take this a step further and explore important words and concepts that were misunderstood and changed to fit into the Roman practices.

---

39 The Latin *uno die et uno tempore per omnem orbem* means "on the same day and at the same time throughout the world."
40 Schaff, *History of the Christian Church*, vol. 3, p. 405.

SETTING THE TABLE 2

WORDS AND CONCEPTS CHANGED

Over time, the meaning of words and concepts can change a great deal. The farther removed from the original context they are, the more their meaning can drift from the original intent. As Rome took over the early Messianic movement, many words and concepts changed, with others evolving much later as the English language originated. So it is important to look closely at the original context of the first-century scriptures to gain a true picture of what was meant at the time.

After the Jewish disconnect, the Roman Church continued to gain in strength and followers. Yet the only things that many Jewish people knew about Christianity was that they were not welcome in it, and that it contained lots of strange rituals and beliefs to which they could not relate. Remember that Constantine called Christianity "our religion," declaring that it was to have nothing in common with the Jews. Much truth was lost in the process, and many concepts were drastically changed.

Since the Bible prophecies show that God is drawing the Jewish people back to Himself in our time, no one should have a problem with returning some of these words and concepts to the first-century Jewish idioms to which Jewish people today might more easily relate. This is not to say that everyone should wear a *yarmulke* (*kippah* or skullcap), because Abraham, Moses, David, and the first-century Jewish believers did not; the wearing of *yarmulkes* was a rabbinic injunction and not from the scriptures. Nor should we all wear robes and sandals as the first-century Jews did. It's only to say that to understand the Jewish Messiah's words and his disciples' teachings in the first-century scriptures, we have to view them from within the Jewish idioms of their day.

In this chapter, we will examine a few terms (such as "church," "communion," "Christian," "saints," and even the name of Jesus) to see how their meanings changed as time went on. And when these meanings change, a false view of history can result.

For example, in the 1862 Young's Literal Translation, James 2:2 is written as follows (with James teaching that we should not show partiality between the wealthy and the poor):

> YLT James 2:2 for if there may come into your synagogue a man with gold ring, in **gay raiment**, and there may come in also a poor man in vile raiment,

In 1862 it was completely acceptable to compliment a Protestant on his attire as being "gay," meaning "colorful" or "bright." However, in our day, this would carry a very different connotation. This is one way that language can change over time to mean completely new things. By taking the original Jewish words and concepts out of the idioms in which they were spoken, believers can end up with meanings that the Jewish Messiah never intended.

Did the Jews Before Paul Share in "Communion" or Partake in the "Eucharist"?

Most Christians (and Jews) today would be shocked if you told them that the Jews who lived a few hundred years before Jesus and Paul shared in "Communion" and partook in the "eucharist."

The Greek word *koinonia*, often translated as "communion" in English Bibles, was also used in the Greek Septuagint (the translation of the Hebrew Old Testament into Greek by the Jewish scholars). Thus it was familiar to Jews a few hundred years before Jesus or Paul even lived. This Greek word meant "fellowship" or "sharing," and of course this Jewish sharing and fellowshipping had nothing in common with the Roman ritual of Communion that came hundreds of years later.

The religious-sounding English word "eucharist" comes from the Greek word *eucharistia*, meaning "thanksgiving." It, too, often appeared in the Septuagint and was therefore common among Jews living before the time of Jesus and Paul. To them, the word simply meant "thanksgiving," and they often "partook in thanksgiving" to God. As with the word "communion," their use of the word "eucharist" certainly had no connection with any kind of Communion rite or Blessed Eucharist ritual that was kept later in Rome.

So when first-century Jews like Paul use these same Greek words in the New Testament, we must be careful not to overlay them with what they later came to mean in Roman theology. The Jewish nation used these words for hundreds of years before Paul, and we should therefore consider his words from that perspective, not from that of a later ritual in Rome.

The true Jewish communion—what this Greek word meant in the Jewish idiom and how it applied to the Jewish festivals, communal meals, and the Last Supper—will be more fully covered in the Twelve Courses.

Did the First-Century Jews Really Go to "Church"?

Today, the word "church" can evoke various emotions among Jewish people, and for the most part they are not warm and fuzzy. If anything, "church" is considered a place where you would not find many Jewish people, which is easy to understand after reading the history that led to the Jewish disconnect. This also explains why many Messianic congregations do not use the term "Messianic Church."

This English word "church" (from the Greek *ekklesia*) can incorrectly portray first-century Jewish believers as no longer being Jewish (i.e., having no Jewish identity), but rather as "Christians" going to "church." However, this Greek word *ekklesia* was used by first-century Jewish writers of scripture to indicate the place where the Jews would "congregate" or "assemble." It was the same word that appeared in the Septuagint and was commonly used among Jews for hundreds of years before the New Testament to mean "called-out ones." It referred to the "assembly" or those "called out" by God.

When first-century Jewish Messianic followers continued using the Greek word *ekklesia*, it connected directly back to the assembly under Moses. They did not picture themselves going to a new place called "church," but rather they understood the Greek word in the sense that they were those "called out" by God.

Did you know that Moses spoke the words of his song to the "church"?

> NAS Deuteronomy 31:30 Then Moses spoke in the hearing of all the **assembly** of Israel the words of this song, until they were complete:

> LXT Deuteronomy 31:30 καὶ ἐλάλησεν Μωυσῆς εἰς τὰ ὦτα πάσης ***ἐκκλησίας*** Ισραηλ τὰ ῥήματα τῆς ᾠδῆς ταύτης ἕως εἰς τέλος

English translations make a distinction between the Old Testament and the New Testament. In the former, this gathering together is translated as "assembly" or "congregation"; in the latter, it is translated as "church." But in fact the Messianic Jews made no such distinction. Above in Deuteronomy, we see that the *exact same* Greek word is used in the Septuagint for the assembly under Moses, which is almost always translated from the Greek New Testament into English as "church," as it is here:

> KJV Hebrews 2:12 Saying, I will declare thy name unto my brethren, in the midst of the **church** will I sing praise unto thee.

> GNT Hebrews 2:12 λέγων, Ἀπαγγελῶ τὸ ὄνομά σου τοῖς ἀδελφοῖς μου, ἐν μέσῳ ἐκκλησίας ὑμνήσω σε,

Notice that the writer to the Hebrews is quoting David from the Psalms. However, was David really going to "church" to sing? Definitely not as most people would think today.

When the King James Bible translates this same scripture from the Psalms, David does not sing praise in "church," for that word was reserved for Christians. Instead, David sings his praise in the "congregation."

> ᴷᴶⱽ Psalm 22:22 I will declare thy name unto my brethren: in the midst of the **congregation** will I praise thee.

If you asked a Jewish follower of Moses living a hundred years before Jesus if he would like to go into the midst of an *ekklesia* and sing praise, he would be glad to do it. However, if you used the English translation of this Greek word and asked a Jewish follower of the Old Covenant living today if he would like to sing in the midst of a *church*, his reaction would likely be very different.

English translations never use this English word in the Old Testament, because to them "church" is the place where "Christians" go. However, the first-century Jews did not make such a distinction; they used the same Greek word the Jews had used for hundreds of years that connected directly to the assembly under Moses, Samuel, David, and the other Jewish leaders, as the Septuagint shows:

> ᴺᴬˢ 1 Samuel 17:47 and that all this **assembly** may know that the LORD does not deliver by sword or by spear; for the battle is the LORD's and He will give you into our hands."

> ᴸˣᵀ 1 Samuel 17:47 καὶ γνώσεται πᾶσα ἡ **ἐκκλησία** αὕτη ὅτι οὐκ ἐν ῥομφαίᾳ καὶ δόρατι σῴζει κύριος ὅτι τοῦ κυρίου ὁ πόλεμος καὶ παραδώσει κύριος ὑμᾶς εἰς χεῖρας ἡμῶν

> ᴺᴬˢ Psalm 26:12 My foot stands on a level place; In the **congregations** I shall bless the LORD.

> ᴸˣᵀ Psalm 25:12 ὁ γὰρ πούς μου ἔστη ἐν εὐθύτητι ἐν **ἐκκλησίαις** εὐλογήσω σε κύριε

Although most English translations (of the Old Testament) are from the Hebrew Bible and not from the Greek Septuagint, the change from using "assembly/congregation" to using "church" is yet another one that has aided in portraying the New Testament as being disconnected from Jewish roots. Picturing "church" in first-century Jerusalem as a modern-day church with a steeple would simply be wrong. We would not picture Samuel and King David going to "church," nor did the first-century Jewish believers see themselves going to a new place called "church."

Many believers today are not aware that the early Protestants also had a problem with this English word "church," because in their idiom it was directly connected to the "one universal church" that was understood to be the Roman Catholic Church. (Note that the word "catholic" means "universal.")

William Tyndale (c. 1492–1536), the first scholar to translate large parts of the Greek New Testament into English, rejected the English word "church" and used the word "congregation" instead. In his day, this more accurately pointed to *any gathering* of believers rather than to the one Roman Catholic Church.

In this example of Tyndale's use of "congregation" in 1 Corinthians 10:32, notice how much the English language has changed since then:

> Se that ye geve occasion of evell nether to ye Iewes nor yet to the gentyls nether to ye **cogregacion** of god:

> KJV 1 Corinthians 10:32 Give none offence, neither to the Jews, nor to the Gentiles, nor to the church of God:

The Catholic Church became angry with Tyndale and his English translation because now the scriptures were accessible in the language of the common man, whereas before they had been in Latin, a language reserved for the higher, better educated classes.

Tyndale responded to a Catholic cleric who challenged him concerning his English translation by saying, "I will cause the boy who driveth the plow to know more of the scriptures than thou."

Tyndale was imprisoned in a dungeon and later burned at the stake. The Roman Catholic Church did not say this was because he had translated the Bible into English or because he had left out the word "church," but rather it claimed he was a heretic (as the Fourteenthers were called). The Messiah never said to kill those who do not believe the same way you do, so this was definitely the wrong spirit at work.

Several English (Protestant) translations—such as Young's Literal Translation (1862) and The Darby Bible (1884)—would follow Tyndale's lead by not using the word "church" anywhere in the scriptures. Instead, they used the word "assembly" where Tyndale had used "congregation." Since these believers were protesting (hence the term "Protestants") the doctrines and practices of the "one universal church," they did not want to use a word that seemed connected to that church.

In turn, the Roman Catholic Church disliked the word "congregation," and in the King James translation (which kept about 85 percent of Tyndale's original translation), it was changed back to "church." After all, in Catholic theology they were the "one Catholic Church" that the Messiah had built. This word "church" became the accepted term for the place where Christians gather, right down to our day.

Giving this word a different nuance in English is another change in word and concept that helped separate the Jewish people from hearing about the Messiah, as well as to separate them from the Gentiles who believe in the Messiah.

Did the Early Jews Who Believed in the Messiah Become "Christians"?

Many Christians today believe that when Peter, Paul, and the early Jews found Jesus to be the Messiah, they saw themselves as Christians and thus part of a new religion. Yet this is a false picture of their true experience. Those earliest Jewish believers accepted that they had found the Messiah, and yet initially most everything else remained the same; they did not see themselves as members of a new religion.

When the Holy Spirit came down at Pentecost and certain other events transpired (such as Peter's vision in Acts 10), they began to understand that they were now in the promised New Covenant of which many Jewish prophets had spoken. However, they continued to participate daily in the Temple, performing the requisite ritual *mikvah* immersions as well as appropriate sacrifices each year, such as the Passover. Some Christians today might not like this reality, but if one understands Jewish law and God's law, they would realize that in those days one could not enter the Temple without being "right with God" as per the sacrifices and ritual cleansings; the Temple authorities would never have allowed it. We see this with Paul as late as Acts 21, when he needs to be ritually prepared to enter the Temple, offer up the appropriate sacrifices, and give notice to the Temple authorities of having been thus ceremonially purified:

> ^{NAS} Acts 21:26   Then Paul took the men, and the next day, **purifying himself** along with them, went into the temple, **giving notice** of the completion of the days of purification, until **the sacrifice was offered for each one of them**.

Paul already understood New Covenant truths, but he knew that to enter the Temple certain requirements of the law (such as appropriate sacrifices and cleansings) had to be adhered to because the Temple authorities still enforced the law of Moses.

We see Peter also gradually coming into new truth, for he would have continued to refuse to eat with Gentiles had the Lord not given him the vision in Acts 10 to bring him further into the New Covenant. Not all the apostles had the same understandings initially, but because they were open to God's spirit leading them, they did gradually come into the new truths from the Lord as they went along. For example, this new truth that Peter came to understand—that it was okay to eat with Gentile believers and to no longer consider them as unclean—came years after the Resurrection. The apostles clearly did not see all truth immediately but were led into it as they yielded to God's spirit.

As New Covenant Jewish believers were eventually rejected from Judaism and as various persecutions drove them out of Israel, they adopted these new truths to the point that Paul—understanding they were now under the New Covenant and the Sabbath was part of Old Covenant law—would teach that it was no longer necessary to obey the Old Covenant laws (Colossians 2:16, 17; Romans 14:5). However, it wasn't as simple as that for Messianic Jews who assembled in the Temple in Jerusalem, where the authorities there were not lenient with those who did not obey the Old Covenant laws concerning the Sabbath and the sacrifices.

The law was clear that anyone not offering up the Passover sacrifice at the proper time would be cut off from the nation. The Jews in the Temple were even going to kill Paul for bringing a man they mistakenly believed to be uncircumcised into the Temple and for teaching against the law of Moses (Acts 21:26–31). As strict as the Jewish authorities were, these Messianic believers would not have been able to continue meeting in the Temple as they had been for some years if they had been rejecting the law right in front of the Temple authorities.

It must be reiterated that early Jewish believers did not see themselves as now practicing some new religion, but rather that the promised Messiah had brought them into the promised New Covenant. Originally, Messianic followers were called the "sect of the Nazarene" (probably as a derisive term) by those on the outside. Later, this Jewish Messianic movement was called "the way" (because in John 14:6 Jesus had said he was "the way"), and the believers were called this for some time.[41]

It was not until one or two decades later that some in the Greek city of Antioch began to be called "Christians" (meaning followers of Christ/Messiah, Acts 11:26), and this nickname stuck. At first, the label was not used by Jesus or initially by the apostles, but it arose later and eventually came to be accepted. The term "Messianic" (from "Messiah") is basically the same as "Christian" (from "Christ"); both are from the original Hebrew and Greek words for "anointed."

Although Jewish Messianic believers should, of course, accept all true Christians as brothers and sisters in the Lord, and likewise Christians should accept Messianic believers and not allow any schism in the body of Christ, there is no scriptural command or even a suggestion from the Lord for believers to be called "Christians."

"Christianity," which began as a word referring to those who followed the Jewish Messiah, would later come to not only exclude Jews but be outright hostile to them in Rome. So when we come down to our day, it's hardly surprising that some do not want to use the word "Catholic" when referring to their Christianity, and others prefer the name "Messianic" to Christian.

---

41   Acts 9:2; 18:25, 26; 22:4; 24:14, 22.

Was the Name of the Messiah Really "Jesus?"

Another word that has evolved over time is the English name "Jesus."

In 1985, when I was a graduate student in Bible college, I was part owner of a building that was rented to a group of Jewish Messianic believers. After sharing beliefs with these very nice people and also being impressed by their level of scholarship, I became a touch frustrated by their referring to Jesus as *Yeshua*. My thought was, "Why can't they just call him by his *real* name?" However, after considering this, I soon realized that Jesus was never called by this English name while he lived, nor was he ever called Jesus until only a few hundred years ago.

Even the early English Bibles did not call him Jesus; the 1611 King James Bible called him "Iesus," which is a transliteration of the Greek New Testament name *Iesous* (pronounced *ee-ay-sooce*). The Tyndale original called him *Iesu*. Since the English language did not have its beginnings until many hundreds of years after Jesus lived, the English name "Jesus" was not used until more than 1,600 years later.

Yeshua is the Hebrew name (translated as Joshua in English) that was translated as *Iesous* in Greek. Thus the Messiah's Greek name was the same one as Joshua's, who had led the Israelites into the Promised Land. In the Greek New Testament, both bear the identical name, since it is a translation of the one Hebrew name; it was only in the English translations that Joshua and Jesus were given different names.

Changing his name from "Joshua" to "Jesus" hides certain spiritual connections and truths that might otherwise be seen had the same name continued to be used for both of them. If the Messiah had been called "Joshua" in English, we would see a direct connection to the Jewish man who, after Moses, led the Jews into the Promised Land. Also apparent would be a connection to the Jewish high priest in Haggai, who was commissioned to *build the house of God* (Haggai 1:1, 8, 14), as well as to Joshua, the "Shoot" in chapter 6 of Zechariah:

> NIV Zechariah 6:11 Take the silver and gold and make a crown, and set it on the head of the high priest, **Joshua** son of Jehozadak.
>
> JPS Zechariah 6:12 and speak unto him, saying: Thus speaketh the LORD of hosts, saying: Behold, **a man whose name is the Shoot**, and who shall shoot up out of his place, **and build the temple of the LORD**;

The high priest Joshua pointed to the true Joshua—the "shoot/sprout" out of David, who would build the Lord's true house, a spiritual house (1 Peter 2:5) for those who love God. The Joshua who followed Moses and led Israel into the Promised Land pointed to the true Joshua—the Messiah—who would lead all of God's people into the true ***eternal*** and spiritual Promised Land with fullness of joy and pleasures forever more:

> ^{NAS} Deuteronomy 31:23   Then He commissioned Joshua the son of Nun, and said, "Be strong and courageous, for you shall bring the sons of Israel into the land which I swore to them, and I will be with you."

> ^{NAS} Psalm 16:11   Thou wilt make known to me the path of life; In Thy presence is fulness of joy; In Thy right hand there are pleasures **forever**.

Giving the Messiah a different English name blurs and obscures many of these pictures, further removing him from his true Jewish roots. If you were to call Jesus "Joshua" today, nobody would know to whom you were referring. Even the angel of the Lord directed that the Messiah have the same Greek name as that of Joshua (Matthew 1:20, 21), yet in English we have changed it to a different one that has clouded some of these connections.

For this reason, I will often refer to Christ as "the Messiah" in this book to portray the Jewish sense of who he actually was. Again, it is not that we should never call him "Jesus," for names frequently change from one language to another, but this history must be understood so that no spiritual light is lost in the translation, regardless of whether we call him "Yeshua" or "Jesus."

※※※

If we really wanted to get technical, we would also have to change the way we pronounce the word "Jew," for neither the Hebrew nor the Greek used the "j" sound with these words. Even in early English the "j" sound is not used, as you can see with Tyndale's use of the words "Jesus" and "Jew" boldfaced below:

> Galatians 3:28   Now is ther no **Iewe** nether getyle: ther is nether bonde ner fre: ther is nether man ner woman: but ye are all one thinge in Christ **Iesu**.

> ^{NAS} Galatians 3:28   There is neither **Jew** nor Greek, there is neither slave nor free man, there is neither male nor female; for you are all one in Christ **Jesus**.

The English word "Jew" was derived from the tribe of Judah and from the land that this tribe was given (Judah/Judea). It did not have the "j" sound in Hebrew (pronounced *"Yehudah"*) or in Greek (pronounced *"Iouda"*). Hence in the time of Jesus, they came to be known as "Ioudaians"; the name was first shortened in English to "Iews," then eventually "Jews" or "Judeans." A word spelled or pronounced *"Jew"* is found nowhere in either the Hebrew or Greek scriptures; this is the English translation.

Will the Real "Lion of the Tribe of Judah" Please Stand Up?

The scriptures refer to the Messiah as the lion of the tribe of Judah, which itself was said to be a lionlike tribe. However, the Messiah was set apart as *the* lion, which means he stood above other such mighty men from this lineage such as Caleb, King David, Isaiah, Nehemiah, and others. However, the visual that has been handed down through history often portrays a different picture.

Most people today would immediately recognize the three people below as being Jesus, even though each one is a different person in a different portrait. All that's needed is long, flowing hair and a certain "holy" look, and everyone knows it is Jesus. However, no first-century Jewish believer (whether he had ever seen the Messiah or not) would have picked from these three.

The fact is that the true Messiah had short hair, and Paul actually states that it is a *shame* for a man to have long hair (1 Corinthians 11:14) and that long hair is a covering for the woman to show submission. Paul would not go around saying it was shameful for men to have long hair if the Messiah wore his hair that way.

Another reason Jesus definitely would not have looked like these three men is that he would not have had a pale complexion, for he spent significant time walking under the hot sun of arid Israel before sunscreen was invented. He was a Jew from the tribe of Judah. But as time went by, from the first century when Jesus lived and on into the Middle Ages, he came to be portrayed in paintings as less Jewish and more as a Gentile with the long, flowing hair that became the custom among some European kings and nobility, even down to some of the early American presidents.

Every time something is portrayed falsely, a certain amount of light is lost.

Were the Early Jewish Believers, Like Paul, Really Called "Saints"?

It was through the Roman Catholic Church that the English word "saint" became widely applied to people in the New Testament, as well as to various Catholic "Saints." To first-century Jewish believers, however, the Greek equivalent word *hagios* (from the Hebrew *kadosh*) actually meant "holy" or "set apart to God" (as did *kadosh*). In the Septuagint translation of the Hebrew, *hagios* was often applied to Moses, Aaron, David, and the whole Israelite nation when they walked with God. *Hagios* was later translated into English as "saint."

The use of the English word "saint" for first-century Jewish believers like "Saint Paul" and "Saint Peter" makes them seem more non-Jewish and slightly Catholic. Portraying these Messianic followers as disconnected from their Jewish heritage gives a false impression.

If they are portrayed as Roman Catholic "saints," some might picture them going around Jerusalem (such as in Acts 2:42–46) practicing a Roman ritual of Communion. However, if we think of them correctly—as Jews who were firmly connected to all things Jewish that had gone on before and since Moses, but who now existed in the promised New Covenant—then we see the true Jewish Messianic perspective.

Did the Early Jewish Believers Really Have a "Pastor"?

"Pastor" is another word with no connection to the first-century Jewish idiom. Messianic Jews never had "pastors" as such, but their scriptures often spoke of men who led and guided the people as "shepherds."

It might amaze some believers to know that the English word "pastor" is actually absent from most Bibles. In fact, the word itself does not appear once in the New Testament. To be fair, the plural "pastors" does appear once in some English Bibles (Ephesians 4:11), but the original Greek was the word for "shepherds," and some English Bibles prefer to use that term:

> NAS Ephesians 4:11   And He gave some *as* apostles, and some *as* prophets, and some *as* evangelists, and some *as* **pastors** and teachers,

> DBY Ephesians 4:11   and he has given some apostles, and some prophets, and some evangelists, and some **shepherds** and teachers,

> YLT Ephesians 4:11   and He gave some *as* apostles, and some *as* prophets, and some *as* proclaimers of good news, and some *as* **shepherds** and teachers,

Using the term "shepherd" in a spiritual sense follows the longstanding Jewish idiom of taking a natural (literal) thing and applying it spiritually. As the Jewish people had natural sheep with natural shepherds, so they applied this concept in the New Covenant to spiritual sheep and spiritual shepherds (i.e., those who would shepherd each "flock"). However, it's important to point out that this word was changed, thus becoming something that Jewish people could not relate to, did not feel a part of, and even felt excluded from. That is why it's often better to use words that more authentically convey what the Messiah meant. To most people—especially many Jewish people whom the Lord may be drawing to Himself—"pastor" does not carry the same meaning as a shepherd.

It is true that this word "pastor" means "to shepherd," and this isn't to say that the word should never be used; but again it's important to highlight how the word changed to become something totally foreign to most Jews.

A pastor is typically perceived as the "head" of the "church" (i.e., the "called-out ones"), even though according to scripture the Messiah is to be the head (Ephesians 5:23, 4:15; 1 Corinthians 11:3). Many literal flocks of sheep in Israel would have more than one shepherd, but most churches today do not have more than one pastor.

The mostly Jewish writers of the New Covenant used the same Greek word (ποιμένα) they had been familiar with from the Septuagint for many years, which meant the same as the Hebrew word (רעה) meaning "shepherd":

> ^{NAS}Jeremiah 3:15 "Then I will give you shepherds after My own heart, who will feed you on knowledge and understanding.

We would never think of the Israelites before Christ as having "pastors," so plainly this word took on a new meaning in English:

> ^{NAS}Ezekiel 34:2 "Son of man, prophesy against the shepherds of Israel. Prophesy and say to those shepherds, 'Thus says the Lord God, "Woe, shepherds of Israel who have been feeding themselves! Should not the shepherds feed the flock?"

Changing the Greek word for "shepherds" into the New Testament English as "pastors" is one more thing that has portrayed a whole new religion that was separated from all Jewish history.

What about the Word "Trinity"?

Although many good people believe in both sides of this doctrine, and numerous arguments concerning it exist, one thing cannot be disputed: The word "Trinity" is found nowhere in either the New Testament or the Old Testament. Furthermore, this concept is totally alien from anything the monotheistic Jews ever believed.

While this book's aim is not to argue this doctrine, we do briefly need to examine the word "Trinity," since this chapter is about words and concepts that changed over time. This is one concept that clearly changed in Rome. It was under Constantine at the council of Nicaea in AD 325 that this doctrine was formalized into the "Nicene Creed," whereby God, the Holy Spirit, and Jesus were called "very God" themselves, yet together these three were the one true God.

To believe this doctrine, one would also have to believe that all of God's great leaders throughout history completely missed this "very God" concept. It's untenable that Noah, Elijah, Abraham (who was called the friend of God), and Moses (who spoke "face to face" with God) all missed this *supposed* understanding of God's nature and that there were really three Gods who make up the one God. While it is true that these great Jewish leaders believed in the Father, the Holy Spirit, and in a future Messiah, they never believed this actually made three Gods into one God.

David spoke of the Holy Spirit (*Ruach HaKodesh* in Hebrew), but he did not see it as a second God or one-third of God, otherwise he would have told us:

> NAS Psalm 51:11   Do not cast me away from Thy presence, And do not take Thy **Holy Spirit** from me.

The Jewish writers of the New Covenant used the same Greek words for "Holy Spirit" that the Septuagint used in this Psalm of David. We must not jump to the conclusion that just because they spoke of the Holy Spirit, they were thinking of a third God, or a member of the threefold Trinity of Constantine's Nicene Creed (which did not exist yet). When David spoke of the Holy Spirit, he was simply speaking of God's presence (who is holy and who is spirit) being with him.

First-century Jews had this same understanding. They also believed in a coming Messiah from the tribe of Judah through David, but again they did not consider him to be a third God or a member of a threefold Trinity that together made up the one God. Once again, here is another overlay of Roman theology on the words and idioms of first-century Jewish believers.

It is true, however, that the Jewish scriptures portray the Messiah as having a nature that is like God's. And they do speak of the Messiah in exalted terms, saying his *name* would be called "Mighty God" and "Eternal Father":

> NAS Isaiah 9:6   For a child will be born to us, a son will be given to us; And the government will rest on His shoulders; And His **name** will be called Wonderful Counselor, Mighty God, Eternal Father, Prince of Peace.

Now Jesus was never called the long string of names listed above. In the Jewish idiom, a person's name was often symbolic for his nature, for who he was. Many of the Jewish prophets and others had God's name "Yah" (or "El," meaning God) attached to their name (such as Isa-iah, Jerem-iah, Dani-el, Ezeki-el).

When Abraham was given the promises of God, his name was changed from "Abram" to "Abraham" (meaning "father of a multitude," Genesis 17:5). When Jacob (meaning "one who supplants") wrestled with the angel of the Lord, his name was changed to "Israel" (meaning "prevailed with God," Genesis 32:28). When the ark of God was captured by the Philistines under Eli, and Eli fell over backward and broke his neck, the child to whom his daughter-in-law was giving birth was named Ichabod (meaning "the glory has departed").

It was also written that the Messiah would be called "Immanuel" (meaning "God with us"):

> [DBY] Isaiah 7:14 Therefore will the Lord himself give you a sign: Behold, the virgin shall conceive and shall bring forth a son, and call his **name** Immanuel.

Now Mary did not name Jesus "Immanuel," even though God told her that the coming child was the Messiah; the angel directed her husband Joseph to give him the name that had God's name attached to it. As we saw earlier, the name "Jesus" was the Greek name for "Joshua," a loose transliteration of the Hebrew name to which God's name was attached ("Yah-Oshea" meaning "Yahweh saves").

So why didn't Joseph and Mary call Jesus "Immanuel" to fulfill this prophecy? The answer is that, like the prophecy from Isaiah 9:6 above, the name is not meant literally. Rather, it expresses the nature and essence of the Messiah, who would be "God with us" and would bring salvation. As the scripture says, he was the exact expression of God's nature:

> [NAS] Hebrews 1:3 And He is the radiance of His glory and the exact representation of His nature, and upholds all things by the word of His power. When He had made purification of sins, He sat down at the right hand of the Majesty on high;

Thus, the Messiah was not a second or third God, but because of his nature and being perfectly yielded to God, he was in effect "God with us." You might ask which God was with us? There is only one God, the God of Abraham, Isaac, and Jacob. This one God (often pictured as the Father) would be indwelling him, as the Messiah himself said:

> NAS John 14:10 "Do you not believe that I am in the Father, and the Father is in Me? The words that I say to you I do not speak on My own initiative, but **the Father abiding in Me** does His works.

Jesus said his heavenly Father was the *only* true God, and that he, Jesus, could do nothing by his own initiative:

> NAS John 17:3 "And this is eternal life, that they may know Thee, **the only true God**, and Jesus Christ whom Thou hast sent.

> NAS John 5:30 "I can do nothing on My own initiative. As I hear, I judge; and My judgment is just, because I do not seek My own will, but the will of Him who sent Me.

There are many scriptures that call for answers, and those answers are actually fairly simple when we consider the first-century Jewish idioms and the fact that God sometimes spoke directly through Christ (see "The Logos of God" section in Course 8). Clearly the prophets and other men of God, from Noah and Abraham down to Isaiah and Malachi, did not view God as a Trinity. As this Roman doctrine developed, "Trinity" became another word that caused Jews to know that the "Church" was not a place connected to the God of Abraham.

Some may ask where this word "Trinity" originated, since it is not in the Old Testament, the Septuagint, or the New Covenant scriptures.

It's historically clear that three different gods made up the Roman triad, with Jupiter as the supreme god of the Roman pantheon alongside Juno and Minerva. On Rome's Capitoline Hill stood an elaborate temple where their deities (called the "Capitoline Triad") were worshipped. Earlier in Roman history, a previous version of this Triad—commonly called the "Archaic Triad"—was made up of Jupiter, Mars, and Quirinus.

The Greek *he trias*, which means "the triad," was first used in a Christian sense by Theophilus, the bishop of Antioch (ca. 169–ca. 183) to refer to God, God's *logos*, and God's *Sophia*. It is hard to discern Theophilus's exact meaning; some say he was referring to the Holy Spirit with *Sophia* and to Christ with the *logos*. According to McClintock and Strong, Theophilus "was educated a heathen, and afterwards converted to Christianity.... Having been converted from heathenism by the study of the Scriptures, he wrote an apology for the Christian faith, addressed in the form of a letter to his friend Autolycus."[42]

---

42 McClintock and Strong, *Cyclopedia*, vol. 10, p. 335, s.v. "Theophilus of Antioch."

It was in this letter to Autolycus (*Apology to Autolycus* 2:15) that we have the first Christian usage of the Greek term for "the triad" in connection with God. But it was third-century church writer Tertullian who is credited with coining the term *trinitas*—a Latinization of the Greek *he trias*—which later became "Trinity" in English. Born to a Roman centurion in Carthage, Tertullian later converted to Christianity in Rome and is often called the father of Latin Christianity.

As for the Jewish believers, they never used the Greek term *he trias* in the scriptures, nor did they portray God as a triad, for they knew God was one.

After Rome destroyed the Jewish Temple (AD 70) and then slaughtered Bar Kochba who led the Jewish revolt against Rome (AD 135), the Roman emperor Hadrian forbade the Jews to enter Jerusalem altogether. He not only renamed Jerusalem "Aelia Capitolina" in honor of the Jupiter temple on Rome's Capitoline Hill, but he also subsequently erected another temple to Jupiter on the very site where the Jewish Temple had once stood, blatantly showing that the Roman God (and Triad of Gods) was now in control.

While some readers may not like the history given here, it's important nonetheless to examine the origins of our English word "Trinity" and how this was yet another concept that changed over time.

What about the Word "Apostle"?

One last word that has a different nuance today in English than it did to the first-century Jews is "apostle." As with all of the other words we've so far covered (except "Trinity"), the Greek word *apostolos* (translated into English as "apostle") also appeared in the Septuagint hundreds of years before the time of Jesus and Paul. It simply meant "sent forth."

This Greek word was well established among first-century Jews and did not portray a new concept or part of a new religion to them. However, the English word "apostle" that is in use today seems foreign to most Jews and not at all connected to their history—only to Christianity.

> NAS Exodus 23:20 "Behold, I am going **to send** an angel before you to guard you along the way, and to bring you into the place which I have prepared.

> LXT Exodus 23:20 καὶ ἰδοὺ ἐγὼ ἀποστέλλω τὸν ἄγγελόν μου πρὸ προσώπου σου ἵνα φυλάξῃ σε ἐν τῇ ὁδῷ ὅπως εἰσαγάγῃ σε εἰς τὴν γῆν ἣν ἡτοίμασά σοι

This same Greek word was used for a vine that would "shoot forth" and bear fruit:

> NAS Song of Solomon 4:13 "Your **shoots** are an orchard of pomegranates With choice fruits, henna with nard plants,

> LXT Song of Solomon 4:13 ἀποστολαί σου παράδεισος ῥοῶν μετὰ καρποῦ ἀκροδρύων κύπροι μετὰ νάρδων

The promised Messiah was also pictured as a "shoot" or "branch" coming out of the lineage of David:

> NAS Jeremiah 23:5 "Behold, *the* days are coming," declares the LORD, "When I shall raise up for David a righteous **Branch**; And He will reign as king and act wisely And do justice and righteousness in the land.

> NAS Zechariah 3:8 'Now listen, **Joshua** the high priest, you and your friends who are sitting in front of you—indeed they **are men who are a symbol**, for behold, I am going to bring in My servant **the Branch**.

> NAS Isaiah 11:1 Then a **shoot will spring** from the stem of Jesse, And **a branch** from his roots will bear fruit.

> JPS Isaiah 11:10 And it shall come to pass in that day, that the **root** of Jesse, that standeth for an ensign of the peoples, unto him shall the nations seek; and his resting-place shall be glorious.

When Jesus used this Greek word for root[43] in the scripture below, he referenced this same "root/shoot" that Isaiah prophesied would come from David's lineage.

> NAS Revelation 22:16 "I, Jesus, have sent My angel to testify to you these things for the churches. I am the **root** and the offspring of David, the bright morning star."

---

43   *BDAG* gives a meaning of this Greek word as follows: 2. that which grows from a root, *shoot, scion*, in our lit. in imagery ***descendant***. (Bauer, *A Greek-English Lexicon of the New Testament and Other Early Christian Literature* (*BDAG*), 3rd ed., p. 906, s.v. "ῥίζα.")

The Greek in this scripture is not saying that Jesus was a root that came *before* David, but rather a "root shoot" out of dry ground that was connected back to David by being his promised descendant. The Septuagint uses this same Greek word in Isaiah 11:1, which is translated as "a branch" from Jesse (in Isaiah 11:1 further above).

The Messiah said that he was the true vine, and that the apostles would be sent forth as extended branches:

> ^{NAS} John 15:5 "I am the vine, you are the branches; he who abides in Me, and I in him, he bears much fruit; for apart from Me you can do nothing.

The intention here is that as we stay connected to the Messiah—as branches shooting off from the vine—we will also bear much spiritual fruit.

To summarize, many words and concepts covered in this chapter were blurred or changed when Rome took over the Church. Also, subtle and not-so-subtle changes have occurred through the evolution of the English language. To accurately understand what these scripture writers intended, we must always discern what they meant in terms of the Jewish idioms of the day.

SETTING THE TABLE 3

The Messiah Would Speak in Parables

Parables held a major place in Israelite history. It was even prophesied that the promised Messiah would speak in parables and dark sayings. The word "parable" comes from the Greek παραβολή (*parabolē*), a conjunction of *para* (meaning alongside) and *bolē* (to throw). Hence the true meaning is found in understanding the symbolic or figurative words that were "thrown alongside" the intended meaning.

Speaking in parables is exactly what Jesus did at the Last Supper and on many other occasions, as was prophesied:

> NAS Psalm 78:2 I will open my mouth in a parable; I will utter dark sayings of old,

This scripture was a prophecy concerning the Messiah, who set forth truths and the plan of God "after the manner of a parable and riddle," as the Keil and Delitzsch *Commentary* explains:

> The poet, however, does not mean to say that he will literally discourse gnomic sentences and propound riddles, but that he will **set forth the history of the fathers after the manner of a parable and riddle**, so that it may become as a parable, i.e., a didactic history, and its events as marks of interrogation and nota-bene's[44] to the present age.[45]

Matthew, writing under God's anointing, applies Psalm 78:2 directly to Christ:

> NAS Matthew 13:34 All these things Jesus spoke to the multitudes **in parables**, and **He did not speak to them without a parable**,

> NIV Matthew 13:35 **So was fulfilled** what was spoken through the prophet: "I will open my mouth in parables, I will utter things hidden since the creation of the world."

---

44 *Nota bene* is Latin, essentially meaning to "note well" the instruction at hand.
45 Keil and Delitzsch, *Biblical Commentary on the Old Testament*, vol. 5, p. 363.

The Messiah spoke in parables when he was led by God to do so, which was quite often. In reference to these scriptures, the commentator Lenski remarks how some will understand the parables and others will not:

> This brings out the two features of parables: they are unsolved riddles to some (unbelievers) but are **highly illuminating illustrations for those having or receiving the solutions** (believers).[46]

The Lord desires to reveal truth to the people, and when the time is right, He will do so as long as we are willing to hear:

> NAS Mark 4:11–12   And He was saying to them, "To you has been given the mystery of the kingdom of God; but those who are outside get everything in parables, And with **many such parables** He was speaking the word to them **as they were able to hear it**;

> NAS Mark 4:34   and He did not speak to them without a parable; but He was **explaining everything privately** to His own disciples.

Parables in the Jewish Tradition

Parables were a well-established part of the Jewish idiom. God used parables and figures of speech through the prophets (such as Ezekiel, Daniel, and Zechariah). Samson and many others also spoke in riddles and parables. In fact, God explicitly told various prophets to bring riddles and parables to the house of Israel:

> NAS Ezekiel 17:2   "Son of man, **propound a riddle**, and **speak a parable** to the house of Israel,

> NAS Ezekiel 20:49   Then I said, "Ah Lord God! They are saying of me, 'Is he not *just* speaking parables?'"

> NAS Hosea 12:10   I have also spoken to the prophets, And I gave numerous visions; And through the prophets I gave parables.

God also spoke to the sons of Abraham, Isaac, and Jacob in visions and dreams that often required interpretation. This dream of Joseph prefigured the coming Messiah:

---

46   Lenski, *The Interpretation of St. Matthew's Gospel 15–28*, p. 534.

> ^{NAS} Genesis 37:9   Now he had still another dream, and related it to his brothers, and said, "Lo, I have had still another dream; and behold, the sun and the moon and eleven stars were bowing down to me."

God said that He would not speak in riddles or enigmatic speech to His friend Moses but rather face-to-face. Sometimes God has His people in a special place before Him where He speaks plainly and reveals deeper truths without riddles, such as with Moses:

> ^{NIV} Numbers 12:8   With him I speak face to face, clearly and not in riddles; he sees the form of the LORD. Why then were you not afraid to speak against my servant Moses?"

But some truths are sealed until the time is right and the people are ready. Here Daniel and Isaiah show that God has some truths that even the learned man cannot understand, because they are sealed (and thus reserved) for a future understanding:

> ^{DBY} Daniel 12:8–9   And I heard, but I understood not. And I said, My lord, what shall be the end of these things? And he said, Go thy way, Daniel; for these words are closed and sealed till the time of the end.

> ^{JPS} Isaiah 29:11   And the vision of all this is become unto you as the words of a writing that is sealed, which men deliver to one that is learned, saying: 'Read this, I pray thee'; and he saith: 'I cannot, for it is sealed';

And some of the Messiah's parables concerning the kingdom of God were for his disciples to understand, but not intended to be comprehended by those whose hearts were not for truth:

> ^{NAS} Matthew 13:10–11   And the disciples came and said to Him, "Why do You speak to them in parables?" And He answered and said to them, "To you it has been granted to know the mysteries of the kingdom of heaven, but to them it has not been granted.

Obviously, those who love God—who have hearts receptive to truth, who are willing to do God's will, and who are open to God's leading—receive more truth than those whose hearts are not willing:

^{NAS} John 7:17 "If any man is willing to do His will, he shall know of the teaching, whether it is of God, or *whether* I speak from Myself.

Parables at the Time of the Last Supper

Throughout the time leading up to the Last Supper, Jesus related one parable after another:

^{KJV} Luke 18:1 And he spake a **parable** unto them *to this end*, that men ought always to pray, and not to faint;

^{KJV} Luke 18:9 And he spake this **parable** unto certain which trusted in themselves that they were righteous, and despised others:

^{KJV} Luke 19:11 And as they heard these things, he added and spake a **parable**, because he was nigh to Jerusalem, and because they thought that the kingdom of God should immediately appear.

^{KJV} Luke 20:9 Then began he to speak to the people this **parable**; A certain man planted a vineyard, and let it forth to husbandmen, and went into a far country for a long time.

^{KJV} Luke 20:19 And the chief priests and the scribes the same hour sought to lay hands on him; and they feared the people: for they perceived that he had spoken this **parable** against them.

^{KJV} Luke 21:29 And he spake to them a **parable**; Behold the fig tree, and all the trees;

Then Jesus continued speaking spiritual truth at the Last Supper:

^{NIV} John 13:7 Jesus replied, "You do not realize now what I am doing, but later you will understand."

Jesus gave many parables; yet the scriptures do not always qualify each one by adding, "This is a parable." Here is just one example, spoken on the evening of the Last Supper:

^{KJV} John 15:5 I am the vine, ye *are* the branches: He that abideth in me, and I in him, the same bringeth forth much fruit: for without me ye can do nothing.

Of course Jesus did not mean, "I am really a grapevine, and I want you all to hold hands and pretend to be branches, and to turn this into a new ritual." Nor did he spell out, "Well, actually I'm not *really* a grapevine; this is just a parable," because he expected them to figure out the obvious.

In that same sense, while eating supper earlier that night, Jesus held bread, broke it, and handed the pieces to his apostles saying, "This is my body." Jesus did not elaborate, "Well okay, this really isn't my physical body that we are eating; it's just bread—but you know that because this is a parable." He knew they understood this to be a spiritual teaching:

> KJV Luke 22:19   And he took bread, and gave thanks, and brake *it*, and gave unto them, saying, This is my body which is given for you: this do in remembrance of me.

Thus, contrary to the belief of Roman and other theologians, at the Last Supper Jesus did not *mean* "This bread is really my body; I want you to eat it in a new ritual."

After the apostles died and many of the earliest Jewish and Gentile believers either perished or were martyred, the Church became essentially Rome's domain. As we've seen, the Jews, along with their understandings, customs, and idioms, became despised and were rejected. Roman Emperor Constantine wanted the Church to have *nothing in common* with the Jews, so the Church devolved into many lifeless rituals and doctrines that would never have been taught by the Jewish apostles.

Bizarre Statements Point to Parables

A bizarre-sounding scripture is like a big sign saying "parable." Often in the Bible, a statement that seems strange, such as the following one by the Jewish prophet Isaiah, is intended to be understood figuratively:

> KJV Isaiah 60:16   Thou shalt also suck the milk of the Gentiles, **and shalt suck the breast of kings**: and thou shalt know that I the LORD *am* thy Saviour and thy Redeemer, the mighty One of Jacob.

No Jewish scribe or commentator ever believed that Isaiah meant this to be taken literally. They knew it referred symbolically and figuratively to the provision (whether natural or spiritual) of the nations flowing to Israel.

Another bizarre statement made by the patriarch Jacob comes from a portion of scripture referring to the promised Messiah:

> NAS Genesis 49:11   "He ties *his* foal to the vine, And his donkey's colt to the choice vine; **He washes his garments in wine**, And **his robes in the blood** of grapes.

Everyone knows you cannot wash robes in wine or the "blood" of grapes and expect them to come out clean. Then below, in the context of the Promised Land, Moses follows with a similarly peculiar analogy of the Israelites drinking blood, although it was only the "blood" of grapes:

> NAS Deuteronomy 32:14   Curds of cows, and milk of the flock, With fat of lambs, And rams, the breed of Bashan, and goats, With the finest of the wheat—And **of the blood** of grapes you drank wine.

With all the admonitions God gave to Moses for the Jews to avoid any manner of blood,[47] this verse in the Song of Moses might have seemed bizarre to many Israelites. Why didn't Moses simply write of the "fresh flowing juices of the grapes"? Wouldn't that have been more appealing? Imagine how the Israelites would have reacted if Moses had said to them, "Here, have a cup of blood to drink; this is blood of the grapes." This scripture shows that Moses (and Jacob) spoke a "dark saying" of old.[48]

In the New Testament, Peter (the Jewish follower of the Messiah) made the following statement that would be *very bizarre* if taken in the natural sense. Rome, Martin Luther, and the Protestants all understood this scripture spiritually, and none of them applied it naturally by actually sprinkling each other during their Communion ritual:

> NAS 1 Peter 1:2   according to the foreknowledge of God the Father, by the sanctifying work of the Spirit, that you may **obey Jesus Christ and be sprinkled with His blood**: May grace and peace be yours in fullest measure.

In Acts, chapter 10, through a vision from the Lord, a hungry Peter was told to "kill and eat" various unclean animals (including lizards, in the Greek). Peter responded, "Not so, Lord, for I have never eaten anything common or unclean." However, Peter soon understood what God was showing him—that the believing Gentiles were no longer to be considered as unclean. This bizarre statement was only a parable that gave Peter new truth when he came to understand it (Acts 10:14, 28).

---

47   Leviticus 7:26, 27; 17:10–14, etc.
48   In Course 11 we will explore how these two scriptures tie into the "dark sayings" that the Messiah spoke at the Last Supper.

Why the Messiah Spoke in Parables at the Last Supper

After the many parables the Messiah spoke at the Last Supper, he then said the following:

> ᴺᴬˢ John 16:25 "These things I have spoken to you in **figurative language**; an hour is coming when I will speak no more to you in figurative language, but will tell you plainly of the Father.

The disciples remark on this specifically, showing their understanding that what Jesus had said earlier during supper had been figurative:

> ᴺᴬˢ John 16:29 His disciples said, "Lo, **now** You are speaking plainly, and are not using a figure of speech.

At the Last Supper, Jesus knew his disciples were not yet in a place of discernment to receive deeper spiritual truths, so instead he used parables and figurative language that they would remember. Once they were filled with God's spirit on the soon-coming Day of Pentecost, they were better able to understand:

> ᴺᴬˢ John 14:26 "But the Helper, the Holy Spirit, whom the Father will send in My name, He will teach you all things, **and bring to your remembrance all that I said to you**.

> ᴺᴬˢ John 16:12 "I have **many more things to say** to you, **but you cannot bear** *them* now.

How sad it is that these followers of the Messiah had him right there with them, but their previous traditions and understandings were so ingrained that they could not bear to hear the new truths that the Messiah wanted them to understand. Today, too, we must not let previous traditions, no matter how entrenched they may be, hold us back from anything God intends for us.

What Jesus Said or What He Meant

When interpreting the scriptures, it's not always what Jesus *said* that matters, but what he *meant*. Jesus often spoke from a higher plane or a spiritual point of view. For example, when Jesus spoke of the leaven of the Pharisees, he was referring to their false teachings. At first the disciples did not understand what Jesus *meant*; they thought he was speaking *literally* about the leaven of bread:

> ^{NAS} Matthew 16:6   And Jesus said to them, "Watch out and beware of the leaven of the Pharisees and Sadducees."
>
> ^{NAS} Matthew 16:7   And they began to discuss among themselves, saying, "*It is* because we took no bread."
>
> ^{NAS} Matthew 16:11   "**How is it that you do not understand** that I did not speak to you concerning bread? But beware of the leaven of the Pharisees and Sadducees."
>
> ^{NAS} Matthew 16:12   **Then they understood** that He did not say to beware of the leaven of bread, but of the **teaching** of the Pharisees and Sadducees.

If the disciples took the Messiah's words literally, they would miss his true meaning:

> ^{NAS} John 11:11   This He said, and after that He said to them, "Our friend Lazarus has fallen asleep; but I go, that I may awaken him out of sleep."
>
> ^{NAS} John 11:13   Now Jesus had spoken of his death, **but they thought** that He was speaking **of literal** sleep.
>
> ^{NAS} John 11:14   Then Jesus therefore said to them plainly, "Lazarus is dead,

Often even those closest to Jesus wrongly took his words *literally* when he intended a *spiritual* meaning. This was true when, at the age of 12, Jesus was in the Temple during the Passover and his parents could not find him:

> ^{NAS} Luke 2:46   And it came about that after three days they found Him in the temple, sitting in the midst of the teachers, both listening to them, and asking them questions.
>
> ^{NAS} Luke 2:47   And all who heard Him were amazed at His understanding and His answers.
>
> ^{KJV} Luke 2:49   And he said unto them, How is it that ye sought me? wist ye not that I must be about my Father's business?

> ᴷᴶⱽ Luke 2:50   And **they understood not the saying** which he spake unto them.

> ᴺᴬˢ Luke 2:51   And He went down with them, and came to Nazareth; and He continued in subjection to them; and His mother treasured all *these* things in her heart.

Many times Jesus puzzled his disciples with his use of parables and figurative language. The disciples sometimes asked Jesus to clarify his meaning:

> ᴷᴶⱽ Matthew 15:15   Then answered Peter and said unto him, Declare unto us this parable.

> ᴷᴶⱽ Matthew 15:16   And Jesus said, **Are ye also yet without understanding?**

> ᴷᴶⱽ Matthew 15:17   **Do not ye yet understand**, that whatsoever entereth in at the mouth goeth into the belly, and is cast out into the draught?

> ᴷᴶⱽ Matthew 15:18   But those things which proceed out of the mouth come forth from the heart; and they defile the man.

In the Temple at Jerusalem during the Festival of Sukkot (also called Feast of Tabernacles/Booths/Ingathering), the Messiah called out to the thirsty to come to him and drink. But he did not *mean* this literally, as the second verse below makes clear:

> ᴺᴬˢ John 7:37   Now on the last day, the great *day* of the feast, Jesus stood and cried out, saying, "If any man is thirsty, let him come to Me and drink.

> ᴺᴬˢ John 7:39   **But this He spoke of the Spirit**, whom those who believed in Him were to receive; for the Spirit was not yet *given*, because Jesus was not yet glorified.

Often the scripture leaves it up to the reader to discern if the words are meant literally or not, such as the "yoke" the Messiah mentions below:

> ᴺᴬˢ Matthew 11:28   "Come to Me, all who are weary and heavy-laden, and I will give you rest.

^{NAS} Matthew 11:29 "Take My yoke upon you, and learn from Me, for
I am gentle and humble in heart; and you shall find rest for your souls.

Again, the Messiah said many things that he did not *mean* to be taken literally, and many times he did not qualify that his statements were parables, since he expected his disciples to understand. For instance, Jesus *said* he was the following:

- the door of the sheep—but he did not *mean* door or sheep literally
- the good shepherd—but he did not *mean* of sheep
- the true vine—but he did not *mean* vine literally
- the light of the world—but he did not *mean* literal light
- the bread of life—but he did not *mean* literal bread.

God's spirit will bear witness with our own spirit when something is to be taken literally or spiritually. God also sends us teachers for the equipping of the believers (Ephesians 4:11–13).

To take every scripture *literally* would require belief in the following:

- that the disciples became branches of the grapevine (John 15:5)
- that Jesus was actually a lamb (John 1:36)
- that King Herod was actually a fox (Luke 13:32)
- that Jesus was actually bread, and he literally came down from heaven (John 6:41)
- that Jesus gave bread, that was really his body (Luke 22:19)
- that Jesus held a cup, which was really his blood (Matthew 26:27, 28)
- that the cup at the Last Supper was actually the New Covenant (1 Corinthians 11:25)
- that we should get busy washing each other's feet (John 13:14, 15)
- that Jesus told the Jews to destroy the Temple (John 2:19, 20)
- that Jesus had two flock of sheep somewhere (John 10:16)
- that Jesus was actually eaten up by zeal (John 2:17, KJV)
- that the Lord wanted Peter to eat reptiles, crawling things, and other unclean animals (Acts 10:12, 13, reptiles in Greek)

Numerous other examples exist of Jesus speaking figuratively, metaphorically, or in a parable. It's easy to see how it is not always what the Messiah *said* that is important, but what he *meant*.

SETTING THE TABLE 4

The Jewish Idiom of Natural to Spiritual

^{NAS} 1 Corinthians 15:46 However, the spiritual is not first, but the natural; then the spiritual.

The most important idiom to help understand what Jesus meant at the Last Supper, as well as Paul's interpretation of the Messiah's teachings as given in 1 Corinthians 10–12, is the natural-to-spiritual idiom of the first-century Jews. Its role as another form of parable makes it vital to understanding the Messiah's true teachings.

The Jewish Prophets

Early Jewish Messianic followers often used many terms figuratively, whereby they did not actually mean the natural or literal object, but the spiritual truth or aspect behind it.

The Jewish prophets who came before Christ often used this natural-to-spiritual idiom. Speaking in this idiomatic way was commonplace among the Israelites, as seen here in relation to tasting and eating food:

^{NAS} Ezekiel 3:1 Then He said to me, "Son of man, eat what you find; **eat this scroll**, and go, speak to the house of Israel."

^{NAS} Ezekiel 3:3 And He said to me, "Son of man, **feed** your stomach, and **fill your body with this scroll** which I am giving you." **Then I ate it, and it was sweet as honey in my mouth**.

^{NAS} Ezekiel 3:4 Then He said to me, "Son of man, go to the house of Israel and **speak with My words to them**.

Here Ezekiel speaks of spiritually "feeding" on the word of God ("scroll"), taking it within and then giving it out to the house of Israel. He is speaking a spiritual truth; Ezekiel is of course not saying that he literally ate a wooden scroll with parchment of animal skin on it.

The prophet Jeremiah also uses this spiritual idiom with eating and feeding:

> KJV Jeremiah 15:16   **Thy *words* were found, and I did *eat* them**; and thy word was unto me the joy and rejoicing of mine heart: for I am called by thy name, O LORD God of hosts.

> JPS Jeremiah 3:15   and I will give you shepherds according to My heart, who shall **feed you** with knowledge and understanding.

Jesus Continues Using This Natural-to-Spiritual Idiom

God anointed the Messiah to continue using this same natural-to-spiritual idiom:

> NAS John 4:32   But He said to them, "I have **food to eat** that you do not know about."

> NAS John 4:33   The disciples therefore were saying to one another, "No one brought Him *anything* to eat, did he?"

> NAS John 4:34   Jesus said to them, "**My food** is to do the will of Him who sent Me, and to accomplish His work.

Jesus does not mean that he has a secret food stash, but rather that he is partaking of spiritual nourishment that comes from God. This "food" motivates and gives him strength to do God's will, to teach what God wanted him to teach (John 7:16), and to accomplish His work.

Paul, a former Pharisee who had studied under the famous Rabbi Gamaliel, also frequently used this idiom:

> NAS Hebrews 13:10   We have **an altar**, from which those who serve the tabernacle have no right **to eat**.

In saying that those who serve the tabernacle (i.e., the Old Covenant) have no right to "eat" from this altar, it presupposes that those in the New Covenant do have this authority. However, we in the New Covenant do not interpret this "altar" or "eating" literally; we understand that Paul means the eating to be *spiritual*. We are not searching for the lost altar of Paul so that we can offer sacrifices on it, and neither does Paul qualify his statement by saying, "Oh, I don't mean we literally have an altar," for he expects readers to discern this.

In John 6, Jesus speaks to a particularly stubborn group of people who are following him only for free bread, having partaken of loaves that he had broken and miraculously multiplied the previous day:

> NAS John 6:26 Jesus answered them and said, "Truly, truly, I say to you, you seek Me, not because you saw signs, but because you ate of the loaves, and were filled.

The context of this verse is crucial to understanding the scriptures that follow in John 6, as is knowing that Jesus is speaking to a group that only wanted more bread and didn't understand or care that the Messiah was in their midst or that God was giving them miraculous signs:

> NAS John 6:27 "Do not work for the **food** which perishes, but for the **food** which endures to eternal life, which the Son of Man shall give to you, for on Him the Father, *even* God, has set His seal."

Jesus uses the natural-to-spiritual idiom to refer to spiritual food that endures to eternal life, but this group mainly desires more natural bread and reminds Jesus how God gave them bread in the wilderness. They complain and in effect question why Jesus doesn't also provide bread every day (except the Sabbath), as under Moses:

> NAS John 6:30 They said therefore to Him, "What then do You do for a sign, that we may see, and believe You? What work do You perform?
>
> NAS John 6:31 "Our fathers ate the manna[49] in the wilderness; as it is written, 'He gave them **bread out of heaven to eat.**'"

These men blow right by what Jesus told them in verse 26 and imply that he should be like Moses with the daily manna, so Jesus responds:

> NAS John 6:32 Jesus therefore said to them, "Truly, truly, I say to you, it is not Moses who has given you the bread out of heaven, but it is My Father who gives you the **true bread** out of heaven.

Jesus of course means the spiritual bread here—the word of God—not a ritual with wafers.

---

49   The manna is called the "bread from heaven" in Exodus 16:4.

> NAS John 6:33 "For the bread of God is that which comes down out of heaven, and gives life to the world."
>
> NAS John 6:35 Jesus said to them, "**I am the bread** of life; he who comes to Me shall not hunger, and he who believes in Me shall never thirst.
>
> NAS John 6:51a "I am the **living bread that came down out of heaven**; if anyone eats of this bread, he shall live forever;

After Rome took over and the Jewish disconnect took place, many spiritual understandings were lost. As a result, scriptures intended as spiritual truth were misconstrued as a Roman ritual, and many false concepts have come out of John 6 because of this failure to understand the natural-to-spiritual idiom and the true context in which Jesus speaks.

Jesus is not saying that he used to be a God in heaven but then came down as bread; he is only comparing himself to the manna, the natural bread "out of heaven" that "came down" from God in the wilderness. He is the spiritual fulfillment of what the manna pointed to—he is the "true bread."

Spiritual Eating and Drinking

Let's look at a few more examples of eating and drinking that are meant to be taken spiritually, starting with the letters of Paul. These come just before the scriptures that the Roman Church interpreted as meaning a natural ritual (i.e., 1 Corinthians 10:16, 17; 11:23–34):

> NAS 1 Corinthians 10:1 For I do not want you to be unaware, brethren, that our fathers were all under the cloud, and all passed through the sea;
>
> NAS 1 Corinthians 10:2 and all were **baptized** into Moses in the cloud and in the sea;
>
> NAS 1 Corinthians 10:3 and all **ate** the same **spiritual food**;
>
> NAS 1 Corinthians 10:4 and all **drank** the same **spiritual drink**, for they were **drinking** from a **spiritual rock** which followed them; and **the rock was Christ**.

Here Paul uses the natural word "baptized," but he means it in a spiritual sense. He also speaks of "eating" and "drinking" that pointed forward to the true *spiritual* food and drink.

On their journey out of Egypt, the Israelites became very thirsty and God told Moses to take his rod and strike the rock, causing "rivers" of water to flow in the desert (Psalm 78:16; Exodus 17:1–6). Paul says that the "rock" that gave them drink was Christ, but certainly he is not saying that the rock was really Jesus disguised as a rock in the wilderness. Instead, Paul shows in the above verses that what the Jews did *naturally* under Moses often extends *spiritually* to us in the New Covenant with the *spiritual* eating and *spiritual* drinking that Christ (the true spiritual rock) provides for us.

In this same context (verse 6), Paul uses the Greek word for type (*tupos*), saying that these Old Covenant things he had mentioned were types for the believers in the Messiah:

> ^{YLT} 1 Corinthians 10:6 and those things became **types** of us, for our not passionately desiring evil things, as also these did desire.

Paul shows that the rock (the type) pointed forward to the Messiah (the antitype) who is the true spiritual rock. Jesus knows this event with Moses and the rock foreshadowed him, yet he also applies it to those who believe in him and receive God's spirit:

> ^{NAS} John 7:37 Now on the last day, the great *day* of the feast, Jesus stood and cried out, saying, "**If any man is thirsty, let him come to Me and drink**.

> ^{NAS} John 7:38 "He who believes in Me, as the Scripture said, '**From his innermost being** shall flow **rivers of living water**.'"

> ^{NAS} John 7:39 **But this He spoke of the Spirit**, whom those who believed in Him were to receive; for the Spirit was not yet *given*, because Jesus was not yet glorified.

At the Last Supper, the Messiah spoke of "eating" and "drinking" at his table in the kingdom of God. This concept of a Messianic feast in God's kingdom was a long-standing Jewish one:

> ^{NAS} Luke 22:30 that you may eat and drink at My table in My kingdom, and you will sit on thrones judging the twelve tribes of Israel.

Yet in his letter to the Romans, Paul *seems* to correct Jesus though in fact he is bringing out what Jesus meant—that the believers would be eating and drinking spiritually:

> NAS Romans 14:17   for the kingdom of God is **not** eating and drinking, but righteousness and peace and joy in the Holy Spirit.

Many examples of this common Jewish idiom exist in scripture, such as when Jesus speaks to the Samaritan woman at the well that Jacob had built:

> NAS John 4:10   Jesus answered and said to her, "If you knew the gift of God, and who it is who says to you, 'Give Me a drink,' you would have asked Him, and He would have given you **living water**."

> NAS John 4:14   but whoever drinks of the water that I shall give him shall never thirst; but the water that I shall give him shall become in him a well of water springing up to eternal life."

Jesus says we will never thirst for water, but that is not literally what he means. It doesn't take long for any believer without water to become parched, but Jesus *means* that the believer will not go spiritually thirsty, because living water (the spirit of God) is available to all who receive him.

Similarly, Paul speaks of drinking the spirit:

> NAS 1 Corinthians 12:13   For by one Spirit we were all baptized into one body, whether Jews or Greeks, whether slaves or free, and we were all made to **drink** of one Spirit.

And of us having "tasted" the word of God:

> KJV Hebrews 6:5   And have **tasted** the good word of God, and the powers of the world to come,

He also speaks of "fruit" as a natural thing but means it in a spiritual sense:

> NAS Galatians 5:22–23   But the **fruit** of the Spirit is love, joy, peace, patience, kindness, goodness, faithfulness, gentleness, self-control; against such things there is no law.

And these scriptures below speak of something as being "true" when it is the spiritual fulfillment of the natural object or concept that came before:

> ^{NAS} Hebrews 9:24 For Christ did not enter a holy place made with hands, **a mere copy** of **the true one**, but into heaven itself, now to appear in the presence of God for us;

> ^{NAS} Hebrews 8:2   a minister in the sanctuary, and in the **true tabernacle**, which the Lord pitched, not man.

> ^{NAS} John 6:32   Jesus therefore said to them, "Truly, truly, I say to you, it is not Moses who has given you the bread out of heaven, but it is My Father who gives you the **true bread** out of heaven.

> ^{NIV} John 1:8–9   He himself was not the light; he came only as a witness to the light. The **true light** that gives light to every man was coming into the world.

Even God's law itself was said to be a shadow, meaning that something more real (or "true") caused the shadow:

> ^{NAS} Hebrews 10:1   For the Law, since it has only **a shadow** of **the good things to come** and **not the very form of things**, can never by the same sacrifices year by year, which they offer continually, make perfect those who draw near.

Readers who are familiar with this crucial natural-to-spiritual idiom may wish to just skim through the following list and go right to Course 1. The full list is provided for those who wish to delve deeper into this idiom.

One way to frame *most* of the following list would be as type and antitype, where the type points forward to the antitype, shown below as the natural pointing to the spiritual. We'll see this idiom used time and again in these five areas:

1. The Tabernacle and Temple themselves
2. Services performed in the Tabernacle and Temple
3. The priests and priesthood
4. The altar and sacrifices
5. Jews, Israel, and Jerusalem

List of Natural-to-Spiritual Examples

1. The Tabernacle and Temple Themselves	
Natural Tabernacle pointing to the spiritual heavenly Tabernacle	ᴺᴬˢ Hebrews 8:1–2 Now the main point in what has been said *is this*: we have such a high priest, who has taken His seat at the right hand of the throne of the Majesty in the heavens, a minister in the sanctuary, and in the **true tabernacle**, which the Lord pitched, not man.
Natural Temple pointing to the spiritual Temple	ᴺᴬˢ Ephesians 2:21 in whom the whole building, being fitted together is growing into a holy **temple** in the Lord; ᴺᴬˢ 1 Corinthians 3:16 Do you not know that **you are a temple** of God, and *that* the Spirit of God dwells in you?
Natural house of God pointing to the spiritual house	ᴺᴬˢ 1 Peter 2:5 you also, as living stones, are being built up as a **spiritual house** for a holy priesthood, to offer up spiritual sacrifices acceptable to God through Jesus Christ.
Natural Holy Place in the Temple pointing to the true spiritual Holiest Place (heaven)	ᴺᴬˢ Hebrews 9:24 For Christ did not enter a **holy place made with hands, a *mere* copy of the true one**, but into heaven itself, now to appear in the presence of God for us; ᴺᴬˢ Hebrews 10:19 Since therefore, brethren, we have confidence to enter **the holy place** by the blood of Jesus,

Natural stones (in the natural Temple) pointing to spiritual living stones in the spiritual Temple	NAS 1 Peter 2:5 you also, **as living stones**, are being built up as a spiritual house for a holy priesthood, to offer up spiritual sacrifices acceptable to God through Jesus Christ.
Natural cornerstone of the Temple pointing to Christ being the cornerstone in a spiritual Temple	NAS Psalm 118:22 The stone which the builders rejected Has become the chief corner *stone*. NAS Acts 4:11 "He is the stone which was rejected by you, the builders, *but* which became the very corner *stone*." * * There were the natural builders (stonemasons) of the Temple, and those referred to as builders (masons) in a spiritual sense (i.e., the religious leaders of the Jews), who rejected the chief cornerstone. Then we have the powerful group today called the Masons, but that is a longer story…
Natural kingdom of God pointing to the spiritual kingdom of God	NAS Mark 12:34 And when Jesus saw that he had answered intelligently, He said to him, "You are not far from the kingdom of God." And after that, no one would venture to ask Him any more questions. NAS Luke 17:20–21 Now having been questioned by the Pharisees as to when the kingdom of God was coming, He answered them and said, "The kingdom of God is not coming with signs to be observed; nor will they say, 'Look, here *it is*!' or, 'There *it is*!' For behold, the kingdom of God is in your midst."

2. Services Performed in the Tabernacle and Temple

Natural incense offering in the Temple and our prayers pointing to spiritual incense	ᴺᴬˢ Psalm 141:2 May **my prayer** be counted **as incense** before Thee; The lifting up of my hands as the evening offering. ᴺᴬˢ Revelation 5:8 And when He had taken the book, the four living creatures and the twenty-four elders fell down before the Lamb, having each one a harp, and golden bowls **full of incense, which are the prayers of the saints.** ᴺᴬˢ Revelation 8:3–4 And another angel came and stood at the altar, holding a golden censer; and much incense was given to him, that he might add it to the prayers of all the saints upon the golden altar which was before the throne. And the smoke of the incense, with the prayers of the saints, went up before God out of the angel's hand.
Natural blood of the covenant pointing to spiritual blood of the covenant	ᴺᴬˢ Zechariah 9:11 As for you also, because of **the blood of *My* covenant** with you, I have set your prisoners free from the waterless pit. ᴺᴬˢ Mark 14:24 And He said to them, "This is **My blood of the covenant**, which is poured out for many.
Natural sprinkling of blood pointing to spiritual sprinkling of blood	ᴺᴬˢ Exodus 24:8 So Moses **took the blood and sprinkled *it* on the people**, and said, "Behold the **blood of the covenant**, which the LORD has made with you in accordance with all these words." ᴺᴬˢ 1 Peter 1:2 according to the foreknowledge of God the Father, by the sanctifying work of the Spirit, that you may obey Jesus Christ and **be sprinkled with His blood**: May grace and peace be yours in fullest measure.* * Peter here writing to those of the Diaspora; see verse 1.

Natural drink offering poured out to God in the Temple pointing to a spiritual drink offering	^{NIV} Exodus 29:40 With the first lamb offer a tenth of an ephah of fine flour mixed with a quarter of a hin of oil from pressed olives, and a quarter of a hin of wine as a **drink offering**. ^{NIV} 2 Timothy 4:6 For I am already being poured out like a **drink offering**, and the time has come for my departure.
Natural ritual washing pointing to spiritual washing with God's word	"Make them wash their garments…. for on the third day the LORD will come down on Mount Sinai in the sight of all the people. (paraphrase of Exodus 19:10–11) ^{NAB} John 2:6 Now there were six stone water jars there for Jewish **ceremonial washings**, each holding twenty to thirty gallons. ^{KJV} Ephesians 5:26 That he might sanctify and cleanse it with **the washing of water by the word**, ^{KJV} John 15:3 Now ye are clean through the word which I have spoken unto you.
Natural baptism in water pointing to spiritual baptism by the Holy Spirit	^{NAS} John 1:26 John answered them saying, "**I baptize in water**, *but* among you stands One whom you do not know. ^{NIV} Acts 11:16 Then I remembered what the Lord had said: 'John baptized with water, **but you will be baptized with the Holy Spirit**.'

Natural ritual cleansing and atonement through the blood of animal sacrifices pointing to the shed blood of Christ that provides spiritual cleansing before God	NAS Hebrews 9:22 And **according to the Law**, *one may* almost *say*, all things are cleansed with blood, and without shedding of blood there is no forgiveness. NAS 1 John 1:7 but if we walk in the light as He Himself is in the light, we have fellowship with one another, and the blood of Jesus His Son cleanses us from all sin.
Natural Sabbath rest pointing to the spiritual Sabbath rest	NIV Exodus 31:16 The Israelites are to observe the Sabbath, celebrating it for the generations to come as a lasting covenant. NAS Hebrews 4:9 There remains therefore a Sabbath rest for the people of God.
Natural circumcision on the eighth day pointing to spiritual circumcision of the heart	NAS Deuteronomy 10:16 "Circumcise then your heart, and stiffen your neck no more. NAS Deuteronomy 30:6 "Moreover the LORD your God will circumcise your heart and the heart of your descendants, to love the LORD your God with all your heart and with all your soul, in order that you may live. NAS Romans 2:28–29 For he is not a Jew who is one outwardly; neither is circumcision that which is outward in the flesh. But he is a Jew who is one inwardly; and circumcision is that which is of the heart, by the Spirit, not by the letter; and his praise is not from men, but from God.

3. The Priests and Priesthood

Natural high priest pointing to a spiritual fulfillment of the high priest	ᴺᴬˢ Hebrews 9:11 But when Christ appeared *as* a high priest of the good things to come, *He entered* through the greater and more perfect tabernacle, not made with hands, that is to say, not of this creation;
Natural priesthood pointing to a spiritual priesthood	ᴺᴬˢ 1 Peter 2:5 you also, as living stones, are being built up as a spiritual house for a holy priesthood, to offer up spiritual sacrifices acceptable to God through Jesus Christ.
Natural priests in the natural Temple pointing to spiritual priests in the spiritual Temple	ᴺᴬˢ Revelation 1:6 and He has made **us** *to be* a kingdom, priests to His God and Father; to Him be the glory and the dominion forever and ever. Amen.
Natural priests pointing to those who function as spiritual priests in the spiritual covenant	ᴺᴬˢ Hebrews 8:4–6 Now if He were on earth, He would not be a priest at all, since there are those who offer the gifts according to the Law; who serve a copy and shadow of the heavenly things, just as Moses was warned *by God* when he was about to erect the tabernacle; for, "See," He says, "that you make all things according to the pattern which was shown you on the mountain." But now He has obtained **a more excellent ministry**, by as much as He is also the mediator of a better covenant, which has been enacted on better promises.

Natural priests partaking of the sacrifices at the altar	^{NAS} 1 Corinthians 9:13 Do you not know that those who perform sacred services eat the *food* of the temple, *and* those who attend regularly to the altar have their share with the altar? ^{KJV} 1 Corinthians 10:18 Behold **Israel after the flesh**: are not they which eat of the sacrifices partakers of the altar?
And spiritual priests partaking spiritually from the altar	^{NAS} Hebrews 13:10 **We have an altar**, from which those who serve the tabernacle have no right to eat. ^{NAS} 1 Peter 2:5 you also, as living stones, are being built up as a spiritual house for a holy priesthood, **to offer up spiritual sacrifices** acceptable to God through Jesus Christ.
Natural spots on a priestly garment (from Temple sacrifices) pointing to spiritual spots (from spiritual flesh, sins of the flesh) on spiritual priest's garment	^{DBY} Jude 1:12 These are **spots** in your love-feasts, feasting together *with you* without fear, pasturing themselves; clouds without water, carried along by *the* winds; autumnal trees, without fruit, twice dead, rooted up; ^{DBY} Jude 1:23 but others save with fear, snatching *them* out of the fire; hating even **the garment spotted by the flesh**. ^{KJV} 2 Peter 2:13 And shall receive the reward of unrighteousness, *as* they that count it pleasure to riot in the day time. **Spots *they are*** and blemishes, sporting themselves with their own deceivings **while they feast with you**;

Priests clothed in natural linen pointing to spiritual priests (pictured below as the bride) clothed in the spiritual linen of righteousness	ᴷᴶⱽ Leviticus 6:10 And **the priest shall put on his linen garment**, and his linen breeches shall he put upon his flesh, and take up the ashes which the fire hath consumed with the burnt offering on the altar, and he shall put them beside the altar. ᴷᴶⱽ Revelation 19:8 And to her was granted that she **should be arrayed in fine linen**, clean and white: **for the fine linen is the righteousness of saints**.
Natural priest washing his clothes for ritual cleansing pointing to spiritual priests washing their robes in the spiritual blood of the true Lamb, who provides spiritual cleansing	ᴷᴶⱽ Numbers 8:6–7 Take the Levites from among the children of Israel, and cleanse them. And thus shalt thou do unto them, to cleanse them: Sprinkle water of purifying upon them, and let them shave all their flesh, and let them **wash their clothes**, and *so* make themselves clean. ᴺᴬˢ Revelation 7:14 And I said to him, "My lord, you know." And he said to me, "These are the ones who come out of the great tribulation, and **they have washed their robes and made them white in the blood of the Lamb**.
Natural shepherds leading and guiding the flocks and spiritual shepherds being those called to lead and guide God's people	ᴺᴬˢ Jeremiah 23:4 "I shall also raise up **shepherds** over them and they will tend them; and they will not be afraid any longer, nor be terrified, nor will any be missing," declares the LORD. ʸᴸᵀ Ephesians 4:11 and He gave some *as* apostles, and some *as* prophets, and some *as* proclaimers of good news, and some *as* **shepherds*** and teachers, * Most English translators use "pastors" instead of "shepherds" here in verse 11, but the Greek word is "shepherds."

Natural sheep and people as sheep speaking spiritually	ᴺᴬˢ Jeremiah 50:6 "**My people** have become **lost sheep**; Their shepherds have led them astray. They have made them turn aside *on* the mountains; They have gone along from mountain to hill And have forgotten their resting place.
Natural stars in the firmament give light, and God's people pictured as stars spiritually, called to show forth His light	ᴰᴮʸ Daniel 12:3 And they that are wise **shall shine as the brightness of the expanse**; and they that turn the many to righteousness as the **stars**,* for ever and ever. * Hollywood tries to counterfeit this by designating those who shine in worldly music, movies, and TV as "stars," but in God's eyes stars are those who have Godly wisdom and turn others to righteousness.

4. The Altar and Sacrifices

Natural sacrifices and believers as spiritual living sacrifices	ᴺᴬˢ Romans 12:1 I urge you therefore, brethren, by the mercies of God, to **present your bodies a living and holy sacrifice**, acceptable to God, *which is* your **spiritual service** of worship.
Natural altar and spiritual altar	ᴺᴬˢ Hebrews 13:10 **We have an altar**, from which those who serve the tabernacle have no right to eat.
Natural Passover and spiritual Passover	ᴺᴬˢ Exodus 34:25 "You shall not offer the blood of **My sacrifice** with leavened bread, nor is the sacrifice of the Feast of **the Passover** to be left over until morning. ᴺᴬˢ 1 Corinthians 5:7 Clean out the old leaven, that you may be a new lump, just as you are *in fact* unleavened. For **Christ our Passover** also has been sacrificed.

Natural first-fruits offering and spiritual first-fruits offering	^{NAS} Leviticus 23:10 "Speak to the sons of Israel, and say to them, 'When you enter the land which I am going to give to you and reap its harvest, then you shall bring in **the sheaf** of **the first fruits** of your harvest to the priest. ^{NAS} 1 Corinthians 15:20 But now Christ has been raised from the dead, the first fruits of those who are asleep.
Natural burnt offerings and spiritual burnt offerings seen under the altar	^{NAS} Revelation 6:9 And when He broke the fifth seal, I saw **underneath the altar** the souls of those who had been slain because of the word of God, and because of the testimony which they had maintained;
Natural ritual cleansing by the blood of animals and spiritual cleansing by the blood of Christ	^{NIV} Hebrews 9:13–14 The blood of goats and bulls and the ashes of a heifer sprinkled on those who are ceremonially unclean sanctify them so that they are outwardly clean. **How much more, then**, will the blood of Christ, who through the eternal Spirit offered himself unblemished to God, cleanse our consciences from acts that lead to death, so that we may serve the living God!

5. Jews, Israel, and Jerusalem

Natural Jew and spiritual Jew	ᴺᴬˢ Romans 2:28–29 For he is **not a Jew who is one outwardly**; neither is circumcision that which is outward in the flesh. But he is a Jew who **is one inwardly**; and circumcision is that which is of the heart, **by the Spirit**, not by the letter; and his praise is not from men, but from God.
Natural Israel and spiritual Israel	ᴺᴵⱽ Romans 9:6–8 It is not as though God's word had failed. For not all who are descended from Israel are Israel. Nor because they are his descendants are they all Abraham's children. On the contrary, "It is **through Isaac** that your offspring will be reckoned." In other words, **it is not the natural children** who are God's children, but **it is the children of the promise who are regarded as Abraham's offspring.**
Natural Jerusalem and spiritual Jerusalem	ᴺᴬˢ Revelation 21:2 And I saw the holy city, **new Jerusalem**, coming down out of heaven from God, made ready as a bride adorned for her husband.

Natural covenant and spiritual covenant, in the form of the two women (Sarah and Hagar) by whom Abraham had sons

NAS Galatians 4:21   Tell me, you who want to be under law, do you not listen to the law?

NAS Galatians 4:22   For it is written that Abraham had two sons, one by the bondwoman and one by the free woman.

NAS Galatians 4:23   But the son by the bondwoman was born **according to the flesh**, and the son by the free woman **through the promise**.

NAS Galatians 4:24   This is allegorically speaking: for these *women* **are two covenants**, one *proceeding* from Mount Sinai bearing children who are to be slaves; she is Hagar.

NAS Galatians 4:25   Now this Hagar is Mount Sinai in Arabia, and corresponds to the present Jerusalem, for she is in slavery with her children.

NAS Galatians 4:26   But the Jerusalem* above is free; she is our mother.

NAS Galatians 4:29   But as at that time he who was born according to the flesh persecuted him *who was born* according to the Spirit, so it is now also.

* I.e., heavenly spiritual Jerusalem.

The Twelve Courses on the Last Supper

The Twelve Courses on the Last Supper

By understanding the Jewish idioms of first-century Jerusalem and grasping the truth of what the Messiah *meant* at the Last Supper, many new truths that were previously obscured will become clear. When we consider the bread and wine (fruit of the vine) at this meal from *within* the first-century Jewish idiom, it becomes evident that Jesus was teaching in parables and not a ritual of Communion.

Instead, the Messiah was showing the true spiritual communion that God desires with, and among, His people. His words about the bread and fruit of the vine were parables to be understood within their Jewish idiom of the day.

I do not ask the reader if this is the interpretation you have previously heard, because it will most likely not be. I only ask if this is indeed what the Scriptures prove. The following conclusions are based on what proper logic and reason require when considered through the idioms of the first-century Messianic Jews. I only ask that you keep an open mind and an open heart as these points are proved using the first-century Jewish idioms and, most importantly, the word of God.

COURSE I

Last Supper Ritual or Parable?
The Messiah Held One *Leavened* Bread

The Fourteenthers understood that the Last Supper was not the Passover, and this fits perfectly with the Jewish apostles and original disciples who all taught that Jesus gave them regular leavened bread at this meal. Had it actually been the Passover, serving such "bread" would have been illegal according to the law of Moses. These facts require believers to question the *unleavened* bread ritual that has been handed down from Rome and which the Protestants accidentally continued in a slightly altered form when they departed Catholicism.

For if Jesus shared regular bread at this supper (it not being the Passover), then the *unleavened* bread ritual did not come from his teachings. It was perfectly acceptable to eat regular, leavened bread (*lechem* in Hebrew, *arton* in Greek) instead of unleavened (*matzah* in Hebrew, *azumos* in Greek) only because the Last Supper took place the evening *before* the Passover sacrifice.

The original Jewish believers knew the Messiah was teaching spiritual truths, using figurative language (rather than the Roman ritual), for this is what Jesus explained to them right after supper:

> NAS John 16:25 "These things I have spoken to you in figurative language; an hour is coming when I will speak no more to you in figurative language, but will tell you plainly of the Father.

Uncontested Ritual

Jesus warned believers to beware of man's traditions. Although scripture instructs us to "prove all things," the Communion ritual is rarely questioned. However, it's important to question it, for if this meal was indeed the Passover, then Jesus would have sinned by having regular bread with it. On the other hand, if Jesus used regular bread in a parable, why do most churches (both Catholic and Protestant) keep a ritual with unleavened bread?

According to God's law, to eat leaven during the Passover ***cut one off from Israel, and thus from God's presence***:

> ^{NAS} Exodus 12:15   "Seven days you shall eat **unleavened bread**,[50] but on the first day you shall remove leaven from your houses; for **whoever eats anything leavened** from the first day until the seventh day, that person shall be **cut off from Israel**."

> ^{NAS} Exodus 12:19   "Seven days there shall be no leaven found in your houses; for whoever eats what is leavened, that person shall be **cut off** from the congregation of Israel, whether *he is* an alien or a native of the land."

Yet, all four Gospel writers—Matthew, Mark, Luke, and John—recorded that at the Last Supper, when Jesus said, "This is my body," he held, broke, and then partook of regular *leavened* bread (*arton*).

> ^{KJV} Matthew 26:26   "And as they were eating, Jesus took **bread**, and blessed *it*, and brake *it*, and gave *it* to the disciples, and said, 'Take, eat; this is my body.'"

> ^{KJV} Mark 14:22   "And as they did eat, Jesus took **bread**, and blessed, and brake *it*, and gave to them, and said, 'Take, eat: this is my body.'"

> ^{KJV} Luke 22:19   "And he took **bread**, and gave thanks, and brake *it*, and gave unto them, saying, 'This is my body which is given for you: this do in remembrance of me.'"

> ^{KJV} John 13:18   "I speak not of you all: I know whom I have chosen: but that the scripture may be fulfilled, He that eateth **bread** with me hath lifted up his heel against me."

Paul writes of *spiritually* fulfilling this Jewish feast of Passover with *azumos* (unleavened):

> ^{KJV} 1 Corinthians 5:8   Therefore let us keep the feast, not with old leaven, neither with the leaven of malice and wickedness; but with the **unleavened** *bread*[51] of sincerity and truth.

---

50   The Hebrew word translated as "unleavened bread" does not contain the word "bread" at all; it is *matzah*.

51   The King James Version italicizes the word "bread" to indicate that it is not in the original Greek text; the Greek word used is *azumos* (unleavened).

> ^{GNT} 1 Corinthians 5:8 ὥστε ἑορτάζωμεν μὴ ἐν ζύμῃ παλαιᾷ μηδὲ ἐν ζύμῃ κακίας καὶ πονηρίας ἀλλ' ἐν **ἀζύμοις** εἰλικρινείας καὶ ἀληθείας.

Then in the same letter to the Corinthians, when Paul talks about what Jesus ate at the Last Supper, he uses *arton*, the Greek word for regular daily leavened bread, seven times. Not once does he say it was unleavened (*azumos*):

> ^{KJV} 1 Corinthians 11:23 "For I have received of the Lord that which also I delivered unto you, That the Lord Jesus the *same* night in which he was betrayed took **bread**."

> ^{KJV} 1 Corinthians 11:26 "For as often as ye eat this **bread**, and drink this cup, ye do shew the Lord's death till he come."

> ^{KJV} 1 Corinthians 11:27 "Wherefore whosoever shall eat this **bread**, and drink *this* cup of the Lord, unworthily, shall be guilty of the body and blood of the Lord."

> ^{KJV} 1 Corinthians 11:28 "But let a man examine himself, and so let him eat of *that* **bread**, and drink of *that* cup."

> ^{KJV} 1 Corinthians 10:16b "The **bread** which we break, is it not the communion of the body of Christ?"

> ^{KJV} 1 Corinthians 10:17 "For we *being* many are one **bread**, *and* one body: for we are all partakers of that one **bread**."

As soon as Jesus spoke the following parable about *leaven*, the disciples failed to understand that he was actually speaking spiritual truth. Yet the first word that came to their minds when they thought of leaven was ***bread***, for the two go hand in hand. So when Jesus mentioned *leaven*, they thought he was referring to the fact that the disciples had forgotten to bring the leftover *bread*:

> ^{NAS} Matthew 16:5 And the disciples came to the other side and had forgotten to take bread.

> ^{NAS} Matthew 16:6 And Jesus said to them, "Watch out and beware of the **leaven** of the Pharisees and Sadducees."

> ^NIV Matthew 16:7   They discussed this among themselves and said, "It is because we didn't bring any **bread**."

These very same first-century Jews who equated leaven with bread would never declare to the whole world that the Messiah and his disciples broke God's law by eating bread at Passover. Had this supper truly been the Passover, the apostles would have risked being cut off from Israel for making such a declaration.

In other words, if Jesus had actually eaten *matzah* (*azumos* in Greek), and if the Last Supper had indeed been the Passover, why would they discredit the Messiah by implying that he committed a grievous sin before the nation and before God by eating regular bread?

Additional Punishment for Leaven at Passover

Prior to the Resurrection, believers remained under Old Testament law. The Jewish writers of the Talmud describe the penalty of a high priest being whipped (referred to as "stripes") for eating anything leavened at the Passover, just as if he had consumed blood or unclean meat. This is made clear in the following passage:

> MISHNA *I.*: To the following stripes[52] apply:
>
> …**A high-priest** who was unclean and partook of things belonging to the sanctuary or entered the sanctuary while unclean; and he who consumed illegal fat, blood, or meat left overnight from the sacrifice, or *piggul*, or unclean meat, and also of such which was slaughtered and brought outside of the Temple; **he who ate leaven on Passover**, ate or labored on the Day of Atonement; who compounded oil similar to that of the Temple, or compounded the frankincense of the Temple, or anointed himself with the oil used in the Temple; who ate carcasses or animals preyed by beasts, or reptiles—**to all of them stripes apply**. (piggul—*I. e.*, meat of a sacrifice illegally slaughtered.)[53]

So if the Jewish authorities would whip even their own high priest for eating regular leavened bread at the Passover, certainly the disciples of Christ would also be soundly punished. Yet, when referring to what was eaten at the Last Supper, the scriptures all

---

52   This punishment comes from Deuteronomy 25:1–3.
53   Babylonian Talmud, Book 9, Tract Maccoth, ch. 3, p. 35, http://sacred-texts.com/jud/t09/mac08.htm.

use the Greek word *arton* for daily leavened bread, which once again proves that the Fourteenthers were correct and that this meal was not the Passover.

Some Find It "Dangerous" to Even Question the Ritual

Despite the presence of bread at the Last Supper, English translations of the Gospels *seem* to make it clear that this meal was indeed the Passover, and most churches and fellowships today adhere to this belief. Yet once I understood from the original Greek texts the proper way to translate those scriptures [54] such that all the Gospels harmonize, I became certain that the Last Supper was not the Passover.

Excited by discovering the answers to this longstanding controversy, I wrote to a few local church leaders concerning what Jesus meant when he broke the one *leavened* bread, and what this revealed about the Communion ritual with *unleavened* bread. I received the following response:

> The implications of teaching that Jesus referred to leavened bread when he said, "This is my body," are **dangerous**.

It's not uncommon to see great religious fear and intimidation attached to the Communion ritual, and for some it can be "dangerous" to even question it. However, since the scripture warns us to "prove all things" (1 Thessalonians 5:21), we must see if this ritual and these doctrines hold up to the test of the scriptures. Jesus also cautions us to beware of man's traditions that make the word of God of no effect (Mark 7:13, Matthew 15:6, Colossians 2:8). So at the very least, we should be willing to test this ritual to see if it falls into that category.

So I wrote that pastor back as follows:

> Pastor, if that were true, then why did Jesus use the everyday word for **bread**, which was **leavened**, when he spoke of the bread at the Last Supper? Shouldn't Jesus rather have said, "This holy and pure *azumos*, without leaven, is my body?"
>
> Why would he use the Greek word for common daily leavened bread? Worse yet, why then would Paul, in every instance (seven in all), also use the Greek word for common daily leavened bread when he spoke of what they ate at the Last Supper? Was Paul dangerously sinning in referring to the Lord's body, using the common Greek word for daily bread, rather than the Greek word for unleavened (*azumos*)?

---

[54] The English translations that seem to so clearly have Jesus eating the Passover at the Last Supper will be explained correctly in "Three Keys That Unlock the Gospels."

And I continued:

> In my opinion, Jesus, Matthew, Mark, Luke, John, and Paul were not tainting the Lord's body but they were stating a fact: that Jesus and the Apostles ate bread, and that this bread brings out the truth of what Jesus *meant* at the Last Supper.

Honest questioning as to whether the Messiah wanted an unleavened bread ritual is not dangerous before God. However, to declare you ate bread at Passover in first-century Jerusalem *would* have been dangerous.

I requested a meeting with that pastor and his research assistant to better explain these truths, but it was never granted. I was then invited to a private meeting with the next two men in line of authority under that pastor, and to their credit they saw the truth of this almost immediately. After I laid out these facts showing that the Last Supper was not the Passover, that Jesus did indeed eat bread, and that this ritual was not actually in the scriptures, one elder remarked about the ritual, saying "It's Catholic." Yet they were not about to approach their pastor with these truths, because they knew his reaction would not be good.

We often end up in churches where *man* is in control instead of allowing Christ to be the head of his Church. We need to conduct ourselves more like the Jews did in Acts 15, when reasonable men—various leaders and scholars—met and heard each other and then, led by God's spirit, decided on what the will of God was and whether or not a doctrine was from the Lord. Unfortunately, situations arise where one pastor rules as a sort of "Pope-lite," laying down the law and commanding all to believe, rather than allowing the Messiah to be the rightful head. Setting a leader with papal-style authority[55] over doctrine is not God's will for his assembly.

On a positive note, that pastor's research assistant has since started a new fellowship, and called me to say that he also is seeing some of these same truths and now agrees that the Last Supper was not the Passover.

Jesus Held One Bread, Not Multiple Breads

In every scriptural occurrence where Jesus holds bread at the Last Supper and then breaks it into pieces, the Greek word used for "bread" is always singular.

When Jesus broke the five breads and miraculously multiplied them to be distributed to the multitudes, the Greek plural word is used (Mark 6:41). When Jesus broke and multiplied the seven breads, again the plural word is used (Mark 8:6).

---

55 See "Appendix A: Proper Authority."

However, when the scriptures refer to the Last Supper bread that Jesus broke, in every single instance the Greek singular *arton* ("a bread") is used.

> ᴷᴶⱽ Matthew 26:26   And as they were eating, Jesus took **bread**, and blessed *it*, and brake *it*, and gave *it* to the disciples, and said, Take, eat; this is my body.

> ᴳᴺᵀ Matthew 26:26 Ἐσθιόντων δὲ αὐτῶν λαβὼν ὁ Ἰησοῦς **ἄρτον** καὶ εὐλογήσας ἔκλασεν καὶ δοὺς τοῖς μαθηταῖς εἶπεν, Λάβετε φάγετε, τοῦτό ἐστιν τὸ σῶμά μου.

Paul depicts this clearly when referring to what he understands from the Lord—that the one bread (singular) at the Last Supper and the pieces of it pointed ahead to spiritual truth in the New Covenant:

> ᴺᴬˢ 1 Corinthians 10:17 **Since** there is one bread, **we** who are many are **one body**; for we all partake of the one bread.

Paul received special revelation from the Lord concerning the Last Supper (1 Corinthians 11:23). Paul himself was not present at the Last Supper, but he now understands that the Last Supper parables are spiritual instruction. Paul shows that at the Last Supper, when Jesus held one bread, broke it into pieces, and gave it to his disciples to partake, these individual pieces pointed to the various members that "are one body." The Messiah's breaking of the one bread into pieces was a parable to show that individual believers in the New Covenant would make up the one spiritual body of Christ and receive spiritual sustenance from one another, with God's presence and the Messiah spiritually in their midst.

We can tell Paul understands this from what he teaches throughout Corinthians:

> ᴺᴵⱽ 1 Corinthians 12:27 Now **you** are the **body** of Christ, and each one of you is a part of it.

Since the parts of this one bread represent us—the members of the spiritual body of Christ—it makes sense that the bread was leavened because, spiritually speaking, we are not yet unleavened (i.e., experientially pure and having all truth).

As an aside, some may think it is strange that the pieces of the one bread would represent the believers, but God often used this kind of symbolic teaching through the prophets. God spoke a parable through the Jewish prophet Ezekiel to take two sticks—which he said were Judah and Joseph, representing the divided and scattered kingdom—and make them ***one in a new covenant*** (Ezekiel 37:16–26). In the same way, God led the Messiah at his Last Supper to speak in parables using one bread, which he broke into pieces to show that those individual pieces represented parts/members of his spiritual body[56] and how they would function in the promised New Covenant. Paul shows that this parable meant we would all be **one** (1 Corinthians 10:17, 12:12, 13, 14, 18, 20, 25, etc.).

As with Ezekiel's parable, the parables taught by Jesus show forth aspects of this promised New Covenant and how God would unite all of his people as one.

The English Translations Can Cause Confusion

Original Hebrew and Greek scriptures never connect the word for regular leavened bread to the Feast of Unleavened, and the Jews deliberately kept this bread far away from it. Jewish writers of the Hebrew Old Testament used one word for unleavened: *matzah*. When Jewish scholars translated these Hebrew scriptures into Greek (called the Septuagint), they used the single Greek word for unleavened bread, *azumos*, which was also used by Jewish writers of the New Testament.

Literal words and typological understandings are essential to Last Supper scriptures. Yet, where the Greek and Hebrew simply read "unleavened" (*azumos* or *matzah,* respectively), English translations insert the word "bread," thus rendering "unleavened" as two words: "unleavened ***bread***."

As a result, the Feast of Unleavened (*matzah*) was translated into English as the Feast of Unleavened **Bread**. However, this festival was never called the Feast of *Matzah Lechem* ("unleavened bread" in Hebrew), nor was it called the Feast of *Azumos Arton* ("unleavened bread" in Greek). It was not until 1,500 years or so later that the English translations joined "bread" to the name of this Jewish feast. This English idiom is now so common that it sounds strange in our vernacular to not add the word "bread" to the name of this feast, but this was not so in bible days.

Below we see the English translations join "bread" to the name of this festival by calling it the Feast of Unleavened **Bread**:

> KJV Exodus 12:17 And ye shall observe *the feast of* unleavened **bread**; for in this selfsame day have I brought your armies out of the land of Egypt: therefore shall ye observe this day in your generations by an ordinance for ever.
>
> NIV Exodus 12:17 "Celebrate the Feast of Unleavened **Bread**, because it was on this very day that I brought your divisions out of

---

56 Course 2 will delve deeper into the meaning of the pieces of bread pointing to the members of the spiritual body.

Egypt. Celebrate this day as a lasting ordinance for the generations to come.

Young's Literal Translation does a better job by not adding the word "bread":

> YLT Exodus 12:17   and ye have observed the **unleavened things**, for in this self-same day I have brought out your hosts from the land of Egypt, and ye have observed this day to your generations—a statute age-during.

Although it is not in the original text, most English translations add the word "bread" in referring to **what is eaten** with Passover:

> KJV Exodus 13:7   "Unleavened **bread** shall be eaten seven days; and there shall no leavened bread be seen with thee, neither shall there be leaven seen with thee in all thy quarters."

> NAS Exodus 13:7   "Unleavened **bread** shall be eaten throughout the seven days; and nothing leavened shall be seen among you, nor shall any leaven be seen among you in all your borders."

No fewer than 26 times do the Old Testament Hebrew scriptures mention the name of this festival, what God commanded the Jews to eat at it, or what they actually ate at it.[57] In all occurrences, the word *matzah* is used; not once does *lechem* appear, except in Deuteronomy 16:3 where *matzah* is referred to figuratively as "bread of affliction."

Why do the English translations insert the word "**bread**," when it is not present in either the Hebrew or Greek original scriptures? Is it because their translators see Jesus eating bread at what they *assume* was the Passover, and therefore try to explain it as "unleavened bread"?

Is that also why the King James translates the Greek word for Passover (πάσχα) as "Easter"—to imply that first-century Jews not only ate "bread" at Passover, but also celebrated Easter?[58]

---

57   Exodus 12:8, 15, 17, 18, 20, 39; 13:6, 7; 23:15 (twice); 34:18 (twice); Leviticus 23:6 (twice); Numbers 9:11; 28:17; Deuteronomy 16:3, 8, 16; Joshua 5:11; 2 Chronicles 8:13; 30:13, 21; 35:17; Ezra 6:22; Ezekiel 45:21.

58   The word "Easter" comes from Astarte, the spring goddess of fertility. In Christ's day, bunnies and Astarte eggs had nothing to do with the Jewish Passover. For further reading concerning Astarte shifting to Easter, see Alexander Hyslop's *The Two Babylons*, p. 103.

> ᴷᴶⱽ Acts 12:4   And when he had apprehended him, he put *him* in prison, and delivered *him* to four quaternions of soldiers to keep him; intending after **Easter** to bring him forth to the people.

> ᴳᴺᵀ Acts 12:4   ὃν καὶ πιάσας ἔθετο εἰς φυλακὴν παραδοὺς τέσσαρσιν τετραδίοις στρατιωτῶν φυλάσσειν αὐτόν, βουλόμενος μετὰ τὸ **πάσχα** ἀναγαγεῖν αὐτὸν τῷ λαῷ.

The sad fact is that—whether by accident, idiom, or to bolster existing religious beliefs about Jesus eating bread at what was believed to be the Passover—the English translations can cloud the truth on this issue by adding "bread" to the Feast when it is not in the scripture.

Bread Is Bread?

Concerning the bread at the Last Supper, some wrongly suggest that "bread is bread" in the belief that "bread" and "unleavened bread" are essentially interchangeable. In doing so, they apparently think it would have been normal for Jews to go around Jerusalem declaring to the world that they ate bread at Passover, something that law-observant Jews would not do even in our day. They appeal to a few scriptures where bread is used figuratively for something unleavened, such as referring to *matzah* as "bread of affliction" (Deuteronomy 16:3).

Of the more than 300 times that the word "bread" is used in the scriptures for regular leavened bread, there indeed are a few rare occasions when it is used figuratively for something that was actually unleavened. However, in every single one of these cases, the scriptures fully qualify it, making it obvious that it is not meant literally (those rare occasions when something unleavened is figuratively called "bread" are covered in Course 7). The Jewish scribes never thought it was acceptable to eat bread at Passover because of its figurative uses in Deuteronomy and elsewhere.

Others point to the twelve temple breads (called "Showbread" in English), explaining that although they were always called regular "bread" in scripture, they were made unleavened in Jesus's day. The reason that Moses called them "bread" is they *were* regular bread. And the reason God referred to them as "bread" in scripture and never once as *matzah* (unleavened) is that He never commanded for these "breads" to be made unleavened.

Jesus warned that some doctrines and traditions of the Pharisees made the word of God of none effect:

> ᴷᴶⱽ Mark 7:13   Making the word of God of none effect through your **tradition**, which ye have delivered: and many such like things do ye.

It was only after the Pharisees gained control that these twelve breads were to be made unleavened, as this was not an original command from God. This Pharisaic change to unleavened therefore has no bearing on this argument.[59]

New Ritual or Spiritual Truth in Parables?

It might be a surprise to some that until around the 9th to the 11th centuries, both Western and Eastern churches kept their Communion ritual with regular leavened bread. Those who imagine that the Last Supper was the Passover—at which *matzah* was eaten—must ask themselves, "How did all those early churches get it so wrong by eating regular leavened bread at their ritual?" and "Why did no historian ever record a single shred of the controversy this would have caused?"

If the Jewish apostles all taught the importance of keeping a ritual with unleavened bread, how could both Eastern and Western churches maintain their ritual with regular leavened bread for 900 years—without a single word of the controversy this shocking mistake would have caused? The reason is that the disciples never taught such a ritual, whether unleavened or leavened, for they understood it as spiritual truth in figurative language—something the Messiah was clearly known for.

Sometime after the ninth century, history shows that Rome established the doctrine of "transubstantiation." This is probably why Rome made this late change, and insisted on using *unleavened* bread in their Communion ritual. In this Roman Catholic belief, the ritual bread actually turns into Christ's sinless, human flesh—hence, the need for *unleavened*.

At that time, the Eastern churches derided those in the West for making this change in the ritual by calling them "Azymites" (Greek for "unleavened ones"). To this day, many Eastern churches still use regular *leavened* bread. When the Protestants left the Catholic Church, they accidentally took along the unleavened bread ritual in a slightly altered form, believing it was what the Lord wanted.[60]

Last Supper Prophecy, Betrayed with Bread

In case anyone would like more proof that what Jesus shared at the Last Supper was regular leavened bread, consider the following: The betrayal of the Messiah was prophesied in the Hebrew scriptures to take place with **bread** *(lechem)*, not *matzah*.

---

59 The history of the twelve breads being changed from leavened to unleavened will be covered in Course 7.

60 This history and the beginnings of the ritual are covered in more detail in the chapter "The Ritual—Why Didn't the Jewish Disciples Teach It?"

It was prophesied in the Psalms that the one eating bread (*lechem*) with the Messiah would betray him. God, knowing that this betrayal would occur the evening before the Passover sacrifice, said it would be bread—regular leavened bread—that the betrayer would be eating. Otherwise, if God by His foreknowledge had known the betrayal would occur while eating the Passover, the scripture would say the "one eating my *matzah*," not the "one eating my bread":

> YLT Psalm 41:9   Even mine ally, in whom I trusted, One eating my **bread**, made great the heel against me

The present participle ("eating") used in the Septuagint shows it is the one *presently eating* my **bread**, and at the Last Supper just before the betrayal, Jesus says that this scripture has been written of him:

> NAS John 13:18   "I do not speak of all of you. I know the ones I have chosen; but *it is* **that the Scripture may be fulfilled**, 'He who eats My **bread** has lifted up his heel against Me.'"

Young's Literal Translation brings out the present-tense aspect of the Messiah's words in the Greek in this scripture:

> YLT John 13:18   not concerning you all do I speak; I have known whom I chose for myself; but that the Writing may be fulfilled: He who is **eating the bread** with me, did lift up against me his heel.

> DBY John 13:19   I tell you *it* now before it happens, that when it happens, ye may believe that I am *he*.

To paraphrase: "I tell you now, before it happens, so that you will know that this was written of me. I am he of whom this Psalm was written. I am he who will be betrayed by one 'eating my bread,' for just as soon as I give Judas this morsel/piece of my bread he will go out to betray me."

> NAS John 13:21   When Jesus had said this, He became troubled in spirit, and testified, and said, "Truly, truly, I say to you, that one of you will betray Me."

> NAS John 13:26   Jesus therefore answered, "That is the one for whom I shall dip the **morsel** and give it to him." So when He had dipped the **morsel**, He took and gave it to Judas, *the son* of Simon Iscariot.

> ᴳᴺᵀ John 13:26 ἀποκρίνεται [ὁ] Ἰησοῦς, Ἐκεῖνός ἐστιν ᾧ ἐγὼ βάψω τὸ ψωμίον καὶ δώσω αὐτῷ. βάψας οὖν τὸ ψωμίον [λαμβάνει καὶ] δίδωσιν Ἰούδᾳ Σίμωνος Ἰσκαριώτου.

Obviously Jesus is referring to a morsel of **bread**, as it was indeed a morsel (or "sop") of the bread that he gave to Judas; remember the betrayal was prophesied to happen with bread (not *matzah*). This same Greek word for "morsel" (*psomion*) is used several times in the Septuagint, where it came from the Hebrew scriptures that always denoted a morsel of bread, and never a morsel of *matzah*.

In the following excerpts from the Greek lexicons, consensus exists that the Greek word *psomion* itself means a piece/morsel of bread:

> *UBS:* ψωμίον, ου n: piece of bread[61]
>
> *BDAG:* ψωμίον: (small) piece/bit of bread[62]
>
> *Louw-Nida:* ψωμίον, ου *n*: a small piece or bit of bread – 'a piece of bread, a bit of bread.'[63]

Here we see it used in the scripture:

> ᴺᴬˢ John 13:27 And after the **morsel**, Satan then entered into him. Jesus therefore said to him, "What you do, do quickly."

> ᴳᴺᵀ John 13:27 καὶ μετὰ τὸ ψωμίον τότε εἰσῆλθεν εἰς ἐκεῖνον ὁ Σατανᾶς. λέγει οὖν αὐτῷ ὁ Ἰησοῦς, Ὃ ποιεῖς ποίησον τάχιον.

When Hebrew scholars translated the following scriptures into the Greek Septuagint, they used the Greek word *arton* for regular leavened bread in every occurrence where this morsel is used:

> ᴸˣᴱ Ruth 2:14 And Booz[64] said to her, Now *it is* time to eat; come hither, and thou shalt eat of **the bread**, and thou shalt **dip thy morsel** in the vinegar: and Ruth sat by the side of the reapers: and Booz handed her meal, and she ate, and was satisfied, and left.

---

61   *UBS Greek-English Dictionary*, p. 201.
62   Bauer, *A Greek-English Lexicon of the New Testament and Other Early Christian Literature* (BDAG), 3rd ed., p. 1100.
63   Louw and Nida, *Greek-English Lexicon of the New Testament Based on Semantic Domains*, vol. 1, p. 49.
64   Most translations use the spelling "Boaz."

^{LXT} Ruth 2:14 καὶ εἶπεν αὐτῇ Βοος ἤδη ὥρᾳ τοῦ φαγεῖν πρόσελθε ὧδε καὶ φάγεσαι τῶν **ἄρτων** καὶ **βάψεις τὸν ψωμόν** σου ἐν τῷ ὄξει καὶ ἐκάθισεν Ρουθ ἐκ πλαγίων τῶν θεριζόντων καὶ ἐβούνισεν αὐτῇ Βοος ἄλφιτον καὶ ἔφαγεν καὶ ἐνεπλήσθη καὶ κατέλιπεν

^{LXE} 1 Samuel 28:22 And now hearken, I pray thee, to the voice of thine handmaid, and I will set before thee a **morsel of bread**, and eat, and thou shalt be strengthened, for thou wilt be going on thy way.

^{LXT} 1 Samuel 28:22 καὶ νῦν ἄκουσον δὴ φωνῆς τῆς δούλης σου καὶ παραθήσω ἐνώπιόν σου **ψωμὸν ἄρτου** καὶ φάγε καὶ ἔσται ἐν σοὶ ἰσχύς ὅτι πορεύσῃ ἐν ὁδῷ

^{LXE} 1 Kings 17:11 And she went to fetch it; and Eliu cried after her, and said, Bring me, I pray thee, **a morsel of the bread** that is in thy hand.

^{LXT} 1 Kings 17:11 καὶ ἐπορεύθη λαβεῖν καὶ ἐβόησεν ὀπίσω αὐτῆς Ηλιου καὶ εἶπεν λήμψῃ δή μοι **ψωμὸν ἄρτου** ἐν τῇ χειρί σου

^{LXE} Proverbs 28:21 He that reverences not the persons of the just is not good: such a one will sell a man for a **morsel of bread**.

^{LXT} Proverbs 28:21 ὃς οὐκ αἰσχύνεται πρόσωπα δικαίων οὐκ ἀγαθός ὁ τοιοῦτος **ψωμοῦ ἄρτου** ἀποδώσεται ἄνδρα

In the original Hebrew scriptures it's never called a "morsel of matzah." As we saw earlier in Psalm 41:9, it is clearly stated that Jesus would be betrayed by one eating his bread (*lechem*), and this is what happened:

^{YLT} John 13:18 not concerning you all do I speak; I have known whom I chose for myself; but **that the Writing may be fulfilled**: He who is **eating the bread** with me, did lift up against me his heel.

God knew that His Son would not be present to eat that Passover but would instead die at the legal time and day as the Passovers were to be sacrificed, soon after having been betrayed by one eating his *bread*. If Jesus had been about to eat the Passover, no bread would have been at that table.

The fact is that Jesus and the apostles did eat bread on this night of the Last Supper, just as the scriptures all say, but it was not a sin before God since this was not the night of eating the Passover. Instead, Jesus would die the following day, on which the Jews would always offer up their lambs, being the very time God's foreknowledge had ordained through Moses for them to sacrifice the Passover:

> ^{NAS} Acts 2:23 this *Man*, delivered up by the **predetermined plan** and **foreknowledge of God**, you nailed to a cross by the hands of godless men and put *Him* to death.

After all, how could Jesus have had a Passover lamb slain one day at the legal time, eat it that night with his disciples at the Last Supper, and then die—with he himself fulfilling the Passover sacrifice—the following day?

To summarize, the Fourteenthers witnessed the Roman Church joining the Passover with the Last Supper. However, the earliest historical evidence shows that the Last Supper was not a Passover, and the scriptures confirm this by stating that Jesus held and broke bread at this supper. So we see that something is not right in the theology that places Jesus eating the Passover with *matzah* at the Last Supper, or with his instituting a new ritual using unleavened bread.

COURSE 2

THE BODY OF CHRIST DID NOT MEAN A RITUAL

In this Course we will consider what the Jewish apostles taught concerning the *spiritual* body of Christ. We will also see how this connects to the Last Supper parable, in which the Messiah broke one bread into pieces and spoke of it *figuratively* as his body.

When Rome rejected Jewish idioms and understandings, it used scriptures that the Messiah spoke of in a symbolic sense, but it then misapplied them by interpreting them literally. Below is one scripture that the Messiah meant as figurative spiritual truth that was taken literally in Rome:

> KJV Matthew 26:26 And as they were eating, Jesus took bread,[65] and blessed *it*, and brake *it*, and gave *it* to the disciples, and said, Take, eat; **this is my body**.

The Roman Church eventually came to teach that Jesus wanted us to remember him in a ritual where we partake of bread that is literally the Messiah's body. When the Protestants left the Catholic Church, they continued the ritual, albeit in a slightly different form. First Martin Luther formed his consubstantiation[66] belief, and later Protestants mostly taught that the Messiah only wanted us to remember him as we eat unleavened bread that *represents* his sinless body; the bread does not change into the Messiah's body, as the Catholics taught.

Early Messianic Jews, however, understood that the Messiah was only speaking in parables and figurative language when he broke the one bread into pieces, for right after supper Jesus told them so:

> NAS John 16:25 "**These things I have spoken to you in figurative language**; an hour is coming when I will speak no more to you in figurative language, but will tell you plainly of the Father."

---

65 The Greek word for bread is singular, as in "a bread."

66 Luther's idea of consubstantiation was that the bread in the Communion ritual contained Christ's flesh, yet it did not completely change into it (as the Catholics taught).

Jesus had presented so many parables on the night of the Last Supper that when he finally spoke without them, the disciples noted this change:

> NIV John 16:29 "Then Jesus' disciples said, '**Now** you are speaking clearly and without figures of speech.' "[67]

The early Jewish disciples did not teach a new ritual; of course they never believed that the pieces of the one bread were Christ's physical body, for they understood the Messiah's figurative instruction. They then went out teaching that **we** the believers make up the spiritual body of Christ:

> NAS 1 Corinthians 12:27 Now **you** are Christ's body, and individually members of it.

> NAS Ephesians 5:30 because **we** are members of His body.

Below, Paul shows that he understands the Messiah's figurative teaching, and that when Jesus broke the one bread into pieces, it showed forth how we members will receive spiritual nourishment in the New Covenant:

> NAS 1 Corinthians 10:17 **Since** there is **one bread**, **we** who are many are **one body**; for **we all** partake of the **one bread**.

So where did the Jewish disciples get this teaching that *we* are the body of Christ? When Abraham died, the Jews did not become the "body of Abraham." When the prophet Elisha died, the Jews did not become the "body of Elisha." These New Covenant disciples were teaching that *we* are the spiritual "body of Christ" and individually members of it because this is what they understood from the Messiah's Last Supper instruction.

"This Is My Body," But What Is This?

Sometimes when we attempt to interpret the scriptures, it's best to work backward. By this I mean that we must first examine what the disciples *taught* about the "body of Christ" (i.e., that we believers are the spiritual body of Christ)—then see if this points back to what Jesus himself taught at the Last Supper or elsewhere—to show that they understood the meaning of his parables:

---

67 According to the *UBS Greek-English Dictionary*, the Greek word translated into English as "figures of speech" in the verse above means "parable, figure of speech, proverb."

> ᴷᴶⱽ Matthew 26:26 And as they were eating, Jesus took bread,[68] and blessed *it*, and brake *it*, and gave *it* to the disciples, and said, Take, eat; this is my body.

In the Matthew scripture, Jesus first broke a single bread into pieces, which he gave to his disciples to eat; *then* he told them, "this is my body." Notice that it was *after* Jesus broke the one bread into pieces that he said "**this** is my body."

Mark brings out this progression quite clearly:

> ᴺᴬˢ Mark 14:22 And while they were eating, He took *some*[69] bread, and after a blessing He broke *it*; and gave *it* to them, and said, "Take *it*; this is My body."

So the progression is as follows:

1. Jesus took *a bread*, singular.
2. Then Jesus gave a blessing.
3. After this blessing, *he broke* the one bread into *pieces*.
4. He then gave the pieces of the one bread to the disciples.
5. He **then** said, "take, **this** is my body" as they partook of the bread.

Was Jesus really teaching a ritual of Communion in the way that the Roman Church believed and as the Protestants accidentally took along in a changed form?

Of course, his disciples knew that the pieces of bread were not really pieces of the Messiah's human body; this is evident from what they would later teach about the "one bread" and "the body of Christ."

No, *This* Is Not the Flesh of the Messiah

The details of Rome's (and later Luther's) ritual can be vexing, especially to those not brought up in this ritual, but to understand how we have arrived at where we are today, it is necessary to briefly go over certain aspects of this history.

In reference to Matthew 26:26 above, the Greek scholar and commentator R. C. H. Lenski (1864–1936) acknowledged that the Greek words for "this" and "bread" do **not** agree in gender, and therefore "this"—as in "this is my body"—***cannot refer*** to the one bread that Jesus had previously held:

---

68   The Greek for bread is singular, "a bread."

69   Notice that "*some*" is italicized, showing that it doesn't appear in the Greek; in the Greek language, bread is singular—"a bread."

> we must note that τοῦτο is neuter, and hence cannot grammatically or in thought refer to *αρτος* which is masculine.[70]

The Greek word τοῦτο above means "this" and *αρτος* means "bread." All four scriptural accounts of "this" and "bread" at the Last Supper show the exact same truth (Matthew, Mark, Luke, and 1 Corinthians 11:23–24), for these words do not harmonize grammatically in the Greek. Therefore "this" cannot refer to the singular "bread" that Jesus held before breaking.

According to Lenski and more importantly the established rules of Greek grammar, the Greek word for "this" cannot refer to the one bread; otherwise both words would have the same gender.

Commenting on these Greek words in the Last Supper scripture in Luke 22:19, Lenski added:

> The English "this" and "bread" hide this distinction in gender, yet no real student will ignore it[71]

Despite being an excellent Greek scholar, Lenski was too close to Luther's teachings on the ritual of Communion. As such, he believed that the revelation concerning this distinction in gender was that the bread had actually changed to now contain Christ's flesh, which in his thinking would explain why "this" does not align grammatically with "bread." However, the Jewish disciples in the Messiah's day would not have believed such a thing.

Lenski then went on to quote from Luther's doctrine of *consubstantiation*—the belief that Christ's flesh is somehow contained in the ritual Communion bread:

> "This" means, "this bread which I have now consecrated by blessing and thanksgiving"; or more tersely, "This that I now give to you" .... "It is no longer mere bread of the oven but bread of flesh, or bread of body, that is, bread which is sacramentally one with Christ's body." Luther.[72]

Luther's idea that somehow the bread had turned into "bread of flesh" to be eaten by the faithful certainly does not have a first-century Jewish ring to it. And Lenski's (and Rome's) interpretation does not correctly explain why "this" and "bread" do not harmonize grammatically, because it does not provide a true reason.

---

[70] Lenski, *The Interpretation of St. Matthew's Gospel 15–28*, p. 1025.
[71] Lenski, *The Interpretation of St. Luke's Gospel 12–24*, p. 1047.
[72] Lenski, *The Interpretation of St. Matthew's Gospel 15–28*, pp. 1025–1026.

To put this in some historical context, the writings of the Jewish prophets do contain some things that would be bizarre if interpreted literally. This scripture from the Prophet Isaiah is one such example as we saw earlier:

> ᴷᴶⱽ Isaiah 60:16   Thou shalt also suck the milk of the Gentiles, **and shalt suck the breast of kings**: and thou shalt know that I the LORD *am* thy Saviour and thy Redeemer, the mighty One of Jacob.

The Jewish scribes of course never taught that this should be literally fulfilled. And in the same vein, when we read the Messiah's words at the Last Supper, we need to consider the Jewish idioms and understandings of his first-century followers. Would it make sense that the Messiah would want them to remember him by eating a piece of bread that they were to believe was a part of his human body? Or would it make more sense that they knew it was another parable spoken in figurative language that pointed forward to the intended spiritual truth?

The Lord desired to open their minds to truly understand the scriptures:

> ᴺᴬˢ Luke 24:45   Then He opened their minds to understand the Scriptures.

So what did Jesus mean when, after breaking the one bread into pieces, he said, "***this*** is my body"? What does "this" really refer to?

One reason "this" does not harmonize with "bread" is it was no longer a single bread when Jesus spoke those words, but rather various pieces of what had been the one bread.

As the disciples shared the pieces of what was once the one bread, this act spiritually pointed further to the truth of how the *spiritual* body of Christ would function in the New Covenant. Each believer is symbolically and spiritually a part of the one bread; each is a member of the one spiritual body. As we fellowship together, we spiritually receive Christ in and through one another, the symbolic pieces of the one bread.

Thus, "this" that we are doing—partaking of the pieces of the one bread—points to the New Covenant provision where "this" is the spiritual "body" and the spiritual fellowship among the believers that occurred for them after Pentecost, as we will see in later Courses.

What the Apostles Taught about Us Being the Spiritual Body

In looking at what the disciples taught, we see that the Messiah's use of the word "this" shows figurative truth along these lines:

This act of the believers gathering together and sharing sustenance (spiritually, the one bread, Christ the bread of life) is what my spiritual body is. It's where I will dwell, "for where two or three of you" (as pieces/members of the one bread) "are gathered together in my name" there I am in the midst (Matthew 18:20).

Or:

You, as the believers with God's spirit within, will be my spiritual body on earth. When I am resurrected, and you are filled with God's spirit, I will be with you—even in you—spiritually; you will be members of my spiritual body and I will dwell spiritually in my body. That is what "this" points to.

Clearly, this is what Paul understood and taught:

> NAS 1 Corinthians 12:27   Now **you** are Christ's body, and individually members of it.

So, as individual members gather and partake of the one bread—Christ the bread of life—these believers function figuratively as members (or "pieces") of Christ's spiritual body.

Again, the key here is that it's *not* the one bread that Jesus previously held and now broke into pieces that is "my body." Rather, it's what the pieces of the bread point to and what we are doing—coming together and sharing spiritual sustenance. This sustenance from God is made possible by the shed blood of Jesus, which cleansed all believers and gave us the legal right to enter God's presence. This shed blood was represented at the Last Supper by the fruit of the vine and provided the spiritual life in the New Covenant.[73]

Thus, what Jesus showed in this Last Supper parable points to how his disciples, acting as spiritual members of his body, would operate in the New Covenant and of course, how believers today are to function as members.

On the very evening of his figurative instruction at the Last Supper, Jesus said:

> NAS John 16:12   "I have many more things to say to you, but you cannot bear *them* now.

It must have been a source of some grief to Jesus—the promised Messiah sent from God—that his disciples were not yet in a ready state to receive all that he had for them.

---

[73]   See Course 11 ("Jacob, Moses, and the Fruit of the Vine") for more on this.

It is sad when people cling so steadfastly to their traditions that they shut out even the Messiah when he desires to bring them new truth.

However, when they were later filled with God's spirit at Pentecost, they would come to understand these spiritual concepts and the parables that Jesus had taught them:

> NAS John 16:13 "But when He, the Spirit of truth, comes, **He will guide you into all the truth**; for He will not speak on His own initiative, but whatever He hears, He will speak; and He will disclose to you what is to come.

> NAS John 14:26 "But the Helper, the Holy Spirit, whom the Father will send in My name, He will teach you all things, **and bring to your remembrance all that I said to you**.

Paul was an especially zealous apostle and received abundant revelations from the Lord (2 Corinthians 11:5; 12:7; Galatians 2:1, 6, 9, 11), which included the *one bread* that Jesus held and broke at the Last Supper.

> NAS 1 Corinthians 11:23 For I received from the Lord that which I also delivered to you, that the Lord Jesus in the night in which He was betrayed took bread;[74]

> NAS 1 Corinthians 10:17 **Since** there is one bread, **we** who are many **are one body**; for we all partake of the one bread.

Here, Paul reminds the Corinthians that "since" Jesus held one bread and broke it into pieces at the Last Supper, *we*—the pieces of the one bread, the spiritual members of his body—are spiritually all one body, the body of Christ.

The Messiah's words showing that he was the bread of life (and that believers were pieces/members of the one bread) may seem strange in our modern idiom. However, in Christ's day those who were spiritually minded would have drawn a connection to the twelve temple breads (later called Showbread in English). In the covenant with Moses, the highest order of priests received sustenance every Sabbath from these twelve breads, which represented the twelve tribes. Under the New Covenant, Jesus has made us priests (Revelation 1:6), and we feed spiritually on the one bread that is now many members by sharing God's love and sustenance through spiritual fellowship and in the sharing of His word.

---

74   Again, the Greek version is singular, meaning "a bread."

1 Corinthians 10:17b   For we all partake of the one bread

They also would have recalled the manna that fell under Moses, called the "bread of heaven." When Jesus said that he was the *true* bread (John 6:32), it showed that these various breads throughout Israel's history pointed to his teaching and spiritual provision.[75]

Many more scriptures that come directly from what Paul understood from the Last Supper parables contain the same truths presented in various ways. Here are just a few examples:

> [NAB] Romans 12:5   so **we**, though many, **are one body** in Christ and individually parts of one another.

> [NAS] 1 Corinthians 12:14   For **the body** is not one member, but many.

> [NAS] 1 Corinthians 12:20   But **now** there are **many members**, but **one body**.

When Jesus gives his disciples pieces of the one bread to *feed on*, we see Paul telling the Corinthians that they can all partake of and feed on the one bread in the spiritual sense, as members of the *spiritual* body of Christ:

> [NAS] 1 Corinthians 10:17   Since there is one bread, **we** who are many **are one body**; for **we all partake** of the one bread.

Again, Paul is not speaking to them about a Roman ritual of eating one bread at "Communion," but rather he is teaching the spiritual truths he received from the Lord concerning the Last Supper.

The Spiritual Body, the Spirit of God Dwells within Us

According to John 6:33 and 6:35, Christ is the bread of life. At the Last Supper, he broke one physical bread into pieces, during which he spoke in parables of those pieces representing his (spiritual) body and that we are many members of that body, because he *spiritually* dwells within us.

> [KJV] John 14:17   *Even* the Spirit of truth; whom the world cannot receive, because it seeth him not, neither knoweth him: but ye know him; for **he dwelleth with you**, and **shall be in you**.

---

75   The connection of the Messiah's teaching to the Showbread will be covered more in Courses 3 through 9.

In this scripture above and the verse below, Jesus spoke spiritual truth about things that would take place after they were filled with God's spirit at Pentecost:

> NAS Matthew 18:20 "For where two or three have gathered together in My name, there I am in their midst."

We the believers are now the body of Christ, and the spirit of God dwells within, as it has since the day of Pentecost. Jesus thus was pointing to the soon-coming time after Pentecost when the assembly would function as his anointed spiritual body.

Christ would spiritually dwell in this spiritual body, nourishing the believers in and through one another just as happens in a *natural body*, where joints and ligaments supply nutrients:

> NAS Colossians 2:19 and not holding fast to the head, from whom the entire body, being supplied and held together **by the joints and ligaments**, grows with a growth which is from God.

> NAS Ephesians 4:16 from whom the whole body, being fitted and held together by that which **every joint supplies**, according to the proper working **of each individual part**, causes the growth of the body for the building up of itself in love.

In this clear picture from these two verses, we, as members of the spiritual body, are the joints and ligaments supplying spiritual sustenance. This happens as we fellowship with one another, with the spiritual blood flow bringing sustenance and cleansing to each member in the body:

> NAS 1 John 1:7 but if we walk in the light as He Himself is in the light, we have fellowship with one another, and the blood of Jesus His Son cleanses us from all sin.

This occurs as we pray for one another, and as we allow God's *agape*[76] love to flow to and through one another:

> NAS 1 Peter 1:22 Since you have in obedience to the truth purified your souls for a sincere love of the brethren, fervently **love one another** from the heart,

---

76   Note that *agape* is the Greek word for "love," often used for God's love.

> ^{NAS} 1 John 4:7   Beloved, let us **love one another**, for love is from God; and everyone who loves is born of God and knows God.

> ^{NAS} 1 John 4:12   No one has beheld God at any time; if we **love one another**, God abides in us, and His love is perfected in us.

Thus the giving and receiving in the spiritual body is reciprocal ("one another"). It is to flow both to and out from each member in the body because we are members "one of another":

> ^{NAS} Romans 12:4–5   For just as we have many members in one body and all the members do not have the same function, so we, who are many, are one body in Christ, and individually **members one of another**.

> ^{NAS} Ephesians 4:25   Therefore, laying aside falsehood, speak truth, each one *of you*, with his neighbor, **for we are members of one another**.

> ^{NAS} 1 Corinthians 12:25   that there should be no division **in the body**, but *that* the **members should have the same care** for one another.

These multiple pictures of us being members of the body all originate from the Last Supper parable, where we are the pieces of the one bread that bring spiritual nourishment (Christ dwelling within) for others to partake of. The sharing of the pieces of the one bread at the Last Supper pointed forward to this spiritual sharing and partaking after Pentecost.

Christ provides the spiritual bread and drink, and often this comes through the other members of his spiritual body. The drink that he gives is the Holy Spirit of God:

> ^{NAS} John 6:35   Jesus said to them, "I am the bread of life; he who comes to Me shall not hunger, and he who believes in Me shall never thirst.

> ^{NAS} 1 Corinthians 12:13   For by one Spirit we were all baptized into one body, whether Jews or Greeks, whether slaves or free, and **we were all made to drink of one Spirit**.

> ᴺᴬˢ John 7:37–39   Now on the last day, the great *day* of the feast, Jesus stood and cried out, saying, "If any man is thirsty, let him come to Me and drink. **He who believes in Me**, as the Scripture said, 'From **his** innermost being shall flow **rivers of living water**.'" **But this He spoke of the Spirit**, whom those who believed in Him were to receive; for the Spirit was not yet *given*, because Jesus was not yet glorified.

Thus the "living water" is to flow through each individual believer, providing spiritual drink to and through each member in the body.

"This Do," but Do What—a New Ritual?

The Messiah wanted the disciples to do something in his remembrance:

> ʸᴸᵀ Luke 22:19   And having taken bread, having given thanks, he brake and gave to them, saying, '**This** is my body, that for you is being given, **this do** ye—to remembrance of me.'

"This do" points back to "this" that he said is his body, after he broke the bread and gave them the pieces to share among themselves. In other words, as we gather together in fellowship, as members of his spiritual body, we are to remember him and the sacrifice that he paid, which provides spiritual life for us in God's presence. "This" that he wants us to do in his remembrance is to break bread and share it, just as he had done with his disciples, but he means for the disciples to go forth breaking and sharing the bread of life, the spiritual bread.

When Paul and the other apostles speak of breaking and sharing the *one* bread, they are not saying that the turnout was so low at the ritual that they used only one bread. Instead, they understand Christ's parable; they are gathering and partaking of the *spiritual* bread as members of the one spiritual body:

> ᴺᴬˢ 1 Corinthians 10:17   Since there is **one bread**, we who are many are **one body**; for we all partake of the one bread.

Taking this further still, Paul was also not saying that since they used only one bread at the ritual, it showed they were *one body*, whereas if more people had been present—and used five breads—they would have been *five bodies*. Rather, he is referring to the one bread that Jesus held and broke into pieces at the Last Supper; those pieces showed that *we who are many* are one body.

The book of Acts also speaks of believers breaking and sharing ***the*** bread, singular:

> ^NAS^ Acts 2:42 And they were continually devoting themselves to the apostles' teaching and to fellowship, to the **breaking of bread** and to prayer.

The original Greek for the above verse includes the article "the" before bread (which is missing in most English translations, including the one above). The Greek word for "bread" is singular here ("breaking ***the*** bread"). The believers were not breaking the same "one" communion bread over and over in a ritual. Instead, this shows that they understood the Last Supper parables and were sharing ***the one bread***, the spiritual bread of life, as they gathered together in fellowship with one another.[77]

Remember that when Jesus broke five breads and miraculously multiplied them for the multitudes, the word for "breads" in the Greek scriptures was plural. Later, when Jesus broke and multiplied the seven breads out to the multitudes, again the Greek word was plural in each occurrence. Yet, when Paul speaks about the one bread and when the apostles speak of "breaking ***the*** bread" (singular) in spiritual fellowship (such as in Acts), they are once again showing they understood the parables at the Last Supper.

We Remember the Messiah and the Price That He Paid

As we come together in fellowship and worship as symbolic pieces of the one bread, we remember all that the Messiah has done for us in his paying the price for our atonement and salvation. At the moment Jesus said to do this in "remembrance of me," he was very possibly seeing the full weight of his decision to pay the penalty for all of humanity's sins.

Facing this penalty, he became more distressed:

> ^NAS^ John 12:27 "Now My soul has become troubled; and what shall I say, 'Father, save Me from this hour'? But for this purpose I came to this hour.

The wages of sin were death (Ezekiel 18:4; Romans 6:23), and this did not mean temporary death but eternal death, as in separation from God. Jesus was not so worried about physical death, as many others had faced this, but his anguish of soul was in facing eternal separation from God. The original Greek text means to deliver him

---

[77] Courses 3 and 4 delve much deeper into the longstanding tradition of breaking bread in the Jewish idiom, as well as these scriptures in Acts.

"out of" death; he was not "heard" by God and saved from physical death but rather was saved out of *eternal* death/separation:

> ^{NLT} Hebrews 5:7 While Jesus was here on earth, he offered prayers and pleadings, with **a loud cry and tears**, to the one who could deliver him **out of** death. And God **heard** his prayers because of his reverence for God.

This is why, when the full realization and weight of the decision he was making became clear, Jesus called out with "a loud cry and tears" to be saved out of death. The Greek is more along the lines of "a powerful outcry and tears." When Jesus began to experience that he, who had known no sin, was now to *become* sin (2 Corinthians 5:21), with all penalty for sin being laid upon him, he realized that God was withdrawing completely:

> ^{NIV} Matthew 27:46 About the ninth hour Jesus cried out in a loud voice, "Eloi, Eloi, lama sabachthani?"—which means, "My God, my God, **why have you forsaken me**?"

Before Jesus became sin's ultimate sacrifice, God—who is holy—had to depart from him, resulting in the Messiah's greatest pain, feeling totally forsaken by God. In God's understanding of justice, however, since Jesus was willing to pay the eternal price for our sins, this sacrifice of his life alone was sufficient to pay the penalty. Thus Jesus would be lifted up *out of* death and spiritual separation from God. One just and sinless man's willingness was sufficient to make restitution for a whole world that had fallen short.

With this in mind came the Messiah's final words before his death:

> Father, into thy hands I commit my spirit. (Luke 23:46)

Jesus asked that as often as we "this do" (i.e., fulfill the parables that he gave at the Last Supper, 1 Corinthians 11:24–26), we do this in remembrance of him. Whenever we partake of the cup of New Covenant blessings (God's love, His spirit, etc.) and the bread of life (the word of God and fellowshipping in the spiritual body of Christ), he asks that we remember him. We remember Jesus as we worship, as we partake in the *agape* love from God for one another, and as we partake in God's word. We also remember Jesus because all of this is provided by his sacrifice; thus we keep him in the forefront of all that we do.

This is why God spoke through Jeremiah, declaring that when the New Covenant comes, "I will no longer remember their sins" (Jeremiah 31:31–34), because now the price has been fully paid and no more condemnation remains for the believer. When one has received God's spiritual love from another member in the body, all condemnation is shown to be a lie, and one comes to realize how great indeed His love is for each soul. A move of God's pure love is coming to the true believers, one so powerful that it will be hard to imagine. As we partake and experience that love, we must remember the Messiah and that it was because of him that we can enter God's presence and freely partake of His love.

Challenging times loom ahead, but we are also entering a period that will be "joy unspeakable and full of glory" (1 Peter 1:18) for those who want God. During this time, the spiritual bride will make herself ready (Revelation 19:7). The bride will not be a frigid, legalistic accuser of the brethren but instead will be able to flow—giving and receiving—in God's pure love, thus fulfilling the command of Jesus for those in the New Covenant:

> NAS John 13:34   "A new commandment I give to you, that you **love one another**, even as I have loved you, that you also love one another.

This is the same love that God showed to Israel, of which He wants us all to partake:

> NAS Jeremiah 31:3   The LORD appeared to him from afar, *saying*, "**I have loved you with an everlasting love**; Therefore I have drawn you with loving kindness."

God's plan meant that Jesus would not have to lose out eternally for being willing to pay the price of giving his life and soul (Isaiah 53:10). Because this sinless, righteous man was willing to sacrifice the ultimate for us and because it was also his Father's will that he go to the cross, God raised him from out of death. What possible reason would the Israelite prophet Isaiah write that it would please the Father to bruise[78] the promised Messiah? It was because God knew all the good that would come from His plan being fulfilled:

> KJV Isaiah 53:10   Yet it **pleased the LORD** to bruise him; he hath put *him* to grief: when thou shalt make **his soul an offering for sin**, he shall see *his* seed, he shall prolong *his* days, and the pleasure of the LORD shall prosper in his hand.

---

78   *Strong's Exhaustive Concordance of the Bible* defines this Hebrew word as "to crush, be crushed … be broken."

So as we fellowship with one another and figuratively represent the pieces of the one bread that was broken, we spiritually partake of the living bread as the spiritual body of Christ, with Jesus/Yeshua in our midst.

Isaiah thus wrote of the Messiah's death, but he also showed forth the Resurrection:

> ^{DBY} Isaiah 53:12   Therefore will I assign him a portion with the great, and he shall divide the spoil with the strong: because he hath poured out his soul unto death, and was reckoned with the transgressors; and he bore the sin of many, and made intercession for the transgressors.

God does not "assign a portion" to the dead but to the living, thus showing the Messiah would be resurrected after making his soul an offering for sin. Because Jesus willingly "poured out his soul unto death" and "bore the sin of many," God raised him out of death.

Some may ask why the Messiah, on his last day alive, is suddenly concerned with being raised from out of death—when he had clearly prophesied he would be raised from the dead after three days. I believe the answer is found in what John the Baptist also experienced. John, who clearly knew and taught that Christ was the promised Messiah, said that the Messiah's ministry would increase and that his own must decrease. With John's ministry complete, God's spirit began to lift off of him and with that so did some spiritual understanding, such that when John was in prison and close to death he even sent two of his disciples to ask Jesus if he was really the Messiah (Matthew 11:2, 3).

Similarly, as the Messiah felt God's spirit withdrawing from him, he—who had known no sin and who had experienced unbroken fellowship with God all his life—now felt the eternal reality of becoming the sin sacrifice. Sensing God's presence departing, he cried out to be saved from eternal separation. Thus, things that he understood when God's spirit was with him became clouded when God's presence began to lift.

The Body of Christ as Anointed Tabernacle

Since Paul states that Christ is the head of the body (Colossians 2:19, Ephesians 4:15), shepherds and teachers need to be sure they are allowing him to truly be the head (i.e., leader and decision maker) in bringing forth new truths and understandings to the body.

We must allow God's word to come first and not permit human egos to rise up above the new truths that He will bring to spiritually grow and perfect the believers. Satan works to divide and conquer, but God's will is for the house of the Lord to be a house of prayer for all nations (i.e., all races), and this is what the spiritual body of Christ provides. The Messiah was prophesied to be a light to the nations, and all believers must be prepared to carry out his will since he is the head of the body.

There is one more aspect of the "body" that also applies to the body of Christ. In Greek, the word "Christ" means "anointed" (as does the Hebrew word "Messiah"). Jesus spoke of his body as the temple—meaning the dwelling place of God (John 2:18–22)—for he knew that the God of Abraham was dwelling within him. The believers (the spiritual body of Christ) are later pictured in heaven, where they are called the "tabernacle of God" (Revelation 13:6). And elsewhere the believers are called the "temple of God," for we are now the anointed tabernacle/temple where God's presence dwells (Revelation 21:3; 1 Corinthians 3:16; 6:19).

This "tabernacle/temple of God," consisting of the believers, refers to the true spiritual temple that the Messiah was to build:

> NAS Zechariah 6:11–12 "And take silver and gold, make an *ornate* crown, and set *it* on the head of Joshua the son of Jehozadak, the high priest. Then say to him, 'Thus says the LORD of hosts, "Behold, **a man whose name is Branch**, for He will branch out from where He is; and **He will build the temple of the LORD**.

Joshua, the High Priest mentioned in this scripture, had the same Hebrew name (Yeshua) as Jesus, and both he and Jesus share the same Greek name as well. As we saw in "Setting the Table 2," it was only in the English translations where they were deliberately given two different names: Joshua and Jesus. So this points to the true Branch ("Yeshua" the Messiah), who would "branch out" through his disciples (the "branches," John 15:5) and build the true spiritual temple. Thus the Messiah would be the greater Joshua, as high priest and king, pictured in the scripture above with a crown; he would build God's spiritual house. "Joshua" would later be translated into English as "Jesus."

God had told the Israelites that He would dwell among them and meet them in the tabernacle, which was often called the "**tent of meeting**" or as some translations say "tabernacle of the congregation":

> NAS Exodus 29:4 "Then you shall bring Aaron and his sons to the doorway of the **tent of meeting**, and wash them with water.

> NAS Exodus 29:42 "It shall be a continual burnt offering throughout your generations at the doorway of the tent of meeting before the LORD, **where I will meet with you, to speak to you there**.

This structure where God would meet the people and dwell among them (the tabernacle, then the temple) was also called the "house of God" and sometimes just the "house." The Jews also understood this analogy of the outward man (the body) being a tent (tabernacle or house) for the inner man (soul and spirit) to dwell within. Paul used this idiom:

> NAS 2 Corinthians 4:16 Therefore we do not lose heart, but though our **outer man** is decaying, yet our **inner man** is being renewed day by day.

> NAS 2 Corinthians 5:1 For we know that if the **earthly tent** which is our **house** is torn down, we have a building from God, a house not made with hands, eternal in the heavens.

> NAS 2 Corinthians 5:8 we are of good courage, I say, and prefer rather to be absent from **the body** and to be at home with the Lord.

Peter, speaking of his soon-coming death, refers to putting off his "tabernacle":

> DBY 2 Peter 1:13–14 But I account it right, as long as I am in this tabernacle, to stir you up by putting *you* in remembrance, knowing that the putting off of my tabernacle is speedily *to take place*, as also our Lord Jesus Christ has manifested to me;

Talmudic writers also understood this picture of the human body functioning as the tent or tabernacle in which we dwell. They quoted the scripture in Amos 9:11 that speaks of the raising up of the fallen tabernacle (tent) of David, and they applied this figuratively to the Messiah:

> R. Na'hman said to R. Itz'hak: Have you heard when the fallen son will come? And to the question, Who is it? He answered: The Messiah. And the Messiah you call "**The fallen son**"? And he said: Yea, for it reads [Amos, ix. 11]: "On that day will I raise up the tabernacle of David, which is fallen."[79]

This Talmudic reference states that the Messiah is the promised son of David. By extension, this raised-up tabernacle could also refer to the believers being raised up as the spiritual body of Christ (i.e., anointed) where God's spirit will dwell within.

---

79 Babylonian Talmud, Book 8, Tract Sanhedrin, ch. 11, p. 300, http://sacred-texts.com/jud/t08/.t0814.htm.

When New Testament writers speak of Jesus's dead body, they refer to the "body of Jesus" (Matthew 27:58; Mark 15:43; Luke 23:52; 24:3; John 19:38, 40; 20:12). Yet when they speak of the "body of Christ," they almost always refer to the body of anointed believers (i.e., his spiritual body) as the tent/temple/tabernacle/house of God.

The point is that when the scriptures speak of the body of Christ—with Christ meaning "anointed" in Greek—it can also refer to a tent or tabernacle of the "anointed" congregation where God will meet us and dwell among us. We should keep these Jewish idioms in mind when we examine the scriptures, which also *picture the believers as an extension of the one bread of life, as pieces of the one bread, and as members of the Messiah's anointed spiritual body.*

COURSE 3

The Jewish Idiom of Breaking Bread Among the Early Believers

This Course will focus on proving two main points:

1. The New Testament scriptures that speak of *breaking bread* among early Messianic Jews did *not* mean the supposed Communion ritual, as many commentators have believed since Rome.

2. The idiom of breaking bread has a long Jewish history, originating with the twelve breads that were *broken* and shared each Sabbath in the Temple. We will then see how Messianic Jews understood that the Messiah and his teaching fulfilled this idiom as the *true bread*, the *bread of life*. This is what the New Covenant scriptures on breaking bread refer to, and this was the idiom where the phrase "breaking bread" originated.

Since these scriptures were originally written from a first-century Jewish perspective but later misunderstood by Rome to indicate a ritual, we'll focus first on how breaking bread developed in the Jewish tradition. Then we'll turn to how New Covenant Jewish believers—using their *natural-to-spiritual* idiom—built on the existing Jewish idiom of breaking bread in the Temple and in Jewish homes, and went forth "breaking bread" spiritually.

※※※

The twelve breads that were broken each Sabbath in the Tabernacle were first mentioned in the scripture when God gave the law to Moses. This service continued in the Temple under David and Solomon, with the priests "breaking bread" there as well. They were *broken* rather than cut with a knife, for this occurred on the Sabbath when the use of such instruments was forbidden.[80] Here are two English translations with two different names for the bread:

> NAS Exodus 25:30 And you shall set the **bread of the Presence** on the table before Me at all times.

---

80 Except when absolutely necessary, such as for the animal sacrifices in the Temple.

> KJV Exodus 25:30   And thou shalt set upon the table **shewbread** before me alway.

Calling them "bread of the Presence" indicates that the breads were to continually be in God's presence in the Temple. Although translating them as "Showbread" is common in our day, it can actually be quite misleading since these twelve breads were never called that by Moses, David, Jesus, or Paul, or any other Jews—either before or during the time of Christ. In the original Greek and Hebrew scriptures, they are simply called "bread." It was not until around 1530 AD that Protestant reformer and translator William Tyndale coined the word "Shewbread" (see KJV above) while translating the Greek New Testament into English. Later it became "Showbread."

This change of names from "bread" to "Showbread" may not seem significant, but it is in fact important. In certain scriptures, the words "bread" or "breaking bread" are *historically connected* to the twelve breads broken in the Temple each Sabbath, but because the English translation does not show Jesus or his disciples using the term "Showbread," this connection may be obscured or lost.

To illustrate this, consider the example of Jews breaking bread in their homes on the Sabbath. There is seemingly no spiritual connection between this and Showbread, since Jews do not use the expression "breaking Showbread," and since the Talmud and other Jewish writings never spoke of breaking Showbread—*because the word "Showbread" itself did not yet exist*. However, if it's phrased that the priests "break bread" in the Temple on the Sabbath and the Jewish families "break bread" in their homes, then it's easier to draw a spiritual connection between these two events that otherwise may seem unrelated.

Similarly, when the Messiah miraculously broke and multiplied the twelve breads to feed the multitudes (five then seven), there is seemingly no connection since it does not say he broke Showbread (a nonexistent word in his day). Yet if we consider that God commanded Moses to bring forth *twelve breads* in this Temple service, and the Messiah brought forth *twelve breads* for the Israelites in these miracles, then one is more likely to see a possible historical, spiritual, or typological connection. Additionally, when we see the Jewish disciples speaking of breaking bread in the scriptures and consider their natural-to-spiritual idiom, it becomes clear that they are applying this phrase spiritually. Throughout this Course, we will often refer to the Showbread as the "twelve breads" to maintain this historical connection.

Talmudic writers often spoke of breaking bread as well, and certainly not in the context of a "Blessed Eucharist" ritual. So first we will set the stage for understanding how breaking bread originated within the Jewish idiom.

Washing of the Hands before Eating Bread

During Christ's time, the service of the twelve breads in the Temple was already about 1,500 years old and considered a hallowed event. Only the higher order of priests from Aaron's lineage could partake of these breads, and even they were required to bathe for ritual purification before entering the Temple and breaking and eating these breads. They would also wash their hands at the laver before sharing them, which is probably why the Pharisees in Christ's time washed their hands to the wrist before eating bread (more on this shortly).

In the Jewish tradition, the service of these twelve breads in the Temple was highly revered, and this filtered into other aspects of Jewish home life. While Temple priests were breaking bread on the Sabbath, so were many Jews in their homes breaking bread. And just as the priests washed before eating the bread, so a tradition arose among the Jews in their homes to do the same. This focus on washing the hands before bread is illustrated by the following quote from *The Jewish Encyclopedia* (under "Ablution"):

> The passage, Ps. xxvi. 6, "I will wash mine hands in innocency: **so will I compass thine altar, O Lord,**" also warrants the inference that Ablution of the hands is requisite **before performing any holy act**. This particular form of Ablution is the one which has survived most completely and is most practised by Jews. Before any meal **of which bread forms a part**, the **hands must be solemnly washed** and the appropriate benediction recited.[81]

First-century Jewish historian Josephus tells of a bread ritual adopted by the Essenes—one of the three Jewish factions he mentions (the others are the Sadducees and Pharisees). Clearly their bread service, with its washing for purification, emulated and was derived from the eating of the twelve Temple breads:

> They work until about 11 A.M. when they put on ritual loincloths and **bathe for purification**. Then they enter a communal hall, where no one else is allowed, and eat only one bowlful of food for each man, together with their **loaves of bread**. They eat in silence. Afterwards they lay aside their sacred garment and go back to work until the evening.[82]

Where would the Essenes have come up with such a ritual of bathing before partaking of bread? No likely answer exists other than the longstanding hallowed service in the Temple with the twelve breads, and the communal meals in the Temple.

---

81   *The Jewish Encyclopedia*, vol. 1, p. 68, s.v. "Ablution."
82   Josephus, "Wars," 2.8.5, http://essene.com/History/AncientHistoriansAndEssenes.html.

The Dead Sea Scrolls from Qumran also mention a revered service in which Jews gathered to eat bread after bathing for ritual purification (for more on this, see Course 6).

The fact that various Jewish groups kept services in which they first bathed and then ate bread connects back spiritually to those priests gathering each Sabbath in the Temple to break the twelve breads.

The dining table in the family home was revered and seen as more than just a piece of furniture because of its spiritual connection to the Showbread table and its religious uses in the Temple. This partially explains why Jews have a longstanding tradition of washing hands before eating bread and why certain prayers are prescribed before breaking bread in the home.

The following is from *Gateway to Judaism*:

> The table for the Jewish people, with its unique ceremonials, is an essential part of the Jewish religion. It is around the table that the ideals of Israel's home life find concrete expression. For the Jewish people the table is more than a piece of furniture upon which the daily meals are served. **It is a symbolic altar of God.**
>
> The religious **uses of tables in the Temple lend significance to the table in the Jewish home.** **The Table of Shew-bread** (Leviticus 24:6), the table for the lights (2 Chronicles 4:8), and the table for the sacrifices (Ezekiel 40:39), have a **symbolic counterpart in the home.**[83]

So we see that the Showbread table in the Temple lends significance to the table in the Jewish home in much the same way as breaking bread in the Temple lends significance to breaking bread in the Jewish home. The Jewish family dinner table became **an altar** of sorts, as each family meal was seen as an extension of God's provision in the Temple.

Twelve Sacred Breads Carried Forward in Jewish Daily Life

The Pharisees observed the tradition of washing their hands before eating bread long before the Messiah lived. This tradition was not a law that came from God, but most likely was a Pharisaic injunction that arose as an extension of the laws concerning eating the twelve breads in the Temple.

Mark 7:6–9 points out that the Pharisees were upset at Christ's disciples for not washing before eating bread; however, the Pharisees were following their own

---

83 Shulman, *Gateway to Judaism*, vol. 1, p. 441, s.v. "The table an altar."

traditions rather than God's law or God's heart on this matter. Here the scribes and Pharisees question Jesus concerning this:

> NAS Matthew 15:2 "Why do Your disciples transgress **the tradition of the elders**? For they **do not wash their hands** when they eat **bread**."

> KJV Mark 7:2 And when they saw some of his disciples **eat bread with defiled, that is to say, with unwashen, hands**, they found fault.

> YLT Mark 7:3 for the Pharisees, and all the Jews, if they do not **wash the hands to the wrist**, do not eat, holding the tradition of the elders.

The Pharisees forced this tradition so that all Israelites were to wash their hands before a meal *with bread*, a tradition that has been carried down to this day to some extent, as seen in the earlier quote from *The Jewish Encyclopedia*.

Breaking Bread on Different Occasions

Not only would the highest order of priests break bread in the Temple, but non-priestly Jews would also break bread at various times. It wasn't only on high holy occasions that bread was broken, as Isaiah and Jeremiah show:

> LXE Isaiah 58:7 **Break thy bread** to the hungry, and lead the unsheltered poor to thy house: if thou seest one naked, clothe *him*, and thou shalt not disregard the relations of thine own seed.

> JPS Jeremiah 16:7 neither shall men **break bread** for them in mourning, to comfort them for the dead; neither shall men give them the cup of consolation to drink for their father or for their mother.

The twelve Temple breads were considered a communal meal. Jewish tradition shows that meals that involved bread were set off as significant by the inclusion of special prayers, as explained in the following quotes from *Encyclopedia Judaica*:

> Grace after meals, a central feature of the liturgical service in the Jewish home....Grace after meals consists of four blessings and is recited only after a meal at which **bread** has been eaten.[84]

---

84 *Encyclopedia Judaica*, vol. 7, p. 838, s.v. "Grace After Meals."

> The rabbis ordained that whenever three or more have eaten **bread** together, one of them must summon the others to say Grace with him (Ber. 7:1–5).[85]
>
> The rabbis required a blessing before partaking of food since they considered it sacrilegious to "enjoy of this world without the proper benediction" (Ber. 35a). They instituted separate blessings for the various species of food, of which those over **bread and wine are considered the most important**.[86]
>
> The custom of **communal** grace, originally used only when the participants numbered at least ten, can be traced back to the custom of *havurah* ("community") meals, **held especially on the Sabbaths**.[87]

Even today for some who follow these traditions, different prayers are said when bread is *not* part of the Jewish communal meals:

> **When bread is not eaten** there are two other forms of grace (known as *Berakhah Aharonah*—"final benediction") to be recited, depending on the nature of the food consumed.[88]

When Talmudic scholars wrote of "breaking bread," as they often did, you can be sure they were not taking this reference from the Blessed Eucharist or copying a Roman ritual in any way. They were simply following an ancient Jewish tradition that originated with the breaking of the twelve "breads of the presence" every Sabbath—the same tradition that was handed down in Jewish homes, as seen on the Sabbath and at other times.

> Soncino Talmud Shabbath:
> R. Abba said: On the Sabbath it is one's duty to **break bread** over two loaves, for it is written, twice as much bread. R. Ashi said: I saw that R. Kahana held two [loaves] but **broke bread** over one, observing, 'they gathered' is written, R. Zera broke enough bread for the whole meal.[89]

---

85 *Encyclopedia Judaica*, vol. 7, p. 839, s.v. "Grace After Meals."
86 *Encyclopedia Judaica*, vol. 7, p. 841, s.v. "Grace Before Meals."
87 *Encyclopedia Judaica*, vol. 7, p. 840, s.v. "Grace After Meals."
88 *Encyclopedia Judaica*, vol. 7, p. 841, s.v. "Grace After Meals."
89 The Soncino Babylonian Talmud, Tractate Shabbath, Folio 117b, http://www.come-and-hear.com/shabbath/shabbath_117.html.

> Berakoth soncino Talmud: Folio 46a:
>
> Does not your honour accept the dictum of R. Johanan that **the host should break bread**? So he [R. Abbahu] **broke the bread** for them. When the time came for saying grace he said to him [R. Zera], Will your honour please say grace for us, He replied: Does your honour not accept the ruling of R. Huna from Babylon, who said that the one who **breaks bread** says grace? Whose view then did R. Abbahu accept? — That expressed by R. Johanan in the name of R. Simeon b. Yohai: **The host breaks bread** and the guest says grace. The host **breaks bread** so that he should do so generously, and the guest says grace so that he should bless the host.[90]

All of these quotes on breaking bread demonstrate that this long Jewish history of eating bread with a meal—to be considered a special occurrence—came from the hallowed Temple service with its table holding the twelve breads. Historical evidence certainly supports this, and examining this in more detail will lead us to understand that breaking bread also represented a *spiritual communion* to the Jewish Messianic believers.

Breaking Bread Spiritually

In "Setting the Table 4," we saw a long list of natural (literal) items in the Temple and Tabernacle that were applied spiritually by first-century Messianic Jews. They would frequently speak or write of a natural element or event in the Temple, but its real meaning would be the New Covenant spiritual truth that is pointed to.

Another example we could add to that long list: The *natural* breaking bread and the sharing of it that occurred in the Temple prefigured the *spiritual* breaking bread, the bread of life that was shared among New Covenant believers.

As we've seen before, the natural-to-spiritual idiom was very common among these first-century Jewish believers. Therefore, it should not be a stretch to understand that when Jews who had accepted the Messiah went out breaking bread, they were doing so spiritually; they were not performing a natural ritual that Jesus and his Jewish disciples neither wanted nor taught.

When the priests gathered in the Holy Place with the Showbread to break bread, this also pointed forward to the spiritual bread that **we break**:

> YLT 1 Corinthians 10:16b   the bread that **we** break—is it not the fellowship of the body of the Christ?

---

[90] The Soncino Babylonian Talmud, Tractate Berakoth, Folio 46a, http://www.come-and-hear.com/berakoth/berakoth_46.html.

> NAS 1 Corinthians 10:17   Since there is **one bread**, **we who are many** are **one body**; for we all partake of the one bread.

The priests who fellowshipped and broke the twelve breads in the Temple pointed to the New Covenant believers and the *true bread* that we break and share, just as the manna—the "bread" of heaven—pointed to the true bread of which we spiritually partake:

> NAS John 6:32   Jesus therefore said to them, "Truly, truly, I say to you, it is not Moses who has given you the bread out of heaven, but it is My Father who gives you **the true bread** out of heaven.

Jesus here speaks of himself as the "true bread," the true spiritual bread from God. This is what his disciples would later go out "breaking" and sharing—his words, teachings, and God's presence by His spirit that was dwelling in their midst. This pattern of things in the Tabernacle that God gave to Moses (including the "bread of the presence" or Showbread) reveals spiritual truths that are to be understood in the New Covenant:

> NAS Hebrews 8:4–5   Now if He were on earth, He would not be a priest at all, since there are those who offer the gifts according to the Law; who serve **a copy and shadow** of the heavenly things, just as Moses was warned *by God* when he was about to erect the tabernacle; for, "See," He says, "that you make all things **according to the pattern** which was shown you on the mountain."

We know that Christ is the true pattern that we are to be formed into, and as we partake of the spiritual bread of life, we—as one spiritual body—are growing up into him:

> NAS Ephesians 4:15–16   but speaking the truth in love, we are to grow up in all *aspects* into Him, who is the head, *even* Christ, from whom the whole body, being fitted and held together **by that which every joint supplies**, according to **the proper working of each individual part**, causes the growth of the body for the building up of itself in love.

Returning to Paul's analogy taken directly from the Last Supper teaching of Jesus, "**we** who are many are one body" and "we all partake of the one bread":

> NAS 1 Corinthians 10:17 Since there is one bread, we who are many are one body; for we all partake of the one bread.

This is the bread that **we** break; it is the spiritual fellowship in the spiritual body. As we partake of Christ in and through one another as members of his spiritual body, we are becoming the pattern that God wants for us.

The twelve breads that came from the people's wheat offerings represented the twelve tribes of Israel, and the priests would partake of these twelve breads and receive nourishment from them. So in the same sense, we—as the pieces of the *one* bread that make up the *one* spiritual body of Christ—partake of spiritual food in and through one another and receive spiritual nourishment "by that which every joint supplies." This causes the growth of the body "for the building up of itself in love" (Ephesians 4:16 above).

The "bread that we break"—and share and partake of—is the true "bread of the presence," the true altar of which "we" the believers may partake:

> NAS Hebrews 13:10 **We** have an altar, from which those who serve the tabernacle have no right to eat.

Paul is not speaking of a literal altar or of literal eating; he is speaking figuratively of partaking *spiritually* from a spiritual altar. Earlier we saw Albert Shulman's quote from *Gateway to Judaism*, in which he spoke of the Showbread table in the Temple having a symbolic counterpart in the Jewish home. As we will see shortly from the Book of Acts, early Messianic Jews understood that the spiritual bread they were breaking was the spiritual counterpart to the breaking of the Temple Showbread. Thus, all believers can feed spiritually on the bread of life at the Lord's table:

> NAS 1 Corinthians 10:21 You cannot drink the cup of the Lord and the cup of demons; you cannot partake of **the table of the Lord** and the table of demons.

We partake of the table of the Lord spiritually, and we drink the spiritual cup of the New Covenant that the Lord provides. As Paul says above, we are not to partake of what demons may offer us (also meant spiritually) at their table.

In speaking of the "table of the Lord" just a few verses after mentioning the "bread that *we* break" (verse 16), Paul again connects the Corinthians' spiritual partaking with the Showbread table in the Temple. Clearly, this breaking of bread among early Messianic followers was built upon the long history of breaking bread every Sabbath in the Temple, as they applied it spiritually in the New Covenant, to sharing the true bread of life.

Did "Breaking Bread" Mean Either Common Meals or a Ritual of Communion?

By not considering the existing first-century Jewish idioms, many Bible commentators remain unsure as to precisely what "breaking bread" in Acts 2 and elsewhere means. They erroneously believe it refers to sharing common meals or to celebrating the ritual of Communion (also called the "Lord's Supper" or "Eucharist").

> KJV Acts 2:42 And they continued stedfastly in the apostles' doctrine and fellowship, and in **breaking of bread**, and in prayers.

> KJV Acts 2:46 And they, continuing daily with one accord in the temple, and **breaking bread from house to house**, did eat their meat with gladness and singleness of heart,

Below are the views of various commentators as to what occurred in Acts 2.

Matthew Henry, *Matthew Henry's Commentary on the Whole Bible*:

> They frequently joined in **the ordinance** of the Lord's supper. They continued *in the breaking of bread*, in celebrating that memorial of their Master's death…. They broke bread from house to house; κατ' οικον—*house by house*; **they did not think it fit to celebrate the eucharist in the temple**, for that was **peculiar to the Christian institutes**, and therefore they administered that ordinance in private houses….[91]

Adam Clarke, *Clarke's Commentary*:

> *And in breaking of bread* —Whether this means the holy eucharist, or their common meals, it is difficult to say.[92]

Albert Barnes, *Barnes' Notes on the New Testament*:

> It cannot, however, be determined whether this refers to their partaking of their ordinary food together, or to feasts of charity, or to the Lord's Supper.[93]

---

[91] Henry, *Matthew Henry's Commentary*, vol. 6, p. 28.
[92] Clarke, *Clarke's Commentary*, vol. 3, p. 700.
[93] Barnes, *Barnes' Notes*, p. 392.

Jamieson, Fausset, and Brown, *A Commentary, Critical, Experimental, and Practical, on the Old and New Testaments*:

> ... it seems pretty certain that partaking of the Lord's Supper is what is here meant. But just as when the Lord's Supper was first instituted it was preceded by the full paschal meal, so a frugal repast seems for a considerable time to have preceded the Eucharistic feast.[94]

J. P. Lange, *A Commentary on the Holy Scriptures: Critical, Doctrinal and Homiletical*

> —Breaking bread from house to house—They naturally observe their peculiar holy rite, the Sacrament of the new covenant, apart from the public.[95]

Notice above that Lange, an excellent commentator, realizes the difficulties of conducting such a peculiar ritual in first-century Jerusalem by saying that they observe this rite "apart from the public."

Many otherwise scrupulous commentators, who were good men of God but were nevertheless influenced by some 1,500 years of Roman tradition surrounding the Communion ritual, view these first-century Jews as going around Jerusalem or the Temple celebrating a Roman ritual of the Eucharist. Does this seriously sound right for first-century Jews in Jerusalem? Does this align with the previous Jewish idiom of breaking bread that we've seen?

The answer is no; these interpretations miss the truth. The following English translation gives a closer sense of what the believers were doing in the second chapter of Acts:

> [DBY] Acts 2:42–43 And they persevered in the teaching and fellowship of the apostles, **in breaking of bread** and prayers. And fear was upon every soul, and many wonders and signs took place through the apostles' means.

> [DBY] Acts 2:46 And every day, **being constantly in the temple** with one accord, and **breaking bread in *the* house**, they received their food with gladness and simplicity of heart,

---

94   Jamieson, Fausset, and Brown, *A Commentary*, vol. 3, p. 15.
95   Lange, *A Commentary on the Holy Scriptures,* vol. 4, p. 59.

Notice that Darby translates this verse *not* as breaking bread "at every house" or "from house to house," as most English translations do, but as breaking bread "in *the* house."

Just as the twelve breads were broken in the "house"—often short for the house of God[96]—so are the New Covenant believers gathering to break spiritual bread in the house of God. The spiritual bread is the bread that we break, the true bread, the bread of life.

Additionally, the same Greek word *kat*, when used with "house," is translated as "in" several times in other scriptures (Romans 16:5, Philippians 1:2, etc.). Below, fourth-century theologian John Chrysostom agrees with this aspect of Darby's translation in his Homily 7, on Acts 2:46:

> And this honor too passed over to the place; **the eating in the house**. In what house? **In the Temple**.

We will return to Acts 2:46 shortly. But first, when trying to understand what the Jewish believers were doing here at the Temple and possibly elsewhere in Acts, we have to place ourselves in the first-century Jewish idiom ***of the Temple*** and view these scriptures through these believers' eyes. The *Encyclopedia Judaica* sets out the framework for the Temple service:

> The Daily Service
>
> The essential element of the daily Temple service was the offering of the *tamid*[97] sacrifice of two lambs, one in the morning, with which the service began, and one in the afternoon, with which it concluded....
>
> In the second Temple, prayers, blessing and **Pentateuchal readings** were added to the Temple service. **After the offering of the incense**, the priests gathered together on the steps of the entrance hall and blessed the assembled people with the Priestly blessing (Tam. 7:2)....
>
> **During the offering of the incense the people used to gather in the azarah for prayer.** The libation of wine at the conclusion of every tamid sacrifice was accompanied by levitical singing. After the

---

96   See the Greek in Luke 11:51; also see Psalm 127:1; 1 Kings 6:3, 14, 15.
97   "Tamid" means the "continual" daily lamb offering.

service the members of the division of Israelites deputed to accompany the daily Temple services **gathered for Scripture reading and prayer**.[98]

Notice the main aspects of this Temple service:
- The people assembled together.
- An offering of incense was made (which was symbolic of *the prayers* of the Israelites).
- And they gathered for *sharing the word of God and prayer*.

The New Covenant Jewish believers also assembled in the Temple during the morning and evening sacrifices and for the incense offerings and prayers that followed, but they were also sharing the scriptures and the Messiah's teachings. They referred to this sharing as "breaking bread," which was meant in a spiritual sense.

※※※

Although it is somewhat difficult to interpret and know the exact idiom, another instance in the Talmud clearly connects "breaking bread" to the **reading** of the law in the Temple and Synagogue. It starts by relating that Moses gave the law to the priests:

> GEMARA. [A PRIEST IS CALLED UP FIRST TO **READ THE LAW**]. What is the warrant for this? — R. Mattenah said: Because Scripture says, And Moses wrote this law and gave it to the priests the sons of Levi.

As it continues, it refers to the one who "breaks bread," and the rabbi who comments on this connects it to **the reading** in the Synagogue:

> The one who **breaks bread** helps himself to the dish first, but if he wishes to pay respect to his teacher or to a superior he may do so. **Commenting on this**, the Master said: This applies only to **the table**, but not to the synagogue, since there such deference might lead to quarrelling. R. Mattenah said: What you have said about the synagogue is true only on Sabbaths and Festivals, when there is a large congregation, but not on Mondays and Thursdays. Is that so? Did not R. Huna **read** as kohen even on Sabbaths and Festivals? —

---

98   *Encyclopedia Judaica*, vol. 15, p. 974, s.v. "Temple/The Daily Service."

> R. Huna was different, since even R. Ammi and R. Assi who were the most distinguished kohanim of Eretz Israel paid deference to him. Abaye said: We assume the rule to be that if there is no kohen there, the arrangement no longer holds. Abaye further said: We have it on tradition that if there is no Levite there, a kohen **reads** in his place. Is that so? Has not R. Johanan said that one kohen should not **read** after another, because this might cast a suspicion on the first, and one Levite should not **read** after another because this might cast a suspicion on both? — What we meant was that the same kohen [should **read** in the place of the Levite].[99]

In the mention of the **table** quoted above, clearly an understanding exists, gleaned from the service with the table (of Showbread) in the Temple, that points spiritually to the sharing of the scriptures in the Synagogue.

Jesus often taught in the Temple, as it was common for people to gather and discuss the word of God there:

> DBY Acts 2:42 And they persevered in the teaching and fellowship of the apostles, in **breaking of bread and prayers**.

By backing up His word with miracles, God was powerfully anointing the apostles with His spirit as they shared with all who were willing to hear:

> YLT Acts 2:43 And fear came on every soul, **many wonders also and signs were being done through the apostles,**

> DBY Acts 2:46 And **every day, being constantly in the temple with one accord, and breaking bread in *the* house**, they received their food with gladness and simplicity of heart,

So if Darby's translation conveys the true meaning here in Acts, this would be another proof that it was spiritual bread the apostles were breaking (i.e., sharing the word of God and the bread of life), since they were not allowed to bring their daily meals to the Temple. (For those who have noticed the phrase "they received their food" in

---

99 The Soncino Babylonian Talmud, Tractate Gittin, Folio 59b, http://www.come-and-hear.com/gittin/gittin_59.html.

the scripture above, the Greek word for "food" often refers to spiritual nourishment; we will return to this aspect shortly.)

The different occasions when the people would gather in the Temple were accompanied by the sharing of God's word, as we see in Nehemiah:

> NIV Nehemiah 8:18   Day after day, from the first day to the last, **Ezra read from the Book of the Law of God**. They celebrated the feast for seven days, and on the eighth day, in accordance with the regulation, there was an assembly.

Below in Acts, we see that Peter and John were often going up to the Temple *at the ninth hour*, which was the time that Israelites would be gathered for the evening Temple sacrifice and the prayers and scripture reading that followed:

> YLT Acts 3:1   And Peter and John were going up at the same time **to the temple**, at the hour of **the prayer, the ninth**[100] *hour*,

The Greek imperfect tense here ("were going up") shows this was their habitual custom. Peter and John were going up to the Temple at this time because all the people had gathered there for the daily evening sacrifice and the incense offering that floated heavenward, representing the prayers of the saints being accepted by God. This gave the disciples a chance to teach truth from the Messiah and to share God's word, *spiritually* breaking bread.

As mentioned before, the Temple was often called the *house* (short for "house of God"), with the word of God as the spiritual "food" (Hebrews 5:12, 14; 1 Corinthians 3:2; 10:3) that they were partaking of in Acts 2:46. We see that Jeremiah figuratively ate the word of God:

> NAS Jeremiah 15:16   **Thy words were found and I ate them**, And Thy words became for me a joy and the delight of my heart; For I have been called by Thy name, O LORD God of hosts.

And Ezekiel ate the word of God:

> NAS Ezekiel 3:1–3   Then He said to me, "Son of man, eat what you find; **eat this scroll**, and go, speak to the house of Israel." So I opened my mouth, and He fed me this scroll. And He said to me,

---

[100] Josephus also confirms this time for the evening daily sacrifice, saying it was "about the ninth hour" (Whiston, *The New Complete Works of Josephus*, Antiquities, 14.4.3, p. 459).

"Son of man, feed your stomach, and **fill your body with this scroll** which I am giving you." Then I ate it, and it was sweet as honey in my mouth.

We see another instance of the people gathering for prayer when the priest (who was the father of John the Baptist but prior to John's birth) offers the incense in the Temple:

> NAS Luke 1:8–10 Now it came about, while he was performing his priestly service before God in the *appointed* order of his division, according to the custom of the priestly office, he was chosen by lot to enter the temple of the Lord and burn incense. **And the whole multitude of the people were in prayer** outside **at the hour of the incense offering.**

King David and the more spiritual Jews knew that this incense offering represented God accepting their prayers, having come after the sacrifice:

> NAS Psalm 141:2 May **my prayer** be counted **as incense before Thee**; The lifting up of my hands as the evening offering.

Most scholars agree that the Book of Acts was written around 30 years after the Crucifixion and the pouring out of God's spirit at Pentecost. By this time, this spiritual idiom of breaking bread was commonly understood by the believers.

They Weren't Just Sharing Common "Meals"

We've seen that many commentaries concerning the breaking of bread in the book of Acts suggest that this meant either eating regular meals—akin to church picnics—or celebrating the Communion ritual, also referred to as the "Eucharist" or "Lord's Supper." They interpret the breaking of bread naturally (literally) as a new Lord's Supper ritual, not *spiritually* or within the existing Jewish idiom.

Neither of these natural options—a regular meal or a ritual celebration—was what the first-century spiritual followers of the Messiah had in mind as they entered the New Covenant, were filled with God's spirit, and then witnessed the powerful miracles being done among them. So, let's cover the reasons why these natural options are incorrect, starting with refuting the belief that they were just sharing common "meals."

> YLT Acts 2:42–43 and they were continuing stedfastly in the teaching of the apostles, and the fellowship, and the breaking of the bread,

and the prayers. **And fear came on every soul, many wonders also and signs were being done** through the apostles,

> ᵞᴸᵀ Acts 2:46   Daily also continuing with one accord in the temple, **breaking also at every house bread,** they were partaking of food in gladness and simplicity of heart,

As we saw already, the Darby translation for this verse reads, "breaking bread *in the house*" (short for the *house of God—the Temple*). This is one viable way to translate it:

> ᴰᴮᵞ Acts 2:46   And every day, **being constantly in the temple with one accord, and breaking bread in *the* house**, they received their food with gladness and simplicity of heart,

In the Darby translation, the English word "and" has been *added* just before "breaking bread," but it does not appear in the Greek. This small addition in some translations changes the meaning to "meeting in the Temple *and* breaking bread at their houses":

> ᴷᴶⱽ Acts 2:46   And they, continuing daily with one accord **in the temple, and** breaking bread **from house to house**, did eat their meat with gladness and singleness of heart,

Without the added "and" and when translating the rest of the verse correctly, the meaning could be "constantly in the temple with one accord, breaking bread in the house." My point here is that without the additional "and," the reader more properly connects the house as *being* the temple instead of potentially interpreting "the temple" and "the house" as two different locations. Most commentators connect this breaking bread to the *supposed* ritual, understanding this could not occur in the Temple but that it must have been in private homes, and therefore translate it according to their belief.

Another possible translation from the Greek is "breaking bread *just as* the house," "*corresponding to* the house," or "*according to* the house." The Greek preposition *kat* is translated as "every" (i.e., every house) in many English translations, but the *UBS Greek-English Dictionary* gives the following definition:

> according to, corresponding to, with reference to, just as … [101]

---

101   *UBS Greek-English Dictionary*, p. 92, s.v. "κατά."

Kat is used often with *oikous* (houses) in the Septuagint, where it is often translated as "*according to* the houses," as below:

> ^{LXE} Numbers 1:2   Take the sum of all the congregation of Israel according to their kindreds, **according to the houses** of their fathers' families, according to their number by their names, according to their heads: every male

> ^{LXT} Numbers 1:2   λάβετε ἀρχὴν πάσης συναγωγῆς υἱῶν Ισραηλ κατὰ συγγενείας αὐτῶν **κατ' οἴκους** πατριῶν αὐτῶν κατὰ ἀριθμὸν ἐξ ὀνόματος αὐτῶν κατὰ κεφαλὴν αὐτῶν πᾶς ἄρσην

As the *UBS* points out, *kat* is often translated as "according to" in the New Testament as well:

> ^{NAS} Colossians 3:10   and have put on the new self who is being renewed to a true knowledge **according to** the image of the One who created him

> ^{GNT} Colossians 3:10   καὶ ἐνδυσάμενοι τὸν νέον τὸν ἀνακαινούμενον εἰς ἐπίγνωσιν **κατ'** εἰκόνα τοῦ κτίσαντος αὐτόν,

Returning now to Acts 2:46 with this definition of *kat* in mind, the scripture could then mean that the apostles were spiritually fulfilling the "breaking bread" *according to* the house (i.e., Showbread in God's house).

In other words, since the disciples were constantly in the Temple, it's a distinct possibility that Acts 2:46 is not portraying that the disciples are teaching or breaking bread at *every house*, but rather that they are teaching and breaking bread "according to" or "corresponding to" the breaking of the twelve breads that took place in the house of God. This option would show their understanding that the spiritual bread they were breaking corresponded to the natural bread that was broken and shared in God's house. At the very least, we know they understood that the Messiah was the bread of life, and their breaking bread would have included sharing the word of God that had come through him.

Whether or not the apostles were breaking bread "according to the house," "corresponding to the house," "in the house," or (as many English translations say) at "every house," their focus was not on *natural* bread. At this momentously historical time—when they were now filled with God's spirit—they were breaking and sharing the true bread, the bread of life.

We know that the following historical points are true, so therefore let us consider whether, after taking these facts into account, sharing meals "at every house" is what these first-century Jews were really concerned with and were writing about in Acts 2:

- These Jews had waited hundreds upon hundreds of years for their promised Messiah, who then came and was then crucified.

- The believers thought it was all somehow a mistake (Luke 24:14–27), for they were not expecting the Messiah to die, even though he had told them that he would be crucified.

- They then realized that God had raised the Messiah from the dead, and Jesus walked among them for 40 days, showing forth powerful signs and teaching them before ascending to heaven right in their midst (Acts 1:1–11).

- Just before he ascended, the believers were told by Jesus to tarry in Jerusalem, waiting for the "promise of the Father." This came down on the day of Pentecost when they were all filled with the Holy Spirit of God (with powerful signs and miracles following), fulfilling the promise of God through Joel that He would pour out his spirit upon all flesh (Joel 2:28). Whereas previously only the high priest could enter the holiest place where God's presence dwelt—and only once a year at that—now these common fishermen and other Messianic followers had God's holy presence infill and engulf them daily.

- Then, as Acts 2:43 shows, great fear was falling upon every soul, for God Himself was now right in their midst (see also Acts 5:12–16), and "many wonders and also signs were being done among the Apostles."

- According to Acts 2:46, the believers were partaking of meals (or "nourishment" in the Greek, meaning spiritual nourishment here) in "gladness" and simplicity of heart. The same Greek word translated as "meals" in the *NAS* also denotes spiritual food in Hebrews 5:12. However, the Greek word translated into English as "gladness" (*NAS*) is more correctly translated along the lines of "a piercing exclamation, exultation ... full of exultation, joy" (*BDAG Lexicon*) or as "a state of intensive joy and gladness, often implying verbal expression and body movement (for example, jumping, leaping, dancing)—'to be extremely joyful, to rejoice greatly, extreme gladness.'"[102]

After all this history, we are then told by commentators to picture these spiritual Jews meeting for the purpose of breaking bread in a ritual, or for a regular natural meal.

To further illustrate this common-meal view held by some commentators, here is a hypothetical conversation:

James, the Lord's brother: Wow, isn't this "food" great!

Peter: Yes, these meals sure are great! Could you pass me three more breads to break? This is great stuff; I'm really glad to have such nice meals. Isn't this fun? I feel extremely joyful! Could you pass me the butter?

Stephen: Yes, and wasn't it great being filled with God's spirit at the Temple? Excuse me, John, could you hand me another bread and a leg of lamb? This is incredible food, and I feel glad, too.

James: Growing up with Jesus as my brother, I knew he was very special, but I never considered in those days that he was really the Messiah. Could you pass me a few more breads, some dip, and another lamb shank? This is food is tremendous; I sure feel glad.

Peter: Hey, let's keep going from house to house breaking bread. I'm just really enjoying this. Whose house are we going to break bread at next?

Stephen: I don't know whose house we'll visit next, but I am going to start having to watch my waistline! These breads are just too good... Could you pass me a few more lamb shanks, and another "cup of blessing?" (1 Corinthians 10:16)

Peter: Anyone want to "break bread" and split this last one? This is causing me to feel incredible joy!

---

[102] Louw and Nida, *Greek-English Lexicon of the New Testament Based on Semantic Domains*, vol. 1, p. 303, s.v. "ἀγαλλίασις."

We should not believe for a minute that this is what the Book of Acts is conveying when it speaks of breaking bread. The idea that these Jews who had walked with the Messiah continually "devoted themselves" (Acts 2:46, NAB) to common meals does not fit with reality.

These spiritual followers of the Messiah were breaking *spiritual* bread in a state of "extreme joy and gladness" and, as the *Lexicon* above showed, it may have involved "jumping, leaping, and dancing" before the Lord at times. They were awestruck that God Himself was right in their midst, showing forth signs and powerful miracles through the apostles. They were acting just like David did when the Ark came back into Jerusalem:

> NAS 2 Samuel 6:14–15   And David **was dancing before the LORD with all *his* might**, and David was wearing a linen ephod. So David and **all the house of Israel were bringing up the ark of the LORD with shouting** and the sound of the trumpet.

The breaking of bread in Acts 2 (and also Acts 20:7–11, see Course 4) is spiritual bread, the bread from heaven, and the true bread (John 6:32). The Messiah's followers shared this bread of life in the Temple, where they often met at Solomon's portico (Acts 2:46; 5:12):

> NIV John 6:32   Jesus said to them, "I tell you the truth, it is not Moses who has given you the bread from heaven, but it is my Father who gives you the true bread from heaven.

> NAS John 6:35   Jesus said to them, "**I am the bread of life**; he who comes to Me shall not hunger, and he who believes in Me shall never thirst.

They did not have any New Covenant scriptures yet; instead, they were sharing the words of Christ—"the true bread"—and the many things he said and did, and who he was. They were also sharing great joy that God's presence was among them, after seeing the many Old Covenant scriptures that spoke of Christ and were fulfilled by him. And their experience was nothing less than what the Jews experienced under Solomon, when God's presence came down at the Temple:

> NAS 1 Kings 8:10   And it came about when the priests came from the holy place, that the cloud filled the house of the LORD,

>   ᴸˣᴱ 1 Kings 8:11   And **the priests could not stand to minister** because of the cloud, because the glory of the Lord filled **the house**.

These priests encountered a powerful glory at Solomon's Temple and the first-century Israelites also experienced things that were exceedingly profound. Although they were filled with great joy, fear was also close at hand, for to have God's spirit so closely in their midst was overwhelming and humbling.

The focus was not on fun meals and church picnics, but on the powerful moving of God's spirit and feeding on the Messiah's spiritual nourishment, the word of God, and all that the Last Supper parables pointed to.

They Weren't Partaking in a New Roman Catholic/Christian/Protestant Ritual

So far we've shown that the commentators' theory—that breaking bread (as seen in Acts 2) meant sharing a natural meal—falls short of the reality. Now let's turn to the reasons why these first-century, spirit-filled disciples of the Messiah were not celebrating the Roman ritual of Communion when these believers mentioned breaking bread.

Transport yourself for a few minutes to first-century Israel, with its strict laws and Jewish history, and discern if the following reenactment bears witness to how this might have gone:

> *Knock, knock, knock!* The Jewish followers of the Messiah knock on the door of a Jewish home in Jerusalem and exclaim, "Shalom, we are the apostles! We're here to celebrate a new ritual, the Blessed Eucharist! Here, have a piece of bread: This is the body of Jesus who was recently crucified. And here, have a sip from this cup: This is his blood."
>
> Later that same evening Habib, the eldest son, speaks up: "Why is it, Father, that they kept calling it the Lord's Supper, but all we got was that one morsel of bread? That was barely even a snack. Also, Father, if the morsel and the sip of juice was really what they say it was, will that not render us unclean according to the Jewish kosher food laws that Moses gave us, and therefore prevent us from entering the Temple tomorrow for the services?"
>
> Father responds, "Son, you ask many questions. Your uncle Zedekiah is the highest-ranking Pharisee on the Sanhedrin. He's stopping by on his way to the evening Temple service tomorrow, and surely he will have answers for this new ritual."

Although many people since the days of Rome have thought this is what these scriptures really *meant*, it is clear that this Catholic breaking-bread scenario could not have taken place in first-century Jerusalem. The Jews had been commanded by God to avoid ingesting any manner of blood lest they be cut off from the nation, since the life was in the blood, which was given at the altar to provide atonement. Because of this, Jewish society has always had a great aversion to blood (Leviticus 7:27; 17:10–11, 14).

Consider this quote we saw earlier in Course 1: Even the high priest was to be whipped (stripes applied) if he should ever ingest blood, just as if he had eaten a reptile or consumed leaven during the Passover:

> MISHNA *I*.: To the following stripes apply:
>
> …**A high-priest** who was unclean and partook of things belonging to the sanctuary or entered the sanctuary while unclean; **and he who consumed** illegal fat, **blood**, or meat left overnight from the sacrifice…; **he who ate leaven on Passover**…; who ate carcasses or animals preyed by beasts, or reptiles—**to all of them stripes apply**.[103]

However, the Gentiles had not walked under God's commandments concerning the ingesting of blood. So when the Gentiles started coming to God, Jewish believers in the New Covenant had to warn them to ***avoid blood*** (Acts 15:19–20, 29; 21:25). And the scriptures did not say to abstain from blood "except during the new ritual"; they simply said to abstain from blood, because no such ritual was kept by the Jewish believers to begin with.

The truth of the matter is that no such ritual[104] ever existed in Israel in the first century. It was a later invention created mostly by the Roman Catholic Church as a result of having misunderstood the Jewish idioms concerning breaking bread, communion, and what the Messiah really meant at the Last Supper. Its prevalence would come about only when the Church deliberately forsook traditional Jewish idioms and understandings.

As we have seen, some Gentiles did not share the same Jewish aversion to ingesting blood. Therefore, they misunderstood the Jewish scriptures (John 6 and 1 Corinthians 10 and 11) and eventually ended up believing in the ritual of Communion still held

---

103 Babylonian Talmud, Book 9, Tract Maccoth, ch. 3, p. 35, http://sacred-texts.com/jud/t09/mac08.htm.

104 As seen in the chapter "The Ritual—Why Didn't the Jewish Disciples Teach It?"

today, in which priests are believed to actually change bread and wine into Christ's flesh and blood. Below, *The Catholic Encyclopedia* speaks of the "Mass," a piece of bread that, to Catholics, is the flesh of Christ as a current sacrifice. The following quote shows that they believe this is what is meant by the "breaking of bread" in Acts:

> *1. Precepts for the Promotion of the Dignity of the Sacrifice*
> (a) One of the most important requisites for the worthy celebration of the Mass is that the place in which the all-holy Mystery is to be celebrated should be a suitable one. Since, in the days of the Apostolic Church, there were no churches or chapels, private houses with suitable accommodation were appointed for the solemnization of "**the breaking of bread**" (cf. Acts 2:46; 20:7 sg.; Colossians 4:15; Philemon 2).[105]

This is from *The Catholic Encyclopedia*, under "Holy Communion":

> That Holy Communion may be received not only validly, but also fruitfully, certain dispositions both of body and of soul are required. For the former, a person must be fasting from the previous midnight from everything in the nature of food or drink.[106]

Since the Roman Catholic Church teaches that the bread and wine changes into Christ's flesh and blood during their ritual, they would not want it to mix with common food in the stomach; hence the requirement to abstain from other food before the ritual.

By now, it should be easy to discern if this talk of the Communion ritual sounds first-century Jewish or of Roman origin.

So far, we have seen the following progression:

1. God gave the service of the twelve breads in the temple to Moses, and after the priests washed, these breads were broken and shared on the Sabbath.

2. The Jewish Essenes held a sacred service that involved ritual bathing before eating breads.

---

105 Herbermann et al, *The Catholic Encyclopedia*, vol. 10, p. 20, s.v. "Mass."
106 Herbermann et al, *The Catholic Encyclopedia*, vol. 7, p. 402, s.v. "Holy Communion."

3. The Therapeutae, another Jewish group in Egypt, held a similar service that required ritual bathing before eating breads, and Philo specifically stated that it emulated the Temple breads. (This will be covered in Course 6, pages 194–195.)

4. The Jewish Pharisees washed their hands to the wrist before eating bread.

5. Talmudic writers, who in a sense were spiritual descendants of the Pharisees, often spoke of breaking bread and of special prayers that were to be said before eating any bread.

6. Jewish Messianic followers, with their clear natural-to-spiritual idiom, went forth breaking bread, but we see that they often meant this in the spiritual sense of partaking of the true bread—the bread of life.

7. In Rome, people were instructed to have nothing in common with the Jews (as per Constantine's edict; see "Setting the Table 1"). The Roman Church held its own ritualistic service of breaking bread (the Blessed Eucharist) in the belief that this Communion ritual was what the New Testament scriptures referred to.

In Rome, the sacking of Jerusalem by Roman emperor Titus is commemorated in the Arch of Titus. It depicts the Roman troops carrying off, among other items, the golden table of Showbread to Rome. Not only was this table for the twelve breads taken to Rome, but so were the many truths on breaking bread in the Jewish idiom—gone to Rome and not seen since.

However, with many Jews now coming back into a covenant relationship with God and His spirit moving upon all people who are willing, God is restoring many truths that became obscured (including those surrounding the breaking of bread), so that we may understand their true meaning.

We need to be sure that we are not continuing to view these scriptures through Roman or even Protestant glasses, but understanding them through the original spiritual idiom of first-century Jewish believers. Otherwise we will perpetuate something the Messiah never intended. After all, God is not looking for ritual communion with literal bread, but true spiritual communion with and among His people.

COURSE 4

BREAKING BREAD SPIRITUALLY—
THE PROGRESSION

The events leading up to God's spirit being poured out upon the believers (Acts 2) help to define the *breaking bread* that took place among them. In this Course we will look closely at those events and see the progression that shaped this idiom among early Messianic believers.

Since the scripture tells us that God led the Messiah to almost always speak in parables, wouldn't it make sense that the God-inspired New Covenant scriptures contain truths that are also somewhat hidden but revealed to those whose hearts are open to Him?

In the Old Covenant as well, many of God's teachings could be understood only spiritually. The learned man reads, but he cannot understand:

> JPS Isaiah 29:11   And the vision of all this is become unto you as the words of a writing that is sealed, which men deliver to one that is learned, saying: 'Read this, I pray thee'; and he saith: 'I cannot, for it is sealed';

Paul speaks of this as well:

> YLT 1 Corinthians 2:13   which things also we speak, not in words taught by human wisdom, but in those taught by the Holy Spirit, **with spiritual things spiritual things comparing**,

> YLT 1 Corinthians 2:14   and the natural man doth not receive the things of the Spirit of God, for to him they are foolishness, and he is not able to know *them*, **because spiritually they are discerned**;

In Course 3, we saw the progression from priests breaking bread (Showbread) in the Temple to Jewish families breaking bread in their homes to Jews in the New Covenant breaking bread spiritually. We also saw why Acts 2:42–46 makes no sense when interpreted as a new Roman ritual or as a church picnic.

Now we'll more closely examine the events leading up to the breaking of bread, as written in the Book of Acts (chapters 2 and 20) from the perspective of the Jewish disciples of the Messiah who entered the promised New Covenant. As we go through these scriptures, keep in mind the Jewish history we've covered concerning breaking bread, from the twelve breads of the presence to Isaiah's and Jeremiah's references, all the way to the Talmudic references to breaking bread. Then, we'll overlay this with the New Covenant understanding of how all the natural things in the Tabernacle/Temple were used to bring out spiritual truths (as listed in Setting the Table 4).

An Overview of the Progression

Later in this Course we'll delve into greater detail, but first let's start with a brief overview of breaking bread among first-century Jewish believers, divided into the following five phases. We first see Jesus breaking natural bread, which in the Jewish natural-to-spiritual idiom leads to the understanding of breaking bread spiritually—a sharing of God's word, with His presence and the Messiah spiritually in the midst. Whenever we see the breaking of bread in the New Covenant scriptures, an element of the miraculous is often connected to it.

Phase 1: Jesus Miraculously "Breaks Bread" Twice to Feed the Multitudes

Jesus "broke" five breads (Mark 6:41), then "broke" another seven breads (Mark 8:6), thus breaking twelve breads in total in the two events. He fed the multitudes with these *twelve* breads that he "broke" out to them. At one of these miraculous feedings Jesus compared himself to the manna, the "*bread* from heaven." He then declared that he was the true *bread* and the living *bread*.

Shortly after the second miracle, Jesus spoke of the "leaven" of the Pharisees (meaning their false teachings). The disciples, however, thought he was speaking of natural bread—the remaining bread that they had forgotten to bring along. He then reminded them of the (twelve) breads that he had broken at the two events, and said, "How is it that you do not understand" (Matthew 16:6–12; Mark 8:13–21).

After one of the breaking-bread miracles, Jesus told the people to gather up remaining pieces of bread, "that not any be lost" (John 6:12). This pronoun "any" can mean "anyone, anything, someone, something…".[107] Was Jesus literally caring for the pieces of bread, or was he pointing forward to what the remaining fragments represented—the scattered twelve tribes of the Diaspora?

> [NAB] James 1:1 James, a slave of God and of the Lord Jesus Christ, to the **twelve tribes** in the dispersion, greetings.

---

107 *UBS Greek-English Dictionary*, pp. 182–183, s.v. "τις."

Eventually the twelve apostles (including Judas's replacement, Matthias) would go forth to gather the *spiritual* "pieces" of the bread, the lost sheep of the house of Israel. Before his death, many Jews had believed Jesus was the Messiah (John 12:19), then thousands more came to believe at Pentecost, and then another five thousand (Acts 4:4), as well as a great company of Temple priests (Acts 6:7). Then these disciples wrote letters, calling out to the Jews of the Diaspora (James 1:1, Peter 1:1) as they sought to bring in the pieces of the bread, that "no one be lost." Ultimately this extended to all people being called from all nations.

Phase 2: Jesus "Breaks Bread" at the Last Supper in a Parable

At the Last Supper, Jesus held one bread, then broke it into pieces, gave it to those present to partake of, and then said, "This is my body." The original Greek text clearly shows that Jesus did not mean that the one bread he held was literally his body, but that the broken pieces represented his spiritual body and pointed to the spiritual bread that he would provide in the New Covenant. Christ's spiritual body would be the true presence bread, as he manifests in and through his spiritual body (with the believers as members of his body). From this Last Supper parable, the apostles came to understand what Jesus meant, so they went forth teaching that *we* are now the body of Christ spiritually, and individually members of it (as covered in Course 2).

Phase 3: Jesus Becomes Invisible Just as He "Breaks Bread" Right after His Resurrection

Right after his Resurrection, Jesus walked with some of his disciples, but God withheld their eyes from recognizing who he was (Luke 24). Then Jesus entered their home, and in the moment when he began breaking bread and giving it to them, they immediately recognized him—and he vanished from their sight (Luke 24:30–31).

Phase 4: Jesus Reappears and Is Recognized "in the Breaking of the Bread"

These same disciples then ran to where the apostles were gathered in Jerusalem and explained that they had just seen the resurrected Messiah and that they had recognized him "in the breaking of the bread." Amazingly, at the exact moment they were speaking about recognizing him, Jesus again miraculously appeared in their midst (Luke 24:33–36). So Jesus became invisible in the "breaking of the bread," then appeared again (in their midst) in the "breaking of the bread."

Phase 5: The Disciples Go Forth in God's Spirit "Breaking Bread" Spiritually

Several weeks later at the Festival of Pentecost (Acts 2), the disciples—who were symbolically pieces of the one bread—were filled with God's spirit, essentially becoming what the presence bread/Showbread pointed to. By the time the book of Acts was written some 30 years later, a common idiom and understanding existed that the "breaking of the bread" meant experiencing Christ and the word of God in the fellowship of the believers. This was what the priests sharing the presence bread in the Temple had pointed to. By now the disciples understood that they were living in the promised New Covenant and were fully accustomed to the natural-to-spiritual idiom of breaking bread.

The Bread That *We* Break

Paul speaks of the bread that we break and shows that it is spiritual bread, meaning the fellowship of the believers in the spiritual body of Christ:

> YLT 1 Corinthians 10:16b   the bread that **we** break—is it not the fellowship of the body of the Christ?

In the very next verse, Paul shows that we are (figuratively) pieces of the one bread that Jesus held and then broke at the Last Supper, that we are the members of the one body (of Christ), and that we all—the fellowship of the believers—feed on and partake spiritually of this one spiritual bread:

> NAS 1 Corinthians 10:17   Since there is one bread, we who are many are one body; for we all partake of the one bread.

We must remember that the Bible is a few thousand years of history condensed into one book, and therefore we are given only short bits of conversation. We can be sure that after Jesus became invisible (while breaking bread) and then reappeared just as the disciples were discussing the breaking of the bread, many hours of heated debate would have ensued as to what this all meant. The disciples would surely have talked about the Lord, saying that whenever two or three are gathered in his name he is there in the midst (Matthew 18:20). They would have discussed what Jesus meant when he broke the bread and fed the multitudes in the two miracles with the twelve breads. They would have contemplated what the Messiah really meant when he broke bread at the Last Supper and said its pieces were his body. They would have considered what the twelve breads that the priests broke in the Temple every Sabbath pointed to. They would have come to understand that, as pieces of the one bread, they essentially represented the "breads of the presence," for after Pentecost they knew that God's spirit dwelt within them:

> NAS 1 Corinthians 3:16   Do you not know that you are a temple of God, and *that* the Spirit of God dwells in you?

This is how their natural-to-spiritual idiom of breaking bread would have developed, whereby they would know that God's spirit was present as they gathered together and broke bread spiritually.

As we turn to look at Acts 2, it's worth mentioning again that scholars largely agree that the Book of Acts was written around 30 years after the Crucifixion and God's spirit falling at Pentecost. By this time, the believers were very familiar with the spiritual idiom of breaking bread, which had already been well established long before the Book of Acts was written. These believers would have had those three decades to ponder and discuss these events and to understand the idiom concerning both natural and spiritual breaking of bread.

> ^{NAS} 1 Corinthians 15:46   However, the spiritual is not first, but the natural; **then the spiritual.**

It is essential to understand all the spiritual teachings concerning breaking bread that led up to Acts 2, as well as the more than 1,500 years of this Jewish idiom, for only then can we understand the true meaning of these scriptures:

> ^{NAS} Acts 2:42   And they were continually devoting themselves to the apostles' teaching and to fellowship, to the **breaking of bread** and to prayer.

> ^{GNT} Acts 2:42   ἦσαν δὲ προσκαρτεροῦντες τῇ διδαχῇ τῶν ἀποστόλων καὶ τῇ **κοινωνίᾳ**, τῇ κλάσει τοῦ ἄρτου καὶ ταῖς προσευχαῖς.

The Greek word *koinonia*, translated here as "fellowship," is the same word used above in 1 Corinthians 10:16 for fellowship (sometimes translated as "communion"). The believers were *not* continually devoting themselves to a Communion ritual, but to the true spiritual communion that they were experiencing with God's very presence dwelling among them.

It must be remembered that in the long history of the Jewish nation, the believers had never before experienced God's spirit dwelling directly within them, although He was often with them from a distance. This was a powerful new experience for them. In the Old Covenant, their sins were never fully expiated, and thus the high priest would have to enter the Temple with the blood of the sacrifice each new year on the Day of Atonement. However, in the New Covenant we are sanctified and brought near to God by the true sacrifice of the Messiah. So this would have been a shocking phenomenon in their time when, on the day of Pentecost, God began filling them directly with His Holy Spirit.

Getting back to Acts 2:42, there is only one other place in the Bible where this exact same Greek word for "breaking" occurs, and that is in Luke 24:35, which took place seven weeks earlier, on the day of the Resurrection:

> NAS Luke 24:35 And they *began* to relate their experiences on the road and how He was recognized by them **in the breaking of the bread**.

Young's Literal Translation translates this verse as:

> YLT Luke 24:35 and they were telling the things in the way, and how he was **made known to them** in the breaking of the bread,

Then Jesus immediately appeared again in their midst, right as they were speaking about the breaking-bread experience:

> NAS Luke 24:36 And **while** they were telling these things, He Himself stood in their midst.

The following scriptures relate this account of them first recognizing Jesus as he took out bread and broke it out to them:

> NAS Luke 24:30 And it came about that when He had reclined *at the table* with them, He took the bread and blessed *it*, and breaking *it*, He *began* giving *it* to them.

> NAS Luke 24:31 And their eyes were opened and they recognized Him; and He vanished from their sight.

His invisible presence in the breaking of bread was the beginning of the spiritual fulfillment of the promise he had previously made:

> NAS Matthew 18:20 "For where two or three have gathered together in My name, there I am in their midst."

About seven weeks after the Messiah's Last Supper bread parable and after he was revealed to them in the breaking of bread, we come to Pentecost. Here, God's spirit is poured out on the believers (Acts 2), and again we see them *breaking bread*:

> Acts 2:42 "continually devoting themselves to the apostles' teaching and to the fellowship, to the breaking of bread and to prayer."

So let's look again at Acts 2:42 through the eyes of the first-century Jewish believers who had grown up going to the Temple at the time of the daily sacrifices, and for the morning and evening prayers and the scripture reading that followed. As we saw in Course 3, the *Encyclopedia Judaica* describes this well:

> The Daily Service
>
> In the second Temple, **prayers**, blessing and **Pentateuchal readings** were added to the Temple service. After the offering of the incense, the priests gathered together on the steps of the entrance hall and blessed the assembled people with the Priestly blessing (Tam. 7:2)…
> During the offering of the incense the people used to gather in the azarah for prayer. The libation of wine at the conclusion of every tamid sacrifice was accompanied by levitical singing. After the service the members of the division of Israelites deputed to accompany the daily Temple services **gathered for Scripture reading and prayer.**[108]

This description with prayers and Pentateuchal readings fits perfectly with that given in the Book of Acts, where the fellowship of the believers is described as the "breaking of the bread" (which was a spiritual depiction of sharing God's word) and the prayers:

> YLT Acts 2:42 and they were continuing stedfastly in the teaching of the apostles, and the fellowship, *and* the breaking of the bread, and the prayers.

> GNT Acts 2:42 ἦσαν δὲ προσκαρτεροῦντες τῇ διδαχῇ τῶν ἀποστόλων καὶ τῇ κοινωνίᾳ, τῇ κλάσει τοῦ ἄρτου καὶ ταῖς προσευχαῖς.

In the Greek, there is no "*and*" (italicized by me, above) after "the fellowship"; this has been incorrectly inserted into the English translation. I believe that by dropping "and," this Greek construction is revealed to be appositional,[109] showing that their "fellowship/communion" *was* the "breaking of the bread and the prayers," just as we saw in the quote from the *Encyclopedia Judaica*.

---

108 *Encyclopedia Judaica*, vol. 15, p. 974, s.v. "Temple/The Daily Service."
109 Walvoord and Zuck, *The Bible Knowledge Commentary (New Testament)*, p. 360.

Continuing in the Jewish idiom of drawing out spiritual truths from the natural service in the Temple, believers were now breaking bread figuratively with the Messiah spiritually in their midst as they met at Solomon's Porch in the Temple (Acts 3:11; 5:12)—the same location where the Messiah had often taught (John 10:23).

In his work *Greek Grammar Beyond the Basics*, Daniel B. Wallace examines this Greek construction in Acts 2:42 and shows two options[110] for understanding it. I believe that the first option he gives is the correct one:

> Either this pattern of worship was well known in the early church because it was the *common* manner in which it was done, or…[111]

Wallace writes this not to connect it to Jewish history but to demonstrate a result of the structure and wording of the Greek text. But we see from the earlier quote of the Daily Service in the Temple that this service in the form of Pentateuchal readings and prayers was the common method of worship in first-century Jerusalem. We also know that early believers in the Messiah continued this same method of worship for some time with extra emphasis, revelation, and spiritual understanding. Additionally, they experienced powerful miracles, which often happened among them as God's spirit moved:

> NIV Acts 2:43 Everyone was filled with awe,[112] and many wonders and miraculous signs were done by the apostles.

It is clear that in the natural-to-spiritual idiom of these early believers, the spiritual fellowship/communion (*koinonia*, Acts 2:42) meant the sharing of the word of God (breaking the true bread) and the prayers.[113] And we see that the New Covenant believers used this same idiom by referring to the time of the scripture reading and sharing as "breaking bread," meaning sharing God's word as it came from Moses and the prophets, but also sharing Christ and his words—the bread of heaven, the bread of life.

This term "breaking bread" was so common among the believers that it was also used to denote their gathering together on the first day of the week (our Sunday) to share and hear God's word:

---

110 The other option Wallace gives is "… or Luke was attempting to convey that each element of the worship was the only one deserving of the name (*par excellence*)."
111 Wallace, *Greek Grammar Beyond the Basics*, p. 225.
112 The Greek word translated into English as "awe" can also mean fear, dread, terror, reverence (for God), etc.
113 See also Luke 1:8–17 for the incense offering.

> YLT Acts 20:7 And **on the first of the week**, the disciples having been gathered together **to break bread**, Paul was discoursing to them, about to depart on the morrow, he was also **continuing the discourse till midnight**,

The stated reason for their gathering was "to break bread"; again this did not mean natural but *spiritual* bread, as they could thus delve more deeply into the scriptures while among Messianic believers of like understanding. Many believers were still going to the Synagogue on the Saturday Sabbath[114] and also meeting the following day where they could more freely share their understandings in the Messiah. This was the very purpose of their gathering: to share the word of God and partake of the spiritual nourishment, as verse 11 continues:

> YLT Acts 20:11 and having come up, and having broken bread, and having **tasted**, for a long time also having talked—**till daylight**, so he went forth,

These spiritually minded Jews were not breaking bread in a ritual until daybreak, nor were they sharing an all-night Christian picnic; they were tasting spiritual food and the true bread that Paul was sharing as they gathered together. The *UBS Greek-English Dictionary* shows that this word "tasted" can also mean "experience." This same Greek word translated as "tasted" above is also used in the following scriptures, where it speaks of *spiritually* tasting or experiencing:

> NAS Hebrews 6:4 For in the case of those who have once been enlightened and have **tasted** of the heavenly gift and have been made partakers of the Holy Spirit,

> NAS Hebrews 6:5 and have **tasted** the good word of God and the powers of the age to come,

The Jews were familiar with this Greek word because it was the same one used in the Greek Septuagint when David told the people to "taste" and see that the Lord was good:

> NAS Psalm 34:8 O **taste** and see that the LORD is good; How blessed is the man who takes refuge in Him!

---

114 Acts 9:2, 20; 13:5; 14:1; 26:11, etc.

David speaks again of tasting below, showing their common Jewish idiom of spiritually tasting God's word:

> KJV Psalm 119:103   How sweet are **thy words** unto my **taste**! *yea, sweeter* than honey to my mouth!

These men of God were not gathering together in Acts 20 with the main purpose of eating natural food or to celebrate the "Blessed Eucharist" ritual until daylight. The Greek shows that they were coming together to *spiritually* break bread, and it was their conversing and experiencing the word of God that constituted the breaking bread:

> YLT Acts 20:11   and having come up, and having broken bread, and having **tasted,** for a long time **also** having talked—**till daylight**, so he went forth,

According to the *UBS*, the Greek word translated as "also" above can also mean "and so." This definition fits much better in this context, where it means "***and so*** having discussed till daybreak, so he went forth." Their breaking bread referred to tasting and experiencing the word of God, which they shared and discussed until daylight.

No Roman Church existed at this time, so the ritual of Communion was not something these Jews partook of. Nor did Jesus ever say anything about a Communion ritual. These were men and women of God who had recently been filled with God's spirit, believers who were coming to share the words of the Messiah and to fellowship in spiritual things. Ultimately they came to fully understand that Yeshua (Jesus) and God's spirit would be in their midst in the spiritual breaking of bread.

This also aligns with the spiritual "meals" of which they were partaking in Acts 2:

> NAS Acts 2:46   And day by day continuing with one mind in the temple, and breaking bread from house to house, they were taking their **meals** together with gladness and sincerity of heart,

The Greek word for "meals" was often used for spiritual meals. It is also used in the scriptures below where it is translated as "food," again meaning spiritual food:

> NAS Hebrews 5:12 For though by this time you ought to be teachers, you have need again for someone to teach you the elementary principles of the oracles of God, and you have come to need milk and not solid **food.**

> ᴺᴬˢ Hebrews 5:14   But solid **food** is for the mature, who because of practice have their senses trained to discern good and evil.

Using another Greek word for food, Jesus shows this same concept of spiritual food:

> ᴺᴬˢ John 4:34   Jesus said to them, "My **food** is to do the will of Him who sent Me, and to accomplish His work.

And one more example from Paul:

> ᴺᴬˢ 1 Corinthians 3:2   I gave you milk to drink, not **solid food**; for you were not yet able *to receive it*. Indeed, even now you are not yet able,

Below Paul shows the believers receiving spiritual nourishment as members of the spiritual body stay connected to one another. He further shows that nourishment comes from the head, then to and through the "joints and bands" (the Greek means "ligaments and connections") in the body:

> ᴷᴶⱽ Colossians 2:19   And not holding the Head, from which **all the body by joints and bands** having **nourishment** ministered, and knit together, increaseth with the increase of God.

Once again, this concept of spiritual food was a common idiomatic way of speaking in the New Covenant, one well understood by the early Messianic believers.

As John Lightfoot states:

> "There was nothing more common in the schools of the Jews than the phrase of 'eating and drinking' **in a metaphorical sense**."[115]

It was only as the church was taken over by Rome that these words were reinterpreted as a natural (literal) ritual called Communion, the Blessed Eucharist, or Mass. However, neither God nor the Messiah was seeking a natural ritual, but true spiritual fellowship and communion:

> ᴺᴬˢ John 14:23   Jesus answered and said to him, "If anyone loves Me, he will keep My word; and My Father will love him, and **We will come to him**, and make Our abode with him.

---

[115] Lightfoot, *Commentary on the New Testament from the Talmud and Hebraica,* vol. 3, p. 307.

^NAS^ 1 John 1:3   what we have seen and heard we proclaim to you also, that you also may have fellowship with us; and indeed **our fellowship**[116] **is with the Father, and with His Son Jesus Christ**.

What, Regular Bread during the Festival?

At this point, let's turn our attention to a potentially huge problem that I have never seen addressed. Luke 24 states that Jesus breaks bread, and this occurs right during the Festival of Unleavened Bread. Since the Last Supper was not the Passover,[117] there was no problem with Jesus eating regular bread, as all the scriptures say. However, the events in Luke 24 take place a few days into this seven-day Festival during which, according to the law, all leaven was forbidden lest one be cut off from the nation (Exodus 12:15, 19).

There are a few possible ways to explain this. One plausible explanation is that such a ruckus was happening in the Temple, what with darkness covering the land until the ninth hour, the veil being torn in half, the earth shaking, and rocks splitting (Matthew 27:51), that the authorities decided to choose the option allowed by God to defer the Passover to the second month. The Talmud gives an example of a Passover being thus put off for a month when a man was crushed in the Temple.[118] Because of his death and the ritual uncleanness it caused, the Passover was celebrated on the 14th day of the second month instead (Numbers 9:1–14).

However, another option exists that I believe is the actual answer to this problem. We know that the disciples eventually understood that, after the Resurrection, they were no longer under Old Covenant law since the shed blood of Christ had now brought them into the promised New Covenant. The most obvious way that Jesus could show them this on the day of his Resurrection was by bringing out regular leavened bread and breaking it out to them. It was during this time of shock in seeing regular bread during the Passover Festival that God opened their eyes to recognize Jesus, and then, before they could even react, he disappeared. Then these two disciples ran out of the house to tell the apostles in Jerusalem how Jesus was made known to them during the *breaking of the bread*, and as they said this, he immediately appeared in their midst, just in case there were any questions!

This breaking of regular bread would not have been a sin, for after the Resurrection, the believers were no longer under the law of Moses but the promised New Covenant.

---

116   The Greek word for "fellowship" is *koinonia*, which is often translated as "communion."
117   See "Course 1: Last Supper Ritual or Parable? The Messiah Held One *Leavened* Bread," "The Three Major Greek Keys That Unlock the Gospels," and "50 Reasons the Last Supper Was Not the Passover."
118   Babylonian Talmud, Book 3, Tract Pesachim (Passover), ch. 5, pp. 119 and 121, http://sacred-texts.com/jud/t03/psc09.htm.

This would have been the most obvious sign that they were no longer under the restrictions of the ceremonial law with all its sacrificial offerings, purification rituals, and other regulations for the body (Hebrews 9:10). Jesus really did not need to say anything more, for the disciples would eventually put all these spiritual clues together and understand them as they went forward. No one could accuse the disciples of sinning, for they had run out of the house as soon as they saw the bread; if the authorities had wanted to accuse the resurrected Jesus of sin, they would have had to find him first.

Although the disciples were slowly coming to understand that they were no longer under the law of Moses, for some time they continued their activities in the Temple as they had always done, offering the same required sacrifices and purifications before entering. Here we see Paul giving notice of such:

> NAS Acts 21:26 Then Paul took the men, and the next day, purifying himself along with them, went into the temple, **giving notice of the completion of the days of purification**, until the sacrifice was offered for each one of them.

For these spiritual Jews, their entire lives had revolved around the Temple, and when the Messiah and the New Covenant came, this did not change immediately. Eventually, however, they would understand that they were no longer under the law of the first covenant, yet to enter the Temple they still needed to follow protocol according to the law, as enforced by the Temple authorities.

Many commentators think this was all just a plan to make it look like Paul and the Jewish believers really kept the law when in actuality they were not keeping it. They think the transition from the Old Covenant into the New Covenant was immediate. I do not believe this, since the believers clearly did continue keeping various aspects of the law for some time, and the big debate in Acts 15 was only whether the *Gentiles* should be circumcised—not whether the Jews should continue this practice. It was Paul who moved most quickly out of the ceremonial law, as he had received the most revelation.

It was true, as he was accused of doing (Acts 21:20, 21), that Paul taught Jews in foreign lands that they did not need to be circumcised or to follow the law of Moses, for he understood better than those in Jerusalem just how far out of the law the believers were to come. Those living in Jerusalem would not have fared well if they had boycotted the sacrifices (those refusing the Passover were cut off according to the law), taught against circumcision, refused the Sabbaths, or tried to enter the Temple in any kind of ritually impure state. So while he was teaching and sharing the word of God in Jerusalem, the Jewish Paul also observed the tenets of the law as required by the authorities for any Jews entering the Temple:

> NAS 1 Corinthians 9:20 And to the Jews I became as a Jew, that I might win Jews; to those who are under the Law, as under the Law, though not being myself under the Law, that I might win those who are under the Law;

The First-Fruits Offering Before Eating the Bread in the Promised Land

Under the law of Moses, when the Israelites entered the Promised Land, they were to give a sheaf of wheat as a first-fruits offering to God *before* they could eat any grain or **bread** from the Promised Land. This offering was to come soon after Passover, on the morrow of the first Saturday Sabbath that followed (i.e., Sunday). Thus, this would have happened in the Temple on the very same morning that Christ was raised. Christ arose sometime before sunrise on the third day after his crucifixion, just as he had told his disciples he would (Luke 24:1 and 21; Mark 16:9).

> NAS 1 Corinthians 15:20 But now Christ has been raised from the dead, the **first fruits** of those who are asleep.

This scripture reveals that the Messiah's Resurrection actually fulfilled the "first-fruits" offering. At some point, the Pharisees changed this offering from the morrow of the Saturday Sabbath to the morrow of the 15th-day Sabbath of the Passover Festival (i.e., the 16th day of Nisan). But God raised the Messiah as the true first fruits on the morrow of the Saturday Sabbath, as He had intended from the beginning.

This first-fruits offering and the subsequent ability to eat of "bread" in the *natural* Promised Land points forward to the spiritual bread of which the believers would soon begin partaking in the *spiritual* Promised Land. Only after the first-fruits offering (consisting of Christ himself) had been accepted by God could the believers partake of the true spiritual bread from the Promised Land:

> NAS Leviticus 23:10–11 "Speak to the sons of Israel, and say to them, 'When you enter the land which I am going to give to you and reap its harvest, then you shall bring in the sheaf of the **first fruits** of your harvest to the priest. 'And he shall wave the sheaf before the LORD **for you to be accepted**; on the day after the sabbath the priest shall wave it.

> NAS Leviticus 23:14 '**Until this same day**, until you have brought in the offering of your God, **you shall eat neither bread nor roasted grain nor new growth**. It is to be a perpetual statute throughout your generations in all your dwelling places.

Thus Christ fulfilled the first-fruits typology[119] at his Resurrection, just as a few days previously he had also fulfilled the type of the Passover, having been slain on that predetermined 14th day of Nisan according to God's plan (Acts 2:23). The bread that he broke out to them on this morrow of the Sabbath (Luke 24:30, 31), after which he disappeared but remained spiritually in their midst, pointed to the true spiritual bread that they could now share and partake of from the true Promised Land.

The Lost Tribes of the Diaspora

Many people today are descended from the Israelites without realizing it. In our day this does not make anyone closer to God, but it's only to say that many were dispersed from the tribes in Israel to other nations during various wars and persecutions, and later they became a part of the countries in which they settled.

Diaspora is a Greek word that means "dispersion" or "scattered." It was used to refer to the Jews who lived outside the borders of Israel and Judah. We see the first-century Jewish writers of the New Testament reaching out to these dispersed Jews probably as a result, at least in part, of the parables Jesus taught when he broke bread, miraculously multiplied the twelve breads out to the hungry, and told the disciples to gather up the remaining pieces. Here we see James writing to the Israelites of the dispersion:

> YLT James 1:1 James, of God and of the Lord Jesus Christ a servant, to the **Twelve Tribes** who are in the **dispersion**: Hail!

> GNT James 1:1 Ἰάκωβος θεοῦ καὶ κυρίου Ἰησοῦ Χριστοῦ δοῦλος ταῖς δώδεκα φυλαῖς ταῖς ἐν τῇ **διασπορᾷ** χαίρειν.

And here is Peter writing to these dispersed Israelites:

> NAB 1 Peter 1:1 Peter, an apostle of Jesus Christ, to the chosen sojourners of the **dispersion** in Pontus, Galatia, Cappadocia, Asia, and Bithynia,

> GNT 1 Peter 1:1 Πέτρος ἀπόστολος Ἰησοῦ Χριστοῦ ἐκλεκτοῖς παρεπιδήμοις **διασπορᾶς** Πόντου, Γαλατίας, Καππαδοκίας, Ἀσίας καὶ Βιθυνίας,

---

119 In typology, the *type* is an element or event in the Old Testament that prefigures the fulfillment of it (the *antitype*) in the New Testament. Adapted from *Theopedia.com*, s.v. "Biblical typology."

In the two miracles when Jesus broke the twelve breads (five at the first miracle, then seven at the next), there may reside a few truths in these figurative pieces of bread that pointed to this gathering of the dispersed tribes.

The Talmud states that the high priest had authority over *five* loaves of the Showbread (see also 1 Samuel 21:3). After he took his portion for him and his sons, the remaining *seven* loaves were divided (broken out) among the other priests (Tractate Yoma). This is noteworthy because these numbers five and seven are echoed in the two miracles of Jesus breaking and multiplying bread. The disciples would later picture Jesus as a high priest after the order of Melchizedek (Psalm 110:4; Hebrews 5 and 7).

Was Jesus referring to the scattered tribes of Israel when he said to be sure to gather up the (twelve) baskets of bread fragments? (Note that in Greek the word *klasmata*, which is translated below as "fragments," literally means "pieces of the break.")

> NAS John 6:12 And when they were filled, He said to His disciples, "**Gather up** the leftover **fragments** that nothing may be lost."

> GNT John 6:12 ὡς δὲ ἐνεπλήσθησαν, λέγει τοῖς μαθηταῖς αὐτοῦ, Συναγάγετε τὰ περισσεύσαντα **κλάσματα**, ἵνα μή τι ἀπόληται.

If Jesus did not intend this as a parable, why is he so concerned with gathering up the leftover bread? Also, the word he uses for "gather up" is the Greek word for "synagogue," which means "gather together" as defined by the *UBS Greek-English Dictionary*. So Jesus says to "synagogue" (assemble or gather together) the pieces of the "break."

Jesus has his disciples gather up the fragments of bread so that not "anything/any one" be lost. He is not concerned about the remaining bits of bread in a literal sense, but about the dispersed twelve tribes that represent the scattered fragments of the *spiritual* bread.

> KJV John 17:12 While I was with them in the world, I kept them in thy name: those that thou gavest me I have kept, **and none of them is lost**, but the son of perdition; that the scripture might be fulfilled.

We should not be surprised by how many baskets are filled when the disciples gather together all the remaining pieces of bread:

> DBY John 6:13 They **gathered** *them* therefore together, and filled **twelve** hand-baskets full of fragments of the five barley loaves, which were over and above to those that had eaten.

When Jesus would again break bread at the Last Supper, this would take on another meaning, for in that parable Jesus showed them that as believers, they were the pieces of the one bread, as Paul understood:

> ᴺᴬˢ 1 Corinthians 10:17   Since there is one bread, **we who are many** are one body; for we all partake of the one bread.

During the Messiah's three-and-a-half-year ministry, God sent him only to the house of Israel:

> ᴺᴬˢ Matthew 15:24   But He answered and said, "I was sent only to the lost sheep of the house of Israel."

But in the New Covenant, after his death he became a light to the Diaspora and also to the Gentiles:

> ᴺᴬˢ John 10:16   "And I have other sheep, which are not of this fold; I must bring them also, and they shall hear My voice; and they shall become one flock *with* one shepherd.

Isaiah shows how the Messiah will be a light to the Gentiles and also gather the dispersed of Israel:

> ᴸˣᴱ Isaiah 11:10   And in that day there shall be **a root of Jesse**, and he that shall arise to rule over the Gentiles; **in him shall the Gentiles trust**, and his rest shall be glorious.

> ᴺᴬˢ Isaiah 11:12   And He will lift up a standard for the nations, And will **assemble the banished ones of Israel**, And will **gather the dispersed of Judah** From the four corners of the earth.

When the Messiah broke and multiplied the twelve breads, the apostles came to understand that Jesus was alluding to this aspect of his ministry of reaching out to those of the Diaspora (dispersed). This coincided with their understanding that the bread they were then breaking and multiplying was the spiritual bread:

> ʸᴸᵀ Acts 6:7   And **the word of God did increase**, and **the number of the disciples did multiply** in Jerusalem exceedingly; **a great multitude** also of the priests were obedient to the faith.

> NAS Acts 12:24   But **the word of the Lord** continued to grow and to be **multiplied**.

They comprehended that the Messiah was the word (*logos*) of God manifested (John 1:14, Revelation 19:13), and by extension so was his spiritual body, the pieces of the one bread.

⁂

After the second miracle of breaking breads out to the hungry multitude had occurred and the disciples had forgotten to bring along the leftover bread fragments, the Lord shows no concern for the lost *natural* bread. However, he seems to shed additional light on the twelve breads being symbolic, possibly first connecting to the Showbread and by extension to the twelve tribes of Israel:

> NAS Mark 8:8   And they ate and were satisfied; and they picked up seven large baskets full of what was left over of the broken pieces.

> KJV Mark 8:14   Now *the disciples* had forgotten to take bread, neither had they in the ship with them more than one loaf.

> NAS Mark 8:15–20   And He was giving orders to them, saying, "Watch out! Beware of the **leaven** of the Pharisees and the **leaven** of Herod." And they *began* to discuss with one another *the fact* that they had no bread. And Jesus, aware of this, said to them, "Why do you discuss *the fact* that you have no bread? **Do you not yet see or understand?** Do you have a hardened heart? "Having eyes, do you not see? And having ears, do you not hear? And do you not remember, when I broke the **five** loaves for the five thousand, how many baskets full of broken pieces you picked up?" They said to Him, "**Twelve**." "And when *I broke* the **seven** for the four thousand, how many large baskets full of broken pieces did you pick up?" And they said to Him, "Seven."

> NAS Mark 8:21   And He was saying to them, "**Do you not yet understand?**"

Twelve and seven were, of course, symbolically important numbers among the Jews. When one apostle (Judas) died, why not leave it at just eleven apostles? No; it was decided that it was important to add another, so there would be twelve (Acts 1:15–26).

When men full of the Holy Spirit were needed for a certain ministry, the apostles appointed seven (verse 3 below).

> ^{KJV} Acts 6:1   And in those days, when the number of the disciples was multiplied, there arose a murmuring of the Grecians against the Hebrews, because their widows were neglected in the daily ministration.

> ^{NAS} Acts 6:2   And **the twelve summoned** the congregation of the disciples and said, "It is not desirable for us to neglect the word of God in order to serve tables.

> ^{NAS} Acts 6:3   "But select from among you, brethren, **seven** men of **good reputation, full of the Spirit and of wisdom**, whom we may put in charge of this task.

They chose *seven* men to fulfill this ministry, and these chosen seven were not waiters cleaning the tables but men of God with special talents.

> ^{NAS} Acts 6:5–7   And the statement found approval with the whole congregation; and they chose Stephen, **a man full of faith and of the Holy Spirit**, and Philip, Prochorus, Nicanor, Timon, Parmenas and Nicolas, a proselyte from Antioch. And these they brought before the apostles; and after praying, they laid their hands on them. And **the word of God kept on spreading**; and the number of the disciples continued to increase greatly in Jerusalem, and a great many of the priests were becoming obedient to the faith.

Notice that these seven men were performing powerful miracles and evangelizing:

> ^{NAS} Acts 6:8   And Stephen, full of grace and power, **was performing great wonders and signs among the people**.

> ^{NAS} Acts 21:8   And on the next day we departed and came to Caesarea; and entering the house of **Philip the evangelist, who was one of the seven**, we stayed with him.

Among the believers, being an evangelist was one of the leadership positions that the Lord gave as a gift for the perfecting of those called out:

> ^{NAS} Ephesians 4:11   And He gave some *as* apostles, and some *as* prophets, and some *as* evangelists, and some *as* pastors and teachers,

These seven men were certainly not just serving *natural* food at tables (Acts 6:2 further above), as the translation seems to imply, because they held anointed positions with God flowing through them in miracles and evangelizing. You do not need seven "men of good reputation, full of the Spirit and of wisdom" to serve natural food or to clean the tables. The "Grecians" mentioned in Acts 6:1, meaning Greek-speaking Jews here (according to commentator Lightfoot), could have done those things themselves.

The same Greek word translated as "ministration" (Acts 6:1 above) is translated as "ministry" ***of the spirit*** in 2 Corinthians 3:8 (NAS). Remember that the Messianic believers had been assembling in that part of the Temple called Solomon's Porch, where many signs and wonders were taking place (Acts 3:11; 5:12). The apostles may have been studying the Hebrew scrolls in the Temple, or even teaching from the Hebrew, and therefore needed others to go minister the word to those Greek-speaking Jews.

The Promise of the Messiah Was to Recover Those Who Were Scattered

In the Greek Septuagint, which was commonly read by Jews in the first century, we see God's promises to the Diaspora (these twelve tribes of Israel who would be scattered):

> ^{JPS} Deuteronomy 30:4   If any of thine that are **dispersed** be in the uttermost parts of heaven, from thence will the LORD thy God gather thee, and from thence will He fetch thee.

> ^{LXT} Deuteronomy 30:4   ἐὰν ᾖ ἡ **διασπορά** σου ἀπ' ἄκρου τοῦ οὐρανοῦ ἕως ἄκρου τοῦ οὐρανοῦ ἐκεῖθεν συνάξει σε κύριος ὁ θεός σου καὶ ἐκεῖθεν λήμψεταί σε κύριος ὁ θεός σου

> ^{NAS} Nehemiah 1:9   but if you return to Me and keep My commandments and do them, though those of you who have been **scattered** were in the most remote part of the heavens, I will gather them from there and will bring them to the place where I have chosen to cause My name to dwell.'

^{LXT} Nehemiah 1:9   καὶ ἐὰν ἐπιστρέψητε πρός με καὶ φυλάξητε τὰς ἐντολάς μου καὶ ποιήσητε αὐτάς ἐὰν ᾖ ἡ **διασπορὰ** ὑμῶν ἀπ᾽ ἄκρου τοῦ οὐρανοῦ ἐκεῖθεν συνάξω αὐτοὺς καὶ εἰσάξω αὐτοὺς εἰς τὸν τόπον ὃν ἐξελεξάμην κατασκηνῶσαι τὸ ὄνομά μου ἐκεῖ

Isaiah showed that the Messiah would be *the covenant* to a family/nation, which the Messiah revealed would be from one father—God—and that the family/nation would then receive spiritual light to see and be a part of His kingdom.

^{LXE} Isaiah 49:6   And he said to me, *It is* a great thing for thee to be called my servant, to establish the tribes of Jacob, and **to recover the dispersion** of Israel: behold, I have given **thee for the covenant** of a race, for **a light of the Gentiles**, that thou shouldest be for salvation to the end of the earth.

^{LXT} Isaiah 49:6   καὶ εἶπέν μοι μέγα σοί ἐστιν τοῦ κληθῆναί σε παῖδά μου τοῦ στῆσαι τὰς φυλὰς Ιακωβ καὶ τὴν **διασπορὰν** τοῦ Ισραηλ ἐπιστρέψαι ἰδοὺ τέθεικά σε εἰς διαθήκην **γένους** εἰς φῶς ἐθνῶν τοῦ εἶναί σε εἰς σωτηρίαν ἕως ἐσχάτου τῆς γῆς

The Greek word for "race" above speaks of family, nation, or ancestral stock coming from one father such as Abraham. Jesus uses a similar word that the English scriptures usually translate as "born again":

^{NAS} John 3:3   Jesus answered and said to him, "Truly, truly, I say to you, unless one is **born again**, he cannot see the kingdom of God."

^{GNT} John 3:3   ἀπεκρίθη Ἰησοῦς καὶ εἶπεν αὐτῷ, Ἀμὴν ἀμὴν λέγω σοι, ἐὰν μή τις **γεννηθῇ ἄνωθεν**, οὐ δύναται ἰδεῖν τὴν βασιλείαν τοῦ θεοῦ.

The Greek word translated here as "again" actually means "from above." It does not really mean "born again" but instead speaks of being birthed or generated from above by God's spirit and then becoming part of His family/nation, whereby one's sins are forgiven and one's spirit, which was "dead" in sin (Isaiah 59:2), is given new life.

When Jewish writers of the New Testament wrote to these Jews of the Diaspora, they did not compel them to return to the land of Israel, for they knew that this was not how the Messiah was leading. One example was his response to the Samaritan woman who speaks at the start of this scripture:

> ᴺᴬˢ John 4:20 "Our fathers worshiped in this mountain, and you *people* say that in Jerusalem is the place where men ought to worship."
>
> ᴺᴬˢ John 4:21–23 Jesus said to her, "Woman, believe Me, an hour is coming when **neither in this mountain, nor in Jerusalem**, shall you worship the Father. "You worship that which you do not know; we worship that which we know, for salvation is from the Jews. "But an hour is coming, and now is, when the true worshipers shall worship the Father **in spirit and truth**; for such people the Father seeks to be His worshipers.

The disciples knew that the Messiah was not called to gather all the Jews back to Israel, but rather to fulfill the covenant with Abraham by bringing them back into a spiritual relationship with God. The Jewish high priest, speaking by the spirit, confirmed that the Messiah would gather those scattered "into one":

> ᴺᴬˢ John 11:50–52 nor do you take into account that it is expedient for you that one man should die for the people, and that the whole nation should not perish." Now this he did not say on his own initiative; but being high priest that year, he prophesied that Jesus was going to die for the nation, and not for the nation only, but that He might also **gather together into one** the children of God **who are scattered abroad**.

God's spirit gave this unction through the high priest to show that the Messiah would gather together into *one* the children of God who are scattered, and this is what the one bread at the Last Supper and the other breaking bread parables pointed to. Thus, the children of God are no longer pictured as twelve breads but as pieces of the one bread.

Initially the disciples continued speaking the Messiah's words only to those who were Jewish, but later they would realize that the New Covenant was intended for all nations:

> ᴷᴶⱽ Acts 11:19 Now they which were scattered abroad upon the persecution that arose about Stephen travelled as far as Phenice, and Cyprus, and Antioch, **preaching the word to none but unto the Jews only.**

In Paul's letter to the Romans, he declares:

> ^{NIV} Romans 1:16 I am not ashamed of the gospel, because it is the power of God for the salvation of **everyone** who believes: first for the Jew, then for the Gentile.

Paul, of course, does not mean that one should always share the good news of the Messiah with a Jew first; rather he means that the word of God concerning the New Covenant came through the Messiah to the Jews first, but after that it goes out to all equally. And Peter came to understand that when God filled the Gentiles with the Holy Spirit, He did not show partiality; as the King James Bible reads, "God is no respecter of persons" (Acts 10:34).

COURSE 5

Paul, 1 Corinthians, and the Last Supper

> KJV 1 Corinthians 2:14 But the **natural man** receiveth not the things of the Spirit of God: for they are foolishness unto him: neither can he know *them*, **because they are spiritually discerned**.

It is spiritual communion—not a ritual of Communion—that Paul speaks of in his first letter to the Corinthians. In this letter, Paul writes to a group of believers among whom he had previously taught and fellowshipped for 18 months (Acts 18:11). This fellowship had begun in a house next door to the local synagogue in Corinth. During this time, Crispus (the synagogue leader), his family, and many others came to know the Messiah (see Acts 18:1–17 for how this fellowship developed). It appears that Sosthenes, Crispus's successor as the synagogue's leader, also became a believer (Acts 18:17; 1 Corinthians 1:1).

As the power base shifted to Rome and Jewish idioms and understandings were then rejected, certain scriptures in Paul's letter (1 Corinthians 11:17–34) and elsewhere were wrongly interpreted as a Roman ritual of Communion. In this Course, we'll consider those verses within the idioms of the first-century assembly and how they would have been understood at that time.

Looking from the viewpoint of first-century Messianic Jews, we'll see that Paul was not teaching the Corinthians a Communion ritual, but rather the true spiritual communion that God desires for His people. Paul was an especially zealous apostle who received abundant revelations from the Lord (2 Corinthians 11:5; 12:7; Galatians 2:1, 6, 9, 11), including the understanding of the parable of the *one bread* that Jesus held and broke at the Last Supper:

> NAS 1 Corinthians 11:23 For **I received from the Lord** that which I also delivered to you, that the Lord Jesus in the night in which He was betrayed took bread;

The revelations that Paul ***received from the Lord*** concerning the Last Supper create the framework for most of 1 Corinthians 10, 11, and 12. Thus, it's vital to understand these scriptures from the first-century Jewish perspective, not the Roman-style ritual of Communion that arose over a hundred years later, unintended by either the Lord or Paul.

If you've grown up accustomed to seeing a Communion ritual within these scriptures, it may be quite disconcerting to view this anew through the eyes of first-century Jewish believers. However, since these Jews were not Roman Catholics, the scriptures need to be interpreted using their own idioms.

Some may think a spiritual explanation of the "bread" in 1 Corinthians 11 to be in error or even shocking. They may insist on believing that the Jewish Messiah wanted a literal ritual instead of realizing that he was using a parable to teach spiritual truths, as he so often did. But before we delve further into Paul's spiritual meanings in chapter 11, let's consider the immediate context of Paul's teachings in chapters 10 and 12, where he is also speaking spiritually.

1 Corinthians Chapter 10: Eating and Drinking Spiritually

In chapter 10, Paul refers back to the Israelites under Moses, saying they ate and drank *spiritually*:

> NAS 1 Corinthians 10:3–4   and all ate the same **spiritual food**; and all drank the same **spiritual drink**, for they were drinking from a **spiritual rock** which followed them; **and the rock was Christ**.

Their food and drink was "spiritual" in the sense that it was provided by God (manna from heaven and water from the rock), but more importantly in that it pointed to the true spiritual food and drink that the Messiah would provide. Spiritually speaking, Paul says that the rock that gave the Israelites drink was Christ (10:4), meaning a type of the Messiah (a "type" being a copy or image that points to something else). As a type, it foreshadowed the Messiah as the true spiritual rock who gives us spiritual drink (and spiritual bread, as Paul goes on to say).

At the time of Paul's letter to the Corinthians, their church was falling into various sins and thus partaking of the one (spiritual) bread in an "unworthy manner" (1 Corinthians 5:1; 6:18; 7:2; 11:27, 29). Knowing this, Paul illustrates how the Israelites under Moses were also eating spiritual food and drinking spiritual drink (1 Corinthians 10:3, 4) and were similarly falling short of what God wanted by engaging in sin:

> NAS 1 Corinthians 10:5   Nevertheless, with most of them God was not well-pleased; for they were laid low in the wilderness.

> NAS 1 Corinthians 10:6   Now these things happened **as examples for us**, that we should not crave evil things, as they also craved.

^KJV^ 1 Corinthians 10:8 **Neither let us commit fornication**, as some of them committed, and fell in one day three and twenty thousand.

^NAS^ 1 Corinthians 10:11 Now these things happened to them **as an example**, and they were written **for our instruction**, upon whom the ends of the ages have come.

In verse 11, Paul juxtaposes the Israelites' behavior in the wilderness (eating and drinking spiritually yet falling into fornication) with the poor behavior of the Corinthians, who were doing the same thing. He warns the Corinthians not to continue making the same mistakes for which he had rebuked them earlier (1 Corinthians 5:1; 6:13, 18; 7:2).

A few verses later (verse 17 below), he speaks about the "one bread" that Jesus held at the Last Supper, saying "we all partake of the one bread."

^YLT^ 1 Corinthians 10:16b the **bread** that **we** break—is it not the fellowship of the body of the Christ?

^NAS^ 1 Corinthians 10:17 Since there is **one bread**, we who are many are one body; **for we all partake of the one bread.**

This links the Corinthians *spiritually* partaking of the one bread in the New Covenant to the Israelites under Moses *spiritually* partaking of the "**bread** from heaven" (called "***spiritual food***" by Paul in 10:3 above), referring to the manna from God.

^NIV^ Exodus 16:4 Then the LORD said to Moses, "I will rain down **bread from heaven** for you. The people are to go out each day and gather enough for that day. In this way I will test them and see whether they will follow my instructions.

^NAB^ John 6:32 So Jesus said to them, "Amen, amen, I say to you, it was not Moses who gave the bread from heaven; my Father gives you the **true bread from heaven**.

The bread that *we* break is spiritual bread. It is the bread of heaven, the bread of life. As we partake of Christ in and through one another—as pieces of the bread and members of his body—this is the true spiritual fellowship that we share.

Paul understood that when the Lord broke the one bread into pieces at the Last Supper and gave them to his disciples to partake of, those pieces pointed to them being members in the one body, the spiritual body of Christ. Paul knew the Messiah was showing how he would provide spiritual nourishment in the New Covenant, and he understood that true communion lies in fellowship among the believers, those in the *spiritual* body of Christ:

> ^{YLT} 1 Corinthians 10:16b   the bread that **we** break—**is it not the fellowship** of the **body** of the Christ?

The spiritual "bread" that the Corinthians "break" is also what the twelve Temple breads pointed to. It is their spiritual fellowshipping as believers in God's presence—as they partook of God's spirit, His word, His love, and Christ as the spiritual bread of life.

The King James Version translates this verse using the word "communion" instead of "fellowship," for those translators understood the bread as applying to Christ's **natural** body (thus referring to their Communion ritual). They didn't view the bread from the figurative perspective of the first-century Jews:

> ^{KJV} 1 Corinthians 10:16b   The bread which we break, is it not the **communion** of the body of Christ?

It's acceptable to translate this Greek word *koinonia* in verse 16 as "communion," as long as one considers it in the sense that first-century Jewish believers used it. *Koinonia* was commonly used by the Jews in the Septuagint for 150 years before either Jesus or Paul ministered. To them, it meant having a common bond of fellowship and of communing with God and one another, such as during the festivals (covered more in Course 6). It never meant a ritual as later taught by Rome.

1 Corinthians Chapter 11: What Paul Received from the Lord

Many of the scriptures that Rome interpreted as a ritual of Communion are found in 1 Corinthians chapter 11 (verses 17–34). However, we must determine if that is really what the Jewish Paul intended.

When Paul speaks of the bread that Jesus held, broke, and said was his body, was he really speaking of a Roman ritual in which bread was Christ's human body, or was he speaking spiritually as Jesus did at the Last Supper? If this is difficult to determine, it only shows how strong a hold this Roman ritual has over us.

> ^{NAS} 1 Corinthians 11:23   For I received from the Lord that which I also delivered to you, that the Lord Jesus in the night in which He was betrayed took **bread**;

> NAS 1 Corinthians 11:24 and when He had given thanks, He broke it, and said, "**This** is My body, which is for you; do this in remembrance of Me."[120]

> NAS 1 Corinthians 11:27 Therefore whoever eats the bread or drinks the cup of the Lord **in an unworthy manner**, shall be guilty of the body and the blood of the Lord.

> NAB 1 Corinthians 11:29 For anyone who eats and drinks without discerning the **body**, eats and drinks judgment on himself.

Drawing on what we saw earlier in Corinthians chapter 10 with Paul's warnings to the Corinthians to stop falling into sin, here we see Paul speaking plainly of not eating the one bread "in an unworthy manner." As members of Christ's spiritual body (i.e., pieces of the one bread), we must keep this partaking of the bread pure. This does not mean upholding a ritual in which we literally eat morsels of unleavened bread, but rather partaking of *spiritual* bread as we fellowship with one another in Christ's spiritual body.

When Protestants left the Roman Catholic Church, they brought with them an altered ritual of Communion, believing they were doing what the Lord wanted. However, once one fully breaks free from the Roman ritual, it becomes clear that Paul is teaching to partake of the one bread as the spiritual body of Christ. Nowhere in these chapters or anywhere else does he teach a Roman or Protestant Communion ritual.

1 Corinthians Chapter 12: *We* Are the Body of Christ

The *spiritual* bread that Paul speaks of in chapters 10 and 11 fits perfectly with the *spiritual* body of Christ that he mentions throughout chapter 12.

> YLT 1 Corinthians 12:1 And **concerning the spiritual things**, brethren, I do not wish you to be ignorant;

As Paul continues, notice how often he speaks of the "body" of Christ in this chapter, and how in every single instance it refers to the *spiritual body* and ***not once*** to Christ's human body:

---

[120] In verses 23 and 24, the Greek words "this" and "bread" are not in grammatical agreement in the original Greek; therefore Jesus clearly cannot be saying "this **bread** is my body" as the ritual teaches. For a full explanation, see Course 2.

^{NAS} 1 Corinthians 12:12   For even as the **body** is one and *yet* has many members, and all the members of the **body**, though they are many, are one **body**, so also is Christ.

12:13   For by one Spirit we were all baptized into one **body**, whether Jews or Greeks, whether slaves or free, and we were all made to drink of one Spirit.

12:14   For the **body** is not one member, but many.

12:15   If the foot should say, "Because I am not a hand, I am not *a part* of the **body**," it is not for this reason any the less *a part* of the **body**.

12:16   And if the ear should say, "Because I am not an eye, I am not *a part* of the **body**," it is not for this reason any the less *a part* of the **body**.

12:17   If the whole **body** were an eye, where would the hearing be? If the whole were hearing, where would the sense of smell be?

12:18   But now God has placed the members, each one of them, in the **body**, just as He desired.

12:19   And if they were all one member, where would the **body** be?

12:20   But now there are many members, but one **body**.

12:21   And the eye cannot say to the hand, "I have no need of you"; or again the head to the feet, "I have no need of you."

12:22   On the contrary, it is much truer that the members of the **body** which seem to be weaker are necessary;

12:23   and those *members* of the **body**, which we deem less honorable, on these we bestow more abundant honor, and our unseemly *members come to* have more abundant seemliness,

12:24   whereas our seemly *members* have no need *of it*. But God has *so* composed the **body**, giving more abundant honor to that *member* which lacked,

> 12:25 that there should be no division in the **body**, but *that* the members should have the same care for one another.
>
> 12:26 And if one member suffers, all the members suffer with it; if *one* member is honored, all the members rejoice with it.
>
> 12:27 Now **you** are Christ's **body**, and individually members of it.

If you counted, that makes 18 times when Paul speaks of the spiritual *body* of Christ in chapter 12, and not a single time does he talk of Christ's human body in this context.

Furthermore, Paul's words about the bread being Christ's *spiritual* body (10:16) lead up to this same spiritual understanding that Paul focuses on throughout chapter 12. This is that the pieces of the one bread Jesus broke show that we the believers are the members of the one ***body***:

> 12:20 But now there are many members, but **one body**.
>
> 12:27 Now **you** are Christ's **body**, and individually members of it.

As we've seen, all of chapter 12 references the *spiritual* body of Christ; obviously chapter 11 did not mean the literal eating of Christ's body in a ritual. Often the immediate context is important when interpreting scriptures. Now that we have seen that Paul is speaking spiritually of the "body" in Corinthians chapter 12 and that he spoke spiritually of the "food," "drink," and "one bread" in chapter 10, it's easier to see that the "bread" in chapter 11 is also meant spiritually.

Figurative Use of "Eating" and "Drinking"

Before delving into the significance of the "eating" of the bread and the "drinking" of the cup of the New Covenant (11:23–29) and what this meant within the Jewish idiom of Paul's day, let's first consider the understandings of some Jewish and Talmudic scholars:

> "There was nothing more common in the schools of the Jews than the phrase of 'eating and drinking' **in a metaphorical sense**."[121]

---

121 Lightfoot, *Commentary of the New Testament from the Talmud and Hebraica*, vol. 3, p. 307; the quote refers to John 6:51.

The famous rabbinic scholar Moses Maimonides wrote in *The Guide for the Perplexed* about how Jews in the Talmud and in scripture use these words idiomatically:

> **This figurative use of the verb "to eat"** in the sense of "acquiring wisdom" is frequently met with in the Talmud, e.g., "Come, eat fat meat at Raba's" (Baba Bathra 22a); comp. "All expressions of 'eating' and 'drinking' found in this book (of Proverbs) refer to wisdom," or, according to another reading, "to the Law" (Koh. rabba on Eccl. iii. 13) Wisdom has also been frequently called "water," e.g.,"Ho, every one that thirsteth, come ye to the waters" (Isa. lv. 1).
>
> **The figurative meaning of these expressions has been so general and common**, that it was almost considered as its primitive signification, and led to the employment "of **hunger**" and "thirst" in the sense of "absence of wisdom and intelligence"[122]

Maimonides had not received the Messiah; he did not enter the New Covenant, and thus he was not filled with the Holy Spirit. Therefore he didn't experience the *spiritual* eating and drinking of the New Covenant Jews as Paul did. However, these quotes—even from the Talmud—clearly show this common Jewish idiom of eating and drinking in a spiritual or metaphorical sense.

Many examples illustrate this point. Below we see "drink" used in the Proverbs to mean confining sexual relations to one's wife and not straying beyond marriage:

> NAS Proverbs 5:15 **Drink** water from your own cistern, And fresh water from your own well.

> NAS Proverbs 5:16 Should your springs be dispersed abroad, Streams of water in the streets?

> NAS Proverbs 5:17 Let them be yours alone, And not for strangers with you.

> NAS Proverbs 5:18 Let your fountain be blessed, And rejoice in the wife of your youth.

Similarly, the adulterous woman is portrayed negatively as "eating":

---

[122] Maimonides, *The Guide for the Perplexed*, ch. 30, p. 40, http://sacred-texts.com/jud/gfp/gfp040.htm.

^{NAS} Proverbs 30:20   This is the way of an adulterous woman: She **eats** and wipes her mouth, And says, "I have done no wrong."

Wisdom is also personified, but as a good woman who (figuratively) gives forth good bread to "eat" and wine to "drink":

^{DBY} Proverbs 9:1   Wisdom hath built her house, she hath hewn out her seven pillars;

^{DBY} Proverbs 9:4   Whoso is simple, let him turn in hither. To him that is void of understanding, she saith,

^{DBY} Proverbs 9:5   Come, **eat** ye of my **bread**, and **drink** of the wine that I have mingled.

Jewish believers were not ignorant of these scriptures or of the common idioms. They knew that words such as "eating," "drinking," "**bread**," and "wine" (fruit of the vine) were often used figuratively to convey separate truths, either positively or negatively, depending on the context. Keep this in mind as we move on to what the Jewish Paul *meant* when he wrote to the Corinthians about partaking from the *one* bread.

Here, eating bread is used figuratively in a negative sense:

^{KJV} Psalm 14:4   Have all **the workers of iniquity** no knowledge? **who eat up my people *as* they eat bread**, and call not upon the LORD.

In these two verses below, Jesus also speaks of eating bread figuratively in a positive sense:

^{NAS} John 6:51   "**I am the living bread** that came down out of heaven; if anyone **eats of this bread**, he shall live forever; and the bread also which I shall give for the life of the world is My flesh."

^{NAS} John 6:35   Jesus said to them, "**I am the bread** of life; he who comes to Me **shall not hunger**, and he who believes in Me **shall never thirst**.

The disciples knew from the parables and lessons Jesus had previously taught them that he was the *bread* of life, the true *bread* from God. Therefore in 1 Corinthians, we shouldn't be surprised if Paul says "partake of the one bread" or speaks of eating the bread, and means it spiritually in a positive sense, or if he uses "hungering" or "eating" and intends it figuratively in a negative way. If it indicates something done correctly as God desired (1 Corinthians 10:17), then eating bread is positive; but if it is in the ungodly sense of hungering or eating "unworthily" (1 Corinthians 11:21, 27, 34), then it carries a negative connotation.

Paul's Intended Meaning in 1 Corinthians Chapter 11

All through chapter 11, Paul is only building on what he had *previously taught the Corinthians* when he was with them those 18 months:

> ᴺᴬˢ 1 Corinthians 11:23   For I received from the Lord that **which I also delivered to you**, that the Lord Jesus in the night in which He was betrayed took bread;

Since Paul had previously shared these truths with them, he therefore does not completely re-teach them but instead uses short statements to remind them about the one bread and that we believers are all one body.

But before commencing with more Last Supper instruction, Paul chastises the Corinthians for having divisions and other sins among them, and thus not "eating" the supper *pertaining to the Lord*. We see this rebuke in the verses leading up to verse 23:

> ʸᴸᵀ 1 Corinthians 11:18   for first, indeed, ye coming together in an assembly, **I hear of divisions being among you**, and partly I believe *it*,

> ᴺᴵⱽ 1 Corinthians 11:20   When you come together, it is not the Lord's Supper you eat,

> ᴳᴺᵀ 1 Corinthians 11:20   Συνερχομένων οὖν ὑμῶν ἐπὶ τὸ αὐτὸ οὐκ ἔστιν **κυριακὸν** δεῖπνον φαγεῖν·

The Greek word translated in verse 20 as "Lord's" Supper is actually the supper "*pertaining to the Lord*." The *Louw-Nida Lexicon* defines the Greek word translated "Lord's" as:

> **pertaining to the Lord** – 'belonging to the Lord,[123]

---

123   Louw and Nida, *Greek-English Lexicon of the New Testament Based on Semantic Domains*, vol. 1, p. 139, s.v. "κυριακός."

The NIV further above leaves out the translation for the Greek word "οὖν" (which means "therefore" or "thus"), and so verse 20 would be better translated as, "When you come together, **thus**, it is not the supper *pertaining to the Lord* that you eat." In saying "thus," Paul points back to the Corinthians' divisions and sins, indicating that their fellowship and spiritual sharing is not the supper pertaining to the Lord.

Remember that "eat" (and therefore "supper") can easily signify instruction or spiritual food in the Jewish idiom, as we saw earlier in the words of Lightfoot and Maimonides. Paul reproves the Corinthians for not carrying out the *spiritual* "supper that was pertaining to the Lord" in a pure way, as the Lord would have wanted:

> NAS 1 Corinthians 11:21 for **in your eating** each one takes his own supper first; and **one is hungry** and another is drunk.

> NAS 1 Corinthians 11:22 What! **Do you not have houses in which to eat and drink? Or do you despise the church of God, and shame those who have nothing?** What shall I say to you? Shall I praise you? In this I will not praise you.

Roman and Protestant theologians missed Paul's intended meaning in these scriptures. They thought Paul was saying that these believers were bringing big meals to church (for some strange reason) for the supposed Communion ritual. They misunderstood Paul to mean that instead they should eat these big meals at home, so the hungry and starving wouldn't have to watch them eat. However, when we examine this interpretation logically, it quickly breaks down, for why wouldn't Paul simply tell those people to share their big meals with those who are so hungry?

⁂

The Roman Catholic Church views these scriptures through a natural (literal) interpretation, therefore teaching that one should not eat before taking the ritual (thus, the Lord's flesh will not be in the stomach digesting alongside other food). Quoting from *The Catholic Encyclopedia* on "Holy Communion":

> That Holy communion may be received not only validly, but also fruitfully, certain disposition both of body and of soul are required. For the former, a person must be **fasting from the previous midnight from everything in the nature of food or drink**.[124]

---

124 Herbermann et al, *The Catholic Encyclopedia*, vol. 7, p. 402, s.v. "Holy Communion."

Does this explanation have a first-century Jewish ring to it?

There's a big problem with the interpretation of Paul wanting the Corinthians to refrain from eating because of the ritual. The problem is that Jesus, whom many believe to have supposedly taught this ritual at the Last Supper, actually spoke his instructions "***while they were eating***" supper. So why is Paul condemning these Corinthians for *supposedly* doing the same thing?

> NAS Matthew 26:26   And **while they were eating**, Jesus took *some* bread, and after a blessing, He broke *it* and gave *it* to the disciples, and said, "Take, eat; this is My body."[125]

Remember that in the previous chapter (10:17), Paul had reiterated to the Corinthians some of his earlier teachings to them, such as "we being many" (members) of the one body ***all partake out of the one bread***. He also warned the Corinthians not to fall into sin as the Israelites had done in the wilderness (and as the Corinthians had done previously), but to be pure in the partaking of the spiritual bread—the spiritual body of Christ. Here in chapter 11, Paul continues to build on that understanding by stressing the importance of keeping the spiritual partaking pure:

> NAS 1 Corinthians 11:27   Therefore whoever **eats the bread** or **drinks** the cup of the Lord **in an unworthy manner**, shall be guilty of the body and the blood of the Lord.

Verse 27 shows that if we partake in the New Covenant unworthily, we are essentially committing an injustice to the blood of the covenant. Paul does not speak of a new ritual but instead warns us not to act in a way that disrespects the blood of the covenant, just as he does in his letter to the Hebrews:

> NAS Hebrews 10:29   How much severer punishment do you think he will deserve who has trampled under foot the Son of God, **and has regarded as unclean the blood of the covenant by which he was sanctified**, and has insulted the Spirit of grace?

Paul also speaks along these lines in his first letter to the Thessalonians:

> NAS 1 Thessalonians 4:4   that each of you know how to possess his own vessel in sanctification and honor,

---

125   "Body" means the pieces of the broken bread representing my spiritual body.

> NIV 1 Thessalonians 4:5   not in passionate lust like the heathens, who do not know God;

> NAS 1 Thessalonians 4:6   *and* that **no man transgress and defraud his brother** in the matter because the Lord is *the* avenger in all these things, just as we also told you before and solemnly warned *you.*

In Corinthians, the theme of keeping the partaking pure is stressed repeatedly. Paul says that by not "discerning the body," many among them are weak and sick, and a number are asleep (meaning either spiritually asleep or dead). Paul explains that by not recognizing each believer as part of Christ's spiritual body (i.e., discerning the body) and by not treating each person properly, sin can enter, causing weakness, sickness, or worse. Paul warns the Corinthians not to reject others, to have divisions among them, or to allow the sharing of God's love to become tainted through sensuality or sin, as they had previously done:

> KJV 1 Corinthians 11:28   But **let a man examine himself**, and so let him eat of *that* bread, and drink of *that* cup.

> KJV 1 Corinthians 11:29   For he that eateth and drinketh unworthily, eateth and drinketh damnation to himself, **not discerning the** Lord's[126] **body**.

> NAS 1 Corinthians 11:30   For this reason many among you are weak and sick, and a number sleep.

> NAS 1 Corinthians 11:31   But if we **judged**[127] ourselves rightly, we should not be judged.

> GNT 1 Corinthians 11:31   εἰ δὲ ἑαυτοὺς διεκρίνομεν, οὐκ ἂν ἐκρινόμεθα·

---

126 The word "Lord's" is not in the best Greek manuscripts; it is added here in the King James Version, probably because in the 1600s the translators thought this referred to the Roman ritual. The best Greek manuscripts merely say, "not discerning the **body**," which refers to the spiritual body—not the "Lord's" human body, as Rome believed.

127 The word "judged" is not used here in a negative sense but rather to "discern" that our motives and actions are what the Lord would want. The *UBS Greek-English Lexicon* shows the Greek word διεκρίνομεν can also mean "discern, **evaluate, make a distinction, consider**."

In verse 31 above, two different Greek words are both translated into English as "judged." The first one, διεκρίνομεν, is not referring to "judging ourselves" negatively, but instead means "*discerning*" or "*evaluating* ourselves" to keep our motives aligned with what the Lord wants—properly caring for other members. Paul wants to make sure that our motives remain proper, knowing that God wants us to partake of His love (and share it among the body), but to keep the sharing of that love both spiritual and pure. Remember that earlier Paul said to "not despise the church of God" with improper eating and drinking, and to "eat at home" if any sensual hungers or desires arose for things that are not spiritual (11:21–22).

The other Greek word ἐκρινόμεθα, translated as "judged" in the two different translations below, carries a more negative meaning, as in "judging in a trial":

> YLT 1 Corinthians 11:31   for if ourselves we were discerning, we would not be being **judged**,
>
> NAS 1 Corinthians 11:32   But when we are **judged**, we are disciplined by the Lord in order that we may not be condemned along with the world.

This shows that as we enter further into the coming move of God's love, the Lord will also be present with those shepherds He calls (like Paul) to discipline and correct so that we stay on the right path. As such, Paul is bringing the Lord's discipline to the Corinthians in a firm but loving way.

The scripture says that in the New Covenant, we the believers are the "house of God" and His Tabernacle (Hebrews 3:6, 1 Peter 2:5, NAS Revelation 13:6).

God wants His dwelling place to be sanctified and revered:

> KJV Leviticus 19:30b   **reverence my sanctuary: I *am* the LORD**.

Paul knew and wrote that now *we* are Christ's body. Paul never dreamed that Jesus intended any such ritual, for he understood that Jesus was speaking spiritual truth, as he so often did. Paul was not talking about actual bread or any ritual; he was speaking metaphorically in the way that he and all Jews so often did.

It is true that, as Peter said, some of Paul's letters were difficult to understand (2 Peter 3:14–16). However, if we consider his statements within the context of first-century Jewish idioms and examine them in a spiritual sense, we can then comprehend Paul's true *meaning*.

That true meaning is that when we partake spiritually of the one bread (Christ's spiritual body), we are not to take it into sensuality as the Israelites under Moses did (1 Corinthians 10:1–8). Nor are we to do as the Corinthians did by falling into sin (1 Corinthians 5:1; 2 Corinthians 12:21). Instead, we are to keep the spiritual partaking pure, as the Lord intends, by allowing His *agape* love and acceptance to flow in, through, and to one another.

One more detail that supports Paul's meaning of "eating" and "drinking" in a *spiritual* sense is the fact that he often uses the Greek *subjunctive* mood in reference to these activities. The following words are all subjunctive in these scriptures: drink (11:25), eat and drink (11:26), eats and drinks (11:27).

Greek scholars Dana and Mantey[128] state that the subjunctive mood can refer to that which is *unreal*, saying "While the indicative assumes reality, the subjunctive assumes **unreality**." Thus in this context, Paul was showing that this was not *real* eating and drinking; in fact, it was literally unreal, because he meant *spiritually* eating and drinking.

In the following scripture, Jesus also uses the Greek subjunctive for "may eat" with an obvious spiritual meaning:

> YLT John 6:51a 'I am the living bread that came down out of the heaven; if any one **may eat** of this bread he shall live—to the age

Spiritual Communion and Reciprocal Communal Meals

One particular verse ties everything together in Corinthians 11, but because of inaccurate translations from the original Greek, its true meaning has been obscured. This scripture in question is verse 33. Let's start by examining the common but *inaccurate* English translation of this verse:

> NAB 1 Corinthians 11:33 Therefore, my brothers, when you come together to eat, **wait for one another**.

Those who follow the Roman ritual say that "wait for one another" refers to not beginning the Communion ritual until everyone has arrived. English translations that used this wording "wait for one another" follow the legacy of those steeped in this ritual; they are attempting to make sense of what Paul is saying. But the result is a fallacious interpretation of Paul's words to mean, "Don't start the ritual until everyone arrives."

---

128 Dana and Mantey, *A Manual Grammar of the Greek New Testament*, p. 170.

Back in the days when Paul was writing to the Corinthians, no phones existed, so how would the Corinthians know just who would be coming to each supposed Communion ritual? They might wait all day for the Goldstein family to arrive without knowing that they couldn't make it because their daughter was ill. If we think Paul is talking about eating meals and having rituals, waiting until everyone arrives really doesn't make sense, not to mention the fact that Paul doesn't even tell them what time to start.

As we saw, those who teach this ritual often believe the surrounding verses indicate to stop bringing meals to the assembly, so as to not connect this ritual to a common meal. The famous commentator Lenski wrote the following about this:

> "This wretched conduct, which even made the Sacrament impossible, the Corinthians should by all means avoid." [129]

He speaks of the "wretched conduct" of these people, who were supposedly eating some of their dinner along with the ritual of Communion. I am not poking fun at Lenski, because he was an excellent Greek scholar and a man of God's word. I am only showing how this ritual has held such sway over people.

It's important to remember that Paul often used words like "food" and "milk" symbolically when he meant them *spiritually* to teach and share God's word. Here are some examples:

> [NAS] 1 Corinthians 3:2   I gave you **milk** to drink, not **solid food**; for you were not yet able *to receive it*. Indeed, even now you are not yet able,

> [NAS] Hebrews 5:12   For though by this time you ought to be teachers, you have need again for someone to teach you the elementary principles of the oracles of God, and you have come to need **milk** and not **solid food**.

> [NAS] Hebrews 5:14   But **solid food** is for the mature, who because of practice have their senses trained to discern good and evil.

Jesus used the same idiomatic technique when he spoke of himself as the true bread and the spiritual bread from heaven, as well as the fact that his disciples should "eat" from (or partake of) this bread from heaven. His parables set the tone and understanding among the New Covenant Jews for the concept of their eating bread in a *spiritual* sense:

---

[129]   Lenski, *The Interpretation of St. Paul's First and Second Epistles to the Corinthians*, p. 487.

^NAS^ John 6:58 "This is the bread which came down out of heaven; not as the fathers ate, and died, he who **eats** this **bread** shall live forever."

So getting back to 1 Corinthians 11:33, is Paul really saying we are to come together **to eat** a little Communion wafer? Is an unleavened wafer, along with a tiny cup of grape juice, the "supper" that the Lord intends for us?

No, a wafer is not "supper"; at best it would be a snack or a morsel. The "supper" that is "pertaining to the Lord" is a *spiritual supper*. Paul speaks of eating spiritual bread, coming together to share God's love, hearing His word, and fellowshipping with one another. He is definitely not referring to a ritual.

What then *is* the correct translation of 1 Corinthians 11:33? For that, we have to return to the original Greek. The important Greek word below (and the faulty English translation of it) appears in boldface:

> ^GNT^ 1 Corinthians 11:33 ὥστε, ἀδελφοί μου, συνερχόμενοι εἰς τὸ φαγεῖν ἀλλήλους **ἐκδέχεσθε**.

> ^NAB^ 1 Corinthians 11:33 Therefore, my brothers, when you come together to eat, **wait for** one another.

A more *accurate* English translation of ἐκδέχεσθε would be "***receive from***" or "receive ***out of***."

This Greek word ἐκδέχεσθε is a combination of two words: ἐκ (meaning "out from" or "out of") and δέχεσθε (meaning "receive"). Hence the true meaning here is to **receive out from one another**. The *New Analytical Greek Lexicon* defines this Greek word as follows:

> "*to receive from* another; *to expect, look for ... to wait for ...*"[130]

To receive out from one another fits perfectly with partaking out of the one bread and receiving Christ and God's love in and through the other members in the *spiritual body*, as we saw Paul show in Corinthians chapters 10 and 12. We receive out from one another as the spiritual pieces of the one bread, or in the parallel picture, as members of the one body.

Even if we consider secondary definitions from *The New Analytical Greek Lexicon*, we would still apply them in the proper sense that Paul means:

> "*to expect, look for ... to wait for ...*"

---

130 Perschbacker, *The New Analytical Greek Lexicon*, p. 125.

In other words, as we worship or dance in the spirit before the Lord (as David did) or minister Christ in any capacity, we're *expecting, looking for, waiting for* Christ to be seen in, through, and out from one another in the spiritual body. In the process, we're spiritually giving and receiving God's love, which often comes through one another as we fellowship and share testimonies, God's word, worship, etc.

Tying this all together, Paul in effect means, "So then my brethren, when you come together to spiritually partake of the bread of life, receive Christ and the spirit of God out from one another in the spiritual fellowship." This spiritual feast (the *agape* feast or feast of God's love as we will see shortly) is the spiritual fulfillment of both the Lord's supper and the Lord's new commandment to love one another (John 13:34, 35). This is what Paul truly meant when he said that "**we** who are many are one body, for we all partake of the one bread" (1 Corinthians 10:17).

As we've seen, the natural-to-spiritual idiom was very common. Many words and natural (literal) activities of first-century Jews (breaking bread, sprinkling blood, eating at the altar, etc.) were understood as *spiritually* fulfilling various aspects of the Old Covenant. Therefore in 1 Corinthians 11:33 their spiritual partaking and receiving out from "**one another**" with God's presence in their midst spiritually fulfilled the Old Covenant communal meals[131] that were shared in the Temple (which also had God's presence in the midst).

> NAS 1 Corinthians 11:33 So then, my brethren, when you come together to eat, wait for **one another**.

Before we examine the reciprocal nature of these Temple communal meals, note that the Greek word (ἀλλήλων) translated above as "one another" is ***reciprocal***, as the *UBS Greek-English Dictionary* shows:

> ἀλλήλων, οις, ους **reciprocal** pro. *one another, each other*;[132]

So, keeping in mind the accurate translation of "receive out from," this shows that Paul wanted reciprocal, spiritual giving and receiving among the believers ("one another, each other").

The Jewish Encyclopedia describes the reciprocal nature of the Temple communal meals that Paul had grown up with:

---

131 Such as Showbread, eating at the altar, etc.
132 *UBS Greek-English Dictionary*, p. 8.

> The meals were in general of a joyful character, wine being freely indulged in. Meat that was unconsumed might not be profaned. That which was left over from the "praise-offering" had to be consumed on the same day (ib. verse 15); the residue of the other **communal** sacrifices had to be disposed of on the second day; and all that then remained had to be disposed of outside the camp on the third day (Lev. vii. 16 et seq., xix. 6).
>
> Inasmuch as **community** was expressed at these sacrifices by **reciprocal giving and accepting, God must have been considered as more than a mere guest**.
>
> Through the **common-meal** sacrifice the members of the family or gens (I Sam. xx. 6), as likewise an army at the beginning of a campaign, were brought into **communion** with God.[133]

When we see *The Jewish Encyclopedia* speak of "communion" and "reciprocal giving and accepting" at these communal meals, we never for a moment dream that they mean a Roman Communion ritual. Giving Paul the same consideration, we would see that he is drawing spiritual truths from the Temple communal meals that he and the other Jewish apostles had grown up with.[134]

Paul also speaks of spiritual eating for those in the New Covenant:

> [NAS] Hebrews 13:10 **We have an altar**, from which those who serve the tabernacle have no right to eat.

And the scriptures often point out the reciprocal aspect (one another) of the *agape* love that comes from God (1 John 4:7), as this was the Messiah's commandment for the New Covenant:

> [NAS] John 13:34 "A new commandment I give to you, that you love **one another**, even as I have loved you, that you also love one another.

> [NAS] John 13:35 "**By this** all men will know that you are My disciples, if you have love for **one another**."

> [NAS] 1 John 4:7 Beloved, let us love **one another**, for **love is from God**; and everyone who loves is born of God and knows God.

---

133 *The Jewish Encyclopedia*, vol. 9, pp. 566–567, s.v. "Peace-Offering."
134 More on these Israelite communal meals and how they connect to Paul's teachings will be covered in Course 6.

> ^{NAS} 1 John 4:12   No one has beheld God at any time; if we love **one another**, God abides in us, and His love is perfected in us.

Notice in verse 7 that this love is ***from God*** (the Greek word for "love" here is *agape*). This powerful spiritual love that comes from Him and the act of sharing it with one another is what will cause His love to be perfected in us.

Jesus said that the spiritual flow was to come ***out from each believer*** as rivers of living water, meaning a flow of God's spirit:

> ^{NAS} John 7:38   "**He who believes in Me**, as the Scripture said, 'From **his innermost being** shall flow **rivers of living water.**'"

> ^{NAS} John 7:39   But **this He spoke of the Spirit**, whom those who believed in Him were to receive; for the Spirit was not yet *given*, because Jesus was not yet glorified.

The scriptural picture of God's provision in the body of Christ is not that of one man (pastor, priest, or rabbi) bringing spiritual sustenance to the people. Instead the Messiah is the head, and the sustenance comes from God through the Messiah, then to and through the members in the spiritual body. The various God-appointed positions (pastors/shepherds, teachers, etc.; Ephesians 4:11) are important of course, but the reciprocal sharing among all the members is also essential.

This spiritual "flow" in the scripture above would begin to take place after the believers were filled with God's spirit on the day of Pentecost. The "rivers of living water" that the Messiah mentions spiritually fulfills the event where Moses gets "rivers" of water from the rock for the Israelites in the desert (Psalm 78:16; Exodus 17:1–6).

We saw that Paul said the "rock" that gave them drink was Christ, but certainly he was not saying that the rock in the wilderness was really Jesus disguised as the rock. Rather, Paul was showing that what the Jews did *naturally* under Moses often extends *spiritually* to us in the New Covenant with the *spiritual* eating and drinking that Christ (the true spiritual rock) provides for us. So, as believers and members in his spiritual body, these living waters are to flow out from each member to one another. Paul was a spiritual Jew who saw the coming together for fellowship and the partaking of the one bread as spiritual fulfillment of the Israelites' communal meals. Paul was not extolling a church picnic or a Roman ritual.

God and Christ must always remain as the primary focus of our spiritual communion, not just *our* love for other people in the body of Christ. Although we do receive God's love from individual members in the body, this spiritual *agape* love first and foremost comes from God because of Christ, so we are also to remember him in all that we do.

Paul was expecting spiritual experiences in which Christ would be in the midst, just as Jesus had promised (Matthew 18:20). To experience God's pure love from another member in the body gives a special insight and depth into the Messiah's promise about being in the midst when two or more are gathered together in his name. This *agape* love also breaks down all legalism and condemnation, because you see the reality of how much God loves us when we experience His love for another.

Eating Unworthily

Right after Paul says we come together "to eat" in verse 33, he then declares that if anyone is hungry, to eat at home!

> ^{NAS} 1 Corinthians 11:34   If anyone is hungry, let him eat at home, so that you may not come together for judgment. And the remaining matters I shall arrange when I come.

Paul is not confused; he is speaking again about those who are "hungry" for sensual desires, a reference he also made earlier to what Israel had done under Moses (1 Corinthians 10:5–9). He is saying that the Corinthians should keep those desires at home and not allow such hungers to surface in the house of God, where they would "despise" or disrespect the assembly of God (11:21–22).

These people of whom Paul now speaks (those hungering for fleshly desires, not discerning the body, etc.) also appear in various other scriptures. Below, Jude (and further below Peter) speak of those who sometimes came to the *agape* feasts (feasts of God's love) but "ate" unworthily on purpose, referring to them as "spots":

> ^{KJV} Jude 1:7   Even as Sodom and Gomorrha, and the cities about them in like manner, **giving themselves over to fornication**, and going after strange flesh, are **set forth for an example**, suffering the vengeance of eternal fire.

> ^{DBY} Jude 1:12   These are **spots** in your **love-feasts**,[135] **feasting together *with you*** without fear, pasturing themselves; clouds without water, carried along by *the* winds; autumnal trees, without fruit, twice dead, rooted up;

---

135   The Greek word translated as "love feasts" is *agapais*, which refers to the feasts of God's pure love they were experiencing. Yet some who attended sought sensual pleasure (i.e., the "spots") and took things out of the realm of God's love and into indulgence of the flesh.

God's love was to be shared and kept fervent, because His love for us is fervent and high above our human love. However, it was also to be kept pure. Those who refused to keep it pure were "feeding" from the one bread, the body of Christ, *in an unworthy manner.* Some were allowing it to become sensual by not discerning the body or respecting each member as a part of Christ's spiritual body.

For those who were weak and fell short to one degree or another, there was much grace and mercy, but those who came to the love feasts with impure motives were called "spots" (Jude 1:12 above). The Greek word for "spot" comes from the spots that sometimes stained the garments of the priests who cooked or roasted the sacrifices at the altar. So New Covenant Jews once again applied their natural-to-spiritual idiom *spiritually* to those working with the "spiritual sacrifices" (Romans 12:1, 1 Peter 2:5), showing that we should avoid getting our *spiritual garments* spotted:

> ᴷᴶⱽ Jude 1:23 And others save with fear, pulling *them* out of the fire; hating even the **garment spotted** by the flesh.

Peter comes out very strongly against these "spots":

> ᴺᴬˢ 2 Peter 2:10 and especially those who **indulge the flesh** in *its* corrupt desires and despise authority. Daring, self-willed, they do not tremble when they revile angelic majesties,

> ᴷᴶⱽ 2 Peter 2:12 But these, as natural brute beasts, made to be taken and destroyed, speak evil of the things that they understand not; and shall utterly perish in their own corruption;

> ᴷᴶⱽ 2 Peter 2:13 And shall receive the reward of unrighteousness, *as* they that count it pleasure to riot in the day time. **Spots** *they are* and blemishes, sporting themselves with their own deceivings **while they feast with you**;

> ᴷᴶⱽ 2 Peter 2:14 Having eyes full of adultery, and that cannot cease from sin; beguiling unstable souls: an heart they have exercised with covetous practices; cursed children:

Jude shows below that those "spots" who are "feasting together with you **without fear**" (or "without reverence," according to the *UBS Greek-English Dictionary*) do not care that they are taking advantage of the members of Christ's spiritual body:

> ^{DBY} Jude 1:12   These are **spots in your love-feasts, feasting together *with you* without fear**, pasturing themselves; clouds without water, carried along by *the* winds; autumnal trees, without fruit, twice dead, rooted up;

Paul states unequivocally that those who purposely partake unworthily of the *spiritual* bread risk damnation:

> ^{KJV} 1 Corinthians 11:29   For he that eateth and drinketh **unworthily**, eateth and drinketh **damnation to himself**, not discerning the Lord's body.

Paul is not saying to the Corinthians that those who eat a little too much "Communion" bread face damnation from God, or that those who supposedly brought their supper to church face damnation. Nor are these verses about those who may have fallen into sin, yet repent and keep their hearts right before God, as King David did.

Rather, they are about those who eat of the *bread* in a despicable manner by continually taking advantage of others in the body and not caring that they feast unworthily. The "spots" who were coming to their *agape* feasts were of a sensual nature, not seeking God's love or God's spirit:

> ^{KJV} Jude 1:19   These be they who separate themselves, **sensual**, having not the Spirit.

> ^{KJV} 1 Corinthians 6:15   Know ye not that your bodies are the members of Christ? shall I then take the members of Christ, and make *them* the members of an harlot? God forbid.

> ^{KJV} 1 Corinthians 6:18   **Flee fornication**. Every sin that a man doeth is without the body; but he that committeth fornication sinneth against his own body.

> ^{NAS} 1 Corinthians 6:19   Or do you not know that your body is a temple of the Holy Spirit who is in you, whom you have from God, and that you are not your own?

Paul is obviously not saying that they cannot show normal affection and love, for that is what God wants. Paul writes in both letters to the Corinthians (and to the Romans as well) to greet one another with a holy kiss, and Peter also writes of greeting with a kiss of *agape* (a kiss of God's love, 1 Peter 5:14). They are not writing these letters for the purpose of shutting down the *agape* love, but rather to keep His love pure and never allow the spiritual sharing to degrade into sensual hunger in God's house.

※※※

At this point, some may agree with the scriptures that clearly show the position of an assembly as a bride without a "spot" that God is calling us to (Ephesians 5:27). Yet they may be wondering and asking *how*, in our undisciplined generation, can we possibly allow God's love to flow and still keep it pure, to accomplish this high calling?

This is the same basic question the Israelites asked when they faced the giants in the *natural* Promised Land. How could they, a ragtag army with no weaponry, possibly go in and take the land from the heavily armed giants who were dwelling there?

They did not know exactly how it was going to be accomplished—they knew only that God had called them to accomplish it and that He would be with them, guiding them along the way and providing powerful miracles when necessary. Paul also gives some common-sense advice to the Corinthians a few chapters earlier so as to avoid sin (fornication and adultery). For instance, he instructs those who are burning with desire to find a spouse, and for spouses to get their marriages in order and not defraud one another but to meet each other's needs as God intended (1 Corinthians 7). If we do our part to keep things pure, we know that God will do His part, because the perfecting of the spiritual bride will be accomplished by His spirit:

> KJV Zechariah 4:6b   Not by might, nor by power, but **by my spirit**, saith the LORD of hosts.

> KJV Galatians 5:16   *This* I say then, **Walk in the Spirit**, and ye shall not fulfil the lust of the flesh.

> KJV Galatians 5:22   But the **fruit of the Spirit** is love, joy, peace, longsuffering, gentleness, goodness, faith,

In the Old Covenant, the Israelites were commanded by God to *not* offer their sacrifices out in the unsanctified (common or profane)[136] hills or valleys, but to bring those sacrifices dedicated to God into the sanctified precincts of God's house (Deuteronomy 11). But it is also true that, under certain circumstances, prophets

---

136   That which was common or profane did not mean evil or dirty, but referred to that which was not set apart and sanctified to God.

and others would offer sacrifices outside the house of God (Elijah on Mt. Carmel, etc.).

The antitype of this (what it points to in the New Covenant) would be along the lines of keeping the full expression of *agape* love in the house of God where it is public among the fellowship of believers, and not moving things dedicated to God (*agape* love, another member of the body of Christ, etc.) out of the spiritual realm. The reason for this would be to protect marriages against the ever-present weakness of the flesh. This would not be a hard, fast rule of law, but rather a common-sense general principle. Paul said that he had a gift whereby, due to the persecution-filled ministry that he was called to, he could remain unmarried. Yet at the same time he said it was necessary to bring his body into subjection (i.e., to God's will), lest he be disapproved (1 Corinthians 9:27).

This would, of course, have somewhat different applications for single people looking toward marriage, for God's deep spiritual love can be a nice segue into marriage. Nothing on earth compares to experiencing God's love, and the giving and receiving of this love among the believers can involve very strong emotions. Therefore, singles would need to exercise wisdom, for you can feel and experience God's powerful love for another person with whom you would never be compatible in a marriage.

Paul says that the marriage bed is undefiled, and Proverbs 5:19 tells the husband to be ravished (the Hebrew word can mean "intoxicated") by his wife's love. The pleasure and intimacy for marriage pointed forward to the eternal union, which is the powerful and passionate **spiritual** love in God's presence for eternity. God's love is a much higher spiritual love, not a natural or earthly one, yet by the same token, marital commitment and love is an earthly type that points forward to what we will experience spiritually with His love. This higher love was what God had for Israel, and it is the love pictured between the Messiah and the assembly. God wants us to experience His *agape* love now, yet to keep it sanctified and handle it properly.

Although we thoroughly enjoy God's love, we do not take His *agape* love out of the spiritual realm for our own personal benefit, but we handle it skillfully and appropriately for His intended purposes. His purposes include helping us to know the depths of His love, teaching us to love one another with His love, and uniting the spiritual body of believers.

Growing into the Perfected Bride

We've seen that God's love is to be shared and kept fervent, and that our goal should be to keep our intentions and actions completely pure as we grow into the spiritual bride without spot or wrinkle. We will now consider some scriptures that show the importance of this spiritual giving and receiving among members of the spiritual body, and how this is so important in perfecting the bride:

> ^{NAS} Ephesians 5:27   that He might present to Himself the church in all her glory, having no spot or wrinkle or any such thing; but that she should be holy and blameless.

Paul teaches in various ways that we are one body in Christ:

> ^{NAS} Ephesians 5:31   For this cause a man shall leave his father and mother, and shall cleave to his wife; and the two shall become **one** flesh.

> ^{YLT} Ephesians 5:32   this secret is great, and **I speak in regard to Christ and to the assembly**;

This is the "great mystery" of which Paul spoke. Part of Paul's teaching comes from what Jesus *meant* at the Last Supper when he said the pieces of the one bread were his body:

> ^{NIV} Ephesians 5:30   for **we are members of his body**.

In another analogy, Paul shows that, as members of the spiritual body, we are the joints and ligaments that give and receive nourishment, and this is how the body grows:

> ^{NAS} Colossians 2:19   and not holding fast to **the head, from whom the entire body, being supplied** and held together **by the joints and ligaments**, grows with **a growth which is from God**.

So, all these verses together demonstrate that when we assemble in the spiritual body as pieces of the one bread, we should give and receive spiritual sustenance to and from one another. Whether receiving the ministry of God's anointed word, being blessed by anointed music, singing and spiritually dancing before the Lord, experiencing miracles, hearing and giving testimonies, fellowshipping, sharing God's love, comforting one another, or praying for one another—in all these things and more, we are giving and partaking of Christ in and through one another, with God's spirit in our midst. We do not shut down this love, fearing that some might take it to excess, but allow it to flow because God's love is what will build and nurture the body into maturity and perfection.

Consider the extreme hypothetical example of a teenage boy confined by his parents in a windowless room from the age of 13 until 20, with his meals slid under the door. Certainly he would be sheltered from many temptations. He would never be tempted to watch a bad movie, play an unsavory video game, or be in the company of undesirable people. However, when he finally emerged from that confinement, he'd be damaged and unable to cope in the real world, and he would be hindered from having the spiritual growth that God would have wanted.

Of course this doesn't mean that parents shouldn't shelter their children from evil influences; it is only making a point that we must not shut down God's love so that no one might ever sin. Similarly, God does not want us to be locked in a legalistic room, but to flow in His love and grow into His likeness as we give and receive in the spiritual body. It is the teaching and guidance led by God's spirit that will help cause the spiritual bride to be made ready.

> NAS 1 Peter 4:8 **Above all, keep fervent in your love for one another**, because love covers a multitude of sins.

Just after speaking his Last Supper parables, Jesus gave a new commandment for the New Covenant—that we *love (agape) one another*. God wants us to keep this pure, allowing His love to shape us into the spiritual bride. Jesus also showed that as we treat one another in the body, it's as if we are treating him that same way (Matthew 25:34–44). He does not want those members in the spiritual body who are hurting, lonely, or needy to go without God's love. Nor does the Messiah desire a frigid, legalistic, or judgmental bride who is unable to love spiritually.

> NAS John 13:34 "A **new commandment** I give to you, that you love one another, even as I have loved you, that you also **love one another**.

> NAS John 13:35 "By this all men will know that you are My disciples, if you have love for one another."

We have seen before the concept of believers being the joints and ligaments of the spiritual body (Colossians 2:19). In his letter to the Ephesians, Paul gives another spiritual picture of the "body of Christ," with each member pictured as a "joint" in the body that supplies sustenance to the other members, which causes the body to grow into Christ for the building up of itself in love (*agape*).

> NAS Ephesians 4:15–16 but speaking **the truth in love, we are to grow up in all** *aspects* **into Him**, who is the head, *even* Christ, from whom the whole **body**, being fitted and held together by that which

> **every joint supplies,** according to **the proper working of each individual part,** causes the growth of the **body** for the **building up of itself in love.**

This growing and building itself up *in love* is what God wanted in the Assemblies of the believers, and Paul explains the need to keep it pure. It was the Messiah's command (not a superficial wish or a hope) that we "love one another." This was his new **commandment** for the New Covenant. We must not run in disbelief from this commandment, as some will want to do. Fulfilling this commandment will perfect and complete the bride.

In his commandment, Jesus used the same reciprocal "one another" that we saw earlier. He also used the same Greek word *agape* for "love" that Peter would later use, understanding what Jesus wanted for the believers who would eventually become God's spiritual bride:

> KJV 1 Peter 1:22 Seeing ye have **purified your souls** in obeying the truth **through the Spirit** unto unfeigned love of the brethren, *see that ye* **love one another** with a **pure heart fervently**:

> NAS Revelation 19:7 "Let us rejoice and be glad and give the glory to Him, for the marriage of the Lamb has come and **His bride has made herself ready.**"

※※※

The truths in God's word are for all people. Lest anyone feel these truths are adverse to Catholic people by pointing out that the ritual missed the Messiah's intended meaning, we can turn to one of the most revered Catholics—Mother Teresa—to see the importance of loving and caring for those around us:

> We think sometimes that poverty is only being hungry, naked and homeless. The poverty of being unwanted, unloved and uncared for is the greatest poverty. We must start in our own homes to remedy this kind of poverty ... Love begins by taking care of the closest ones—the ones at home.[137]

The powerful move of God's love is coming—both in the Jewish Messianic movement and in many churches and assemblies throughout the world—and this means that

---

137 Mauriello, *Mercies Remembered*, p. 278.

these truths will be important to understand. Comprehending them and properly carrying them out will help the whole body of Christ to grow into the perfected bride, without spot or wrinkle. God is revealing these truths now because He wants the bride to understand the Messiah's true meaning in the parables spoken at the Last Supper and the figurative words used by Paul in Corinthians. God is bringing these understandings to light now because the hour is late, and the world empire beast prophesied by the prophet Daniel (and by John in the Book of Revelation) is forming, and the bride must be made ready. (This will be covered in more detail in Course 12.)

The first-century Jewish believers understood that the first two annual Jewish festivals, Passover and Pentecost, were fulfilled spiritually in the New Covenant. However, the assembly has not yet entirely fulfilled the third and final Israelite festival, called both "Ingathering" (to celebrate the final harvest) and "Tabernacles" (Booths/Sukkot). This will be carried out as we do God's will and enter into the spiritual wedding feast as the bride is made ready.

I believe it is clear that the *agape* feasts of God's love were the beginning of fulfilling Tabernacles, the third and final Israelite festival, but as a body those first-century believers did not fully enter in because of problems and fears (just as natural Israel failed to enter the Promised Land on the first try). That attempt under Moses was at the time of the first ripe grapes (Numbers 13:20). The *final* Feast of the Ingathering—with the spiritual grape harvest—will be fulfilled as we enter in as one body and as one spiritual bride.

This third festival took place in the Jewish month called "Tishri" (which means "to begin"). The first day (new moon) of this month is often called the "blowing of trumpets," yet the word "trumpets" is not in the Hebrew (the word means "shouting," Leviticus 23:24; Numbers 29:1). This Hebrew word for "shouting" was used for a joyful sound (Psalm 89:15) or as a battle cry (Joshua 6:5, 20).

Thus prior to this third festival, there was a shouting among the people that signaled something new was beginning; within the next two weeks the Day of Atonement would occur and this third and final feast, the Festival of Ingathering, would begin.

This same Hebrew word is translated as a great "shout" below:

> NAS 1 Samuel 4:5 And it happened **as the ark of the covenant of the LORD came into the camp**, that all Israel **shouted with a great shout**, so that the earth resounded.

> NAS 1 Samuel 4:6 And when the Philistines heard the noise of the shout, they said, "What *does* the noise of this great shout in the camp of the Hebrews *mean*?" **Then they understood that the ark of the LORD had come into the camp.**

The Ark of the Covenant (or ark of the Lord) mentioned in these scriptures is a type of the presence of God coming into the assembly of believers in our day, when we align with His will.

While it is true that, as a body, those first-century followers of the Messiah did not fully enter in, yet in their *agape* love feasts they were indeed partaking of the first ripe fruit of Tabernacles:

> NAS Galatians 5:22–23 But the fruit of the Spirit is love, joy, peace, patience, kindness, goodness, faithfulness, gentleness, self-control; against such things there is no law.

We must fully take the land as God commanded, producing the fruit of the spirit and celebrating the final fruit harvest. The Lord was not teaching a ritual at the Last Supper; the ritual was rather a tradition of man. We must now move beyond the ritual and fulfill what the Lord truly intended—the spiritual sharing of God's *agape* love and the partaking among the pieces of the one bread. The scriptures we have covered concerning the reciprocal sharing of God's *agape* love, along with the Messiah's words at the Last Supper, show forth the road map that will fulfill God's high calling for us.

COURSE 6

The True Jewish Communion and the Messianic Feast

As we've seen, the true communion that Paul spoke of was based on 1,500 years of Israelite communal meals in the Tabernacle and the Temple, not on a Roman Communion ritual that did not yet exist. This Course will cover much ground, from the communal meals often seen in the Tabernacle and Temple to the ultimate communal meal in heaven, for which the parables at the Last Supper prepare us. We will see how, throughout history, the Israelites under the Old Covenant viewed their communal meals as "preenactments" of a heavenly feast with the Messiah. The Messianic Jews in the New Covenant then lived this out through their *agape* feasts, thus fulfilling this natural-to-spiritual idiom.

Course 5 showed that these truths were necessary for the spiritual bride to be made ready. Now we will see how the Israelite bread-and-wine communal meals align with the Last Supper in pointing forward to the Messianic Feast. From the Showbread to various sacrifices, these communal meals all foreshadow the true spiritual communion that God desires with every person.

The First Bread-and-Wine "Communal" Meal

In the scriptures, the first bread-and-wine communal meal (at least symbolically communal) is that in which Melchizedek, the king of Salem and priest of God, brought out ***bread and wine to Abraham***, who returned victorious from battle:

> NAS Genesis 14:18   And Melchizedek king of Salem brought out **bread and wine**; now he was a **priest of God** Most High.

Paul later speaks of how great Melchizedek was because Abraham, the inheritor of God's promises, gave him a tithe. He states that Melchizedek had no father or mother, meaning only that his genealogy was not traced from the Levitical priestly lineage (Hebrews 7:6). Paul furthermore states that Melchizedek's name means "king of righteousness," and since this man was king over Salem, it also shows him as "king of peace." (Note that "Salem" means "peace," and the city of Salem was later named "Jeru-salem," meaning "foundation of peace.")

Melchizedek was a type of Christ in various ways, such as through his priestly ministry. Although Jesus was from the tribe of Judah and thus could not hold the rank of high priest according to the law of Moses, he was spiritually called a high priest after the order of Melchizedek. In this priesthood what mattered was the calling of God, not the genealogy from the tribe of Levi (Hebrews 6:20; 7:11, 12).

Several hundred years later King David acknowledged this when, under God's anointing, he spoke concerning the future Messiah: "Thou art a priest forever, according to the order of Melchizedek."

> NAS Psalm 110:4 The LORD has sworn and will not change His mind, "Thou art a priest forever According to the order of Melchizedek."

Although David was also from the tribe of Judah, he had a revelation on one occasion that he himself could go right into the Temple and ask the high priest for a portion of the twelve breads (Showbread). According to God's law, only priests from Levi's lineage (through Aaron) were to partake of these breads, which were made from the Israelites' grain offerings. These breads were to continually abide in God's presence in the Temple, and the higher order of priests would partake of them every Sabbath.

David was likely also applying the concept of the Melchizedek priesthood to himself and thus had the confidence to ask for the Showbread on this one occasion. Samuel's account of this event with David refers to the priestly need to be ritually pure before partaking of the Showbread (1 Samuel 21:1–6). This purity requirement pointed to the Showbread (breads of the presence) as a *communal* meal at which God Himself was considered to be present. David (from the tribe of Judah) giving out the Showbread to those with him is a type of Christ giving out the true bread to those with him. This typology could also explain why David's sons were called priests (*kohen* in Hebrew, 2 Samuel 8:18). These Jewish communal meals involved *communion* with God and one another as members of the Jewish nation who were following the covenant and law of Moses.

Many Israelites were excluded from this Showbread meal, as this represented a future high calling for only those who desired to be closest to God and dwell in His intimate, most direct presence.

So what was God showing back in Melchizedek's day? Why did God lead that great king and priest to bring **bread and wine** out to Abraham, just a stone's throw from the location where David would later be directed to build the Temple?

Many years after Melchizedek brought out bread and wine to Abraham, and after the Israelites returned to Israel from the captivity in Egypt, God instructed Moses to build the Tabernacle. One of the first things God commanded for this Tabernacle was the gold-overlaid table on which the **breads** of the presence were set (and the cups/bowls for the *wine* libations, Exodus 25:23–30). Since the Israelites had re-entered this same Promised Land where Melchizedek had lived, this history of Melchizedek bringing out bread and wine to Abraham would have been part of their understanding. David showed this many years later in his statement in Psalm 110:4 (above) about Melchizedek. Thus, some of God's commandments to Moses (including the Showbread and its wine) would point forward to both the literal and spiritual Promised Land while also reflecting back on the event with Melchizedek.

What we'll see throughout Jewish history is a common thread linking the communal meals—beginning with the bread and wine of Melchizedek, then the twelve breads and wine in the Tabernacle (and later in the Temple), and then through the solemn bread-and-wine services of the Dead Sea Sect and other Jewish groups. The bread and wine the Messiah served at the Last Supper also pointed forward, for all of these communal meals point to the same Messianic feast or banquet with the king and priest.

The Three Annual Festivals as Communal Meals

The three annual festivals that God commanded through Moses were also communal. The first of these festivals was Passover, the second was Pentecost or Weeks (Shavout), and the final festival was often called Ingathering, Tabernacles, or Booths (Sukkot). They were not open to strangers outside of the covenant given to Moses; among Israelites, those who were ritually clean could attend and partake. However, the festivals were also open to Gentile proselytes who would be circumcised and thus enter the covenant; these proselytes were to be treated as those born in the land (Exodus 12:45).

These festival communal meals at the Tabernacle and Temple involved *bread and wine* with rejoicing as the bread was broken and the wine—either new wine or wine diluted with water—was shared. These meals were not regarded as worldly parties but rather as reverent but joyful celebrations in God's presence, and they pointed forward to the spiritual feasting in the New Covenant and to the Messianic banquet envisioned by many Jews throughout history.

God commanded the Israelites to attend these three annual festivals in the place where the ark—symbolic of His presence—would dwell.

> NAS Deuteronomy 16:16–17 "Three times in a year all your males shall appear before the LORD your God in the place which He chooses, at the Feast of Unleavened Bread and at the Feast of Weeks and at the Feast of Booths, and they shall not appear before the LORD empty-handed. Every man shall give as he is able, according to the blessing of the LORD your God which He has given you.

These three festivals were communal in nature—intended for the whole nation of Israel to commune as a united people in God's presence in the place He had chosen. God commanded these festivals because they pointed forward to future spiritual truths that would be revealed by the Messiah. It is the spiritual fulfillment of these three festivals that will produce the image and likeness that we are called to (covered in Course 8). This is what will mature the spiritual fruit that God seeks in His people, thus preparing the believers to be caught up into God's presence as the spiritual bride.

Two of these annual festivals were spiritually fulfilled among the New Covenant Jewish believers. The first—the true Passover—was accomplished when Christ was crucified at the exact time and day of Passover. The second—the Festival of Weeks or Pentecost—was spiritually fulfilled on the exact day of Pentecost (Acts 2) after the 50-day counting of the Omer (the sheaf), when God filled the Messiah's disciples with His spirit. This individual infilling of God's spirit had never happened before, and it fulfilled Joel's prophecy that God would pour out His spirit on all people (Joel 2:28).

The third annual festival was the Festival of Ingathering (Booths), in which the Israelites would rejoice and give thanks for all the produce of the land, including the "ingathering" of the grape harvest with its new wine:

> ^{NAS} Deuteronomy 16:13–14   "You shall celebrate the Feast of Booths seven days after you have gathered in from your threshing floor and your **wine** vat; and **you shall rejoice in your feast**, you and your son and your daughter and your male and female servants and the Levite and the stranger and the orphan and the widow who are in your towns.

The scriptures show that this festival included great celebration and joy.

> ^{NAS} Deuteronomy 16:15   "Seven days you shall celebrate a feast to the LORD your God in the place which the LORD chooses, because the LORD your God will bless you in all your produce and in all the work of your hands, **so that you shall be altogether joyful**.

Unlike the first two festivals, however, nothing in the scriptures indicates that this third annual festival was spiritually fulfilled within that same year. However, they do indicate that the disciples were entering this third festival's spiritual fulfillment because they were sharing the feasts of God's love (called *Agapais* in Greek), as we saw in Course 5. It is in the spiritual fulfillment of this third festival that the believers who enter in will be perfected as a spiritual bride, completing the picture of the ripened fruit and the harvest.

The joy experienced in these Old Covenant festivals was even greater in their New Covenant spiritual fulfillment. This is evident after God's spirit began to fill the Messiah's disciples on the day of Pentecost and beyond:

> NAS 1 Peter 1:8 and though you have not seen Him, you love Him, and though you do not see Him now, but believe in Him, you greatly rejoice with **joy inexpressible** and full of glory,

Keil & Delitzsch Commentary further speaks of the joy concerning the third festival:

> The leading character of the feast of Tabernacles . . . was to consist in "joy before the Lord." As a "feast," i.e., a feast of joy . . . (חַג, from חָגַג = חוּג, **denoting the circular motion of the dance**, 1 Sam xxx.16), it was to be kept for seven days; so that Israel **"should be only rejoicing,"** and give itself up entirely to joy (Deut xvi.15).[138]

We saw in Course 3 that the breaking of bread (with "gladness") experienced by the Messiah's followers after Pentecost (Acts 2:42, 46) was not mere gladness as the English translation indicates, but rather an incredibly ecstatic joy as God moved powerfully among them. The *Louw-Nida Lexicon* defines the Greek word translated as "gladness" in Acts 2:46 as "a state of intensive joy and gladness, often implying verbal expression and body movement (for example, jumping, leaping, dancing)...."[139] According to this definition, these joyous emotions were so powerful that they needed to be expressed with exuberant physical movement, just as when David danced as the ark was coming into Jerusalem.

Communal Meals and Communal Sacrifices

For many hundreds of years in the Mosaic covenant, the Israelites partook of certain communal meals and communal sacrifices, which formed a deep part of Jewish idiom. Under Moses, sacrifices and offerings brought Israel into *communion* with God. Some of these were communal in the sense of being offered up for the whole nation, while others were offered as individual sacrifices. The Babylonian Talmud often speaks of the communal sacrificial offerings:

---

138 Keil and Delitzsch, *Biblical Commentary on the Old Testament* (see his commentary concerning Leviticus 23:33–43 on p. 449).
139 Louw and Nida, *Greek-English Lexicon of the New Testament Based on Semantic Domains*, vol. 1, p. 303, s.v. "ἀγαλλίασις."

MISHNA. (a) What was done with this money drawn? The daily sacrifices, the additional sacrifices, and the drink-offerings belonging to them were bought therewith; also the Omers (sheaves), the two loaves, **the showbreads**, and **communal** sacrifices in general. The watchmen who had to guard the after-growth on the Sabbatical year were paid out of this money. R. Jose says: "One who so desired could undertake the guarding (of the after-growth on Sabbatical years) without pay." The sages answered him: "Thou wilt admit thyself, that the sacrifices (from the after-growth on Sabbatical years) must be brought only from **communal** property."[140]

One example of a communal sacrifice brought on behalf of the whole nation was the Tamid—the daily morning and evening burnt offerings in the Temple. These offerings provided communion with God for the nation as a whole, with both the animal's flesh and blood extremely important for the Israelites' atonement, as Moses had made clear.

Properly understanding the communal meals and sacrifices helps illustrate the true spiritual communion that Paul wrote about in 1 Corinthians (Course 5), and how the spiritual partaking among the believers fulfilled what these communal meals pointed to. We saw in Courses 3 and 4 (with more coming in Course 9) that the breaking of the twelve Temple breads was a communal meal that points forward to the spiritual meal that God has for us. We also saw that after Pentecost, Messianic Jews went forth "breaking bread"—meaning the spiritual bread, the bread of life.

As was mentioned in the previous Course, *The Jewish Encyclopedia* described the nature of these ***communal*** gatherings under "Peace-Offerings":

> It is difficult to determine whether Yhwh was regarded as the guest at these sacrificial meals, or the sacrificers were considered guests of God, to whom the sacrifice was being devoted.
>
> Inasmuch as community was expressed at these sacrifices by reciprocal giving and accepting, God must have been considered as more than a mere guest.[141]

What a powerful picture—that God Himself was considered as partaking with the Israelites in these meals and offerings in the "reciprocal giving and accepting."

The Jewish Encyclopedia continues:

---

140 Babylonian Talmud, Book 2, Tract Shekalim, ch. 4, p. 15, http://sacred-texts.com/jud/t02/shk08.htm.
141 *The Jewish Encyclopedia*, vol. 9, p. 566, s.v. "Peace-Offering."

> Through the common-meal sacrifice the members of the family or gens (I Sam. xx. 6), as likewise an army at the beginning of a campaign, were brought into **communion** with God.[142]

From the Jewish idiom shown here, the communion with God clearly came about "through the common-meal sacrifice," and it was the shed animal blood that provided this communion. This is important to keep in mind when Paul says what "our communion" is for those in the New Covenant (1 Corinthians 10:16). "Our communion" is not a Roman ritual, because no Catholic Church or Roman ritual existed yet. Instead, Paul speaks of these meals that involved communing with God through sacrifices from a 1,500-year-old Israelite experience. Now in the promised New Covenant, however, Paul shows that our communion is based on a different type of shed blood and a spiritual communal meal.

When Jewish writers mention "communion" as in the encyclopedic reference above or in Talmudic quotes we've seen, it is obviously not in the context of a Roman Communion ritual or the Blessed Eucharist. We must approach the Jewish Paul, the former Pharisee taught under Gamaliel, in a similar way. Paul speaks from the Jewish idiom of his day, with its clear understanding of communal meals, communal Temple sacrifices, and how communion with God was achieved under those sacrifices in the Mosaic covenant. Paul also knew that all this pointed forward to the spiritual experience in the promised New Covenant.

Common Bond for the Communal Meals

The root of the word "communion" (*koinonia* in Greek) is "common," and this aspect of the word relates to having things in common. The common bond of the people of the Israelite nation was that they were all sons of Israel walking in the covenant of Moses as a separated nation unto God. Their common bond was being part of the nation in good standing with God, having offered the appropriate sacrifices; this was their "commun-ion."

When Paul and John speak of our "communion" (also translated as "fellowship," 1 Corinthians 10:16; 1 John 1:3), they point out that the New Covenant communion is based on the common bond of having accepted the Messiah and his sacrifice. Accepting God's plan through the Messiah—who willingly offered his soul (Isaiah 53:10, YLT)—and accepting his shed blood as payment of our trespasses and partaking of the spiritual bread of life creates our common bond of fellowship, and thus our communion.

---

142 *The Jewish Encyclopedia*, vol. 9, p. 567, s.v. "Peace-Offering."

In Leviticus 10 and elsewhere, the two things that most concerned Moses were the shedding of the blood of the sacrifice and the consuming of its flesh for our atonement. Moses became angry when he discovered that Aaron and his sons had not eaten the flesh of the atoning sacrifice. Taken in context with the Jewish natural-to-spiritual idiom, the Messiah's shed blood is what provides the fellowship and communion in God's presence, and his body (who he was, as God's word expressed) is the bread that *we* break and feed upon (Christ the "bread of life"). In the New Covenant as spiritual members in Christ's spiritual body, the common bond of fellowship between God and man is based on and fulfills these same two aspects.

> ᴷᴶⱽ 1 Corinthians 10:16   The cup of blessing which we bless, is it not the **communion** of the blood of Christ? The bread which we break, is it not the **communion** of the body of Christ?

> ʸᴸᵀ 1 Corinthians 10:16   The cup of the blessing that we bless—is it not the **fellowship** of the blood of the Christ? the bread that we break—is it not the **fellowship** of the body of the Christ?

> ᴳᴺᵀ 1 Corinthians 10:16   τὸ ποτήριον τῆς εὐλογίας ὃ εὐλογοῦμεν, οὐχὶ **κοινωνία** ἐστὶν τοῦ αἵματος τοῦ Χριστοῦ; τὸν ἄρτον ὃν κλῶμεν, οὐχὶ **κοινωνία**[143] τοῦ σώματος τοῦ Χριστοῦ ἐστιν;

> ᴺᴬˢ John 6:51   "I am the **living bread** that came down out of heaven; if anyone eats of this bread, he shall live forever; and **the bread also which I shall give** for the life of the world **is My flesh**."

Natural Communion to Spiritual Communion

In the communal sacrifices, the Jews shared, communed, and fellowshipped in the shed blood in the sense that they shared in the atonement, the forgiveness, and the other benefits it represented. This sacrificial blood provided communion with God and one another, as well as the blessings and protections of being in covenant with God and having one's sins forgiven. God explained that it paid the price for the atonement of the people:

---

143   The Greek word *koinonia* is translated into English in various ways, usually as "fellowship," "communion," or "sharing." Additionally, the Greek word for "blessing" could also be translated as "praise"; indeed, *Strong's* lists "praise" as the first meaning for the word and *BDAG* defines εὐλογίας "to say someth. commendatory, speak well of, praise, extol."

>^{NAS} Leviticus 17:11 'For the **life** of the flesh **is in the blood**, and I have given it to you on the altar **to make atonement** for your souls; for it is the blood by reason of the life that makes atonement.'

The Israelites also shared in the food and nourishment from some of the animal sacrifices and bread offerings. Part of these offerings went to the officiating priests for food and another part often went to the one making the offering. Paul points to this when he says "the bread that *we* break" (spiritual bread) and "*we* have an altar" (Hebrews 13:10), which he means spiritually. Paul is showing that the New Covenant communion with God is no longer based on common genealogical bonds or animal sacrifices, but on believing in God's plan for atonement through the Messiah.

The same Greek word for communion (*koinonia*) was used by the Jews in the Septuagint, which was written more than 150 years before Jesus and Paul ministered, and four or five centuries before the Roman Catholic Church took over. When Jewish scholars used this Greek word in the Septuagint, it obviously did not refer to a Roman Communion ritual or a "Blessed Eucharist." These Jewish writers did not intend any such ritual when they translated Leviticus using the Greek word *koinonia* for "fellowship":

> ^{LXE} Leviticus 6:2 The soul which shall have sinned, and willfully overlooked the commandments of the Lord, and shall have dealt falsely in the affairs of his neighbour in the matter of a deposit, or concerning **fellowship**, or concerning plunder, or has in anything wronged his neighbour,

> ^{LXT} Leviticus 5:21 ψυχὴ ἐὰν ἁμάρτῃ καὶ παριδὼν παρίδῃ τὰς ἐντολὰς κυρίου καὶ ψεύσηται τὰ πρὸς τὸν πλησίον ἐν παραθήκῃ ἢ περὶ **κοινωνίας** ἢ περὶ ἁρπαγῆς ἢ ἠδίκησέν τι τὸν πλησίον

In Christ's day, Jews like Paul were familiar with these Greek words. In fact, the majority of the Old Testament verses quoted in the New Testament come from the Septuagint. Therefore, we should not mentally leap to a Roman ritual when we see those same Greek words used by the Jews in the New Testament.

In Corinthians 10:16, Paul contrasts the New Covenant communion with that under the law given through Moses. By saying in Greek that "the cup of the praise which we praise" is a "communion/sharing/fellowship" of the blood of Christ, Paul points back to what Jesus taught at the Last Supper—that the cup of which they were partaking symbolically represented the New Covenant:

> NAS Luke 22:20 And in the same way *He took* the cup after they had eaten, saying, "**This cup** which is poured out for you **is the new covenant** in My blood.

While the first covenant was based on the blood of the sacrifices (Exodus 24:6–8), the Messiah shows here that the New Covenant is based on his own shed blood.

Below, Paul speaks of the "bread that **we** break" and shows it as spiritual fellowship (communion) in Christ's spiritual body, in and through its members:

> YLT 1 Corinthians 10:16b the bread that **we** break—is it not the fellowship of the body of the Christ?

Here, Paul refers back to what the Lord had revealed to him and to what he had previously taught the Corinthians about the Last Supper teachings and the Messiah's parables (1 Corinthians 11:23). Paul understood by revelation from the Lord that when Jesus "broke" one bread and gave his disciples the pieces and said this was his body (see Course 2), he was showing them how the believers—the spiritual body of Christ—would function in the promised New Covenant.

Paul also taught that as the symbolic pieces of the one bread, we also partake of it, and receive sustenance from it, for we are the members of the one spiritual body:

> NAS 1 Corinthians 10:17 Since there is one bread, we who are many are one body; for we all partake of the one bread.

This is how God will give us spiritual provision, as we fellowship and commune with one another in His spirit.

Notice how verse 17 connects to what we just saw in verse 16, so that immediately after speaking of our communion, fellowship, and the bread that we break, Paul mentions the spiritual bread that the believers were sharing in Corinth. This spiritual partaking in God's presence fulfills what the Israelite communal meals had pointed to.

Then, in the following verse, Paul compares the Old Covenant communion with the New Covenant communion:

> DBY 1 Corinthians 10:18 See Israel according to flesh: are not they who eat the sacrifices in **communion** with the altar?

Paul was not teaching a Roman ritual here, but simply comparing the two covenants and how they both share and commune from the altar. In the New Covenant, we have an altar and we partake of the bread and wine offering of the people, just as the

Israelites did under the first covenant. But this time our partaking is from a *spiritual* altar, from which only those in proper New Covenant communion can partake:

> ^{NAS} Hebrews 13:10 **We have an altar**, from which those who serve the tabernacle have no right to eat.

In the previous chapter of Corinthians, Paul had also contrasted the Old Covenant priests sharing and eating in the Temple with our *spiritual* sharing and eating in the New Covenant:

> ^{NAS} 1 Corinthians 9:13 Do you not know that those who perform sacred services **eat** the *food* of the temple, *and* those who attend regularly to the altar have their share with the altar?

> ^{YLT} 1 Corinthians 9:14 **so also** did the Lord direct to those proclaiming the good news: of the good news to live.

In other words, those who partake in the New Covenant receive their sustenance from the spiritual provisions that God provides (i.e., in the spiritual sharing and fellowshipping of the pieces of the one bread). This is what the bread and wine offerings throughout Jewish history pointed to, and also what the Messiah showed by the bread and the wine at the Last Supper. (This also refers to the *natural* offerings of the people, such as providing financing and support for the natural needs of the New Covenant teachers and ministers.)

Jewish Groups Emulate the Showbread

Through the Dead Sea Scrolls and other writings, historians have understood that various Jewish groups held services that emulated the Showbread service in the Temple. In Course 3, we saw the following quote that was part of the evidence proving that the Jewish idiom of breaking bread came from the Showbread; this was also presumably how the table in the home came to be considered as a symbolic altar:

> The table for the Jewish people, with its unique ceremonials, is an essential part of the Jewish religion. It is around the table that the ideals of Israel's home life find concrete expression. For the Jewish people the table is more than a piece of furniture upon which the daily meals are served. **It is a symbolic altar of God.**
> The religious uses of tables in the Temple lend significance to **the table in the Jewish home. The Table of Shew-bread** (Leviticus

24:6), the table for the lights (2 Chronicles 4:8), and the table for the sacrifices (Ezekiel 40:39), have a **symbolic counterpart in the home**.[144]

The Jewish biblical philosopher Philo, who lived in the Egyptian city of Alexandria at the time of Christ, wrote of the Therapeutae, a Jewish group in Egypt that held a holy meal with bread that emulated the Showbread table in the Temple:

> Philo reported that the Therapeutae's central meal was intended to emulate the holy table set forth in the sacred hall of the temple, but though the Qumran community are portrayed in the Dead Sea Scrolls as viewing the Jerusalem service as having failed to achieve priestly holiness, Philo describes the Therapeutae as deliberately **introducing slight differences** in their practices from those at the Temple, **as a mark of respect for the Temple's shewbread**.[145]

Philo put it thus:

> (81) And when each individual has finished his psalm, then the young men bring in the table which was mentioned a little while ago, on which was placed that most holy food, **the leavened bread**, with a seasoning of salt, with which hyssop is mingled, **out of reverence for the sacred table,** which lies thus in the holy outer temple; for on this table are placed loaves and salt without seasoning, and the bread is unleavened, and the salt unmixed with anything else, (82) for it was becoming that the simplest and purest things should be allotted to the most excellent portion of the priests, as a reward for their ministrations, and that the others should admire similar things, but should abstain from the loaves, in order that those who are the more excellent person may have the precedence.[146]

Although these two quotes make it appear that the twelve Temple breads (Showbread) were to be unleavened, in the following Course (7) it will be shown that this change to unleavened happened after the Pharisees gained control.

---

144 Shulman, *Gateway to Judaism*, vol. 1, p. 441.
145 *Wikipedia*, s.v. "Therapeutae."
146 Yonge, *The Works of Philo Judaeus*, "On the Contemplative Life or Suppliants," 10:81–82, http://earlyjewishwritings.com/text/philo/book34.html.

Philo also mentioned that the Therapeutae drank the *pure wine of God's love*:

> Then, when each chorus of the men and each chorus of the women has feasted separately by itself, like persons in the bacchanalian revels, **drinking the pure wine**[147] **of the love of God**, they join together, and the two become one chorus, an imitation of that one which, in old time, was established by the Red Sea, on account of the wondrous works which were displayed there;[148]

Thus here is more proof of the continuing thread through Jewish history of a hallowed bread service derived initially from Melchizedek, and then from the Showbread that always pointed to the Messianic banquet, which the Last Supper also pointed to (as we'll see further below).

Josephus, a first-century Jewish historian, wrote of the Essenes—another Jewish group that lived in Israel in his day that also held a solemn service with breads:

> They work until about 11 A.M. when they put on ritual loincloths and **bathe for purification**. Then they enter a **communal** hall, where no one else is allowed, and eat only one bowlful of food for each man, **together with their loaves of bread**. They eat in silence. Afterwards they lay aside their sacred garment and go back to work until the evening. At evening they partake dinner in the same manner. During meals they are sober and quiet and their silence seems a great mystery to people outside.[149]

Their timing also seems to emulate the workings of the Temple, as they *bathe for ritual purification* at 11 AM to be ready by the after-noon period. Josephus noted elsewhere that at noon the priests (having already bathed) would be ready at the Temple to begin the process toward the evening offering.[150]

---

147 Philo's mention of the pure wine here may initially refer to new wine, the fresh fruit of the vine, which he then shows points to God's love.
148 Yonge, *The Works of Philo Judaeus*, "On the Contemplative Life or Suppliants," 11:85, http://earlyjewishwritings.com/text/philo/book34.html.
149 Josephus, "Wars," 2.8.5, http://essene.com/History/AncientHistoriansAndEssenes.html.
150 Whiston, *The New Complete Works of Josephus*, "Against Apion," 2.8.105, p. 966.

The discovery of the Dead Sea Scrolls brought to light that this Jewish sect there also had a reverent service with bread and wine that most likely emulated the Showbread and certainly pointed to a Messianic banquet. Most scholars agree that Josephus's account of the Essenes shows a close and similar belief system to the sect at Qumran, where the Dead Sea Scrolls were found. In Josephus's brief mention of the Essenes, he did not say that they drank wine (or water) with their breads. But they would have needed to drink something with the breads, which they ate in the heat of the day. When we consider their similarity to the Qumran sect who did partake of wine with their hallowed meals, one could easily draw a speculative parallel.

The following quote from the Dead Sea Scrolls can be a little difficult to follow, because of the age of the scroll and its missing letters, but its main points remain clear. The quote is about the coming Messianic banquet when the believers will share bread and wine, which this sect at Qumran also did at their own communal meals:

> The procedure for the [mee]ting of the men of reputation [when they are called] to the **banquet** held by the society of the *Yahad,* when [God] has fa[th]ered(?) **the Messiah** (or, when the Messiah has been revealed) among them: [the priest,] as head of the entire congregation of Israel, shall enter first, trailed by all [his] brot[hers, the Sons of] Aaron, those priests [appointed] **to the banquet** of the men of reputation. They are to sit be[fore him] by rank. Then **the [Mess]iah of Israel** may en[ter] and the heads of the th[ousands of Israel] are to sit before him by rank, as determined by [each man's comm]ission in their camps and campaigns. Last, all the heads of [the con]gregation's cl[ans], together with [their] wis[e and knowl-edgeable men], shall sit before them by rank.
>
> [When] they gather [at the] **communal** [tab]le, [having set out bread and w]ine so the **communal table is set** [for eating] and [the] **wine** (poured) for drinking, none [may re]ach for the first portion of **the bread** or [the wine] before the priest. For [he] shall [bl]ess the first portion of the **bread and the wine**, [reac]hing for the bread first. Afterw[ard] **the Messiah of Israel** [shall re]ach for the bread. [Finally,] ea[ch] member of the whole congregation of the *Yahad*[151] [shall give a bl]essing, [in descending order of] rank.
>
> This procedure shall govern every me[al], provided at least ten me[n are ga]thered together.[152]

---

151 *Yahad* means "unity," in this context referring to the community together, in unity.
152 Wise, Abegg, and Cook, *The Dead Sea Scrolls: A New Translation*, p. 147.

Talmudic and Dead Sea Scrolls scholar Lawrence Schiffman writes about this Messianic meal at Qumran and the difference between it and other rabbinic depictions of the Messianic banquet:

The Sectarian Communal Meal

Although the messianic banquet of rabbinic sources was envisioned as a onetime affair inaugurating the messianic era, the Dead Sea community looked forward to a regular series of such banquets, as is evident from the words "whenever {the meal} is a{rranged} when as many as ten {meet} together." The sectarian practice of **acting out the future messianic banquet** in their everyday lives indicates the **messianic overtones that were ever present** during their frequent communal meals.[153]

Schiffman also states:

Whereas the sects communal meal described in Rule of the Community {6:2–5} required either **bread or wine**, the **messianic banquet** would require **both**.[154]

He then gives a powerful statement regarding the Dead Sea Scrolls that we can apply *spiritually* in the New Covenant:

The sect's **communal meals**, conducted regularly as part of its everyday life, **were preenactments of the final messianic banquet** at the End of Days. Thus we again see that the contemporary life of the sect reflected its dreams for the age to come.[155]

Having received instruction at the Last Supper through the bread and wine parables, the New Covenant followers of the Messiah essentially went forth "acting out the future messianic banquet." However, these Messianic Jews never regarded this as a natural or literal meal but understood it as a spiritual partaking from a spiritual altar. Their meals of *agape*, where they shared God's love, His word, and His spiritual sustenance, were not the same "preenactments of the final Messianic banquet," as Schiffman says of the Dead Sea Sect. For the Messianic believers, the *agape* feasts

---

153 Schiffman, *Reclaiming the Dead Sea Scrolls*, p. 334–335.
154 Schiffman, *Reclaiming the Dead Sea Scrolls*, p. 334.
155 Schiffman, *Reclaiming the Dead Sea Scrolls*, p. 338.

were *spiritual* meals that would prepare the believers to be made ready as a spiritual bride, which Israel had always been called to.

They knew Paul was not intending a new ritual when he quoted Christ, saying, "For *whenever* you eat this bread and drink this cup ...." (1 Corinthians 11:26 NIV). Instead, Paul's teachings in that regard concerned the feasts of *agape* or God's love into which the early believers were entering, and which he and others were trying to keep pure (as Course 5 highlighted).

The Messiah, of course, also knew this was to be a spiritual banquet among the believers, and it would lead to a spiritual wedding feast (Revelation 19:7, 9). The Messiah's Last Supper parables, along with his new commandment given right after this supper to love (*agape*) one another, showed the plan for such a spiritual partaking. This is what would make the bride ready for a wedding feast and thus for the eternal Messianic banquet, which begins on earth with the preenactments (the *agape* feasts) and continues forever.

Some Christians have wrongly claimed an analogy between the bread and wine meal at Qumran and the Roman ritual called the "Blessed Eucharist" by quoting text such as the following from Qumran:

> Whenever they arrange the table to eat or the wine to drink, the priest shall extend his hand first to bless the first (portion) of the bread or the wine. (*Rule of the Community 6:4–5*)[156]

Schiffman addresses this supposed analogy with the Eucharist:

> Claiming an analogy between this description and the Christian Eucharist, dominant scholarly opinion has tended to characterize the sect's communal meals as sacral. In fact, some even consider the sacral meal of bread and wine central to Qumran fellowship, tracing its origins back to the priestly traditions of the Temple. By that analogy, the communal meal would effectively have replaced the sacrificial rituals in the Temple from which the sectarian Zadokite priests had withdrawn.[157]

---

156 Schiffman, *Reclaiming the Dead Sea Scrolls*, p. 335.
157 Schiffman, *Reclaiming the Dead Sea Scrolls*, p. 335.

Schiffman then states that these meals at Qumran were not connected to the Eucharist because the Dead Sea meals were not "sacral" (pages 335–336). I would agree that anyone claiming an analogy between the Roman Eucharist and the Dead Sea Sect would be wrong, because the Roman ritual was completely different. Since the emperor Constantine wanted nothing in common with the Messianic Jews, Rome changed the Jewish spiritual communion that Paul spoke of into its own version, which was their literal Communion ritual.

A huge line of separation needs to be drawn between the spiritual truth that the Messiah brought out at the Last Supper and that of the Roman Blessed Eucharist established a few hundred years later. Later in this book (in the chapter "The Ritual—Why Didn't the Jewish Disciples Teach It?") we document that this Roman ritual was later changed to using unleavened bread, and then the Protestants morphed it in other ways when they pulled away from Rome. The picture subsequently painted of a long-haired Jesus at the Last Supper presiding over a Roman sacramental ritual is inaccurate and has greatly confused the true connections that the Messiah's teachings had to all of Jewish history.

Although no link exists between the bread and wine of the Dead Sea Sect and that of the Roman Communion ritual, this does not change the true connection between all of Jewish history and the Last Supper. There is no question that the bread and wine given by the Messiah at the Last Supper is connected to the longstanding Jewish tradition of similar Messianic meals—from Melchizedek bringing out the bread and wine to Abraham to the Showbread service in the Temple to the Messianic meals observed by the Jewish groups such as the Essenes and the Dead Sea Sect.

Christian commentators who see these meals at Qumran as somehow connected to the Blessed Eucharist have been overly influenced by the Roman ritual. The Last Supper was not sacramental, nor was it meant to be a continuing *ritual*. Rather, it pointed to the spiritual banquet in God's spiritual kingdom—the true Messianic banquet. Such a portrayal of the Last Supper as a Roman ritual has alienated many who may otherwise have seen the connection of this Messianic meal to all of Jewish history.

The Last Supper and the Messianic Feast/Banquet

The Messiah's Last Supper was a *communal* meal, for it was held among ritually pure Israelites the evening before the Passover would be sacrificed. It was also a Messianic meal since it was a meal with the Messiah. Although the Last Supper was not intended as a feast or banquet, the parables spoken at it did point forward to the spiritual feast that the Lord would provide (Luke 22:29–30). This Messianic banquet is for all the victorious believers who enter the promised New Covenant and partake from the Lord's table.

This is not to say that the disciples understood the Last Supper as a Messianic preenactment of this ultimate heavenly banquet at the time they were eating, but soon enough they would understand what the bread and wine at the Last Supper were pointing to. We will now see that when the nuances of the Greek language are considered, along with the Jewish idioms of the day, it becomes clear that Paul understood that the Last Supper parables (with the bread and fruit of the vine) pointed to this Messianic banquet.

The term "Last Supper" is found nowhere in the scripture; however, the "Lord's Supper" does appear, right where Paul speaks about the *spiritual banquet* of which the Corinthians should have been partaking:

> NIV 1 Corinthians 11:20   When you come together,[158] it is not the Lord's Supper you eat,

> GNT 1 Corinthians 11:20 Συνερχομένων οὖν ὑμῶν ἐπὶ τὸ αὐτὸ οὐκ ἔστιν **κυριακὸν δεῖπνον** φαγεῖν·

We already saw in Course 5 that the Greek word translated as "Lord's" meant *pertaining to the Lord*, or *belonging to the Lord*.[159] And now the *UBS Greek-English Dictionary* shows some possible meanings for the Greek word translated as "Supper"—the correct English word to use would depend on the context:

> δεῖπνον ου ν **feast, banquet**; supper, main meal

Together then, these two Greek words could easily be translated as "Banquet pertaining to the Lord" or "Feast pertaining to the Lord." And since the "Lord" spoken of here was the Messiah, then the English translation of "Lord's Supper" would more accurately refer to this long Jewish history of a coming "Messianic feast" or "Messianic banquet." The term "Messianic" means *pertaining to the Messiah*, so this would be a perfectly good meaning of Paul's words.

Many English translations translate this same Greek word δεῖπνον as "feast" or "banquet" in various scriptures, such as in the verses below speaking of the coming wedding "feast" and then another great "feast":

> NAB Revelation 19:9   Then the angel said to me, "Write this: Blessed are those who have been called to the **wedding feast** of the Lamb."

---

158 We saw in Course 5 that the Greek here rather reads along the lines of "when you come together *thus, or thusly*" ... referring to their improper conduct.

159 Louw and Nida's *Greek-English Lexicon* for κυριακός ή όν (vol. 1, p. 139).

And he said to me, "These words are true; they come from God."

> ^{NLT} Luke 14:16 Jesus replied with this illustration: "A man prepared a **great feast** and sent out many invitations.

Translators often have different opinions on which word to use in a given scripture, as we see in the verse below:

> ^{DBY} Matthew 23:6 and love the chief place in **feasts** and the first seats in the synagogues,

> ^{NAS} Matthew 23:6 "And they love the place of honor at **banquets**, and the chief seats in the synagogues,

In the verses below, this same Greek word is again translated as "banquet." This is the parable in which Jesus pictured many who were invited to a great banquet but then made excuses as to why they could not come, essentially rejecting the man who invited them. Jesus showed that by disregarding this invitation, they would miss out on the coming Messianic banquet:

> ^{NIV} Luke 14:16 Jesus replied: "A certain man was preparing a **great banquet** and invited many guests.

> ^{NIV} Luke 14:24 I tell you, not one of those men who were invited will get a taste of **my banquet**.'"

Another example of this same Greek word translated as "banquet" involves Herod holding a great banquet for his lords and military commanders:

> ^{NAS} Mark 6:21 And a strategic day came when Herod on his birthday gave a **banquet** for his lords and military commanders and the leading men of Galilee;

These translations show that it's no stretch to say that when Paul spoke to the Corinthians of the "Lord's supper"—and that their "coming together thusly" was *not* the supper pertaining to the Lord—the word could just as easily have been translated as the Lord's "feast" or the Lord's "banquet." Either of these two words would better fit the context in which Paul spoke, whereby he connected the longstanding Jewish idea of a Messianic banquet or feast to what the Corinthians should have been partaking of *spiritually*. Paul was not speaking of a ritual with a morsel of unleavened bread, but rather of the Messiah's banquet with the spiritual feasting in God's presence.

This recognition of what the Last Supper pointed to fits perfectly with a coming Messianic communal banquet or feast with bread and wine—a concept long understood by various Jewish groups throughout history. Although the Last Supper before the Messiah's atoning death was not actually this Messianic banquet, it pointed forward to it.

Using parables and figurative language at the Last Supper, the Messiah communicated to his disciples the future spiritual banquet of which they would partake in the promised New Covenant. This is the Lord's banquet that Paul refers to in Corinthians 11. The fruit of the vine (new wine) in the Messiah's instruction pointed to the spiritual drink of the Holy Spirit (and of God's love) that would be poured out for the believers in the New Covenant at Pentecost. And the breaking bread pointed to the spiritual bread that the believers would be sharing as they gather, share the word of God, and fellowship with one another in His love with His spirit in their midst.

On the night of his last meal, the Messiah spoke of this future heavenly banquet in the kingdom of God:

> NAS Luke 22:29 and just as **My Father has granted Me a kingdom**, I grant you

> NAS Luke 22:30a that you may **eat and drink at My table** in My kingdom,

Jesus had already taught his disciples that they should not look for an outward sign concerning the kingdom of God. When the Pharisees asked Jesus when God's kingdom would come, he seems to say that it was more along the lines of an inward spiritual kingdom that would emerge as the believer yielded to God's will:

> DBY Luke 17:20–21 And having been asked by the Pharisees, When is the kingdom of God coming? he answered them and said, **The kingdom of God does not come with observation;** nor shall they say, Lo here, or, Lo there; for behold, the kingdom of God is in the midst of you.

Paul, of course, understood this. After all, he had also taught the Jewish idea of a coming Messianic banquet and showed what Jesus *meant* when he spoke about eating and drinking at his table in the kingdom of God. Paul shows in his teachings that this is a *spiritual* banquet that the believer can enter into now. He also knew that the

Lord's Supper/Banquet/Feast alluded to a spiritual banquet for all those in the New Covenant who would enter in and take the land:

> ^{NAS} Romans 14:17   for the kingdom of God is **not eating and drinking**, but righteousness and peace and **joy in the Holy Spirit**.

This Messianic kingdom would begin at Passover when the Messiah paid the ultimate price, and after the Resurrection, which showed God's acceptance:

> ^{NAB} Luke 22:16   for, I tell you, I shall not eat it (again)[160] until there is fulfillment in the kingdom of God."

This Messianic kingdom and its spiritual banquet would enter a new phase when the Holy Spirit was poured out at Pentecost 50 days later as the ***new wine*** of God's spirit and His love, which Jesus said he would share with his disciples in the coming kingdom:

> ^{NAS} Matthew 26:29   "But I say to you, I will not drink of this fruit of the vine from now on until that day when I drink it **new with you in My Father's kingdom**."

> ^{NAB} Mark 14:25   Amen, I say to you, I shall not drink again the **fruit of the vine** until the day when I **drink it new** in the kingdom of God."

The Bread and Wine of the High Priest Melchizedek

Here is a man about whom we know very little. We know only that Melchizedek, the High Priest of God, brought bread and wine to Abraham when the latter returned victorious over his enemies. Before we tie that bread and wine to the bread and wine the Messiah shares with parables at the Lord's Supper, let's first build out this typology.

Here are the verses where Moses writes of Melchizedek:

> ^{NIV} Genesis 14:18–20   Then Melchizedek king of Salem brought out **bread and wine**. He was priest of God Most High, and he blessed Abram, saying, "Blessed be Abram by God Most High, Creator of heaven and earth. And blessed be God Most High, who

---

[160] The word "again" is given in parentheses, the translators thus showing it is not in the Greek text.

delivered your enemies into your hand." Then Abram gave him a tenth of everything.

Paul says to observe how great this man Melchizedek was:

> ^{NAS} Hebrews 7:4 Now observe how great this man was to whom Abraham, the patriarch, gave a tenth of the choicest spoils.

Moses, the law giver, wrote of Melchizedek. King David, the greatest Jewish king, also wrote of him. Saul (later called Paul), the greatest scholar to follow the Messiah, wrote of him in three different chapters in his letter to the Hebrews (Hebrews 5:6, 10; 6:20; 7:1–21). Both Josephus and Philo wrote of him, as did those Jews at the Dead Sea and the writers of the Talmud. So who was Melchizedek really and what did his early bread and wine point to? And why is this short portion of scripture so vital in Jewish history, such that all these major people and historians write of him?

We saw at the beginning of this Course that his name meant "king of righteousness" and that he was king and priest over Salem, later called Jerusalem. In the following scriptures, King David at first is speaking of the Messiah, whom he calls "my Lord":

> ^{NAS} Psalm 110:1 *A Psalm of David.* The LORD[161] says **to my Lord**: "Sit at My right hand, Until I make Thine enemies a footstool for Thy feet."

Knowing that it applied to himself as Messiah, Jesus tested the Pharisees on the above scripture (seen in Matthew 22:41–46) by asking them this: If David called the coming Messiah "Lord" (Adonai), how could he be David's son? Within the Jewish idiom, the father did not call the son Lord. In one sense the Messiah *was* David's son, since he was from his line, and in another sense he was David's Lord, as the promised Messiah.

While still in the context of this coming Messiah, David speaks prophetically of the future Messiah as the coming priest after the order of Melchizedek, as we saw earlier:

> ^{NIV} Psalm 110:4 The LORD has sworn and will not change his mind: "You are a priest forever, in the order of Melchizedek."

---

[161] When "LORD" is in capital letters, it refers to the Hebrew word *YAHWEH*, whereas "Lord" refers to the Hebrew word *Adonai*.

Paul also applies this to the Messiah in the following verse. He asks that if perfection was to come from the first covenant given to Moses and its Levitical priesthood, then why would David later speak (by the spirit) about another priesthood that was not according to genealogy from Aaron?

> [NAS] Hebrews 7:11 Now if perfection was through the Levitical priesthood (for on the basis of it the people received the Law), what further need *was there* for another priest to arise according to the order of Melchizedek, and not be designated according to the order of Aaron?

Interestingly, the Dead Sea Scrolls writers also wrote of Melchizedek, portraying him as bringing a "jubilee" as a forgiveness of sins:

> And concerning what Scripture says, "In [this] year of jubilee [you shall return, every one of you, to your property" (Lev. 25:13) and what is also written, "And this] is the [ma]nner of [the remission]: every creditor shall remit the claim that is held [against a neighbor, not exacting it of a neighbor who is a member of the community, because God's] remission [has been proclaimed" (Deut. 15:2): [the interpretation] is that it applies [to the L]ast Days and concerns the captives, just as [Isaiah said: "to proclaim the jubilee to the captives, (Isaiah 61:1) .... Just] as [....] and from inheritance of **Melchizedek**, f[or ... Melchize]dek, who will return them to what is rightfully theirs. **He will proclaim to them the jubilee, thereby releasing th[em from the debt of a]ll their sins.**[162]

Whether they meant this spiritually, picturing a future Messiah as a king and high priest whose arrival would bring a release from the penalty of sins, or if they meant a resurrected Melchizedek literally doing this, either way the Messiah would achieve this remission of sins when he fulfilled God's plan in providing the promised New Covenant:

> [NIV] Hebrews 1:3 The Son is the radiance of God's glory and the exact representation of his being, sustaining all things by his powerful word. After he had **provided purification for sins**, he sat down at the right hand of the Majesty in heaven.

---

162 Wise, Abegg, and Cook, *The Dead Sea Scrolls: A New Translation*, p. 456.

So we see the various Jewish groups—from Moses and David to the Dead Sea Sect and others—speaking about Melchizedek and the completed picture of him sharing bread and wine at a Messianic feast among the righteous. When understood correctly, this is also what the Messiah pointed to at the Last Supper concerning himself.

<hr />

At this point, we've seen how Jewish groups throughout history emulated the service of the Showbread, how the twelve Temple breads pointed to the spiritual breaking of bread in the New Covenant, and how the bread and the wine at the Last Supper pointed to the spiritual fulfillment of the Showbread. Now, to complete the circle, we'll connect the bread and wine of Melchizedek to the Showbread under Moses, and then to the spiritual bread and wine of the Messiah as seen in the Last Supper parables.

1. Melchizedek, king of Salem and priest of God, is directed by Him to bring out bread and wine to Abraham. Melchizedek ministered in a location where God would later direct David to build the Temple, in the Promised Land. This mention of the bread and wine does not refer to Melchizedek coming out for a mere church picnic with Abraham, because the same sentence connects it to his being "priest (Kohen) of God Most High" (Genesis 14:18). As with Jacob speaking prophetically of the Messiah and the blood of the grape, so does Melchizedek's bread and wine prophetically prefigure the Messianic banquet.

2. Hundreds of years later, before entering the Promised Land, Moses the law giver was directed by God in the service of the twelve Temple breads and the accompanying wine libations. The high priest divided out the breads to the high order of priests (sons of Aaron). This service with bread and wine reflected back on the hallowed event where the High Priest Melchizedek had brought out bread and wine to Abraham, which happened shortly after God promised Abraham the land (Genesis 12:7). It also pointed forward to the future Messianic banquet that so many Jewish groups understood and looked for. If we believe that God directed Melchizedek as high priest to bring out bread and wine to Abraham in Salem, then we can see the connection to the bread and wine that God directed Moses to bring. This service with twelve breads would later be continued in the Temple under David and Solomon. The Temple was built in the location where God directed, just a stone's

throw from where this event with Melchizedek and Abraham occurred. This connection may have been part of the reason God instructed it be built there.

3. On his last night before the Crucifixion, the Messiah gave out bread and new wine in Jerusalem to his closest followers, who were sons of Abraham. This bread and wine pointed to the Messianic banquet, the true Promised Land, and a spiritual inheritance. He showed that these things pointed further to spiritual truths: the wine as the cup of spiritual blessings in the New Covenant and the bread as the spiritual fellowship among the believers with God's presence in their midst. Jesus (Yeshua) thus showed that the bread and the wine—beginning with Melchizedek, then the Showbread, and then to and through the Last Supper—pointed to the Messiah and to the spiritual partaking he would provide.

When we put all these facts together, we see that the new wine is the New Covenant and its provisions, the infilling of God's spirit, the joy and rejoicing, the *agape* love of God. The bread is the living word of God, the bread of life, the Messiah's spiritual provision provided among the believers as we partake together, with God as "more than a mere guest." By fulfilling what the bread and wine pointed to, the assembly will complete the plan of the ages by coming into God's image and likeness, prepared to have the bridal relationship with God that Israel and all people are called to.

Feasts of God's Love

In Course 5 we saw that it would take a proper partaking in the feasts of God's love to bring about what Jesus was teaching for the Messianic banquet. Jude speaks of these love-feasts, as well as of certain people whose intentions were not pure and were thus pictured as "spots" in the feasts:

> DBY Jude 1:12 These are spots **in your love-feasts**, feasting together *with you* without fear, pasturing themselves; clouds without water, carried along by *the* winds; autumnal trees, without fruit, twice dead, rooted up;

Jude did not suggest that the love-feasts be stopped or that God's love be prevented from flowing because of these spots, but as Timothy pointed out, the believers should "turn away from such as these" (2 Timothy 3:5, 6) and as Jude said to abide in the love of God:

> ^{NIV} Jude 1:19–21   These are the men who divide you, who follow mere natural instincts and do not have the Spirit. But you, dear friends, build yourselves up in your most holy faith and pray in the Holy Spirit. **Keep yourselves in God's love** as you wait for the mercy of our Lord Jesus Christ to bring you to eternal life.

Peter gave similar instruction to keep the love flowing:

> ^{NAS} 1 Peter 4:8   **Above all**, keep **fervent in your love for one another**, because love covers a multitude of sins.

The Lord wants his bride to be perfected in love. This spiritual bride will be a people capable of receiving *agape* love from God, loving Him and one another in the same powerful way, and keeping that love as pure as it should be in the family of God:

> ^{DBY} 1 John 4:12   No one has seen God at any time: if we love one another, God abides in us, and his love is perfected in us.

> ^{NAS} Ephesians 4:16   from whom the whole body, being fitted and held together by that which every joint supplies, according to the proper working of each individual part, causes the growth of the body **for the building up of itself in love**.

> ^{NAS} 1 Peter 1:22   Since you have in obedience to the truth purified your souls for a sincere love of the brethren, fervently love one another from the heart,

The love between Christ and the bride is mirrored in the love between Solomon, the king of Israel, and his Shulamite bride:

> ^{NAS} Song of Solomon 2:4   "He has brought me to *his* **banquet** hall, And his banner over me is love.

The true (spiritual) communal meal—partaking of God's love with His spirit in the midst—is to be reciprocal, in and through one another, with God and the Messiah as much more than mere guests!

When the Messianic-based assembly was steamrolled by the Roman Church, which was backed by the power of Rome's military to convince all on "acceptable" doctrine, many of these first-century Jewish idioms, scriptural understandings, and nuances were lost. However, God has promised a latter-day rain, a teaching rain whereby many of these original truths (as well as new ones) will pour down from Him. The truths will be based on the word of God, but not as it has been understood through the Roman filter that we have inherited.

Was the Fruit of the Vine Partaken of with the Showbread?

The twelve breads were a communal meal that pointed forward to the true spiritual communal meal and the Messianic banquet. We've seen the Jewish history of hallowed meals with bread and wine (including the Lord's Supper/Banquet/Feast), as well as their allusion toward a Messianic banquet or feast. If all this connects back to the Showbread and Melchizedek as has been considered, then it would make sense that the priests partook of wine with these twelve breads. If the Tabernacle and Temple priests did indeed partake of the fruit of the vine with the Showbread, what would this have pointed to?

> ^{YLT} Exodus 25:29–30 and thou hast made its dishes, and its bowls, and its covers, **and its cups, with which they pour out**; of pure gold thou dost make them; and thou hast put on the table bread of the presence before Me continually.

The Jewish Encyclopedia shows some uncertainty from Jewish sources about the usage of these cups, bowls, and dishes that are listed above as part of the Showbread offering:

> Among the vessels enumerated as belonging to the table of the showbread are "ke'arot" (dishes, or, probably, the "forms" in which the cakes were baked) and "kappot" (hand-like bowls). These were the "bezikin" for the incense, "kesawot" (σπόνδεια) **for the wine-libations**, and "menakkiyyot" (probably dippers). **But according to** the Jerusalem and Samaritan Targumim, the kesawot were intended to cover the loaves.[163]

I have come to the conclusion that, at least in the times of Moses, King David, and Solomon, the priests would have partaken of wine with the Showbread. This wine would be either "mixed" (wine diluted with water) or fresh "fruit of the vine" (grape juice or "new wine"). Here are the reasons for this:

---

163 *The Jewish Encyclopedia*, vol. 11, p. 313, s.v. "Showbread."

1. We have seen that these Temple meals were pictured by the Israelites as occasions where God was more than a mere guest, and that He was actually partaking in the bread with them. Course 7 will show that God had His bread in the Temple (the bread of God) and the priests had their bread as well. We also know that some of the new wine from the people's tithes was to be poured out at the altar as a libation to God, so wouldn't it make sense that the priests, as His guests, would also share in some of this new wine with Him, just as they shared in the bread? On those hot summer days, they would have needed to drink something with the Showbread, and God did not command them to drink water in any scripture. If He had wanted them to drink only water or nothing at all, He could have commanded it, but He did not. The twelve breads were a blessing to the priests, and God did not intend their consumption as something they could not enjoy. Fresh fruit of the grapevine (or mixed wine) would also have been a blessing for the priests, making the partaking of the twelve breads more enjoyable while also fulfilling the type.

2. We saw that most of the later Jewish groups who held hallowed services that emulated this eating of the Showbread often partook of wine with their breads. The Dead Sea Scrolls confirm this, as does Philo, who wrote about the Therapeutae in Egypt, among others. These Jewish groups considered their service as symbolic of the Messianic banquet that they believed was to come.

3. If Lawrence Schiffman and other scholars are correct in believing that the Dead Sea Sect descended from the Sadducees, then their use of wine in their Showbread-like service would align with my belief that they consumed wine with the Showbread when the Sadducees (whose name descended from Zadokites) had full control over all aspects of the Temple (before the Pharisees gained much authority).

4. Before Moses gave out the law of the Showbread, the first "king priest"—Melchizedek—brought forth bread and wine to Abraham near the site where God would later direct David to build the Temple. It was also near to where the Messiah would pay the final penalty for remission of sins.

5. The Messiah, who was pictured as a spiritual high priest after the order of Melchizedek, also gave out bread and new wine to Abraham's sons, prefiguring the spiritual Messianic banquet that was to come.

It is true that Nadab and Abihu—the sons of Aaron—became drunk, offered strange incense on the fire to God, and were then slain (Leviticus 10). After this event, it was forbidden to drink "wine, the strong drink" (Leviticus 10:9). However, this was not among God's commands given to Moses as part of the law but was commanded later, after this incident. The command itself does not prohibit drinking new or mixed wine, but in the Hebrew it appears to forbid only the consumption of intoxicating wine or strong drink when entering the Tabernacle. After all, God did not want the priests to become inebriated and thus lose the carefulness and sobriety of the ministry they were carrying out.

It is probably because of this prohibition that mixed or new wine was often used at the festivals and elsewhere. This way, if the fruit of the vine had fermented to a state of being highly alcoholic, the mixing of the wine was sufficient to keep one from losing his senses and reverence while still retaining the good flavor of the fruit of the vine.

Below we see Wisdom personified as a woman who sets her table with **bread** and **wine**:

> JPS Proverbs 9:1–2   Wisdom hath builded her house, she hath hewn out her seven pillars; She hath prepared her meat, she hath **mingled**[164] **her wine**; she hath also furnished her table.

> JPS Proverbs 9:5   'Come, eat of my bread, and **drink of the wine which I have mingled**.

In another example, the navel of Solomon's bride (the Shulamite) is pictured figuratively (and positively) as never lacking mixed wine:

> NAS Song of Solomon 7:2   "Your navel is *like* a round goblet Which never lacks mixed wine; Your belly is like a heap of wheat Fenced about with lilies.

Remember also that at Qumran the wine was mixed. The Dead Sea Scroll text reads as follows:

> and when they gather to the table of the community and to the drinking of the wine and when the table of the community is made

---

164   Notice that Wisdom has "mingled" (meaning "mixed") her wine.

ready and the wine has been mixed for drinking, then no one is to touch the first portion of the bread and the wine before the priest.[165]

The book of Jubilees shows that the priests were to ***drink the wine*** with joy before the Lord, which came from the tithes of the people:

> Jubilees 13:25–27   for Abram, and for his seed, a tenth of the first fruits to the Lord, and the Lord ordained it as an ordinance for ever that they should give it to the priests who served before Him, that they should possess it for ever. And to this law there is no limit of days; for He hath ordained it for the generations for ever **that they should give to the Lord the tenth of everything**, of the seed **and of the wine** and of the oil and of the cattle and of the sheep. And He gave (it) unto His priests to eat **and to drink with joy before Him**.

Speaking to the priests in Deuteronomy, God says they are to partake of the new wine *in His presence*:

> [NAS] Deuteronomy 14:23   "And **you shall eat in the presence of the LORD** your God, at the place where He chooses to establish His name, the **tithe of your grain, your new wine**, your oil, and the first-born of your herd and your flock, in order that you may learn to fear the LORD your God always.

Clearly, it was not wrong for these priests to drink new wine or fruit of the vine in the presence of the Lord in the Temple, or God would not have directed them to do it. After all, would God encourage the priests to drink the new wine before Him and then forbid it from the higher order of priests as they partook of the breads of His presence?

Philo also wrote about the instruction of Moses concerning the drinking of wine and how in certain instances (such as the Nazirite vow), God commanded abstinence, while at other times He commanded the priests to drink:

> …for in many places of his history of the giving of the law **he mentions wine**, and the plant which produces wine, namely the vine; and he commands some persons to drink it, but some he does not permit to do so; and at time he gives contrary directions to the same people, ordering them sometimes to drink and some times to abstain. These therefore are the persons who have taken the great

---

165   Stendahl, *The Scrolls and the New Testament*, p. 71.

> vow, to whom it is expressly **forbidden to drink unmixed wine,** being the priests who are engaged in offering sacrifices. **But those who drink wine are numerous beyond all calculation, and among them are all those who are especially praised by the lawgiver for their virtue.**[166]

Notice that Philo wrote that the priests who were engaged in offering sacrifices were forbidden from drinking *unmixed* wine while ministering, but this rule did not extend to *mixed* wine or fresh "fruit of the vine" (grape juice) with the Showbread.

Some scriptures concerning Solomon's Temple speak of *the* table (singular) on which the Showbread was set (1 Kings 7:48; 2 Chronicles 29:18), while other scriptures mention tables in the plural (ten tables) with the Showbread on them, with ten bowls on each table (1 Chronicles 28:16; 2 Chronicles 4:8; 2 Chronicles 4:19). Were these other tables for when the priests would gather together and partake of the Showbread? If so, it would make sense to have ten bowls for the new wine on each table, assuming ten men were at each table. But if these bowls were intended for the drink offering poured out at the altar, you would not think that ten would be placed on each table.

The sect at the Dead Sea also mentioned bread and new wine being set out at a table for *ten* men, which would align with these ten bowls on each table in Solomon's Temple:

> By these rules they are to govern themselves wherever they dwell, in accordance with each legal finding that bears upon communal life. Inferiors must obey their ranking superiors as regards work and wealth. They shall eat, pray, and deliberate communally. Wherever **ten men** belonging to the society of the *Yahad* are gathered, a priest must always be present. The men shall sit before the priest by rank, and in that manner their opinions will be sought on any matter. When **the table** has been set for eating or the **new wine** readied for drinking, it is the priest who shall stretch out his hand first, blessing the first portion of the **bread** or the **new wine**. In any place where is gathered **the ten-man quorum**, someone must always be engaged in study of the Law, day and night, continually, each one taking his turn. The general membership will be diligent together for the

---

[166] Yonge, *The Works of Philo Judaeus*, "On Drunkenness," 1:2, http://earlyjewishwritings.com/text/philo/book13.html.

first third of every night of the year, **reading aloud from the Book, interpreting Scripture, and praying together.**[167]

Notice that they also connected this partaking of bread and wine to their scripture reading and prayer. As we saw in Courses 3 and 4, these were the various elements of the Temple service as seen in Acts 2: the spiritual breaking of bread (sharing the word of God) and the prayers.

When the nation backslid from God and wealthy priests were still living the high life while people were being afflicted, the Lord raised up the prophet Amos to speak against those priests who were drinking wine *in bowls*:

> KJV Amos 6:6   That **drink wine in bowls**, and anoint themselves with the chief ointments: but they are not grieved for the affliction of Joseph.

The Hebrew word *mizraq* that Amos uses for "bowls" is the same word used for the hundred golden "bowls" mentioned earlier that Solomon made for the tables of Showbread (2 Chronicles 4:8). Amos was not against the priests drinking wine in bowls or anointing each other per se, as God commanded; he spoke against their doing these things while not caring for the affliction of their brothers.

Some of these libations were poured out at the altar, and since these meals and offerings were seen as a partaking with God, it would make sense that the priests also partook of the wine from these bowls, as Amos showed above. Zechariah also had an interesting prophecy in which the Messiah comes and the Israelites are figuratively pictured with him as these same bowls of wine (Hebrew *mizraq*, i.e., as the priestly bowls filled with the new wine of rejoicing and God's love). Zechariah thus pictures the Israelites as drinking and filled with wine and rejoicing, and this leads into Zechariah's teaching on the latter rain (Zechariah 9:9–10:1).

> JPS Zechariah 9:9   Rejoice greatly, O daughter of Zion, shout, O daughter of Jerusalem; behold, thy king cometh unto thee, he is triumphant, and victorious, lowly, and riding upon an ass, even upon a colt the foal of an ass.

> JPS Zechariah 9:15   The LORD of hosts will defend them; and they shall devour, and shall tread down the sling-stones; and they shall drink, and make a noise as through wine; and they shall be filled like the basins,[168] like the corners of the altar.

---

167   Wise, Abegg, and Cook, *The Dead Sea Scrolls: A New Translation*, pp. 133–134.
168   The word "basins" above is this same Hebrew word *mizraq*, for bowls.

Wine and God's Love

If it is true that the priests originally shared with God in the wine offerings that accompanied the Showbread, what would this point to? While much of this will be answered in Course 11 regarding the fruit of the vine, let's see here how it foretells the Messianic banquet of God's love.

In Israel, wine was often compared to love. Below is a picture of Solomon and his bride that prefigures the Messiah and his own last-days bride:

> JPS Song of Solomon 1:2   Let him kiss me with the kisses of his mouth—for **thy love is better than wine**.

> JPS Song of Solomon 1:4   Draw me, we will run after thee; the king hath brought me into his chambers; we will be glad and rejoice in thee, we will find **thy love more fragrant than wine!** sincerely do they love thee.

> JPS Song of Solomon 4:10   How fair is thy love, my sister, my bride! **how much better is thy love than wine!** and the smell of thine ointments than all manner of spices!

Paul spoke of not overdoing it with natural wine, but rather being filled with what the new wine spiritually pointed to—God's spirit:

> NIV Ephesians 5:18   Do not get drunk on wine, which leads to debauchery. Instead, be filled with the Spirit.

Philo also saw the symbolic link between *pure* wine and God's love mirrored in the description of the Therapeutae, that reverent Jewish group in Egypt, with their service that emulated the Showbread. He wrote that they were "**drinking the pure wine of the love of God**."[169]

Not only did the Song of Solomon compare wine with love, and Philo speak of pure wine as God's love, but the Messiah also shared and then poured out the fruit of

---

169   Yonge, *The Works of Philo Judaeus*, "On the Contemplative Life or Suppliants," 11:85, http://earlyjewishwritings.com/text/philo/book34.html.

the vine as a symbol of his own love. After the Last Supper, Jesus said man can show no greater love than when he lays down his life for his friends (John 15:13). He also showed that the fruit of the vine he poured out (symbolizing his shed blood) would provide the New Covenant. This great love was intended not only for his friends but for all people throughout history. God's love is also shown in this sacrifice, for God so loved the world that He allowed His own son to suffer as the true Passover, which God called His sacrifice:

> JPS Exodus 34:25   Thou shalt not offer the blood of **My sacrifice** with leavened bread; neither shall the sacrifice of the feast of the passover be left unto the morning.

> NAS John 3:16   "For God **so loved** the world, that He gave His only begotten Son, that whoever believes in Him should not perish, but have eternal life.

> NAS John 15:13   "Greater love has no one than this, that one lay down his life for his friends.

COURSE 7

THE SHOWBREAD: WHO THEY REPRESENT, WERE THEY UNLEAVENED, AND WHY IT MATTERS

Historians tell us that in the time of Jesus the twelve breads (later called the "Showbread" in English) were actually unleavened—even though they were always called "breads" in scripture. Made from the grain offerings of the Israelites, these breads were always present in the Temple. In this Course, we will consider if God really meant for these twelve breads to be made unleavened when He gave His commandment to Moses, or if He intended something else. Along these same lines, we will consider if making the Showbread unleavened was one of the doctrines of the Pharisees who, as the Messiah said, made void the word of God by their traditions (Mark 7:13).

The twelve breads were a part of the pattern that God gave to Moses and, just like other aspects of the Tabernacle and Temple, they point forward to spiritual truth in the New Covenant:

> NAS Hebrews 8:5   who serve a **copy and shadow** of the heavenly things, just as Moses was warned *by God* when he was about to erect the tabernacle; for, "See," He says, "that you make all things according to the pattern which was shown you on the mountain."

> NAS Hebrews 10:1   For the Law, **since it has *only* a shadow of the good things to come** *and* not the very form of things, can never by the same sacrifices year by year, which they offer continually, make perfect those who draw near.

Before we look at what these breads foreshadow and the "good things" to which they point, it's crucial to first see what these breads were in the natural or literal sense.

> NAS 1 Corinthians 15:46   However, the spiritual is not first, but **the natural; then the spiritual.**

The reason it's so critical to see what these twelve natural breads in the Temple pointed to is they show forth God's plan and pattern for the *spiritual* bread, being all those who love Him and are filled with His spirit.

Important doctrines have been clouded by a failure to understand the difference between the word "bread" in its normal usage as daily *leavened* bread and its figurative usage, when on rare occasions it refers to something that is actually *unleavened*. This Course sets out to make this difference clear, because understanding it will help shed light on many scriptures and therefore on various truths. These truths include what Jesus intended with the Last Supper bread, what the twelve Temple breads pointed to spiritually, and what "breaking bread" referred to for early Jewish believers. It even sheds more light on how the modern-day ritual of Communion (or "Blessed Eucharist") with unleavened bread was inherited from Rome and was not a ritual kept by the early Messianic Jews.

The Twelve Breads in the Natural Sense

These twelve breads, or Showbread, were made from the grain that the Israelites would harvest from their fields and bring into the Temple as tithes and offerings in "an everlasting covenant for the sons of Israel" (Leviticus 24:8). In King David's day, they were baked by the Levite family of the Kohathites (1 Chronicles 9:32) and brought fresh each Sabbath into the Holy Place within the Temple. There, the priests would divide and partake of the previous week's twelve breads that were now replaced by the new ones.

God commanded that this offering be continually in His presence, near to where He symbolically dwelt. The new breads were placed in two rows on the golden overlaid table of Showbread.

The *McClintock and Strong Cyclopedia* explains the various items in the Holy Place of the Temple, including the twelve breads:

> The table stood in the sanctuary, together with the seven branched candlestick and the altar of incense. Its position, according to Josephus (*Ant*. iii, 6, 6), was on the north side of the sanctuary, not far from the veil that opened into the most holy place. Besides the twelve loaves, the showbread table was adorned with dishes, spoons, bowls, etc., which were of pure gold (Exod. XXV, 29). These, however, were evidently subsidiary to the loaves, the preparation, presentation, and subsequent treatment of which manifestly constituted the *ordinance* of the showbread.[170]

A container of frankincense was initially set upon each of these two rows of bread; later its contents were placed on the altar in the fire (Leviticus 24:5–9) as a memo-

---

170 McClintock and Strong, *Cyclopedia*, vol. 9, p. 710.

rial offering to God. Aaron and his descendants would then eat the bread. Together, the Showbread and frankincense were called a "fire offering," even though only the frankincense actually went into the fire (Leviticus 24:9).

※

The table itself upon which these twelve hallowed breads were placed had a turbulent history; the scriptural and historical details remain somewhat uncertain. It was most likely taken away when Babylon destroyed the Temple in 586 BC; then after the Babylonian captivity it was probably restored to Jerusalem around 519 BC (Ezra 5:14; 15: 6:5).

The first-century Jewish historian Josephus further explained the table's history that took place a few centuries after the Jews returned from their captivity in Babylon. He wrote that the king of Egypt, Ptolemy Philadelphus (283 BC–246 BC), was seeking to procure all the books of the world for a library in Alexandria. Ptolemy wanted the Old Testament Hebrew scriptures translated into Greek so they would be accessible to most people. To encourage the High Priest Eleazar to be amenable to this, he freed approximately 120,000 Jews who, years before, had been taken captive by the Persians and were later brought to Egypt as slaves. He also ordered that an elaborate Showbread table be made out of solid gold, along with other vessels as gifts for the Temple in Jerusalem.[171]

To fulfill Ptolemy's translation request, the Israelite High Priest Eleazar sent 72 Jewish scholars (six from each tribe) to perform this task. The result—the Septuagint—pleased Ptolemy and all Greek-speaking Jews living in Alexandria, Israel, and throughout the Diaspora.

The solid gold table ordered by Ptolemy was meant to replace the wooden table (which was overlaid with gold) that was still in the Temple (Antiquities 12.2.8). This may explain why the Old Testament Hebrew scriptures say the table was wood overlaid with gold (Exodus 25:23, 24), yet the Greek Septuagint translation for these verses leaves out the wood, saying it was pure gold.

Years later the Maccabees wrote of the evil king Antiochus Epiphanes attacking Israel and taking the vessels from the house of the Lord (around 167 BC), including the Showbread table (1 Maccabees 1:20–25). Subsequently the Maccabees brought in a new table for the Showbread (1 Maccabees 4:48, 49).

In 70 AD, when Israel was conquered by Rome and the Temple that had been rebuilt by Herod was destroyed, the Showbread table was carried to Rome and placed in a new temple built by the emperor Vespasian. McClintock and Strong write that the table later survived a fire there and then was subsequently taken by the Vandals

---

171 Whiston, *The New Complete Works of Josephus*, "Jewish Antiquities," 2.2.1–11, pp. 388–393.

to Africa. Later it was then said to have been taken to Constantinople (520 AD) and from there eventually remitted back to Jerusalem.[172]

The Twelve Breads Are Symbolic of the Twelve Tribes

Josephus and the first-century Jewish philosopher Philo both believed that the twelve breads symbolized the twelve months of the year. However, no scriptural basis exists for this belief. In the law given to Moses, God repeatedly directed him to use the number twelve in the Tabernacle to represent the twelve tribes of Israel.

> Albert M. Shulman in his *Gateway to Judaism* states the reason for twelve breads: "for the twelve tribes of Israel"[173]

The *McClintock and Strong Cyclopedia* concurs with this understanding of the Showbread:

> The twelve loaves plainly answer to the twelve tribes (comp. Revelation 22:2). But, taking this for granted, we have still to ascertain the meaning of the rite, and there is none which is left in Scripture so wholly unexplained.[174]

Since we always want to prove our doctrine using the scriptures, let's see what they show. Notice below in all of these scriptures given to Moses and in many concerning the Tabernacle, the number twelve keeps appearing in reference to the twelve tribes:

> NAS Exodus 24:4 And Moses wrote down all the words of the LORD. Then he arose early in the morning, and built an altar at the foot of the mountain with **twelve** pillars **for the twelve tribes** of Israel.

> NAS Exodus 28:9 "And you shall take **two onyx stones** and engrave on them **the names of the sons of Israel,**

> NAS Exodus 28:10   **six** of their names **on the one stone**, and the names of the remaining **six on the other** stone, according to their birth.

---

172 McClintock and Strong, *Cyclopedia*, vol. 10, p. 153.
173 Shulman, *Gateway to Judaism*, vol. 1, p. 41, s.v. "The Table of Showbread."
174 McClintock and Strong, *Cyclopedia*, vol. 9, p. 711, s.v. "Showbread."

The names of these twelve tribes of Israel were also engraved like seals on these twelve stones on the high priest's garment:

> NAS Exodus 28:15   "And you shall make a breastpiece of judgment, the work of a skillful workman; like the work of the ephod you shall make it: of gold, of blue and purple and scarlet *material* and fine twisted linen you shall make it.

> NAS Exodus 28:17   "And you shall mount on it four rows of stones; the first row *shall be* a row of ruby, topaz and emerald;

> NAS Exodus 28:21   "And the **stones shall be according to the names of the sons of Israel: twelve**, according to their names; they shall be *like* the engravings of a seal, each according to his name **for the twelve tribes**.

This description of the high priest with twelve stones on his garment points forward to Christ in type (John 15:13) as the true high priest, keeping the sons of Israel (the twelve stones) close to his heart as he yields to God in the ministry that he was called to:

> NAS Exodus 28:29   "And Aaron **shall carry the names of the sons of Israel** in the breastpiece of judgment **over his heart** when he enters the holy place, for a memorial before the LORD continually.

> NAS Exodus 28:38   "And it shall be on **Aaron's forehead**, and Aaron shall take away the iniquity of the holy things which the **sons of Israel** consecrate, with regard to all their holy gifts; and it shall always be on his forehead, **that they may be accepted** before the LORD.

Time and time again we see this number twelve pointing back to the Israelite people—the nation descended from Abraham that was walking in the covenant:

> NAS Numbers 1:44   These are the ones who were numbered, whom Moses and Aaron numbered, with the leaders of Israel, **twelve** men, each of whom was **of his father's household**.

> NAS Numbers 7:84   This *was* the dedication *offering* for the altar from the leaders of Israel when it was anointed: **twelve** silver dishes, **twelve** silver bowls, **twelve** gold pans,

> ^{NAS} Deuteronomy 1:23 "And the thing pleased me and I took **twelve** of your men, **one man for each tribe**.

> ^{NAS} Joshua 4:8 And thus the sons of Israel did, as Joshua commanded, and took up **twelve** stones from the middle of the Jordan, just as the LORD spoke to Joshua, **according to the number of the tribes of the sons of Israel**; and they carried them over with them to the lodging place, and put them down there.

From this, it's abundantly clear that these twelve breads point to the twelve tribes. This is assuredly not to cause anyone who is not of Israel to feel excluded from God's plan, for God is no respecter of persons. God did not call Abraham because of his DNA, but because of his heart for God and his willingness to be led by Him.

When God summoned Abraham, nobody else was willing to walk with Him. God called him in part because He knew Abraham would command his children after him (Genesis 18:19). Although the Israelites often fell short of God's will, such as in the wilderness, they were the only nation that sought to truly walk with God, and His mercy was with them. A necessary part of God's plan was to have a separated people out of which to bring the Messiah. Other nations were unwilling to walk with God at this time, but His plan was to use Israel and the Messiah as a light to the nations (Isaiah 42:6, 49:6, 60:3). Keeping Israel separate from the ungodly nations was crucial so that it would not become corrupted before the Messiah could fulfill God's plan of redemption for all people.

This requirement for separation from the nations changed after the Messiah came and fulfilled God's plan; this removed the wall of separation between the Jewish New Covenant believers and the believers among the nations (Galatians 3:28, Ephesians 2:14). For several years after the Resurrection, Peter refused to eat with Gentiles until the Lord gave him a vision, which he understood to mean that the believing Gentiles were no longer to be considered unclean (Acts 10). He realized this after the Holy Spirit was poured out on those uncircumcised Gentiles who believed (Acts 10:44–46; 11:1–18) and he was then able to move forward in New Covenant understanding.

Now returning to the number twelve, the Messiah also chose twelve sons of Israel, probably as a spiritual fulfillment of what the twelve tribes were called to:

> ^{NAS} Matthew 10:1 And having summoned His **twelve** disciples, He gave them authority over unclean spirits, to cast them out, and to heal every kind of disease and every kind of sickness.

> ^{NAS} Matthew 10:2 Now the names of the **twelve** apostles are these: The first, Simon, who is called Peter, and Andrew his brother; and James the *son* of Zebedee, and John his brother;

And concerning heaven and the New Covenant description of it, we see the twelve tribes represented there as well:

> NAS Revelation 21:12 It had a great and high wall, with **twelve** gates, and at the gates **twelve** angels; and names *were* written on them, which are *those* of the **twelve tribes of the sons of Israel**.

When Judas died, Peter considered it important to keep the number of apostles at twelve, so one more apostle—Matthias—was chosen (Acts 1:15–26).

Why It Matters Whether These Twelve Breads Were Leavened or Not

Now that we've seen that the twelve breads definitively point to the twelve tribes of Israel, let's turn our attention to why it matters whether the breads were leavened or not.

Some argue that Jesus eating bread at the Last Supper (which they believe was the Passover) would have been fine, because in the Old Testament scriptures matzah was sometimes called "bread." They say that the "bread of God," which was given as a fire offering on the altar to God, was commanded by Him to be made unleavened; yet it was sometimes referred to figuratively as "bread."

Others also argue that, since they believe the Showbread was matzah and was always called "bread" in scripture, it would have been normal for the Jewish disciples to announce that they and Jesus had eaten bread at Passover. These people claim that bread is bread, which can mean either unleavened or leavened. But even today, one would never go around the orthodox sections of Jerusalem announcing they were eating *bread* during Passover, and in Jesus's day the Jewish nation was much more strict concerning the laws of Moses.

These twelve breads were a commandment of God that pointed to spiritual truths in the New Covenant, just as those things in the first covenant under Moses (the Passover, three Festivals, sacrifices, altar, lamp stand, etc.) point forward and show spiritual truth in the New Covenant.

If the Last Supper was not the Passover, and Jesus was therefore eating regular bread as all the scriptures show, then it shows that someone else came up with the ritual of Communion using *unleavened* bread; it was not Jesus or the Jewish disciples.

Jesus said some of the Pharisees' traditions made the word of God void. One of these traditions was likely their making of the twelve breads unleavened. This changed the breads to matzah, voiding the word of God by leaving no typology that could accurately be drawn out.

> Typology is a method of biblical interpretation whereby an element found in the Old Testament is seen to prefigure one found in the

New Testament. The initial one is called the *type* and the fulfillment is designated the *antitype*. Either type or antitype may be a person, thing, or event, but often the type is messianic...[175]

A simple example would be the lamb sacrifices being a "type" of Christ, who was called the "lamb of God" and also Christ "our Passover." He was the fulfillment of what these sacrificial lambs prefigured.

Below we will see which typology fits better for these twelve breads that represent the twelve tribes: regular leavened breads or matzah.

Moses, David, and all the scriptures continually refer to these loaves as "bread." The Messiah and Paul also called them bread. If these twelve breads were commanded by God to be *unleavened*, that would point out certain spiritual truths. If they were *leavened*, that would indicate other spiritual truths and types.

But the fact is that in the scriptures, He does not command for them to be either unleavened or leavened. God leaves this mysteriously unspoken. Therefore, it would have been the legal decision of the Israelite leaders throughout history to decide how the twelve breads were made.

However, while many scriptures refer to these twelve breads as "bread" (*lechem* in Hebrew), not a single scripture calls them "matzah" (unleavened). This alone is a huge hint as to their original makeup at the time the instruction was given to Moses. If God had expected the twelve breads to be made as matzah, He would not have called them "bread" without qualifying that they were to be unleavened. If God required this, clearly He would have commanded it to Moses and made it unambiguous for future leaders and other believers.

While it is true that certain rare offerings were referred to *figuratively* as "bread" when they were actually matzah, we will see later in this Course that in each of those instances, God clearly qualified the "bread" to be matzah.

The twelve Temple breads (Showbread) are different, though, because they were never once called "matzah," nor were they commanded to be made without leaven, whereas the "bread of God" (such as in Leviticus 21:6) that was placed directly on the altar as a fire offering to the Lord was commanded by God always to be made **without leaven**. Therefore, the word "bread" in the phrase "bread of their God" is obviously being used figuratively.

---

175 Adapted from *Theopedia.com*, s.v. "Biblical typology."

> NAS Leviticus 2:11   'No grain offering, which you bring to the LORD, shall be made with leaven, for you shall **not offer up in smoke any leaven** or any honey as an offering by fire to the LORD.

> NAS Leviticus 21:6   'They shall be holy to their God and not profane the name of their God, for they present the offerings by fire to the LORD, **the bread of their God**; so they shall be holy.

The difference is this: The twelve breads (Showbread) were not offered in the fire to God, but rather they were eaten by the priests. Only the frankincense in the bowls on top of the breads actually went in the fire to God (Leviticus 24:7), so no commandment or any inferred command existed for these twelve *breads* to be made unleavened.

Pharisaic Tradition That the "Breads" Are to Be Unleavened

If you read Josephus or Philo, who both lived near the time of Christ, you'll notice that these breads were unleavened at that time, as the authoritative *McClintock and Strong Cyclopedia* relates:

> II. *The Bread and its Significance.* — **Whether the bread was to be leavened or unleavened is not said**. The Jewish tradition holds it to have been unleavened (Josephus, *Ant.* iii, 6, 6; 10, 7; Philo, *De Congr.* V, 1); and as Josephus and Philo could scarcely be ignorant of what on such a matter was customary in their time, it is not to be doubted that, **according to the later practice at least**, the bread was unleavened, affording ground for the inference that the same was the case also in earlier times.[176]

McClintock and Strong Cyclopedia says that since (according to Josephus and Philo) the breads were unleavened at that time, it could be inferred that they were also unleavened in earlier times. Our concern is not with how these breads were made during the rule of the Pharisees, but with how they were made under the more spiritual leaders such as Moses and David before the legalism of the Pharisees was established.

Josephus and Philo both lived during the time when the Pharisees exercised much control, and Jesus often rebuked the Pharisees and their scribes because they forced certain traditions on the people that were not from God. Jesus spoke of this as he quoted from the Jewish prophet Isaiah:

---

176 McClintock and Strong, *Cyclopedia*, vol. 9, p. 711, s.v. "Showbread."

> NAS Mark 7:7   'But in vain do they worship Me, Teaching as doctrines the precepts of men.'

Josephus and other sources documented the Pharisees' great power over their people during the time of Christ. The Sadducees, descended from the high priestly lineage of Aaron through Zadok, were given authority over the twelve breads according to God's law. They were seen as a wealthy ruling class who had some authority as ministers in the Temple, but the Pharisees exerted even more control, which they used to instill their doctrines, as Josephus relates:

> What I would now explain is this, that the Pharisees have delivered to the people **a great many observances by succession** from their fathers, **which are not written in the law of Moses**; and for that reason it is that the Sadducees reject them and say that we are to esteem those observances to be **obligatory which are in the written word**, but are **not to observe** what are derived **from the tradition** of our forefathers;
>
> and concerning these things it is that great disputes and differences have arisen among them, while the Sadducees are able to persuade none but the rich, and have not the populace obsequious to them, **but the Pharisees have the multitude on their side**;[177]

Jesus also bears witness to this, telling how the scribes and the Pharisees inserted themselves into the place of authority by taking the "chair" of Moses:

> NAS Matthew 23:2   saying, "The scribes and the Pharisees have seated themselves in the chair of Moses;

It must also be remembered that the Pharisees were jealous of the Sadducees and greatly despised them (this can be seen both in the New Testament and in the Talmud). The Pharisees may have been jealous of the Sadducees' authority over these hallowed breads (see also Ezekiel 44:15, 16), and this jealousy probably led in part to the eventual making of the twelve breads as matzah, without leaven.

The legalistic Pharisees could have felt justified in wanting these breads to be more "holy" by making them unleavened. This would also have forced the Sadducees to then eat the much less flavorful matzah (i.e., the "bread of affliction" as mentioned in Deuteronomy 16:3). This parallels the Roman Catholic Church changing the

---

[177] Whiston, *The New Complete Works of Josephus*, "Jewish Antiquities," 13.10.6, p. 441.

Communion bread from leavened to unleavened after the ninth century.[178] These two disparate groups both preferred the unleavened bread of affliction—the bread of liturgy and ritual—over the more pleasing (leavened) breads of God's presence and true spiritual communion with Him.

Below, Josephus writes of the Essenes and their *regular bread* (not matzah) service which, as we saw in Course 6, emulated the Showbread:

> They work until about 11 A.M. when they put on ritual loincloths and **bathe for purification**. Then they enter a **communal** hall, where no one else is allowed, and eat only one bowlful of food for each man, **together with their loaves of bread**. They eat in silence. Afterwards they lay aside their sacred garment and go back to work until the evening. At evening they partake dinner in the same manner. During meals they are sober and quiet and their silence seems a great mystery to people outside.[179]

A historical connection runs from the Zadokite priests under David (who I believe ate their Showbread leavened as it had been since the time of Moses) all the way down to the Sadducees, then to the Essenes, and thus to the Dead Sea Sect (who all ate regular leavened bread in their service that emulated the Showbread).

Course 6 documented that the Dead Sea sect was another Jewish group that held a reverent service with *bread and wine* that most likely emulated the Showbread and definitely pointed to a Messianic banquet. Most scholars agree that Josephus's account of the Essenes shows a close and similar belief system to the Dead Sea Sect.

Judaic scholar Lawrence Schiffman states that the Dead Sea Sect was probably started by Sadducees.[180] The Sadducees derived their name from Zadok (meaning "righteous"), the high priest who remained faithful to David. (The Greek word for "Zadok" is **Saddouk**, and for "Sadducee" is **Saddoukaios**.)

If it is true that the Showbread was made as regular leavened bread in David's day, then the Zadokite priests—the forerunners of the Sadducees—would have passed down this same understanding of the breads being leavened to the Essenes as well as the Dead Sea Sect. This would explain why all these groups ate regular leavened breads that emulated the Showbread.

---

178 See the chapter "The Ritual—Why Didn't the Jewish Disciples Teach It?" for more on this.
179 Josephus, "Wars," 2.8.5, http://essene.com/History/AncientHistoriansAndEssenes.html.
180 Schiffman, *Reclaiming the Dead Sea Scrolls*, p. 75.

Naturally, the requirement to eat these breads as the far less appetizing *matzah* would have angered some Sadducees. This could have played a part in their eventual withdrawal from Pharisaic control at the Temple services. Hence, these sects that withdrew from the Temple services to protest the Pharisaic injunctions would continue with their own communal bread service using regular leavened breads, which is what we see.

Philo (20 BC–AD 50), who lived in Alexandria, Egypt, wrote of another Jewish group in Egypt called the Therapeutae. They also held a holy meal with regular leavened bread (as mentioned in Course 6) that emulated the Showbread table in the Temple:

> … Philo describes the Therapeutae as deliberately **introducing slight differences** in their practices from those at the Temple, **as a mark of respect for the Temple's shewbread.**[181]

Philo put it thus:

> (81) And when each individual has finished his psalm, then the young men bring in the table which was mentioned a little while ago, on which was placed that most holy food, **the leavened bread**, with a seasoning of salt, with which hyssop is mingled, **out of reverence for the sacred table,** which lies thus in the holy outer temple….[182]

Philo, who lived when the Pharisees were in control (and the twelve breads were unleavened), asserted that the Therapeutae ate their bread *leavened* out of reverence for the table of Showbread in the Temple (i.e., to be slightly different). However, another possibility is that they were a similar offshoot of the Zadokites/Sadducees/Essenes/Dead Sea Sect. And if this were true, it would explain the true reason their breads were leavened. Otherwise, it would make no sense for the Therapeutae and the other groups to "taint" God's plan by making their breads leavened.

One further point: In the Talmud (which was written by rabbinic successors of the Pharisees), there is discussion and debate among the rabbis about a previous rabbinic school's decision concerning not having "large loaves" during the Passover. They deliberate over what this meant and what size is considered "large," to which one rabbi responds that it meant the size of the Showbread. Another retorts that it would not have meant this because the Showbread bakers were very careful (using

---

181 *Wikipedia*, s.v. "Therapeutae."
182 Yonge, *The Works of Philo Judaeus*, "On the Contemplative Life or Suppliants," 10:81, http://earlyjewishwritings.com/text/philo/book34.html.

many oscillations, hot ovens, etc.) to ensure that these breads remained unleavened; thus, the prohibition of "large" more likely applied to the breads made by the common people, who might not be skilled enough to keep larger loaves unleavened.[183]

However, it is also possible that this previous rabbinic school's writing referred to an earlier time when the twelve breads were made leavened ("large loaves" would thus have referred to the risen Showbread). If this is accurate, then what was actually intended was that the breads were not to be made as the usual "large loaves" but rather unleavened during the Passover Festival (when all leaven was forbidden). Jewish scholars often had to decide which law superseded or took precedence when a conflict occurred. Since God did not command the Showbread to be either leavened or unleavened, it would have been acceptable to have them unleavened during Passover.

It is true that the Mishnah (the first major written record of Jewish oral traditions) mentions a complex contraption with 28 ventilation tubes placed on the Showbread table to prevent the twelve matzahs from leavening. However, God never gave Moses instruction for such a device in the scripture, so it would have been a later addition by the Pharisees when they changed these breads to unleavened (matzah). Most likely the Pharisees took a few scriptures out of context (such as Ezekiel 4:13, Hosea 9:4, or Malachi 1:7) to justify making the twelve breads as matzah; in these scriptures the Hebrew speaks of "defiled bread."

Since God never commanded these breads to be unleavened, it makes sense that the priests who lived in those earlier, less legalistic days would have preferred the more flavorful leavened breads to matzah. Knowing the true nature of God's heart as to this offering, the leaders like Moses, Samuel, and David would have made the breads leavened, as this was both allowable and more appetizing for the priests. They would have understood that the truths God was showing in the twelve breads did not require them to eat these breads unleavened. The fact that they were called "breads" in the Torah without ever being qualified as matzah would have strengthened this understanding.

The scripture continually refers to these twelve breads in the Temple as "bread" (*lechem* in Hebrew), and *not once* as "matzah" (unleavened). Even the English term for them is "Show-*bread*," not "Show-*matzah*." So we should consider the possibility that this making of the twelve breads unleavened in the time of Jesus was a tradition forced by the Pharisees, one that actually made void God's word by painting a false picture and invalidating what these breads pointed to:

> NAS Mark 7:13 ***thus* invalidating the word of God** by your tradition which you have handed down; and you do many things such as that."

---

183 This debate is covered in the Babylonian Talmud, Book 4, Tract Betzah or Yom Tob [Feast Days] ch. 2, pp. 41–43, http://sacred-texts.com/jud/talmud.htm#t04.

With this invalidation of God's word by making these breads matzahs, the spiritual truths these breads pointed to became lost to the Jewish scholars who followed. For instance, here is what prominent Jewish Torah scholar Moses Maimonides wrote concerning these twelve breads in his book *The Guide for the Perplexed*:

> "The use of the altar for incense and the altar for burnt-offering and their vessels is obvious; but I do not know the object of the table with the bread upon it continually, and up to this day I have not been able to assign any reason to this commandment."[184]

It is very possible that the forcing of these breads to be made unleavened, when God's commandments did not require it, hid their true spiritual meanings to successive generations.

God Commanded Certain Breads to Be Made with Leaven

Let us consider two other Tabernacle and then Temple offerings that were commanded by God to be baked *with leaven*. Like the twelve breads, they too were always called "bread" and never "matzah." The original Hebrew referred to them as *lechem* and in the Greek Septuagint as *arton* (i.e., regular bread).

The first of these was a sacrificial offering of thanksgiving that was commanded to be made **with leaven** and was called "bread":

> [NAS] Leviticus 7:12 'If he offers it by way of thanksgiving, then along with the sacrifice of thanksgiving he shall offer unleavened cakes mixed with oil, and unleavened wafers spread with oil, and cakes *of well* stirred fine flour mixed with oil.

> [NAS] Leviticus 7:13 'With the sacrifice of his peace offerings for thanksgiving, he shall present his offering with cakes of **leavened bread**.

The other offering, also called "bread," was for the Festival of Pentecost (Shavout) and was commanded to consist of two **leavened** breads. The Greek word *Pentecost* means "50," as this festival under Moses happened after the 50 days counting from the morrow of the first regular Sabbath after Passover:

---

184 Maimonides, *The Guide for the Perplexed*, ch. 45, p. 356,
   http://sacred-texts.com/jud/gfp/gfp181.htm.

> NAS Leviticus 23:16 'You shall count fifty days to the day after the **seventh sabbath**; then you shall present a new grain offering to the LORD.

It was on this day, following the true Passover of Christ, that God began to pour out His spirit on all flesh (Joel, Acts 2, 10), causing the two leavened "breads" (Jews and Gentiles) to become "one bread," i.e., the spiritual body of Christ (Acts 2:16).

These two breads were made with the same measure of flour as the Showbread and were baked with leaven. And like the Showbread, and the leavened sacrifice for thanksgiving, they were never called "matzah" but always "bread":

> NAB Leviticus 23:17 For the wave offering of your first fruits to the LORD, you shall bring with you from wherever you live two loaves of **bread** made of two tenths of an ephah of fine flour and **baked with leaven.**

> NAS Leviticus 23:18 'Along with the **bread**, you shall present seven one year old male lambs without defect, and a bull of the herd, and two rams; they are to be a burnt offering to the LORD, with their grain offering and their libations, an offering by fire of a soothing aroma to the Lord.

Since the thanksgiving offering (also called "thank offering") and the Festival of Pentecost offering are both made with leaven, it makes sense that they are never called "matzah" (unleavened). Along the same lines, since the twelve breads were called "bread" and never "matzah," this affords some proof that in the time of Moses they were made as regular leavened bread. Some say that the leaven in bread *always* refers symbolically to malice and wickedness, but then this would have God commanding offerings to Him of malice and wickedness.

At some point in history an argument began between the Pharisees and the Sadducees concerning the true starting point for the countdown to Pentecost, which began with the waving of the sheaf (Leviticus 23:12) and the *first-fruits offering*.

The Pharisees argued that this 50-day counting was to begin after the Sabbath of the Passover (i.e., the Sabbath of the 15th special day of rest when the Israelites came out of Egypt). The Sadducees argued that since in Hebrew the regular word for the Sabbath (i.e., Saturday Sabbath) was used, that the first Saturday Sabbath in the Festival is what was meant.

God decided the matter by raising Christ from the dead on the morrow of the Saturday Sabbath, and Paul called Christ our "first fruits." Thus Pentecost also would always fall on a Sunday. The scriptures also bear this out, because Leviticus 23:16 says to count 50 days until the "day after the seventh Sabbath," and for that 50-count to end on the day after a Sabbath, it had to begin on the day after a regular Saturday Sabbath.

It is possible that the Pharisees changed this date so that events did not align so closely with Christ being both sacrificed at the 14th-day Passover and then resurrected, fulfilling the unleavened first-fruits offering on the morrow of the Sabbath (i.e., Sunday). This change to the Pharisaic doctrine probably took place sometime shortly after Christ fulfilled this first-fruits offering, but either way the change was not scriptural.

God Also Clearly Commanded When Unleavened Was Required

As we saw in Course 1, God commanded to eat only matzah during the Passover and the seven-day Festival of Unleavened *Bread*—26 Old Testament verses listed there bore this out. So the question to ask is why the twelve Temple breads were always called "bread" and never "matzah" if they were really matzah under Moses?

When comparing the two leavened bread offerings (the thank offering and those breads at the Feast of Pentecost) to the Festival of Unleavened *Bread,* we see a marked contrast. Although the English translations add the word "Bread" to this Festival of Unleavened, the original Hebrew and Greek scriptures never connected the word "bread" at all to this festival name.

Here are a couple of examples where the Hebrew text simply says "matzah" (unleavened) and the Greek Septuagint says *azumwn* (unleavened), but the word "bread" has been *added* to the English translation:

> ᴷᴶⱽ Leviticus 23:6   And on the fifteenth day of the same month *is* the feast of unleavened **bread** unto the LORD: seven days ye must eat unleavened **bread**.

> ᴸˣᵀ Leviticus 23:6   καὶ ἐν τῇ πεντεκαιδεκάτῃ ἡμέρᾳ τοῦ μηνὸς τούτου ἑορτὴ τῶν ἀζύμων τῷ κυρίῳ ἑπτὰ ἡμέρας ἄζυμα ἔδεσθε

> ᴷᴶⱽ Exodus 12:8   And they shall eat the flesh in that night, roast with fire, and unleavened **bread**; *and* with bitter *herbs* they shall eat it.

> ᴸˣᵀ Exodus 12:8   καὶ φάγονται τὰ κρέα τῇ νυκτὶ ταύτῃ ὀπτὰ πυρὶ καὶ ἄζυμα ἐπὶ πικρίδων ἔδονται

Whether or not the word "bread" was added to bolster the translator's concept of Jesus supposedly eating bread at what the translator believed to be the Passover, it has created confusion. In reality, bread had nothing to do with this seven-day festival.

So you would have to ask yourself why is the *exact opposite* true with the Showbread? Why are they never called "matzah" in any scripture (Hebrew or Greek)? And why are they never qualified by God or any prophet as being unleavened? On the contrary, they are simply called breads (*lechem* in Hebrew), just like the other two *leavened* grain offerings seen earlier—the thank offerings and the Feast of Pentecost bread offerings.

Are we to believe that this exact opposite usage is just a coincidence?

One more thing—in addition to all the times the twelve breads are called "bread" in scripture, there is an occasion when they are called "cakes" or *challah* in Hebrew (Leviticus 24:5). However, this doesn't add much to our investigation since "cakes" in the Temple offerings were either leavened or unleavened depending on God's direction, but the scripture specifically qualifies them each time as either leavened or unleavened (Leviticus 7:13; Exodus 29:2).

Twelve Breads Show Forth Aspects of God's Plan for His People

Let's now consider this picture through a typological, symbolic interpretation—in other words, how certain elements in the Old Covenant prefigure those in the New Covenant. We'll start with the possibility that the twelve breads were leavened and what this would symbolically portray for the twelve tribes, and then consider the same if the breads were *unleavened*.

In the first scenario we would see that the twelve tribes of Israel were still leavened in the figurative sense since they fell short of God's will at times (read any book in the Jewish Bible to confirm this). Yet God still accepted them in His presence because they performed the legally commanded blood sacrifices, and their heart was to walk in God's covenant and in the light He had shown. Thus, the Showbread that symbolized the twelve tribes was placed face-to-face before Him, in His presence:

> NAS Exodus 25:30 "And you shall set the **bread of the Presence** on the table **before Me** at all times.

> LXT Exodus 25:30 καὶ ἐπιθήσεις ἐπὶ τὴν τράπεζαν ἄρτους ἐνωπίους ἐναντίον μου διὰ παντός

These two rows of six breads sat side by side in the first room (Leviticus 24:6) facing the second room, which contained the Ark of the Covenant, where God was considered to reside; thus they were symbolically situated toward His face in the place where He said He would dwell (Exodus 25:22). However, a veil hung between these two rooms, separating the innermost sacred room from the room containing the Showbread portion. This was true in the movable Tabernacle and later in the fixed

Temple. The priests would enter into the larger room called the Holy Place (where the Showbread dwelt). And when the High Priest passed beyond the veil on the Day of Atonement into the Most Holy Place (also called the Holy of Holies), he would see the Ark of the Covenant, considered the dwelling place of God.

> NIV Hebrews 9:7   But only the high priest entered the inner room, and that only once a year, and never without blood, which he offered for himself and for the sins the people had committed in ignorance.

> DBY Hebrews 9:8   the Holy Spirit shewing this, that the way of the *holy of* holies has not yet been made manifest while as yet the first tabernacle has *its* standing;

So Paul is saying that under the law and the first covenant, only the high priest could enter the Holy of Holies, and never without blood. This kept the other priests (and symbolically the twelve breads) away from the direct presence of God in this holiest place. Paul then explains that the Holy Spirit was showing that the way directly into God's presence was not yet available while the first covenant law still had its legal standing. When the Holy Spirit tore this veil in half at the time of the Messiah's death, it showed that the way into God's direct presence was now fully available because the full price had just been paid:

> NAS Matthew 27:50   And Jesus cried out again with a loud voice, and yielded up *His* spirit.

> NAS Matthew 27:51   And behold, the veil of the temple was torn in two from top to bottom, and the earth shook; and the rocks were split,

With the veil torn in two, the twelve breads were now face-to-face with God, showing that all who believed in the Messiah's sacrifice had direct access to God's presence. In fact, not only could believers enter directly into the holiest place where His full presence dwells, but His spirit could actually infill them.

After the 50-day counting following the sheaf offering (Leviticus 23:15) that we discussed earlier and the coming of the Day of Pentecost, the Holy Spirit was poured out for all believers to receive, and anyone—male, female, and proselytes (Acts 1:14, 15; 2:10)—could now be filled with God's spirit:

> NAB Acts 2:1   When the time for Pentecost was fulfilled, they were all in one place together.

> NAB Acts 2:4 And they were all filled with the holy Spirit and began to speak in different tongues, as the Spirit enabled them to proclaim.

Then an event occurred that was quite shocking to these Jewish Messianic believers: God actually filled **uncircumcised Gentile believers** (Acts 10 and 11) with the Holy Spirit:

> NAS Acts 10:45   And all the circumcised believers who had come with Peter were amazed, because the gift of the Holy Spirit had been poured out upon the Gentiles also.

They were all filled with the spirit of God (with the evidence of speaking in tongues). Peter says that this fulfilled what Joel had prophesied (Acts 2:16; see also Isaiah 28:9–12): that a time was coming when God would pour out His spirit on all people—not just the high priest, but on everyone from fishermen to tax collectors to uncircumcised Gentiles—anyone who would receive His forgiveness and His gift. Thus God's Spirit would be poured out on all mankind:

> NAS Joel 2:28   "And it will come about after this That I will pour out My Spirit on all mankind; And your sons and daughters will prophesy, Your old men will dream dreams, Your young men will see visions.

In the New Covenant, whosoever desires to enter God's house through the door may come in (the Messiah said he is the door, John 10:9). Thus the prophecy was fulfilled that God's house would be a house of prayer for all nations:

> NIV Isaiah 56:7   these I will bring to my holy mountain and give them joy in my house of prayer. Their burnt offerings and sacrifices will be accepted on my altar; **for my house will be called a house of prayer for all nations.**"

In Course 2 we saw what Jesus was referring to with the pieces of the one regular *leavened* bread that he broke: that we are the body of Christ. Remember that when interpreting typology or figurative teachings, only the portion of the teaching that fits and is *meant* by the spirit of God should be applied. When something is in question, Jesus said the Holy Spirit will lead us into all truth, so we always of course want to be led by God's spirit. The word of God comes first, and typology can be gleaned from what is already true in God's word.

So when Jesus refers to himself as the living "bread" in John 6, he obviously does not mean anything negative by using the Greek word for regular leavened "bread." He is only pointing to bread as daily sustenance, and in this context comparing himself to the true manna (the spiritual provision sent from God) called the "bread of heaven." The same is true when John refers to Jesus as the "lamb of God." Lambs often have white curly hair and are easily led astray. However, you could not apply those traits to the Messiah, because that is not what John meant in the type or symbolic language that he used. John was using "lamb" typologically in the positive sense, that Christ was perfectly led by God, never resisting (Isaiah 53:7), and also pointing to Christ as the true Passover lamb.

Jesus warned the disciples about the "leaven" of the Pharisees (Matthew 16:6–12), and eventually they understood that he was not referring to the leaven of bread but to the Pharisees' *teachings*. Paul uses leaven figuratively in a much harsher sense in referring to the man who commits gross sin (1 Corinthians 5). Paul figuratively equates this sin to having leaven at Passover, saying malice and wickedness should not be a part of this spiritual feast that they, and we, have entered into.

None of this presents the twelve tribes symbolized by the Showbread as bad people containing leaven. It only acknowledges that all have sinned, and no one is righteous by himself or able to perfectly keep the law. This is why the virgin birth was needed (Isaiah 7:14)—to bypass the genetic disposition toward sin that is in every son and daughter of Adam. The natural man at his best is not perfectly subject to God and the law, neither can he be (Romans 8:7, as seen in the original Greek text). However, God loves and accepts us into His presence when we follow His commandments and are covered by the blood. This was true in the Old Covenant, and it remains so in the New Covenant, yet with a different blood.

If the Twelve Breads Were Unleavened…

We have considered the typological truths seen in the twelve Temple breads being leavened. Now we will examine the typology if the twelve breads were matzah and what symbolic picture this would show forth.

If the twelve breads were really matzah (unleavened), then in this typological picture the twelve tribes would be without sin, malice, pride, or any false doctrine. They would always make the right choice as God leads them and they would represent His finished plan revealed—holy and complete, never once falling short of the law but ready to ascend as an unleavened fire offering to God.

Now the Jewish writers of scripture deserve a great deal of credit because they do not hide what really happened. The ups and the downs, the good and the bad—it's all there for us to read. In both Testaments of the Bible, you can open pretty much any book and see that the tribes of Israel (as well as the believers in the Messiah) were not yet perfected.

Bible history clearly shows that from a typological figurative picture, regular leavened bread fits better for the twelve breads, so let's consider why God did not specify whether they should be leavened or not, and yet He still called them "breads."

We could say that God did not command that these twelve breads be leavened because He was showing that, for the believers, a time would come when they would be unleavened before Him (legally or by experience). Leaving this one offering unsaid as to leaven could indicate that God was symbolically showing that the believers could become spiritually unleavened one day.

God knew the twelve tribes under the law would symbolically still have leaven; therefore these twelve breads were called "breads" (*lechem* in Hebrew—regular leavened breads) and never *matzah* (unleavened). God did not command for these twelve breads to be made unleavened, for this could wrongly imply that God saw the twelve tribes as holy and pure in and of themselves at that time.

By not directly commanding that the breads be made unleavened or leavened, God shows that the twelve tribes had free will before Him to strive individually to be holy and clean under the law, without implying that they had actually succeeded in this. Calling them "breads" in the scriptures is just being real with what they represented—and that they were not yet completely unleavened.

Through the blood sacrificial system, God saw the twelve tribes as consecrated and acceptable before Him and thus able to come into His presence, but only because this same system pointed forward to the true deliverer from sin—Messiah the true Passover.

In addition, by not giving Moses any direct command to make the twelve breads without leaven, it would have been legal to bake them as the priests saw fit. If they decided it was God's will to make them unleavened (bread of affliction), then they could do that. And if they felt that the leavened breads were much more appetizing and did not oppose the spirit of any of the commandments, then they could bake them as the more flavorful loaves that would be a blessing to the priests from Aaron every Sabbath.

Later, under the Pharisees' legalistic leadership (and thus not led by God's spirit to understand what God, Moses, and David meant in calling the twelve loaves "bread" without any qualifying description), the Sadducee ministers could be forced to eat them unleavened, as matzah, every Sabbath.

Figurative Uses of Bread

Before we get to the one figurative occurrence of bread used during the Festival of the Unleavened (Deuteronomy 16:3), let's first look at some other figurative uses of bread in the Jewish idiom.

Some have tried to argue that because manna was called "bread"—and in their logic it would have been unleavened—they think this is another example of bread being actually unleavened. However, this misses the fact that manna was only figuratively called "bread." It was obviously not baked in an oven in heaven, with or without leaven, so this does not apply to the argument as to whether or not the Showbread was leavened.

> [NAS] Exodus 16:4 Then the LORD said to Moses, "Behold, I will **rain bread** from heaven for you; and the people shall go out and gather a day's portion every day, that I may test them, whether or not they will walk in **My instruction**.

> [NAS] Deuteronomy 29:5–6 "**And I have led you forty years in the wilderness**; your clothes have not worn out on you, and your sandal has not worn out on your foot. **You have not eaten bread**, nor have you drunk wine or strong drink, in order that you might know that I am the LORD your God.

Thus the scriptures say they ate no bread for 40 years in the wilderness, but they did eat the manna that was called "bread"; but this is not a contradiction as manna was called "bread" only in a figurative sense.

> [JPS] Numbers 21:5 And the people spoke against God, and against Moses: 'Wherefore have ye brought us up out of Egypt to die in the wilderness? **for there is no bread**, and there is no water; **and our soul loatheth this light bread**.'

So the people first say "there is no bread," then they say they loathe this "light bread." The Hebrew word for "light" means "contemptible, worthless, wretched," and each mention of bread in this verse is *lechem*, the normal Hebrew word for "bread." So when they declare that there is no "bread," this does not contradict the fact that they loathe the bread, because manna was not actual bread—it was only called "bread" in a figurative sense.

Several other verses exist in which "bread" appears in the figurative sense. For instance:

> [NAS] Psalm 80:5 Thou hast fed them with the bread of tears, And Thou hast made them to drink tears in large measure.

This, of course, doesn't mean that people cried bread or breadcrumbs, but it is used in a symbolic, figurative, and descriptive sense.

Many more such examples exist:

> ᴷᴶⱽ Psalm 127:2 *It is* vain for you to rise up early, to sit up late, to eat the **bread of sorrows**: *for* so he giveth his beloved sleep.

> ᴷᴶⱽ Proverbs 4:17 For they eat the **bread of wickedness**, and drink the wine of violence.

> ᴷᴶⱽ Proverbs 20:17 **Bread of deceit** *is* sweet to a man; but afterwards his mouth shall be filled with gravel.

In the verse below, the Canaanite woman came to Jesus for healing, and he symbolically spoke of healing as the "children's bread," meaning that healing from God was symbolically "bread" for those who are in covenant with God:

> ᴷᴶⱽ Matthew 15:26 But he answered and said, It is not meet to take the **children's bread**, and to cast *it* to dogs.

Although this Canaanite woman was outside of the covenant, she did not retreat but instead pressed forward, asking the Messiah to heal her daughter:

> ᴺᴬˢ Matthew 15:27 But she said, "Yes, Lord; but even the dogs feed on the crumbs which fall from their masters' table."

> ᴺᴬˢ Matthew 15:28 Then Jesus answered and said to her, "O woman, your faith is great; be it done for you as you wish." And her daughter was healed at once.

Bread of sorrows, bread of wickedness, bread of deceit, children's bread, and other such figurative usages for bread were commonly spoken and understood in the idiomatic sense among the Jews.

"Bread of Affliction" Used Figuratively in Deuteronomy 16:3

In the original Hebrew or Greek scriptures, neither the Hebrew nor the Greek words for "bread" are ever connected to the name of the feast that we call the Festival of Unleavened *Bread*. Yet there is *one* time when the matzah is figuratively called "bread" (as in the "bread of affliction") in connection with this Festival:

> ^{DBY} Deuteronomy 16:3   Thou shalt eat no leavened *bread* along with it; seven days shalt thou eat unleavened *bread* with it, **bread of affliction**; for thou camest forth out of the land of Egypt in haste,— that thou mayest remember the day when thou camest forth out of the land of Egypt, all the days of thy life.

In the verse above, the first two instances of "bread" are italicized (by me) to indicate that they do not appear in the original Hebrew or Greek text but were added to the English translation. Then we see the term "bread of affliction," which clearly describes the matzah (badly translated above as "unleavened **bread**"). Thus the matzah is figuratively called "bread of affliction." No reputable Jewish scholar of the Torah would cite this scripture as affirmation that it's acceptable to eat bread at Passover, or that it's fine for the Jews to go around Jerusalem saying they ate bread at Passover.

In both Hebrew and Greek the words for *matzah* and *azumwn* are plural, whereas "bread" (as in the "bread" of affliction) is singular. If this verse were referring to matzah as actual "bread," the grammatical rules (of Greek at least) would require "bread" to be plural, too. Instead, the sentence structure confirms that God is referring to the *matzah* **figuratively** as the "bread" of affliction.

Those who think that the Last Supper was the Passover regard the Messiah's eating of bread at that meal as normal behavior. They look at this scripture in Deuteronomy and say, "See, bread is bread."

However, the Jewish scribes were never confused as to this one figurative use of the word "bread." They knew that "bread of affliction" described the matzah only in a figurative sense; they never proclaimed, "I guess it's fine to go around Jerusalem saying we eat **bread** during Passover now."

This verse in Deuteronomy is a prime example that some commentators cite to prove that "bread is bread." Although Jesus ate bread at what they believe was the Passover, they insist the bread was unleavened because of rare cases like this, where "bread" refers to something that was unleavened.

It doesn't occur to them that under no circumstances would Jewish Messianic followers proclaim to the Jewish nation that they, together with Jesus, ate bread at the Passover (had the Last Supper actually been the Passover). The Talmud is clear that if even the high priest ate leaven at the Passover, he would be taken out and whipped.[185] To go around Jerusalem saying they had eaten bread at the Passover would have been shocking in the first-century Jewish idiom, and then to leave it unqualified—by not clarifying that it was supposedly matzah—could have led to whippings and worse.

---

185   Babylonian Talmud, Book 9, Tract Maccoth, ch. 3, p. 35, http://sacred-texts.com/jud/t09/mac08.htm.

Why was it not qualified as matzah? Because it was regular leavened bread served at this Last Supper meal—which actually took place on the night *before* the Passover sacrifice.

"Bread of God" Is Used Figuratively

As we have seen before in this Course, the Levitical fire offering to God, called the "bread of God," was clearly commanded to be unleavened since God specified that nothing leavened was ever to be placed on the altar in the fire to Him:

> ᴺᴬˢ Leviticus 2:11 'No grain offering, which you bring to the LORD, shall be made with leaven, **for you shall not offer up in smoke any leaven** or any honey as **an offering by fire to the LORD.**

Some of the grain offerings from the people would be made into the Showbread, and some of that same grain (ground into flour) went directly on the altar as a fire offering to God. Thus God was showing Himself as partaking with His people by referring figuratively to His portion in the fire as "bread." God plainly qualified that these fire offerings to Him be unleavened, so the priests would not be confused or accidentally break a commandment (even though He loosely referred to them as His "bread").

As was already mentioned, several scriptures appear where the word "bread" is used *figuratively* for the matzah that went into the fire offering to God:

> ᴺᴬˢ Leviticus 21:6 'They shall be holy to their God and not profane the name of their God, for they present **the offerings by fire** to the LORD, **the bread of their God**; so they shall be holy.

> ᴺᴬˢ Leviticus 21:8 'You shall consecrate him, therefore, **for he offers the bread of your God**; he shall be holy to you; for I the LORD, who sanctifies you, am holy.

> ᴺᴬˢ Leviticus 21:21 'No man among the descendants of Aaron the priest, who has a defect, is to come near to offer the LORD's offerings by fire; *since* he has a defect, he shall not come near to offer **the bread of his God.**

The previous Course discussed that Jewish communal meals during the festivals were not just meals among the Jews, but that God Himself was regarded more than just a guest since the entire Temple was God's house. Thus in the Showbread communal meal they partook of bread together, the priests with their "presence breads" and

God with His "bread" in the fire offering on the altar, both of which came from the same grain tithes of the people.

With God's commandment that nothing leavened was ever to be offered in the fire to Him, it is clear that His bread was only figuratively called "bread," just as the manna was. God could then also refer to His portion of the sacrifices figuratively as His "bread," partly to show *that He was joining in the communal meals with them*. The Jews were not confused by God calling his portion "bread"; they did not say, "Oh, I guess this means bread is bread and we can offer it in the fire to God either leavened or unleavened."

Below, in Leviticus 3, the Hebrew word for "bread" is used figuratively *for the kidneys* from the animal sacrifice that went in the fire to God, as this was God's portion:

> ᴺᴬˢ Leviticus 3:10   and the two kidneys with the fat that is on them, which is on the loins, and the lobe of the liver, which he shall remove with the kidneys.

> ʸᴸᵀ Leviticus 3:11   and the priest hath made it a perfume on the altar—**bread of a fire-offering to Jehovah**.

The "bread of God" also points to Christ, the only man who could be said to be unleavened, who ascended to God directly through the fire. Christ was the only sinless one that this offering pointed to. And Jesus also referred to himself as the "bread of God"—as in the true spiritual manna (also itself figuratively called "bread," Psalm 105:40). He figuratively comes down as manna from God bringing God's teaching and spiritual provision:

> ᴺᴵⱽ John 6:33   For **the bread of God** is he who **comes down** from heaven and gives life to the world."

So we cannot use these figurative occurrences of bread in the scriptures to claim that "bread is bread" and therefore the twelve breads were unleavened, or that the bread Jesus ate at the Last Supper was unleavened. We cannot do this because, when it was important to know, God always qualified in the scriptures whether something was unleavened or not. Of the more than 300 times that "bread" is used in the scriptures for regular leavened bread, only on a few rare occasions does it refer loosely or figuratively to something unleavened. But as we cover each one, we will see that every single time *it is clearly qualified in the text*.

Other Figurative Uses of Bread

Now we will examine the remaining scriptures used by some people to try to prove that bread is bread, since these unleavened items mentioned below are occasionally referred to figuratively or in a loose, generic sense as "bread." There's one important distinction, however: God clearly qualifies that each of them are to be made *unleavened*.

"Bread" is used a few rare times to refer to a basket of various unleavened things (cakes, wafers, etc.) that are all called "matzahs," some of which will go in the fire to God. These are figuratively called "breads." However, just as with the unleavened "bread of God" that went in the fire to Him, God always indicates specifically when something is actually to be unleavened, as in this priestly ordination service:

> NAS Exodus 29:1 "Now this is what you shall do to them to consecrate them to minister as priests to Me: take one young bull and two rams without blemish,

> NAS Exodus 29:2 and **unleavened bread** and unleavened cakes mixed with oil, and unleavened wafers spread with oil; you shall make them of fine wheat flour.

> NAS Exodus 29:3 "And you shall put them in **one basket**, and present them in the basket along with the bull and the two rams.

> NAS Exodus 29:23 and one cake of bread and one cake of bread *mixed with* oil and one wafer **from the basket of unleavened bread**[186] which is *set* before the LORD;

> NAS Exodus 29:25 "And you shall take them from their hands, **and offer them up in smoke on the altar** on the burnt offering for a soothing aroma before the LORD; **it is an offering by fire to the LORD**.

I counted 36 times where most English translations say "unleavened bread" in the Old Testament, but in 35 of them the original Hebrew only says "matzah." Verse 2 above is the only instance where both words— *matzah* and *lechem* (unleavened bread)—actually appear together. However, three points make it obvious that once again "bread" is being used *figuratively* for this basket of matzah.

---

186 In the original Hebrew of the above verse, the text reads "basket of **matzah**" instead of "basket of unleavened bread."

First of all, in the Greek Septuagint text, "bread" is a noun, whereas *unleavened* (*azumos*) is an adjective. Therefore the Jewish scholars who translated the Septuagint show that "unleavened" qualifies that this is not regular bread. Secondly, as we see in verse 23, these breads that were placed in a basket were already called the "basket of *matzah*" in Hebrew, leaving no question that they were unleavened. Thirdly, each of the items in the basket was placed on the altar as a fire offering to God (as seen in verse 25) and, as we know, fire offerings were commanded to be unleavened (Leviticus 2:11).

So for any scholar to say, "See, bread is bread, and in these scriptures it's unleavened so that proves the twelve breads must have been unleavened" does not accurately reflect the meaning of these scriptures. Taking figurative uses of the word "bread" to prove that the twelve breads were therefore matzah does not logically follow.

Likewise, you cannot extend these figurative uses to insist that it was normal for Jesus to eat bread at Passover, or that the disciples went around Jerusalem telling everyone that they and Jesus ate bread during Passover. When it was important to know, God always qualified the type of bread (as we saw in the scriptural examples above). During Passover, knowing the difference between matzah and bread was critical, lest one be cut off from the nation (Exodus 12:15, 19); God made it especially clear that only matzah was allowed.

This same priestly ordination service we just saw in Exodus was also mentioned in Leviticus, where the items again were figuratively called "bread," yet placed on the fire to the Lord—and therefore necessarily unleavened (Leviticus 2:11)—as the "bread of God":

> NAS Leviticus 8:2 "Take Aaron and his sons with him, and the garments and the anointing oil and the bull of the sin offering, and the two rams and the **basket of unleavened bread**;

In the Hebrew for this scripture, the word "bread" does not appear; it's just the basket of matzahs. Similarly, in verse 26 below the Hebrew says "basket of matzah"; the word "bread" is inserted in most English translations:[187]

> NAS Leviticus 8:26 And from the **basket of unleavened bread** that was before the LORD, he took one unleavened cake and one cake of bread *mixed with* oil and one wafer, and placed *them* on the portions of fat and on the right thigh.

---

[187] I have found the NAS to be a very good translation overall, but in our English idiom, saying "unleavened bread" has become so common that it sounds strange to not add the word "bread."

Verse 28 refers to this same basket of matzahs, with Moses offering one of each as a *fire offering* to the Lord:

> ^{NAS} Leviticus 8:28   Then Moses took them from their hands **and offered them up in smoke on the altar with the burnt offering**. They were an ordination offering for a soothing aroma; **it was an offering by fire to the LORD**.

Remember we saw in the previous "bread of God" section that when matzah went up to God as a fire offering, it was referred to figuratively as the "bread of God." In verse 31, Aaron and the priests partook of the remaining matzah in the basket after God's portion of this fire offering went up in the smoke to Him, showing a joint participation. Since God symbolically partook of this offering with them, it is referred to as "bread" in a generic or figurative sense:

> ^{NAS} Leviticus 8:31   Then Moses said to Aaron and to his sons, "Boil the flesh at the doorway of the tent of meeting, and eat it there together with the **bread** which is **in the basket** of the ordination offering, just as I commanded, saying, 'Aaron and his sons shall eat it.'

The Jewish priests were never confused about this figurative usage of the word "bread." Only later was this usage clouded by those who said that the Showbread was to be unleavened, and by others who said that the Last Supper bread was unleavened.

As we've seen, many of the figurative uses of the word "bread" were taken out of context and used as apparent proofs that bread is bread. For the true meaning to emerge, the scriptures must be understood from within the Jewish idiom and by ascertaining whether God meant "bread" literally or figuratively, by qualifying it.

One portion of scripture sums it all up: The angel of the Lord (i.e., God manifesting as an angel) comes down to Manoah and his wife, having already promised that they would have a son, Samson, who would deliver Israel. The angel of the Lord then speaks about man's "bread":

> ^{KJV} Judges 13:15   And Manoah said unto the angel of the LORD, I pray thee, let us detain thee, until we shall have made ready a kid for thee.

> ᴋᴊᴠ Judges 13:16   And the angel of the LORD said unto Manoah, Though thou detain me, **I will not eat of thy bread**: and if thou wilt offer a burnt offering, thou must offer it unto the LORD. **For Manoah knew not that he *was* an angel of the LORD**.

> ɴɪᴠ Judges 13:19   Then Manoah took a young goat, **together with the grain offering**, and sacrificed it on a rock to the LORD. And the LORD did an amazing thing while Manoah and his wife watched:

> ɴɪᴠ Judges 13:20   As the flame blazed up from the altar toward heaven, the angel of the LORD ascended in the flame. Seeing this, Manoah and his wife fell with their faces to the ground.

So when Manoah speaks of having an earthly meal with this angel of the Lord (i.e., God manifesting as an angel), the Lord in effect says, "I do not eat of man's bread." The "bread of God" is that which goes in the fire to God. God has given regular bread to man as a provision of food, but God does not eat man's bread (or man's food). The bread of God is pure and unleavened, and while the bread of man is good and flavorful (not necessarily evil), God only partakes of man's bread figuratively.

Christ was the true "bread of God" that He was looking for, and God sees Christ in those of us who have received him, which makes us acceptable in God's presence. Because the penalty was paid, He is no longer mindful of our sin as to require payment (Jeremiah 31:34). He casts it away "as far as the east is from the west," never to remember it against us (Psalm 103:12).

Jesus figuratively called himself "bread," for he was "made like unto his brethren" (i.e., the twelve "breads" of Israel, Hebrews 2:17), yet without sin. Jesus was the sinless "bread of God" without leaven that can go right up in the fire to God; he was "bread" in the sense of the manna (the "bread of heaven"). He is "bread" because he is our daily sustenance.

Those who are "caught up" to God without seeing death (1 Thessalonians 4:17, Revelation 12:5) can go straight to Him, because they are the spiritual "body of Christ" and legally unleavened. They represent the spiritual fulfillment of what the twelve breads pointed to, and Christ—as the true frankincense that went in the fire to God—sanctified them, thus making the whole offering an acceptable fire offering to Him.

In the Old Covenant, 11 of the Israelite tribes were excluded from partaking of these breads, as were all Gentiles and many Levites (except those of Aaron's lineage). This shows that partaking of the twelve breads was a high calling, yet it is something we are all invited to fulfill in the spiritual sense.

In the New Covenant all are called, but not all will hear the calling and move into it. Jesus showed this in the parables of Matthew (22:1–14) and Luke (14:16–24) when many began to make excuses as to why they could not come to the Lord's wedding feast. The Lord will have a bride, however, and in the New Covenant this position is open to everyone (John 6:37).

COURSE 8

GOD'S OVERALL PLAN AND PATTERN FOR MANKIND

In this Course we will step back and examine the bigger picture of God's plan for mankind from the beginning. This will then set the stage for a deeper look into the twelve breads to see what God was showing in this Temple bread service. After all, God has a purpose and a plan for His people, and the pattern for this has been shown throughout history.

In the scriptures, we first see this plan in Genesis 1:26:

> NAS Genesis 1:26a Then God said, "Let Us make man in Our image, according to Our likeness;

This pattern (form, model, figure) and plan is also later seen in Noah, Moses, King David, and symbolically in the twelve breads (Showbread). The plan shows the path to coming into God's likeness and the way of escape from the hour of tribulation that will soon come upon the world (as was pictured through Noah and the Ark).

God's Plan from the Beginning

From the beginning God kept showing His plan, and throughout history He revealed a pattern that pointed to His own image and likeness that He wanted man to come into. For instance, He made Adam in His own image:

> NAS Genesis 1:26a Then God said, "Let Us make man in Our image, according to Our likeness;

> NAS Genesis 1:27 And God created man in His own image, in the image of God He created him; male and female He created them.

We see this plan fulfilled in the Messiah, who was the *true* plan and pattern of the Showbread (as we will see in Course 9). God's will is that we also come into this same image that Christ came into, as the following scriptures show:

> ^{NAS} 2 Corinthians 4:4   in whose case the god of this world has blinded the minds of the unbelieving, that they might not see the light of the gospel of the glory of **Christ, who is the image of God**.
>
> ^{NAS} 2 Corinthians 3:18   But **we all**, with unveiled face beholding as in a mirror the glory of the Lord, **are being transformed into the same image** from glory to glory, just as from the Lord, the Spirit.
>
> ^{NAS} Ephesians 4:13   until we all attain to the unity of the faith, and of the knowledge of the Son of God, to a mature man, **to the measure of the stature which belongs to the fulness of Christ**.

As a side note, it is probably true that in Genesis 1:26 God is speaking to Christ *prophetically*, and in a sense also to all those who work with God toward this end of fulfilling this scripture, both before and after Christ (John 5:17; Hebrews 4:11; Revelation 19:7). In the same way that God spoke prophetically to King Cyrus more than a century before Cyrus was born (Isaiah 45:1–6), God also speaks to the Messiah prophetically in Isaiah and in the Psalms:

> ^{NIV} Isaiah 42:6   "I, the LORD, have called you in righteousness; I will take hold of your hand. I will keep you and will make you to be a covenant for the people and a light for the Gentiles,
>
> ^{NIV} Psalm 110:1   Of David. A psalm. The LORD says to my lord: "Sit at my right hand until I make your enemies a footstool for your feet."

It is clear that this statement in Genesis 1:26 ("Let Us make man in Our image, according to Our likeness") was spoken before Adam was created, and God was not speaking to another God for there is only one God (Isaiah 45:5, 6, 21). Nor was God conversing with angels, for they are not in His image and likeness and are only a little above man in this realm (Psalm 8:4–6; Hebrews 2:7–9).

Whether one agrees with the prophetic nature of Genesis 1:26 or not, it cannot be disputed that it was God's desire to make man *in His image*, and that is what He did with Adam (Genesis 1:27). The "likeness" was to come as Adam walked with God and dwelt in His presence.

This theme keeps playing out in various generations in various ways, until the coming of the true pattern for God's plan—the Messiah—who was not only in God's image but also His likeness.

The Pattern Given to Noah in Type

When God told Noah to construct an ark in which he and his family would be saved, He was also pointing ahead and using the type of Noah to warn us of future things for which we should prepare and make ready:

> NAS Genesis 6:15a "And this is how you shall make it:

Then God went on to give Noah the *pattern* for the natural ark, which, when built as commanded, would provide safety for Noah and his family to escape the coming flood.

> NAS Genesis 6:22 Thus Noah did; according to all that God had commanded him, so he did.

This natural ark is a *type* that prefigures the spiritual ark to come in the promised New Covenant time. Jesus (Yeshua) tells us below that his next coming will be just like the days of Noah. This means that we will be constructing a *spiritual* ark, just as Noah built a *natural* ark, and that by doing this exactly according to the pattern that God wants (i.e., Messiah, the true pattern), we will be taken safely away into His presence:

> NAS Matthew 24:37 "For the coming of the Son of Man will be **just like** the days of Noah.

> NAS Matthew 24:38 "For as in those days which were before the flood they were eating and drinking, they were marrying and giving in marriage,[188] until the day that Noah entered the ark,

> NAS Matthew 24:39 and **they** did not understand until the flood came and **took** them[189] all away; so shall the coming of the Son of Man be.

In verse 39, "they" who "did not understand" refers to those left behind in the flood. It is also important to understand that "took them away all" (see footnote 189) does not refer to those drowned in the flood, as we might expect, but rather to those taken away safely in the Ark with Noah. The Greek word *airw*, translated as "took," means "to elevate, lift up, or carry away" (our English word "air" stems from this). Those who were taken away safely were those sons of Noah and their wives who remained faithful and worked on the Ark with Noah.

---

[188] There is, of course, nothing wrong with eating, drinking, or marrying; it just shows that outward life was taking place as normal until the flood came.

[189] The word "them" is not in the Greek. It reads "took away all," referring to those in the Ark.

Jesus thus shows that Noah and the Ark were a *type* of the spiritual ark—those who allow the spirit of God to shape them into the pattern that He wants. Noah's sons and their wives simply had to continue working with Noah as God gave direction. They did not have to be great in themselves or possess any super qualities, only be willing to follow God and to work on the Ark according to His pattern.

God used the flood to take Noah and his family safely away; in connecting the last half of verse 39 with verse 40, Jesus then continues this same theme in the scriptures that follow in reference to the future catching away of the believers, the spiritual ark:

> NAS Matthew 24:39   and they did not understand until the flood came and took them all away; so shall the coming of the Son of Man be.
>
> NAS Matthew 24:40   "Then there shall be two men in the field; one will be **taken**, and one will be left.
>
> NAS Matthew 24:41   "Two women *will be* grinding at the mill; one will be **taken**, and one will be left.
>
> NAS Matthew 24:42   "Therefore be on the alert, for you do not know which day your Lord is coming.

The Greek word for "coming" in verse 39 above is *parousia*, which can also mean "presence," either physically on earth or by the Lord's presence in the air. Here it refers to the Messiah's presence in the air, which will occur at the rapture (or at the "catching away," for those who do not like the term "rapture"). Those *taken* in verses 40–41 correspond to those taken away safely to God in verse 39.

Parousia is also translated as "coming" in 1 Thessalonians 4:15 in the same context of our being "caught up" (4:17) to meet the Messiah in the **air** at the rapture:

> NAS 1 Thessalonians 4:15   For this we say to you by the word of the Lord, that we who are alive, and remain until the coming of the Lord, shall not precede those who have fallen asleep.
>
> NAS 1 Thessalonians 4:16   For the Lord Himself will descend from heaven with a shout, with the voice of *the* archangel, and with the trumpet of God; and the dead in Christ shall rise[190] first.

---

190   "Rise" here refers to believers who have died yet will rise out of their graves upon the earth first, before then being caught up.

> NAS 1 Thessalonians 4:17   Then we who are alive and remain shall be **caught up together with them** in the clouds[191] **to meet the Lord in the air**, and thus we shall always be with the Lord.

Some may dismiss this as pie in the sky, but there is no pie here at all; this is people rising up in the air to be with the Lord forever. This is not the second coming, which will follow later, but the Lord's presence (*parousia*) in the air and our being safely caught up to meet him. The book of Revelation (3:10; 12:5) symbolically pictures this same event where the man child (or "male child," NIV) is caught up to God, which we will get to shortly. Another picture of this spiritual ark preparing is the bride of Christ making herself ready (Revelation 19:7).

Returning to Noah, Peter also speaks of him:

> NAS 1 Peter 3:19   in which also He went and made proclamation to the spirits *now*[192] in prison,

> NAS 1 Peter 3:20   who once were disobedient, when the patience of God kept waiting in the days of Noah, during the construction of the ark, in which a few, that is, eight persons, **were brought safely through** *the* **water**.

Jesus said that the last days would be just like in the days of Noah (Matthew 24:37), so we should now be building the true spiritual ark and the pattern that God has given us. This will provide our escape when the devil's "flood" of iniquity and lawlessness arrives. We will then be lifted up and "brought safely through" if we follow God's pattern and plan and do not become "disobedient," as many were in Noah's day.

We see from Peter's verses above that some who were righteous—although they were disobedient to God's high calling, did not believe Noah, and therefore died in the flood—still received good news of salvation from the Messiah. This is made clear in Ephesians 4:8, which says "he took captivity captive," a figure of speech meaning he delivered those righteous who died from the time of Adam and took them to heaven, which the Messiah was prophesied to do (Psalm 68:18).

---

191 "In the clouds" actually reads as "in clouds" in Greek, and it refers to large numbers of people going up in the air.

192 The italicizing of the word "now" shows it does not appear in the original Greek.

The Pattern and Plan Shown to Moses for the Dwelling Place of God

God shows His plan again in another picture in type when he directs Moses to construct the Tabernacle. This time His plan points forward to the spiritual tabernacle that the Messiah would build:

> ^{NAS} Exodus 25:8 "And let them construct a sanctuary for Me, **that I may dwell among them**.
>
> ^{NAS} Exodus 25:9 "According to all that I am going to show you, *as* the **pattern** of the tabernacle and the **pattern** of all its furniture, just so you shall construct *it*.
>
> ^{NAS} Exodus 25:40 "And see that you make *them* **after the pattern** for them, which was shown to you on the mountain.
>
> ^{NAS} Exodus 26:30 "Then you shall erect the tabernacle **according to its plan** which you have been shown in the mountain.
>
> ^{NAS} Exodus 25:22 "And **there I will meet with you**; and from above the mercy seat, from between the two cherubim which are upon the ark of the testimony, I will speak to you about all that I will give you in commandment for the sons of Israel.

In verse 8 God told Moses to construct a sanctuary, "that I may dwell among them." We see in the scriptures that Messiah is the true sanctuary and true tabernacle that God was pointing to (John 2:19–22), and that we—the believers who fulfill God's pattern by having Christ formed in us—are also this tabernacle. Revelation 13:6 shows the Antichrist railing at this "tabernacle" of God (those who had been caught up to heaven):

> ^{NAS} Revelation 13:6 And he opened his mouth in blasphemies against God, to blaspheme His name **and His tabernacle**, *that is*,[193] **those who dwell in heaven**.

---

[193] The italicized words "*that is*" do not appear in the original Greek, so a more accurate reading of this passage is "to blaspheme His name and His tabernacle, those who dwell in heaven." In this case, "His tabernacle" consists of those people pictured in heaven in John's vision of a future time yet to come.

The *UBS Greek-English Dictionary* gives several meanings for this Greek word that is translated into English as "tabernacle," including "dwelling place," "tabernacle," and "house."[194] Thus, the believers collectively are pictured as the "house" of God (1 Peter 2:5), while the body of the individual spirit-filled believer is called "the temple" because the spirit of God dwells within (1 Corinthians 6:19). This helps explains why, in the scripture above, the believers—"those who dwell in heaven"—are called His **tabernacle**.

The true tabernacle of God as pictured above (Revelation 13:6) consists of those who had previously been caught up to God, as we see in the scripture below (Revelation 12:5). These are God's people who have fulfilled His plan and pattern, and are symbolically pictured here as a man child born from the woman:

> KJV Revelation 12:5 And she brought forth a **man child**, who was to rule all nations with a rod of iron: and her child was **caught up** unto God, and *to* his throne.

> NAS Revelation 21:3 And I heard a loud voice from the throne, saying, "Behold, the **tabernacle** of God is among men, and **He shall dwell among them**, and they shall be His people, and God Himself shall be among them,

This man child represents the nation that is born out of this woman who represents the visible church (Revelation 12:1–5). This man child/nation was also spoken of by the prophet Isaiah in the scriptures that follow, but first let's see how Isaiah sets up the context for these people who will serve as God's dwelling place or house of rest:

> NAS Isaiah 66:1 Thus says the LORD, "Heaven is My throne, and the earth is My footstool. **Where then is a house** you could build for Me? **And where is a place that I may rest?**

Then God goes on to say where and with whom His resting place will be (i.e., those who tremble at His word):

> NAS Isaiah 66:2 "For My hand made all these things, Thus all these things came into being," declares the LORD. "But to this one I will look, To him who is humble and contrite of spirit, and who trembles at My word.

---

194   *UBS Greek-English Dictionary*, pp. 163–164, s.v. "σκηνή."

> NAS Isaiah 66:5   Hear the word of the LORD, you who tremble at His word: "Your brothers who hate you, who exclude you for My name's sake, Have said, 'Let the LORD be glorified, that we may see your joy.' But they will be put to shame.
>
> KJV Isaiah 66:7   Before she travailed, she brought forth; before her pain came, she was delivered of a **man child**.
>
> NAS Isaiah 66:8   "**Who has heard such a thing?** Who has seen such things? Can a land be born in one day? **Can a nation be brought forth all at once?** As soon as Zion travailed, she also brought forth her sons.

In Isaiah's strange prophecy ("who has heard such a thing"), it was *before* the woman's pain came that she brought forth this man child/nation. Then in the book of Revelation, we again see this man child (who is eventually caught away to God) being born of the woman[195] ***before*** her pain fully came (Revelation 12:5, 17).

༺❋༻

Once again, those who build the true spiritual tabernacle according to God's pattern will be taken up and away to safety, fulfilling what He said to Moses concerning His plan:

> NAS Exodus 25:8   "And let them construct a sanctuary for Me, **that I may dwell among them.**

And to repeat, these scriptures in Revelation show that we are fulfilling this plan given to Moses by becoming the true tabernacle of God before getting caught up to Him.

> KJV Revelation 12:5   And she brought forth a **man child**, who was to rule all nations with a rod of iron: and **her child was caught up unto God**, and *to* his throne.
>
> NAS Revelation 13:6   And he opened his mouth in blasphemies against God, to blaspheme His name **and His tabernacle,** *that is,* **those who dwell in heaven.**

---

195   Here the woman represents the outward church. After the man child has been born and caught up, the remnant of her seed is attacked by the beast after the rapture (Revelation 12:17). See Course 12 for more on the beast.

Willing believers both small and great from all over the world will fulfill God's plan and receive His love as they follow His pattern (including the new commandment to love one another, seen in John 13:34), just as Noah and Moses followed the pattern given to them. They will come into His image and likeness by becoming the promised spiritual bride:

> NIV Revelation 19:7 Let us rejoice and be glad and give him glory! For the wedding of the Lamb has come, and his bride has made herself ready.

This profound spiritual union is what God has always desired for Israel and for all those who love Him; consequently, this "nation" will be caught up to God and kept out of the hour of testing:

> NAS Revelation 3:8 'I know your deeds. Behold, **I have put before you an open door which no one can shut**, because you have a little power, and have kept My word, and have not denied My name.

> NAS Revelation 3:9 'Behold, I will cause *those* of the synagogue of Satan, who say that they are Jews,[196] and are not, but lie—behold, I will make them to come and bow down at your feet, and to know that I have loved you.

> NAS Revelation 3:10 'Because you have kept the word of My perseverance, **I also will keep you from the hour of testing**, that *hour* which is about to come upon the whole world, to test those who dwell upon the earth.

The Plan and Pattern Given to David for the Dwelling Place of God

Now that we have seen God's plan and pattern applied to Noah with the Ark and Moses with the Tabernacle, we will consider King David and the plan for building the Temple. Not only was David given a pattern of God's plan for the Temple, but from Genesis he also understood God's desire to make men in His likeness, and that motivated him to fulfill His plan.

> NAS 1 Chronicles 28:10 "Consider now, for the LORD has chosen you to build **a house** for the sanctuary; be courageous and act."

---

[196] Those who are truly Jewish in heart will not fight against what God is doing.

> NAS 1 Chronicles 28:11   Then David gave to his son Solomon the **plan** of the porch *of the temple*, its buildings, its storehouses, its upper rooms, its inner rooms, and the room for the mercy seat;
>
> NAS 1 Chronicles 28:12   and the **plan** of all that he had in mind, for the courts of the house of the LORD, and for all the surrounding rooms, for the storehouses of the house of God, and for the storehouses of the dedicated things;
>
> KJV 1 Chronicles 28:18   And for the altar of incense refined gold by weight; and gold for the **pattern** of the chariot of the cherubims, that spread out *their wings*, and covered the ark of the covenant of the LORD.

David said that the Lord gave him understanding in all the details of this pattern:

> NAS 1 Chronicles 28:19   "All *this*," *said David*, "the LORD made me understand in writing by His hand upon me, all the details of this pattern."

Although David received these plans from God, later God said that David would not build the Temple but his son Solomon would. Many years after Solomon's death, Isaiah, Zechariah, and Jeremiah were still talking about the coming son of David, the "Branch," who would build the Temple. This showed that Solomon was not the *true* fulfillment of the promised son of David that was prophesied, nor therefore was Solomon's Temple the building of which God spoke.

Then we see in Zechariah that the one whose name is "Branch" would build the temple, meaning the true *spiritual* temple (and soon we will see that we the believers are built into this spiritual house):

> NAS Zechariah 6:12   "Then say to him, 'Thus says the LORD of hosts, "Behold, a man whose name is Branch, for He will branch out from where He is; and **He will build the temple of the LORD.**
>
> NAS Zechariah 6:13   "Yes, it is He who will build the temple of the LORD, and He who will bear the honor and sit and rule on His throne. Thus, He will be a priest on His throne, and the counsel of peace will be between the two offices.'"

Jeremiah and Isaiah also mentioned this "Branch," the chosen one from the House of David, in reference to the coming Messiah:

> NAS Jeremiah 23:5 "Behold, *the* days are coming," declares the LORD, "When I shall raise up for David a righteous Branch; And He will reign as king and act wisely And do justice and righteousness in the land.

> NAS Jeremiah 33:15 'In those days and at that time I will cause a righteous Branch of David to spring forth; and He shall execute justice and righteousness on the earth.

> NAS Isaiah 11:1 Then a shoot will spring from the stem of Jesse, And a branch from his roots will bear fruit.

> NAS Isaiah 11:2 And the Spirit of the LORD will rest on Him, The spirit of wisdom and understanding, The spirit of counsel and strength, The spirit of knowledge and the fear of the LORD.

> NAS Isaiah 4:2 In that day the Branch of the LORD will be beautiful and glorious, and the fruit of the earth *will* be the pride and the adornment of the survivors of Israel.

The temple that the Messiah (the Branch) would build would be a *spiritual* temple ("house"), as Peter says below. This temple would consist of living stones and would be built without hands (Daniel 2:34, 35; Mark 14:58). Peter shows the people offering up *spiritual* sacrifices in this spiritual house:

> NAS 1 Peter 2:5 you also, as **living stones**, are being built up as **a spiritual house**[197] for a holy priesthood, **to offer up spiritual sacrifices** acceptable to God through Jesus Christ.

Peter, quoting Psalm 118:22, continues picturing the Messiah as the very cornerstone of the spiritual temple:

---

197 The Jews often called the Temple the "house," short for the "house of God." In the Greek, "house" is used in 2 Chronicles 3:15–17 and Luke 11:51. In the King James Version it is translated into English as "temple," thus showing it refers to this.

^{NAB} 1 Peter 2:7   Therefore, its value is for you who have faith, but for those without faith: "The stone which the builders rejected has become the cornerstone,"

^{NAS} Hebrews 3:6   but Christ *was faithful* as a Son over His house **whose house we are**, if we hold fast our confidence and the boast of our hope firm until the end.

David knew that it was God's plan for us to be in His image and likeness and thus be a habitation and dwelling place of His presence; and for Him to fully dwell in us, we must grow into the pattern that is His likeness:

^{JPS} Psalm 17:15   As for me, I shall behold Thy face in righteousness; I shall be satisfied, **when I awake, with Thy likeness**.

God desires to dwell in His people, to tabernacle in and among those He loves, and in turn we are His house and tabernacle. If we allow Him to form us into the pattern He gives, then He will fully dwell among and within us:

^{NAS} Psalm 132:13   For the LORD has chosen Zion; He has desired it for His habitation.

^{NAS} Psalm 132:14   "This is My resting place forever; Here I will dwell, for I have desired it.

We have seen that God's will is that He finds habitation among His people. Another important aspect of His dwelling in and among His people lies in musical praise, as David understood:

^{KJV} Psalm 22:3   But thou *art* holy, O *thou* that **inhabitest the praises**[198] of Israel.

This soon-coming, last-days assembly will offer songs of praise to God. The spiritual worship offerings will not be "leavened" in the sense of "Jesus rock" music or soulful melodies, but they will be pure, very powerful spiritual "fire offerings" directly

---

198   The Hebrew word for "praises" can also refer to "songs of praise."

to God, since He will be in the midst of these praises. In other words, these will be incredibly moving, captivating *spiritual* songs of praise that will sweep lovers of God up into spontaneous praise and worship. Just as the daily offerings (Tamid) in the Temple were accompanied by singing and musical instruments, so is the spiritual worship in God's spiritual house.

Those with musical gifts must be seeking God to receive the spiritual songs that will be coming. They must also use discernment, for Satan is pictured with his own music that he would like to inject into the congregation (Isaiah 14:11–13). God will be dwelling in His people in powerful ways, inhabiting their praises, and songs will be born of the spirit as musicians wait on God to receive them, as David did.

As Jesus said to the Samaritan woman at Jacob's well:

> NAS John 4:21   Jesus said to her, "Woman, believe Me, an hour is coming when neither in this mountain, nor in Jerusalem, shall you worship the Father.

> NAS John 4:22   "You worship that which you do not know; we worship that which we know, for salvation is from the Jews.

> NAS John 4:23   "But an hour is coming, and now is, when the true worshipers shall worship the Father in spirit and truth; for such people the Father seeks to be His worshipers.

> NAS John 4:24   "God is spirit, and those who worship Him must worship in spirit and truth."

David understood that God inhabits the praises of the people. The true worship that accompanies the coming spiritual music will help perfect the people into the pattern that God wants, fulfilling the picture of the spiritual bride.

Stephen Gives the Progression of God's Plan in Acts, but His Message and Life Were Cut Short

Stephen, one of the seven chosen (Acts 6:3, 5) and "a man full of faith and of the Holy Spirit," speaks about God's pattern and plan just before he is martyred, saying:

> NAS Acts 7:44   "**Our fathers had the tabernacle** of testimony in the wilderness, just as He who spoke to Moses directed *him* to make it according to the **pattern** which he had seen.

> NAS Acts 7:47 "But it was Solomon who built a **house** for Him.
>
> NAS Acts 7:48 "However, the Most High does not dwell in *houses* made by *human* hands; as the prophet says:
>
> NAS Acts 7:49 'Heaven is My throne, And earth is the footstool of My feet; What kind of **house** will you build for Me?' says the Lord; 'Or what place is there for My repose?

Below are the scriptures Stephen references from Isaiah—where God says with whom He will dwell—which we saw earlier when discussing the pattern and plan shown to Moses:

> NAS Isaiah 66:1 Thus says the LORD, "Heaven is My throne, and the earth is My footstool. Where then is a house you could build for Me? And where is a place that I may rest?
>
> NAS Isaiah 66:2 "For My hand made all these things, Thus all these things came into being," declares the LORD. "But to this one I will look, To him who is humble and contrite of spirit, and who trembles at My word.

This will be the line of demarcation between those who are formed into the image and likeness of God and the Messiah, and those who refuse God's *agape*[199] love. As with Noah's example, some will be caught up and others will stay. Those who are contrite and humble and tremble at God's word are those He will be able to lead into the new truths that the Holy Spirit will bring (John 16:13). God's spirit, as well as those called by Him to minister, will correct and teach if any doctrinal error arises. These truths from God's word will help perfect the assembly into the bride of Christ as she makes herself ready (Revelation 19:7).

God does not say He is looking to those who tremble at the word of a pastor, a rabbi, or a priest, yet count God's own word as small in comparison. On the contrary, God is seeking those who will put His word first. All other authorities are to be extensions of God's word, not of their own favorite doctrines or ideas.

Thus, the pastors, priests, and rabbis who refuse God's truths will not be among those in the ark who are caught up; they will be left behind. However, God promises to bring forth those who will properly feed His people:

---

199 *Agape* is the Greek word often applied to the highest form of love—God's love.

^{NAS} Jeremiah 3:15   "Then I will give you shepherds after My own heart, who will feed you on knowledge and understanding.

The Logos of God Shows This Plan and Pattern

To the first-century Messianic Jews, the Greek word *logos* (usually translated as "word") often referred to an important communication coming from God. In "Setting the Table 2" we examined many Greek words that took on new meanings as the power base shifted to Rome. *Logos* is another one we could add to that list; this Greek word came to be misunderstood in a very important passage of scripture.

In this section, we'll first see how Roman theology viewed this word and then examine what it meant in the idiom of the first-century Messianic Jews. First-century Romans believed in gods and families of gods, and even their own caesars were considered to be gods. When Christianity became Rome's religion, Jesus of course could be nothing less. But this history must be taken into account to understand how the meaning of certain Greek words changed over time.

What the Logos Came to Mean in Rome

Since Emperor Constantine's time, many have taught that the *logos* was actually Jesus as a pre-existent being who was himself God, and who was in the beginning with God. This idea mostly comes from misinterpreting the *logos* in the Gospel of John, translated as "Word" below:

> ^{NAS} John 1:1   In the beginning was the **Word**, and the **Word** was with God, and **the Word was God**.

> ^{NAS} John 1:2   **He was in the beginning with God**.

And here are two versions of verse 3:

> ^{KJV} John 1:3   **All things were made by him**; and without him was not any thing made that was made.

> ^{NAS} John 1:3   **All things came into being by Him**, and apart from Him nothing came into being that has come into being.

Then we come down to verse 14:

> ^{NAS} John 1:14 And the **Word became flesh, and dwelt among us**, and we beheld His glory, glory as of **the only begotten from the Father**, full of grace and truth.

When we examine these scriptures outside of the Jewish idioms and only through the Roman concepts handed down, it's easy to see that an incorrect belief such as the following could arise: Since Jesus was the Word (*logos* verse 14), and the Word was God (verse 1), and the Word was in the beginning with God (verse 2), and made all things (verse 3), therefore Jesus was mistakenly thought to be a pre-existent God (called *logos*) who made all things. To add to this confusion, the Jewish Mary was also exalted by Rome, for she had given birth to this pre-existent God and therefore was regarded as the Mother of God.

This misunderstanding of what the *logos* was gave rise to faulty translations of other scriptures that also *appear* to say things along this same line—that Jesus made the worlds and was the firstborn of all creation as a pre-existing God:

> ^{KJV} Hebrews 1:2 Hath in these last days spoken unto us by *his* Son, whom he hath appointed heir of all things, **by whom also he made the worlds**;

> ^{DBY} Colossians 1:15 who is image of the invisible God, **firstborn of all creation**;

Logos to the First-Century Messianic Jews

During the time of Jesus, Greek was the most commonly spoken language. Alexander the Great (ca. 356–323 BC), the king of Macedon (ancient northern Greece), had conquered the known world about 300 years earlier, and thus Greek became the dominant language throughout his empire. The first-century Jewish historian Josephus wrote in Greek, as did his contemporary, the Jewish biblical philosopher Philo. All the original New Testament scriptures were written in Greek. Even the holy gathering places of the Jews, located throughout Israel and among the nations, were called by a Greek name (*sunagogais*, or later "synagogues" in English) rather than a Hebrew or Aramaic name. The common Bible in use among the Jews was the Greek Septuagint, and the majority of Old Testament scripture quotes in the New Testament came from it, and not from the original Hebrew scriptures.

So to understand what John meant, we must accept how Jews used this word *logos* for hundreds of years before he wrote these scriptures. Both before and during the time of Jesus, Jews were familiar with *logos* (λόγος) because it was used often in the Septuagint (the Greek below) when the Prophets would bring a "word" from the Lord:

> ^{NAS}Jeremiah 13:8 Then the **word** of the LORD came to me, saying,

> ^{LXT}Jeremiah 13:8 καὶ ἐγενήθη **λόγος** κυρίου πρός με λέγων

> ^{NAS}Jeremiah 13:9a "Thus says the LORD …

So in this scripture above, Jeremiah says "the word [*logos* in the Septuagint] of the LORD came to me, saying"; then in the next verse he speaks forth what God wanted to express, starting with, "Thus says the Lord …".

When first-century Jews read in Ezekiel of the dry bones connecting together and coming alive because of the "word" of the Lord, they would have seen this same word for *logos* in their Greek scriptures:

> ^{NAS}Ezekiel 37:4 Again He said to me, "Prophesy over these bones, and say to them, 'O dry bones, hear the **word** of the LORD.'

> ^{NAS}Ezekiel 37:5 "**Thus says the Lord God** to these bones, 'Behold, I will cause breath to enter you that you may come to life.

You will see this same wording over and over in the Prophets:

> ^{NAS}Jeremiah 24:4 Then the **word** of the LORD came to me, saying,

> ^{LXT}Jeremiah 24:4 καὶ ἐγένετο **λόγος** κυρίου πρός με λέγων

> ^{NAS}Jeremiah 24:5a "Thus says the LORD God of Israel …

When a *logos* came from "the LORD," it was "saying" that something was coming from God, be it a truth, a warning, or something else. It was God expressing Himself; thus the word (*logos*) was pictured figuratively as speaking for God, "saying" this or that. Naturally, in the above scripture, Jeremiah was not saying, "The pre-existing Son of God, Jesus, came to me saying …".

Therefore when the Jewish scripture writer John uses this word *logos*, we must not read this kind of interpretation into the text. Instead we must look at the actual meaning of the Greek word *logos* and see how it was understood within the Jewish idiom of John's day.

Within the Jewish idiom, *logos* often referred to *an inward thought and an outward expression*. The *BDAG Greek-English Lexicon* definition for it covers a few pages, but this is the first and clearest definition that they give:

> λόγος a communication whereby the mind finds expression, *word*[200]

So the *logos* in John was God's inward thought that would be outwardly expressed. It was God's *plan and pattern* for His people, just as we saw was *in the beginning* in Genesis 1:26 and right on through Noah, Moses, David, and the Messiah.

> NAS John 1:1 In the beginning was the **Word**, and the **Word** was with God, and **the Word was God**.

The English translations capitalize "Word" because they mostly see it as referring to Jesus as the pre-existent God, but John himself does not capitalize it. The proper way to interpret this verse is that God's plan and pattern (*logos*) was in the beginning with God, and it "was God" in the sense that the *logos* was God Himself expressed. The fulfillment of God's plan and pattern for man is to have man in His image and likeness, as we saw at the beginning of this Course concerning Genesis.

When the Messiah was born, he began to grow into God's image and likeness:

> NIV Luke 2:52 And Jesus grew in wisdom and stature, and in favor with God and men.

As he grew older, he fulfilled God's pattern to such a degree that he became the perfect expression of God's nature:

> NAS Hebrews 1:3 And He is the radiance of His glory and **the exact representation of His nature**, and upholds all things by the word of His power. When He had made purification of sins, He sat down at the right hand of the Majesty on high;

> NAS Colossians 1:15 And He is **the image of the invisible God**, the **first-born** of all creation.

---

200 Bauer, *A Greek-English Lexicon of the New Testament and Other Early Christian Literature* (*BDAG*), 3rd ed., pp. 598–601.

Again, this verse above does not mean that Jesus was "first born" as a pre-existent God before all creation; it rather means that he is the firstborn son in the Jewish sense of having inherited the position of authority handed down by the Father. He is also the firstborn of the new spiritual creation that God had in mind, and he is called the "first born out of the dead" (Revelation 1:5, YLT), for his Resurrection opened the door through which others may escape death. He is also the firstborn in the sense of being the first[201] man born who came into God's exact image and likeness.

The Messiah was not *literally* in the beginning with God, but he was in God's mind, the central focus of His plan, and the one who would fulfill His plan and pattern. So here is another look at what John meant from within the Jewish idioms and understandings of his day:

> ᴺᴬˢ John 1:1 In the beginning was the Word, and the Word was with God, and the Word was God.

> ᴺᴬˢ John 1:2 He was in the beginning with God.

The Greek word οὗτος, translated as "He" in the above verse, is usually translated as "this." The original Greek here means "this was in the beginning." This *logos*, this thought and plan was in God's mind from the very beginning. While *logos* here initially refers to God's inward thought and outward expression, as John continues toward verse 14, the focus slowly changes to the one who fulfills this *logos*—the Messiah.

> ᴺᴬˢ John 1:14 And the Word became flesh, and dwelt among us, and we beheld His glory, glory as of the only begotten from the Father, full of grace and truth.

All the things God created were made with the Messiah and God's plan of redemption in mind. Since the *logos* was not another God, we can see John's real meaning in these scriptures—that the *logos* is another way of showing God's plan and pattern for His people. So John's Gospel must be interpreted correctly in this context:

> ᴷᴶⱽ John 1:3 **All things were made by him**; and without him was not any thing made that was made.

Notice how the King James Version translated this as "All things were made by him," since many believed that the *logos* was the "pre-existent" Christ (Messiah) who made

---

201 Some may consider Adam to be the first son (Genesis 1:26–7), but he was not "born" and although he was in God's image, the scripture does not say he came into God's likeness.

all things. But the Greek word above for "by" is *dia*, which can also mean "through" or "with." In other words, "all things were made" **with** the *logos*—God's plan—in mind.

As the future perfect expression of His *logos*, the Messiah was in God's mind from the beginning. The sun, moon, twelve constellations, seven days of creation, Adam, then Eve coming from his side, and the marriage relationship were all made with Christ and God's plan for mankind *in mind*. So were all things that were built on earth under God's direction—the Ark, Tabernacle, Temple, Showbread, etc. As the second half of John 1:3 says, "without him was not any thing made that was made," meaning that the Messiah and God's plan were in His mind when God spoke and created all these things (Genesis 1:1; 2:4; Hebrews 1:2; 11:3).

This is the proper way to understand the following scripture as well:

> NAS Hebrews 1:2   in these last days has **spoken to us in *His* Son**, whom He appointed heir of all things, **through whom also He made the world**.

The Greek word translated into English as "world" is actually plural and is more accurately translated as "ages." And "through" is the Greek word *dia*, which here refers to God's plan *through* Christ—namely that the ages of mankind were set forth by God with a view to His plan through Christ to bring the people into His likeness. After all, God's son did not yet exist back in Genesis since the Messiah would be born many years later, so he could not have made the "worlds."

It was God doing the speaking and God who created everything in Genesis, and the Jews understood this. It was only in Rome where these idioms were misunderstood, giving rise to the concept of Jesus rolling up balls of dirt to make the planets. The scripture states irrevocably that God spoke and it was He who made the heavens:

> NAS Genesis 1:1   In the beginning **God created** the heavens and the earth.

> NAS Psalm 33:6   By the word of the LORD[202] the heavens were made, And by the breath of His mouth all their host.

---

202 "LORD," when spelled in capital letters, is "YAHWEH" in Hebrew.

When the Messiah came, this *logos* took on its fullest expression because in Christ we see the clearest example of God's pattern and plan. John pointed this out in the verse we saw earlier, showing that Christ was this Word *(logos)* of God being expressed:

> ᴺᴬˢ John 1:14   And the Word became flesh, and dwelt among us, and we beheld His glory, glory as of the only begotten from the Father, full of grace and truth.

God and scripture writers alike often speak figuratively in the Bible. Some theologians who came later jumped to the conclusion that John 1:1–3 was speaking of a second or third God who formed part of the one God. Jewish people, however, had always known that only one God existed, and He was not divided into halves or thirds.

As Isaiah wrote:

> ᴺᴬˢ Isaiah 44:6   "Thus says the LORD, the King of Israel And his Redeemer, the LORD of hosts: 'I am the first and I am the last, And **there is no God besides Me**.

> ᴺᴬˢ Isaiah 44:8   'Do not tremble and do not be afraid; Have I not long since announced it to you and declared it? And you are My witnesses. **Is there any God besides Me**, Or is there any *other* Rock? **I know of none**.'"

God did not ask, "Is there any God besides *us*?" Instead He asked if there was any God "besides Me" and further emphasized this by saying "I know of none," clearly proclaiming that He Himself is the only God. God did not answer Isaiah saying, "the Messiah (Jesus) is another God that I know," because no Messiah existed until God placed the seed in the virgin and she gave birth, as was prophesied by Isaiah (7:14).

When God revealed Himself to Moses, He said "I AM"; He did not say "We are." When David, the king of Israel, spoke of the "Holy Spirit" in the verse below, he did not mean that the Holy Spirit was another God, for the Jews knew definitively that only one God existed.

> ᴺᴬˢ Psalm 51:11   Do not cast me away from Thy presence, And **do not take Thy Holy Spirit from me**.

The Jews understood the Holy Spirit (*Ruach HaKodesh* in Hebrew) was the one true God, who is holy and who is spirit. They never dreamed that the Holy Spirit was a second God or a third of God. They understood this verse from Psalms to be speaking of God's presence, of His spirit dwelling with David.

Jesus also spoke of his heavenly Father as the only true God:

> NAS John 17:3 "And this is eternal life, that they may know Thee, **the only true God**, and Jesus Christ whom Thou hast sent.

It is true that the Messiah was to be called "Immanuel" (Isaiah 7:14, Matthew 1:23), and that this Hebrew name means "God with us." But when someone asks which God was "with us," the answer is that, since there is only one God, it was He who was with us and He who was dwelling in Christ, as the scriptures say.

> NAS 2 Corinthians 5:19 namely, that **God was in Christ** reconciling the world to Himself, not counting their trespasses against them, and He has committed to us the word of reconciliation.

When people speak of the "Deity of Christ," this must also be qualified. Yes, God was dwelling in Christ, but this did not make Christ a second or third Deity; rather, it fulfilled the above scripture of God being "in Christ."

God stated unequivocally that there was no other God besides Him, and the scriptures also clearly state that Jesus was a man:

> NIV 1 Timothy 2:5 For **there is one God** and **one mediator** between God and men, **the man Christ Jesus**,

You cannot be a man and also be a God, because only one God exists, and He is not a man:

> NIV Numbers 23:19 **God is not a man**, that he should lie, nor a son of man, that he should change his mind. Does he speak and then not act? Does he promise and not fulfill?

No man ever existed—*except* for the Messiah—who was the perfect expression of God. This is why the prophet Isaiah pictured the Messiah in such a close position to God that his *name* would be called "Mighty God" and "Eternal Father":

> NAS Isaiah 9:6 For a child will be born to us, a son will be given to us; And the government will rest on His shoulders; And **His name will be called** Wonderful Counselor, **Mighty God, Eternal Father**, Prince of Peace.

Notice it says that "His **name** will be called" these things. When Moses saw the calling of God upon Joshua—who would lead the Jews into the Promised Land—he added part of God's name (Yahweh) to Oshea, making it Yah-Oshea (Numbers 13:16). In English, we call this name "Joshua," but in Hebrew and Greek it was the very same name that Jesus had. Of course, this did not mean that Joshua became another God, but only that he was worthy to bear God's name.

Both Isaiah 9:6 (above) and Isaiah 7:14 (which says the Messiah's name would be Immanuel) state basically the same thing, but in a greater measure with the Messiah. The Messiah would have the one true God dwelling within him; he would be the true tabernacle/temple of God (John 2:19–21), and in this sense he would literally be "God with us."

God Speaks Through the Logos

The Israelites understood that the *logos* of God was *an aspect* of God being expressed, not a separate, pre-existent being. When I searched for the phrase "Thus says the Lord," it appeared about 400 times as spoken by the prophets. However, the Messiah never once uses this phrase, for when God spoke through the Messiah, He spoke in the first person. The Messiah so perfectly yielded to his Father that God would often speak through him directly:

> NAS Hebrews 1:2a   in these last days has spoken to us **in** *His* Son,

Jesus said that the words he spoke were not just from himself, but often those his Father was speaking through him:

> DBY John 14:10   Believest thou not that I *am* in the Father, and that the Father is in me? **The words which I speak to you I do not speak from myself; but the Father who abides in me**, he does the works.

> NAS John 14:24   "He who does not love Me does not keep My words; and **the word which you hear is not Mine, but the Father's** who sent Me.

One example of God speaking through His Son is when Jesus saw the multitude coming with swords and clubs to arrest him, and said to them, "I AM." Upon hearing this, the people fell backward to the ground, because God was anointing him and speaking through him in power:

> ^{NAB} John 18:6   When he said to them, "I AM," they turned away and fell to the ground.

The Greek wording says they went backward and fell to the ground. Most translations say "I am **he**," but "he" does not exist here in the original Greek. God was speaking in the first person through Christ, just as He did when He spoke to Moses out of the fiery bush, saying "I AM" hath sent me (Exodus 3:14).

Another example of God speaking through Christ is found in John 2:19, which reads "Destroy this temple and in three days **I** will raise it up." According to a following scripture (2:21), these words concerned his earthly body and not the natural Temple as some thought. These words were not Jesus speaking but his Father within him, for later the scripture says that God raised him from the dead, and Jesus of course did not raise himself (Acts 10:40).

God has always wanted to reveal Himself, His love, and His nature to His people, and Christ is the fullness of that expression; he is the perfect expression of this *logos*. The Messiah fully yielded to his Father and spoke the words that God gave him (John 14:10). In all the things that the Messiah said and did, we see God's heart and His nature expressed. This is how he "declared" the Father:

> ^{KJV} John 1:18   No man hath seen God at any time; the only begotten Son, which is in the bosom of the Father, he hath **declared**[203] *him*.

The Logos Is the Plan, the Messiah Is the Expression and Pattern

We've seen that the Messiah was the firstborn to fulfill God's plan and pattern. Yet God desires to bring many into this same pattern, image, and likeness:

> ^{NIV} Romans 8:29   For those God foreknew he also predestined **to be conformed to the likeness of his Son**, that he might be the **firstborn among many brothers**.

We were created in God's image and were to then grow into His likeness. When Adam sinned, some of that image and likeness fell short for future generations, but God's plan was to restore us through the Messiah and thus to redeem us back to Himself.

In the beginning of this Course, we considered whether God was speaking to Christ prophetically in Genesis 1:26 ("Let us make man in our image" …). This

---

203   The Greek word ἐξηγήσατο, translated as "declared," means "to reveal or explain, or make known."

would fit with John saying that the *logos* was in the beginning with God (John 1:1–3), because God's inward thought and then His outward expression are what Genesis chapter 1 is all about. And this *logos* was fulfilled in Christ when the *logos* became flesh and dwelt among us (John 1:14).

When we come into this image and likeness that God desires, we will be a habitation for God. His presence will abide within us, just as the "presence breads" (Showbread) pointed to. This is the true tabernacle that John speaks of—God dwelling in and among His people. It is the people who are caught up to heaven (Revelation 3:10, 12:5, 13:6, 21:3) and who escape the hour of tribulation; they are the true tabernacle of God.

It is probably normal to look at this high calling that God has for us, then examine ourselves and exclaim, "How can we possibly get there?" We must always remember that God's love and mercy will encourage us along the way:

> NAS Proverbs 24:16a   For a righteous man falls seven times, and rises again,

> NAS Psalm 103:11   For as high as the heavens are above the earth, So great is His loving kindness toward those who fear Him.

> NAS Psalm 103:12   As far as the east is from the west, So far has He removed our transgressions from us.

> NAS Psalm 103:13   Just as a father has compassion on *his* children, So the LORD has compassion on those who fear Him.

> NAS Psalm 103:14   For He Himself knows our frame; He is mindful that we are *but* dust.

The spiritual body of Christ will be truly merciful toward all those who have fallen short and still have weaknesses—in other words to all who are not perfected yet—for that is God's heart.

One verse used to bring me a lot of comfort when I was a new believer. Having lived my first 22 years apart from God and then afterward as a believer, the road ahead seemed difficult. There was a scripture that spoke of a bruised reed, and while I didn't know what a bruised reed was, I knew that I was one:

> NAS Isaiah 42:3a   "A bruised reed He will not break, And a dimly burning wick He will not extinguish;

We must remember that, as we stay connected to the spiritual body of Christ and yield to all God brings, He will form us into His image and likeness as the spiritual bride. God has promised to raise up shepherds having His heart, and they will bring the true teaching from God's word that will help us. This support, along with God's spirit and His love in and through the members of the spiritual body, will grow us into the spiritual habitation that He desires. He has given us precious promises that we must hold on to and never let go:

> ^{NAS} 2 Peter 1:4   For by these He has granted to us His precious and magnificent promises, in order that **by them you might become partakers of *the* divine nature**, having escaped the corruption that is in the world by lust.

We must not allow our focus to be only on ourselves or only on how we are doing, but to look to the Messiah as the author and he who perfects:

> ^{NAS} Hebrews 12:1   Therefore, since we have so great a cloud of witnesses surrounding us, let us also lay aside every encumbrance, and the sin which so easily entangles us, and let us run with endurance the race that is set before us,

> ^{NAS} Hebrews 12:2   fixing our eyes on Jesus, **the author and perfecter** of faith, who for the joy set before Him endured the cross, despising the shame, and has sat down at the right hand of the throne of God.

We must also realize that we will not be perfected overnight, but it will be a process from glory to glory:

> ^{NAS} 2 Corinthians 3:18   But we all, with unveiled face beholding as in a mirror the glory of the Lord, are being transformed into the same image **from glory to glory**, just as from the Lord, the Spirit.

As someone once said concerning the above verse, the "glory" part is what we like, but it is the "to" period that can be tough.

As we look to Christ as "the author and finisher" (KJV Hebrews 12:2) and seek to understand God's word, yielding as God's spirit leads, His *agape* love will perfect us into the bride:

^{NAS} 1 John 3:2   Beloved, now we are children of God, and it has not appeared as yet what we shall be. We know that, **when He appears, we shall be like Him**, because we shall see Him just as He is.

^{NIV} Galatians 4:19   My dear children, for whom I am again in the pains of childbirth **until Christ is formed in you**,

^{NAS} Ephesians 4:13   until we all attain to the unity of the faith, and of the knowledge of the Son of God, to a mature man, **to the measure of the stature which belongs to the fulness of Christ.**

The Messiah was the image and likeness of God, and while we individually will never fully be his equal, as a group of believers we shall be like him, fulfilling God's pattern and plan.

COURSE 9

God's Plan as Seen in the Showbread

The main focus of this Course will be on the twelve Temple breads (breads of the presence) and on God's intended spiritual meanings when He commanded this natural service. In Course 8 we saw God's plan to make mankind into His image and likeness so that He could dwell among and within His people. Now we'll turn our attention to how God's plan was seen in the weekly Sabbath service with the twelve breads in the Temple:

> NAS Exodus 25:8 "And let them construct a sanctuary for Me, that I may **dwell among** them.

> NIV Psalm 27:4 One thing I ask of the LORD, this is what I seek: that I may dwell in the house of the LORD all the days of my life, to gaze upon the beauty of the LORD and to seek him in his temple.

> DBY Psalm 17:15 As for me, I will behold thy face in righteousness; I shall be satisfied, **when I awake, with thy likeness**.

The law, the sacrifices, the Temple, and the Tabernacle all pointed forward to spiritual truths in the New Covenant, as did the service with the twelve breads:

> NAS Hebrews 8:4b–5 since there are those who offer the gifts according to the Law; who serve **a copy and shadow of the heavenly things**, just as Moses was warned *by God* when he was about to erect the tabernacle; for, "See," He says, "that you make all things according to the pattern which was shown you on the mountain."

> NAS Hebrews 9:24 For Christ did not enter a holy place made with hands, **a *mere* copy** of the **true one**, but into heaven itself, now to appear in the presence of God for us;

^NAS^ **Hebrews 8:2**   a minister in the sanctuary, and in the true tabernacle, which the Lord pitched, not man.

^NAS^ **Hebrews 10:1**   For the Law, since it has *only* a shadow of the good things to come *and* **not the very form of things**, can never by the same sacrifices year by year, which they offer continually, make perfect those who draw near.

As the scripture shows, the Showbread service (as a part of the law) was **a shadow** of the good things to come and "not the very form" or substance of those things. The Showbread thus pointed to a spiritual position (the substance) that the twelve tribes were called to. In the New Covenant, we are all called to this position that was foreshadowed by these twelve breads.

Names Used for These Breads Reveal Spiritual Truths

To ascertain what God was revealing through this Showbread service and learn what He wants to show us in the New Covenant, we will first look at the names used for these breads since these names can help us to see the true spiritual meaning:

- The "bread of the presence" is the most common name. In Hebrew, the literal meaning is "bread of the face" or "faces." However, many other slightly different meanings exist, such as "face to face" (Exodus 25:30; 35:13; 2 Chronicles 4:19). If you are face-to-face with someone, you are in his or her "presence."

- The "bread of the row" or "row bread" referred to the two rows on the golden table in the Temple on which these breads were stacked (1 Chronicles 9:32; 23:29; 2 Chronicles 13:11; Nehemiah 10:33).

- The name "continual bread" was used because these fresh breads were continually set in the second most holy room of the Temple, near the holiest place where God said He would dwell. Every Sabbath the priests would bring in twelve new breads, and "break bread" by eating the previous week's twelve loaves (Numbers 4:7).

- The twelve "cakes" or challah (they are called this one time in Leviticus 24:5).

- The "breads of the purpose" or "breads of the plan." They are often called this in the Greek of the Septuagint (1 Samuel 21:6; Exodus 40:23; 1 Chronicles 9:32). Jesus used this same Greek wording, calling them the "breads of the purpose" or "plan" (Matthew 12:4; Mark 2:26; Luke 6:4).

- The "purpose of the breads" or "plan of the breads." Paul gives a slightly different nuance by reversing the order of the Greek words that Jesus used when he refers (in Greek) to these twelve breads as the "plan of the breads" or the "purpose of the breads" (Hebrews 9:2).

In Course 7 we saw that these breads represented the twelve tribes of Israel, but we also know that many other things in the Tabernacle/Temple pointed forward to spiritual truths in the New Covenant.

The Hebrew names of these breads ("face," "presence," etc.) help reveal their true meaning, but let's now consider how the Greek words that the Messiah and Paul used shed additional light on them (the breads of the purpose/plan, and the plan/purpose of the breads). These various meanings in the list above are not really dissimilar, for when you are face-to-face with someone, you are before them, or in their presence. Also, a person's face can reveal their purpose, their plan, or their will.

When the time was drawing near for Christ's suffering, death, and ascension, he "set his face" to go to Jerusalem. The Messiah understood the totality of what his sacrificial death would involve, and his face showed his determination to do what God had called him to:

> NAS Luke 9:51 And it came about, when the days were approaching
> for His ascension, that He resolutely **set His face** to go to Jerusalem;

Isaiah, speaking of the Messiah, said he would "set his face" as a flint stone. In other words, his face revealed his unmovable determination to fulfill God's will, and strikes from the enemy did not cause him to shrink back. His resolute face revealed that this was his plan and purpose:

> JPS Isaiah 50:7 For the Lord GOD will help me; therefore have I
> not been confounded; therefore have **I set my face like a flint**, and
> I know that I shall not be ashamed.

Speaking harshly of the man who would eat blood among the Israelites, God also said that He would set His face against anyone who went against this command. God's "face" figuratively showed his plan and purpose:

> ^{NAS} Leviticus 17:10 'And any man from the house of Israel, or from the aliens who sojourn among them, who eats any blood, I will **set My face** against that person who eats blood, and will cut him off from among his people.

We Who Abide in God's Presence Are to Be Made into Spiritual Presence Breads

Although the English translations do not convey this, the words Jesus spoke in Greek should be translated as "breads of the purpose" or "breads of the plan." And Paul's words should be translated as "purpose of the breads" or "plan of the breads." The exact same Greek word spoken by Jesus in connection with the Showbread appears in only one other place in New Testament scripture (aside from when referring to the twelve breads), and it means "purpose" or "plan":

> ^{NAS} Acts 27:13 And when a moderate south wind came up, supposing that they had gained their **purpose**,[204] they weighed anchor and *began* sailing along Crete, close *inshore*.

The similar Greek word (this time in the accusative case) is translated as both "plan" and "purpose" in the following translations of this verse in Ephesians:

> ^{NAS} Ephesians 1:11 also we have obtained an inheritance, having been predestined according to His **purpose** who works all things after the counsel of His will,

> ^{NIV} Ephesians 1:11 In him we were also chosen, having been predestined according to the **plan** of him who works out everything in conformity with the purpose of his will,

In Course 8 we saw that God revealed His purpose and plan for mankind down through the ages, beginning in Genesis 1:26, then through men such as Noah, Moses, David, and also the Messiah. And God has called us to become partakers in the divine nature:

> ^{NAS} 2 Peter 1:4 For by these He has granted to us His precious and magnificent promises, in order that by them **you might become partakers of *the* divine nature**, having escaped the corruption that is in the world by lust.

---

204 *Barnes' Notes* (p. 531) describes "purpose" in this verse as the "object of their desire."

Just as the Showbread continually abides in God's presence, so did David understand that being in His presence was a position the upright were called to:

> NAS Psalm 140:13 Surely the righteous will give thanks to Thy name;
> The upright will dwell in Thy presence.

As the Showbread would be permeated symbolically by God's presence, so does the believer have God's spirit continually indwelling him. We have this treasure dwelling in our earthen vessels (i.e., our bodies):

> NAS 2 Corinthians 4:7 But we have this treasure in **earthen vessels**, that the surpassing greatness of the power may be of God and not from ourselves;

> NIV 1 Corinthians 6:19 Do you not know that your body is a temple of the Holy Spirit, who is in you, whom you have received from God? You are not your own;

David knew the fullness of joy that came from abiding in God's presence:

> NAS Psalm 16:11 Thou wilt make known to me the path of life; **In Thy presence is fulness of joy**; In Thy right hand there are pleasures forever.

The Jewish scholars who translated the Septuagint from Hebrew into Greek used these same Greek words that Jesus and Paul used for the twelve breads, so this was not a completely new concept or understanding. The "bread of the face/presence" was sometimes translated into Greek as "breads of the purpose/plan."

Many of these spiritual truths were lost after the Pharisees gained control among the people. They were not geared toward spirituality and the love of God, but instead were more interested in rigidly enforcing their interpretations of the law, doctrines, and traditions on their subjects.[205]

Although some who were more spiritually minded understood prophecies and deeper truths to various degrees, the Messiah told his disciples that many prophets and kings had desired to look into some of the truths that he was showing forth, yet they could not see them:

---

205 Whiston in his *New Complete Works of Josephus* ("Jewish Antiquities," 13.10.6 [p. 441] and 18.1.3–4 [p. 586]) translates this history written by Josephus.

> NAS Luke 10:24   for I say to you, that many prophets and kings wished to see the things which you see, and did not see *them*, and to hear the things which you hear, and did not hear *them*."

The Making of the Twelve Breads Shows God's Process to Make Us into His Image and Likeness

Now we'll look at the making of the Showbread from a spiritual, typological perspective to see how God's plan is shown through these twelve breads. This is not meant to be a full dissertation on this subject; it is only intended to spur more discussion.

> **Typology** is a method of biblical interpretation whereby an element found in the Old Testament is seen to prefigure one found in the New Testament.[206]

Typology does not prove doctrine, but on numerous occasions it was used by Paul, John, and other writers of the scripture to bring out spiritual truth from elements in the Old Testament.

One of the elements in the Tabernacle that pointed forward was the Showbread. The priests who made these twelve breads served "a copy and shadow" of the heavenly spiritual things to come, including the making of man into God's image and likeness.

Building on this analogy of the priests preparing the Showbread, we see that three main elements go into God's process of making us into His image and likeness: God's part, man's part, and the priest's part. We will examine this in further detail in a moment, but it's worth stating first that some overlap existed between the priest's part and man's part. For instance, the people of Israel were to remove the *natural* (or literal) chaff and the priests (i.e., shepherds and teachers) in the New Covenant are to use God's word to carefully remove the *spiritual* chaff. Part of this overlap between the people's functions and the priestly functions exists because God wanted the Israelites to be a kingdom of priests.

The fact that all twelve breads are pictured as abiding in God's presence shows that His will was for all Israelites (and by extension all nations) to dwell in His presence and be as priests before Him, once the Messiah's mission was completed:

> NAS Exodus 19:6   and **you shall be to Me a kingdom of priests** and a holy nation.' These are the words that you shall speak to the sons of Israel."

---

206   Adapted from *Theopedia.com*, s.v. "Biblical typology."

This is fulfilled in the New Covenant believers:

> ^{NAS} Revelation 1:6   and **He has made us *to be* a kingdom, priests** to His God and Father; to Him *be* the glory and the dominion forever and ever. Amen.

We will now turn to the reciprocal aspects in the making of the Showbread to see that God, the people, and the priests were all involved in giving and receiving in His house.

God's Part in the Process

The rain from God must come for the wheat crops to grow

There is natural rain that God sends upon the earth for the growing of crops, and there is spiritual rain (also called the "teaching" rain) that God sends to spiritually grow the crops of people. Moses showed that the rain coming down parallels the teaching that comes from God:

> ^{NAS} Deuteronomy 32:2   "Let my **teaching** drop as the rain, My speech distill as the dew, As the droplets on the fresh grass And as the showers on the herb.

The rains were, of course, extremely important in Israel. There was a spring rain that happened around Passover, and a winter (latter) rain that came around the time of the Festival of Ingathering (Tabernacles/Sukkot):

> ^{NAS} Joel 2:23   So rejoice, O sons of Zion, And be glad in the LORD your God; For He has given you the early rain for *your* vindication. And He has poured down for you the rain, The early and latter rain as before.

The Hebrew word for "rain" above can also mean "teacher," seen below in Young's Literal Translation of this same verse as "Teacher of righteousness":

> ^{YLT} Joel 2:23   And ye sons of Zion, joy and rejoice, In Jehovah your God, For He hath given to you the **Teacher for righteousness**, And causeth to come down to you a shower, Sprinkling and gathered—in the beginning.

What is probably meant here is that God would give the rain in righteous or just measure, but this could also have a secondary application pointing to the Messiah. The teaching that comes down from God is what prepares us for the third and final Festival of the Ingathering (Sukkot/Tabernacles). Unlike Passover and Pentecost, this is a festival that has not yet been completely fulfilled in its spiritual aspect:

> ᴺᴬˢ Deuteronomy 11:14   that He will give the rain for your land in its season, the early and late rain, that you may gather in your grain and your new wine and your oil.

> ᴷᴶⱽ Hosea 6:3   Then shall we know, *if* we follow on to know the LORD: his going forth is prepared as the morning; and **he shall come unto us as the rain**, as the latter *and* former rain unto the earth.

We are dependent upon God for this spiritual teaching rain, which He has promised us. Without natural rain there could be no wheat for the Showbread, and without spiritual rain the final third festival will not be fulfilled:

> ᴺᴬˢ James 5:7   Be patient, therefore, brethren, until the coming of the Lord. Behold, the farmer waits for the precious produce of the soil, being patient about it, until it gets the early and late rains.

Believers must remember that if the Lord is bringing a latter teaching rain to correctly grow our crops, we must be willing to receive His new truths and not assume that we already have all that we need to know and therefore do not need the rain. The truth behind the following scripture in Amos is that God will send His teaching rain upon those assemblies who are willing, but those who refuse His truth will not receive His rain:

> ᴺᴬˢ Amos 4:7   "And furthermore, I withheld the rain from you While *there were* still three months until harvest. Then I would send rain on one city And on another city I would not send rain; One part would be rained on, While the part not rained on would dry up.

While some may say that doctrine is divisive, and that we should just love, the Messiah and his disciples taught the importance of true doctrine:

> ᴷᴶⱽ Matthew 15:9   But in vain they do worship me, teaching *for* doctrines the commandments of men.

> ^{NIV} Titus 1:9   He must hold firmly to the trustworthy message as it has been taught, so that he can encourage others **by sound doctrine** and refute those who oppose it.

> ^{NAS} 1 Thessalonians 5:21   But examine everything *carefully*; hold fast to that which is good;

> ^{DBY} 1 Timothy 4:1   But the Spirit speaks expressly, that in latter times some shall apostatise from the faith, giving their mind to deceiving spirits and **teachings of demons**.

> ^{NAS} Acts 2:42   And **they were continually devoting themselves to the apostles' teaching** and to fellowship, to the breaking of bread and to prayer.

The sunlight from God is needed to grow the crops

The land needed the sunlight, for without it, the wheat crops would not grow and there would then be no Showbread. God sent forth the Messiah, who grew into the exact representation of God's nature, giving us spiritual light and showing us the pattern that we are to come into:

> ^{NAS} John 12:46   "I have come *as* light into the world, that everyone who believes in Me may not remain in darkness.

> ^{NAS} 2 Corinthians 4:6   For God, who said, "Light shall shine out of darkness," is the One who has shone in our hearts to give the light of the knowledge of the glory of God in the face of Christ.

> ^{NAS} Hebrews 1:3   And He is the radiance of His glory and **the exact representation** of His nature, and upholds all things by the word of His power. When He had made purification of sins, He sat down at the right hand of the Majesty on high;

As long as wheat receives both water and sunlight, it will grow into the finished product; this is built into the DNA of wheat. So it is with the believer: as long as we stay willing to receive God's teaching and sunlight, it is within our *spiritual* DNA to grow into the intended product—the image and likeness of God (Genesis 1:26) that Christ showed forth.

Man's Part in the Process

The Israelite needed to till the ground

Israeli wheat growers had to till their land so that it could receive the grain seed during planting. Through a parable, the Lord showed that if the ground was not first prepared, the seed would not bring forth as intended (Matthew 13:3–9). Jesus told several parables along this line, applying tilling in the spiritual sense of preparing one's heart to receive the teaching he was bringing from God.

God used this figurative language through the prophets:

> NAS Jeremiah 4:3 For thus says the LORD to the men of Judah and to Jerusalem, "Break up your fallow ground, And do not sow among thorns.

And Jesus taught along these lines:

> NAS Luke 8:15 "And **the *seed* in the good soil**, these are the ones who have heard the word in an honest and good heart, and hold it fast, and bear fruit with perseverance.

When the ground of our heart is prepared, it can properly accept the seed during the planting.

As the proverb below says, we are to buy the truth and never let go of it. We are not to reject truth just because it's uncomfortable in society or it does not align with our traditions, but to always hold on to it:

> NAS Proverbs 23:23 Buy truth, and do not sell *it, Get* wisdom and instruction and understanding.

The wise man planted the seed that came from God

One of the Lord's parables likened the kingdom of heaven to a man who planted good seed:

> NAS Matthew 13:24 He presented another parable to them, saying, "The kingdom of heaven may be compared to **a man who sowed good seed** in his field.

Some say that, in terms of our doctrine, we need to submit to our pastor, priest, or rabbi. However, the Messiah is the highest authority under God, and we must hear his voice and hold on to any good seed that he gives. He provides teachers and shepherds to teach us his word, yet we must yield to the Holy Spirit when new truth is brought, rather than think, "Well, I believe this teaching is from the Lord, but my pastor/priest/rabbi and my social club do not approve, so I cannot keep it."

The Israelite needed to harvest and then winnow the wheat

Ruth met Boaz at the winnowing area (called the "threshing floor," where the chaff was removed from the grain) after he had spent a long day winnowing barley (Ruth 3:2). Boaz would have brought the priests a tithe of the barley and the wheat that he grew, harvested, and winnowed from his land, and the priest would have used some of this wheat to create the twelve breads in the Temple.

One grandchild from the eventual union of Boaz and Ruth was King David, son of Jesse the Bethlehemite (1 Samuel 16:1). It was prophesied that the Messiah was to be a *son* of David (meaning from David's lineage) and to be born in Bethlehem (Micah 5:2), which means "house of bread." Both prophecies were fulfilled exactly when the Messiah was born in Bethlehem of David's lineage (Matthew 2). Those who are made into his image will spiritually come from the "house of bread" as they partake of the bread of life that the Messiah gives.

This winnowing process removed the chaff so that only the good, edible grain would remain. The New Covenant states that we are to be a kingdom of priests (Revelation 1:6), which points to all believers being involved in both the spiritual winnowing and meshing of that grain into flour.

We do this as we encourage one another daily in the house of God. We share His love. We are merciful as chaff comes to the surface and is blown away, knowing that we ourselves also have chaff and God is covering us in the process. We do not point to one grain and say, "Look, Sam has chaff!" but instead we cover one another in the process. The devil stands near to accuse, and although some brethren will join him, we do not listen to those voices; rather, we hear the Lord's voice that promises mercy. The Messiah knew that the Pharisees did not really understand mercy and God's love, of which the prophet Hosea spoke:

> KJV Hosea 6:6 For **I desired mercy, and not sacrifice**; and the knowledge of God more than burnt offerings.

Quoting a portion of this verse in Hosea, the Messiah specifically told them to go and learn about God's mercy:

> NIV Matthew 9:13 But **go and learn what this means**: 'I desire mercy, not sacrifice.' For I have not come to call the righteous, but sinners."

And later in Matthew, similar words:

> ^{NIV} Matthew 12:7   If you had known what these words mean, '**I desire mercy, not sacrifice**,' you would not have condemned the innocent.

Christians can also be Pharisaic—legalistically condemning others who may still have sin, instead of learning mercy—so we all need to learn what these scriptures are saying. At the same time, the scripture is clear that when one (including an elder) continues in blatant, willful sin, such as those "spots" in Course 5, there is a time for open rebuke (1 Timothy 5:19–20).

Yet all of the grains need chaff to be removed, and all who are willing deserve God's mercy. Figuratively speaking, the grains should not attack other grains when they see chaff but rather cover one another during the perfecting process. The grains do not highlight the weaknesses of another grain when it is sometimes failing but still trying to walk with God; instead they show forth God's mercy with an understanding that each grain has chaff that needs to be removed. God brings the winds of adversity to help blow away the chaff during the winnowing process, and the people, like Boaz, also do their part to help the grains be separated from the chaff:

> ^{NIV} Hebrews 3:13   But **encourage one another daily**, as long as it is called Today, so that none of you may be hardened by sin's deceitfulness.

> ^{NAS} Galatians 6:1 Brethren, even if a man is caught in any trespass, **you who are spiritual**, restore such a one in a spirit of gentleness; *each one* looking to yourself, lest you too be tempted.

> ^{NAS} Proverbs 24:16   For a righteous man **falls seven times, and rises again**, But the wicked stumble in *time of* calamity.

God also takes part in the spiritual winnowing

> ^{NAS} Matthew 3:12   "And His winnowing fork is in His hand, and He will thoroughly clear His threshing floor; and He will gather His wheat into the barn, but He will burn up the chaff with unquenchable fire."

In Israel, the people would look for a hill with wind as a good spot for the winnowing. God showed the importance of spiritual winnowing by choosing a threshing floor for the site of His house, the Temple. The very site where He directed David to build the Temple had been used previously for winnowing wheat:

> NAS 1 Chronicles 21:18   Then the angel of the LORD commanded Gad to say to David, that David should go up and build an altar to the LORD on the **threshing floor** of Ornan the Jebusite.
>
> NAS 1 Chronicles 22:1   Then David said, "**This is the house of the LORD God**, and this is the altar of burnt offering for Israel."

When the winnowing was complete, the people would bring their grain tithe into the house of God, demonstrating reciprocal giving and receiving. They were to bring their grain offerings as fine flour, which the Showbread required; thus they first needed to grind the grain into this flour before bringing it into the Temple.

In a spiritual sense, we must be willing to be formed into flour so that we can be joined to our brethren and made into one bread; otherwise the priests do not have the proper substance from which to make the Showbread. God's ministers can work only with what we give them; we must prepare our hearts to be changed when they bring His teaching, or else we will remain alone and not bear the proper fruit:

> NAS John 12:24   "Truly, truly, I say to you, unless a grain of wheat falls into the earth and dies, it remains by itself alone; but if it dies, it bears much fruit.

This parable shows that to grow more wheat the grain must fall into the ground and break open (in other words "die" or germinate). So too, to be made into spiritual Showbread, the grain must be willing to be broken and combined into one flour, then into one bread (the spiritual body).

The Priest's Part in the Process

The Showbread service was considered one of the communal meals for Temple priests, and the first-century historian Josephus wrote that the Showbread came from the *commom* (communal) offerings of the people.[207]

The priest was required to enter the house of God in a state of holiness, for he was doing God's will in his ministry by making the required offerings and sacrifices, many of which kept the nation sanctified and set apart unto Him. Another reason he had to enter the sanctuary in holiness was that he ate the "bread of God." The priest could eat from the holy and the most holy offerings:

---

[207] Whiston, *The New Complete Works of Josephus*, "Jewish Antiquities," 3.10.7, p. 133.

> ^{NAS} Leviticus 21:22   'He may eat the bread of his God, *both* of the most holy and of the holy,

The Showbread was a required and "most holy" offering, because the frankincense was placed on the fire (thus making it a fire offering) before the bread was shared by the priests descended from Aaron:

> ^{NAS} Leviticus 24:9   "And it shall be for Aaron and his sons, and they shall eat it in a holy place; for it is most holy to him from the LORD's offerings by fire, *his* portion forever."

Under the law of Moses, the priest was to live off of the people's tithes and offerings. This is how he would receive his sustenance in the house of God and be able to do the work in the Tabernacle/Temple. In the New Covenant, we receive spiritual sustenance from one another as members in the spiritual body of Christ when we gather together in spiritual fellowship:

> ^{NAS} Ephesians 4:15–16   but speaking the truth in love, we are to grow up in all *aspects* into Him, who is the head, *even* Christ, from whom the whole body, being fitted and held together **by that which every joint supplies**, according to the proper working of each individual part, **causes the growth of the body** for the building up of itself in love.

> ^{NAS} Colossians 2:19   and not holding fast to the head, from whom the entire body, **being supplied and held together by the joints and ligaments**, grows with a growth which is from God.

> ^{NAS} 1 Corinthians 12:25   that there should be no division in the body, but *that* **the members** should have **the same care for one another**.

The Greek word translated as "one another" in the scripture above is a reciprocal pronoun, showing the reciprocal nature of the members of the spiritual body caring for one another.

While addressing who should be taken care of financially by the assembly, Paul in his letter to Timothy writes not of spiritual provision but of natural provision, stating that elders who labor in God's word are worthy of double wages:

> ^{NJB} 1 Timothy 5:17   Elders who do their work well while they are in charge earn double reward, especially those who work hard at preaching and teaching.

> NAS 1 Timothy 5:18 For the Scripture says, "You shall not muzzle the ox while he is threshing," and "The laborer is worthy of his wages."

For the ministry to continue, the people's offerings must help the ministers and those who are called to labor in the word of God. Unlike some teachings today that still insist on the 10 percent tithe, Paul understood that the tithe was a requirement of the law, but that in the New Covenant we are no longer under this law. Paul knew that in the New Covenant, the giving is not by compulsion (as it was under the law), but something that comes from the heart after seeing the ministry's need:

> NIV 2 Corinthians 9:7 Each man should give what he has decided in his heart to give, not reluctantly or under compulsion, for God loves a cheerful giver.

In the Temple, priests would share the bread, and God's word was also shared among the people gathered together. Jesus often spent time teaching in the Temple:

> NAS Luke 21:37 Now during the day He was teaching in the temple, but at evening He would go out and spend the night on the mount that is called Olivet.

> NAS Nehemiah 8:1 And all the people gathered as one man at the square which was in front of the Water Gate, and they asked Ezra the scribe to bring the book of the law of Moses which the LORD had given to Israel.

> NIB Nehemiah 8:8 They read from the Book of the Law of God, making it clear and giving the meaning so that the people could understand what was being read.

The priest would then add water and mix it with the flour

The water that is mixed with flour to make the twelve breads can represent the Holy Spirit of God—the water of life—as well as the teaching rain, as we saw previously:

> NAS Revelation 22:17 And the Spirit and the bride say, "Come." And let the one who hears say, "Come." And let the one who is thirsty come; let the one who wishes take the **water of life** without cost.

Jesus speaks of the Holy Spirit as (living) water, which would later be poured out because of his sacrifice:

> ᴺᴬˢ John 4:13–14   Jesus answered and said to her, "Everyone who drinks of this water shall thirst again; but whoever drinks of the water that I shall give him shall never thirst; but **the water that I shall give** him shall become in him a well of water springing up to eternal life."
>
> ᴺᴬˢ John 7:37   Now on the last day, the great *day* of the feast, Jesus stood and cried out, saying, "If any man is thirsty, let him come to Me and drink.
>
> ᴺᴬˢ John 7:39   **But this He spoke of the Spirit**, whom those who believed in Him were to receive; for the Spirit was not yet *given*, because Jesus was not yet glorified.

Adding warm water to the flour would initiate the natural leavening process, which, once heat was applied, would cause the dough to rise into bread. It is also possible that the priests added leaven to make the twelve breads, since that was the normal way to make bread. (Just because God did not say to add leaven does not mean it was not added, for neither did He say to add water. The way the Israelites made *bread* was to add leaven and water to the flour, then mix it, and bake it.)

Without adding water to the flour, the resulting product at the end of the baking process would not be bread, but rather burned flour. The spiritual priest in the New Covenant must always add the water of life, because the letter of the law without the spirit does not bring life, but only burns the flour without producing the true bread that God wants:

> ᴺᴬˢ 2 Corinthians 3:6   who also made us adequate *as* servants of a new covenant, not of the letter, but of the Spirit; **for the letter kills**, but the Spirit gives life.

Again, God's plan through the Messiah was to make man into His image and likeness, into which the Messiah himself was made perfectly:

> ᴺᴬˢ Genesis 1:26   Then God said, "Let Us make man in Our image, according to Our likeness;
>
> ᴺᴬˢ 2 Corinthians 4:4   in whose case the god of this world has blinded the minds of the unbelieving, that they might not see the light of the gospel of the glory of Christ, who is the image of God.

^{DBY} 1 Corinthians 15:49   And as we have borne the image of the *one* made of dust, we shall bear also the image of the heavenly *one*.

As we abide in God's presence (as the presence breads did), it is in our *spiritual* DNA to grow into His likeness as long as we become sifted as flour, partake of the water, remain in fellowship and harmony with the other willing breads, and allow God's process to perfect us.

The priests would oversee the baking of the Showbread

After mixing the water with the fine flour, the priests had the duty to oversee the baking process. Placed in the heat, the breads would rise into the "image" of the pans that contained them. The form of the pan represents Christ/Messiah, the image and pattern of God's plan that we are to come into.

In the New Covenant, the fiery trials (spiritual baking process) help perfect us, and as we rise above them, we become like Christ in the process. The trials that we face in this world work to perfect us into what God wants:

^{NAS} 1 Peter 4:12   Beloved, do not be surprised at the fiery ordeal among you, which comes upon you for your testing, as though some strange thing were happening to you;

^{DBY} 1 Peter 1:7   that the proving of your faith, much more precious than of gold which perishes, though it be proved by fire, be found to praise and glory and honour in *the* revelation of Jesus Christ:

^{DBY} Romans 8:17   And if children, heirs also: heirs of God, and Christ's joint heirs; if indeed we suffer with *him*, that we may also be glorified with *him*.

^{NIV} John 16:33   "I have told you these things, so that in me you may have peace. In this world you will have trouble. But take heart! I have overcome the world."

God knows those who love Him, and those whom He knew ahead of time by his foreknowledge, He predestined to live at the proper time when the people would be conformed to the image of His son. This is what the scripture says:

^{NAS} Romans 8:29   For whom He foreknew, He also predestined *to become* conformed to the image of His Son, that He might be the first-born **among many brethren;**

God did not want only one son to come into His image, but to have Christ be the firstborn *among many brethren*. For as soon as Zion travailed, she gave birth to many sons:

> ^{NAS} Isaiah 66:8 "Who has heard such a thing? Who has seen such things? Can a land be born in one day? Can a nation be brought forth all at once? As soon as Zion travailed, she also brought forth her sons.

The priests were to place the breads on the golden table in God's presence

It was the priests' duty to place the twelve breads on the golden table before God, in His presence, on the other side of the veil from where the ark of His presence resided. The veil that separated the Showbread from the holiest place showed that the way into God's direct presence had not been made while the Old Covenant law (Tabernacle/Temple) still had a legal standing:

> ^{NIV} Hebrews 9:7 But only the high priest entered the inner room, and that only once a year, and never without blood, which he offered for himself and for the sins the people had committed in ignorance.

> ^{YLT} Hebrews 9:8 the **Holy Spirit this evidencing** that not yet hath been manifested the way of the holy *places*, the first tabernacle having yet a standing;

The picture of the Showbread in the New Covenant is this: When Christ paid the penalty for sin, the veil in the holiest place was torn in two. The Holy Spirit was thus "evidencing" that, because of Christ, the *spiritual* Showbread is now face-to-face with God in His very presence.

> ^{NIV} Hebrews 10:19 Therefore, brothers, since we have confidence to enter the Most Holy Place by the blood of Jesus,

The New Covenant teacher should seek to place the spiritual Showbread in God's presence, where it can be transformed inwardly (speaking spiritually). In the New Covenant we can move spiritually beyond this veil into God's very presence.

The priest from Aaron must partake of the breads

As we partake of the one bread in the body of Christ, we partake of Christ in one another:

> NAS 1 Corinthians 10:17   Since there is one bread, we who are many are one body; for we all partake of the one bread.

We see Christ within each member of his body. We share Christ—the bread of life—whenever two or three are gathered in his name (Matthew 18:20). God is then flowing to and through each member in the spiritual body.

Some of the best sharing of scriptures I have experienced was in the master's class in Bible college. In certain areas of research or understanding where I might have been weak, another student was strong, and together all the students' talents and knowledge combined to enable us to delve much deeper into select studies. Similarly, when the body of Christ unites, Jewish and Hebrew scholars who are like the righteous scribes in David's day will come together in God's house with various Gentile scholars, and together they will find many treasures in His word. What a glorious day that will be, as we can then explore even deeper truths that await us. Just as the priests shared the twelve breads, so will God's people share new truths from His word, and together we will gather new truths from the Old and New Testaments:

> NAS Matthew 13:52   And He said to them, "Therefore every scribe who has become a disciple of the kingdom of heaven is like a head of a household, who brings forth out of his treasure **things new and old**."

After seeing this high calling that God has for us, some might feel overwhelmed and think, "How can we possibly get there?"

In these times, we must remember that all we need to do is stay connected to the spiritual body of Christ and yield to all that God brings in His word and by His spirit—then He will bring us into His image and likeness.

And we must not allow the focus to be only on ourselves—condemning ourselves for falling short of God's high calling—but look away to Christ as the author and finisher (Hebrews 12:1–2). Our perfection will not happen overnight, but it will be a process from glory to glory:

> NAS 2 Corinthians 3:18   But we all, with unveiled face beholding as in a mirror the glory of the Lord, are being transformed into the same image from glory to glory, just as from the Lord, the Spirit.

Bread Is Instruction from God

Just as we saw earlier that the rains from God typify His teaching, so did the manna (the bread of heaven) typify His divine instruction coming down:

> ^{NAS} Exodus 16:4   Then the LORD said to Moses, "Behold, **I will rain bread from heaven** for you; and the people shall go out and gather a day's portion every day, that I may test them, whether or not they will walk in **My instruction**.

When Jesus miraculously "broke bread" out to the multitudes using only five breads, a group approached him the following day wanting him to provide bread again, just as Moses had provided manna continually (John 6). Jesus went on to relate many things on this, but essentially he said that he represented the "true bread" (i.e., spiritual manna) being given out from heaven, which was the Father's teaching coming through him.

> ^{NAS} John 6:32   Jesus therefore said to them, "Truly, truly, I say to you, it is not Moses who has given you the bread out of heaven, but it is My Father who gives you the **true bread** out of heaven.

> ^{NAS} John 6:51   "I am the living **bread that came down out of heaven**; if anyone eats of this bread, he shall live forever; and the bread also which I shall give for the life of the world is My flesh."

In this parable, Jesus declaring that he will give his "flesh" as bread partly refers to the people who make up his body on earth—the spiritual body of Christ, or his bride. Genesis 2:24 speaks of two—a man and his wife—becoming *one flesh*. Paul, teaching about a man loving his wife (as his own flesh), showed this was a great mystery that concerns Christ and the Church/assembly:

> ^{NAS} Ephesians 5:29–32   for no one ever hated his own flesh, but nourishes and cherishes it, just as Christ also *does* the church, because we are members of His body. For this cause a man shall leave his father and mother, and shall cleave to his wife; and the two shall become one flesh. This mystery is great; but I am speaking with reference to Christ and the church.

So John 6:51 above is possibly also showing that Jesus has given us—his spiritual body (his flesh, his bride, the assembly)—to also be as spiritual bread that brings his teaching and spiritual nourishment to the world:

> ^{NAS} John 6:58   "This is the bread which came down out of heaven; not as the fathers ate, and died, he who eats this bread shall live forever."

Jesus thus spoke of himself (and his "flesh") being bread that he would give in the future—statements that were to be understood spiritually:

> ᴺᴬˢ John 6:63   "It is the Spirit who gives life; the flesh profits nothing; **the words that I have spoken to you are spirit and are life.**

※⚜※

It was not a new concept to Jews that God's words were spiritual bread to eat; many would have understood this connection. It was because of the rain (teaching rain) that they would have bread:

> ᴷᴶⱽ Isaiah 55:10–11   For as the rain cometh down, and the snow from heaven, and returneth not thither, but watereth the earth, and maketh it bring forth and bud, that it may give seed to the sower, and **bread** to the eater: **So shall my word be** that goeth forth out of my mouth: it shall not return unto me void, but it shall accomplish that which I please, and it shall prosper *in the thing* whereto I sent it.

Isaiah spoke of a future new covenant in which the true bread and wine that brings satisfaction is found in listening carefully to God and His instruction:

> ᴺᴬˢ Isaiah 55:1–3   "Ho! Every one who thirsts, come to the waters; And you who have no money come, buy and eat. Come, buy **wine** and milk Without money and without cost. "Why do you spend money **for what is not bread**, And your wages for what does not satisfy? **Listen carefully to Me**, and **eat what is good**, And **delight yourself in abundance**. "Incline your ear and come to Me. Listen, that you may live; And **I will make an everlasting covenant** with you, *According to* the faithful mercies shown to David.

Paul quotes Isaiah 55:10 below and speaks of **bread** for food, giving it a spiritual application as a *spiritual* harvest of righteousness:

> ᴺᴬˢ 2 Corinthians 9:10   Now He who supplies seed to the sower and **bread for food**, will supply and multiply your seed for sowing and increase the **harvest of your righteousness**;

God anointed Moses to write that man does not live by natural bread alone, but by every word of God, which is the true spiritual bread:

> ^{NAS} Deuteronomy 8:3 "And He humbled you and let you be hungry, and fed you with manna which you did not know, nor did your fathers know, that He might make you understand that man does not live by **bread alone**, but man lives by everything that proceeds out of the mouth of the LORD.

As we saw earlier, the word of God was shared in the Temple during the festivals, Sabbaths, and often throughout the week:

> ^{NIV} Nehemiah 8:18 Day after day, from the first day to the last, Ezra read from the Book of the Law of God. They celebrated the feast for seven days, and on the eighth day, in accordance with the regulation, there was an assembly.

> ^{NAS} Matthew 26:55 At that time Jesus said to the multitudes, "Have you come out with swords and clubs to arrest Me as against a robber? **Every day I used to sit in the temple teaching** and you did not seize Me.

Reciprocal Giving and Receiving in the House of God

Now we've seen how the making and sharing of the Showbread demonstrated reciprocal giving and receiving in God's house, and how this in turn showed forth His purpose and plan for those in the New Covenant.

As with the twelve breads in the Temple, the three annual festivals (and communal meals in general) all require reciprocal giving and receiving. During these festivals, no one is to appear before God without bringing some of their harvest or a similar offering:

> ^{NAS} Deuteronomy 16:16 "Three times in a year all your males shall appear before the LORD your God in the place which He chooses, at the Feast of Unleavened Bread and at the Feast of Weeks and at the Feast of Booths, and **they shall not appear before the LORD empty-handed**.

In this giving and receiving, all were involved. The Showbread also embodies this, since it was made from the communal grain tithes that came from the produce and labors of the people.

The people had their part: to till the ground and then plant the seed, grow and harvest the wheat, and bring their tithes into the Temple. God had His part: to provide the water and sunlight, without which the wheat could not grow. The priests had their part: to provide the sacrifices required to keep the whole nation sanctified before God, and to partake of the breads. They would also teach in the Temple and other leaders in the synagogues, so the people would know the will of God. The priests received food and sustenance from the tithes and sacrificial offerings of the people, and in return the people received atonement and forgiveness provided for the whole nation as a result of the sacrifices performed by the priests; these sacrifices kept the nation in right standing before God.

God took an active part in reciprocally giving and receiving as well; He was always in the midst of the Temple activities as long as the people's hearts were right and they walked with Him. God would then provide His portion and blessing in the rain and teachings that He sent down.

In these communal Temple meals, Israelites knew that God was more than just a distant guest; He was actually a participant, spiritually dwelling right in their midst (as was covered in Courses 5 and 6).

In Matthew 18:20, Jesus said that wherever two or three are gathered in his name, there "I am" in the midst; he was showing how the believers would soon function in the New Covenant. This is the perfect picture of the spiritual Showbread—the believers are the presence bread, for they are pieces of the one bread that have Christ within and dwell in God's presence. The grains of wheat are combined together in fellowship by sharing God's word with Christ and God's spirit in their midst. The two or three show the reciprocal aspect of giving and receiving in the body of Christ.

The one new commandment that Jesus gave also displays this reciprocal giving and receiving in the New Covenant:

> NAS John 13:34–35 "A new commandment I give to you, that you love **one another**, even as I have loved you, that you also love one another. By this all men will know that you are My disciples, if you have love for one another."

> NAS Romans 13:8 Owe nothing to anyone except to love **one another**; for he who loves his neighbor has fulfilled *the* law.

The *UBS Greek-English Dictionary* makes it clear that the Greek word translated as "one another" in both scriptures above is a reciprocal pronoun, showing that the Lord wants us to *both give and receive* His *agape* love. This will be a prominent feature in the powerful move of God's spirit that is now beginning. It is the teaching rain and the spirit, along with reciprocal giving and receiving of God's love in the body of Christ, that will produce the spiritual fruit that God is seeking.

> ^{YLT} 2 Corinthians 3:18   and **we all**, with unvailed face, the glory of the Lord beholding in a mirror, **to the same image are being transformed**, from glory to glory, even as by the Spirit of the Lord.

The Greek word translated into English as "beholding in a mirror" means "beholding, reflecting" according to the *UBS*, and both meanings fit this context. This Greek word is often translated into English as "mirror," because in a mirror you behold and reflect at the same time. "We all" behold and reflect the Lord's image as we share His *agape* love and allow His spiritual sustenance to flow from one member to another as we fellowship and worship.

Whether in worshipping, singing, dancing before the Lord, or fellowshipping in God's love, *we all* are being transformed from glory into glory by God's spirit as we follow His plan.

Twelve Breads, Now One Spiritual Bread

As he broke the one bread at the Last Supper, Jesus showed that in the New Covenant we are no longer twelve breads, but we are made one bread and one body in the Messiah, the bread of life. This is what the apostles understood from the Last Supper parables:

> ^{NAS} 1 Corinthians 10:17   Since there is **one bread**, we who are many are one body; for we all partake of the one bread.

> ^{NAS} Galatians 3:28   There is neither Jew nor Greek, there is neither slave nor free man, there is neither male nor female; for **you are all one** in Christ Jesus.

When Jesus held one bread at the Last Supper, broke it, and gave the pieces to the disciples, the Greek word used is singular. Similarly, when the disciples went forth "breaking bread" in Acts 2:42, the Greek reads "Breaking *the* bread" (singular). In Acts 2:46, once again "breaking bread" is singular, as it is in Acts 20:7 and 20:11, showing that the disciples now understood and were "breaking bread" in the spiritual sense.

We no longer approach God in the old way through blood sacrifices, nor do we partake of the twelve breads of the presence in the Temple. This is because now we can enter God's direct presence through the one bread—the Messiah—and by being pieces of the one bread that he broke, the true presence bread, the spiritual body of Christ with Christ in the midst. It is he who provides the bread of life. We who are his spiritual body also break and share this bread.

The *McClintock and Strong Cyclopedia* quotes the German scholar Carl Bahr, who makes some excellent points about the bread being spiritual food whereby God is seen and experienced:

> The 'bread of the face' is, therefore, that bread through which God is seen; that is, with the participation of which the seeing of God is bound up, or through the participation of which man attains the sight of God. Hence it follows that we have not to think of bread merely as such, as the means of nourishing the bodily life, but as spiritual food, as a means of appropriating and retaining that life which consists in seeing the face of God. Bread is therefore here a symbol, and stands, as it generally does in all languages, both for life and life's nourishment; but by being entitled the bread of the face, it becomes a symbol of a life higher than the physical. They who eat of it and satisfy themselves with it see the face of God" (Bahr, Symbolik, bk. 1, ch. 6, § 2).

The article continues:

> Bahr proceeds to show very beautifully the connection in Scripture between seeing God and being nourished by God, and points, as the coping stone of his argument, to Christ being at once the perfect image of God and the bread of life.[208]

To this excellent writing of Bahr, I would only add that we also see God's face in our brethren (pieces of the one bread) during spiritual fellowship, as we gather together and share the bread of life in and through one another. That is what the reciprocal aspects of the making of the twelve breads and the sharing of these breads in the Temple showed forth.

---

208 McClintock and Strong, *Cyclopedia*, vol. 9, p. 712, s.v. "Showbread."

COURSE 10

The Symbolic "Cup" and the Promised New Covenant

The concept of a symbolic "cup" was common in the Jewish idiom, often referring to one's portion or lot. "Cup" was used in a metaphorical sense, as described in the following excerpt from *The Jewish Encyclopedia*:

> "Cup" is frequently used in metaphors of good or of ill fortune, as in "My cup runneth over" (Ps. xxiii. 5, xvi. 5); "the cup of his fury" (Isa. li. 17, 22); "the bowl of the cup of staggering" (Zech. xii. 2, Hebr.); "the cup of astonishment and desolation" (Ezek. xxiii. 33). Babylon is a "golden cup in the Lord's hand that made all the earth drunken" (Jer. li. 7). The "cup of consolation" (Jer. xvi. 7) is one offered to mourners; while the "cup of salvation" (Ps. cxvi. 13) is a cup of thanksgiving for deliverance, in allusion, perhaps, to the wine of the peace-offering ("shelamim"), or to the cup of praise and thanksgiving.[209]

Many examples exist of the cup used in a positive sense, symbolizing blessing or abundance:

> [NAS] Psalm 16:5 The LORD is the portion of my inheritance and my **cup**; Thou dost support my lot.

> [KJV] Psalm 23:5 Thou preparest a table before me in the presence of mine enemies: thou anointest my head with oil; my **cup** runneth over.

> [KJV] Psalm 116:13 I will take the **cup** of salvation, and call upon the name of the LORD.

The cup was also used in a negative symbolic sense to indicate punishment, anger, or God's vengeance. Sometimes it was the nations that would drink this figurative cup of judgment:

---

[209] *The Jewish Encyclopedia*, vol. 4, p. 384, s.v. "Cup."

> KJV Jeremiah 25:15   For thus saith the LORD God of Israel unto me; Take the wine **cup** of this fury at my hand, and cause all the nations, to whom I send thee, to drink it.
>
> KJV Jeremiah 25:17   Then took I the **cup** at the LORD'S hand, and made all the nations to drink, unto whom the LORD had sent me:
>
> KJV Zechariah 12:2   Behold, I will make **Jerusalem** a **cup** of trembling unto all the people round about, when they shall be in the siege both against Judah *and* against Jerusalem.

Then when Israel rejected God's ways and walked in unrighteousness, as a nation it was given this cup of judgment:

> KJV Isaiah 51:17   Awake, awake, stand up, O Jerusalem, which hast drunk at the hand of the LORD the **cup** of his fury; thou hast drunken the dregs of the **cup** of trembling, *and* wrung *them* out.
>
> KJV Ezekiel 23:31   Thou hast walked in the way of thy sister; therefore will I give her **cup** into thine hand.[210]

Given this long Jewish history of using "cup" metaphorically, it's not surprising that when early Messianic believers spoke of it, they understood its meaning to often be symbolic, figurative, or pointing out a certain truth. Paul was among many who spoke of a symbolic cup:

> NAS 1 Corinthians 10:21   **You cannot drink** the **cup of the Lord** and the **cup of demons**; you cannot partake of the table of the Lord and the table of demons.

Demons, of course, do not have actual cups filled with drink for us; Paul is speaking both spiritually and figuratively, not of natural or literal cups.

So when we examine the Last Supper scriptures, it is imperative to keep in mind this metaphorical use of "cup" and the symbolic nature of the Messiah's words:

> NAS Matthew 20:22–23   But Jesus answered and said, "You do not know what you are asking for. Are you able to drink the **cup** that I am about to drink?" They said to Him, "We are able." He said to

---

210   Ezekiel 23 here is speaking to Judah as Israel's figurative "sister."

them, "My **cup** you shall drink; but to sit on My right and on *My* left, this is not Mine to give, but it is for those for whom it has been prepared by My Father."

^KJV John 18:11   Then said Jesus unto Peter, Put up thy sword into the sheath: the **cup** which my Father hath given me, shall I not drink it?

^NAS Matthew 26:39   And He went a little beyond *them*, and fell on His face and prayed, saying, "My Father, if it is possible, let this **cup** pass from Me; yet not as I will, but as Thou wilt."

The Last Supper cup was slightly different in that an actual cup was involved; however, the Messiah used the cup and its contents (the fruit of the vine) to symbolize aspects of the promised covenant, for he said the cup was the *new covenant*:

^NAS 1 Corinthians 11:25   In the same way *He took* the cup also, after supper, saying, "This cup is the **new covenant** in My blood; do this, as often as you drink *it*, in remembrance of Me."

Some translations say *new testament* instead:

^KJV 1 Corinthians 11:25   After the same manner also *he took* the cup, when he had supped, saying, This cup is the **new testament** in my blood: this do ye, as oft as ye drink *it* [211] in remembrance of me.

In Greek, the word for "in" (as "in my blood") can mean "in the sphere of" or "in the realm of." Since the New Covenant could only come through the shed blood of Christ, here Jesus means, "This cup is the New Covenant which is *in the realm of* (and provided by) my shed blood."

Spiritual Truth and Not a New Ritual

The Messiah's words about the cup at the Last Supper clearly portrayed the New Covenant cup as a *spiritual* picture, not as instruction to perform a Communion ritual, as the Roman Church misconstrued it. The Greek scholar and commentator Lenski believed in some of Luther's doctrine, such as consubstantiation, where the flesh and blood of Christ are supposedly within the bread and wine of the ritual. But even Lenski admitted that the Greek predicate is "the new covenant in My blood,"

---

211   The italicized "it" shows that this word does not appear in the original Greek.

and that the phrase "in My blood" modifies "New Covenant" (*not* "this cup"), as he states concerning the 1 Corinthians 11:25 scripture above:

> The predicate is "the new testament in my blood," and the ἐν[212] phrase modifies "testament" and not "this cup."[213]

In other words, the Messiah is certainly not saying, "This cup *has* my blood in it" (as the Roman ritual teaches). Instead, the ἐν phrase (referring to "in my blood") reveals that the "cup" of the *New Covenant* of which we partake *has its legal basis* in his shed blood, not in the blood of the animal sacrifices under the Old Covenant. He is showing that the New Covenant will come about and have its authority and be effectual *because of* his shed blood. The disciples came to understand this truth, and eventually they went out teaching that the Messiah's shed blood is what provides *communion* with God in the promised New Covenant.

John wrote about this:

> NAS Revelation 1:5   and from Jesus Christ, the faithful witness, the first-born of the dead, and the ruler of the kings of the earth. To Him who loves us, **and released us from our sins by His blood**,

Paul wrote to the Ephesian assembly about this:

> NAB Ephesians 1:7   In him we have redemption **by his blood**, the forgiveness of transgressions...

He wrote about this same truth to the Hebrews:

> NAB Hebrews 9:12   he entered once for all into the sanctuary, not with the blood of goats and calves but with his own blood, **thus obtaining eternal redemption**.

> NAS Hebrews 10:4   For it is impossible for the blood of bulls and goats to take away sins.

Then Paul quoted King David (Psalm 40:6–8), showing that God had really taken no pleasure in the animal sacrifices, and that those sacrifices pointed further to the one who would come to do His will:

---

212 The Greek ἐν means "in," and here Lenski refers to the "in my blood" phrase.
213 Lenski, *The Interpretation of St. Paul's First and Second Epistles to the Corinthians,* p. 470.

> ᴺᴬˢ Hebrews 10:5–6   Therefore, **when He comes into the world**, He says, "Sacrifice and offering Thou hast not desired, But a body Thou hast prepared for Me; In whole burnt offerings and *sacrifices* for sin Thou hast taken no pleasure.
>
> ᴺᴬˢ Hebrews 10:7   "Then I said, 'Behold, I have come (In the roll of the book it is written of Me) To do Thy will, O God.'"
>
> ᴺᴬˢ Hebrews 10:8   After saying above, "Sacrifices and offerings and whole burnt offerings and *sacrifices* for sin Thou hast not desired, nor hast Thou taken pleasure *in them*" (which are offered according to the Law),

Continuing below, we see that He takes away the first covenant to establish the second one—the promised New Covenant—which would have its legal basis in a different shed blood, not that of sacrificed animals:

> ᴺᴬˢ Hebrews 10:9–10   then He said, "Behold, I have come to do Thy will." **He takes away the first in order to establish the second**. By this will we have been sanctified through the offering of the body of Jesus Christ once for all.

The phrase "as often as you drink," which we saw earlier in 1 Corinthians 11:25, refers to the drink that was the spiritual fruit of the vine (Matthew 26:29) and foreshadows spiritual partaking and fellowshipping with other believers. The fruit of the grapevine refers to that which is provided in the New Covenant, and here the Messiah points forward to the time just ahead of them at Pentecost, when the believers will be "drinking" the spiritual drink—the "new" wine that points to God's spirit and His love:

> ᴺᴬˢ John 7:37   Now on the last day, the great *day* of the feast, Jesus stood and cried out, saying, "If any man is thirsty, **let him come to Me and drink**.
>
> ᴺᴬˢ John 7:39   **But this He spoke of the Spirit**, whom **those who believed in Him were to receive**; for the Spirit was not yet *given*, because Jesus was not yet glorified.

The Promised New Covenant

We've seen that when Jesus said, "This cup is the *New Covenant*," he was referring to the promised New Covenant. This had been foretold by many Jewish prophets, including Isaiah, Ezekiel, Jeremiah, Daniel, and Malachi.

Through Isaiah, God speaks of an everlasting covenant, indicating that it will take place in the future by saying the words, "*I will*." The Jewish scholars who translated the Hebrew into Greek in the Septuagint also used a *future* form of the Greek to express "I will make an everlasting covenant."

> NAS Isaiah 55:3 "Incline your ear and come to Me. Listen, that you may live; And I **will** make **an everlasting covenant** with you, *According to* the faithful mercies shown to David.

> NAS Isaiah 61:8 For I, the LORD, love justice, I hate robbery in the burnt offering; And I will faithfully give them their recompense, And I **will** make **an everlasting covenant** with them.

The following verse is big, with God speaking prophetically to the promised Messiah before he comes:

> NAS Isaiah 42:6 "I am the LORD, I have called you in righteousness, I will also hold you by the hand and watch over you, And **I will appoint you as a covenant** to the people, **As a light to the nations**,

This is just one more proof of who the Messiah really was. Only Jesus could bring in the promised New Covenant, for God appointed *him* and his sacrifice to bring it in. He is the sole Jewish man from the line of David who could truly be called a "covenant to the people" and a "light to the nations." Each Sunday, the nations gather to read God's word. They have learned of Moses and Abraham and to walk with God, all because of the Messiah. There have been many false Messiahs, but they are revealed as false since they were not appointed as a covenant, nor did they bring in the promised New Covenant, nor were they a light to the nations.

For example, during the Jewish uprising (AD 132–135) against the Roman occupation and Emperor Hadrian, who had erected a pagan temple to Jupiter on the Temple Mount, the famous rabbi Akiva endorsed Bar Kochba as the Messiah. Many believed him to be the Messiah, based on the rabbi's proclamation. However, Bar Kochba did not have a promised New Covenant and therefore could not have been the Messiah. Nearly 600,000 Jews were killed by Rome in this uprising.

Christ is the seed of Abraham in which **all nations** will be blessed, as promised in Genesis:

> ^{NAS} Genesis 22:18 "And in your **seed all the nations** of the earth shall be **blessed**, because you have obeyed My voice."

Paul explains this further:

> ^{NAS} Galatians 3:16 Now the promises were spoken to Abraham and to his **seed**. He does not say, "And to seeds," as *referring* to many, but *rather* to one, "And to your seed," that is, Christ.

God also spoke through Ezekiel about this future covenant. Ezekiel begins chapter 16 with God showing him that Jerusalem (as the capital of Judah representing all Israel as the covenant nation) had broken the previous covenant. God then continues by speaking of the promised New Covenant:

> ^{NAS} Ezekiel 16:59–60 For thus says the Lord God, "I will also do with you as you have done, you who have despised the oath **by breaking the covenant**. Nevertheless, I will remember My covenant with you in the days of your youth, and I **will** establish **an everlasting covenant** with you.

God, too, speaks plainly about the New Covenant through Jeremiah, saying that it will *not* be according to the covenant under Moses:

> ^{NAS} Jeremiah 31:31–32 "Behold, days are coming," declares the LORD, "when I will make a **new covenant** with the house of Israel and with the house of Judah, **not like the covenant which I made with their fathers** in the day I took them by the hand to bring them out of the land of Egypt, **My covenant which they broke**, although I was a husband to them," declares the LORD.

> ^{NAS} Jeremiah 31:33–34 "**But this is the covenant which I will make with the house of Israel after those days**," declares the LORD, "I will put My law within them, and on their heart I will write it; and I will be their God, and they shall be My people. And they shall not teach again, each man his neighbor and each man his

brother, saying, 'Know the LORD,' for they shall all know Me, from the least of them to the greatest of them," declares the LORD, "for I will forgive their iniquity, **and their sin I will remember no more**."

Under the Old Covenant there was a remembrance of sin (Hebrews 10:3), so why would God say here that He would no longer remember their sin when the New Covenant came? It is because the price for atonement has been fully paid, something that the animal sacrifices could never fully do.

God Showed That the Messiah Would Make a Firm Covenant, yet Be Cut Off

God spoke through Daniel, declaring that the Messiah would "***make a firm covenant***," but He also shows that he would be cut off in the middle of the "week."

> NAS Daniel 9:26 "Then after the sixty-two weeks **the Messiah** will be **cut off** and have nothing, and the people of the prince who is to come will destroy the city and the sanctuary. And its end *will come* with a flood; even to the end there will be war; desolations are determined.

> NAS Daniel 9:27 "And he will make a firm **covenant** with the many for one week, but **in the middle of the week** he will **put a stop to sacrifice and grain offering**; and on the wing of abominations *will come* one who makes desolate, even until a complete destruction, one that is decreed, is poured out on the one who makes desolate."

Christ was cut off in the middle of the week, which is exactly in the middle of the "week" of seven years that Daniel meant. This happened in AD 30,[214] when Christ was crucified as God's Passover lamb, thus paying the price that brought in the New Covenant. From God's perspective, the "sacrifice and grain offering" ceased at the Crucifixion (Isaiah 66:3), and He would no longer accept animal sacrifices for sin.

Then, as the first-century historian Josephus explains, all the people who were still offering sacrifices were walled up in the city at Passover when Roman troops at-

---

[214] Astronomical science shows that a Passover full moon occurred on Thursday, the 14th of Nisan, in the year AD 30. Jesus was approximately 33½ years old at death, having begun his 3½-year ministry at about age 30 (Luke 3:23). Scholars mostly agree that Rome was off by a couple of years in estimating the beginning date of our calendar, so when taking into account the "zero year" (between 1 BC and AD 1), Jesus would have been born around 4 BC. He did not make it to his 34th birthday, which would have been around September or October of 30 AD.

tacked the Temple[215] (which occurred 40 years to the day later, in AD 70). Thus the sacrifice and grain offerings that ceased to be efficacious in God's eyes at Passover in AD 30 ceased *literally* during that Roman attack 40 years later. So whether Daniel was speaking of the sacrifices and grain offering as no longer valid in God's eyes after the Crucifixion, or whether he was speaking of them ceasing literally when the Temple was destroyed, both meanings could fit.

The number "40" is often meaningful in the scriptures: It rained 40 days and 40 nights in the flood during Noah's day, the Israelites wandered 40 years in the wilderness, and there are many other examples. The Messiah spoke of the generation of those who rejected him, saying they would be given the sign of Jonah (Luke 11:29–30). Jonah, who had spent three days and three nights in the belly of the whale, warned the people of Nineveh that they would be destroyed in *40 days*, but they repented and God turned away His wrath. It appears that the generation of people who rejected the Messiah were given *40 years*, but many failed to repent, and Jerusalem was then attacked by Rome at Passover.

As an aside, the scriptures show there was a definite Messianic expectancy during Christ's time, for Jewish scholars understood that the prophecies pointed to that time for the Messiah's coming. The following passage from the Talmud, written a few hundred years later by a rabbinic scholar, confirms this:

> Said Rabh: All the appointed times for the appearance of the Messiah have already ceased.[216]

God also spoke through Malachi concerning the promised covenant:

> NAS Malachi 3:1 "Behold, I am going to send My messenger, and he will clear the way before Me. And the Lord, whom you seek, will suddenly come to His temple; and **the messenger of the covenant**, in whom you delight, behold, He is coming," says the LORD of hosts.

In Isaiah 42:6, God said that He would appoint the Messiah as a covenant (i.e., New Covenant) to the people. God's son, the Messiah, would give up his very life and soul (Isaiah 53:10–12) as the true sacrificial offering that Abraham's example pointed to when he was ready to obey God and offer his chosen son, Isaac. However, God knew

---

215 Whiston, *The New Complete Works of Josephus*, "The Jewish War," 6.9.3–4, pp. 906–907.
216 Babylonian Talmud, Book 8, Tract Sanhedrin, ch. 11, p. 305, http://sacred-texts.com/jud/t08/t0814.htm.

that He would provide the true lamb (Genesis 22:8, 13) and Isaac—as the promised son—was a type of this.

God referred to the Passover sacrifice personally as "My sacrifice" (Exodus 34:25). The shed blood of the true lamb of God would be the true sacrifice that God would accept to bring us out of *spiritual* Egypt; hence Christ was crucified on the same day as the Passover lambs. This Mount of the Lord (Moriah) where God directed Abraham to offer Isaac is the same mount where He would later direct David to locate the Temple with its sacrifices. It was also very close to where the Crucifixion would take place.

Christ came to a place of commitment before God where he was willing to offer up not just his earthly life but his eternal soul to bear the sins of his brethren and all people, and thus pay the full eternal penalty for transgressions that the animal sacrifices could only point to:

> NAS Isaiah 53:3 He was despised and forsaken of men, A man of sorrows, and acquainted with grief; And like one from whom men hide their face, He was despised, and we did not esteem Him.

> NAS Isaiah 53:4 Surely our griefs He Himself bore, And our sorrows He carried; Yet we ourselves esteemed Him stricken, Smitten of God, and afflicted.

> NAS Isaiah 53:5 But He was pierced through for our transgressions, He was crushed for our iniquities; The chastening for our well-being *fell* upon Him, And by His scourging we are healed.

Isaiah continued to show the Messiah as the lamb sacrifice—the true Passover lamb who would be crucified on the very day that natural lambs were offered:

> NAS Isaiah 53:6 All of us like sheep have gone astray, Each of us has turned to his own way; But the LORD has caused the iniquity of us all To fall on Him.

> NAS Isaiah 53:7 He was oppressed and He was afflicted, Yet He did not open His mouth; **Like a lamb that is led to slaughter**, And like a sheep that is silent before its shearers, So He did not open His mouth.

> NAS Isaiah 53:8 By oppression and judgment He was taken away; And as for His generation, who considered That He was cut off

out of the land of the living, For the transgression of my people to whom the stroke *was due*?

^{NAS} Isaiah 53:9   His grave was assigned with wicked men, Yet He was with a rich man in His death, Because He had done no violence, Nor was there any deceit in His mouth.

^{KJV} Isaiah 53:10   Yet it pleased the LORD to bruise him; he hath put *him* to grief: when thou shalt make **his soul an offering for sin**, he shall see *his* seed, he shall prolong *his* days, and the pleasure of the LORD shall prosper in his hand.

Why on earth would the Lord be "pleased" to "bruise" (or crush) the Messiah? The answer is that, as the true lamb, the Messiah's willingness completed God's plan of redemption by paying the price for all transgressions. God was thus pleased with the outcome. He was now able to bring the people—all who would appropriate this offering by faith —into complete, unending communion with Himself. This was something the animal sacrifices could not fully accomplish.

^{KJV} Isaiah 53:11   As a result of the anguish of His soul, He will see *it* and be satisfied; By His knowledge the Righteous One, My Servant, will justify the many, As He will bear their iniquities.

Isaiah knew that the Messiah must first face death but he also foresaw the Messiah's Resurrection, that he would "divide the spoil with the mighty." Here we see that the Messiah would be resurrected, for God does not "divide him a portion" to the dead but to the living:

^{JPS} Isaiah 53:12   Therefore will **I divide him a portion among the great**, and **he shall divide the spoil with the mighty**; because he bared his soul unto death, and was numbered with the transgressors; yet he bore the sin of many, and made intercession for the transgressors.

At the Last Supper (which was the evening before the Passover lambs would be slaughtered and Christ would be crucified), the Messiah taught the disciples with a parable that they would later fully understand—that his *shed blood* is what provides the *New Covenant*:

> ^{NAS} Luke 22:20   And in the same way *He took* the cup after they had eaten, saying, "This cup which is poured out for you is the **new covenant in My blood.**

Theologians in Rome would later misunderstand these words and think that the Messiah was creating a new ritual.

God Said He Would Draw the Israelite People Back into a Relationship with Him

God said that in the last days He would draw the Israelites back into a covenant relationship with Him, and this is happening in amazing ways in our day.

> ^{NAS} Jeremiah 23:3–5   "Then I **Myself** shall gather the remnant of My flock out of all the countries where I have driven them and shall bring them back to their pasture; and they will be fruitful and multiply. I shall also raise up shepherds over them and they will tend them; and they will not be afraid any longer, nor be terrified, nor will any be missing," declares the LORD. "Behold, *the* days are coming," declares the LORD, "**When I shall raise up for David a righteous Branch**; And He will reign as king and act wisely And do justice and righteousness in the land.

> ^{NAS} Jeremiah 31:10   Hear the word of the LORD, O nations, And declare in the coastlands afar off, And say, "**He who scattered Israel will gather him, And keep him as a shepherd keeps his flock**."

> ^{NAS} Isaiah 44:3   'For I will pour out water on the thirsty *land* And streams on the dry ground; **I will pour out My Spirit on your offspring**, And My blessing on your descendants;

Although God wanted to draw the Jews back into a relationship with Him, the Devil had other ideas—to alienate them from their promised New Covenant. By being portrayed as "Judaizers" and connected to the "perjury of the Jews," as Roman Emperor Constantine had proclaimed, the Jews were essentially forced out of the promised New Covenant. This history should not be used to create animosity toward Catholics today, who had nothing to do with these events, and who mostly believe they are following the Lord; it is only so that we can accurately understand the effects of an all-powerful Roman government.

Remember, as we discussed in "Setting the Table 1," these Jewish believers were later derisively called "Quartodecimans," meaning "Fourteenthers," since they honored the day the Messiah was crucified as the true Passover by keeping the 14th day of Nisan special. The Messianic believers did not yield to Roman doctrines and this angered certain Roman leaders.

The Roman Church eventually introduced new doctrines that most Jews would never believe. These new teachings included the woman Mary becoming God's mother, a ritual where people were to ingest flesh and blood, and the worshipping of three Gods who make up the one God. These doctrines alienated the Jews from the New Covenant and helped to usher them back under the authority of the Pharisaic rabbis.

So instead of following the heart of the Jewish Messiah, who wept over Israel and desired to take her under his wing as a hen does her chicks (Luke 13:34), the Roman Church of the day and its world military power at that time rejected all things Jewish, including its idioms. This completed the Devil's plan of alienating the Jews from the New Covenant that had been promised to them by their own prophets.

In fact, the Quartodecimans were not "Judaizers," for they only wanted to continue to keep the 14th day special as their ancestors had done before them for many hundreds of years. The real Judaizers were those trying to bring the people back under the authority of the previous covenant and back under the law of Moses, a teaching that Paul spoke against:

> NAS Galatians 3:10 For as many as are of the works of the Law are under a curse; for it is written, "Cursed is everyone who does not abide by **all** things written in the book of the law, to perform them."

Paul shows that the law was only the schoolmaster (Galatians 3:24) that disciplined us until we could find justification in Christ, because none of us can keep the law perfectly.

> NAS Galatians 3:11 Now that no one is justified by the Law before God is evident; for, "The righteous man shall live by faith."[217]

> NAS Galatians 3:13 Christ **redeemed us from the curse of the Law**, having become a curse for us—for it is written, "Cursed is everyone who hangs on a tree."[218]

---

217 Paul is referencing Habakkuk 2:4.
218 Paul is referencing Deuteronomy 21:22–23; "tree" can also mean a wooden plank or stake.

And, as the quote from Peter in the book of Acts points out, they should not put the yoke of the law on the Gentile disciples who were coming to the Lord:

> NAS Acts 15:10 "Now therefore why do you put God to the test by placing upon the neck of the disciples a yoke which neither our fathers nor we have been able to bear?

Paul shows how the promises to Abraham were given prior to the law of Moses, and therefore that law that came later cannot invalidate these promises:

> NAS Galatians 3:17 What I am saying is this: the Law, **which came four hundred and thirty years later**, does not invalidate a covenant previously ratified by God, so as to nullify **the promise**.

> NAS Galatians 3:18 For if the inheritance is based on law, it is no longer based on a promise; **but God has granted it to Abraham by means of a promise**.

> NAS Galatians 3:19 Why the Law then? **It was added because of transgressions**, having been ordained through angels by the agency of a mediator, **until the seed should come** to whom the promise had been made.

Abraham, Isaac, and Jacob did not have the law of Moses, and they still walked with God. Paul, a scholar in the law educated under the famous rabbi Gamaliel, said in verse 19 above that this law came into existence only because of transgressions in the wilderness.

> NAS Galatians 3:2 This is the only thing I want to find out from you: **did you receive the Spirit by the works of the Law, or by hearing with faith?**

> KJV Galatians 3:24–25 Wherefore the law was our schoolmaster *to bring us* unto Christ, that we might be justified by faith. But after that faith is come, **we are no longer under a schoolmaster**.

Paul could not state more clearly that the law was the schoolmaster until Christ came to pay the price for all of the people's sins. And by putting our faith in him (i.e., believing that he paid the price), we are no longer justified before God by keeping the law of Moses with its sacrifices, Sabbath laws, unclean people outside the camp, circumcision, festivals, etc. After all, the law with its various animal sacrifices and ritual washings was never God's complete plan from the beginning, but rather it pointed forward and served as the schoolmaster until His plan would be revealed:

> ^{JPS} Jeremiah 7:22–23 For I spoke not unto your fathers, nor commanded them in the day that I brought them out of the land of Egypt, concerning burnt-offerings or sacrifices; but this thing I commanded them, saying: 'Hearken unto My voice, and I will be your God, and ye shall be My people; and walk ye in all the way that I command you, that it may be well with you.'

We are no longer under the schoolmaster because now we look to Christ and what he did for our justification. Certain nonceremonial aspects of the law (do not steal, kill, commit adultery, etc.) do endure, for they are now written by the Lord in our hearts (Jeremiah 31:33). We fulfill the law as we walk in *agape* (Romans 13:10) and as we walk according to the spirit (Romans 8:4). Although we are not under condemnation from the law, we do not despise the blood of the covenant through wanton behavior (Hebrews 10:29).

※※※

In the book of Revelation, the Old Covenant is pictured as a moon with no light of its own but only reflected light from the sun—God's sunlight in the New Covenant shown through the Messiah. The New Covenant assembly is pictured as a woman with the moon (law) under her feet, still visible and undergirding her but no longer with the same legal standing; now she is clothed with the sun (New Covenant):

> ^{NAS} Revelation 12:1 And a great sign appeared in heaven: **a woman clothed with the sun, and the moon under her feet**, and on her head a crown of twelve stars;

> ^{YLT} Hebrews 10:1 For **the law having a shadow of the coming good things—not the very image of the matters**, every year, by the same sacrifices that they offer continually, is never able to **make perfect** those coming near,

"Make perfect" above refers at least partially to being perfect in conscience before God. The conscience always knew that the proper price for sin had not been paid with animal sacrifices:

^{YLT} Hebrews 9:9   which *is* a simile in regard to the present time, in which both gifts and sacrifices are offered, which are not able, **in regard to conscience**, to make perfect him who is serving,

As Hebrews 10:1 (above) shows, the law was only a "shadow" of the good things to come. It was never meant to be the be-all and end-all of what God wanted for His people. For those who still want to walk under it, the following scriptures should dissuade them:

^{NAS} James 2:10   For whoever keeps the whole law and yet stumbles in one *point*, he has become guilty of all.

^{NAS} Deuteronomy 27:26   'Cursed is he who does not confirm **the words** of this law by doing them.' And all the people shall say, 'Amen.'

In other words, if you're seeking to be justified by the law and thus avoid the curse that Moses spoke of, then you must keep the whole law perfectly.

The New Covenant Is Not Like the One under Moses

As we've discussed, Abraham, Isaac, and Jacob walked with God and in His promises hundreds of years before the law of Moses (Torah/instruction) was given. So below Paul shows that since God's promises to Abraham were not based on law, the law that came later under Moses did not make void the previous promises to Abraham.

In writing his letter to the Hebrews, Paul quotes Jeremiah 31:31–34 (i.e., concerning the promise of the new covenant), then makes his point:

^{NAS} Hebrews 8:8   For finding fault with them, He says, "Behold, days are coming, says the Lord, When **I will effect a new covenant** With the house of Israel and with the house of Judah;

^{NAS} Hebrews 8:9   **Not like the covenant which I made with their fathers** On the day when I took them by the hand To lead them out of the land of Egypt; For they did not continue in My covenant, And I did not care for them, says the Lord.

^{NAS} Hebrews 8:10   "For this is the covenant that I will make with the house of Israel After those days, says the Lord: I will put My laws into their minds, And I will write them upon their hearts. And I will be their God, And they shall be My people.

> ^{NAS} Hebrews 8:12   "For I will be merciful to their iniquities, And I will remember their sins no more."
>
> ^{NAS} Hebrews 8:13   When He said, "A new *covenant*," **He has made the first obsolete. But whatever is becoming obsolete and growing old is ready to disappear**.

When Jesus (Yeshua) spoke of his blood and the New Covenant, he was simply pointing back to what God had instituted through Moses when He commanded the animal sacrifices. He was bringing the fulfillment that allowed many believing Jews to enter into the promised New Covenant, which would no longer require sacrifices because Christ paid the final penalty for sin for all who receive him:

> ^{NAS} Mark 14:23   And when He had taken a cup, *and* given thanks, He gave *it* to them; and they all drank from it.
>
> ^{NAS} Mark 14:24–25   And He said to them, "This is My blood of the covenant, which is **poured out for many**. Truly I say to you, I shall never again drink of **the fruit of the vine** until that day when I drink it new in the kingdom of God."

Above we see that it was probably after the disciples drank it that Jesus said, "This is My blood…which is poured out." Jesus thus speaks of the fruit of the grapevine in the cup in a symbolic parable that the disciples would later understand.

It is very possible that Jesus here was "pouring out" the remainder from the cup, since the Greek is a present participle and since it was a symbolic comparison to the Old Covenant sacrifices in which animal blood was poured out at the altar. When the Passover lambs were slain, such as would have happened the day following this Last Supper, some of the blood of each lamb was *poured out* at the altar to be efficacious. Jesus uses the same Greek word for "pouring out" as that used in the Septuagint for sacrificial blood (this will be covered more in Course 11).

Whatever the full meaning of the Messiah's words and actions, the scriptures make clear that this cup held only the "fruit of the vine," which *represented* the New Covenant and the blood that God would now accept. The fact that Jesus says it was poured out for *many* indicates that his actions and words had a much bigger application (Mark 10:45).

Do his words spoken on his final night sound similar to anything Moses had said?

> ^{KJV} Hebrews 9:19   For when **Moses** had spoken every precept to all the people according to the law, **he took the blood** of calves and of

goats, with water, and scarlet wool, and hyssop, **and sprinkled both the book, and all the people**,

^{NAS} Hebrews 9:20 saying, "**This is the blood of the covenant** which God commanded you."

^{NAS} Exodus 24:7 Then he took the book of the covenant and read *it* in the hearing of the people; and they said, "All that the LORD has spoken we will do, and we will be obedient!"

^{NAS} Exodus 24:8 So Moses took the blood and **sprinkled** *it* **on the people**, and said, "**Behold the blood of the covenant**, which the LORD has made with you in accordance with all these words."

Below, Peter's words to the Jews of the Diaspora spiritually tie Christ's blood back to Moses by speaking of "obedience" and "sprinkling" blood. Peter knew that this was what the Messiah was referring to at the Last Supper teachings:

^{NAB} 1 Peter 1:1 Peter, an apostle of Jesus Christ, to the chosen sojourners of the **dispersion** in Pontus, Galatia, Cappadocia, Asia, and Bithynia,

^{NAS} 1 Peter 1:2 according to the foreknowledge of God the Father, by the sanctifying work of the Spirit, that you may **obey** Jesus Christ and **be sprinkled with His blood**: May grace and peace be yours in fullest measure.

This was a common method of speaking among spiritual New Covenant Jews, who would say something in the natural or literal sense (often something connected to the first covenant) but intend the spiritual truth behind it—its New Covenant application.

Last Supper Parables Were Shocking in the Natural Sense so They Would Be Remembered, Discussed, and Understood Later

Scriptures like those from Peter above may not have meant a lot in Rome, but they held very clear meaning to Jews within their first-century idiom. The Messiah's somewhat shocking parables from the Last Supper would have stuck with them, and eventually after discussion, prayer, and God's spirit leading, they would understand their full meanings. This is what Jesus knew would happen.

^{NAS} John 14:26 "But the Helper, the Holy Spirit, whom the Father will send in My name, **He will teach you** all things, **and bring to your remembrance all that I said to you**.

The Jewish Peter was not writing about sprinkling one another with literal blood during a ritual of Communion (1 Peter 1:2), because no such ritual was kept. Peter understood that Jesus was speaking spiritual truth at the Last Supper, and therefore of applying blood *spiritually*, whereas under the Old Covenant the blood was sprinkled *naturally*.

Today, the members of the various churches that keep the Communion ritual do not sprinkle one another with the wine in an attempt to follow this verse, for they correctly interpret this verse *spiritually*, and not as something to do as a natural ritual.

In Course 2, we saw how the disciples taught that *we* are the body of Christ, which proves that they understood the parables concerning the one bread at the Last Supper. The same is true for the parables Jesus taught that night concerning his blood. By the disciples' eventual teachings, we know they came to understand that they would *spiritually* apply the blood in the New Covenant:

^{NAS} Hebrews 10:19   Since therefore, brethren, we have confidence to enter the holy place **by the blood of Jesus**,

^{NAS} Ephesians 1:7   In Him we have redemption **through His blood**, the forgiveness of our trespasses, according to the riches of His grace,

Jesus does not say at the Last Supper that this is **the** blood of the covenant, as Moses did (Exodus 24:8); instead Jesus says this is **my** blood of the covenant. Not just any blood sacrifice, animal or otherwise, could pay the full price for all sin; it had to be the precious blood of God's own son.

^{NIV} Matthew 26:28   This is **my blood of the covenant**, which is poured out for many for the forgiveness of sins.

The Messiah and the Ritual Purification

The symbolic cup containing the fruit of the vine (grapevine) symbolized the New Covenant, and Christ's shed blood provided the cup of spiritual blessings available in the New Covenant. This spiritual life flows through the spiritual body of Christ, joining the believers in true communion with God and one another.

> NAS 1 John 1:7   but if we walk in the light as He Himself is in the light, we have fellowship with one another, and the blood of Jesus His Son **cleanses** us from all sin.

The word "cleanses" above (*katharize* in the Greek) is often used to indicate ritual cleansing of the Jews. The Jews understood this Greek word in this context because various forms of it also often appear in the Septuagint, such as the four boldfaced words in the following two scriptures:

> LXE Leviticus 14:7   And he shall sprinkle seven times upon him that was **cleansed** of his leprosy, and he shall be **clean**; and he shall let go the living bird into the field.

> LXE Leviticus 14:11   And the priest that **cleanses** shall present the man under **purification**, and these *offerings* before the Lord, at the door of the tabernacle of witness.

These first-century Jews were very familiar with the Greek Septuagint. This translation of the Hebrew Old Testament by Jewish scholars often used the same Greek words for ritual cleansings or washings, such as when the leper above is pronounced healed and ritually clean.

At the Last Supper, Jesus spoke of the required Jewish practice of immersion in water (needed before entering the Temple), telling Peter he did not need another complete washing. Using this same Greek word *katharoi*, he then declared that not all of the disciples were ritually *clean* (this was because of what was in the heart of Judas—his plan to betray Christ):

> NAS John 13:10   Jesus said to him, "He who has bathed needs only to wash his feet, but is completely **clean**; and you are **clean**, but not all *of you*."

> NAS John 13:11   For He knew the one who was betraying Him; for this reason He said, "Not all of you are **clean**."

After the Last Supper, Jesus points further to the coming New Covenant by explaining that it was because of God's word coming through him and being accepted that the disciples were *ritually* clean (again using this same Greek word *katharoi*):

> ^{NAS} John 15:3 "You are already **clean** because of the word which I have spoken to you.

Paul also brings out this aspect of the New Covenant below as he explains that the Messiah spiritually "cleanses" the assembly of believers, "washing" her (the bride) with the water that is really the word of God. The word "cleansed" *(katharison)* comes from the same Greek root as the other words ("cleanses," "clean," etc.):

> ^{NAS} Ephesians 5:26 that He might sanctify her, having **cleansed** her by the **washing of water with the word**,

Below, this Greek word *(katharismon)* is used to describe one of the Jewish ceremonial washings:

> ^{NIV} John 2:6 Nearby stood six stone water jars, the kind used by the Jews for **ceremonial washing**, each holding from twenty to thirty gallons.

In the New Covenant, the disciples came to understand from the Messiah's teachings that they would no longer need ritual cleansings in water, but that they would be "washed" by the word of God that he brought to them. John showed that in the new covenant God will cleanse *(katharisy)* us as we confess (or admit) our sin to God and ask for His forgiveness:

> ^{NAS} 1 John 1:9 If we confess our sins, He is faithful and righteous to forgive us our sins and to **cleanse** us from all unrighteousness.

> ^{NAS} Acts 3:19 "Repent therefore and return, that your **sins may be wiped away**, in order that times of refreshing may come from the presence of the Lord;

While discussing the Pharisees' requirement of washing hands before eating bread, Jesus showed his disciples that the things that come from outside and enter into man do not defile, but those things that defile him come *out* of man as a result of thoughts of the heart that are sometimes acted upon:

> ^{KJV} Mark 7:18–23 And he saith unto them, Are ye so without understanding also? Do ye not perceive, that whatsoever thing from without entereth into the man, *it* cannot defile him; Because it entereth not into his heart, but into the belly, and goeth out into

the draught, purging all meats? And he said, That which cometh out of the man, that defileth the man. For from within, out of the heart of men, proceed evil thoughts, adulteries, fornications, murders, thefts, covetousness, wickedness, deceit, lasciviousness, an evil eye, blasphemy, pride, foolishness: All these evil things come from within, and defile the man.

The Messiah's sacrifice brought the fulfillment of the ritual cleansings that were required under the Mosaic covenant:

> NAS Hebrews 1:3b   When He had made **purification** of sins, He sat down at the right hand of the Majesty on high;

The Greek word for "purification" above is again *katharismon*, and this shows that through the sacrifice Jesus made and by us accepting his shed blood as the penalty for our forgiveness, we become ritually clean before God if we, by faith, receive this truth and apply it. This makes us fully able to enter God's presence and receive spiritual sustenance.

※❁◦❁※

Jesus was often somewhat contrary to some of the ritual washings and traditional cleansings when they were not originally from God, or if God was leading him otherwise. The Pharisees were upset when his disciples did not first wash before eating bread (Matthew 15:2). These disciples also baptized people in water, although Jesus himself refrained from this (John 4:1).

When Jesus turned the water into wine at the wedding in Cana of Galilee (after the wine ran out), he directed the water to be placed in the pots used for ritual purification. By turning this water into wine, he made the pots temporarily unfit for ritual purification according to rabbinic law (John 2:6). Thus the servants feared telling the head steward where the excellent wine came from (John 2:9), knowing that the pots of purification had been used.

In another example, the Lord almost seems to sport with the kosher Peter by giving him a parable in the form of a vision of unclean animals—which he tells the hungry Peter to "kill and eat"—knowing Peter's strict adherence to the Jewish laws of never eating anything unclean (Acts 10 and 11). Indeed, most Jews who followed the law of Moses strictly avoided eating anything unclean. Peter said "Not so, Lord, for I have **never** eaten anything common or unclean," but Peter later came to understand what the vision really meant—that God was cleansing the Gentile believers. The Messiah had also reached out and touched the unclean leper, immediately healing him (Matthew 8:3).

The Messiah knew that some of the rules for ritual purification were traditions of man and not from God, while others pointed further to New Covenant truth. So consider this: We see the strong will of Peter in saying—even to the Lord—"Not so Lord" when he felt very strongly about the kosher food laws given under Moses. Yet according to the Roman ritual, are we to believe that, at the Last Supper, the kosher Peter was fine with ingesting flesh and blood in a supposed ritual? It's sad that this point has to be argued or even discussed, but to show the error of the long-lasting traditions of man, these first-century Jewish idioms must be considered.

The Apostles Grew in New Covenant Understandings After Receiving the Holy Spirit

The disciples would come to understand that it was the shed blood of the Messiah that now brought them ritual cleansing before God, and that in the New Covenant, forgiveness and cleansing were no longer found in Temple offerings or ritual washings. It is the Messiah's blood and the acceptance of it—by spiritually placing it on the doorposts of our hearts (as in the Passover in Egypt)—that allows us to share in communion and fellowship with God and the assembly.

But the disciples did not fully understand these things at the Last Supper, as they did not yet comprehend that Jesus was really going to die and be resurrected (Luke 18:33–34; Matthew 16:21–22). Even on the day of the Resurrection, some of the disciples still did not understand. Having thought that Jesus was going to redeem Israel, they were distraught and very sad after the Crucifixion, thinking it had all been in vain (Luke 24:13–15, 21, 26). They made the following remarks to a man they did not recognize to be the risen Lord:

> [NAS] Luke 24:21 "But we were hoping that it was He who was going to redeem Israel. Indeed, besides all this, it is the third day since these things happened.

The resurrected Jesus, still unrecognized by them, reproved them for their slowness of heart:

> [NAS] Luke 24:25–27 And He said to them, "O foolish men and slow of heart to believe in all that the prophets have spoken! Was it not necessary for the Christ to suffer these things and to enter into His glory?" And beginning with Moses and with all the prophets, He explained to them the things concerning Himself in all the Scriptures.

Even when the remaining 11 apostles were told by Mary Magdalene and the other women that Jesus had risen from the dead, they dismissed the news, thinking their words to be nonsense (Luke 24:10, 11). Jesus then reproached the apostles for their hardness of heart and unbelief concerning the women's eyewitness testimony:

> NAS Mark 16:14   And afterward He appeared to the eleven themselves as they were reclining *at the table*; and He reproached them for their unbelief and hardness of heart, because they **had not believed** those who had seen Him after He had risen.

This is probably a primary reason why Jesus left the disciples with these parables at the Last Supper. He knew they could not yet handle the new truths and that it would take God's spirit flowing through them later, starting with Pentecost, to begin to understand how they would soon be operating under the promised New Covenant. Just after the Last Supper, Jesus told them:

> NAS John 16:12   "I have many more things to say to you, **but you cannot bear *them* now**.

Some years later they came further into another major New Covenant truth that initially shocked them: God led them to no longer consider uncircumcised Gentile believers in the Messiah to be ritually unclean (Acts 10:28, 45; 11:1–3).

The doctrines that the apostles would teach later show that they came to understand the Messiah's parables. Having already understood the symbolic cup, they would later comprehend the symbolism of the fruit of the grapevine—and see that they were now under a New Covenant provided by *his* shed blood.

Throughout this Course, we've seen that the words of Jesus concerning the symbolic "cup" and the New Covenant at the Last Supper—when understood in light of the Jewish idioms of that day—led the disciples into new truths.

COURSE 11

Jacob, Moses, and the Fruit of the Vine

We've seen that during the Last Supper, Jesus taught that *he* was the true grapevine. But long before the Messiah's words at this momentous event, the fruit of the vine (or grapevine in the Greek) played an important role in Jewish tradition.

Israel's Historic Connection to the Grapevine

Israel had a longstanding connection to grapes and the grapevine, which is shown below in a historic artifact—the last coin minted in Israel before the final crushing of Bar Kochba, the Jewish leader who fought against the Roman occupation (AD 135):

A cluster of grapes hangs from a vine on the front of the coin (left image), and on the reverse is a lyre surrounded by a Hebrew inscription that reads "for the freedom of Jerusalem."

When those whom Moses sent to "spy out" the Promised Land of Israel later returned, they brought back a large vine with grapes on it (Numbers 13:20–23). Thus grapes and the grapevine became symbolic of the Promised Land:

> NAS Numbers 13:17 When Moses sent them to spy out the land of Canaan, he said to them, "Go up there into the Negev; then go up into the hill country.

> NAS Numbers 13:20 "And how is the land, is it fat or lean? Are there trees in it or not? Make an effort then to get some of the fruit of the land." Now the time was the time of the first ripe grapes.

> NAS Numbers 13:23   Then they came to the valley of Eshcol and from there cut down a branch with a single cluster of grapes; and they carried it on a pole between two *men*, with some of the pomegranates and the figs.

The spies returned to Moses with this tremendous cluster of grapes, which was so big that it took two men with a pole to carry it. In addition, the scripture says the spies brought back an "evil" or "bad" report of the existence of giant-sized men in the land who were too strong for them (13:32). It was not evil in the sense that it was a false report, only that it put fear and unbelief into the people as to accomplishing what God had called them to. They cried out, saying that it would have been better if they had stayed in Egypt instead of following God and Moses.

Joshua and Caleb were of a different spirit, though; they wanted to go in and take the land that God had promised. Because this report caused the multitudes to be fearful, however, the Israelites had to wander in the wilderness for 40 years until all those who were over 20 at the time—and thus should have known better (Numbers 32:11)—had died. Forty years later, under Joshua, the next generation finally entered the Promised Land.

Jesus and Joshua have identical names in both Hebrew and Greek; however, English translators changed "Joshua" into "Jesus" (as we saw in "Setting the Table 2"). Thus Joshua leading the multitude into the Promised Land points forward to the true Joshua (Yeshua/Jesus) leading us into the spiritual Promised Land.

Going back earlier to the father of the Israelite nation, we see that Jacob spoke in enigmatic parables about **grapes** and the **grapevine** in a prophecy concerning the Messiah:

> NAS Genesis 49:10   "The scepter shall not depart from Judah, Nor the ruler's staff from between his feet, **Until Shiloh comes**, And to him *shall be* the obedience of the peoples.

> NAS Genesis 49:11   "He ties *his* foal **to the vine**, And his donkey's colt to the choice vine; He washes his garments in wine, And his robes **in the blood of grapes**.[219]

If we view this scripture through our natural or literal senses, we would ask how and why one would ever wash his robes in wine, the "blood" of a "grape," or the blood of a single cluster "of grapes"? And how could such a thing possibly tie into the

---

[219] The Greek Septuagint uses the word "grape" in the singular, but this can also refer to a separate cluster. In Hebrew and the Septuagint, the word used for "vine" is "grapevine."

promised Messiah? No one would wash a garment in the fruit of the vine, for in the natural sense it would become stained.

What would later men of God, such as Moses or David, think of this prophecy? What could Jacob's prophetic words possibly mean?

In the Psalms, David referred to the Messiah coming with parables to bring forth "dark sayings" *that were from old*. Jacob's prophesy was one such ***dark saying***.

> NAS Psalm 78:2   I will open my mouth in a parable; I will utter **dark sayings of old**,

Or, as Young's Literal Translation has it:

> YLT Psalm 78:2   I open with a simile my mouth, I bring forth **hidden things of old**,

And Jesus fulfills this prophecy from the Psalms:

> NAS Matthew 13:35   so that what was spoken through the prophet might be fulfilled, saying, "I will open My mouth in parables; **I will utter things hidden since the foundation of the world**."

You will not see much written in the Torah commentaries about Jacob's statement of washing his robes in the "***blood*** of grapes," because how could this be explained?

John Gives the Spiritual Fulfillment of Jacob's Washing of Robes in Wine

One of the closest Jewish followers of Christ was John, who when writing the Book of Revelation used this saying of Jacob, yet with a slightly different application. John pictured this same spiritual concept of washing robes in "blood" and making them white, but he showed this being done not in the blood of a grape, but in the Messiah's blood. This is what Jacob's "dark saying" pointed to:

> NAS Revelation 6:11   And **there was given** to each of them a **white robe**; and they were told that they should rest for a little while longer, until *the number of* their fellow servants and their brethren who were to be killed even as they had been, should be completed also.

> NAS Revelation 7:14   And I said to him, "My lord, you know." And he said to me, "These are the ones who come out of the great tribu-

lation, and **they have washed** their robes and **made them white** in the **blood of the Lamb**.

You cannot literally make a robe clean or "white" by washing it in wine or in blood, so of course these statements are intended to be interpreted spiritually.

Those who are familiar with Jewish writings know that God was firm through Moses in requiring the Jews never to ingest any manner of blood. However, what may surprise some is that Moses also spoke of drinking blood in a positive sense. Moses, like Jacob, also spoke of the *blood* of the grape:

> NAS Deuteronomy 32:13–15 "He made him ride on the high places of the earth, And he ate the produce of the field; And He made him suck honey from the rock, And oil from the flinty rock, Curds of cows, and milk of the flock, With fat of lambs, And rams, the breed of Bashan, and goats, With the finest of the wheat—And **of the blood of grapes you drank** wine. But Jeshurun grew fat and kicked—You are grown fat, thick, and sleek—Then he forsook God who made him, And scorned the Rock of his salvation.

Moses was speaking of the blessings that pointed to the Promised Land, of God's provision, and drinking from the *blood* of a grape ("grape" is singular in Hebrew, referring to either a single grape or a single bunch of grapes). This "Song of Moses" not only spoke of the Israelites drinking of the fruit of the vine in the Promised Land, but also of their eventual forsaking of the Lord and the exile that occurred.

Whosoever Ingests Any Blood Is to Be Cut Off

But why would Moses speak of *drinking* blood in any form, especially here as a positive experience? Wouldn't this be improper, and at least slightly distasteful, given all of God's commands through Moses to never ingest blood?

> KJV Leviticus 7:27 Whatsoever soul *it be* that eateth any manner of blood, even **that soul shall be cut off** from his people.

> NAS Leviticus 17:10–11 'And any man from the house of Israel, or from the aliens who sojourn among them, **who eats any blood, I will set My face against that person who eats blood, and will cut him off from among his people.** For **the life** of the flesh **is in the blood**, and I have given it to you on the altar **to make atonement** for your souls; **for it is the blood** by reason of the life **that makes atonement.**'

Couldn't Moses have just said that the Israelites drank **cool, refreshing grape juice**? Why put the word "blood" in there? Do we really want to equate the Promised Land with drinking natural blood of any kind, even if it is the blood of a grape? We know that Moses must have had a good reason for including it, for he was a friend of God with whom God spoke face-to-face.

Torah commentators, as well as New Covenant commentators, often avoid this verse altogether since there's no question that the idea of ingesting blood, even the "blood" of a grape, is disturbing.

Since God had said that the "life" is in the blood (Leviticus 17:11), let's assume for now that Moses was speaking spiritually. He gave an analogy about the "life" of the grape from which they were drinking and "the life" that God would provide in the Promised Land. Moses spoke of drinking blood for the same reason that the Messiah spoke of it—both meant it to be understood in a figurative, spiritual sense.

The Messiah and the Spiritual Lifeblood of the New Covenant

The Old Testament contains some scriptures that may seem bizarre, and this is also true of the New Testament. Often a bizarre scripture is a signpost that the speaker is giving a parable that must be understood spiritually. One of the strangest Bible scriptures happens to be spoken by the Messiah himself, and just as with the figurative statement made by Moses, it relates to taking in the lifeblood of the grape in the Promised Land:

> [NAS] John 6:53–54 Jesus therefore said to them, "Truly, truly, I say to you, unless you eat the flesh of the Son of Man and drink His blood, you have **no life in yourselves**. He who eats My flesh and drinks My blood **has eternal life**, and I will raise him up on the last day."

If ever Jesus spoke a parable that needed to be properly interpreted, this was it. Yet when these Jewish scriptures were brought to Rome, it was decided that they meant a new Communion ritual.

Early Jewish believers knew, however, that Jesus was speaking another parable, as he had done so often before. Every statement a person makes must be taken in context, and much needs to be understood about the context of John chapter 6 that leads up to verses 53 and 54, so let's take a closer look.

First of all, this was a particularly stubborn group that was following the Messiah only for "loaves and the fishes" (verse 26), as Jesus had miraculously fed the hungry multitude the previous day by *breaking bread* and multiplying it out to them. Some people from this previous day were waiting for more free bread, and were subtly tempting Jesus to be like Moses and provide bread continually, as Moses did with the manna in the wilderness (verses 30–31). Jesus responded that it was not the decision of Moses that gave them the provision of the manna, but God's miracle (verse 32). Jesus then compared himself to the manna that came down, showing that he was sent by God as the true spiritual provision to which the manna pointed.

Secondly, Jesus taught those present not to labor for food that perishes, but to seek the spiritual food that will bring everlasting life in God's presence. However, they resisted and did not really hear him (verse 27). This is partly what led up to the shocking statement that caused even many of his disciples to forsake him (John 6:66). It must be remembered that Jesus spoke the words that his Father gave him to speak (John 7:16, 17; 14:10; Hebrews 1:1, 2), and at this time God did not want a large group of people only interested in free bread to follow the Messiah. So Jesus gave a parable that would separate out those who were only seeking free bread, and that would later be understood spiritually by the disciples as they came fully into the promised New Covenant.

His disciples who remained loyal knew that this was another parable or "dark saying," and never thought this was something that Jesus wanted in any natural or ritualistic sense. They did not obediently walk over to him and begin nibbling on his leg and drinking his blood as it flowed out. It was only in Rome where this parable would be interpreted naturally as a new Communion ritual that they took literally.

The Blood of the Two Covenants Compared

The reason God stated for not ingesting blood was that He had given the blood of the sacrifice to the Israelite people "to make atonement for your souls" (Leviticus 17:11). But remember that John had shown the blood of the lamb to be what washed the believers' robes and made them white. This pictured the atonement and ritual cleansing, as God had commanded the Israelites to wash their garments when they approached His presence (Exodus 19:10, 11).

It was a longstanding Jewish requirement to have one's garments and body washed when approaching God, and also to have the blood of the appropriate sacrifice applied before entering His presence. Only the high priest was permitted to enter where God's direct presence dwelt, in the Holy of Holies, and never without having first applied the sacrificial blood. One would never want to stand before God and be in His presence having refused the provision that He laid out.

In the book of Hebrews, Paul compares the blood of the animal sacrifices under the Old Covenant to how the shed blood of Christ brought us into the New Covenant, whereby we could be cleansed and go into God's direct presence:

> [DBY] Hebrews 9:6 Now these things being thus ordered, into the first tabernacle the priests enter at all times, accomplishing the services;

> ^{DBY} Hebrews 9:7   but into the second, the high priest only, once a year, **not without blood**, which he offers for himself and for the errors of the people:

> ^{DBY} Hebrews 9:8   **the Holy Spirit shewing this**, that the way of the *holy of* holies has not yet been made manifest while as yet the first tabernacle has *its* standing;

In other words, these verses indicate that the way into God's direct presence was blocked while the first Tabernacle under Moses had its *legal standing*. Paul is showing what the Holy Spirit "is signifying" with these laws from the Tabernacle concerning the Holy of Holies, the veils, and only the high priest entering, and never without the blood. Under the New Covenant, those laws and regulations no longer have a legal standing to keep believers out of God's direct presence. This is why the disciples could be filled directly with God's spirit on the day of Pentecost; the veil had been torn in two at the Crucifixion (Matthew 27:51), signifying that the way into His direct presence had now been provided.

Paul continues:

> ^{NAS} Hebrews 9:9–10   which *is* a symbol for the present time. Accordingly both gifts and sacrifices are offered which cannot make the worshiper perfect in conscience, since they *relate* only to food and drink and various washings, regulations for the body **imposed until a time of reformation**.

The two Greek words that are translated "reformation" in verse 10 actually mean until the "new order of things" was brought in, referring to the promised New Covenant. Paul continues in Hebrews 9 (in NAS):

> 9:11   But when Christ appeared *as* a high priest of the good things to come, *He entered* through the greater and more perfect tabernacle, **not made with hands**, that is to say, not of this creation;

> 9:12   and not through the blood of goats and calves, **but through His own blood**, He entered the holy place once for all, having obtained **eternal redemption**.

> 9:13   For if the blood of goats and bulls and the ashes of a heifer sprinkling those who have been defiled, sanctify for the cleansing of the flesh,

> 9:14   how much more will the blood of Christ, who through the eternal Spirit offered Himself without blemish to God, cleanse your conscience from dead works to serve the living God?
>
> 9:15   And for this reason He is the mediator of a new covenant, in order that since a death has taken place for the redemption of the transgressions that were *committed* under the first covenant, those who have been called may receive the promise of the eternal inheritance.

Paul talks about blood in the Old Covenant:

> 9:18   Therefore even the first *covenant* **was not inaugurated without blood**.
>
> 9:19   For when every commandment had been spoken by Moses to all the people according to the Law, **he took the blood** of the calves and the goats, with water and scarlet wool and hyssop, **and sprinkled both the book itself and all the people**,
>
> 9:20   saying, "**This is the blood of the covenant** which God commanded you."
>
> 9:21   And in the same way he sprinkled both the tabernacle and all the vessels of the ministry with the blood.
>
> 9:22   And according to the Law, *one may* almost *say*, **all things are cleansed with blood**, and **without shedding of blood there is no forgiveness**.

Then he turns to the New Covenant, which Christ's sacrifice ushered in:

> 9:23   Therefore it was necessary for the **copies of the things** in the heavens to be cleansed with these, but the heavenly things themselves with better sacrifices than these.
>
> 9:24   For Christ did not enter a holy place made with hands, a *mere* copy of the true one, but into heaven itself, now to appear in the presence of God for us;

9:25 nor was it that He should offer Himself often, as the high priest enters the holy place year by year with blood not his own.

9:26 Otherwise, He would have needed to suffer often since the foundation of the world; but now once at the consummation of the ages He has been manifested to put away sin by the sacrifice of Himself.

Old Covenant Blood Applied Without; New Covenant Blood Applied Spiritually Within

Under the Old Covenant, God did not want the Israelites to take the "life" (i.e., blood) of the animal sacrifice within them in any form, because He did not want them to *symbolically* take the life of *an animal* within. It is not the life of the animal that God wants *within* us but rather the spiritual life from the Messiah.

Moses, however, did sanctify the people and set them apart unto God by sprinkling sacrificial blood **on the outside** of the people:

> NAS Exodus 24:6 And Moses took half of the blood and put *it* in basins, and the *other* half of the blood he sprinkled on the altar.

> NAS Exodus 24:8 So Moses took the blood and sprinkled *it* **on the people**, and said, "Behold the blood of the covenant, which the LORD has made with you in accordance with all these words."

When God then inaugurated the priesthood under Aaron and his sons, he again told Moses to apply the blood externally. Each priest was to apply the blood on his right ear (symbolically showing that he must hear what this means), the thumb of his right hand (showing the work of his hands is set apart to God), and the toes of his right foot (showing a walk that is set apart to God). Thus the blood atonement would always be pictured as the priests were ministering in His presence.

> NAS Exodus 29:20 "And you shall slaughter the ram, and take some of its blood and put *it* on the lobe of Aaron's right ear and on the lobes of his sons' right ears and on the thumbs of their right hands and on the big toes of their right feet, and sprinkle the *rest of the* blood around on the altar.

All of these blood applications *were on the outside of their bodies*; nothing went within. We know that these animal sacrifices pointed further to New Covenant truths, and at the Last Supper, Jesus showed that the fruit of the grapevine in the cup represented his blood *of the New Covenant* (as we saw in Course 10). Again, when his blood was shed, the Jewish disciples eventually came to know that they were now in the promised New Covenant, with the previous covenant no longer having legal standing over them (Jeremiah 31:31, 33). The promised New Covenant was not based on sacrificial animal blood but on the shed blood of the promised Messiah.

After his disciples eventually came to understand the parables and New Covenant truths that Jesus had been speaking to them, they went out teaching based on this understanding:

> YLT Revelation 5:9   and they sing a new song, saying, 'Worthy art thou to take the scroll, and to open the seals of it, because thou wast slain, **and didst redeem us** to God **in thy blood**, out of every tribe, and tongue, and people, and nation,

In the New Covenant the *spiritual* "priests" (referring to the believers, for "he has made **us** to be a kingdom and priests," Revelation 1:6, 5:10, NIV) understood that they were sanctified to God in a blood that was not from an animal sacrifice:

> DBY 1 Peter 1:18–19   knowing that ye have been redeemed, not by corruptible *things, as* silver or gold, from your vain conversation handed down from *your* fathers, but by precious blood, as of a lamb without blemish and without spot, *the blood* of Christ,

> KJV Revelation 1:5   And from Jesus Christ, *who is* the faithful witness, *and* the first begotten of the dead, and the prince of the kings of the earth. Unto him that loved us, and **washed us from our sins in his own blood**,

This was the blood of the grape(s) that Jacob spoke of concerning the coming of the Messiah and the washing of the robes, and this was the blood of the grape(s) that Moses spoke of as a blessing from God for the Promised Land.

God's Spirit to Indwell the Believer

As we've seen, the blood of sacrificial animals in the Old Covenant was not enough to make the full atonement, and thus God's spirit did *not dwell within* the Israelites yet.

However, the Messiah, having redeemed them and us by his shed blood, does provide for us all to be filled with God's spirit, thus fulfilling the prophecy of Joel that God would pour out His spirit on all flesh. To enter the New Covenant, we spiritually apply the blood of the true Passover *within*—in our hearts—by accepting the Messiah. We allow his sacrifice and atoning death to enter in and touch our hearts.

We have no record that Jesus ever told his disciples, "I am the true Passover," but his Last Supper parables made the connection between his body and blood such that his disciples (who knew the Jewish idiom of applying sacrificial blood) would soon understand that he was the true Passover to which the sacrifices pointed.

These two aspects of the Passover—its body and its blood—were very important under the first covenant, as God required the Israelites to always eat the flesh of the Passover, which was part of the atonement (that also pointed forward). Both aspects were needed to keep the death angel away when God "passed over" and spared the Israelites that first Passover, after blood was applied to the doorposts. The Israelites were never to ingest the blood of any of the animal sacrifices, but they were required *to apply* the blood, such as by pouring it out at the altar of God in the Temple.

On the last night before the Messiah's sacrifice as the true Passover, he applied the two Passover aspects—its body and its blood—to himself. At the Last Supper, Jesus spoke of *his body* figuratively as pieces of the bread, meaning that we would partake of him as we spiritually fellowship with other believers who are filled with God's spirit. Then he spoke of *his blood* being "poured out" for many, just as the Passover blood was always poured out at the altar for the Israelites. His parable also showed that his blood was applied *within his disciples*, because after they drank some of the grape juice, he then appears to pour out the remainder (as if figuratively at the altar) to show that it represented his New Covenant blood:

> NAS Mark 14:24   And He said to them, "This is My blood of the covenant, which is poured out[220] for many.

The Greek word Jesus used for his blood being "poured out" is the same word used in the Septuagint for the sacrifices, whose blood was similarly "poured out" at the altar. The Messiah was showing the fulfillment of the inauguration of the first covenant under Moses, when, after the Israelites had left Egypt, half of the blood was "poured out" at the altar and half was sprinkled *on* the people.

In the book of Ezekiel, God spoke of a time when He would place His spirit within the Israelites:

> NAS Ezekiel 36:26–27   "Moreover, **I will give you a new heart** and put a new spirit within you; and I will remove the heart of stone from your flesh and give you a heart of flesh. "**And I will put My**

---

[220] The Greek for "poured out" is a present tense participle, showing it was "being poured out."

Spirit within you and cause you to walk in My statutes, and you will be careful to observe My ordinances.

For God's spirit to indwell the believer, and, as God promised in Jeremiah regarding the New Covenant, to "put my law *in their inward parts*" and write the law "*in their hearts*," the blood must be applied *within*:

> ^{JPS}Jeremiah 31:33 But this is the covenant that I will make with the house of Israel after those days, saith the LORD, I will put My law **in their inward parts**, and **in their heart** will I write it; and I will be their God, and they shall be My people;

The blood at the first Passover was to be applied on the outside doorposts to spare the Israelites from the coming judgment on Egypt:

> When I see the blood I will pass over you. (Exodus 12:13).

In our day, talking about blood may be distasteful to many. However, the Israelites' religious life *revolved around these sacrifices* and the *blood being applied* for them to walk in God's forgiveness. They viewed blood very differently than we do today, thoroughly understanding the concept of the life being in it and the atonement it provided. One of the rare times that Moses became angry was when Aaron's sons had not eaten the flesh of the sin offering (Leviticus 10:16, 17). Moses understood that this partaking of the sacrificial flesh was the second part of what provided the atonement—not just the shed blood.

The parables Jesus spoke in John 6 show the fulfillment of the two Passover aspects—partaking of the lamb (i.e., Christ's "body") and applying its blood—yet Christ's blood was to be applied in a different way. In these parables, *Jesus showed that his blood must go within, spiritually*, to make way for the soon-coming spiritual life from God, whereby the disciples would be filled with God's spirit and have God Himself dwelling within:

> ^{NAS}John 6:53 Jesus therefore said to them, "Truly, truly, I say to you, unless you eat the flesh of the Son of Man and drink His blood, **you have no life in yourselves**.

Now Jesus was not speaking to dead people here; those listening certainly had *natural* "life" in themselves, so we know that he was speaking of *spiritual* life from God.

He spoke this truth in the form of a parable, as he so often did and as the Messiah was prophesied to do. God's dwelling must be sanctified and set apart, and for God to indwell the believer He must see the atoning blood applied. Similarly, the sacrifice of the Messiah must touch the heart, sanctifying the person within.

Right after Jesus spoke those shocking words in John 6:53 and many of his disciples left him, he made it especially clear to his closest remaining disciples that his words were to be *taken spiritually*. However, they still did not understand:

> ^{NAS} John 6:63 "It is the Spirit who gives life; the flesh profits nothing; **the words that I have spoken to you are spirit** and **are life**.

Jesus was not a Roman Catholic priest teaching a new ritual; indeed, no Roman Catholics even existed yet. Nor was he teaching Luther's ritual of Consubstantiation or the Protestant "Communion-lite" (i.e., without the actual flesh and blood) that came later.

Jesus was a Jewish man from the line of David, living at a time when Jews were familiar with applying the blood of various sacrifices. His disciples were first-century kosher Jews who were well acquainted with his frequent method of speaking to them in parables, whether they fully understood his meaning each time or not.

It's important for us Protestants (and Catholics as well) to realize that we have been led astray by various Communion rituals, so that we can move past these rituals into the true communion that God desires for us. We must unite together, all Jews and Gentiles who love God and His Messiah, as one body under Christ the head. We must allow him to bring the new truths that he has for his people, his spiritual body of believers. We must allow the Holy Spirit to bring new truths, as in Acts 15. We must not allow egos or positions of authority to hamper any truths that the Messiah wants to bring to his people. Christ seeks to cleanse and prepare his bride, and woe unto the men who stand in the way of the truth that he desires to bring (Ephesians 5:26).

Christ Is the Grapevine—His Shed Blood Is the Spiritual Life Flow to the Branches

The promise of the Father in the New Covenant is that His spirit will indwell the believer. At the Last Supper, just before Jesus was slain as the true Passover that God called "My sacrifice" (Exodus 23:18), he spoke of the fruit of the grapevine. There is actually no mention of "wine"[221] at the Last Supper, but fresh fruit of the vine is spoken of. The grape juice in the cup—the fruit of the vine—linked directly into the parable that he spoke after supper, in which he said that he was the grapevine:

---

221 Nor is there mention in the Bible of four cups of wine at Passover; this was a later tradition.

> NAS John 15:1 "I am **the true vine**,[222] and My Father is the vinedresser."

The *natural* fruit of the vine was the lifeblood flowing through the vine, and in the New Covenant it was the Messiah's "lifeblood" (his sacrificial blood) that would provide the spiritual life flow to the connected branches. The Jews understood the concept of the lifeblood of the grape, for they were familiar with the Song of Moses. They were also familiar with Isaiah's analogy of treading the wine press, where the "lifeblood" of the people is pictured as the juice from the trodden grapes (Isaiah 63:3, 6, NAS). Israel was often pictured as the grapevine.[223] However, many of these idioms were not understood in Rome.

Jesus said "I am the true vine" (John 15:1) on the same evening as his Last Supper parables, after he had shown his disciples that the fruit of the grapevine in his cup represented his blood of the New Covenant being poured out. Then later that night he said that *he* was the true grapevine and his disciples were the branches; if they would abide in him, they would bear much *spiritual* fruit. Of course, when they heard this, they did not literally hold out their arms pretending to be branches in a new ritual, because they knew that the Messiah was not creating new rituals at the Last Supper.

So the overall picture created when the two parables are joined—the bread and the fruit of the grapevine during the Last Supper, and the grapevine right after supper—is of Christ as the grapevine and his shed blood providing the spiritual life flow into the vine that spreads to the branches. The spiritual life flow would be the Holy Spirit of God and His *agape* love.

In scripture, the nation and land of Israel are often pictured as a grapevine. And it was a grapevine bearing an enormous clump of grapes that those spies sent by Moses brought back when they first explored this Promised Land. Jesus declared that *he* was *the* true grapevine from which the spiritual essence of the spiritual Promised Land emanated. In effect, he was the grapes and the grapevine branch that the spies under Moses brought back in type, which pointed to the true provision in the spiritual Promised Land, as depicted on the Israelite coin at the beginning of this Course. This was the lifeblood of the grape that Moses spoke of and the blood of the grape mentioned by Jacob (and later John) that would ritually cleanse the believer.

---

222 In the Greek, the word translated into English as "vine" is actually "grapevine."

223 This is in scriptures such as Psalm 80:8–14, Isaiah 5:1–13, etc. See also the parable of Israel as the vineyard, given a few days before the Last Supper in Mark 12:1–10.

Abide in Him and Stay Connected to the Spiritual Flow

Later the apostles would bear much fruit from their ministry by abiding in this spiritual grapevine and allowing this life flow to spread to one another, as thousands came to the Lord through their ministry. They fulfilled what Moses had spoken concerning the Promised Land and the blood (life flow) of the grape—namely that the spiritual life from God would soon be flowing through and within them:

> NAS John 7:37–39   Now on the last day, the great *day* of the feast, Jesus stood and cried out, saying, "If any man is thirsty, let him come to Me and drink. He who believes in Me, as the Scripture said, 'From his innermost being shall flow rivers of living water.'" **But this He spoke of the Spirit**, whom those who believed in Him were to receive; for the Spirit was not yet *given*, because Jesus was not yet glorified.

This picture of the fruit of the vine at the Last Supper and the grapevine parable afterward taught the necessity of "abiding in him":

> NAS John 15:4   "**Abide in Me, and I in you**. As the branch cannot bear fruit of itself, unless it abides in the vine, so neither *can* you, unless you **abide in Me**.

We cannot naturally or literally abide in him, but *spiritually* we abide and stay connected to the spiritual flow that comes from God, because of Christ, so we do not dry up and die spiritually.

> NAS John 15:6   "If anyone does not abide in Me, he is thrown away as a branch, and dries up; and they gather them, and cast them into the fire, and they are burned.

> NAS John 15:9   "Just as the Father has loved Me, I have also loved you; abide in My love.

> NAS John 15:10–11   "If you keep My commandments, you will **abide in My love**; just as I have kept My Father's commandments, and **abide in His love**. These things I have spoken to you, that **My joy may be in you**, and *that* your joy may be made full.

Shortly thereafter on that same night, Jesus spoke similar words again:

> ᴺᴬˢJohn 17:21 that they may all be one; even as Thou, Father, *art* in Me, and I in Thee, that they also may be in Us; that the world may believe that Thou didst send Me.

> ᴺᴬˢJohn 17:23 I in them, and Thou in Me, that they may be perfected in unity, that the world may know that Thou didst send Me, and didst love them, even as Thou didst love Me.

The Holy Spirit of God would be poured out after Christ's sacrifice on the day of Pentecost, which came 50 days later, counting from the Resurrection. A powerful new experience and closeness to God opened up to these Jewish believers, whereby God was no longer distant but was actually *dwelling within them* by His spirit (Acts 2). This life of Christ, symbolized by his shed blood, pictured the spiritual life that is found only in the New Covenant, and now it was flowing spiritually through the believers.

After the Last Supper and shortly after the disciples had taken some of the bread and the fruit of the vine *within them* (thus spiritually applying the two aspects of the Passover—its flesh and blood), Jesus said more about *dwelling within them*:

> ᴺᴬˢJohn 14:16–18 "And I will ask the Father, and He will give you another Helper, that He may be with you forever; *that is* **the Spirit of truth**, whom the world cannot receive, because it does not behold Him or know Him, *but* you know Him because **He abides with you, and will be in you**. I will not leave you as orphans; I will come to you.

> ᴺᴬˢJohn 14:20 "**In that day you shall know** that I am in My Father, and **you in Me, and I in you**.

Jesus said that the Holy Spirit would be sent *in his name*, meaning that it was *because of him* that God's spirit would be coming:

> ᴺᴬˢJohn 14:26 "But the Helper, **the Holy Spirit**, whom the Father will send in My name, He will teach you all things, and bring to your remembrance all that I said to you.

And this "Helper" (or "comforter" in some translations) and "spirit of truth" is the Holy Spirit of God that would soon indwell them:

> NAS John 14:17 *that is* **the Spirit of truth**, whom the world cannot receive, because it does not behold Him or know Him, *but* you know Him because **He abides with you, and will be in you**.

Our Fellowship Is with the Father, Christ, and One Another

As the branches of the grapevine, our fellowship is with the Father, the Messiah, and one another:

> NAS 1 John 1:3 what we have seen and heard we proclaim to you also, that you also may have fellowship[224] with us; and indeed our fellowship is with the Father, and with His Son Jesus Christ.

The disciples realized that in Christ's spiritual body, blood flows spiritually to its every member, cleansing and atoning. This blood was never meant to be applied in the natural sense—in a new ritual—for the Jews understood these things spiritually:

> NAS 1 John 1:7 but if we walk in the light as He Himself is in the light, **we have fellowship**[225] **with one another,** and **the blood** of Jesus His Son **cleanses us** from all sin.

We spiritually commune with God through His spirit that dwells within us, and God has provided that we also commune spiritually with His son. We see this in the new heaven and new earth, where Jesus is pictured as the "lamp" and God is the light that flows through that lamp. Jesus shows forth God's nature, such as His glory and His love, and God has the same plan for all who love Him:

> NAS Revelation 21:23 And the city has no need of the sun or of the moon to shine upon it, for the **glory of God has illumined it**, and **its lamp** *is* the Lamb.

> NAS 2 Corinthians 4:6–7 For God, who said, "Light shall shine out of darkness," is the One who has shone in our hearts to give the light of the knowledge of **the glory of God in the face of Christ**. But **we** have this treasure in earthen vessels, that the surpassing greatness of the power may be of God and not from ourselves;

---

224 The Greek word *koinonia* is translated as "fellowship"; it is sometimes translated as "communion."
225 Same as footnote 224 above.

^{NAS} Hebrews 1:3   And He is the radiance of His glory and **the exact representation of His nature**, and upholds all things by the word of His power. When He had made purification of sins, He sat down at the right hand of the Majesty on high;

We Inherit the Lifeblood from Christ and Grow into His Likeness

In Israel, humanity was often spoken of as "flesh and blood" (Ephesians 6:12). When Paul came to the Lord, the scripture says that he did not first consult with "flesh and blood" (Galatians 1:16) because Paul knew his calling was from God. Of course this did not refer to some bread as literal human flesh and some natural wine in a cup with which he consulted, but rather of humanity. Thus Paul did not feel led to consult with the other disciples right after his conversion, and yet the Lord showed him what the Last Supper meant (1 Corinthians 11:23).

The children of Israel were said to share or partake in the "flesh and blood" of their parents, whose life flow and DNA passed down to them (Hebrews 2:14). This flesh and blood referred to the parents from whom the child was born.

^{NAS} Hebrews 2:13   And again, "I will put My trust in Him." And again, "**Behold, I and the children whom God has given Me**."

^{NAS} Hebrews 2:14   Since then the children **share in flesh and blood**, He Himself likewise also partook of the same, that through death He might render powerless him who had the power of death, that is, the devil;

^{KJV} Hebrews 2:14   Forasmuch then as the **children are partakers of flesh and blood**, he also himself likewise took part of the same; that through death he might destroy him that had the power of death, that is, the devil;

Of course, this Jewish manner of speaking means that children partake in the flesh and blood of their parents by being born of them. As God's children, we inherit the same *spiritual* DNA that Christ had, such that we'll grow into the same image and likeness if we partake of God's spiritual food and spiritual drink, fulfilling His plan:

^{NIV} Genesis 1:26   Then God said, "Let us make man in our image, in our likeness…"

> ᴺᴬˢ Ephesians 4:13   until we all attain to the unity of the faith, and of the knowledge of the Son of God, to a mature man, **to the measure of the stature which belongs to the fulness of Christ**.
>
> ᴺᴬˢ Ephesians 4:16   from whom **the whole body**, being fitted and held together by that which every joint supplies, according to the proper working of each individual part, **causes the growth of the body** for the building up of itself in love.

Even in our modern idiom, we often speak of those in our own family as our "own flesh and blood."

John P. Lange, in his *Commentary on the Holy Scriptures*, uses a phrase in reference to John 6 that I think is perfect here. He says, "But flesh and blood elsewhere denotes **inherited nature**"[226] (boldface mine). So with "Christ our Passover," we partake spiritually of Christ's humanity, "the man, Christ Jesus," as he is called in the scripture. When we read about him and receive his word, we partake of who he was (and is), what he did, and the things that he said. We partake of his life and love that he showed forth. This is the *spiritual* DNA that we inherit. We grow into that same likeness by the spirit:

> ᴺᴬˢ 1 Corinthians 15:49   And just as we have borne the image of the earthy, we shall also bear the image of the heavenly.
>
> ᴺᴬˢ 1 Corinthians 15:47   The first man is from the earth, earthy; the second man is from heaven.
>
> ᴺᴬˢ 1 Corinthians 15:48   As is the earthy, so also are those who are earthy; and as is the heavenly, so also are those who are heavenly.

Just as Eve came out of Adam's side, so did the spiritual bride emerge from Christ's side when his blood was shed (Christ is pictured as the second Adam in 1 Corinthians 15:45–49). Thus we have within us his *spiritual* DNA that is programmed to grow us into his likeness, as long as we receive the nourishment from above.

God's spirit and His word affect our hearts and transform us into His likeness, as we yield:

---

[226]   Lange, *A Commentary on the Holy Scriptures* (Gospel of John), p. 223 (John 6:53).

> ᴵᴸᵀ 2 Corinthians 3:18   and we all, with unvailed face, the glory of the Lord beholding in a mirror, **to the same image are being transformed**, from glory to glory, even as **by the Spirit of the Lord**.

> ᴺᴬˢ Romans 8:29   For **whom He foreknew, He also predestined** *to become* **conformed to the image of His Son**, that He might be the first-born **among many brethren**;

Why is it that so many Jewish believers are coming to know the Messiah in our day? The scripture above says, "whom he did foreknow he predestined to be conformed to the image of his Son." Israel has also been brought back to become a nation, and these things happening at the same time are not by accident. God is doing special work to form all the believers—those who will enter in—into the image and likeness of His son.

Jesus was the first man born who yielded perfectly to God, and who grew into the exact image and likeness of God. He is the firstborn in the Jewish sense; he has the pre-eminent position before God, and in a certain sense he is our elder brother. This scripture says he is the firstborn among *many brethren* whom God will bring into His image and likeness by His spirit, fulfilling Genesis 1:26.

> Genesis 1:26   Then God said, "Let us make man in our image, in our likeness…."

COURSE 12

THE MESSIANIC FEAST, THE BRIDE, AND THE BEAST

To transition from the joys of God's love in the final feast to the workings of the beast system can be a little disconcerting, and yet the scriptures show these two events happening in the same time frame. In this Course, we will first touch on the Messianic feast and the bride, then in more detail examine the scriptural warnings concerning the coming global beast empire. Then we will finish this Course with the open door into God's presence that awaits us.

The Messianic feast or banquet is the spiritual feast that will prepare and make ready the spiritual bride (those who fulfill God's calling):

> NAS Revelation 19:7 "Let us rejoice and be glad and give the glory to Him, for the marriage of the Lamb has come and **His bride has made herself ready**."

> NAB Revelation 19:9 Then the angel said to me, "Write this: Blessed are those who have been called to the **wedding feast** of the Lamb." And he said to me, "These words are true; they come from God."

In the Song of Solomon, we see a prefiguring of the Messiah and the last-days spiritual bride. All people are called to this banqueting table to feast on God's love:

> KJV Song of Solomon 2:3–4 As the apple tree among the trees of the wood, so *is* my beloved among the sons. I sat down under his shadow with great delight, and his fruit *was* sweet to my taste. He brought me to the **banqueting house**, and **his banner over me *was* love**.

As the Song of Solomon continues, it shows that this bride will have two aspects to her nature. She'll be a warrior in the sense of battling spiritually against encroaching darkness, yet a bride because of her great love for God, for the Messiah, and for one another. Below we see these two aspects of this last-days bride: She is as ***beautiful*** as Jerusalem and yet ***terrible*** as an army, not in terms of a wild temper but because of her spiritual power with God:

> KJV Song of Solomon 6:4   Thou *art* **beautiful**, O my love, as Tirzah, comely as Jerusalem, **terrible** as *an army* with banners.

> DBY Song of Solomon 6:9   My dove, mine undefiled, is but one; She is the only one of her mother, She is **the choice one of her that bore her**. The daughters saw her, and they called her blessed; The queens and the concubines, and they praised her.

> NJB Song of Solomon 6:10   'Who is this arising like the dawn, fair as the moon, **resplendent as the sun, formidable as an army?**'

Thus, the Lord is preparing a table before us in the presence of many enemies, just as God prepared a table and a cup for David:

> NAS Psalm 23:5   Thou dost prepare **a table** before me in the presence of my enemies; Thou hast anointed my head with oil; My cup overflows.

The enemies we face are spiritual forces working within the last-days beast empire, of which God informed Daniel (Daniel 2:40–45; 7:7–28) and which was also pictured by John in the book of Revelation (chapters 12, 13, 17, and elsewhere). When all of these prophecies are combined, it becomes clear that the bride will be perfected in the midst of troublesome times. The Messiah was perfected (completed) by the things that he suffered (Hebrews 2:10), and this may apply to us as well, for in this world we will have tribulation (John 16:33; 1 Peter 5:10).

This last-days world empire is the final one in a series of world empires that have warred against those who love God. John pictures all seven of these empires together as a seven-headed dragon (also called a "beast," Revelation 12 and 13).

These seven world empires all have a common thread. Here they are in order:

1. Egypt, where Pharaoh kept Israel in slavery until the Passover.
2. Assyria with Sennacherib, during which the ten tribes of Israel were taken captive.
3. Babylon with Nebuchadnezzar, which leveled Israel and destroyed the Temple.
4. Medo-Persia during which Haman lived, who tried to kill all the Jews.
5. Greece, which ruled Israel and in Daniel's visions extended to Antiochus Epiphanes, attacker of the Jews.

6. Rome, which destroyed Israel and demolished the rebuilt Temple.
7. And the final world empire[227] that is building now.

Israel itself could also have been considered a world empire under David and Solomon, but this seven-headed dragon represents only empires that Satan uses to attack God's people, which is what all seven heads have in common. Why does the beast keep amassing empires to war against Israel? Is Satan anti-Semitic? No, he is actually an equal opportunity employer, and all who give over to the dark side of evil are accepted. He may even prefer to place Israelites in high positions in his system, partly so he can subtly mock God and say "See, those who you called follow me now." One reason he attacks the Jewish people is that Israel was prophesied to bring forth the Messiah, something the devil did not want. There are many scriptural promises of Israel returning to God in the last days, and the seventh empire will fight to resist this.

Some of the following symbolism may be difficult, or even bizarre for new students of prophecy, but we'll get through this section shortly and then on to more positive scriptures and events.

The Soon-Coming Seventh Head of the Beast

This final seventh empire will be no different from its predecessors in that it also makes war with anyone who loves God. In the following scriptures, it is pictured as the seventh head of the dragon with a crown, ready to devour the collective group of people who fulfill God's calling. In Course 8 we saw that these believers are made into the image and likeness that God has called us to (Genesis 1:26). They are pictured symbolically as the "man child," the nation of people to whom the woman (the visible church) gives birth:

> KJV Revelation 12:1   And there appeared a great wonder in heaven; a woman clothed with the sun, and the moon under her feet, and upon her head a crown of twelve stars:

> KJV Revelation 12:2   And **she being with child cried, travailing in birth**, and pained to be delivered.

> KJV Revelation 12:3   And there appeared another wonder in heaven; and behold a great red dragon, having seven heads and ten horns, and **seven crowns upon his heads**.

---

227 Daniel lived during the captivity in Babylon (which was the third empire). Looking forward, he wrote of four future empires, and called the final empire the "fourth beast" (from his time frame). John pictures all seven world empires combined as a seven-headed dragon that includes Egypt and Assyria, which came before Babylon.

> ᴷᴶⱽ Revelation 12:4   And his tail drew the third part of the stars of heaven, and did cast them to the earth: and **the dragon stood before the woman** which was ready to be delivered, for **to devour her child** as soon as it was born.

Notice that the dragon (also called "the beast") stands menacingly before the woman, focused on devouring the man child (or nation of people, Isaiah 66:6–8) that is about to come forth from her. The woman is in travail and discomfort because of what is being birthed out of her, and because this child causes her to be uncomfortably close to the dragon's focus. But this child/nation that is born, who is indwelt by the lion of the tribe of Judah, does not shrink back, for it knows it has God's will to accomplish, and that this plan will indeed be completed. Just as David ran to meet Goliath and hurled the stone into his head, so will the spiritual David come forth (when the time is right and not sooner) to deliver a spiritual death wound to this seventh head of the beast.

This man child[228] will come forth out of the woman and will eventually—after its ministry is accomplished—be caught up to God:

> ᴷᴶⱽ Revelation 12:5   And she brought forth **a man child**, who was to rule all nations with a rod of iron: and **her child was caught up unto God**, and *to* his throne.

This man child born of the woman depicts the spiritual warrior aspect of the bride. This promise of being caught up is also seen in other scriptures:

> ʸᴸᵀ Revelation 3:10   'Because thou didst keep the word of my endurance, **I also will keep thee from the hour of the trial** that is about to come upon all the world, to try those dwelling upon the earth.

> ᴺᴬˢ 1 Thessalonians 4:15   For this we say to you by the word of the Lord, that we who are alive, and remain until the coming of the Lord, shall not precede those who have fallen asleep.

> ʸᴸᵀ 1 Thessalonians 4:16   because the Lord himself, in a shout, in the voice of a chief-messenger, and in the trump of God, shall come down from heaven, and the dead in Christ shall rise first,

---

228   This man child is not Jesus as some suppose, for this all takes place during the final seventh world empire (Revelation 12:3 pictures the seventh head with a crown and thus that this seventh empire is now in effect).

^{YLT} 1 Thessalonians 4:17   then we who are living, who are remaining over, together with them **shall be caught away in clouds to meet the Lord in air**, and so always with the Lord we shall be;

^{NAS} 1 Thessalonians 4:18   Therefore comfort one another with these words.

Course 8 contained many examples of Noah, Moses, King David, and others that pointed to a pattern and plan that God desires for His people. In that Course, we saw Jesus explaining Noah's Ark as an example of the spiritual ark (the bride/man child) that will be erected in the last days to safely lift up and catch away many in the rapture.

Isaiah also spoke of this group of people who would fulfill God's plan of coming into His image and likeness, with God saying they would provide the place of His rest by being "humble and contrite of spirit, and who trembles at My word" (Isaiah 66:1–2). Then Isaiah continued:

^{KJV} Isaiah 66:6–8   A voice of noise from the city, a voice from the temple, a voice of the LORD that rendereth recompence to his enemies. Before she travailed, she brought forth; before her pain came, **she was delivered of a man child**. Who hath heard such a thing? who hath seen such things? Shall the earth be made to bring forth in one day? *or* **shall a nation be born at once**? for as soon as Zion travailed, she brought forth her children.

It is this man child/nation group of people who delivers the death wound to the dragon's seventh head with God's word, which is called the ***sword*** of the spirit in scripture.[229] Below, we see this seventh head having received a death blow from this sword:

^{NAS} Revelation 13:3   And *I saw* **one of his heads as if it had been slain**, and his fatal wound was healed. And the whole earth was amazed *and followed* after the beast;

^{NAS} Revelation 13:14   And **he deceives those who dwell on the earth** because of the signs which it was given him to perform in the presence of the beast, telling those who dwell on the earth to make an image to the beast **who had the wound of the sword** and has come to life.

---

229   Ephesians 6:17.

Verse 14 above shows that this beast *deceives* those on the earth. Daniel also warned of deception with this beast (Daniel 11:21, 23, 32). His prophecy initially referred to Antiochus Epiphanes, then moved to the Antichrist. The Messiah also warns of this last-days deception in Luke 21:8 with the words, "Watch out, that you are not deceived…." Timothy mentions a similar last-days deception (2 Timothy 3:1, 13), and finally, John states the deception involved in this final empire several times (Revelation 12:9, 13:14, 19:20, etc.). John also shows that the last-days deception will include *pharmakia*, using the Greek word for pharmaceuticals and drugs, which has various applications in our day with the proliferation of such items (Revelation 18:23). The scripture shows that in order to avoid this deception, one must receive a love for the truth (2 Thessalonians 2:10–12).

The beast crushes many nations (Daniel 2:40, 7:7), and part of its deception is its pretense of actually protecting people, for how else could it persuade enough people on its side to attain global control? This could be considered "phase one" of this world empire, the supposedly kinder, gentler phase.

However, shortly after the beast's seventh head receives this death wound, and the man-child group of people (the bride) is caught up to God, the beast's fatal wound is healed. Then the mask comes off, revealing its true nature, and "phase two" begins. This beast no longer remains hidden in the sea because of the complete power it now has, and it emerges for all to behold. The Antichrist also takes his position as world leader. At this point in John's picture, no one on earth can oppose the beast (Revelation 13:4).[230] When it rises up from the water (which represents peoples and nations, Revelation 17:5), it is confident and unafraid:

> KJV Revelation 13:1a And I stood upon the sand of the sea, and saw a **beast rise up out of the sea**, having seven heads…

> KJV Revelation 13:4 And they worshipped the dragon which gave power unto the beast: and they worshipped the beast, **saying**, Who *is* like unto the beast? **who is able to make war with him?**

The dragon here is Satan (Revelation 12:9), and the beast is the powerful world-control system that he has labored to put in place, and that is essentially a manifestation of his nature. These prophecies are coming true in our modern day, when tremendous power and control are wielded over the nations' money supplies through their debts. It's not much of a stretch to consider whether this control would include

---

[230] After the death wound (from the sword of the spirit, Revelation 13:3, 14) and after the rapture, the world system quickly revives ("his fatal wound was healed," Revelation 13:3). It is then pictured by John as an eighth head of the beast (see Revelation 17:9–14 for more on this).

all regulatory agencies as well as politicians (left or right), the military, police forces, not to mention the world's food supplies. When big banks control the state, you have fascism. Most large corporations, which are controlled by the same money powers, would also be in lockstep with the beast. The beast-owned and complicit media would bring forth "programming" to dumb down and corrupt the people, for a dumbed-down and corrupted people are more easily led and deceived, and are less likely to be covered by God's protection.

Whether right or left, this mainstream media would seek to shepherd the people into agreeing with the beast's policies on war, as well as giving up their constitutional rights. Truth can still be found in alternative media, but the powers that be will seek to shut down these outlets, declaring that it's for our safety. These are some possible things to be alert for, as John says often in the book of Revelation "he that hath an ear, let him hear…."

It's not necessarily that all these people are in cahoots and communicating with one another, but it's the same spirit of darkness that is working within them that guides things along:

> NAS Ephesians 2:2 in which you formerly walked according to the course of this world, according to the prince of the power of the air, **of the spirit that is now working** in the sons of disobedience.

> NIV 2 Thessalonians 2:7 For the secret power of lawlessness is already at work; but the one who now holds it back will continue to do so till he is taken out of the way.

When we first saw the man child ready to come forth from the woman, the seventh head of the beast had a crown, but at that earlier point the ten horns had no crowns (Revelation 12:3). However in Revelation 13, when the beast is out of the water for all to see, the beast's ten horns now have their ten crowns:

> KJV Revelation 13:1 And I stood upon the sand of the sea, and saw a beast rise up out of the sea, having seven heads and ten horns, and **upon his horns ten crowns**, and upon his heads the name of blasphemy.

Both Daniel (7:24) and John (in Revelation 17:12) say that these ten horns represent ten kings, and John adds that they have *no kingdom as yet* but will rule for a certain period with the beast (i.e., when they receive their crowns). Whoever heard of a king with no kingdom? Certainly in the first century when John lived, kings had kingdoms over which they ruled. But these ten "kings" are now ruling the nations with financial power[231] given by the dark side, and their crowns symbolize outward authority as the new world leaders under the Antichrist.[232]

The devil tempted the Messiah by offering him control over the nations if the Messiah would only worship him:

> [NAS] Luke 4:5 And he led Him up and showed Him all the kingdoms of the world in a moment of time.
>
> [NAS] Luke 4:6 And the devil said to Him, "I will give You all this domain and its glory; for it has been handed over to me, and I give it to whomever I wish.
>
> [NAS] Luke 4:7 "Therefore **if You worship before me, it shall all be Yours**."

Thankfully for us, the Messiah did not succumb to this temptation to worship Satan for the glory of his kingdoms. Other men, however, when tempted with great wealth and power, not only yield to the beast but also worship the dragon in exchange for the massive riches and authority they receive. Many American presidents and politicians of long ago actually resisted these powerful forces seeking to take control, as Andrew Jackson's farewell address in 1837 warned:

> It is one of the serious evils of our present system of banking that it enables one class of society—and that by no means a numerous one—by its control over the currency, to act injuriously upon the interests of all the others and to exercise more than its just proportion of influence in political affairs.[233]

The Jewish prophet Daniel pictured the final kingdom and these same ten horns as John (in Revelation 13:1), but with another horn coming up in the midst of them:

---

231 As the prime minister of Britain, Benjamin Disraeli wrote in his novel *Coningsby*, "…the world is governed by very different personages to what is imagined by those who are not behind the scenes."

232 For more information on the history of those building out this seventh head system, I recommend the following two books: *Wall Street and the Rise of Hitler*, by Antony C. Sutton, and *Illuminati, the Cult that Hijacked the World*, by Henry Makow, PhD.

233 Jackson, *Farewell Address*, online at The American Presidency Project.

> ^{NAS} Daniel 7:8   "While I was contemplating the horns, behold, **another horn, a little one, came up among them**, and three of the first horns were pulled out by the roots before it; and behold, this horn possessed eyes like the eyes of a man, and a mouth uttering great *boasts*.
>
> ^{DBY} Daniel 7:20   and concerning the ten horns that were in its head, and the other that came up, and before which three fell: even that horn that had eyes, and a mouth speaking great things, and **whose look was more imposing** than its fellows.

Daniel said that this little horn had a look "more imposing" than even the ten kings. This is because the little horn is the Antichrist. So, just as Christ was indwelt by God and was the express image of His nature, so will the Antichrist be indwelt by and manifest Satan. The Messiah was called to bring God's light and love to the nations as we saw in Course 10, but the "Anti-Messiah" brings war and death under the guise of keeping us all safe:

> ^{NAS} 1 Thessalonians 5:3   While **they** are saying, "**Peace and safety**!" then destruction will come upon them suddenly like birth pangs upon a woman with child; and they shall not escape.

Unlike the true Messiah, this false Messiah will not be a light to the nations, nor will he bring in the promised New Covenant. After the man child[234] has been caught up to God, the Antichrist outwardly blasphemes God and His tabernacle (i.e., those who were caught away to God), then pictured in heaven:

> ^{NAS} Revelation 13:6   And he opened his mouth in **blasphemies against God**, to blaspheme His name and His tabernacle, *that is*, those who dwell in heaven.

Why is the Antichrist so angry here? You would think that with this centuries-old plan now fulfilled—with him in place as the world's ruler supported by the ten crowned kings—that this would be a time of celebration for him and those working with him.

I believe the answer for this anger is that by this point in time, God's latter rain has poured down upon His willing people, preparing them with a Messianic feast to

---

[234] The man child is one picture, and the bride made ready is another picture of the same group of people who yield to God and fulfill the pattern and plan that He has called us to.

be made ready as the bride, and this spiritual revival among the people is enough to temporarily put a death wound to the seventh-head system. The devil is especially angry that Jewish believers are a major part of this last-days revival, for he knows that Jacob had referred to Judah's tribe as strong and lion-like (Genesis 49:9), and he did not want to have to deal with them. He preferred the time when he was able to veil their eyes, but those days are over (2 Corinthians 3:15, 16).

After the catching away of the bride (man child), this seventh head quickly comes back to life. If the long history of the other six beast heads teaches us anything, it is that when Satan has control over the nations' governments, we will see Israel and all who love God come under attack. Although the beast is set up under the guise of being "pro-Israel," things quickly change once it has gained its needed police-state control. It should be clear that the beast first portrayed the Muslims as the enemy, but this was only to control resources and attain world domination.

Instead of the dragon thanking those Christians and Jews who unknowingly supported him in his global warfare (believing they were fighting for freedom), he now shows that these two groups are, in fact, his next target. In our day the term "Israel" also extends to those who are *spiritual* Israel—those who believe in the Messiah. Once world domination is achieved, they will be portrayed as the new enemy. We saw that his focus was on the man child (Revelation 12:4, 5), but this group of people escapes by being caught up to God. He now attacks the remaining Christians (the seed of the woman, church)—those believers who had refused to become part of the bride and remained behind (Isaiah 66:5; Revelation 12:17).

He (the Antichrist) knows that all are commanded in scripture to refuse the mark of the beast, and the scriptures show he uses this to put them to death when they refuse to take the mark and join him (Revelation 20:4).

The Antichrist moves quickly to install the beast's control system, so that no one can buy or sell without joining his ungodly system and accepting his mark (whether a literal mark like a computer chip, or a figurative mark as in joining with and assenting to the beast system, Revelation 13:7–18). As part of his continuing deceit, he probably accomplishes this under the guise of keeping everyone safe, such as going cashless and paperless to lovingly protect the environment, or keeping all the people united and on the same team. Whatever ruse is put forth, the true reason will be *complete control* over the nations and the destruction of those on the beast's enemy list, beginning with the remaining believers.

The dragon then turns its focus to the final enemy on his list—Israel itself. Finally, he feels that his long-desired destruction for this nation is coming to pass. Around the same time that this system of control is fully implemented, the Antichrist and his ten financial "kings" establish a presence in Israel to show they are "pro-Israel." As this deception continues, the Antichrist seeks to be seen as the true Messiah. The scripture below says he will even enter the Temple in hopes of being pictured as God. Paul shows that the rapture (our gathering together unto the Lord) will not occur until the apostasy comes (when the devil's tail takes down a third of the stars, representing the believers, Revelation 12:4) and this Antichrist is revealed:

> ^{YLT} 2 Thessalonians 2:1   And we ask you, brethren, in regard to the **presence** of our Lord Jesus Christ, and of **our gathering together unto him**,

> ^{NAS} 2 Thessalonians 2:3   **Let no one in any way deceive you**, for *it will not come* unless the apostasy comes first, **and the man of lawlessness is revealed**, the son of destruction,

> ^{NAS} 2 Thessalonians 2:4   who opposes and exalts himself above every so-called god or object of worship, **so that he takes his seat in the temple of God**, displaying himself as being God.

It appears that verse 3 is a first revealing for those who have their spiritual eyes open to see. And then, after the rapture ("he who now restrains is taken away"), the Anti-Messiah is revealed again, but this time openly for all the world to see:

> ^{NAS} 2 Thessalonians 2:7   For the mystery of lawlessness is already at work; only **he who now restrains *will do so* until he is taken out of the way**.

> ^{NAS} 2 Thessalonians 2:8   And **then that lawless one will be revealed** whom the Lord will slay with the breath of His mouth and bring to an end by the appearance of His coming;

At about this same time, this beast's mask has come off further, showing that in reality it is like the previous six beast systems before it, only more powerful. John then shows that these demon spirits under Satan's direction are working within the kings, causing them to bring war upon Israel (Armageddon):

> ^{NAS} Revelation 16:14   for **they are spirits of demons**, performing signs, which go out to the kings of the whole world, **to gather them together for the war** of the great day of God, the Almighty.

> ^{NIV} Revelation 16:16   Then **they gathered the kings together** to the place that in Hebrew is called **Armageddon**.

It is very possible that these nations gathered together by the demons are attacking Israel in retaliation for events instigated by the Antichrist, under Satan's direction. The devil whips up the people into a rage over events that *he* actually caused, resulting in war on Israel. The prophet Zechariah (chapter 12) spoke of this time as did many others, such as Ezekiel (chapters 38, 39) and Jeremiah (chapter 30), who refers to it as the time of Jacob's trouble. As many scriptures foretell, a charade of lies and deception will be on constant parade, and God's people will have to be on guard to "be not deceived."

The sons of Israel followed the ark of God's presence, miraculously crossing the Jordan river (on dry land) into the Promised Land under Joshua (Yeshua). They were to cross over about "2,000 cubits behind the ark" (Joshua 3:4). So will it be with the spiritual sons of Israel (the bride/man child) who will cross over spiritual Jordan (into the Promised Land at the rapture) without touching death. If this type is accurate, this will occur about 2,000 years after the true ark of God's presence (the Messiah) spiritually passed over Jordan into the Promised Land (in 30 AD). This catching away would then occur about 2030 AD, give or take several years. We do not know the day or the hour, but if we look at the signs we will know the season (1 Thessalonians 5:4).

The Bride Keeps Her Focus on God's Leading

As this seventh empire is forming, the bride does not fixate on the beast, for her focus is on preparing to be what God wants and yielding to Him as He leads her. Yet she is not ignorant of Satan's schemes and devices (2 Corinthians 2:11).

As this world empire gains more power and control over the people, things may not look good in the natural sense. This was also true for Noah building the Ark, Moses facing the Red Sea, and David facing Goliath. But as we keep our focus on God's leading and those truths He reveals in His word, we will accomplish His work.

The Song of Solomon pictures the bride leaning on her beloved, she who came forth out of her mother who had labored to give birth. In this same context, he mentions the great strength,[235] power, and fierceness of God's *agape*[236] love:

> NAS Song of Solomon 8:5–6 "Who is this coming up from the wilderness, Leaning on her beloved?" "Beneath the apple tree I awakened you; There your mother was in labor with you, There she was in labor *and* gave you birth. "Put me like a seal over your heart,

---

235 The Hebrew word translated as "strength" can also mean "power" or "fierceness."
236 The Septuagint uses the Greek word *agape* here for "love," a word with which first-century Jewish believers were very familiar.

Like a seal on your arm. **For love is as strong as death**, Jealousy is as severe as Sheol; **Its flashes are flashes of fire, The *very* flame of the LORD**.

We must keep the *agape* love burning, for the Messiah warned that lawlessness in the last days would cause the love (*agape*) of the many to grow cold:

> YLT Matthew 24:12   and because of the abounding of the lawlessness, the love of the many shall become cold;

Daniel shows that none of the wicked will understand what is really going on, which probably includes most who are serving the beast:

> NAS Daniel 12:10   "Many will be purged, purified and refined; but the wicked will act wickedly, and none of the wicked will understand, but those who have insight will understand.

Some of this may be as it was with Elijah, where at first many sons of Israel were deceived into serving the wicked King Ahab (1 Kings 21:25) and his occultist wife Jezebel. Some even fought against Elijah and sought to kill other Jewish prophets (1 Kings 19:10), thinking they were fighting for God and country. The scripture shows some of these prophets were hidden away in caves (1 Kings 18:4). However, in bringing forth His power through His people in these last days, God will show many which side He is really on, just as had occurred with Elijah:

> NAS 1 Kings 18:37   "Answer me, O LORD, answer me, that this people may know that Thou, O LORD, art God, and *that* Thou hast turned their heart back again."

> NAS 1 Kings 18:38   Then the fire of the LORD fell, and consumed the burnt offering and the wood and the stones and the dust, and licked up the water that was in the trench.

> NAS 1 Kings 18:39   And when all the people saw it, they fell on their faces; and they said, "The LORD, He is God; the LORD, He is God."

Throughout Israel's history a picture existed of a coming battle between the sons of darkness and the sons of light:

> NAS 1 Thessalonians 5:4 But you, brethren, are not in darkness, that the day should overtake you like a thief;

> NAS 1 Thessalonians 5:5 for **you are all sons of light** and sons of day. We are not of night nor of darkness;

Judaic scholar Lawrence Schiffman explains that the Dead Sea Scrolls picture this battle as a Messianic war that (in their belief) presumably precedes the ultimate Messianic banquet[237] for the victorious sons of light:

> This new community would then gather together for the messianic banquet, presumably in the aftermath of the great war between the sons of light and the sons of darkness.[238]

The Dead Sea Sect held these beliefs as a result of putting together all the biblical events and prophecies for Israel in the end of days. I believe that the Messianic banquet[239] will be partaken of in the midst of battle, just as a table was prepared before David in the presence of his enemies (Psalm 23:5).

Some will take up natural weapons and attempt to fight the beast using natural force, but they will quickly be crushed, for the beast defeats entire nations under its feet (Daniel 2:40; 7:7). God wants us to put on *spiritual* armor, for this will be a spiritual battle with spiritual enemies (2 Corinthians 10:3, 4) and we will overcome by His spirit:

> NAS Romans 13:12 The night is almost gone, and the day is at hand. Let us therefore lay aside the deeds of darkness and put on the armor of light.

> NAS Ephesians 6:11–17 Put on the full armor of God, that you may be able to stand firm against the schemes of the devil. For our struggle is not against flesh and blood, but against the rulers, against the powers, **against the world forces of this darkness**, against the spiritual *forces* of wickedness in the heavenly *places*. Therefore, take up the full armor of God, that you may be able to resist in the evil day, and having done everything, to stand firm. Stand firm therefore, having girded your loins with truth, and having put on the

---

237 Schiffman, *Reclaiming the Dead Sea Scrolls*, pp. 333–335.
238 Schiffman, *Reclaiming the Dead Sea Scrolls*, p. 331.
239 The *Agape* meals were preenactments of this heavenly feast, as seen in Courses 5 and 6.

> breastplate of righteousness, and having shod your feet with the preparation of the gospel of peace; in addition to all, taking up the shield of faith with which you will be able to extinguish all the flaming missiles of the evil *one*. And take the helmet of salvation, and the sword of the Spirit, which is the word of God.

> ᴷᴶⱽ Ephesians 6:10   Finally, my brethren, be strong in the Lord, and in the power of his might.

The beast may act like Goliath and arrogantly challenge the people who dare to stand with God. He will outwardly mock God's people, but this will be a sign of the soon-coming spiritual death wound to the beast's seventh head.

When Israel was captive in Babylon (the beast's third head), a time came when King Belshazzar overstepped his bounds. The king was throwing a big feast and when he tasted the wine, he decided to bring out the gold and silver vessels of the Lord that had been removed from the Temple when Jerusalem was taken and use them in his own ungodly feast. This was a big mistake, and the scriptures relate what happened:

> Daniel 5:5–6   Suddenly the fingers of a man's hand emerged and began writing opposite the lampstand on the plaster of the wall of the king's palace, and the king saw the back of the hand that did the writing. Then the king's face grew pale, and his thoughts alarmed him; and his hip joints went slack, and his knees began knocking together.

The words *"Mene Mene Tekal Upharsin"* that the hand of God wrote essentially meant "God has numbered your kingdom and put an end to it, and you have been weighed in the balance and found wanting" (Daniel 5:25–28). Kings and rulers may be confident to the point of arrogance; yet when God's presence comes forth, these most powerful rulers tremble.

The Lord Provides an Open Door

In the midst of all this, God provides a way of escape, just as He did with Noah and the Ark:

> ᴺᴬˢ Revelation 3:8   'I know your deeds. Behold, **I have put before you an open door** which no one can shut, because you have a little power, and have kept My word, and have not denied My name.

> ^{NAS} Revelation 3:10 'Because you have kept the word of My perseverance, **I also will keep you from the hour of testing**, that *hour* which is about to come upon the whole world, to test those who dwell upon the earth.

> ^{NAS} Malachi 3:16–17 Then those who feared the LORD spoke to one another, and the LORD gave attention and heard *it*, and a book of remembrance was written before Him for those who fear the LORD and who esteem His name. "And they will be Mine," says the LORD of hosts, "on the day that I prepare *My* own possession, and I will spare them as a man spares his own son who serves him."

The open door is the promise of a bride made ready; it is the promise of being caught up to be with the Lord forever:

> ^{NAS} 1 Thessalonians 4:16 For the Lord Himself will descend from heaven with a shout, with the voice of *the* archangel, and with the trumpet of God; and the dead in Christ shall rise first.

> ^{NAS} 1 Thessalonians 4:17 Then we who are alive and remain shall be caught up together with them in the clouds to meet the Lord in the air, and thus we shall always be with the Lord.

> ^{NAS} 1 Thessalonians 4:18 Therefore comfort one another with these words.

A great move of God is coming that will perfect us into what He desires for His people:

> ^{NAS} Psalm 132:14 "This is My resting place forever; **Here I will dwell**, for I have desired it.

> ^{NIV} Jeremiah 31:3 The LORD appeared to us in the past, saying: "**I have loved you** with an everlasting love; I have drawn you with loving-kindness.

> ^{NAS} Psalm 16:11 Thou wilt make known to me the path of life; **In Thy presence is fulness of joy**; In Thy right hand there are **pleasures forever**.

God desires a bride, and in Jeremiah he referred to Israel as his bride in the making:

> NAS Jeremiah 2:2 "Go and proclaim in the ears of Jerusalem, saying, 'Thus says the LORD, "I remember concerning you the devotion of your youth, **The love of your betrothals**, Your following after Me in the wilderness, Through a land not sown.

God said he was a husband to the Israelites:

> NAS Jeremiah 31:32 not like the covenant which I made with their fathers in the day I took them by the hand to bring them out of the land of Egypt, My covenant which they broke, **although I was a husband to them**," declares the LORD.

Some may wonder why Israel was pictured in the Old Covenant as being betrothed to God, with God saying He was a husband to Israel (Jeremiah 2:2; 31:32), yet in the New Covenant spiritual Israel is pictured as the bride of Christ (the Messiah). These images of the people as a bride are only natural pictures that point forward to the spiritual fulfillment. The Messiah gives us an example of how to love God, for he is a visible expression of God's nature. This example further enables us to love God, whom we cannot see.

In one sense we are the Messiah's spiritual bride. In another sense, after we are caught up to meet the Messiah in the air, he then gives up the whole kingdom to God, that God might be all in all (1 Corinthians 15:24). We will then be spiritually one with God, one with the Messiah, and one with each other in the spiritual realm for all eternity (John 17:20–26).

This powerful move of God's spirit is coming to all who are willing to enter into it. Many Messianic fellowships and many churches will enter in; we'll all be one in the Messiah. We need to prepare ourselves to allow God's *agape* love to flow, yet keep all things pure before Him. This moving of God's spirit will cause the assembly to grow into the bride, without spot or wrinkle:

> YLT Ephesians 5:27 that he might present it to himself **the assembly in glory**, not having spot or wrinkle, or any of such things, but that it may be holy and unblemished;

The (mostly Jewish) scripture writers of the New Testament all came to understand that the festivals and communal meals from the Old Covenant pointed forward to the promised New Covenant in which they now found themselves. Thus the spiritual banqueting that they were experiencing was the sharing of God's love (*agape*).

For example, Paul shows below that the giving and receiving ("every joint supplies") of the individual members of the body causes the body to be built up in love:

> ^{NAS} Ephesians 4:16   from whom the whole body, being fitted and held together by that which **every joint supplies**, according to the proper working of each individual part, **causes the growth** of the body for the building up of itself **in love**.

Along similar lines, Peter refers to *spiritual* "living stones" being built up to become the house of God, where His spirit will dwell:

> ^{NAS} 1 Peter 2:5   **you also**, as living stones, **are being built up as a spiritual house** for a holy priesthood, to offer up spiritual sacrifices acceptable to God through Jesus Christ.

The final ingathering of the harvest that God seeks is the fruit of the spirit being manifest in His people, and the first and most important of this spiritual fruit is love:

> ^{NAS} Galatians 5:22–23   But the fruit of the Spirit is **love**, joy, peace, patience, kindness, goodness, faithfulness, gentleness, self-control; against such things there is no law.

> ^{NAS} John 15:5   "I am the vine, you are the branches; he who abides in Me, and I in him, he bears much fruit; for apart from Me you can do nothing.

The scriptures warn that in the last days, perilous times will come (1 Timothy 3:1–5), yet at the same time the Lord is preparing a table for all who love God. The table from which we partake will fulfill the plan as seen in the Showbread. The Lord's table will also fulfill the third and final Feast of Ingathering, whereby the spiritual fruit is ripened within God's people and we become ready as a bride to be caught away to God.

Courses 5 and 6 showed that this feast can be entered into today, as we share God's *agape* love and feast on His word, taking great delight in His spiritual instruction. This is the Messianic feast that all people are called to—filled with unspeakable joy and glory. It is up to us to enter this Promised Land and receive all that God has for us, and the time to enter in is now!

> ^{NAS} Isaiah 25:1   O lord, Thou art my God; I will exalt Thee, I will give thanks to Thy name; For Thou hast worked wonders, Plans *formed* long ago, with perfect faithfulness.

^{NAS} Isaiah 25:6   And the LORD of hosts will prepare **a lavish banquet for all peoples** on this mountain; A banquet of aged wine, choice pieces with marrow, *And* refined, aged wine.

^{NAS} Isaiah 25:7   And on this mountain He will swallow up the covering which is over all peoples, Even the veil which is stretched over all nations.

^{NAS} Isaiah 25:8   He will swallow up death for all time, And the Lord God will wipe tears away from all faces, And He will remove the reproach of His people from all the earth; For the LORD has spoken.

Part 2

Proofs the Last Supper Was Not the Passover

Proofs the Last Supper Was Not the Passover

The majority of this section covers the various proofs that the Last Supper was not the Passover, with additional information that the ritual of Communion was not something the Messiah or the early believers wanted or taught. The "Template Challenge" forces various beliefs to logically lay out certain scriptural events with the Jewish template of the Passover feast. Then the "Three Keys" chapter takes those scriptures that seem to so clearly have Jesus eating the Passover at the Last Supper and shows what they actually mean in the original Greek. This is followed by the "Fifty Reasons" chapter, which attempts to group all the proofs that the Last Supper was not the Passover into a single chapter.

"Between the Evenings" explores various Jewish laws and idioms that show the proper time and day to slay the Passover, which are vital in disproving several false theories. Other important truths are also seen in this chapter. And finally we take a close look at whether the scriptures actually teach a ritual of Communion in the chapter "The Ritual—Why Didn't the Jewish Disciples Teach It?"

PART 2

The Template Challenge

To maintain the integrity of scriptures, the following time-specific events must all align with the Jewish timeline with respect to Passover and the seven-day Festival of Unleavened Bread.

The Challenge

The challenge is to place all 10 events into the template for this Jewish feast:

1. Jesus being in the heart of the earth three days and three nights.
2. The Last Supper.
3. The 14th-day Passover sacrifice.
4. The time of Christ's death.
5. The 15th-day Sabbath that follows the 14th-day Passover sacrifice.
6. The Saturday Sabbath.
7. The seven-day Festival of Unleavened Bread.
8. Sunday—the first day of the week (Luke 24:1).
9. The day Jesus was condemned and crucified, such that it fulfills Luke (24:1, 20, 21), which says Sunday was "the third day since these things happened" (with "these things" being the condemnation and Crucifixion).
10. The day his disciples questioned Jesus about where they should prepare for the Passover (Matthew 26:17; Mark 14:12; Luke 22:9).

In the following pages we will consider various doctrinal beliefs to see which one meets the test. The final templates in this chapter will show how these events had to occur, but first we will consider the template of the Passover and the seven-day Feast/Festival of Unleavened Bread, as commanded by God to Moses:

Figure 1 (diagram)

Each Jewish day ended at sunset, about 6:00 PM; the new day would then begin with the night portion first

The legal time to slay the Passover is between noon and sunset

The first day of the festival is a Holy Convocation (15th-day high Sabbath)

The seventh day of the festival is a Holy Convocation (Sabbath)

THE PASSOVER

SABBATH

Nisan Calendar Date: 13 | 14 | 15 | 16 | 17 | 18 | 19 | 20 | 21

Days of Seven-Day Feast/Festival of Unleavened Bread: 1 | 2 | 3 | 4 | 5 | 6 | 7

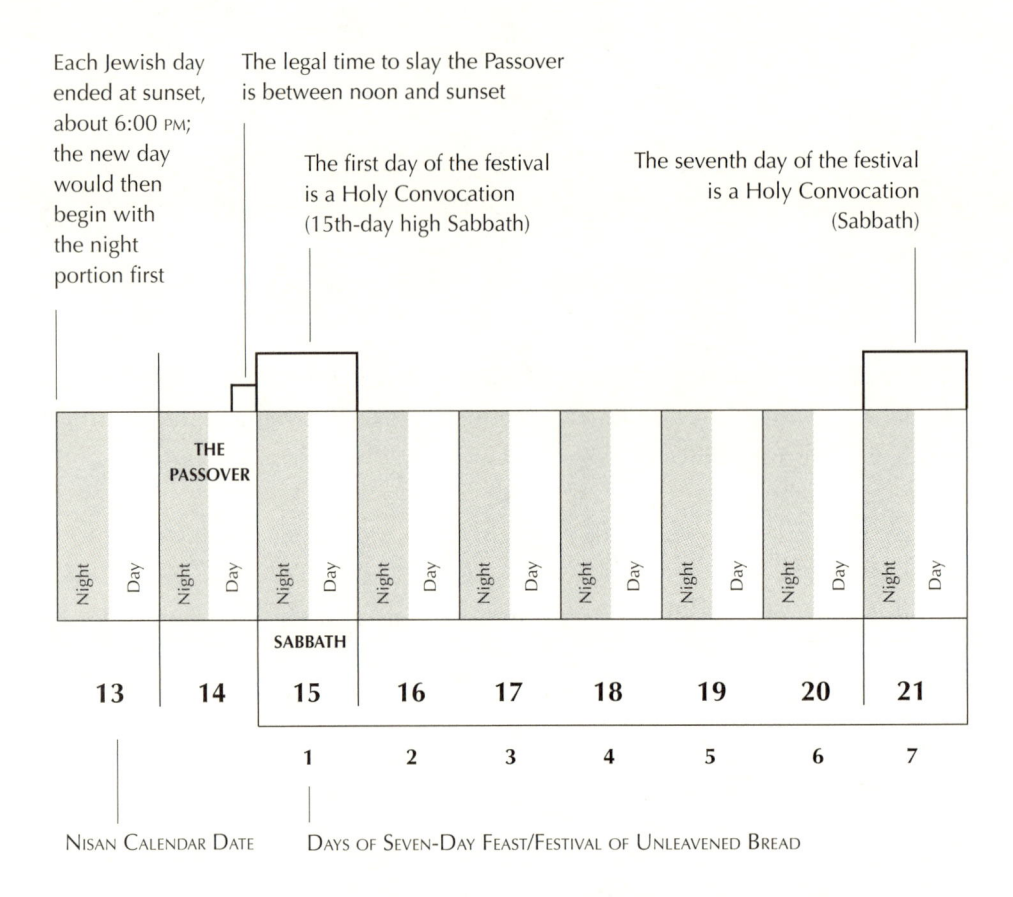

Figure 1. Template challenge: the template of the Passover and the seven-day Feast/Festival of Unleavened Bread, as commanded by God.

> JPS Numbers 28:16–18, 25 And in the first month, on the **fourteenth day** of the month, is the LORD'S **passover**. And on the **fifteenth day** of this month shall be a feast; **seven days** shall unleavened bread be eaten. In the **first day shall be a holy convocation**; ye shall do **no manner of servile work**; And on the seventh day ye shall have a holy convocation; ye shall do no manner of servile work.

Unfortunately, three of the most popular theological doctrines—namely, the Early Roman Catholic Option, the Double Passover Option, and the Saturday Resurrection Option—all violate certain scriptures when overlaid on the template.

As we will see, only one possible option exists to place all these events within the template of this feast, such that no scripture is broken.

But first we will consider these three most popular options.

THE TEMPLATE CHALLENGE | 367

They believed "Good Friday" was the day
"these things happened," i.e., delivered up,
sentenced to death, and crucified

In this option,
Christ eats the Passover
at the Last Supper

Christ then dies at about 3:00 PM
on "Good Friday," being the
15th-day high Sabbath

First day since | Second day since | (In this option, Sunday is not "the third day since" these things happened)

| Night | Day | Night | Day | Night | Day | Night | Day | Night | Day | Night | Day | Night | Day | Night | Day | Night | Day | Night | Day | Night | Day | Night | Day |

THURSDAY | FRIDAY | SATURDAY | SUNDAY
13 | 14 | 15 | 16 | 17 | 18 | 19 | 20 | 21

1 | 2 | 3 | 4 | 5 | 6 | 7

NISAN CALENDAR DATE   DAYS OF SEVEN-DAY FEAST/FESTIVAL OF UNLEAVENED BREAD

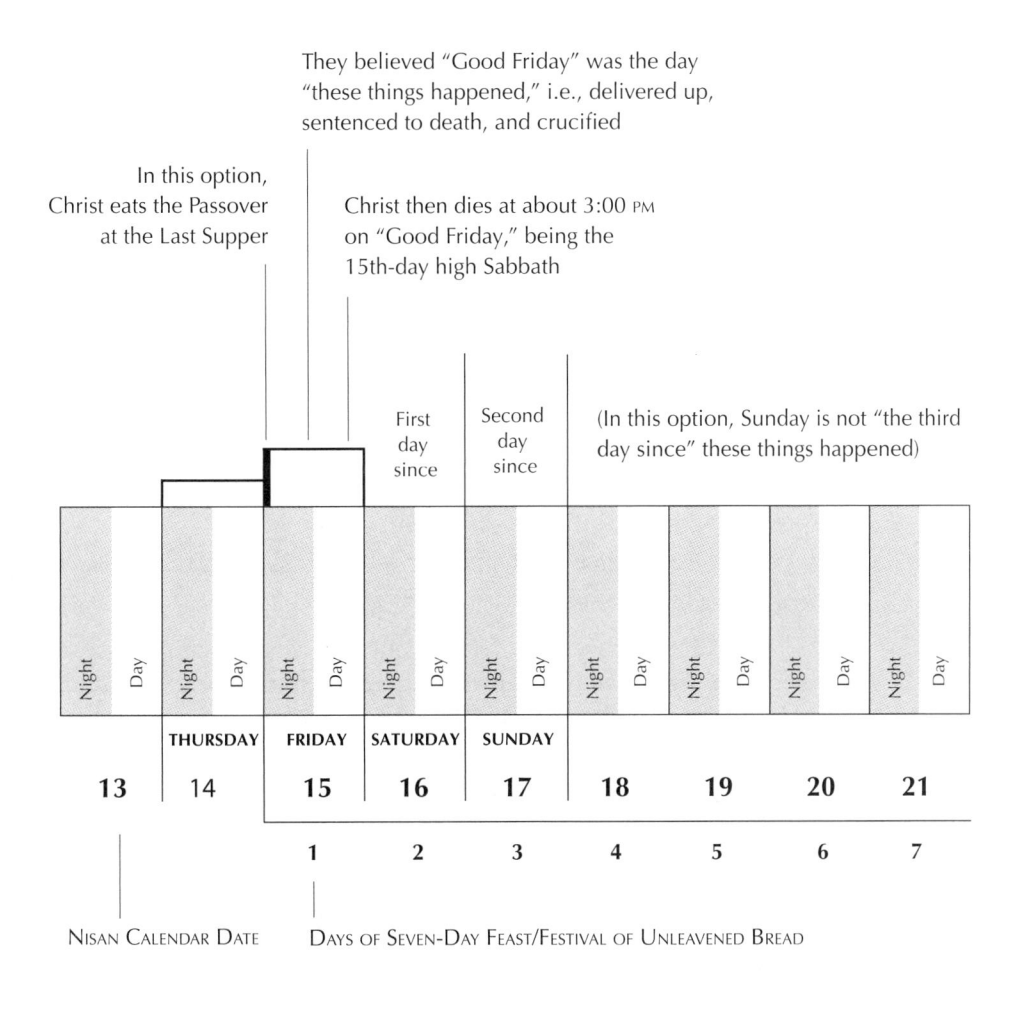

Figure 2. The early Roman Catholic option.

The Early Roman Catholic Option

The first of these popular options is based on Christ being crucified on "Good Friday" after eating the Passover at the Last Supper. By looking closely at the timing of events, it is easy to see that this position cannot be true. This early Roman Catholic option does not fit the scriptures for several reasons:

1. It fails to fit the clear time-specific events in Luke 24, wherein the disciples speak on Sunday—the first day of the week (verse 1)—about Jesus having been delivered up and crucified (verses 19–20). The disciples say that it is now the *third day since* these things happened

(verse 21). Yet if Christ had been crucified on Good Friday, Sunday would only be the *second day since* these things happened.

2. Jesus would have been in the tomb only two (not three) nights. From the first-century Jewish perspective, this would be the night portion of Saturday and the night portion of Sunday (shown in the template diagram above). However, Jesus said he would be in the tomb three days and *three nights* (Matthew 12:40).

3. Had Jesus eaten the 14th-day Passover at the Last Supper, Jewish Sabbath laws would have been completely violated by having the Crucifixion of Jesus on the 15th-day Sabbath.[240]

4. Jesus would have been buried on the 15th-day Sabbath, also completely illegal under Jewish law.

5. It goes against the almost unanimous *early* church history that the Crucifixion was on the 14th day.[241]

6. Having Jesus eat the 14th-day Passover at the Last Supper and believing he was crucified on Good Friday (the 15th day) would contradict God's foreknowledge whereby He instructed Moses to sacrifice the Passover on the 14th day. This option thus implies that Christ was our "one-day-late" Passover.

---

[240] See the chapter "50 Reasons the Last Supper Was Not the Passover" for many more proofs that Christ was not crucified on the 15th-day Sabbath.

[241] As seen in the chapter "Setting the Table 1: The Jewish Disconnect and the Fourteenthers."

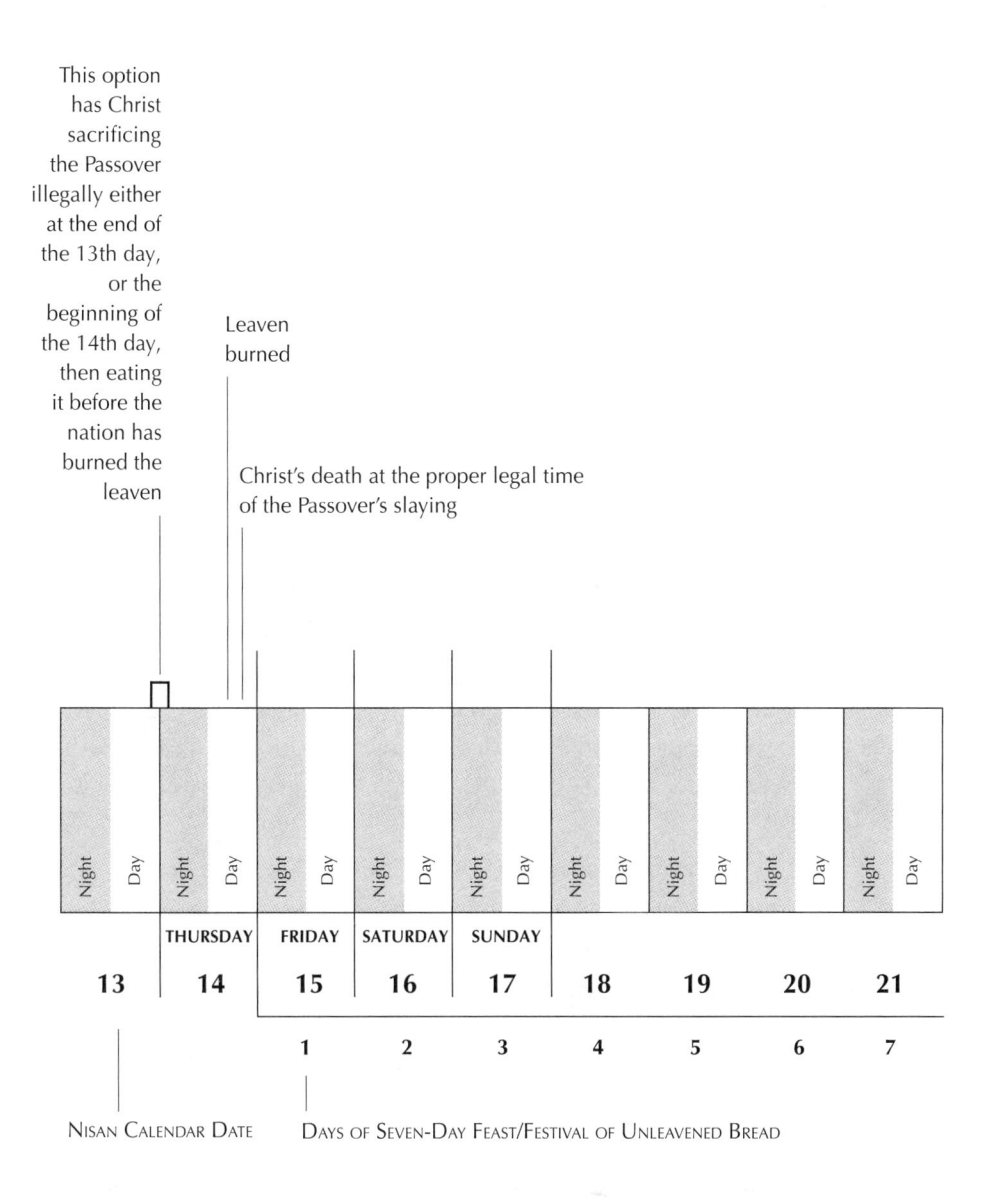

Figure 3. The double Passover option.

The Double Passover Option

Clarke's Commentary on Matthew 26:20[242] espouses a double Passover option. This second of the widely held doctrinal options has Jesus somehow both *eating* a Passover at the Last Supper at the start of the 14th day (i.e., just into the nighttime portion), and then *being crucified as* the Passover in the daytime portion of this 14th day.

---

242 Clarke, *Clarke's Commentary*, vol. 3, p. 248.

Many believe that both are true, not understanding the contradiction that—under Jewish law—if Jesus ate the Passover at the Last Supper, he could not have died at the time of the Passover sacrifice the following day. Those who believe the double Passover concept point out that each Jewish day ended and the new one began at sundown, so if Jesus sacrificed a Passover at the end of the 13th day (just after sundown), it would actually occur on the 14th day.

However, Adam Clarke's double Passover option does not fit the scriptures for the following reasons:

1. God commanded that the Passover be sacrificed on the 14th day between the evenings,[243] and Jewish authorities always understood this time as between noon and sunset. Yet in this option Jesus would be slaying an *illegal* Passover either late on the 13th day or at night as the 14th day began, then roasting and eating it at the Last Supper with his disciples. This would have been completely illegal according to God's laws, and Temple authorities would never have allowed it, because they understood God's commandments that a legal Passover must be sacrificed on the 14th day between noon and sunset. As Alfred Edersheim writes, the idea of sacrificing a Passover early is untenable:

   > Equally untenable is it, that Christ had held the Paschal Supper a day in advance of that observed by the rest of the Jewish world—a supposition not only inconsistent with the plain language of the Synoptists, but impossible, since the Passover Lamb could not have been offered in the Temple, and, therefore, no Passover Supper held, out of the regular time[244]

   By not understanding the correct translation[245] for certain scriptures that portray the Last Supper as the Passover, many commentators (even Edersheim) erroneously defend the long-held tradition that the Last Supper was the Passover. Although Edersheim correctly disputes the double Passover concept, he and most other commentators do believe that Jesus ate the legal Passover at the Last Supper. However, this would then have Jesus crucified the *day after* the Passover lambs were sacrificed,

---

243 See the proof for the legal time to slay the Passover in the chapter "Between the Evenings."
244 Edersheim, *Life and Times*, Book 5, ch. 9, p. 482.
245 See the chapter "The Three Major Greek Keys That Unlock the Gospels" for the correct meaning of the original Greek and how the English translations erred.

and right on the 15th-day high Sabbath, the most holy day of the Festival (which would have been blatantly illegal under Jewish law).

Returning to the double Passover option, Temple authorities would never permit someone to wander in a day early, or after sundown as the 14th day began, and attempt to slay the Passover illegally. The Passover had to be sacrificed in the Temple at the ***appointed time*** and day as specified to Moses by God's foreknowledge:

> NAS Numbers 9:13 'But the man who is clean and is not on a journey, and yet neglects to observe the Passover, that person shall then be cut off from his people, for he did not present the offering of the LORD **at its appointed time**. That man **shall bear his sin**.

The Talmudic and bible scholar John Lightfoot (a believer in the Messiah) also states that eating the Passover at the wrong time would have been "a heinous offense":

> Let them tell me now, who suppose that Christ ate his Passover one day sooner than the Jews did theirs, how these things could be performed by him or by his disciples in the Temple, since it was looked on as a heinous offense among the people not to kill or eat the Passover in the due time.[246]

2. God commanded that the Passover not be sacrificed while leaven was still present among the people (Exodus 23:18; 34:25). Since the legal time to slay the Passover was *after* noon on the 14th day, it was ruled that all leaven must be removed *before* noon on the 14th day.[247]

For Jesus to slay a Passover before all leaven was removed (i.e., any time before noon on the 14th day) was unthinkable, as this would break God's law. The Jewish writer Philo, a contemporary of Christ, further affirmed that sacrifices were not offered at night: "…it was not the custom to offer a sacrifice in darkness…."[248]

---

[246] Lightfoot, *Commentary of the New Testament from the Talmud and Hebraica*, vol. 2, p. 342.
[247] As covered in the quotes from the Talmud in the chapter "Between the Evenings."
[248] Marcus, *Philo Supplement II*, p. 20.

3. All 10 scriptures that refer to "bread" at the Last Supper use the Greek word *arton* for regular leavened bread and not the Greek word for *matzah* (i.e., *azumos*). Had this meal been the Passover, the scriptures certainly would not have presented the Messiah and his disciples eating regular bread with it. Furthermore, had this meal been the Passover, God by His foreknowledge would not have portrayed the Messiah's betrayal with "bread" (Psalm 41:9, *lechem* in Hebrew) but with *matzah*.[249]

4. Those who espouse the double Passover option would still have to explain Luke 22:7, which *seems* to clearly show that the Last Supper was to be the eating of the Passover: "Then came the day…when the passover must be killed" (KJV). Obviously for those who believe the double Passover option, Luke would be saying that this daylight period before the Last Supper was the 14th day when the Passovers were killed. However, this would put the Crucifixion on the 15th-day Sabbath, which would have Christ as our day-late Passover. Luke does not say, "Then came one of the days" or "one of the two days" to kill the Passover, but "**the day**," showing that there was one day to sacrifice the Passovers. (In the "Three Keys" chapter, Luke 22:7 is explained using the accepted rules of Greek grammar.) If adherents to Adam Clarke's double Passover version don't agree, they would still have to explain the verse without breaking the scripture.

5. To slay a Passover before noon on the 14th day would have been an illegal sacrifice. As we saw in Course 1, even a high priest would be whipped if he were to eat meat from a sacrifice slaughtered illegally (referred to as "piggul"). Yet this double Passover option would have us believe that after Jesus and his disciples slaughtered an illegal Passover on the 13th day (or in the darkness of the 14th day), they then ate from that illegal sacrifice at the Last Supper. Are we to believe that the powerful Jewish Temple authorities would soundly whip their own high priest for doing this, but for Jesus and his disciples, they would just wink and let it go?

---

[249] See the section "Last Supper Prophecy, Betrayed with Bread" in "Course 1: Last Supper Ritual or Parable?"

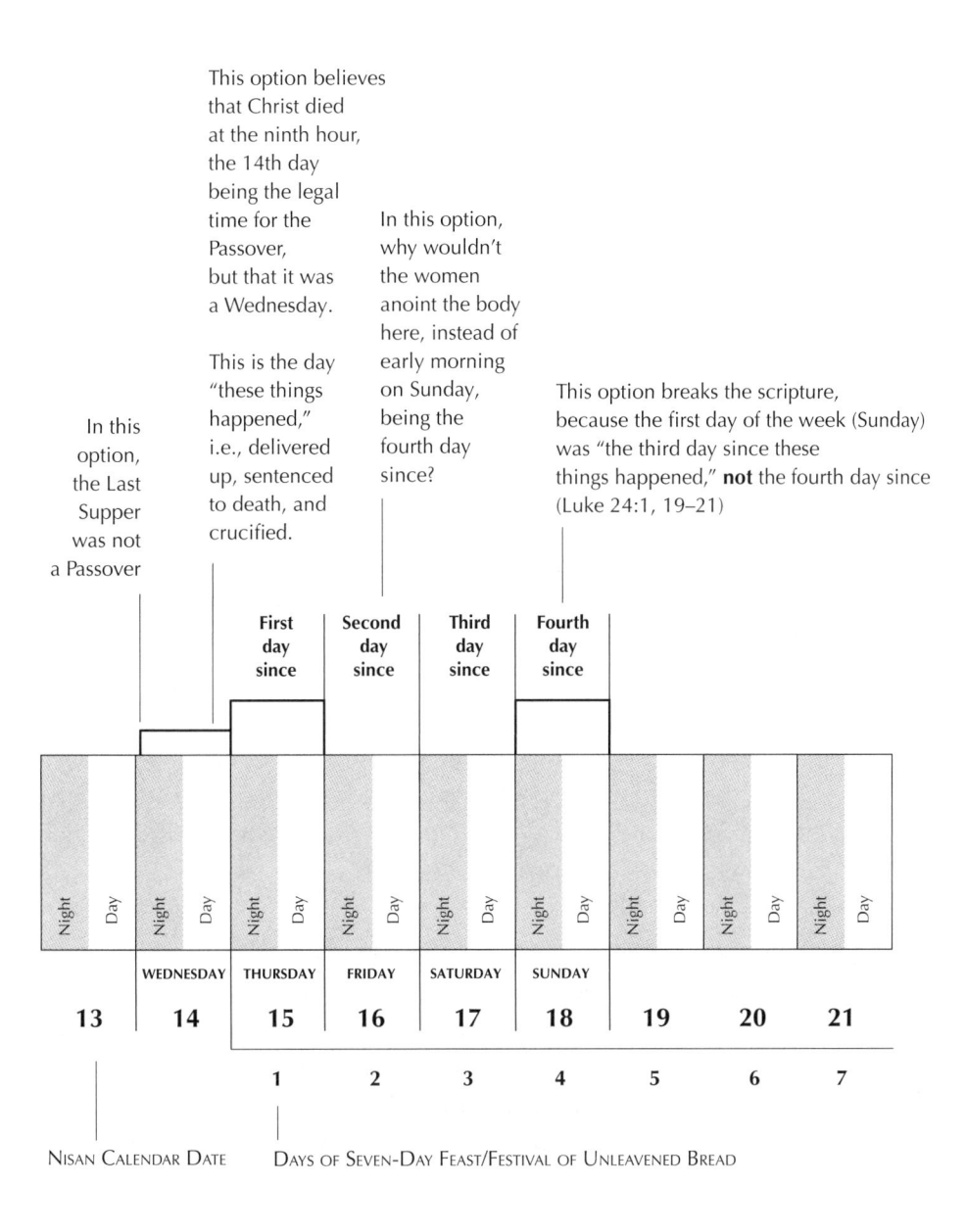

Figure 4. The Saturday Resurrection option.

The Saturday Resurrection Option

The third widely held doctrinal option assumes a Saturday Resurrection and usually teaches a Wednesday Crucifixion (which in this belief was the 14th day that year). The Saturday Resurrection option is popular among those who understand Jewish law concerning the point that Jesus would never have been crucified on the 15th-day high Sabbath.

But here is why this option does not fit the scriptures:

1. *No early historian even mentions a Saturday Resurrection*, because all sides in the early disputes agreed on the Sunday Resurrection. The Messianic Fourteenthers[250] wrote of a Sunday Resurrection, as did those called Church Fathers in Rome. Although the early Fourteenthers disputed the Roman concept of a 15th-day Crucifixion, both sides in these early doctrinal disputes wrote of and agreed on the Sunday Resurrection.

2. Paul called Jesus the "first fruits" because his Resurrection on Sunday (the *morrow of the Sabbath*) fulfilled this offering (Leviticus 23:10–14; 1 Corinthians 15:20, 23). Early church writer Clement of Alexandria, a Fourteenther,[251] wrote that the Resurrection was on the morrow of the Sabbath (i.e., Sunday), when the priest was to offer up this sheaf of the first fruits. In the following quote Clement shows how Christ fulfilled this offering: "He certainly rose on the third day, which fell on the first day of the weeks of harvest, on which the law prescribed that the priest should offer up the sheaf."[252] Forcing a Saturday Sabbath Resurrection would render Christ as our "day-early first-fruits" offering.

3. Those who teach this Saturday Resurrection usually believe in a Wednesday Crucifixion, but this would make Sunday the *fourth day since* Jesus was delivered up, condemned, and crucified instead of the *third* day since "these things" happened (Luke 24:1, 19–21; John 20:1). This Saturday option cannot fit the scriptures, and the Messiah said the scriptures cannot be broken (John 10:35). There is no Greek variant in these verses that would change this timing.

4. Some say that the Saturday Resurrection is the only way to fulfill the three days and three nights *exactly* by having the Messiah resurrected late Saturday afternoon, exactly 72 hours after he entered the "heart of the earth" (Matthew 12:40). But the Jews did not have stopwatches or

---

250 See the chapter "Setting the Table 1: The Jewish Disconnect and the Fourteenthers."
251 Meaning he understood that Jesus was crucified on the 14th day.
252 Roberts and Donaldson, *Ante-Nicene Fathers*, vol. 2, p. 581. The full quote containing additional important information can be found later this chapter in "The 13th-Day Question" subsection.

atomic clocks to mark exact times, so when Jesus said "three days and three nights," he did not mean *exactly* 72 hours to the minute. In Old Testament interpretation, even a portion of a day or night counted as the whole day (such as for ritual cleansings). Jesus said he would be in the "heart of the earth" for three days and three nights just as Jonah was in the whale, and no proof exists that Jonah fulfilled this timing to the exact minute.

5. This option rejects Mark 16:9, which states (in Greek) that Jesus arose early on the first day of the week—our Sunday. Also, if Jesus had arisen on Saturday, why would he have waited more than twelve hours (until the following day) to reveal himself? Some say that the scripture in Matthew 28:1, translated as "in the end of the Sabbath" by the King James Version, shows a Saturday Resurrection. But the Greek actually says "*after* the Sabbaths," with the plural "Sabbaths" probably referring to the 15-day Sabbath (Friday that year) and the Saturday Sabbath that followed it.

6. Luke 24:1 and John 20:1 show Mary Magdalene and the others leaving very early in the morning (while it was still dark) with spices to anoint the body. If Jesus had been crucified on Wednesday, why would these women have risen and left home in the darkness of Sunday morning when they had all day Friday to complete this task? After all, if the 14th-day Crucifixion was Wednesday and the 15th-day Sabbath was Thursday, then Friday would not have been a Sabbath—and that would have been the obvious time to anoint the body, rather than waiting until the fourth day when decay would have set in.

7. Mark 16:1 specifies that the women "bought" the spices and were now coming to anoint the body. Therefore, they probably purchased the spices right after the Crucifixion (as Thursday the 14th day was ending) and before the 15th-day high Sabbath set in, as Luke makes clear (23:55, 56). It would also have been legal to make this purchase anytime after sundown of the Saturday Sabbath.

8. The proof for the Sunday Resurrection is quite strong; it is the only possible way to fit the template challenge, whereby all the scriptural time keys harmonize and make sense (as we will see in the template "Sunday, the Third Day Since"). While it is true that when Mary Magdalene

and the others arrived early Sunday morning, Jesus had already arisen, it must be remembered that anytime *after sundown on Saturday* would then be Sunday.

9. Any option that does *not* have Jesus eating the Passover at the Last Supper would still have to explain Matthew 26:17, Mark 14:12, and Luke 22:7, which on the surface *appear* to show it was the Passover. The "Three Major Greek Keys That Unlock the Gospels" chapter lists what I believe is the proper way to interpret these scriptures, using the accepted rules of Greek grammar.

The True Scriptural Option

Up to now we have looked at the three widely held positions and seen that none of them aligns properly with the scriptures:

1. Early Roman Catholic option
2. Double Passover option
3. Saturday Resurrection option

So here we turn to the one true scriptural option that fits the template for this Israelite feast. The following is a day-by-day explanation (beginning with the 13th day) to show the only way for all the time-specific events listed at the beginning of this chapter to fit the template.

THE TEMPLATE CHALLENGE | 377

The disciples ask Jesus their question on the 13th day, "with reference to" the first day, not "on" the first day of the Feast/Festival of Unleavened Bread

This was the first of the eight unleavened days, for leaven was removed before noon

All leaven must be removed before noon (11:00 AM) as the legal time for the Passovers was afternoon; this led to this day being called the first of the unleavened days, eight days total

15th-day high Sabbath, a Holy Convocation, begins the seven-day Feast/Festival of Unleavened Bread

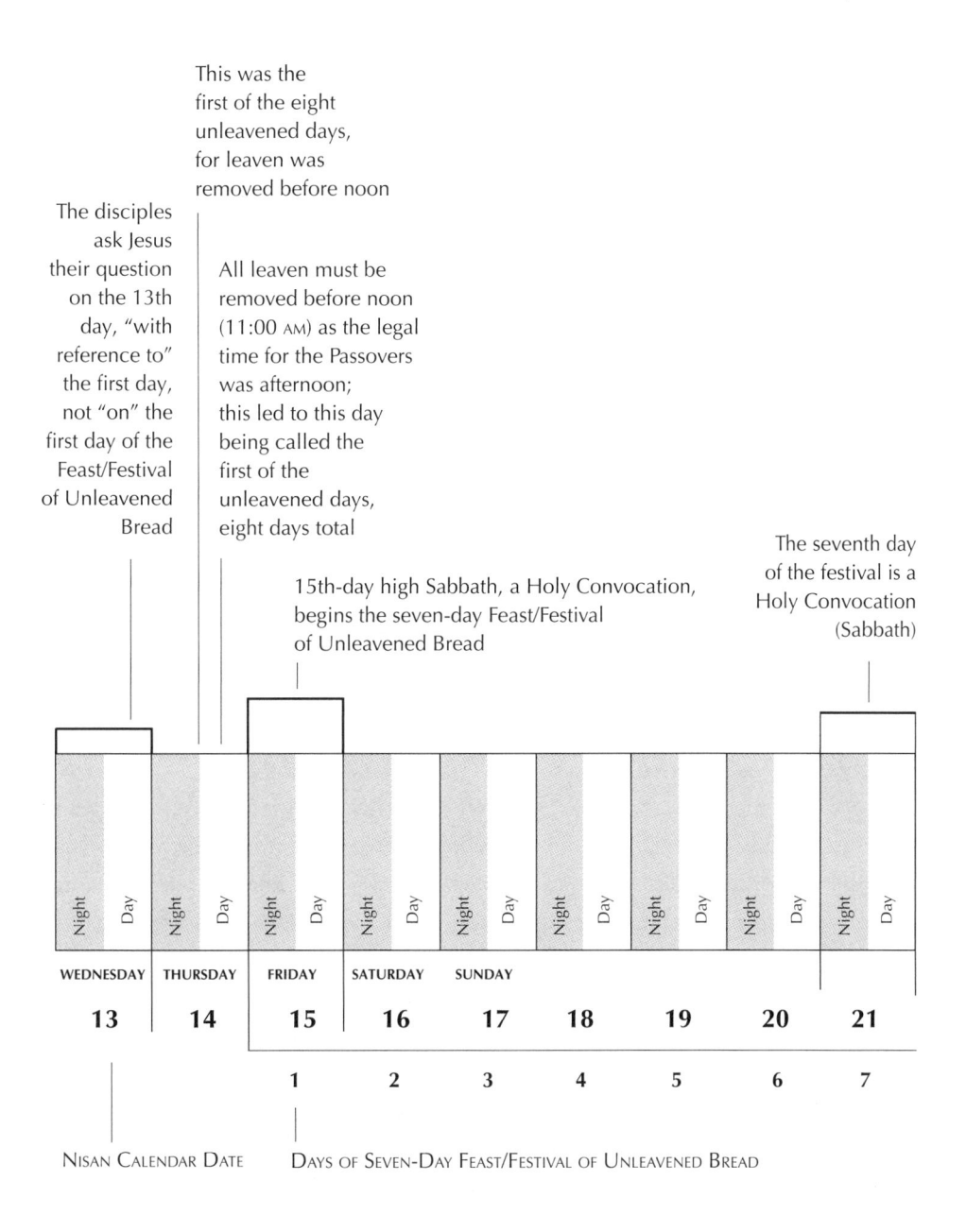

The seventh day of the festival is a Holy Convocation (Sabbath)

WEDNESDAY	THURSDAY	FRIDAY	SATURDAY	SUNDAY				
13	14	15	16	17	18	19	20	21
		1	2	3	4	5	6	7

NISAN CALENDAR DATE   DAYS OF SEVEN-DAY FEAST/FESTIVAL OF UNLEAVENED BREAD

Figure 5. The true scriptural option: the 13th-day question.

The 13th-Day Question

To properly locate the Last Supper on the template, one has to decide which day it was that the disciples asked their question about making preparations for Passover—for it was later this evening that they gathered for what would be the Messiah's final meal. The only possible way to have the 10 time-specific events fit into the template, such that the Crucifixion of Jesus happens on the 14th day and fulfills the Passover sacrifice, is if the disciples asked this question on the 13th day. The Last Supper (which happened later this evening) would therefore not have been a Passover, especially since the Messiah ate regular leavened bread at this meal. (A subsequent chapter details more than 50 such proofs[253] that the Last Supper was not the Passover, notwithstanding the English translations that *appear* to show that it was.)

Therefore, it was on the 13th day of this month that the disciples asked Jesus where to make the necessary preparations[254] for the impending Passover:

> ᴺᴵⱽ Matthew 26:17 **On** the first day of the Feast of Unleavened Bread, the disciples came to Jesus and asked, "Where do you want us to **make preparations** for you to eat the Passover?"

> ᴳᴺᵀ Matthew 26:17 Τῇ δὲ πρώτῃ τῶν ἀζύμων προσῆλθον οἱ μαθηταὶ τῷ Ἰησοῦ λέγοντες, Ποῦ θέλεις ἑτοιμάσωμέν σοι φαγεῖν τὸ πάσχα;

Let us examine what this verse truly says, since the original meaning of the Greek has been altered by most English translations.

This particular translation says it was "On" the first day that the disciples came asking their question. In the Greek, however, the article Τῇ (translated here as "On") does not actually mean "On" the first day in this case but rather "To" the first day. In English this Greek dative should be translated as "With reference to"[255] the first day. Since the deadline for ritual purification is drawing close, the disciples are very concerned *with reference to* the first day, since under Jewish law they need to be ritually prepared before the Passover sacrifice arrives.

The next point concerns two words that have been *added* to the English translation. Neither "Feast" nor "Bread" appears in the Greek of this scripture; Matthew 26:17 just says "first of the unleavened." The English is misleading because the *first day of the Feast of Unleavened Bread* is actually the 15th day—the first day of this seven-day Festival. In contrast, the *first of the unleavened* is the 14th day, because all traces of leaven had to be removed before noon[256] on this Passover day.

So this verse really means that they are now in the 13th day of Nisan, and the Lord has yet to direct his disciples about required preparations (such as finding a location, removing leaven, etc.) for the next day (the 14th-day Passover).

---

253 See the chapter "50 Reasons the Last Supper Was Not the Passover."

254 The chapter "The Three Major Greek Keys That Unlock the Gospels" further explores what the phrase "make preparations" means in the first-century Jewish idiom.

255 This Greek dative and why it should be translated "with reference to" is fully covered in the section "Dative of Reference" in the chapter "The Three Major Greek Keys That Unlock the Gospels."

256 See the chapter "Between the Evenings" for this historical proof.

The English translations cause confusion when they say it was "*on* the first day" instead of "*with reference to* the first day" that the disciples came to Jesus with their question. In the Jewish idiom, the 14th day was often called the "first" of the unleavened because on this day leaven was removed before noon. When combined with the seven-day Feast of Unleavened Bread, this made eight days of unleavened.

Josephus likewise refers to this whole festival as having eight[257] days of unleavened.[258]

Luke also aligns, showing that the 14th day (when the Passovers were sacrificed) was considered one of the eight unleavened days:

> [DBY] Luke 22:7 And **the day of unleavened** bread came, in which the passover was to be killed.[259]

Mark, too, makes it clear that the 14th day (when the Passover was sacrificed) was the **first** of these eight days of unleavened:

> [NAS] Mark 14:12 And **on**[260] the **first day of Unleavened** Bread, **when the Passover *lamb* was being sacrificed**, His disciples said to Him, "Where do You want us to go and prepare for You to eat the Passover?"

※※※

In both Hebrew and Greek, the word "first" can also be translated as "previous." The Talmud makes it clear that when God called the 14th day the "first" day (Exodus

---

257 Some say that Josephus is referring to the rabbinic custom of adding a second day to certain festival high Sabbath days (thus making eight days for Passover), but this is not accurate. Although scripture proclaimed *one day* for the Festival Sabbaths, later history shows that (probably after Rome destroyed the Temple) the rabbis proclaimed that those in the Diaspora were to keep certain Festival holy days for *two days*. This was to avoid desecrating the Sabbath, for those in outlying areas would have no way of knowing which day had been determined by the Sanhedrin as the first of the month (i.e., the new moon, which was always either 29 or 30 days after the previous new moon). Therefore they might not have known which was the 15th-day Sabbath of Passover, so an additional day was to be kept by those in distant locations. However, an extra day was never added in Jerusalem while the Temple existed, so it has no bearing on this Last Supper controversy. Rather, Josephus is counting the 14th day together with the seven-day Festival, which makes eight unleavened days.

258 Whiston, *The New Complete Works of Josephus*, "Jewish Antiquities," 2.15.1, p. 107.

259 Although Luke 22:7 is another scripture that seems to show that the disciples asked this question on the 14th day, it is another of the scriptures that will be correctly interpreted in the chapter "The Three Major Greek Keys That Unlock the Gospels."

260 The Greek word translated as "on" here is also a dative of reference and should have been translated as "with reference to" or "concerning." See "The Three Major Greek Keys That Unlock the Gospels" chapter for more on this.

12:15, the day to remove the leaven), He did not mean the *first* of the seven-day Feast of Unleavened Bread, for if you waited until the 15th day to remove the leaven you would have already broken the law to have no leaven during the seven-day Festival. Therefore the obvious way to understand "first" here is "previous"—the day *preceding* the Feast (i.e., the 14th day):

> GEMARA: We see thus, that at the **commencement of the sixth hour**, all agree, Chometz[261] must be burned. Whence do we adduce this? Said Abayi: From two passages, viz. [Exod. xii. 19]: "Seven days no leaven shall be found in your houses," and [ibid. 15]: "But on the **first day** ye shall have put away leaven out of your houses." According to this, then, on the **first day** there would still be leaven in the house and this would be contrary to the ordinance of the first passage? Hence we must say, that by "the first day" is meant **the day preceding the festival. Then why say the sixth hour?** Say that already early in the morning of the day preceding the festival (leaven should be burned). The word "but" with which the passage commences divides the day into two parts, so that in the morning leavened bread may be eaten **while in the afternoon it must not.**[262]

They continue by explaining that Exodus 34:25 is God's directive of why leaven had to be removed by noon of the 14th day (called the "first" day):

> The disciples of R. Ishmael taught: The reason **that Chometz must be removed on the 14th (of Nissan)** (the eve of Passover) is because that day is referred to as **the first day** (of the festival) in the passage [Exod. xii. 18]: "In the first, on the fourteenth day of the month, at evening shall ye eat unleavened bread," etc.
>
> Rabha said: "The reason may be inferred from the passage [Exod. xxxiv. 25]: **'Thou shalt not offer the blood of my sacrifice with leaven**; neither shall be left unto the morning the sacrifice of the feast of the passover,' **which signifies, that the Passover sacrifice must not be offered up as long as there is yet leaven."** If that be the case, then it might be said that the leaven should be burned by each man immediately before offering his passover sacrifice; **why designate the sixth hour? The passage means to state,**

---

261 "Chometz" refers to that which is fermented or leavened.
262 Babylonian Talmud, Book 3, Tract Pesachim, ch. 1, p. 19, http://sacred-texts.com/jud/t03/psc05.htm.

> that when the *time* for the Passover sacrifice arrives, there must no longer be any leaven on hand.[263]

And now a quote from early church writer and Fourteenther Clement of Alexandria (ca. AD 150 to ca. AD 215), where he describes how the disciples asked their question of Jesus on the **13th day**:

> From the Last Work on the Passover, quoted in the *Paschal Chronicle*:
>
> Accordingly, in the years gone by, Jesus went to eat the Passover sacrificed by the Jews, keeping the feast. But when he had preached He who was the Passover, the Lamb of God, led as a sheep to the slaughter, presently taught His disciples the mystery of the type **on the thirteenth day, on which also they inquired**, "Where wilt Thou that we prepare for Thee to eat the passover?" It was on this day, then, that both the consecration of the unleavened bread and the preparation for the feast took place. Whence John naturally describes the disciples as already previously prepared to have their feet washed by the Lord. And on the **following day our Saviour suffered, He who was the Passover**, propitiously sacrificed by the Jews.

Clement continues, and shows that Christ suffered on the 14th day:

> Suitably, therefore, **to the fourteenth day, on which He also suffered**, in the morning, the chief priests and the scribes, who brought Him to Pilate, did not enter the Praetorium, that they might not be defiled, but might freely **eat the passover** in the evening. With this precise determination of the days both **the whole Scriptures agree**, and **the Gospels harmonize**. The **resurrection also attests it**. He certainly rose on the third day, which fell on the first day of the weeks of harvest, on which the law prescribed that the priest should offer up the sheaf.[264]

John also makes it clear that the disciples came to Jesus on the 13th day when he shows that the day *after* the disciples asked their question was the Crucifixion (the

---

263 Babylonian Talmud, Book 3, Tract Pesachim, ch. 1, pp. 19–20, http://sacred-texts.com/jud/t03/psc05.htm.
264 Roberts and Donaldson, *Ante-Nicene Fathers*, vol. 2, p. 581.

14th day). We know this because on this Crucifixion day the Jewish guards were concerned with the purification required so they could eat the Passover:

> NAS John 18:28 They led Jesus therefore from Caiaphas into the Praetorium, and it was early; and they themselves did not enter into the Praetorium **in order that they might not be defiled, but might eat the Passover**.

With crowds streaming into Jerusalem and time running out, why would Jesus have waited so long to choose a location?

The fact is that Jesus knew very well that he would *not* be present to eat the Passover with his disciples, which is partly why he did not give them direction sooner. Jesus understood himself to be the New Covenant fulfillment of the 14th-day Passover lamb. He also knew he would be cut off in the middle of the week (Daniel 9:24–27, i.e., after three and a half years of ministry). And at the very time the Israelites would have offered their Passovers, Jesus was crucified—between the evenings on the 14th day (Matthew 26:2; 27:46, 50).

To recap, the disciples came to Jesus sometime during the 13th day to ask where they should make preparations for the soon-coming Passover. They did not come asking their question *on* the first day of the Feast of Unleavened Bread or *on* the first of the eight unleavened days (the 14th day in their idiom), but rather *in reference to* this 14th day.

The Last Supper took place
after sunset; Jesus knew
he was now in his final day,
and the "hour" had come
(John 13:1; 17:1);
the "supper" was not a Passover

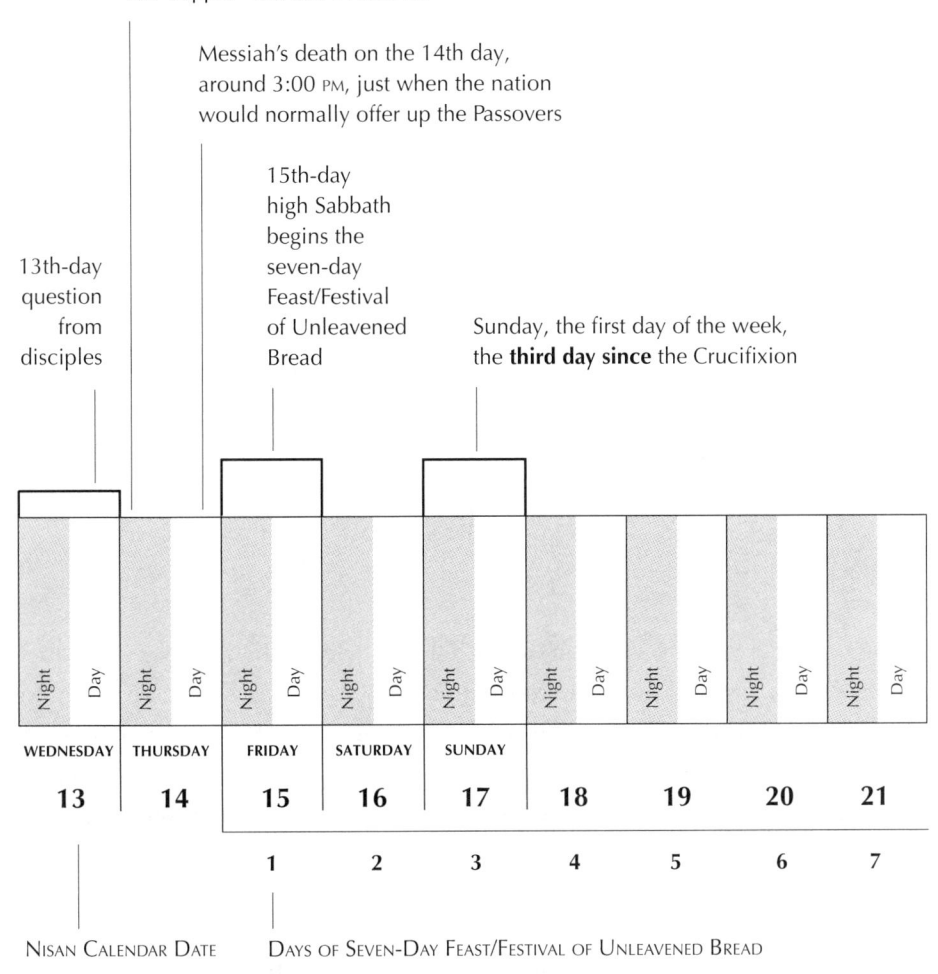

Messiah's death on the 14th day,
around 3:00 PM, just when the nation
would normally offer up the Passovers

15th-day
high Sabbath
begins the
seven-day
13th-day   Feast/Festival
question   of Unleavened   Sunday, the first day of the week,
from   Bread   the **third day since** the Crucifixion
disciples

Night	Day	Night	Day	Night	Day	Night	Day	Night	Day	Night	Day	Night	Day	Night	Day

WEDNESDAY	THURSDAY	FRIDAY	SATURDAY	SUNDAY			
13	14	15	16	17	18	19	20	21

                       1   2   3   4   5   6   7

NISAN CALENDAR DATE   DAYS OF SEVEN-DAY FEAST/FESTIVAL OF UNLEAVENED BREAD

Figure 6. The true scriptural option: the 14th-day true Passover.

The 14th-Day True Passover

God commanded for the Passover to be sacrificed between the evenings (between noon and sunset) on the 14th day of the month called Nisan:

> YLT Leviticus 23:5   in the first month, on the **fourteenth** of the month, **between the evenings**, *is* the **passover** to Jehovah;

> ^{YLT} Leviticus 23:6   and on the **fifteenth** day of this month *is* the **feast of unleavened** things to Jehovah; seven days unleavened things ye do eat;

Moses again shows the 14th day as the Passover in Numbers:

> ^{NAS} Numbers 28:16   'Then on the **fourteenth** day of the first month shall be the LORD's Passover.

> ^{NAS} Numbers 28:17   'And on the **fifteenth** day of this month *shall be* a feast, unleavened bread *shall be* eaten for **seven days**.

As covered in Setting the Table 1, the early Messianic Fourteenthers understood that Jesus was crucified on this 14th day, himself being the true fulfillment of this sacrifice. Of course the Messiah also understood this typology, and in fact just a couple of days before it happened, he said he would be crucified at that soon-coming Passover:

> ^{NAS} Matthew 26:2   "You know that after two days the **Passover** is coming, and the Son of Man is *to be* delivered up for **crucifixion**."

Although some Jewish writings, such as the Talmud, refer to the 15th day as the Passover, Jesus was referring to the more conventional usage of Passover (the 14th day), for he would have known the impossibility of a crucifixion on the 15th-day high Sabbath.

The Sanhedrin also knew the impossibility of arresting and slaying Jesus during this time, and commanded that Jesus **not** be arrested **during** the (seven-day) Festival, lest a riot occur:

> ^{NAS} Matthew 26:4–5   and they plotted together to seize Jesus by stealth, and kill *Him*. But they were saying, "**Not during the festival**, lest a riot occur among the people."

Had Jesus been arrested after eating the Passover at the Last Supper, the arrest would have taken place exactly *during* the Festival. However John shows it was "*before* the Feast," not *during* it, that Jesus and his disciples ate the Last Supper (i.e., shortly into the night-time portion of the 14th day):

> ^{NAS} John 13:1   Now **before the Feast** of the Passover, Jesus knowing that His hour had come that He should depart out of this world to the Father, having loved His own who were in the world, He loved them to the end.

He was arrested that same night and crucified during the daylight that followed, the very predetermined 14th day in which the nation would be ready to sacrifice the Passovers. We see this in the scripture mentioned earlier:

> NAS John 18:28 They led Jesus therefore from Caiaphas into the Praetorium, and it was early; and they themselves did not enter into the Praetorium in order that they might not be defiled, but might eat the Passover.

And this was the very 14th day that God, by His foreknowledge, gave to Moses for the Passover sacrifice, the day that He knew that the Messiah would fulfill this type:

> NAS Acts 2:23 this *Man*, delivered up by the predetermined plan and foreknowledge of God, you nailed to a cross by the hands of godless men and put *Him* to death.

We saw that it was on the 13th day that the disciples asked Jesus their question as to where they should make preparations. According to God's word they needed to prepare a location that was ritually pure by having all leaven removed. Other preparations were also involved (both inward and outward); all these needed to be completed *before noon* of the 14th day. Because of God's commandments that the Passover not be sacrificed while leaven was still present among the people (Exodus 23:18; 34:25), all leaven needed to be removed before this time because after-noon was when the Passover sacrifices could legally begin:

> DBY Exodus 12:6 And ye shall keep it until the fourteenth day of this month; and the whole congregation of the assembly of Israel shall kill it **between the two evenings**.

As Alfred Edersheim correctly explains:

> The period designated as "between the two evenings" when the Paschal lamb was to be slain, was past. **There can be no question** that, in the time of Christ, it was understood to refer to the interval between the **commencement of the sun's decline** and what was reckoned as the hour of his final disappearance (about 6 PM).[265]

---

265 Edersheim, *Life and Times*, Book 5, ch. 9, p. 490.

As referenced earlier in "The 13th-Day Question" subsection, the Talmud also pinpointed the beginning of the sixth hour (around 11 AM) on this 14th day as the time for all leaven to be removed. This makes perfect sense, for it was *after* this sixth hour that the Passover could be legally slaughtered. With Passover blood soon to be shed, no leaven could still be on hand (Exodus 34:25).

※

One of the tricky points regarding this 14th-day Passover presents itself in Luke 22:1, which says the Feast of Unleavened Bread itself is **called** the "Passover":

> NAS Luke 22:1 Now the Feast of Unleavened Bread, which is **called** the Passover, was approaching.

Whenever you see someone writing about the Passover, it is necessary to understand exactly what time period they mean by this. The 14th day was most often referred to as Passover, as seen earlier in scriptures from Moses (Numbers 28:16; Leviticus 23:5) and the Messiah (Matthew 26:2). Yet many Jewish writings often refer to the entire seven-day Feast as the Passover. In calling the seven-day Feast itself the Passover, Luke above indicates that this usage was also common in his day. Still other Jewish writings (such as the Talmud) often refer to the 15th day as the Passover, since it was the high Sabbath and the entrance into the seven-day Feast. It was, after all, the 15th day that the LORD "passed over" after the first Passover sacrifice in Egypt.

Alfred Edersheim describes this duality:

> The cycle of Temple-festivals appropriately opens with 'the Passover' and 'Feast of Unleavened Bread.' For, properly speaking, **these two are quite distinct** …, the 'Passover' taking place on the 14th of Nisan, and the "Feast of Unleavened Bread" commencing on the 15th, and lasting for seven days, to the 21st of the month (Exod. 12:15). But from their close connection **they are generally treated as one**, both in the Old and in the New Testament (Matt. 26:17; Mark 14:12; Luke 22:1); and Josephus, on one occasion, even describes it as "**a feast for eight days**" ….[266]

---

[266] Edersheim, *The Temple*, p. 162.

The following line, excerpted from the Talmudic quote given earlier in "The 13th-day Question" section, shows how Jewish sources often refer to the 14th day as the "eve of Passover":

> The reason that Chometz must be removed on the 14th (of Nissan) (**the eve of Passover**) is because that day is referred to as the first day (of the festival)....

The Messianic Fourteenthers understood the Messiah was crucified on the 14th day. And this meaning of "eve of Passover" shows that even Talmudic scholars agree that Jesus was slain on the 14th day of Nisan:

> On the eve of the Passover Yeshu [the Nasarean] was hanged.[267]

Just as "Christmas Eve" represents the six-hour period before Christmas arrives, so the "eve of Passover" approximates the period of time before the (seven-day Festival called) Passover actually begins. *The Jewish Encyclopedia* elaborates on this:

> The **eve** of Jewish holidays is therefore not the evening of the festival, but **the day preceding it**[268]

The Jewish Encyclopedia continues explaining this eve of Jewish holidays by quoting from the Talmud:

> "He who engages in regular work **late** in the afternoon of the **eve of the Sabbath or holiday** will receive no blessing upon his work" (Pes. 50b)[269]

In other words, to work in the late afternoon of the day before a "holiday" (i.e., one of the seven Festival Sabbaths) or Saturday Sabbath was to show irreverence for the soon-coming Sabbath. Although this was the Talmudic view and not commanded by God, this quote establishes the "eve of the Sabbath" in the Jewish idiom as a period of time the day before a Sabbath. So the "eve of the Passover" denoted this period of time before the 15th-day Sabbath of the Passover Festival.

---

267 The Soncino Babylonian Talmud, Tractate Sanhedrin, Folio 43a, http://www.come-and-hear.com/sanhedrin/sanhedrin_43.html. In this source, next to "Yeshu" is a footnote that says, "Ms.M. adds 'the Nasarean.'"
268 *The Jewish Encyclopedia*, vol. 5, p. 276, s.v. "Eve of Holidays."
269 *The Jewish Encyclopedia*, vol. 5, p. 276, s.v. "Eve of Holidays."

John also shows the 14th day—the day of the Crucifixion—was the day of preparation for the 15th-day Sabbath called Passover:

> NAS John 19:14 Now it was the day of preparation for the Passover; it was about the sixth[270] hour. And he said to the Jews, "Behold, your King!"

With all these nuances and changes in idiom and language, especially with the Jewish disconnect, it's easy to see how these concepts became confused over the last 1,700 years.

---

270 The chapter "Between the Evenings" has a section ("What Does John Mean by the Sixth Hour?") that answers the controversy concerning John portraying Jesus presented to the chief priests at the sixth hour, while Mark (15:25) showed Jesus was crucified at the third hour.

The Template Challenge | 389

[Figure: Timeline diagram showing Nisan calendar dates 13-21 with night/day segments. Annotations indicate:
- Christ's death on the 14th day, the legal time for the Passovers, and Christ is in the tomb sometime before the 15th-day Sabbath arrives
- Seven-day Feast/Festival of Unleavened Bread begins at sundown, with the great Sabbath
- 15th-day Sabbath commemorates God delivering them from Egypt—"no servile labor"
- Christ's Sunday resurrection, being the "morrow of the Sabbath," fulfilled the first-fruits offering that God gave to Moses

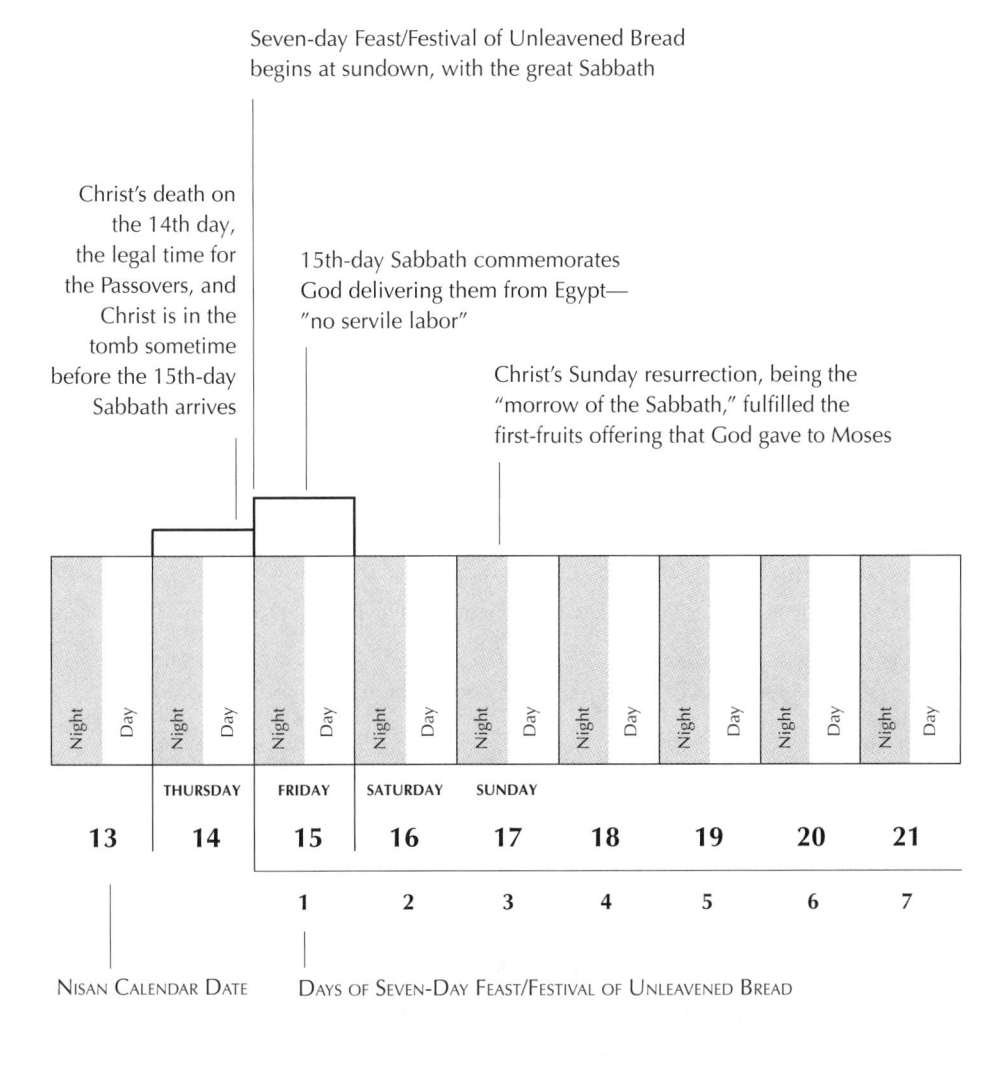

Days labeled: Thursday 14, Friday 15, Saturday 16, Sunday 17. Days of Seven-Day Feast/Festival of Unleavened Bread: 1-7 corresponding to Nisan 15-21.]

Figure 7. The true scriptural option: the 15th-day high Sabbath.

The 15th-Day Sabbath

Jesus was crucified on the 14th day of Nisan as the true Passover, and it was on this preparation day that the Jews rushed to remove the bodies from the crosses and to have the body of Jesus entombed before the revered 15th-day Sabbath began:

> NAS Luke 23:54 And it was the preparation day, and the Sabbath was about to begin.

> NAS John 19:31 The Jews therefore, because it was the day of preparation, so that the bodies should not remain on the cross on the

Sabbath (**for that Sabbath was a high *day***), asked Pilate that their legs might be broken, and *that* they might be taken away.

Clearly the soon-coming Sabbath—the one approaching as Jesus was removed from the cross—was this great 15th day of Nisan Sabbath that always followed the 14th-day Passover sacrifice. The Pharisees and chief priests would never have pushed for his crucifixion *on* this 15th-day Sabbath (Friday that year) nor would they have performed the other illegal activities,[271] then suddenly become concerned with observing tomorrow's Saturday Sabbath as per Jewish law. Even today, many Israeli Jews keep this 15th day as an important Sabbath rest day, and many businesses are closed. The first-century Jews clearly honored it as well.

It was called a high Sabbath ("high" is *megaly* in Greek) because God commanded the Israelites to commemorate this day when He delivered them out of Egypt. It was also called high (or great) because it was one of the seven additional Sabbaths connected to the three annual festivals, as enumerated in Leviticus 23:

1. The 15th day of Nisan (the first day of the seven-day Feast of Unleavened Bread)
2. The seventh day of the Feast of Unleavened Bread
3. Pentecost
4. The first day of Tishri (Rosh Hashanah—this first day of this seventh month)
5. The 10th day of Tishri (Yom Kippur—the Day of Atonement)
6. The 15th day of Tishri (the first day of Tabernacles/Booths/Sukkot)
7. The 22nd day of Tishri (the day following the seven-day Feast of Tabernacles—an eighth day to be kept as a Sabbath, with no servile work)

These sacred assembly days are also referred to as *megaly* (usually translated as "high" or "great") in the Septuagint (Isaiah 1:13). We saw above that John used the Greek word *megaly* to describe the high 15th-day Sabbath (John 19:31) that followed the 14th-day Passover sacrifice (John 18:28). John also uses this Greek word *megaly* for another of these seven additional Sabbaths, this time the eighth-day Sabbath following the seven-day Festival of Tabernacles, translated below as "great":

> NAS John 7:37 Now on the last day, the **great** *day* of the feast, Jesus stood and cried out, saying, "If any man is thirsty, let him come to Me and drink.

---

271 Illegal activities such as carrying torches and clubs, which are all listed in the chapter "50 Reasons the Last Supper Was Not the Passover."

In Leviticus chapter 23, God speaks of both the Saturday Sabbath and of these additional festival-day Sabbaths (referred to as "sacred assemblies" or Holy Convocations):

> ^{NIV} Leviticus 23:2 "Speak to" the Israelites and say to them: 'These are **my appointed feasts**, the appointed feasts of the LORD, which you are to proclaim as **sacred assemblies**.

> ^{NIV} Leviticus 23:3 "'There are six days when you may work, but the **seventh day** is a Sabbath of rest, a day of **sacred assembly**. You are not to do any work; wherever you live, it is a Sabbath to the LORD.

He then returns to these seven other holy days each year that were connected to the three annual festivals and were considered days of no servile labor (i.e., Sabbath rest):

> ^{NIV} Leviticus 23:4 "'These are the LORD's appointed feasts, the sacred assemblies you are to proclaim at their appointed times:

The first of these seven additional Sabbaths mentioned is this 15th-day Sabbath (verses 6, 7), which follows the slaying of the 14th-day Passover:

> ^{YLT} Leviticus 23:5 in the first month, on the **fourteenth** of the month, between the evenings, *is* the passover to Jehovah;

> ^{YLT} Leviticus 23:6 and on the **fifteenth** day of this month *is* the feast of unleavened things to Jehovah; seven days unleavened things ye do eat;

> ^{YLT} Leviticus 23:7 on the first day ye have a holy convocation, **ye do no servile work**;

God commanded this day to be kept special because it marked His delivering of the Israelites out of Egypt:

> ^{JPS} Numbers 33:3 And they journeyed from Rameses in the first month, on the **fifteenth day** of the first month; on the morrow after the passover the children of Israel went out with a high hand in the sight of all the Egyptians,

> ᴶᴾˢ Exodus 12:17   And ye shall observe the feast of unleavened bread; **for in this selfsame day** have I brought your hosts out of the land of Egypt; therefore shall ye observe this day throughout your generations by an ordinance for ever.

> ᴺᴬˢ Exodus 12:42   It is **a night to be observed** for the LORD for having brought them out from the land of Egypt; **this night is for the LORD**, to be observed by all the sons of Israel throughout their generations.

Thus, the Passover was slain on the afternoon of the 14th day, with the 15th-day Sabbath following. Yet on this high Sabbath there was a slight relaxing of the Sabbath laws, but only to prepare food:

> ᴺᴵⱽ Exodus 12:16   On the first day hold a sacred assembly, and another one on the seventh day. **Do no work at all** on these days, except to prepare food for everyone to eat—**that is all you may do**.

To emphasize that the first-century Jews kept the 15th day as a Sabbath, consider the following. God commanded that the sheaf of the first fruits be offered on the "morrow of the Sabbath" ("morrow" meaning the day after). At some point, probably after Christ's death, a dispute arose among the Pharisees and the Sadducees as to which Sabbath the first-fruits offering was to follow—the Saturday Sabbath or the 15th-day Sabbath:

> ᴶᴾˢ Leviticus 23:11   And he shall wave the sheaf before the LORD, to be accepted for you; on the **morrow after the sabbath** the priest shall wave it.

> ᴷᴶⱽ Leviticus 23:15   And ye shall count unto you from the **morrow after the sabbath**, from the day that ye brought the sheaf of the wave offering; seven sabbaths shall be complete:

> ᴷᴶⱽ Leviticus 23:16   Even unto the morrow after the seventh sabbath shall ye number fifty days; and ye shall offer a new meat offering unto the LORD.

While the Pharisees insisted that this offering occur on the morrow of the 15th-day Sabbath, the Sadducees argued that it was to take place on the morrow of the regular Saturday Sabbath. God answered this controversy by raising the Messiah on Sunday, the morrow of the Saturday Sabbath.

The scriptures from Leviticus above showed God's command to count 50 days from the Omer (sheaf offering) to Pentecost (the 50th day). This count was to begin on the morrow of the Sabbath and end on the morrow of the seventh Sabbath. To do this, one would need to begin counting from the day after the Saturday Sabbath (i.e., Sunday) and *not* after the 15th-day Sabbath (as the Pharisees did). This is the only way to have seven complete Sabbaths (49 days), with the following day being the "morrow after the seventh Sabbath." Clearly the Sadducees were correct here.

The point is that the Pharisees' argument holds no weight at all if the 15th was not kept as a Sabbath in their day. (The chapter "50 Reasons the Last Supper Was Not the Passover" covers this 15th day in more detail.)

394 | THE MESSIANIC FEAST

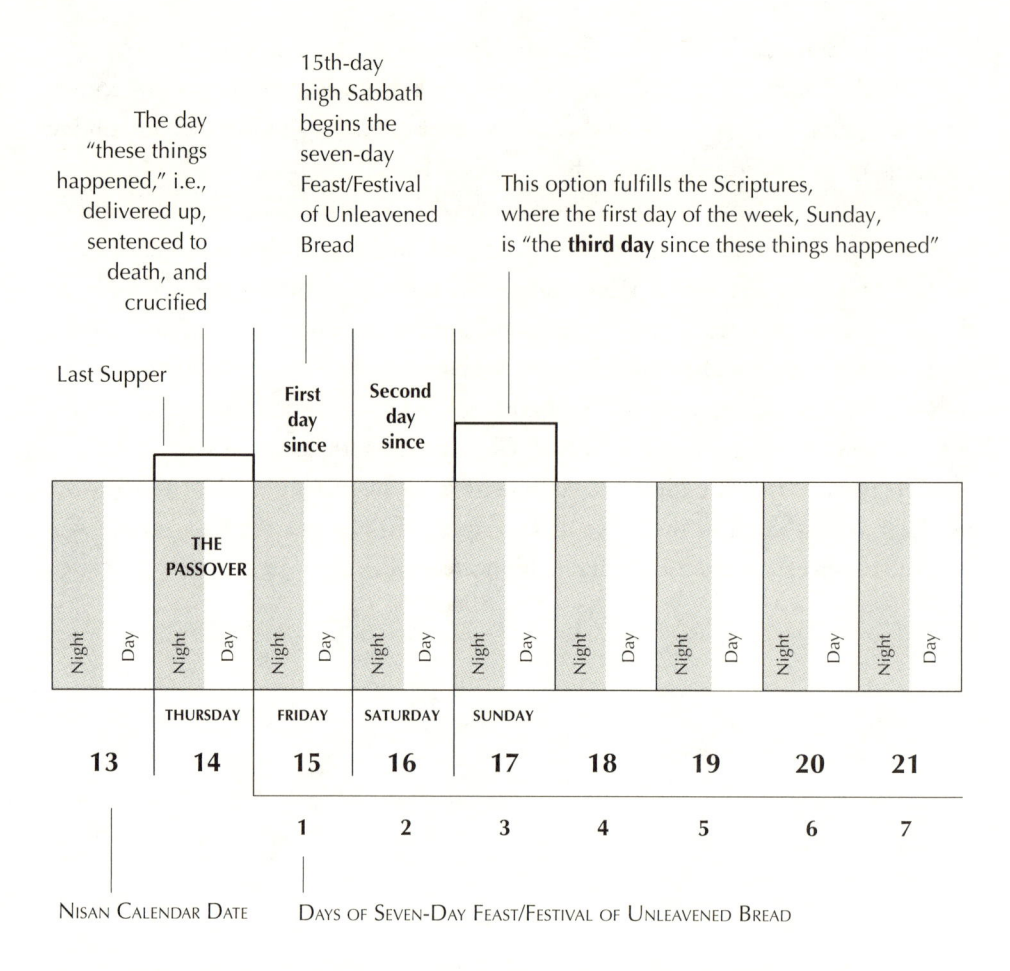

[Figure: Calendar diagram showing Nisan dates 13-21, with Thursday 14 as "THE PASSOVER," Friday 15 as "First day since," Saturday 16 as "Second day since," and Sunday 17 as the "third day since." Labels indicate: "The day 'these things happened,' i.e., delivered up, sentenced to death, and crucified"; "Last Supper"; "15th-day high Sabbath begins the seven-day Feast/Festival of Unleavened Bread"; "This option fulfills the Scriptures, where the first day of the week, Sunday, is 'the **third day** since these things happened'". Days labeled Night/Day across the bottom with "NISAN CALENDAR DATE" and "DAYS OF SEVEN-DAY FEAST/FESTIVAL OF UNLEAVENED BREAD" (1-7).]

Figure 8. The true scriptural option: Sunday, the "third day since."

Sunday the Third Day Since

This final template focuses primarily on the scriptures that show Sunday to be *the third day since* Christ was delivered up and crucified. With Sunday being "the third day *since* these things happened" and the first day of the Jewish week, Thursday had to be the day of Crucifixion. The following several scriptures in Luke make this clear:

> ᴺᴬˢ Luke 24:1 But on **the first day of the week**, at early dawn, they came to the tomb, bringing the spices which they had prepared.

A little later that same day (still Sunday), the disheartened disciples lament Christ's death, their hopes now seemingly dashed. They declare that it is now the "third day since these things happened," with "these things" representing the delivering up, sentence of death, and the Crucifixion:

^{NAS} Luke 24:19 And He said to them, "**What things**?" And they said to Him, "The things about Jesus the Nazarene, who was a prophet mighty in deed and word in the sight of God and all the people,

^{NAS} Luke 24:20 and how the chief priests and our rulers **delivered Him up to the sentence of death, and crucified Him**.

^{NAS} Luke 24:21 "But we were hoping that it was He who was going to redeem Israel. Indeed, besides all this, **it is the third day since these things happened**.

Only one option exists for all these time-specific events to fit this festival template:

- The Crucifixion and burial happen on Thursday with the soon-coming high Sabbath approaching.
- The 15th-day high Sabbath happens on Friday that year.
- The Saturday Sabbath follows.
- Then Christ is resurrected during the night portion (sometime before sunrise) of Sunday, the "third day since" the Crucifixion.

This is the only possible way to maintain the integrity of the scriptures in Luke while also having Jesus in the tomb for (a portion of) three days and three nights.[272]

This explains why the women waited through two Sabbaths (Friday the 15th and Saturday) until very early Sunday morning before rushing out into the darkness to anoint the body. It also explains why the high Sabbath of the 15th day commences at the end of Christ's Crucifixion day (Luke 23:54; John 19:31) and why no Sabbath occurs after the Last Supper.

This true option has Christ crucified on the legal 14th day of the Passovers. It proves that on the previous night at the Last Supper, he would not have eaten the Passover, for the day following the Last Supper was not the 15th-day high Sabbath.

The English translations of Matthew, Mark, and Luke that *seem* to so clearly portray the Last Supper as the Passover are fully explained in the next chapter, "The Three Major Greek Keys That Unlock the Gospels," using proper Greek grammar

---

[272] Jesus saying he would arise from the dead the third day (compare Luke 24:21 with Luke 24:46) does not contradict what he said about being in the heart of the earth for three days and three nights. The former statement meant the third day following his crucifixion, and the latter statement was fulfilled exactly as he meant it (see item 4 in the "Saturday Resurrection Option" section). The same is true for when he said he would arise *after* three days (Mark 8:31), meaning it would occur after *the portion of* three days (and three nights, Matthew 12:40) were fulfilled. Some have attempted to prove a contradiction here, but none exists.

rules. Those Greek language keys truly solve the longstanding controversy as to whether or not the Last Supper was the Passover. They also show that the four Gospels harmonize on this matter and explain why Jesus could legally eat regular bread at the Last Supper. In turn, this opens the door to question the current Communion ritual with unleavened bread at Catholic and Protestant churches.

Later we examine any supposed scriptural proof for a Communion ritual in "The Ritual—Why Didn't the Jewish Disciples Teach It?"

PART 2

The Three Major Greek Keys That Unlock the Gospels

There are three Greek language keys that unlock the truth of the Gospels while solving the apparent contradiction between John and the other Gospel writers as to whether the Last Supper was the Passover or not. There is no question that the English translations of Matthew, Mark, and Luke *seem* to state that the Last Supper *was* the Passover. But one must remember that the Gospels were not originally written in English but in Greek. When Jewish idioms and Passover laws are considered along with original Greek scriptures, it's evident that the story told, after Rome disconnected from these Jewish understandings, is inaccurate. These language keys will help us get back to the truth.

The first key is the Greek **subjunctive mood**, which can imply doubt and uncertainty. The subjunctive mood is used every time Jesus refers to his actual eating of the Passover in the Greek language, but its use does not always carry over into the English translations of the Gospels. This seemingly small change has huge implications for accurately determining whether the Last Supper was the Passover or not.

The second key is the Greek **dative of reference**, which affects the meaning of Greek articles (a common article in English is "the"). In the English language, these Gospel accounts seem straightforward; yet in the original Greek language, the dative case brings additional shades of meaning. This is important because, as Greek scholar Daniel B. Wallace noted in *Greek Grammar Beyond the Basics*, one in seven words in the Greek scriptures is an article.

The third key is the Greek **aorist tense**, which Greek scholar Buist M. Fanning suggests is like a "snapshot" that "presents an occurrence in summary."[273] We will examine how such a snapshot helps us interpret Luke 22:7 in the proper light.

I realize that many readers are not versed in Greek, but please don't think "It's all Greek to me" or assume this will be too difficult. I'll explain these concepts in ways that those without Greek training can understand. So let's start right in with the first key.

---

273 Fanning, *Verbal Aspect in the New Testament Greek*, p. 97.

Key 1: The Subjunctive Mood

The Greek subjunctive mood is often used when there is doubt regarding the accomplishment of an action. It can imply uncertainty—from the speaker's point of view—regarding *the reality* of the action. Many Greek scholars corroborate this as being one aspect of the subjunctive:

> A. T. Robertson, in his *Short Grammar of the New Testament*, writes that the subjunctive can be the mode "of **doubtful** assertion."[274]

> Dana and Mantey offer that "While the indicative **assumes** reality, the subjunctive assumes **unreality**."[275]

> Daniel Wallace writes, "The subjunctive thus, at times, is used for mere *possibility* or even **hypothetical** **possibility** (as well as, at other times, probability)."[276]

So the Greek subjunctive mood can have a range of meanings, including doubt, hypothetical possibility, or even unreality. Let's look at a few examples of the Greek subjunctive in scriptures, with the subjunctive words emphasized in boldface.

Example 1: It is used in the following verse to convey uncertainty:

> NAS John 18:28 They led Jesus therefore from Caiaphas into the Praetorium, and it was early; and they themselves did not enter into the Praetorium in order that they might not be defiled, but **might eat** the Passover.

On the day of the Crucifixion, Jewish guards wouldn't enter the Praetorium judgment hall lest they become ritually unclean according to Mosaic law and thereby unable to eat the Passover. Probably believing that Christ would be killed by the Roman prefect Pilate, a man not known for tolerating dissent (Luke 13:1), the guards refrained from entering a structure that could contain a dead body in order that they "***might*** not be defiled." They did not enter in, so that they "***might*** eat" (subjunctive mood in Greek) the Passover later that day.

Example 2: Jesus uses the subjunctive when he speaks to the woman at Jacob's well, where he refers to "whoever ***may drink***" of the water that he will give. This indicates

---

274 Robertson and Davis, *New Short Grammar*, p. 309.
275 Dana and Mantey, *A Manual Grammar of the Greek New Testament*, p. 170.
276 Wallace, *The Basics of New Testament Syntax,* p. 201.

that the drinking is conditional and based on the choice of each individual; not all will choose to drink. Jesus does not actually have natural water to give but is pointing to spiritual drink:

> YLT John 4:14a but whoever **may drink** of the water that I will give …

Example 3: The subjunctive is also used in John 6:5, when Jesus knows the disciples had nowhere near enough money to buy sufficient bread so that the great multitude "***may* eat**."

> KJV John 6:5–7 When Jesus then lifted up *his* eyes, and saw a great company come unto him, he saith unto Philip, Whence shall we buy bread, that these **may eat**? And this he said to prove him: for he himself knew what he would do. Philip answered him, Two hundred pennyworth of bread is not sufficient for them, that every one of them may take a little.

This is like being on a long hike with only two dollars in your wallet, coming across 5,000 hungry people, and having your friend ask you, "Where should we buy food so all these people might eat?" With no store for miles and hardly any money to buy food, the impossibility of the question would be readily apparent. However, verse 7 above shows that Jesus is only testing Philip, for Jesus knows that he himself will supply the bread. The subjunctive illustrates the unreality of the question.

Example 4: A few more scriptures in John 6 bring out the subjunctive's aspect of unreality particularly well. One of them is verse 51, in which Jesus speaks of himself as being bread that the multitudes "***may eat***."

> YLT John 6:51a 'I am the living bread that came down out of the heaven; if any one **may eat** of this bread he shall live—to the age[277]

Jesus has been dealing with a stubborn group who received the bread that he multiplied out by the thousands the previous day, and who then return the next day wanting more. When Jesus points out that they aren't coming to be close to where God's spirit is moving but only to get more free bread (verse 26), they essentially tempt Jesus to be like Moses and give bread each day, as when the manna came down from heaven (verses 30–32). After he tells them that he is "the living bread that came down from heaven" (the true spiritual manna), Jesus uses the subjunctive

---

277 "To the age" means eternally here.

to say that they "***may*** eat" of this bread—meaning that his teaching is spiritual food from heaven—and live.[278]

Subjunctive Mood Used by Jesus in Reference to Eating the Passover

Notice below how every time Jesus is quoted speaking about actually *eating* the Passover, he uses this Greek subjunctive mood ("may eat" or "might eat") to imply doubt, uncertainty, or even unreality:

> [NAS] Mark 14:14   and wherever he enters, say to the owner of the house, 'The Teacher says, "Where is My guest room in which I **may eat** the Passover with My disciples?"'

> [GNT] Mark 14:14   καὶ ὅπου ἐὰν εἰσέλθῃ εἴπατε τῷ οἰκοδεσπότῃ ὅτι Ὁ διδάσκαλος λέγει, Ποῦ ἐστιν τὸ κατάλυμά μου ὅπου τὸ πάσχα μετὰ τῶν μαθητῶν μου **φάγω**;

Had Jesus truly believed he was going to eat the Passover, he would have used the Greek indicative (the mood of certainty) above to say "will eat" instead of the subjunctive ("may eat").

Remember that Jesus gives his disciples these directions only *after* they finally come to him asking where they should prepare for Passover. In Luke, Jesus is also quoted using the subjunctive (translated below as "may eat"):

> [NAS] Luke 22:8   And He sent Peter and John, saying, "Go and prepare the Passover for us, that we **may eat** it."

> [GNT] Luke 22:8   καὶ ἀπέστειλεν Πέτρον καὶ Ἰωάννην εἰπών, Πορευθέντες ἑτοιμάσατε ἡμῖν τὸ πάσχα ἵνα **φάγωμεν**.

> [NAS] Luke 22:11   "And you shall say to the owner of the house, 'The Teacher says to you, "Where is the guest room in which I **may eat** the Passover with My disciples?"'"

> [GNT] Luke 22:11   καὶ ἐρεῖτε τῷ οἰκοδεσπότῃ τῆς οἰκίας, Λέγει σοι ὁ διδάσκαλος, Ποῦ ἐστιν τὸ κατάλυμα ὅπου τὸ πάσχα μετὰ τῶν μαθητῶν μου **φάγω**;

---

278 John also quotes Jesus using the subjunctive again in verses 53 and 54, where the eating and drinking are obviously unreal in the natural or literal sense but meant as spiritual truth.

Again, Jesus does not say that he *will* eat (indicative) the Passover, but rather he "*may* eat" (subjunctive), implying doubt or unreality. Jesus knows that he is the lamb of God—the true Passover—and therefore that he won't be around to eat the Passover lamb:

> DBY Matthew 26:2 Ye know that after two days **the passover** takes place, **and the Son of man is delivered up to be crucified**.

Although Jesus tells his disciples he will be crucified at Passover, and he had previously mentioned his impending death a few times already, his disciples still cannot fathom that the Messiah is actually going to die:

> NAS Mark 9:31 For He was teaching His disciples and telling them, "The Son of Man is to be delivered into the hands of men, and they will kill Him; and when He has been killed, He will rise three days later."

> NAS Mark 9:32 But **they did not understand *this* statement**, and they were afraid to ask Him.

In Luke, Jesus again expresses these things:

> NAS Luke 18:32–33 "For He will be delivered to the Gentiles, and will be mocked and mistreated and spit upon, and after they have scourged Him, they will kill Him; and the third day He will rise again."

> NAS Luke 18:34 And **they understood none of these things**, and this saying was hidden from them, and they **did not comprehend** the things that were said.

Since his disciples cannot bear to hear about his death at Passover, they come asking him about the all-important preparation for Passover:

> KJV Matthew 26:17 Now the first *day* of the *feast of* unleavened bread the **disciples came to Jesus**, saying unto him, Where wilt thou that **we prepare** for thee to eat the passover?

Because Jewish laws required leaven to be removed and the body and soul to be ritually cleansed before the Passover, the disciples are really asking "at what location do we ***ritually prepare***, so that we all might eat the Passover the following day (the 14th) at the proper time that God commanded (John 18:28)?" They are certainly not asking at which location they should ritually prepare so they can slay an *illegal* Passover today on the 13th day and eat it *illegally* tonight at the Last Supper.

Jesus does not find it necessary to convince his disciples that he will be crucified at Passover, so he partly goes along with their idea of preparing for the Passover. Yet in every scripture he subtly uses the subjunctive mood when he speaks of his "eating" the Passover, in case anyone is willing to hear with spiritual ears. Jesus may also harbor a slight hope that God can find a way out for him, for he prays in the garden to ask that he not have to pay the eternal penalty for sin:

> ^{NAS}Matthew 26:39 And He went a little beyond *them*, and fell on His face and prayed, saying, "My Father, if it is possible, let this cup pass from Me; yet not as I will, but as Thou wilt."

Indicative Mood Used to "Perform" the Passover

Matthew 26:18 contains the only occurrence of Jesus using the indicative mood (the mood of certainty) in the context of his keeping this Passover. However, the crucial difference in this one instance is that the Greek he uses refers to his actual *accomplishing* of the Passover (not his eating of it):

> ^{NIV}Matthew 26:18 He replied, "Go into the city to a certain man and tell him, 'The Teacher says: My appointed time is near. I am going to celebrate the Passover with my disciples **at your house**'" [279]

> ^{YLT}Matthew 26:18 and he said, 'Go away to the city, unto such a one, and say to him, The Teacher saith, **My time is nigh**; **near thee** I **keep** the passover, with my disciples;'

> ^{GNT}Matthew 26:18 ὁ δὲ εἶπεν, Ὑπάγετε εἰς τὴν πόλιν πρὸς τὸν δεῖνα καὶ εἴπατε αὐτῷ, Ὁ διδάσκαλος λέγει, Ὁ καιρός μου ἐγγύς ἐστιν, πρὸς σὲ **ποιῶ** τὸ πάσχα μετὰ τῶν μαθητῶν μου.

The *UBS Greek-Lexicon* shows that the word ποιω can mean "make, do, cause, effect, bring about, *accomplish*, perform, keep, etc." Notice that Jesus ties in "my time is nigh" to the coming Passover that he will accomplish/perform tomorrow on the 14th

---

[279] Many English translations of this scripture portray Jesus saying he will "eat" (or keep/celebrate) the Passover at this man's "house." But you can see that Young's Literal Translation of this verse is more accurate, using "near thee" instead of "at your house," since the Greek word "house" is not in the original scripture.

day. In this one time that he uses the indicative mood, he doesn't say that he will "eat" but rather that he will "*effect, bring about, accomplish, perform*" the Passover.

Note that Matthew 26:18 does not contradict Matthew 26:2 (in which Jesus declared that he would be crucified at the Passover) because Jesus would indeed "accomplish" the Passover when he was crucified as the *true* Passover on the 14th day. As the early Messianic Fourteenthers understood, the Messiah would keep the evening portion[280] of this 14th day with his disciples during the Last Supper and until his arrest. Then he would accomplish/bring about the fulfillment of this 14th-day Passover at his crucifixion. This occurred at the appointed time and day foreknown by God and commanded to Moses:

> NAS Acts 2:23   this *Man*, delivered up by the **predetermined plan** and **foreknowledge of God**, you nailed to a cross by the hands of godless men and put *Him* to death.

In the law of Moses, a first-fruits offering to God would follow the Passover sacrifice on the "morrow of the Sabbath" (i.e., the Sunday following Passover, Leviticus 23:10, 11). Paul called Jesus the Passover (1 Corinthians 5:7) and also the "first fruits" (1 Corinthians 15:20, 23).

Jesus knew that he would be crucified at this Passover as the true lamb of God and rise three days later as the first fruits to God on Sunday, fulfilling this typology. God, by His foreknowledge, knew the time and day that His son would be offered up as the true Passover to pay the price for our sins. God also knew the day He would resurrect him, and He commanded Moses concerning these sacrifices and offerings accordingly.

Double Negative Adds Extra Emphasis

In telling his disciples that he is going to be rejected, killed, and crucified at Passover, Jesus uses the subjunctive mood each time he speaks of his *eating* the Passover. Now, at the Last Supper, we can see that he truly does *desire* to eat the Passover with them:

> KJV Luke 22:15   And he said unto them, **With desire I have desired to eat this Passover** with you **before I suffer**:

> GNT Luke 22:15   καὶ εἶπεν πρὸς αὐτούς, Ἐπιθυμίᾳ ἐπεθύμησα τοῦτο τὸ πάσχα φαγεῖν μεθ' ὑμῶν πρὸ τοῦ με παθεῖν·

---

280   The 12-hour evening portion came first in the Jewish idiom (Genesis 1:5). For more on the early Messianic believers, see the chapter "Setting the Table 1."

404 | The Messianic Feast

The Greek emphasizes his desire to eat the Passover by structuring his words as a double positive ("with desire I have desired"). However, in the next sentence Jesus uses the double negative—the strongest form of Greek negation—to make it clear that he will *not* eat the Passover with his disciples, because tomorrow he will give his life and suffer as the true lamb:

> KJV Luke 22:16 For I say unto you, I will **not** any more **eat** thereof, **until it be fulfilled in the kingdom of God.**

> NAS Luke 22:16 for I say to you, I shall never again eat it until it is fulfilled in the kingdom of God."

> GNT Luke 22:16 λέγω γὰρ ὑμῖν ὅτι οὐ μὴ φάγω αὐτὸ ἕως ὅτου πληρωθῇ ἐν τῇ βασιλείᾳ τοῦ θεοῦ.

Although the two English translations above contain the words "any more" and "never again" respectively, these words do not appear in the original Greek; they were added by English translators. It's important to understand that the vast majority of Bible commentators—from the time the Roman Church gained control until the Protestant Reformation and beyond—believe that Jesus ate the Passover at this Last Supper and was then crucified the following day (on Friday the 15th day). Therefore they needed to translate these verses to fit the theology as they understood it.

This explains how the words "any more" were added to portray that Jesus *did eat* it this time, but that he would not eat it "any more." The big problem is that you cannot simply add words that are not contained in the meaning of the original Greek scripture.

The only translation I've found that does not add "any more," "never again," etc., to this verse is the New Jerusalem Bible:

> NJB Luke 22:16 because, I tell you, I shall **not eat it** until it is fulfilled in the kingdom of God.'

The actual Greek in this scripture reads, "not not *will* I eat it," using the double negative to emphasize the negation. Greek grammar experts Dana and Mantey wrote:

> When special stress is placed upon a negative proposition, the subjunctive is used with οὐ μή.[281]

---

281 Dana and Mantey, *A Manual Grammar of the Greek New Testament*, p. 172.

William D. Mounce also addresses this double negative combination:

> This chapter describes a fascinating combination used by the Greek language to show emphasis: it is the use of the two negatives οὐ μη, with a subjunctive verb to indicate a strong negation about something in the future. The speaker uses the subjunctive verb to suggest a future possibility, but in the same phrase he **emphatically denies** (by means of the double negative) **that such could ever happen**.[282]

This double negative with a subjunctive is the exact combination used in the Greek of Luke 22:16 above.

If Jesus had intended to eat the Passover that night before he suffered, he would instead have said something like, "I've greatly desired to eat this Passover with you before my suffering, and thankfully I'll get to eat it tonight at my Last Supper, because my suffering begins in just over 12 hours. Since my suffering doesn't start until tomorrow, I therefore *will* eat the Passover before my suffering."

However, since his suffering would precede the eating of the Passover, Jesus would no longer be with his disciples when the time came for eating. He would be on the cross at the exact time the nation was preparing to sacrifice its lambs, so how could he possibly be present to eat the Passover? With Jesus using the strongest emphasis the Greek language allows to say he would *not* eat this Passover before his suffering, why do commentators disagree with him and say that he not only *will* but that he *did* eat this Passover before he suffered?

Key 2: The Dative of Reference

The second Greek key that unlocks the Gospels as to whether or not the Last Supper was the Passover is the "dative of reference." We will pay particular attention to the Greek article translated as "on the" in these vital scriptures, where the disciples came to Jesus and asked him their question about preparing for the Passover:

> NAS Matthew 26:17 Now **on the** first *day* of Unleavened Bread the disciples came to Jesus, saying, "Where do You want us to prepare for You to eat the Passover?"

> NIV Matthew 26:17 **On the** first day of the Feast of Unleavened Bread, the disciples came to Jesus and asked, "Where do you want us to make preparations for you to eat the Passover?"

---

[282] Mounce, *Basics of Biblical Greek Grammar*, p. 288.

> ᵞᴸᵀ Matthew 26:17   And **on the** first *day* of the unleavened food came the disciples near to Jesus, saying to him, 'Where wilt thou *that* we may prepare for thee to eat the passover?'

Although the following King James translation of this verse does not say "on the," it still doesn't bring out the true meaning of the Greek dative article here, leaving the reader to think the question was actually posed *on* this day:

> ᴷᴶⱽ Matthew 26:17   Now the first *day* of the *feast of* unleavened bread the disciples came to Jesus, saying unto him, Where wilt thou that we may prepare for thee to eat the passover?

Furthermore, the English translations of Mark *seem* to make the exact day even clearer, saying that the disciples came to Jesus **on the** first day of the unleavened bread, ***when they sacrificed the Passover*** (which would have been the 14th day):

> ᴺᴸᵀ Mark 14:12   **On the** first day of the Festival of Unleavened Bread (**the day the Passover lambs were sacrificed**), Jesus' disciples asked him, "Where do you want us to go to prepare the Passover supper?"

> ᴺᴬˢ Mark 14:12   And **on the** first day of Unleavened Bread, **when the Passover *lamb* was being sacrificed**, His disciples said to Him, "Where do You want us to go and prepare for You to eat the Passover?"

> ᴺᴵⱽ Mark 14:12   **On the** first day of the Feast of Unleavened Bread, **when it was customary to sacrifice the Passover lamb**, Jesus' disciples asked him, "Where do you want us to go and make preparations for you to eat the Passover?"

It's important to know that the words "Festival," "Feast," and "Bread" have been added to certain English translations of Matthew 26:17 and Mark 14:12; these words are not in the original Greek. What the Greek says is, "the first day of the unleavened," which was the day to sacrifice the lamb. This was also the "first" of these eight unleavened days (as is fully explained in the chapter "The Template Challenge" under the subsection "The 13th-Day Question"). However, the insertion of those words into the English translations could even change the meaning from referring to the "first day of the unleavened" (the 14th day) to the "first day of the Feast of Unleavened Bread" (which could have other meanings).

It couldn't be more obvious to those familiar with first-century Jewish idioms and laws that the day to sacrifice the Passover was the 14th day of Nisan between noon and sundown (see the chapter "Between the Evenings"). Yet, if we accept these English translations as accurate, Jesus *would have* eaten the Passover with his disciples that night at the Last Supper, after sacrificing it on the proper 14th day. Jesus would then have been arrested, tried, and crucified on the 15th Jewish day—the special high Sabbath that always follows the 14th-day slaying of the Passover. This is what most commentators have accepted from the time of the Jewish disconnect in Rome. And this is some of what we wrestled with in class in the master's program in Bible college 30 years ago, as mentioned in this book's introduction. These two scriptures (along with the others now explained by the three keys in this chapter) clearly *seemed* to prove that the Last Supper *was* the Passover.

However, on the other side, more than 50 reasons exist (see the next chapter) why the Last Supper *could not* have been the Passover. An understanding of Jewish laws would prove beyond the shadow of a doubt that crucifying Jesus on the 15th-day special Sabbath would have been impossible. This special rest day commanded by God to commemorate the Jews' deliverance from slavery in Egypt was not a legal time to carry clubs and swords to arrest Jesus and then push for his crucifixion to occur (Matthew 26:55). Nor would that 15th-day Sabbath have been a legal time for his Jewish burial. Then there would be the conundrum of Jesus and his disciples eating regular "bread" at what we are told was the Passover (see Course 1).

A few of these points have been debated by scholars for years, with many coming to the conclusion that the Gospel of John (which tells of Jesus *being crucified as* the true Passover lamb) contradicts the other three Gospels that so clearly *seem* to show Jesus *eating* the Passover.

How the Dative of Reference Unlocked the Door

When the Greek is translated as originally intended in Matthew 26:17 and Mark 14:12 using the dative of reference, the text in both scriptures reads "with reference to the" first day. Matthew and Mark were not saying they were currently "on the" 14th day.

One day in 2002, I was in church listening to a sermon when the pastor mentioned that Westcott and Hort's literal translation (as seen in *The Kingdom Interlinear Translation of the Greek Scriptures*) is often much better at staying true to the meaning of the Greek articles and prepositions than many other translations. I had not heard this before and had not previously been using the Westcott and Hort version in my studies, but since I was still learning Greek, I'd begun taking it to church to read along. After hearing his statement, I turned to the problem verses of this Bible controversy that I'd been studying intermittently for some 20 years to see if the *Interlinear Translation* could offer any hints as to the Last Supper being the Passover or not.

To my amazement I found that in *both scriptures* the Greek *Interlinear Translation* said "to the" first day (translating the Greek article τῇ), meaning "with reference to the" and not "on the" first day. This was the only Bible translation where I had ever seen this. I could barely stop myself from jumping out of my seat to go home and research it right away, for after all these years of study and searching I believed that here was finally a major key to solve this controversy. When my eye first saw "to the" in this translation I felt certain I had finally found the key to unlock these scriptures.

Below is the English translation given word for word directly under the Greek text in Matthew 26:17:[283]

Τῇ	δὲ	πρώτῃ	τῶν	ἀζύμων		προσῆλθον	οἱ μαθηταὶ
To the	but	first [day]	of the	unfermented cakes		came toward	the disciples

τῷ	Ἰησοῦ	λέγοντες	Ποῦ	θέλεις	ἑτοιμάσωμέν	σοι
to the	Jesus	saying	where	are you willing	we should prepare	to you

φαγεῖν	τὸ	πάσχα;
to eat	the	Passover?

The same dative article is used in Mark 14:12:[284]

Καὶ	τῇ	πρώτῃ	ἡμέρᾳ	τῶν	ἀζύμων,	ὅτε τὸ πάσχα
And	**to the**	first	day	of the	unfermented (cakes),	when the Passover

ἔθυον,
they were sacrificing,

λέγουσιν	αὐτῷ	οἱ μαθηταὶ	αὐτοῦ	Ποῦ	θέλεις	ἀπελθόντες
are saying	to him	the disciples	of him	Where	are you willing	having gone off

ἑτοιμάσωμεν
we should prepare

ἵνα	φάγῃς	τὸ	πάσχα;
in order that	you might eat	the	Passover?

The article τη ("to the") is in the Greek dative case, as are the words "first" and "day." Here, this dative of reference means "with reference to the" first day, or "concerning

---

283 Westcott and Hort, from the *Kingdom Interlinear*, p. 154.
284 Westcott and Hort, from the *Kingdom Interlinear*, p. 246.

the" first day; it does *not* say it was "**on** the" first day. Despite my initial excitement when I first saw "to the," I was uncertain as to its full meaning, since the dative of reference had never been taught in any Greek class I had attended. After searching a few Greek grammar books to no avail on what "to the" might mean, I eventually found this explained in Daniel Wallace's *Greek Grammar Beyond the Basics*. His excellent book elaborates on this aspect of the dative under the subheading "Dative of Reference/Respect [with reference to]," where he explains:

> Instead of the word *to,* supply the phrase **with reference to** before the dative. (Other glosses are *concerning, about, in regard to, etc.*)[285]

Here is a paraphrase of what the Greek actually means in these scriptures, using the dative of reference and considering the Jewish idioms, God's laws, and the ritual preparations needed for this Festival:

> Matthew 26:17   Now **with reference to the** first of the unleavened the disciples came to Jesus, saying unto him, Where wilt thou that we prepare for thee to eat the Passover?

> Mark 14:12   **With reference to the** first day of the unleavened (**the day the Passover lambs were sacrificed**), Jesus' disciples asked him, "Where do you want us to go to prepare the Passover?"

Or, we could just as correctly translate this dative of reference as "concerning the":

> Mark 14:12   ***Concerning the***[286] first day of the unleavened (**the day the Passover lambs were sacrificed**), Jesus' disciples asked him, "Where do you want us to go to prepare the Passover?"

Translating these scriptures using "with reference to the" or "concerning the"—instead of "on the"—retains the true meaning of this Greek dative here. It was "with reference to" these Jewish ritual purification requirements that the disciples came to

---

285   Wallace, *Greek Grammar Beyond the Basics*, p. 145.

286   Although Τη δε in Matthew 26:17 is sometimes translated as "on the," in Mark 14:12 only τη is in the actual Greek scripture, which can only be translated as "to the" (see the Greek of these scriptures above). Since Matthew 26:17 is the exact same context, it would mean that its correct translation is also "to the," especially when bearing in mind the 50 reasons I give later as to why the Last Supper could not have been the Passover. Thus, both scriptures should be accurately translated using the Greek dative of reference.

Jesus asking where they should ritually prepare so that they may have a legal place to eat the Passover on the following 14th day.

Greek scholar William D. Mounce points out that "to" is the primary word when considering the meaning of the dative.[287] So if you were trying to communicate that Sam went to the store, then "to the" would be a Greek article in the dative case. If you wanted to convey that Sam sat "on the" store, then another Greek construction would be used. And Wallace's Greek work delves deeper by identifying the dative of reference as a separate category within the dative. Thus the dative of reference gives another nuance, such that if Sam visited the store "with reference to" his bounced check, then it would be evident that the Greek article in the dative case was bringing out that aspect of "with reference to."

Wallace also states that the King James Version is weak regarding nuances of the Greek article:

> As a side note, it should be mentioned that the KJV translators often erred in their treatment of the article. They were more comfortable with the Latin than with the Greek. Since there is no article in the Latin, the KJV translators **frequently missed the nuances of the Greek article**.[288]

Most translators follow the same belief held by the King James translators (namely that Jesus ate the Passover at the Last Supper) and therefore they translate this Greek article as "on the."

The Greek scholar A. T. Robertson also comments on the inaccuracy of the King James Version:

> The translators of the King James Version, under the influence of the Vulgate,[289] handle the Greek article loosely and inaccurately.[290]

He continues:

> The vital thing is to see the matter from the Greek point of view and find the reason for the use of the article.[291]

---

287 Mounce, *Basics of Biblical Greek Grammar*, p. 45.
288 Wallace, *Greek Grammar Beyond the Basics*, pp. 208–209.
289 The Vulgate is the Latin translation.
290 Robertson, *A Grammar of the Greek New Testament*, p. 756.
291 Robertson, *A Grammar of the Greek New Testament*, pp. 756–757.

I would add to his statement that, when translating the Greek article, we also need to understand and accept the first-century idioms and laws of the almost exclusively Jewish writers of the Greek New Testament. If commentators believe in the tradition of Jesus eating the Passover at the Last Supper, then they would have an existing bias that would affect their English translations accordingly.

More Dative-of-Reference Examples

Now let's see this dative of reference used in other scriptures:

> ᴺᴬˢ Romans 6:11 Even so consider yourselves to be dead **to sin**, but alive **to God** in Christ Jesus.

> ᴳᴺᵀ Romans 6:11 οὕτως καὶ ὑμεῖς λογίζεσθε ἑαυτοὺς [εἶναι] νεκροὺς μὲν τῇ ἁμαρτίᾳ ζῶντας δὲ τῷ θεῷ ἐν Χριστῷ Ἰησοῦ.

In the above verses, "to sin" and "to God" are in the dative case. An even clearer translation using the dative of reference means "dead *with reference to* sin" (or "*concerning* sin," or "*in regard* to sin") and "alive *with reference to*" or "*concerning* God." However, if we translate this verse the same way that many English translations have done with Matthew 26:17 and Mark 14:12, then it would read "consider yourselves to be dead **on the** sin" and "alive **on the** God."

Here's another example:

> ᴷᴶⱽ Luke 18:31 Then he took *unto him* the twelve, and said unto them, Behold, we go up to Jerusalem, and all things that are written by the prophets **concerning the** Son of man shall be accomplished.

> ᴳᴺᵀ Luke 18:31 Παραλαβὼν δὲ τοὺς δώδεκα εἶπεν πρὸς αὐτούς, Ἰδοὺ ἀναβαίνομεν εἰς Ἰερουσαλήμ, καὶ τελεσθήσεται πάντα τὰ γεγραμμένα διὰ τῶν προφητῶν τῷ υἱῷ τοῦ ἀνθρώπου·

The Greek article translated as "concerning the" is in the dative case. We would not translate this verse as "all things that are written by the prophets **on the** Son of man"; the King James version translated it correctly here, bringing out the nuance of this dative of reference by saying "concerning the Son of man." This is the same way Matthew 26:17 and Mark 14:12 should have been understood and translated.

What Were the Disciples Really Asking?

When Matthew 26:17 and Mark 14:12 are translated correctly, we see that the Jewish disciples find themselves a day before the Passover lamb sacrifice with still no direction from the Messiah on where they should prepare or gather at Passover to eat the lamb. The disciples are likely confused or even hurt by this, for they know how hard it is to find a suitable location at this late hour. They also need time to make preparations as required under Jewish law.

Still today many Orthodox Jews spend huge amounts of time and effort preparing for Passover—even boiling all bowls, utensils, or other items that may have had remote contact with leaven during the year. The Messiah's disciples certainly knew the laws of Moses, the necessary ritual preparations, the bodily immersions in water, and all other requirements for this Festival.

Some English translations bring out this aspect of making ready for Passover:

> NAB Luke 22:8   he sent out Peter and John, instructing them, "Go and **make preparations** for us to eat the Passover."

This was not akin to eating a pilgrim Thanksgiving dinner where "prepare fixin's" would mean to cook the dinner, so we should be careful not interpret this text as "cooking the Passover." The disciples were not asking, "Where should we prepare and cook the Passover lamb for supper tonight?" for they knew the sacrifice and roasting would happen tomorrow, on the 14th day. Instead, their question addressed the need to find and then sanctify a location and themselves. They may have also needed to purchase certain items and have them ready at that location.

This is why they came to Jesus on the 13th day to ask their question that was *with reference to* the first of the unleavened days, (i.e., the 14th day when the Passover was to be sacrificed, which also was the first of those eight unleavened days). They then asked, "Where do you want us to make preparations" (Matthew 26:17 NIV). As Jews under God's laws, certain ceremonial cleansings in body and heart were needed before one was prepared for Passover:

> NIV John 11:55   When it was almost time for the Jewish Passover, many went up from the country to Jerusalem for their **ceremonial cleansing** before the Passover.

We see the same phenomenon in King Hezekiah's day, where a revival of sorts was occurring and letters were written to all in Israel to come and celebrate the Passover. Although it was extremely important that preparations were carried out as prescribed by God, many Israelites had not made the appropriate consecrations and purifications:

> ^{JPS} 2 Chronicles 30:17 For there were many in the congregation that **had not sanctified themselves**; therefore the Levites had the charge of killing the passover lambs for every one that was not clean, to sanctify them unto the LORD.

> ^{JPS} 2 Chronicles 30:18 For a multitude of the people, even many of Ephraim and Manasseh, Issachar and Zebulun, **had not cleansed themselves**, yet did they eat the passover otherwise than it is written. For Hezekiah had prayed for them, saying: 'The good LORD pardon

The disciples who asked Jesus their question were concerned with these same things, as well as the need for the removal of all leaven, which they would have fully completed after the Last Supper (at which they ate regular leavened bread). The quotes from historians in the Talmud[292] showed that the Jews understood all leaven needed to be banished at the start of the sixth hour (11 AM) on the 14th day, because the legal time to begin the Passover sacrifices was *after* noon, as commanded by God. They knew this was the time to remove the leaven because of the scriptures given by Moses, where God directed for no leaven to be on hand when the blood of the Passover was being shed:

> ^{DBY} Exodus 34:25 Thou shalt not offer the blood of my sacrifice with leaven; neither shall the sacrifice of the feast of the passover be left over night until the morning.

The Gospels Do Not Contradict Each Other

The dative of reference has helped show that the Gospels do not contradict each other; therefore we should not be surprised that these anointed scripture writers were also in perfect agreement that the day of the Crucifixion was the 14th day.

The Greek scholar Brooke Foss Westcott points out that all four Gospels agree that the day Jesus was crucified was the day of preparation (*paraskeuy* in Greek).[293] Westcott adds that although many scholars think that *paraskeuy* is the Greek word for "Friday," there was also a preparation day (*paraskeuy*) before each of the seven Festival Sabbaths and depending on the year, these could fall on any day of the week—not just Fridays. *The Jewish Encyclopedia* also makes clear that *paraskeuy* is

---

292 As seen in the subsection "The 13th-Day Question" in the chapter "The Template Challenge."
293 Westcott, *Introduction to the Study of the Gospels*, p. 343.

not only the preparation day before Saturday Sabbaths, but also the preparation day before any of these festival (holiday/holy day) Sabbaths:

> The eve of Jewish holidays is therefore not the evening of the festival, but the day preceding it; in conversation, the expression "'ereb yom tob" is even extended to denote an indefinite period **preceding the holiday**. It is observed as a day on which is prepared (*paraskeuy*) such work as it is not permitted to do **on the holiday or on the Sabbath**.[294]

The writers of the four Gospels agree that the Crucifixion day was a *paraskeuy* (Matthew 27:62; Mark 15:42; Luke 23:54; John 19:14, 19, 31, 42), and therefore it definitely could not have been the 15th-day high Sabbath (that always follows the 14th-day Passover). The 15th-day Sabbath rest would *never* be called the "preparation" for a Sabbath, for it was itself one of the most revered Sabbaths in Jewish history, a day God commanded to be kept in remembrance of His bringing Israel out of Egypt.

Since these Gospel writers all agree that the day following the Last Supper was the *paraskeuy*, they could not possibly have confused the Last Supper with Passover. After all, had the Last Supper been the Passover, they would have known the following day would be the 15th-day Sabbath—and they never would have called it a "preparation" day.[295]

The *BDAG Greek-English Lexicon* also shows that the Greek word translated as "**preparation**" in those scriptures speaks of a definite day:

> "only of a definite day, **as the *day of preparation* for a festival**."[296]

The *Greek-English Lexicon of the New Testament* by Louw and Nida also bears this out:

> 67.201 παρασκευή, ῆς *f*: a day on which preparations were made for **a sacred or feast day** – 'day of preparation, Friday…. The identification of παρασκευή with Friday became so traditional that it eventually came to be the present-day Greek term for 'Friday.'[297]

---

294 *The Jewish Encyclopedia*, vol. 5, p. 276.
295 More information about the above scriptures on the *paraskeuy*, where these verses are written out, can be found in the chapter "50 Reasons the Last Supper Was Not the Passover," in the section "The Gospels All Agree."
296 Bauer, *A Greek-English Lexicon of the New Testament and Other Early Christian Literature (BDAG)*, 3rd ed., p. 771.
297 Louw and Nida, *Greek-English Lexicon of the New Testament Based on Semantic Domains*, vol. 1, p. 654.

Roman Catholic theologians and others have argued that *paraskeuy* means "Friday" in these scriptures and that Jesus was therefore crucified on "Good Friday." By being unaware that this Jewish day of preparation happens before *any* Sabbath (not just the day before the Saturday Sabbath), they have misguidedly taken this Greek word as proof that Jesus was crucified on Friday. All seven of the special high Sabbaths connected to the Festivals—including the Day of Atonement—are preceded by a day of preparation.

To continue, Liddell and Scott's *A Greek-English Lexicon* states how the Jews use this Greek word *paraskeuy*:

> **among the Jews**, *the day of Preparation,* **the day before the sabbath of the Passover**,[298]

The following verses from John fit perfectly with Liddell and Scott's definition, showing that the Crucifixion day was not just any *paraskeuy*, but the preparation for (the 15th-day high Sabbath of) the Passover:

> NAS John 19:14   Now it was the day of **preparation** for **the Passover**; it was about the sixth hour. And he said to the Jews, "Behold, your King!"

> GNT John 19:14   ἦν δὲ **παρασκευὴ** τοῦ πάσχα, ὥρα ἦν ὡς ἕκτη. καὶ λέγει τοῖς Ἰουδαίοις, Ἴδε ὁ βασιλεὺς ὑμῶν.

> NAS John 19:31   The Jews therefore, because it was the day of **preparation**, so that the bodies should not remain on the cross on the Sabbath (**for that Sabbath was a high *day***), asked Pilate that their legs might be broken, and *that* they might be taken away.[299]

> GNT John 19:31   Οἱ οὖν Ἰουδαῖοι, ἐπεὶ **παρασκευὴ** ἦν, ἵνα μὴ μείνῃ ἐπὶ τοῦ σταυροῦ τὰ σώματα ἐν τῷ σαββάτῳ, ἦν γὰρ μεγάλη ἡ ἡμέρα ἐκείνου τοῦ σαββάτου, ἠρώτησαν τὸν Πιλᾶτον ἵνα κατεαγῶσιν αὐτῶν τὰ σκέλη καὶ ἀρθῶσιν.

---

298   Liddell and Scott, *A Greek-English Lexicon*, p. 1324.

299   For those who may not be familiar with the timing of this scripture, it is occurring on the day of the Crucifixion, and the 15th-day high Sabbath is soon coming and begins at sundown.

The following scripture bears this out as well, showing that this 14th-day Crucifixion was the day before the (15th-day festival) Sabbath, where the preparation was *pro-sabbaton* (προσάββατον), meaning "before Sabbath":

> ᴺᴬˢ Mark 15:42   And when evening had already come, because it was the preparation day, that is, the day before the Sabbath,³⁰⁰

> ᴳᴺᵀ Mark 15:42   Καὶ ἤδη ὀψίας γενομένης, ἐπεὶ ἦν **παρασκευὴ** ὅ ἐστιν **προσάββατον**,

To recap, the dative of reference shows that the disciples came to ask Jesus their question on the 13th day (Wednesday that year) and that he was crucified on the 14th day (Thursday). This 14th day was the preparation day (*paraskeuy*) for the 15th-day high Sabbath (Friday that year), which was shown coming at the end of this Crucifixion day. When the original Greek in these scriptures is understood correctly, we see the four Gospels are in complete agreement, as we should expect.

❦

Before we move on to the third key, one more point should be clarified, because it can get confusing in English. Many translations use the word "prepare" for what Jesus and his disciples were speaking about on the 13th day:

> ʸᴸᵀ Luke 22:8   and he sent Peter and John, saying, 'Having gone on, **prepare** to us the passover, that we may eat;'

> ᴺᴬˢ Mark 14:15   "And he himself will show you a large upper room furnished *and* ready; and **prepare** for us there."

The Greek word translated as "prepare" (*etoimazo*³⁰¹) in these scriptures is different from "preparation day" (*paraskeuy*). This *etoimazo* is not the Greek word used for preparing for a Sabbath but a more generic word for getting things ready. On the 14th day many Jewish people would have been at the Temple for the morning offering and the incense and prayers that would accompany it. Then, when the Temple

---

300   The Greek word translated into English as "evening" above actually means "late," i.e., late in the Jewish day, which ended at sunset.
301   The *BDAG* (*A Greek-English Lexicon of the New Testament and Other Early Christian Literature*, 3rd ed.) defines *etoimazo* as "to cause to be ready, *put/keep in readiness, prepare*" (p. 400).

doors re-opened at noon, they would be busy arriving with their washed Passover lambs. Many things would have been made ready in advance—on this 13th day—so the people could focus on the Passover sacrifice and roasting the following day. The 14th day was not a Sabbath, and the word translated as "prepare" in these scriptures was *etoimazo* (not the *paraskeuy* day that occurs before a Sabbath).

As was mentioned, the disciples are also concerned about becoming ceremonially clean to enter the Temple for tomorrow's Passover sacrifice and preparing the location (possibly also beginning the process of removing leaven).

> NAS Mark 14:16 And the disciples went out, and came to the city, and found *it* just as He had told them; and **they prepared the Passover**.

> NAS Mark 14:17 And **when it was evening** He came **with the twelve**.

In saying that they prepared (*etoimazon*) the Passover, verse 16 could imply to some that Peter and John sacrificed and cooked an illegal Passover on this 13th day, then went out to be with Jesus and the others during the remainder of that day (supposedly leaving the roasted Passover on the table). Then in verse 17, all of them came back later to the Passover that had been "prepared" and roasted earlier and was supposedly cold and waiting for them on the table.

However, this is not what these Greek words convey here; they only mean that Peter and John prepared the location and had certain things in order, possibly including their own required ceremonial cleansings for tomorrow's Passover sacrifice. After Peter and John finished these preparations, they went to where Jesus and the others were gathered, and sometime toward the end of that day, they all returned to that location for the Last Supper.

Key 3: The Aorist Tense

One final verse needs to be explained for the scriptures to harmonize with the Jewish feast template and to align with the many proofs that the Last Supper was not the Passover. That verse is Luke 22:7:

> NIV Luke 22:7 **Then came** the day of Unleavened Bread on which the Passover lamb had to be sacrificed.

> GNT Luke 22:7 Ἦλθεν δὲ ἡ ἡμέρα τῶν ἀζύμων, [ἐν] ᾗ ἔδει θύεσθαι τὸ πάσχα·

In the English above, the aorist "*Ἦλθεν*" has been translated as "Then came." In English this implies that the day "then came," and that the disciples sacrificed the Passover that same day, and ate it that night at the Last Supper.

The Greek aorist tense unlocks this important verse so we can correctly understand it. Buist M. Fanning offers this explanation:

> Instead, the aorist tense "**presents an occurrence in summary**, viewed as a whole from the outside, **without regard for the internal make-up of the occurrence**."[302]

In other words, the aorist tense in Greek can set forth a major statement "without regard for the internal make-up" as to the *timing* "of the occurrence" in the narrative by presenting the "occurrence in summary" and then going backward in time to fill in the details.

We can do this in English as well. For example, let's say Grandpa died on Christmas day, and a week later at the memorial service, his son Joe is speaking to a large group of friends and relatives who already know the details of Grandpa's passing. Joe could first give a summary statement and then backfill the details, which all those gathered would understand:

> **Then came** that fateful Christmas day when Grandpa died. All you friends and relatives came from far and wide to spend time with Grandpa and celebrate Christmas. The kids were so excited as we drove through the country picking out the tree, and then we decorated it while Grandma was baking up batches of cookies. At Christmas Eve dinner, all the family rejoiced to be together with Grandpa. As we grown-ups stayed up late making the final preparations and wrapping gifts, the kids lay in bed, dreaming of opening the toys that Santa left for them. As we awoke and shared breakfast, and then later as the children began opening presents, none of us thought that this would be Grandpa's last day.

So you see that Joe gives the initial summary statement ("**Then came** that fateful Christmas day when Grandpa died"), then goes back in time to fill in the details (picking out a tree, decorating, Christmas Eve dinner, etc.) that had taken place *before* the day came that Grandpa died. Since the audience already knows the timeline of Christmas events, they are not confused. They are not thinking that since Joe started with, "Then came that fateful Christmas day when Grandpa died," that he

---

302 Fanning, *Verbal Aspect in New Testament Greek*, p. 97.

was suggesting Grandpa died *before* all those other things had happened (picking out a tree, etc.). "Then came" is the aorist tense at work, "without regard for the internal make-up of the occurrence," as Fanning stated above.

Along this same line, here is a quote from Wallace's excellent *Greek Grammar*:

> The aorist normally views the action *as a whole*, taking no interest in the internal workings of the action. It describes the action in summary fashion, **without focusing on the beginning or end of the action specifically**. This is by far the most common usage of the aorist, especially in the indicative mood. The constative aorist covers a multitude of actions. The event might be iterative in nature, or durative, or momentary, **but the aorist says none of this**.[303]

Before we reconsider the meaning of this aorist tense in Luke 22:7, let's look at some other examples in scripture. We see the same Greek aorist construct in the famous account of Josiah's Passover, which first-century Jews would have been very familiar with from the Greek Septuagint:

> NAS 2 Chronicles 35:1 Then Josiah **celebrated** the Passover to the LORD in Jerusalem, and they **slaughtered** the Passover *animals* on the fourteenth *day* of the first month.

> LXT 2 Chronicles 35:1 καὶ **ἐποίησεν** Ιωσιας τὸ φασεχ τῷ κυρίῳ θεῷ αὐτοῦ καὶ **ἔθυσαν** τὸ φασεχ τῇ τεσσαρεσκαιδεκάτῃ τοῦ μηνὸς τοῦ πρώτου

Notice the way the English translation words this aorist: "Then Josiah celebrated the Passover... and they slaughtered the Passover... on the fourteenth day." Although both words "celebrated" and "slaughtered" are in the aorist tense, these two events did not happen sequentially or simultaneously in verse 1. As in the Grandpa story, the summary statement comes first (verse 1 above), followed by verses relating the preparations and other activities that actually took place *before* the celebration and slaughter of the Passover lamb:

> NAS 2 Chronicles 35:2 And **he set the priests in their offices** and encouraged them in the service of the house of the LORD.

---

303 Wallace, *Greek Grammar Beyond the Basics*, p. 557.

> NAS 2 Chronicles 35:3   He also said to the Levites who taught all Israel *and* who were holy to the LORD, "Put the holy ark in the house which Solomon the son of David king of Israel built; it will be a burden on *your* shoulders no longer. Now serve the LORD your God and His people Israel.
>
> NAS 2 Chronicles 35:4   "And **prepare *yourselves* by your fathers' households in your divisions**, according to the writing of David king of Israel and according to the writing of his son Solomon.
>
> NAS 2 Chronicles 35:5   "Moreover, **stand in the holy place according to the sections of the fathers' households** of your brethren the lay people, and according to the Levites, by division of a father's household.
>
> NAS 2 Chronicles 35:6   "**Now** slaughter the Passover *animals*, sanctify yourselves, and **prepare for your brethren to do according to the word of the LORD by Moses**."

So down here in verse 6, the Passover has *still not been slaughtered*, even though in verse 1 we were *seemingly* told it was already slaughtered (i.e., if we erroneously force the aorist to mean past tense in the "internal workings of the action" without other considerations).

The scriptures that follow in this same chapter show that, again, the people still haven't actually slaughtered the Passover:

> NAS 2 Chronicles 35:7   And **Josiah contributed to the lay people,** to all who were present, flocks of lambs and kids, all **for the Passover offerings**, numbering 30,000 plus 3,000 bulls; these were from the king's possessions.
>
> NAS 2 Chronicles 35:8   **His officers also contributed** a freewill offering to the people, the priests, and the Levites. Hilkiah and Zechariah and Jehiel, the officials of the house of God, gave to the priests for the Passover offerings 2,600 *from the flocks* and 300 bulls.
>
> NAS 2 Chronicles 35:10   **So the service was prepared, and the priests stood at their stations** and the Levites by their divisions according to the king's command.

By now we're way down in verse 10 and the Passover has still not been sacrificed. But we can look back at the summary statement in verse 1 as just that—a summing up of events "without regard for the internal make-up of the occurrence," as Fanning described earlier.

Finally in verse 11, what was described in verse 1 actually happens:

> NAS 2 Chronicles 35:11 **And they slaughtered the Passover animals**, and while the priests sprinkled the blood *received* from their hand, the Levites skinned *them*.

The Passover is now slaughtered and we're taken into the time frame within the narrative. Some could try to argue that—according to the English—the Passover had already been slaughtered in verse 1, but the Greek aorist clearly did not mean that in this passage.

Another excellent example of this particular usage of the aorist tense is Matthew 10:4, where Jesus is calling his 12 disciples to follow him. As Matthew lists them, he mentions the betrayal of Christ by Judas:

> NAS Matthew 10:4   Simon the Zealot, and Judas Iscariot, **the one who betrayed Him**.

> GNT Matthew 10:4   Σίμων ὁ Καναναῖος καὶ Ἰούδας ὁ Ἰσκαριώτης ὁ καὶ παραδοὺς[304] αὐτόν.

Here with Jesus first calling the 12, we are given a summary picture of the betrayal that doesn't actually take place until a few years after the time related in this verse. What's critical to note is that "betrayed" is aorist, and in this instance it means past time *from the writer's perspective*, not past time within the narrative. If we erroneously forced the aorist to mean past time *within* the narrative (as the English could imply), it would incorrectly state that Judas had *already* betrayed Jesus when in fact the betrayal happened much later. Matthew could have used the future tense, saying "the one who years from now will betray him," but the Greek aorist tense was also a perfectly good way to express his point. Thus, the aorist tense often sets up the narrative and leaves the reader to properly put together the events and timing.

The Aorist Tense in Luke 22:7

Let's consider again how the aorist tense works in Luke 22:7. The English translations *seemingly* make it obvious that the day before the Crucifixion was the day the Passovers had to be sacrificed, with Jesus therefore eating the Passover later at the Last Supper as that *supposed* 14th day ended:

---

304 Note that παραδοὺς, translated as "betrayed," is aorist.

> NIV Luke 22:7 **Then came** the day of Unleavened Bread on which the Passover lamb had to be sacrificed.

> GNT Luke 22:7 Ἦλθεν δὲ ἡ ἡμέρα τῶν ἀζύμων, [ἐν] ᾗ ἔδει θύεσθαι τὸ πάσχα·

The English translation of this aorist "Then came" plainly implies that it is now the 14th day, the day to slay the Passover. However, we know that on the following day—the day of the Crucifixion—the Jews need to stay ritually pure so that they might eat the Passover, and God's commandments don't allow for a Passover two days in a row. Remember from our discussion of the subjunctive mood in Key 1 that the Jewish guards did not enter the Praetorium on that day, lest they be defiled and unable to eat the Passover:

> NAS John 18:28 They led Jesus therefore from Caiaphas into the Praetorium, and it was early; and they themselves did not enter into the Praetorium in order **that they might not be defiled**, but might **eat the Passover**.

Let's make sure we understand the context of Luke 22:7, since no scripture occurs in a vacuum. The following points demonstrate that this verse does *not* mean that the Jews were *currently* in the day of sacrificing the Passover (the 14th day). For one thing, the next two verses of Luke show that they're still in the 13th day—the day when the disciples asked Jesus where they should go and prepare (as we saw in Key 2)—and when Jesus told them to make the preparations:

> NAS Luke 22:8 And He sent Peter and John, saying, "Go and prepare the Passover for us, that we **may eat** it."

> NAB Luke 22:9 They asked him, "Where do you want us to make the preparations?"

Back in Key 1, we saw that Jesus—by using the double negative—emphasized that he would *not* eat the Passover before his suffering (Luke 22:15–16), so Luke 22:7 cannot mean it was the day to sacrifice the Passover. Otherwise Jesus *would have* eaten the Passover that night *before his suffering*. If Jesus and his disciples were actually *in* the day to slay the Passover, this would have Luke writing of a preparation day occurring *after* the day to slay the Passover (i.e., on the 15th-day Sabbath), which makes no sense since the preparation day always precedes a Sabbath:

> NAS Luke 23:54   And it was the **preparation** day, and **the Sabbath was about to begin**.

Notice how Luke shows that this Crucifixion day was the preparation day (*paraskeuy*). As we covered earlier, this *paraskeuy* was the 14th day; it was the preparation for the 15th-day Sabbath. Therefore the events in Luke 22:7–9, which occurred on the previous day (i.e., 13th) before the Last Supper, could not have meant that they were then in the 14th day. The time frame of verse 54 is the Crucifixion day, and as the other Gospels show, they are rushing to get the body of Jesus down from the cross and into the tomb *before* this 15th-day high Sabbath begins.

Most commentators argue that Jesus ate the 14th-day Passover following Luke 22:7 (Last Supper), and that Luke 23:54 (the Crucifixion) occurred on the 15th day. However, this high Sabbath, which always came the day after the 14th-day Passover sacrifice, would never be considered a "preparation" day in the Jewish realm. And this is just one final proof that the aorist tense used by Luke in 22:7 doesn't mean that the day to slay the Passover *had actually come* right then in that context, just as the aorist tense of Matthew 10:4 wasn't saying that Judas betrayed Christ in the time frame of verse 4. Remember that the Gospel of Luke was written years after the events took place (as were the other three Gospels), so many events are portrayed as aorist because they are past time *from the Gospel writer's perspective.*

The English translation of Luke 22:7 says that the day "came," but the aorist tense isn't stating that it had actually come at that point. Rather, it's making a summary statement that the most amazing day in history was now before them—the fulfillment of God's plan of the ages concerning the true Passover. Then Luke goes back and relates the events that actually happened *before* the Passover sacrifice occurred.

One Additional Possibility for Luke 22:7

Another possibility for Luke's intended meaning in 22:7 is as follows. The Greek word translated as "Then" (in "Then came") can just as easily be translated "And," making it "And came." The BDAG *Greek-English Lexicon* shows that this Greek word connects two clauses and thus can be translated as "now, then, **and**, so," etc.[305] Adding to this, since this Greek word Ἦλθεν (translated as "came" in English) is in the third person, it can mean he, she, or "it came."

The following scripture from Acts contains an example of this exact same Greek word translated into English as "**it came**":

---

[305] Bauer, *A Greek-English Lexicon of the New Testament and Other Early Christian Literature (BDAG)*, 3rd ed., p. 213.

> ^{NAS} Acts 11:5 "I was in the city of Joppa praying; and in a trance I saw a vision, a certain object coming down like a great sheet lowered by four corners from the sky; and **it came** right down to me,

Therefore, when we use the *BDAG Lexicon*'s accepted meanings in Luke 22:7 and if we connect this with the previous verse (6), we see that Judas is seeking a good opportunity to betray Jesus ("And it came"):

> ^{NAS} Luke 22:6 And he consented, and *began* seeking a good opportunity to betray Him to them apart from the multitude.
>
> Luke 22:7 **And it came** the day of unleavened on which the Passover had to be sacrificed.

So in this perfectly acceptable Greek translation option, Luke shows how Judas was seeking a good opportunity to betray Jesus, "And it came" on the very day it was necessary to sacrifice the Passover (i.e., in the first half of this 14th day—the night period). In this option, Luke subtly connects Christ's betrayal to the Passover sacrifice. Whether we translate this as "And it came" or "Then it came," either way could fit this option and still have the same meaning. This is not to say that Greek is totally plug-and-play, where one can take any definition found in any Greek language lexicon and directly apply it, because each context is important and other considerations must be taken into account. But in this case, "And it came" is a totally acceptable translation of what Luke wrote.

Going from one language to another often presents difficulties, and as we've seen, many Greek words have nuances that do not always precisely translate to a single English word. In an English translation of Luke 22:7, a real difference can exist between "Then" and "And." "*Then* it happened" would indicate a fixed time aspect, whereas "*And* it happened" could be more open-ended, not necessarily meaning it happened right then before the next thing mentioned. Similarly, if someone wrote, "Sally was joyful, *and* she got married," a slightly different meaning could be read into these words than if it said, "Sally was joyful; *then* she got married," implying that perhaps her attitude changed after the marriage. So when we examine English translations, we must always keep these nuances, however slight, in mind.

More Greek Grammar and Hermeneutics as Applied to Luke 22:7

Biblical hermeneutics deals with the methods for properly interpreting scripture. One such guideline is that if you have a majority of scriptural facts that point to one truth, you do not overturn that solid truth because of one obscure verse but rather you interpret that obscure verse in light of well-established scriptural truth (such as interpreting the aorist in Matthew 10:4 correctly). These rules have been used and accepted by a wide range of scholars, from Talmudic writers to Christian researchers.

In this same spirit I would like to offer one final option for Luke 22:7 that is geared more for students of biblical Greek. The *Greek-English Lexicon* by Louw and Nida brings out an additional aspect the Greek aorist Ἦλθεν, translated as "Then **came**" in Luke 22:7. This Greek word has a dictionary form of ἔρχομαι, which they say "involves a highly generic meaning of **movement** from one place to another, **either coming or going**."[306] Louw and Nida categorize it as a verb of "linear movement," explicitly stating that the "lingual subdomain" to which it belongs is "without any special reference to a point in space."[307]

Many Greek words involve concepts that do not correspond exactly to English words. For example, our English word "came," when used by itself, does not imply linear movement but rather something that arrived and is finished moving; this is not the same meaning as "coming or going." If Luke is focusing on this linear movement, he would then be picturing this most important day in history moving on toward its fulfillment and then backfilling the details to set the stage for this momentous Passover. In essence, the aorist tense of Luke 22:7 would then have the shade of meaning that the day in which the Passover must be killed "approached."

One example of this is when Nicodemus "came" to the tomb to bring items for the burial:

> [NAB] John 19:39 Nicodemus, the one who had first come to him at night, also **came bringing** a mixture of myrrh and aloes weighing about one hundred pounds.

This verse also uses the same Greek aorist word translated as "came" in Luke 22:7, but here he *came* bringing the myrrh and aloes. This essentially pictures him "approaching." In contrast, if you already "came" (past tense), you could not still be "bringing" (present tense participle).

Louw-Nida gives other examples of the Greek aorist tense that imply this movement from one place to another, and not as a fixed point. One example given is Luke 3:3 (NAS), where it says Jesus "**came** into all the district around the Jordan, preaching a baptism of repentance for the forgiveness of sins." The Greek word for "came" uses the same Greek aorist tense as in Luke 22:7, and here it clearly has movement attached to it.

---

306 Louw and Nida, *Greek-English Lexicon of the New Testament Based on Semantic Domains*, vol. 1, 15.7, p. 183.

307 Louw and Nida, *Greek-English Lexicon of the New Testament Based on Semantic Domains*, vol. 1, p. 181.

Regardless of the best translation for Luke 22:7, proper hermeneutics require that we interpret it in light of the well-established facts that the Last Supper could not have been the Passover.

In "The Template Challenge" chapter, we saw a verse that Talmudic writers explained with hermeneutics. God had commanded not to have any leaven present during the seven-day Festival (Exodus 12:19), and in another verse He commanded to remove all leaven on the "first" day (Exodus 12:15). The writers explained that although the Hebrew word used in that verse *normally* means "first," here it conveyed the lesser-used meaning of "preceding" the Festival; otherwise the Israelites would be breaking scriptural law by having leaven still present on the first day of the feast.

※※※

I have shown a few possibilities as to how Luke 22:7 could be translated while still fitting in with the myriad of other proofs that confirm it cannot mean that the 14th day had already come. A translator must understand the overall picture and not translate any verse in a vacuum, but always consider the laws of hermeneutics and use proper Bible interpretation. If many solid, logical proofs exist that a scripture cannot mean what it may *seem* to on the surface, one does not throw out the strong evidence and accept the single translation that seems contrary to well-established truth. Instead, one investigates if there is a way to interpret the one scripture in light of many other proofs so that the scriptures harmonize.

Using the intended Greek grammar, we now understand that Luke 22:7 employs the aorist tense in a summary fashion and not to show that the day had *actually* come at that time in the narrative. Anyone who refuses to consider this and forces Luke 22:7 to occur on the 14th day (thus having Jesus eat the Passover at the Last Supper) would have to explain why the Jewish nation forgot to keep their 15th-day high Sabbath the day after the Last Supper. They would need to explain why Jesus broke God's laws by eating regular bread at what they say was the Passover (see Course 1). They would also have to explain how Jesus could be crucified on the 15th-day Sabbath, and they would have to fit their doctrine into the Template Challenge and somehow answer to the multiple proofs listed in the chapter "50 Reasons the Last Supper Was Not the Passover."

Given the huge Jewish disconnect that took place in Rome[308] and how the English translations appear to make it obvious that the time frame before the Last Supper was the 14th day (the day to slay the Passover), it's not surprising that this doctrine has been so confused. However, when we examine it against other proofs and

---

308 See the chapter "Setting the Table 1: The Jewish Disconnect and the Fourteenthers."

understand the original Greek words used by Luke, it's easy to see that the true way to interpret Luke 22:7 is aorist in summary; it did not mean that the 14th day had actually come.

PART 2

50 Reasons
the Last Supper Was Not the Passover

The purpose of this chapter is to list, in one location, many of the reasons why the Last Supper could not have been the eating of the Passover. While some reasons are very clear to see, others require more historical and biblical background to be fully understood. One of the strongest proofs stems from the fact that the day following this supper was *not* kept as the 15th-day great or high Sabbath. Many commentators don't seem to fully comprehend the consequences of this timing—that if the 14th-day Passover were eaten at the Last Supper, then the Crucifixion day would illegally land on this 15th-day Sabbath of the Passover Festival.

The Jewish nation revered the 15th day of Nisan, for it commemorated God delivering the Israelites from bondage in Egypt. God proclaimed that it be kept as an important Sabbath rest day, when "no work at all shall be done"; the only work allowed was preparing and eating the meals (Exodus 12:16, 17, 41, 42; Leviticus 23:7; Numbers 33:3). In the Old Covenant, He told the Israelites that "throughout your generations you are to celebrate it as a permanent ordinance" (Exodus 12:14). Even today Jews in Jerusalem celebrate this 15th day as a very special Sabbath.

Therefore, to determine which day was actually the 14th-day Passover, all we have to do is examine the events listed in the Gospels to see which day was kept as the 15th-day high Sabbath. But first let's turn to the use of leavened bread at the Last Supper as solid proof that this meal was not and could not have been the eating of the Passover.

Bread Is Good, But Not During the Passover!

The scriptures tell us over and over again that bread was eaten at the Last Supper by using *arton*, the standard Greek word for their daily leavened bread. This would have been both shocking and illegal had that meal been the Passover. According to God's commands, anyone who ate leaven at Passover or during this seven-day Festival was to be cut off from the nation (Exodus 12:15, 19). Even today observant Jews do not go around saying that they ate "bread" during Passover, but rather *matzah* (Hebrew for "unleavened"). How much more serious would this have been when Jesus lived? After all, according to the Talmud (Tract Maccoth, ch. 3, Mishna), even the high priest would be whipped for eating anything leavened during this seven-day Festival.

The truth is that the Last Supper was not the Passover, for it occurred at the end of the 13th day when bread was perfectly legal, and that is why the scriptures all say Jesus and his disciples ate bread at that supper.

It's important to understand that it was on the 13th day when the disciples asked Jesus where they should make ready for the Passover (Matthew 26:17; Mark 14:12), and then they ate the Last Supper that night—at the end of the 13th day. In "The Three Major Greek Keys That Unlock the Gospels," we examined those two scriptures using the Greek dative of reference and saw that the disciples did not ask this question "*on*" the first day of the unleavened but "*with reference to* the first of the unleavened" (that is, to the soon-coming 14th day of the Passover sacrifice). The Last Supper couldn't possibly have been a Passover because under Jewish law, the 13th day would be an illegal time for the Passover.[309]

If the disciples had come to Jesus on the 14th day asking where they should prepare for the Passover, then obviously they would have eaten the Passover that night. But if that were the case, the disciples would not have done Jesus or themselves the injustice of portraying to everyone that they eaten leavened bread at it. Jesus certainly would not have remained the spotless lamb if he had sinned before God and the nation by eating regular bread at the Passover:

1. Matthew tells of Jesus eating **bread** at the Last Supper (Matthew 26:26) without qualifying it to be *matzah*. (Had this bread been unleavened, he would have used the Greek word *azumos*.) If the Jewish readers believed that the Last Supper was the Passover, it would have been shocking to them to think that Jesus and his disciples had actually been eating bread.

2. Mark also tells of Jesus eating **bread** at the Last Supper (Mark 14:22) and does not qualify it by showing that it was actually *matzah* (unleavened), which would have been required if the Last Supper had been the Passover.

3. Luke also shows Jesus eating **bread** at the Last Supper (Luke 22:17). The disciples would not risk portraying the Messiah and themselves as committing a major sin before God by eating regular bread, had the Last Supper been the Passover.

---

309 The chapters "The Template Challenge" and "The Three Major Greek Keys That Unlock the Gospels" contain many proofs of this question being asked on the 13th day. When the disciples "made ready" the Passover, this did not refer to slaying and cooking the lamb, but to the Jewish ritual preparations that were required before the Passover. The scriptures that *seem* to so clearly show Jesus eating the Passover at the Last Supper are explained in "The Three Major Greek Keys That Unlock the Gospels."

4. John also shows the disciples eating **bread** at the Last Supper (John 13:18, 19) and quotes Jesus, who was quoting Psalm 41:9 concerning himself, saying that "the one eating my bread" would betray him. In this Psalm, God anointed David to use the Hebrew word for bread (*lechem*), not the word for unleavened (*matzah*). If God had known Christ would be betrayed at the Passover, this prophecy would have said "the one eating my *matzah*." God knew that the Messiah would be betrayed by the one presently *eating* his bread (the Septuagint and New Testament both express this in the present tense). So when Jesus gives Judas the "sop" of bread, Judas goes out to betray him (John 13:30). Had the Last Supper been the Passover, no one would have been eating bread.

5. Most Greek dictionaries (including *BDAG*, *UBS*, and *Louw-Nida*) define the Greek word (*psomion*) usually translated as "sop" or "morsel" (in John 13:26, 27, 30) as a morsel "of bread." The Jewish scholars who translated the Old Testament into the Greek Septuagint used the same Greek word for morsel of bread several times; it was never once used as a morsel of *matzah* (Ruth 2:14; 1 Samuel 28:22; 1 Kings 17:11; Proverbs 28:21). (This is fully covered in Course 1.)

6. Then Paul, who was not present at the Last Supper, says that he received special revelation from the Lord concerning the Last Supper, and we see he understood what Jesus meant with the one bread (1 Corinthians 11:23, 10:17). Paul uses the word "bread" seven times in six different scriptures to refer to what Jesus shared and ate at the Last Supper, but never once says that it was unleavened (1 Corinthians 11:23, 26, 27, 28, and indirectly in 1 Corinthians 10:16,17).

7. At the Last Supper, Jesus held one "bread," broke it into pieces, and then said, "This is my body." Paul, receiving special revelation from the Lord, states that **we** (the believers) are the body of Christ, and members of the spiritual body, as represented by the pieces of the one **bread** (1 Corinthians 10:17, 12:27, and throughout 1 Corinthians chapter 12).

   Since the *pieces* of bread represent us—the members of the spiritual body who are not yet perfected—it fits typologically that the bread is leavened. If the Messiah had been eating the Passover at the Last Supper and was therefore teaching a ritual with *matzah* (i.e., unleavened), then the "bread" in this supposed Jewish ritual would also have been *matzah* (unleavened).[310] The fact is, however, that the Messiah did not mean for a ritual[311] to be kept when he broke one regular leavened bread but was speaking spiritual truth instead.

8. At the Last Supper there was no mention of the three key ingredients of a Passover: a lamb, bitter herbs, and *matzah* (unleavened). However, **bread**—the one thing that must be avoided by all means at the Passover—is mentioned in the scripture 10 times in reference to what was eaten at this meal!

Commentators Attempt to Shoehorn the Passover into the Last Supper

There are some excellent commentators (like Adam Clarke) who see many of the problems associated with the day *after* the Last Supper not being a Sabbath. They see the impossibility of Jesus *slaying* a Passover on the 14th day and then *being slain himself* as the Passover the following day—yet with both days somehow still being the 14th day.[312]

So they came up with the idea that Jesus sacrificed a Passover at the end of the 13th day (or during the night portion of this 14th day) and then ate it during this first half of the 14th day. Remember that the Jewish day ended at sundown. Thus the new day began with this dark period, just as in Genesis 1:1–5 where there was darkness (night), then there was light (day), and together this was the first day.

However, huge problems loom with this belief that Jesus sacrificed a Passover when the 14th day was just beginning, then ate it at the Last Supper. We will see in the following reasons why this double Passover option would have been impossible under the law of Moses:

9. This idea would involve Jesus and the disciples sacrificing an illegal Passover at a time other than that commanded by God. The Talmud is clear that a Passover slain before noon on the 14th day would not be valid,[313] and as the first-century Jewish biblical philosopher Philo

---

310 For more on this important history, see the chapter "The Ritual—Why Didn't the Jewish Disciples Teach It?"

311 This is covered in the chapter "The Ritual—Why Didn't the Jewish Disciples Teach It?"

312 See "The Double Passover Option" section in the chapter "The Template Challenge" for more proof that this option does not fit God's commandments for this Jewish Feast.

313 Babylonian Talmud, Book 3, Pesachim, ch. 5, p. 113, http://sacred-texts.com/jud/t03/psc09.htm.

wrote, the Jews did not offer their sacrifices at night.[314] Furthermore, according to the Talmud, anyone eating meat from an illegal sacrifice ("piggul") would be whipped.[315] Jesus would not have broken God's law concerning the appointed time to slay the Passover, even if the Jewish authorities had allowed it. It is written of any man who would not offer the Passover in its "appointed time" that "that man shall bear his sin" (Numbers 9:13).

10. Jesus could not have sacrificed an illegal Passover at the beginning of this 14th day (as the 13th day ended), because leaven was not required to be removed from Israel until noon of the 14th day. This would have broken God's strict commandment to not eat the Passover while leaven was still on hand in the nation.[316] Additionally, no Jewish historian writes of any change in the law of Moses that supposedly allowed the Passover to be sacrificed early, or of any new law that would be required for the nation to now remove the leaven early—on the 13th day—in time for early Passover sacrifices.

11. Another attempt to solve this controversy are the various two-calendar theories put forth by Anne Jaubert and others. Some of them believe Jesus used a *supposed* Pharisee calendar (slaying the Passover on its 14th day) and the rest of the Jews adhered to a *supposed* Sadducee calendar (sacrificing the Passover **the following day**, aligning with the book of John).

This idea may sound intriguing to some, but it quickly breaks down since these two supposed calendars (offset by one day) would have led to tremendous confusion around Jerusalem and the Temple as one person who carried a load on the Sabbath was accosted by the authorities, only to explain, "Oh, I keep the Sabbath of the other group." Not to mention the fact that at Passover one group would still be eating bread because it was only **their** 13th day, while the other group was sacrificing the Passover with all leaven removed on **their** 14th day.

The idea of two 14th-day Passovers (and two 15th-day Sabbaths) in a row was never mentioned in the New Testament, the Talmud, or in the writings of Josephus, Philo, or any other early historian. This change

---

314 Yonge, *The Works of Philo Judaeus*, "Special Laws II," 27:145, http://www.earlyjewishwritings.com/text/philo/book28.html.

315 Babylonian Talmud, Book 9, Tract Maccoth, ch. 3, p. 35, http://sacred-texts.com/jud/t09/mac08.htm.

316 For more on this, see the subsections "The 13th-Day Question" and "The 14th-Day True Passover" in the chapter "The Template Challenge."

would have been such a huge ordeal, requiring letters to be sent throughout Israel instructing that leaven be removed early from now on, and that two different calendars would now be followed for the Temple services, depending on which sect you followed. Yet this subject was never even debated by the Pharisees, the Sadducees, or those early historians. The only conclusion we can draw is that this two-calendar theory for first-century Jerusalem is a creation mostly out of thin air.

The Dead Sea Scrolls were written by a Jewish group who had withdrawn from participating in the Temple sacrifices and lived at Qumran, near the Dead Sea. These scrolls actually do portray that this group followed a slightly different calendar for some aspects of the festivals, but this has no bearing on what happened in Jerusalem, for the Temple authorities always knew when the 14th day was, in which to slay the Passover. Among Jews in Jerusalem, who carried out God's laws concerning these sacrifices, the 14th day of the month was counted from the sighting of each new moon, and there were never two different ways of counting to 14.

The scriptures clearly confirm that when Jesus lived, only one specific day existed to slay the Passovers in the Temple (then came the day to sacrifice the Passover, not then came one of the various days to slay the Passover, depending on which group you followed; 2 Chronicles 35:1; Luke 22:7).

Too Much Illegal Activity for This to Be the 15th-Day Sabbath

If the Last Supper had been the eating of the 14th-day Passover, then of course the following day would have been the 15th-day Sabbath, which the Jews always kept as a special day of rest.

Different types of Sabbaths were observed under the law of Moses. There was the standard Saturday Sabbath, but others, such as the Day of Atonement, were connected to the three annual festivals, and these could fall on other days of the week. These festival Sabbaths were strictly observed, and no God-fearing Jew in first-century Israel would violate these special rest days. In all, seven Holy Convocation Sabbaths were connected to the three annual festivals (Leviticus 23), and this 15th-day Sabbath is one of the more prominent.[317]

However, as we will see below, the day *after* the Last Supper was definitely not kept as the 15th-day Sabbath, since it was filled with activities that were illegal for

---

317 For a complete list of these festival Sabbaths and additional information, see the subsection "The 15th-Day Sabbath" in the chapter "The Template Challenge."

a Sabbath (proving again that the Last Supper could not have been the Passover). While it is true that various English translations[318] portray the Last Supper as the Passover, remember that they were translated by those who inherited this belief from the Roman Church.

Some commentators have accused first-century Jewish leaders of gross hypocrisy for neglecting Sabbath laws by arresting and pushing for Christ's Crucifixion on the Sabbath. However, the fact is that all these acts, such as carrying swords and clubs, took place on the 14th day—which was not a Sabbath—and therefore no such laws would have been broken. Since the Last Supper was not the eating of the Passover, but rather took place as the 13th day ended (i.e., at sundown), these activities that occurred later on that 14th day did not break any Sabbath laws.

So, had the Last Supper been the eating of the 14th-day Passover, then all these events on the day following would have occurred illegally on their 15th-day Sabbath:

12. When Judas left the Last Supper, the other disciples assumed he was going out to ***buy something*** needed for the Festival (John 13:29). If the Last Supper had indeed been the eating of the Passover, then the period after supper would have been *in* the 15th-day Sabbath rest (which starts at sundown); thus, going out to make purchases would have been illegal according to Jewish Sabbath law.

13. The concept that the chief priests, elders, and Pharisees would all ***leave their homes*** and their gathered families to go out and arrest Jesus—just after eating the Passover on this most holy night that celebrates God delivering them from Egypt—***does not fit the Jewish idiom*** of this 15th-day Sabbath of the Passover, which represented being released from bondage.

14. It would have been illegal for chief priests, Temple officers, and Jewish elders to ***carry swords*** on the 15th-day Sabbath, yet they are pictured using them to go and arrest Jesus (Luke 22:52).

15. It would have also been illegal for these same people to ***carry clubs*** on the 15th-day Sabbath when they went outside the city to arrest Jesus (Luke 22:52), yet they are pictured carrying clubs.

16. The Sabbath laws would preclude these Jewish authorities from going out and ***arresting a criminal*** on the Sabbath, especially on the most

---

318 Those English translations and how they misunderstood the original Greek are covered in the chapter "The Three Major Greek Keys That Unlock the Gospels."

holy 15th-day Sabbath when God set the Israelites free from bondage in Egypt (Exodus 12:17, 42; 31:15; Numbers 33:3).

17. The chief priests made a covenant to pay Judas (Matthew 26:15) 30 pieces of silver—fulfilling the prophecy in Zechariah (11:10–13)—to lead them to a successful arrest of Jesus. Then, *after* Judas led them to make that arrest, they **paid him** the silver. (Judas is later pictured throwing the money back to them in the Temple.) The fact that the chief priests paid Judas *after* the Last Supper shows that the Last Supper was not the 14th-day Passover, for *after* sunset of the 14th day would then have been the 15th-day Sabbath, when making such a payment would have been illegal.

18. Jewish laws were in place to prohibit exceeding the legal distance of walking on the Sabbath. If Jesus had been crucified on the holy 15th-day Sabbath, this commandment surely would have been broken by the chief priests, Temple officers, and Jewish elders as they left their homes to meet on this most holy night, then journeyed outside the city to arrest Jesus, then over to the house of Annas, then to where Caiaphas was, then to Pilate at the judgment hall, and finally back to their homes. Some suggest (and it is most likely true) that on festival days the Jewish commandment of a Sabbath-day's journey was relaxed; however, **walking all around the city** (especially while carrying torches and clubs to make an arrest and hold a trial) would take any relaxing of this law to an extreme.

19. A **fire was kindled** right in the court of the high priest (John 18:8) on this supposed 15th day, even though it was illegal to kindle a fire on the Sabbath (Exodus 35:3). While it is true that God made a special allowance for the preparation of food on this Sabbath (Exodus 12:16), it does not appear that this was the purpose of the fire in this court.

20. Under Jewish law it would have been illegal to **hold a trial** on the 15th-day Sabbath; even Roman law did not require the Jews to break the Sabbath in this way. Josephus relates that the Jews could not be compelled to go to court on the Sabbath, nor on the preparation day before the Sabbath after the ninth hour, which was around 3 PM.[319]

---

319 Whiston, *The New Complete Works of Josephus*, "Jewish Antiquities," 16.6.2, p. 536.

21. Jesus was compelled to ***carry his cross*** on the day of the Crucifixion, an activity that would have been illegal had this been the 15th-day Sabbath.

22. As Jesus carried his cross through the city, a great multitude of people followed, and women openly mourned and lamented (Luke 23:27, 48). According to Jewish history, ***mourning was not allowed on a festival day*** because it was considered a ***duty to rejoice*** at the festival (Deuteronomy 16:11–15; Ezra 6:22; Babylonian Talmud[320]). Therefore, the Last Supper couldn't have been the Passover since this would mean that all these Jewish people—with their open mourning and lamentation (Luke 23:27)—were breaking what they considered a commandment to rejoice during this 15th-day Festival Sabbath.

23. Simon was compelled to ***carry the cross*** when Christ no longer could. Again, this would be illegal on the Sabbath.

24. The Jews asked Pilate for the ***legs of those crucified*** (but not yet dead) ***to be broken*** so they wouldn't escape once they were let down. According to Jewish law, the bodies could not be on the cross during the sooncoming Sabbath (John 19:31). This is total and complete proof that the day of the Crucifixion was not a Sabbath, for if it had been the Sabbath the priests would not have pushed for Pilate to put the bodies up on crosses in the first place.

25. Had Jesus somehow been crucified on the 15th-day Sabbath, it also would have been illegal to ***carry his body*** to the burial site, as carrying any load was illegal on the Sabbath. But since the day *following* the Crucifixion was the 15th-day Sabbath, it's understandable that the disciples were rushing to move his body off the cross and into the tomb ***before*** that high Sabbath arrived (John 19:31; Luke 23:54).

26. Joseph of Arimathea was a wealthy Jewish man who was a disciple of Christ (but kept it somewhat quiet until the Crucifixion, John 19:38). He was said by Luke to be a good and just man (Luke 23:50, 51) and by Mark to be a prominent member of the council (i.e., Sanhedrin, Mark 15:43). Yet had the day of Christ's Crucifixion been a Sabbath,

---

[320] Babylonian Talmud, Book 3, Pesachim, ch. 10, p. 227, http://www.sacred-texts.com/jud/t03/psc14.htm.

Joseph would have been seen publicly breaking the Sabbath laws by ***purchasing*** and ***carrying fine linen*** for a Jewish burial on this day (Matthew 27:57–60; Mark 15:46; John 19:40), activities that would have been illegal on the 15th-day Sabbath.

27. Nicodemus, a Jewish man and a Pharisee said by John to also be a "ruler of the Jews," had previously come to Jesus privately, admitting that he knew Jesus had to be from God because of the miracles he was doing (John 3:1–9). Yet Nicodemus would then be pictured breaking the Sabbath laws by ***carrying about 75 pounds of myrrh*** to assist in the burial of Jesus (John 19:39) on what would have been the 15th day.

28. Concerning these burial laws, the Talmud and other Jewish writings state that it would be illegal to ***bury anyone*** on the Sabbath. The designation of "Sabbath" also includes the seven Festival Sabbaths, which are often called Holidays (Holy days).[321]

29. Had the Last Supper been the Passover, then this would have Joseph of Arimathea, a prominent member of the Sanhedrin, ***rolling the large rock*** down to close up the tomb (after laying the body of Jesus into the burial tomb) on this most holy 15th-day Sabbath (Matthew 27:60). Moving this large rock on the Sabbath would be illegal under Jewish law.

Jesus Was Not to Be Arrested in or during the Seven-Day Feast—the Festival Called Passover

The illegal activities listed in the previous section could never have been carried out on the Sabbath, and of course the powerful Jewish Sanhedrin understood this. This is why we see them, a few days before the Crucifixion, commanding that Jesus not be arrested "during the Festival" lest there be a riot among the people:

> [NAS] Matthew 26:3–5 Then the chief priests and the elders of the people were gathered together in the court of the high priest, named Caiaphas; and they plotted together to seize Jesus by stealth, and kill *Him*. But they were saying, "**Not during the festival, lest a riot occur among the people**."

---

[321] Shulman, *Gateway to Judaism*, vol. 1, p. 571.

This time period was very specific to the Jews; this seven-day Festival began just after the Passover sacrifices with the setting of the sun, which marked the entrance into this 15th-day special Sabbath.

30. It would have been unfathomable for these chief priests, elders, and Temple officers to disregard the command of the Sanhedrin given just a few days earlier by *arresting Jesus right during the Feast/Festival* (Luke 22:52). Nor would they have publicly rebelled against God's Sabbath laws in this way by *arresting Jesus on this 15th-day Sabbath*, the highest holy day of the Festival (Exodus 23:15; Leviticus 23:6–8; Numbers 28:17).

31. The Sanhedrin understood that the people would riot if such an arrest were made during the Festival. However, we see *no disturbance at all among the people* at the time of Christ's arrest, trial, and Crucifixion. This is proof that his arrest and Crucifixion happened on the 14th day (which was not a Sabbath) instead of the 15th-day Sabbath, which would have been during the Festival.

32. By establishing the time at the Last Supper—while they were eating—as "before" the Feast of the Passover, John confirms that the arrest was not in or "during" the Feast/Festival:

    > NAS John 13:1–2 Now **before** the Feast of the Passover, Jesus knowing that His hour had come that He should depart out of this world to the Father, having loved His own who were in the world, He loved them to the end. And **during supper**, the devil having already put into the heart of Judas Iscariot, *the son* of Simon, to betray Him,

33. Later John shows that *the day of Christ's arrest, trial, and Crucifixion was the 14th-day Passover* since the Jews were concerned about ritual purity so that they "might eat the Passover" later that same day:

    > NAS John 18:28 They led Jesus therefore from Caiaphas into the Praetorium, and it was early; and they themselves did not enter into the Praetorium in order that they might not be defiled, but might **eat the Passover**.

Had the Last Supper been the Passover, Jesus would have been arrested "during the Feast," and in the above scripture John would not have pictured the Jews eating the Passover the day following.

Some commentators, who rely on the English translations that portray Jesus as eating the Passover at the Last Supper, claim that John is referring to a Chagigah (or Hagigah) Festival offering instead. They are forced into this view in an attempt to explain this scripture that contradicts the idea of Jesus eating the Passover the previous night. However, the Greek word *Pascha* is correctly translated into English above as "the Passover." Paul said Christ was "our Passover" in 1 Corinthians 5:7; he did not say Christ was our "Chagigah."

34. Furthermore, John links Christ to the 14th-day Passover sacrifice, saying that **not a bone of his was broken** (John 19:36). Having no bones broken was a requirement of God for the Passover sacrifice only (Exodus 12:46), which would have had no meaning if Jesus had been crucified as the fulfillment of the Passover sacrifice a day late, on the 15th day of Nisan (which was **during** the Festival). If Jesus *had* eaten the Passover at the Last Supper and then been crucified the following day, he could not have been said to be the Passover, but rather Christ our "Chagigah" (as mentioned above). The requirement to not break a bone pertained to the Passovers; there was no such command for the Chagigah offerings.

35. Jesus could not have been slain as the Passover the day *after* he sacrificed and ate the Passover with his disciples. He could not slay the Passover one day, then eat it that night at the Last Supper, and then have his death fulfill the 14th-day Passover the following day. **Both of those days could not be the God-commanded 14th day** for the Passover to be slain.

36. God had Jesus in mind when He commanded Moses to slay the Passover on **this 14th day** of Nisan, which was **not** "during the Festival" (the Festival always began when the 14th day ended). Therefore it makes sense that Jesus was crucified on this 14th day just as God commanded Moses for the Passover. The scripture below says that Jesus was delivered up "by the predetermined plan and foreknowledge of God":

> NAS Acts 2:23 this Man, delivered up by the predetermined plan and foreknowledge of God, you nailed to a cross by the hands of godless men and put Him to death.

37. Even the *time* of day that God commanded to slay the Passovers was fulfilled when Jesus died at the proper legal time at the ninth hour (around 3 PM). Josephus states that the Jewish nation sacrificed the Passovers in the Temple from the ninth to the eleventh hour.[322] The Passovers were to be slain "between the evenings," which meant between noon and sundown on the 14th day, and this was the exact time of the Messiah's death. And the Passover was always sacrificed *before* the seven-day Festival, not in or during it.

The Hypothetical Last-Supper-Passover Story

As an intermission to the 50 reasons, imagine the following scenario:

Many prominent Jewish leaders in Jerusalem, including chief priests, are gathered with their relatives in their homes to partake of the Passover lamb and to tell stories of Moses bringing the Jews out of Egypt on this holy night—the 15th-day Sabbath that begins this Festival. Having eaten their Passovers, many of these Jews supposedly take up weapons and torches, and get ready to leave their families on this highly revered night to go out into the dark through the city to find this "deceiver" Jesus. First they knowingly violate God's Sabbath laws, and then they disregard the Sanhedrin's command that they not arrest Jesus "in the Festival." The following hypothetical conversation arises in various Jewish homes:

> *Son:* Father, where are you going on this most special holy 15th-day Sabbath after we have just eaten the Passover?
>
> *Father:* Oh, I'm just heading out to Gethsemane with a group of chief priests, elders, and officers of the Temple to arrest that Jesus who has been causing so much trouble.
>
> *Son:* But Father, will not such an activity break the meaning of this most holy Sabbath that God commanded?
>
> *Father:* Listen son, don't embarrass me in front of all the relatives. We can't follow God's laws all the time, and this is important.
>
> *Son:* But Father, you are carrying a torch and a weapon; you always taught us against carrying such things on the Sabbath, and how much more on this most holy Sabbath when our people were

---

322 Whiston, *The New Complete Works of Josephus*, "Jewish Wars," 6.9.3, p. 906.

delivered from Egypt? You always told me not to lift anything that weighed more than a dried fig on this day, and now you pick up a weapon and a torch?

Father: Son, you know I have strictly kept God's Sabbaths. I even rebuked the man that Jesus healed on the Sabbath, for he carried his bed after the miracle healing. Son, you know that I have never even carried a dry fig on the Sabbath, but tonight, in front of all my Sabbath-obeying relatives, I am throwing all of those laws out the window. As the heathens say, "Sabbath be darned!"

Then Cousin Habib speaks up: Surely you know that the powerful Sanhedrin held court just the other day, and they kept commanding that this man ***not*** be arrested ***in*** the Festival, and surely you understand that having just eaten the Passover, we are now ***in*** the Festival, do you not?

Father: I know, I know. Multitudes of us—elders, chief priests, and Pharisees—all understood the Sanhedrin's commandments the other day, but we've decided to break God's laws concerning the Sabbath and also ignore the Sanhedrin, and go out and arrest Jesus right during the Festival. What's the big problem?

Considering God's laws and the Jews' strict adherence to these Sabbath laws in first-century Jerusalem, it could not be more obvious that such a scenario would have been impossible (had the Last Supper been the Passover). The 15th day was a holy day of rest as commanded by God, and the Jewish nation always commemorated it as a very special day. Since Jesus was arrested several hours after his Last Supper by these chief priests and Temple officers carrying clubs and torches (activities that would have been illegal on the 15th-day Sabbath that follows the 14th-day Passover), it is clear that the Last Supper was not the Passover.

The 15th-Day Great Sabbath Was the Day after the Crucifixion

As we've seen before, if the Last Supper had been the eating of the 14th-day Passover, then the Crucifixion would have been on the 15th-day Sabbath.

The Jews always observed God's commands to keep the 15th day as a special Sabbath rest, and even today in Israel the Sabbath-following Jews still faithfully observe this day. Anyone who would try to deny that the 15th day was not kept as a Sabbath does not understand Jewish history.

The Pharisees argued that this 15th day of Nisan was the Sabbath spoken of in Leviticus (23:11, 15), in which God commanded the Israelites to make the firstfruits sheaf offering (the Omer) "on the morrow of the Sabbath." The Sadducees countered that it referred instead to the morrow of the regular Saturday Sabbath (the first Saturday after the Passover). The Pharisees had their way in this debate, at least during the time of Josephus, because we can see from his writings that this offering occurred on the 16th day of Nisan, the "morrow" of the 15th-day Festival Sabbath.[323] The history is clear that the first-century Jews understood the 15th day to be a Sabbath; therefore, had the Last Supper been the Passover, the following day would have been kept throughout Israel as this Sabbath.

However, the Gospels establish that the 15th-day Sabbath did ***not*** occur on the day ***following*** the Last Supper. Instead this high Sabbath is seen coming at the end of the Crucifixion day, which aligns with Christ being crucified as the true Passover on the 14th day.

38. Mark shows that ***Jesus was on the cross the day before the Sabbath***, not on the 15th-day Sabbath:

    NIV Mark 15:42 It was Preparation Day (that is, the day before the Sabbath). So as evening approached,

39. John, too, shows that the ***day of Crucifixion was not a Sabbath***, as the Jews rushed to take the bodies down from the crosses and move them into a tomb for a proper Jewish burial before the soon-coming Sabbath arrived:

    NAS John 19:31 The Jews therefore, because it was the day of preparation, so that the bodies should not remain on the cross on the Sabbath (**for that Sabbath was a high *day***), asked Pilate that their legs might be broken, and that they might be taken away.

    Jewish law would not allow for bodies to remain on the cross during a Sabbath, and therefore it makes no sense that Jesus and the other two would be crucified and put up on the cross for several hours on this hallowed 15th-day "Holy Convocation" Sabbath. The scriptures agree with Jewish law.

---

323 Whiston, *The New Complete Works of Josephus*, "Jewish Antiquities," 3.10.5, p. 133.

40. The women who had left the scene after seeing Christ's body put in the tomb first went and *prepared spices and perfumes*; then when the Sabbath arrived "they rested according to the commandment."

   > NAS Luke 23:56 And they returned and prepared spices and perfumes. And on the Sabbath they **rested** according to the commandment.

   If the Last Supper had been the eating of the Passover, then the next day would have been the 15th-day Sabbath when no mundane work (such as preparing spices and ointments) was allowed. These women would not have labored on the 15th-day Sabbath and then rested the following day, proving again that the Crucifixion was not on the 15th-day Sabbath.

41. Luke makes it clear that the *day of the Crucifixion was not this 15th-day Sabbath*, for after Jesus's body was taken down he says, "the Sabbath was about to begin":

   > NIV Luke 23:54 It was Preparation Day, and the Sabbath **was about to begin**.

   The chief priests would never push to crucify people on the 15th-day Sabbath, and then show concern later in the day that another Sabbath was about to begin. The fact that the day *following* the Crucifixion was the soon-coming 15th-day Sabbath fits perfectly with Jesus being crucified as the true Passover on the 14th day.

The Gospels All Agree

Much has been written about the supposed contradiction between John's Gospel and the Synoptic Gospels (Matthew, Mark, and Luke) concerning the Last Supper and the Passover. However, since God anointed these scripture writers to give us the truth, it makes sense that they were not confused as to whether the Last Supper was the Passover or not. It should be no surprise, then, that John agrees with the other three Gospels that **the day of the Crucifixion** was the **preparation** day (*paraskeuy* in Greek) for the soon-coming 15th-day Sabbath (which begins the seven-day Festival *called* Passover, Luke 22:1).

Had the Gospel writers somehow believed that the Last Supper was the eating of the 14th-day Passover, how could they all agree in stating that the following day was one of preparation?

A Sabbath day is never mistakenly called a "preparation," because preparation always takes place the day ***before*** a Sabbath. This is the day when all necessary work is done to make ready for the Sabbath (when work was forbidden). The first-century Jewish historian Josephus used this same Greek word for preparation (*paraskeuy*), stating that even the Roman authorities did not compel the Jews to appear in court on the Sabbath day "or on the ***preparation*** for it after the ninth hour" (Antiquities 16.6.2). Roman authorities knew that on the day ***preceding*** the Sabbath, the Jews would be busy in the afternoon ("ninth hour," i.e., around 3 PM) "preparing" for the coming Sabbath.

The Jewish Encyclopedia also speaks of *paraskeuy*, indicating that it was the day before ***any*** Sabbath—including the Festival Sabbaths—and not just the day before the Saturday Sabbath, as many theologians have believed:

> The eve of Jewish holidays is therefore not the evening of the festival, but the day preceding it; in conversation, the expression " 'ereb yom tob" is even extended to denote an indefinite period **preceding the holiday**. It is observed as a day on which is prepared (*paraskeuy*) such work as it not permitted to do **on the holiday or on the Sabbath.**[324]

The *BDAG Greek-English Lexicon* shows that the Greek word translated as "***preparation***" (*paraskeuy*) speaks of a definite day:

> only of a definite day, **as the *day of preparation* for a festival**[325]

The *Louw-Nida Greek-English Lexicon of the New Testament* also bears this out:

> παρασκευή, ῆς *f*: a day on which preparations were made for **a sacred or feast day** – 'day of preparation, Friday ....' The identification of παρασκευή with Friday became so traditional that it eventually came to be the present-day Greek term for 'Friday.'[326]

Roman theologians assumed the Greek word *paraskeuy* meant "Friday" (i.e., "Good Friday"), the day they believed Christ was crucified.[327] But in first-century Israel,

---

324 *The Jewish Encyclopedia,* vol. 5, p. 276, s.v. "Eve of Holidays."
325 Bauer, *A Greek-English Lexicon of the New Testament and Other Early Christian Literature (BDAG),* 3rd ed., p. 771.
326 Louw and Nida, *Greek-English Lexicon of the New Testament Based on Semantic Domains,* vol. 1, p. 654, s.v. "παρασκευή, ῆς."
327 See the section "The Roman Catholic Option" in the chapter "The Template Challenge."

the day before the Saturday Sabbath was known as the sixth day of the week (the Jews did not call it Friday), and this sixth day was always a preparation day for the Saturday Sabbath. In contrast, preparation for the 15th-day Sabbath of the Passover could fall on a different day of the week each year.

Our discussion here focuses on this preparation day for the high 15th-day Sabbath of the Passover. The following scriptures show that all four Gospels agree that the Crucifixion day was the preparation day (*paraskeuy*):

> 42. Matthew shows that the day Christ was crucified was called the ***preparation***, where we see the chief priests and Pharisees gathered the day ***after*** his death:
>
>> NAS Matthew 27:62 Now on the next day, which is *the one* after the preparation, the chief priests and the Pharisees gathered together with Pilate
>
> 43. Mark agrees with Matthew, showing that the day Christ was crucified was the ***preparation***, and that this preparation was the day ***before*** the Sabbath:
>
>> NIV Mark 15:42 It was Preparation Day (that is, **the day before** the Sabbath). So as evening approached,
>
> 44. Luke agrees with Matthew and Mark that the day of the Crucifixion was the ***preparation***, and he also states that the Sabbath was about to begin:
>
>> NIV Luke 23:54 It was Preparation Day, and the Sabbath was about to begin.
>
> 45. John gives us the added information that the day of the Crucifixion was not just the preparation for any Sabbath, but that it was specifically the "preparation of the Passover":
>
>> NAS John 19:14 Now it was the day of **preparation** for **the Passover**; it was about the sixth hour.[328] And he said to the Jews, "Behold, your King!"

---

328 The controversy as to this being called the sixth hour is explained in the section "What Does John Mean by the Sixth Hour?" in the chapter "Between the Evenings."

This was the preparation for the great or high[329] Sabbath (depending on the translation):

> YLT John 19:31 The Jews, therefore, that the bodies might not remain on the cross on the sabbath, since it was the **preparation**, (for that sabbath day was a **great** one,) asked of Pilate that their legs may be broken, and they taken away.

> NAS John 19:31 The Jews therefore, because it was the day of **preparation**, so that the bodies should not remain on the cross on the Sabbath (for that Sabbath was a **high** *day*), asked Pilate that their legs might be broken, and *that* they might be taken away.

Then John writes that because it was the day of preparation and the Sabbath was soon coming, they put Jesus in the nearby tomb:

> NAS John 19:42 Therefore on account of the Jewish day of preparation, because the tomb was nearby, they laid Jesus there.

So while some commentators argue that the Gospels are at variance, what we really see is that all four Gospels are in perfect agreement[330] when the Greek is fully understood. For more on the Greek word *paraskeuy* and on the different preparations, see the chapter "Three Major Greek Keys that Unlock the Gospels."

The Third Day Since

When we take all of the scriptures into account and consider the Jewish idioms for this Festival and the meaning of the original Greek, here is what we see. The church tradition of Jesus eating the Passover at the Last Supper on our Thursday evening and being crucified on "Good Friday" does not fit either the Gospels or the Jewish template for this Festival, as the following reasons show:

---

329 The Greek word translated "great" and "high" in these verses is *megaly*, which is the same Greek word John uses for another of the seven Holy Convocation Festival Sabbaths—the Sabbath of the eighth day of the Festival of Tabernacles (John 7:31).

330 Credit is due to Brooke Westcott (*Introduction to the Study of the Gospels,* p. 343) for seeing that all the Gospel writers harmonize as to this preparation day, and that they all use this Greek word *paraskeuy* for the preparation day on which the Crucifixion occurred.

46. Beginning in Luke 24:1 is the account of Jesus walking with the disciples on the first day of the week (Sunday) after the Resurrection. God had withheld their eyes from recognizing Jesus, whom they told of "these things" that happened concerning Christ, such as his being delivered up to death and being crucified:

> KJV Luke 24:20 And how the chief priests and our rulers delivered him to be condemned to death, and have crucified him.

And they said that it was now "the third day since these things happened":

> NAS Luke 24:21 "But we were hoping that it was He who was going to redeem Israel. Indeed, besides all this, **it is the third day since** these things happened.

As per Catholic Church tradition, if Jesus had sacrificed a Passover on Thursday, eaten it that night at the Last Supper, and then been condemned and crucified on "Good Friday," then Saturday would have been the "first day since" these things happened (i.e., him being delivered up, condemned, and crucified). Following on from that, Sunday would only be the "second day since."[331]

However, since the Last Supper was **not** the Passover and Jesus was instead crucified on Thursday (the 14th of Nisan that year, AD 30), then Friday (the 15th-day Sabbath) would have been the "first day since" he was tried, condemned, and crucified. The Saturday Sabbath would have been the "second day since," and Sunday would have been the "third day since these things happened," just as the scripture says in Luke 24:21.

Additional Scriptural Proofs

47. Right along with this point is the declaration by Jesus that he would be in the tomb three days and three nights (Matthew 12:40). The Thursday Crucifixion fits this perfectly, but the church tradition of Jesus eating the Passover at the Last Supper and being crucified on Good Friday

---

[331] See the sections "The Early Roman Catholic Option" and "Sunday the Third Day Since" in the chapter "The Template Challenge" for more on why this option does not fit.

allows him to be in the tomb only **two** nights—Friday and Saturday—because he was resurrected early Sunday morning before sunrise. Some try to shoehorn this as well, but you cannot make two nights be three nights.[332]

48. Luke also quotes Jesus using the Greek double negative (the strongest negation in Greek[333]) to say that he would **not** eat this Passover **before his suffering**, even though he greatly desired to do so. Jesus is speaking of the soon-coming Passover that would be sacrificed during the "afternoon" of what was the 14th Jewish day. The Last Supper was not the Passover, otherwise Jesus **would have** eaten the Passover before his suffering (Luke 22:15, 16). For Jesus to *refuse* to eat it (had the Last Supper been the Passover) would have been a sin before God and the nation; being in Jerusalem and refusing to partake of the Passover was not an option (Numbers 9:13).

49. Also, if Jesus really planned to be there to eat the Passover, why does he use the Greek subjunctive mood—which often implies unreality or doubt—***every time*** he speaks of his *eating* of the Passover? In Greek, the indicative mood is used to make a statement that you are certainly going to do something; yet when Jesus refers to his *eating* of the Passover that year, he always uses the subjunctive mood. And the single time he uses the indicative (the mood of certainty), he does not say that he will "eat" the Passover but that he will "perform, accomplish" the Passover.[334]

50. Jesus said he would be crucified at the Passover:

> [DBY] Matthew 26:2   Ye know that after two days **the passover takes place**, and the Son of man is **delivered up to be crucified**.

If he understood that he was the true Passover as God intended, and he meant the 14th-day Passover, then he could not have sacrificed a Passover the previous day for the Last Supper. He obviously meant and understood that he himself would be crucified on the 14th day, which

---

332 As covered in the section "Sunday the Third Day Since" in the chapter "The Template Challenge."
333 For more on this Greek double negative, see the chapter "The Three Major Greek Keys That Unlock the Gospels."
334 For more on this, see the chapter "The Three Major Greek Keys That Unlock the Gospels."

was called the Passover in the Israelite scriptures (Leviticus 23:5; Numbers 9:5; 28:16, Joshua 5:10; 2 Chronicles 30:15; 35:1; Ezra 6:19, Ezekiel 45:21) and which was the legal time to slay the Passovers.

Jesus intended the more traditional sense of the word "Passover" (the 14th day). He would not have meant the 15th day, which was also sometimes *called* Passover.[335] He would have known the impossibility of being crucified on the 15th-day Sabbath since all Jewish laws forbade such a thing (John 19:31). He also would have known it was impossible to be crucified at any time during the seven-day Festival called Passover, for this would cause a riot among the people, according to the Sanhedrin. He surely knew that he was the 14th-day Passover in type, and from the prophesies in Daniel[336] and elsewhere, he knew that his time had come. This is part of why he knew this 14th-day Passover (Matthew 26:2 above) was his last day, as John also shows:

> [DBY] John 13:1 Now before the feast of the passover, Jesus, **knowing that his hour had come** that he should depart out of this world to the Father, having loved his own who were in the world, loved them to the end.

Extra-Credit Reasons

The following evidence strengthens the findings that Jesus did not eat the Passover at the Last Supper.

51. The history is clear that the Messianic believers living in Asia (to whom John wrote in Revelation 1:4) continued to keep the 14th of Nisan as a special time to commemorate the day Christ finished the work. Called "Quartodecimans" (a Latin word meaning "Fourteenthers") by Rome, these Asiatic believers fasted on this day *until* the ninth hour (the time Jesus was on the cross); then *at* the ninth hour—the time of Christ's death—they rejoiced in the fact that Christ's finished work had provided redemption (see "Setting the Table 1").

   These early Jewish followers knew that Jesus died on the 14th day and could not have eaten a Passover at the Last Supper. They continued to

---

[335] This is explained in the subsection "The 14th-Day True Passover" in the chapter "The Template Challenge."

[336] Daniel shows that the Messiah was to be cut off in the midst of the week (meaning a week of years), and Christ was crucified after a 3½-year ministry.

observe the 14th day of Nisan—regardless of which day of the month it fell—as their Jewish day of the Passover and especially to commemorate the day of the Crucifixion, when Christ fulfilled the Passover.

52. Renowned biblical and Greek scholar Brooke Foss Westcott states that the earliest church history is nearly unanimous in agreeing that the Last Supper was ***not*** the Passover, but that Jesus was crucified on the 14th day:

> "Now, as far as it appears, early tradition is **nearly unanimous** in fixing the **Crucifixion on the 14th**, and in **distinguishing the Last Supper from the legal Passover**. This distinction is expressly made by Apollinaris, Clement of Alexandria, Hippolytus, Tertullian, Irenaeus, who represent very different sections of the early Church."[337]

53. Even the Talmud says Christ's death was on the 14th day: "on the eve of the Passover Yeshu [the Nasarean] was hanged."[338] "Yeshu" is the shortened form for Yeshua (Jesus), and "hanged" refers to being hung upon a tree (or any wooden plank) in Deuteronomy 21:23. It is clear from *The Jewish Encyclopedia* and the Talmud that the "eve of Passover" is the 14th day, so the Talmud agrees with all the other timing we have seen in the scriptures.

54. God bringing darkness over the land from noon until 3 PM (Matthew 27:45) fits perfectly with Jesus being slain on the 14th day, for at noon the legal time began to sacrifice the Passovers. It also may have been a sign that God would no longer look upon or accept the Passover sacrifices or any of *the animal sacrifice*s. This also fits with Amos 8:9–10 where God said that in that day He would make the sun go down at noon and "make the earth dark in broad daylight." (For more on this period of darkness, see the following chapter "Between the Evenings.")

---

[337] Westcott, *Introduction to the Study of the Gospels*, p. 347. See "Setting the Table 1" for more on this.

[338] The Soncino Babylonian Talmud, Tractate Sanhedrin, Folio 43a, http://www.come-and-hear.com/sanhedrin/sanhedrin_43.html. In this source, next to "Yeshu" is a footnote that says, "Ms.M. adds 'the Nasarean.'"

PART 2

Between the Evenings—
the Legal Time to Slay the Passover

Some of the confusion as to whether the Last Supper was the Passover or not comes from the English translations of the original Hebrew words meaning "between the evenings." The Jewish sources are clear that this period—the time to slay the Passovers—was to be in the afternoon of the 14th day. However many English translators and commentators, believing that Jesus ate the Passover at the Last Supper (and that he also died at the proper time for the Passover sacrifice), portray the period of "between the evenings" as either evening or twilight, which can imply after sunset.

This notion does not fit with Jewish history, which shows the legally allowed time for the Passover sacrifice to be between noon and sunset. Famous Jewish commentator Alfred Edersheim agrees with this, writing:

> The period designated as 'between the two evenings' when the Paschal lamb was to be slain, was past. **There can be no question** that, in the time of Christ, it was understood to refer to the interval between the **commencement of the sun's decline** and what was reckoned as the hour of his final disappearance (about 6 p.m.).[339]

The Jewish Encyclopedia verifies this same time frame:

> The time "between the two evenings" ("ben ha-'arbayim") was construed to mean **"after noon and until nightfall"**[340]

The chart below illustrates the sun ascending (from 6 AM to noon) and descending (from noon to 6 PM, around sunset). If you picture the sun in relation to the vertical line and the horizontal line in the chart below, this line is "even" with the horizon at noon, and is again "even" with the horizon at sunset. Thus, between the even-ings is the time between noon and sunset, as both Edersheim and *The Jewish Encyclopedia* noted.

---

339 Edersheim, *Life and Times*, p. 490.
340 *The Jewish Encyclopedia*, vol. 9, p. 553, s.v. "Passover/Paschal Lamb."

452 | THE MESSIANIC FEAST

12:00 Noon

During this period, all leaven was cleared and had to be burned by 11:00 AM

John 11:9: Jesus answered, Are there not twelve hours in the day?

| First hour | Second hour | Third hour | Fourth hour | Fifth hour | Sixth hour | Seventh hour | Eighth hour | Ninth hour | Tenth hour | Eleventh hour | Twelfth hour |

6 AM 7 8 9 10 11 **12 Noon** 1 2 3 4 5 **6 PM**

Third hour is hour of Crucifixion

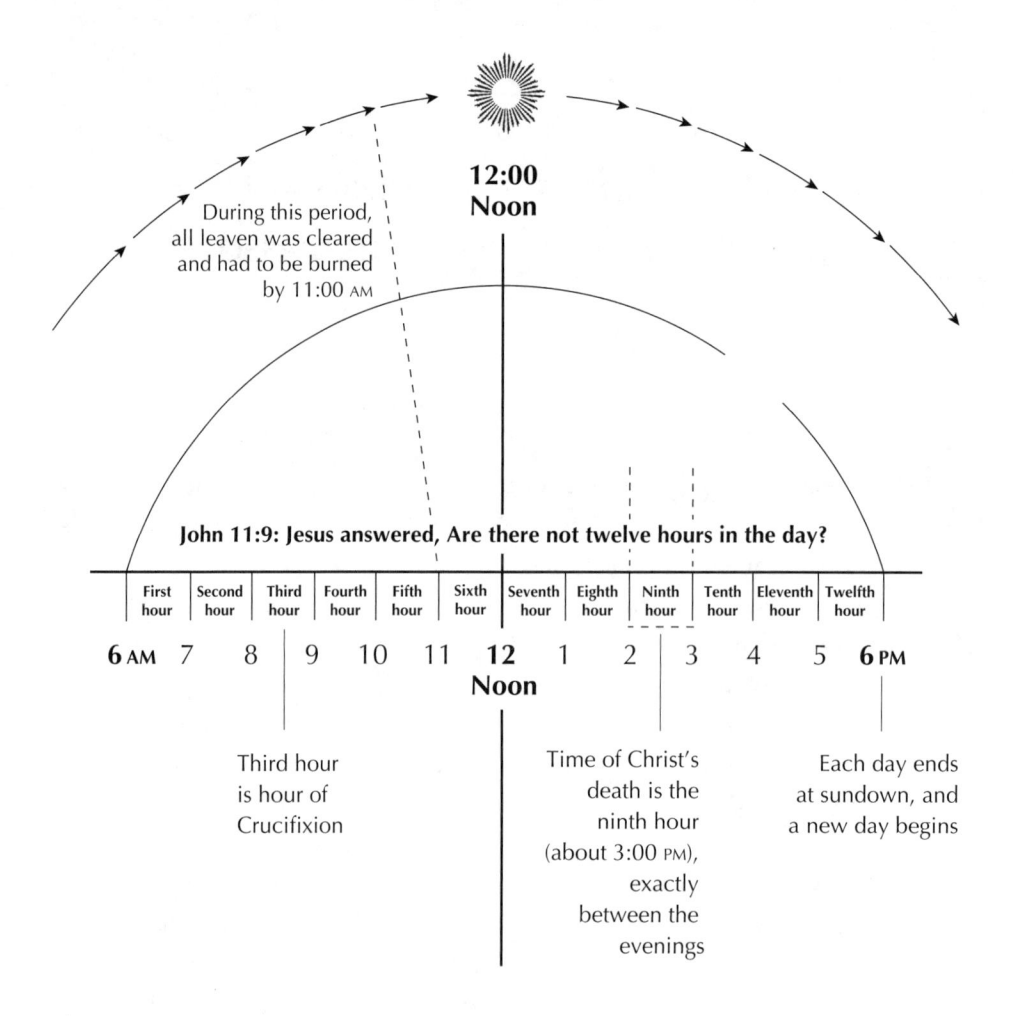

Time of Christ's death is the ninth hour (about 3:00 PM), exactly between the evenings

Each day ends at sundown, and a new day begins

Figure 9. Between the evenings.

Part of the confusion as to whether the Last Supper was the Passover comes from the flexible meaning of the English word "evening," for which most dictionaries include a definition of the "early part of the night." Notice how the six English translations below give six variations (in boldface) of what began as the Hebrew phrase meaning "between the evenings":

> KJV Exodus 12:6   And ye shall keep it up until the fourteenth day of the same month: and the whole assembly of the congregation of Israel shall kill it **in the evening**.

> NAS Exodus 12:6   'And you shall keep it until the fourteenth day of the same month, then the whole assembly of the congregation of Israel is to kill it **at twilight**.

> LXE Exodus 12:6   And it shall be kept by you till the fourteenth of this month, and all the multitude of the congregation of the children of Israel shall kill it **toward evening**.

> YLT Exodus 12:6   'And it hath become a charge to you, until the fourteenth day of this month, and the whole assembly of the company of Israel have slaughtered it **between the evenings**;

> NAB Exodus 12:6   You shall keep it until the fourteenth day of this month, and then, with the whole assembly of Israel present, it shall be slaughtered **during the evening twilight**.

> JPS Exodus 12:6   and ye shall keep it unto the fourteenth day of the same month; and the whole assembly of the congregation of Israel shall kill it **at dusk**.

We must understand how the Jews understood this Hebrew phrase and how they passed it down to successive generations, while of course giving the strongest weight to the original God-anointed Hebrew and Greek scriptures of the Bible.

Overlaying our English understanding of "evening" with its various shades of meaning onto the Hebrew and Greek scriptures can cause problems. We see this, for instance, on the day of the Crucifixion when the 15th-day high Sabbath is soon coming—the following English verse says that evening had already come (although the body of Jesus was not yet moved to the tomb):

> NAS Mark 15:42   And when **evening had already come**, because it was the preparation day, that is, the day before the Sabbath,

> GNT Mark 15:42   Καὶ ἤδη ὀψίας γενομένης, ἐπεὶ ἦν παρασκευὴ ὅ ἐστιν προσάββατον,

> NAS Mark 15:43   Joseph of Arimathea came, a prominent member of the Council, who himself was waiting for the kingdom of God; and he gathered up courage and went in before Pilate, and asked for the body of Jesus.

If we think of verse 42 as being correct and interpret "evening" as occurring after sundown, it would mean that prominent Jews like Joseph of Arimathea (a member of the Sanhedrin) publicly broke the Sabbath by carrying the Messiah's body to the tomb after the 15th-day Sabbath had set in. In this particular verse the solution is easy, for the Greek word ὀψίας, translated as "evening," means "late"; it clearly refers to "late in the Jewish day" (which ended at sunset).

This is just one example of how the time to sacrifice the Passover became confused among commentators since Roman times. When they tried to reconcile the longstanding tradition of Jesus somehow eating the 14th-day Passover at the Last Supper, then fulfilling the 14th-day Passover at the Crucifixion the following day, this idea of sacrificing the Passover in the evening gained acceptance among some. Most Jewish sources correctly state that the Passovers were sacrificed in the afternoon and not after sunset.

The Jewish word for "eve" refers to the part of the day after noon and before sunset, as we saw in the subsection "The 14th-Day True Passover" in the chapter "The Template Challenge." The irrefutable history as detailed below will show that the legal time to slay the Passover was indeed between noon and sunset. We will first consider the historical statements from the Talmud, then look at other Jewish sources (such as Josephus and Philo) to see that the Old Testament evidence perfectly aligns with these other sources. Then we will see that the New Testament scriptural evidence also harmonizes perfectly with these other Jewish writings.

What the Talmud Says

Although as believers in the God-anointed scriptures, we do not get doctrine from the Talmud, it does contain a wealth of accurate information concerning the festivals that the Jewish scholars wanted to preserve and pass down to future generations. Granted, one has to sometimes weed out certain subjects where there was an ax to grind (the Talmud written by the descendants of the Pharisees, who despised the Sadducees and also the Messiah), but there is still much of value regarding the festivals.

First of all, a reminder that the scriptures show unequivocally that the Passover was on the 14th day, and that the seven-day Festival started as the 15th day began (at sundown of the 14th day) and lasted seven days:

> [JPS] Numbers 28:16   And in the first month, **on the fourteenth day** of the month, is the LORD'S **passover**.

> [YLT] Numbers 28:17   and **in the fifteenth day** of this month *is* a festival, **seven days unleavened** food is eaten;

Now let's turn to the Talmudic discussion concerning the time for the Jews to throw away the leaven, which gives us a major point of demarcation as to the legal time to slay the Passover (since it could not be sacrificed on the 14th day until all leaven was burned in Israel):

GEMARA: We see thus, that at the **commencement of the sixth hour**, all agree, Chometz must be burned. Whence do we adduce this? Said Abayi: From two passages, viz. [Exod. xii. 19]: "Seven days no leaven shall be found in your houses," and [ibid. 15]: "But on the first day ye shall have put away leaven out of your houses." According to this, then, on the first day there would still be leaven in the house and this would be contrary to the ordinance of the first passage? Hence we must say, that by "the first day" is meant **the day preceding the festival. Then why say the sixth hour?** Say that already early in the morning of the day preceding the festival (leaven should be burned). The word "but" with which the passage commences divides the day into two parts, so that in the morning leavened bread may be eaten while in the afternoon it must not.

The disciples of R. Ishmael taught: The reason **that Chometz must be removed on the 14th (of Nissan)** (the eve of Passover) is because that day is referred to as the first day (of the festival) in the passage [Exod. xii. 18]: "In the first, on the fourteenth day of the month, at evening shall ye eat unleavened bread," etc.

Rabha said: "The reason may be inferred from the passage [Exod. xxxiv. 25]: **'Thou shalt not offer the blood of my sacrifice with leaven**; neither shall be left unto the morning the sacrifice of the feast of the passover,' which signifies, that the Passover sacrifice must not be offered up as long as there is yet leaven." If that be the case, then it might be said that the leaven should be burned by each man immediately before offering his passover sacrifice; **why designate the sixth hour?** The passage means to state, that **when the *time* for the Passover sacrifice arrives, there must no longer be any leaven on hand.**[341]

There are two particularly important points to take from this passage above. First, these writers understood Exodus 34:25 to mean that leaven (or "Chometz" above, meaning that which is leavened) must be removed by the sixth hour (which commences at 11 AM and ends at noon) since God commanded to not sacrifice the Passover with leaven (meaning while leaven still remained among the people). The *legal* time to slay the Passover was *after* noon, so all leaven had to be removed prior to this time.

The second important point these writers make is that the "first day" (in Exodus 12:15) refers to the 14th day on which the Passover is sacrificed. They reason that if

---

341 Babylonian Talmud, Book 3, Tract Pesachim, ch. 1, pp. 19–20, http://sacred-texts.com/jud/t03/psc05.htm.

no leaven is to be in the land for the whole seven-day Festival (the 15th through the 21st), and if the "first day" of the Festival meant the 15th day of Nisan, then they would have already broken the law by still having leaven to remove during the 15th day.

The Hebrew word can mean either "first" or "previous/preceding," as can the Greek word used here in the Septuagint. They correctly say, therefore, that in this case it means the day *preceding* the Festival (i.e., the 14th day), and they add that Exodus 12:18 calls the 14th day the "first day" as more proof. This was the common Jewish understanding, which fits perfectly with the Gospels, where in the Greek the 14th day is referred to as the "first of the unleavened" (the original Greek of Matthew 26:17 and Mark 14:12).[342]

Remember, God had said that not bringing the Passover in its appointed time would cause one to be *cut off* from Israel. God had given the Israelites a set time for a legal Passover sacrifice, and this time never confused them:

> NAS Numbers 9:13 'But the man who is clean and is not on a journey, and yet neglects to observe the Passover, that person shall then be cut off from his people, for **he did not** present the offering of the LORD **at its appointed time. That man shall bear his sin**.

Would Jesus really have gone against the laws of God and the Temple to somehow sacrifice a Passover outside of its appointed time and thus "bear his sin"?

The following passage from the Talmud goes a step further in defining the time for an acceptable Passover sacrifice, saying that one brought before noon would ***not be valid***:

> MISHNA: If the paschal lamb be slaughtered **before noon, it is not valid,** because it is written [Exod. xii. 6]: "Toward the evening."[343]

This passage is interesting because it does not quote the Hebrew "between the evenings" but rather the Greek Septuagint, which reads "toward evening":

---

342 The 14th day, being the first of the eight unleavened days, is covered in the subsection "The 13th-Day Question" in the chapter "The Template Challenge" and also in the chapter "The Three Major Greek Keys That Unlock the Gospels."

343 Babylonian Talmud, Book 3, Tract Pesachim, ch. 5, p. 113, http://sacred-texts.com/jud/t03/psc09.htm.

> ^{LXE} Exodus 12:6   And it shall be kept by you till the fourteenth of this month, and all the multitude of the congregation of the children of Israel shall kill it **toward evening**.

> ^{LXT} Exodus 12:6   καὶ ἔσται ὑμῖν διατετηρημένον ἕως τῆς τεσσαρεσκαιδεκάτης τοῦ μηνὸς τούτου καὶ σφάξουσιν αὐτὸ πᾶν τὸ πλῆθος συναγωγῆς υἱῶν Ισραηλ **πρὸς ἑσπέραν**

The two words boldfaced in the Greek above are literally "toward evening." In marked contrast to the Greek Septuagint, the English King James translation below says "*in* the evening":

> ^{KJV} Exodus 12:6   And ye shall keep it up until the fourteenth day of the same month: and the whole assembly of the congregation of Israel shall kill it **in the evening**.

You can see from the Talmudic quotes above that their writers understood this time to sacrifice the Passover differently than the translators of the King James Version, which gives the false impression that the Passover is to be sacrificed "***in the evening***." This would not be a problem if "evening" were understood in the first-century Jewish sense—when the sun was moving down in the sky ***toward even-ing*** with the horizon—but the English translations usually convey a different sense.

A big difference can exist between "in" and "toward," for if Daniel (in Babylon) prayed toward Jerusalem, that doesn't mean the same thing as him praying in Jerusalem. These Jewish Talmudic scholars who quoted from the Septuagint understood "toward the evening" (in Greek) to have the same meaning as "between the evenings" (in Hebrew), beginning after noon "when the sun commences to move towards the west."

Young's Literal Translation gives us the meaning of the Hebrew:

> ^{YLT} Exodus 12:6   'And it hath become a charge to you, until the fourteenth day of this month, and the whole assembly of the company of Israel have slaughtered it **between the evenings**;

The evidence shows that the Jews saw this Greek term "toward evening" to mean the *exact same thing* as the after-noon period, a fact that the Talmudic passage below confirms:

CHAPTER V.
REGULATIONS CONCERNING THE SACRIFICE OF THE PASCHAL LAMB.

MISHNA: The continual (daily) offering was slaughtered half an hour after the eighth hour, and sacrificed half an hour after the ninth hour; but on the day before Passover, whether that day happened to be a week-day or a Sabbath, it was slaughtered half an hour after the seventh hour, and sacrificed half an hour after the eighth hour. When the day before the Passover happened to be a Friday, it was slaughtered half an hour **after the sixth hour**, sacrificed half an hour after the seventh hour, **and the Passover sacrifice celebrated (immediately) afterwards.**

GEMARA: Whence do we know all this? Said Rabha: Because it is written [Numbers xxviii. 4], "**toward evening**," we know that this religious duty must be discharged **when the sun commences to move towards the west (evening)**. Then again, on all ordinary days, in respect to vow and voluntary offerings, as it is written [Lev. vi. 5]: "And he shall burn thereon the fat of the peace-offering." And the master said that this signifies that all the other offerings must be sacrificed before the daily offering. Hence this latter was slaughtered half an hour after the eighth hour (two and one half hours after noon); but on the **day before Passover, when the paschal lamb had to be slaughtered after the daily offering, the latter was slaughtered an hour sooner.** If the eve of Passover, however, fell on Friday, when the paschal lamb must be roasted before the Sabbath set in, the literal text of the passage in the Scriptures is abided by, and the daily offering is slaughtered **as soon as the sun commences setting towards the west,** *i.e.***, half an hour after noon**.[344]

We see several important facts in the above writing:

Numbers 28:4 is explained as "toward evening" (quoted from the Greek Septuagint) and interpreted as the time "the *sun commences to move towards the west (evening)*." These Talmudic scholars would also have known that in Hebrew, this verse says "between the evenings." Therefore, they knew that "toward evening" conveys the same meaning as "between the evenings."

To be extra careful to stay within the legal time, the Talmudic writers say that when the 14th day fell on a Friday, the daily (even-ing) offering was brought half an hour after noon. God had also commanded the daily evening offering to be brought "between the evenings" (Exodus 29:39), so the Talmudists correctly state that the daily (evening) offering happens during the same time period as the Passovers are brought.

---

[344] Babylonian Talmud, Book 3, Tract Pesachim, ch. 5, p. 106,
http://sacred-texts.com/jud/t03/psc09.htm.

Although the scriptures usually refer to the 14th day as the Passover, the Talmud and other Jewish writings often speak of "Passover" as the 15th-day Sabbath—which commemorates the day God "passed over" and brought the Israelites out of Egypt—and not the 14th day when the Passovers were slain. One reason the 15th day came to be called the Passover is that it was the entrance into the seven-day Festival, which itself was *called* Passover (Luke 22:1). Another reason for this is that after the Temple was destroyed in AD 70, Passover lambs were no longer sacrificed, so the 14th day was less important. Thus, when Talmudic writers speak of the "day before Passover" in this passage above, they mean the 14th day (which they show is the day the Passover was sacrificed).

Therefore, when the Talmudic writers state that "**on the eve of Passover** Yeshu was hanged,"[345] they mean that he died as the 14th day was closing. This is much as we use the term "Christmas eve" (the 24th) as the time period before Christmas (the 25th). Such idiomatic changes that occurred over time as well as the use of the term "Passover"—sometimes for different days—have probably greatly contributed to the confusion on the timing of the Passover and the Last Supper.

The Jewish Encyclopedia also concurs with this time to slay the Passover:

> In Temple times the paschal lamb was offered **during the afternoon of the eve of Passover**[346]

Where did the Talmudic writers get the idea that "between the evenings" (Hebrew) and "toward evening" (Greek Septuagint) indicate the same time as "When the sun commences to move towards the west?" The answer is from Deuteronomy 16:6 from the Greek Septuagint, where the God-commanded time to slay the Passover is on the 14th day "toward west sun" (πρὸς δυσμὰς ἡλίου). Notice the English translation of this scripture says, "**in the evening at** sunset":

> NAS Deuteronomy 16:6 but at the place where the LORD your God chooses to establish His name, you shall sacrifice the Passover **in the evening at sunset**, at the time that you came out of Egypt.

> LXT Deuteronomy 16:6 ἀλλ' ἢ εἰς τὸν τόπον ὃν ἐὰν ἐκλέξηται κύριος ὁ θεός σου ἐπικληθῆναι τὸ ὄνομα αὐτοῦ ἐκεῖ θύσεις τὸ πασχα ἑσπέρας **πρὸς δυσμὰς ἡλίου** ἐν τῷ καιρῷ ᾧ ἐξῆλθες ἐξ Αἰγύπτου

---

345 The Soncino Babylonian Talmud, Tractate Sanhedrin, Folio 43a, http://www.come-and-hear.com/sanhedrin/sanhedrin_43.html. *Yeshu* is the Hebrew name that is translated into English as "Jesus."

346 *The Jewish Encyclopedia*, vol. 5, p. 277, s.v. "Eve of Holidays."

The original Hebrew in the above scripture speaks of the **going in of the sun** (which begins its descent at noon). The Jewish scholars who translated this verse from Hebrew into Greek used a Greek phrase that says "toward west sun," which is boldfaced on the previous page. The Jewish *ArtScroll* commentary (Stone Edition, the Chumash), agrees with this timing from Deuteronomy 16:6 of "afternoon" when the sun descends:

> except at the place that Hashem, your God, will choose to rest His Name, there shall you slaughter the pesach-offering **in the afternoon, when the sun descends**, the appointed time of your departure from Egypt[347]

Jewish history from the time of Christ is unanimous that the proper time to slay the lambs was from noon until sunset. It is at noon when the sun begins its descent toward the western horizon or, as the Talmudists wrote, "when the sun commences to move towards the west." This is also why the Talmudic writers were so certain that all leaven had to be removed and burned prior to noon on the 14th day of Nisan, because from noon until sunset was the time in which the Passovers could legally be sacrificed. We saw that a sacrifice brought *before noon would not be a valid sacrifice*. This history from the Talmud is crucial, as it sheds light on why Jesus could not have sacrificed an early, invalid Passover while leaven was still on hand in Israel, and also why it would have been fine for him to eat bread at the Last Supper.

What Other Jewish Sources Say

The eminent Jewish scholar and historian Josephus, who was born around 7 years after the Crucifixion (AD 37), gives the time when the Passovers were sacrificed in his day:

> So these High Priests, upon the coming of that feast which is called the Passover, when they slay their sacrifices, **from the ninth hour until the eleventh**, but so that a company not less than ten belong to every sacrifice, (for it is not lawful for them to feast singly by themselves), and many of us are twenty in a company...[348]

Josephus gives us a time that is *after noon* for the proper slaying of the Passovers, in clear agreement with the legal time as given in the Talmud. Obviously it was not the

---

347 Scherman, Nosson. *The Chumash, the Stone Edition*. Brooklyn: Torah Educational Software, 1993. CD-ROM.
348 Whiston, *The New Complete Works of Josephus*, "Jewish Wars," 6.9.3, p. 906.

Jews who were confused on this issue. As we see from the chart near the beginning of this chapter, "from the ninth hour to the eleventh" would mean from around 2 to 5 PM.

God commanded several Temple duties to take place "between the evenings": Passover, evening offering, incense offering (the time of prayer), and the lighting of the lamps. These were all carried out in the Temple after noon; none of them occurred after sunset.

Let's look more closely at the *daily evening sacrifice*. Remember that the Jewish day ended at sundown (around 6 PM), and the time translated into English as "evening" actually meant "toward west sun" or "toward evening." The Jewish scholars who translated the Hebrew Old Testament into the Greek Septuagint used the word "***afternoon***" here in Exodus, but first we see two English translations:

> NIV Exodus 29:39   Offer one in the morning and the other **at twilight**.

> YLT Exodus 29:39   the one lamb thou dost prepare in the morning, and the second lamb thou dost prepare **between the evenings**;

Notice Young's (YLT above) accurately translates this as "between the evenings," which is the exact same Hebrew phrase God used in Exodus 12:6 when He commanded the proper time to slay the Passover lambs.

And here is what the Greek Septuagint has:

> LXT Exodus 29:39   τὸν ἀμνὸν τὸν ἕνα ποιήσεις τὸ πρωὶ καὶ τὸν ἀμνὸν τὸν δεύτερον ποιήσεις τὸ δειλινόν

The Greek adjective δειλινόν means "***in the afternoon***," as defined by *Friberg Greek Lexicon* and *BDAG Lexicon* (as an adverb it means "toward evening"). In the verse from the Septuagint (LXT), the Jewish scholars knew what they were doing when they translated this phrase into Greek as "after-noon." Notice how the English (NIV above) usually translates it with words such as "twilight," which is sometimes considered as the time after sunset. The English translations never say ***afternoon***, which was the meaning of the Greek word the Septuagint translators used, as well as the meaning of the Hebrew phrase "between the evenings," which also harmonizes with all of Jewish history.

Sacrificing a Passover "after sunset" of the 13th day would be invalid, because it was brought before noon of the 14th day, and because leaven would still be present in Israel. Sacrificing the Passover "after sunset" of the 14th day would be the next Jewish day (i.e., the 15th) and therefore would also be an invalid Passover.

Josephus, in regard to this daily *evening* sacrifice, wrote of the priests coming to the Temple at noon to begin this sacrificial duty:

> ... but for the most sacred place, none went in but the high priests, clothed in their special garments. Now there is so great caution used about these offices of religion, that the priests are appointed to go into the temple but at certain hours: for, in the morning, at the opening of the inner temple, those that are to officiate receive the sacrifices, **as they do again at noon**, till the doors are shut.[349]

He also wrote about the Temple morning and evening daily offerings:

> And any one may thus learn how very great piety we exercise towards God, and the observance of his laws, since the priests were not at all hindered from their sacred ministrations by their fear during this siege, but did still twice a day, in the morning **and about the ninth hour**, offer their sacrifices on the altar;[350]

Thus Josephus shows that this "evening" offering was sacrificed at "about the ninth hour" (around 2 to 3 PM), which was "between the evenings" (as per the Hebrew) and "in the afternoon" (as per the Greek Septuagint). In other words, it was right between the evenings. Josephus does not contradict himself—as some have thought—when he says elsewhere that the incense was offered at "sun-setting":

> ... but incense was to be offered twice a-day, both before sun-rising and at **sun-setting**.[351]

Remember that those who translate Josephus into English often have a set theological viewpoint as to when to slay the Passover (because they are sure that the Last Supper was the Passover, and that Jesus was also somehow crucified as the 14th-day Passover). Again we must return to the original Greek to see what Josephus said. His actual words (translated above as "sun-setting") are πρὸς (toward) and δυσμαὶς (west). So Josephus actually said that incense was offered twice each day: before "sun-rising" (probably meaning before the sun had fully risen) and ***toward west***. This is essentially the same rendering of Deuteronomy 16:6 from the Septuagint, which speaks of the time to slay the Passover as πρὸς δυσμὰς ἡλίου (***toward west sun***).

---

349 Whiston, *The New Complete Works of Josephus*, "Against Apion," 2.8.105, p. 966.
350 Whiston, *The New Complete Works of Josephus*, "Jewish Antiquities," 14.4.3, p. 459.
351 Josephus, *Antiquities*, 3.8.3, http://earlyjewishwritings.com/text/josephus/ant3.html.

These sources all agree with the timing mentioned in the Talmud.

Another famous Jewish writer and biblical philosopher from this time was Philo, who plainly stated that the Jews were to slay their Passovers "beginning at noonday" and "continuing till evening":

> Special laws, II:
>
> THE FOURTH FESTIVAL
> XXVII. (145) And after the feast of the new moon comes the fourth festival, that of the **passover**, which the Hebrews call pascha, on which the whole people offer sacrifice, **beginning at noonday** and continuing **till evening**.[352]

Philo also writes:

> Why is the Passover sacrificed πρὸς ἑσπέραν?[353] Perhaps because good things were about to befall at night. **It was not the custom to offer a sacrifice in darkness**, and for those who were about to experience good things at night it was **not proper to prepare it before the ninth hour**. Therefore it was not at random but knowingly that the prophet set a time between the turning πρὸς ἑσπέραν.[354]

So Philo completely agrees with the timing we saw earlier in the Talmud, which states "If the Paschal lamb be slaughtered before noon, *it is not valid*, because it is written [Exodus 12:6]: "***Toward the evening***.""[355] Philo also agrees with the timing of Josephus, who said the Passovers were sacrificed from the ninth to the eleventh hour (Wars 6.9.3), and he agrees with what we saw from the Jewish translation of the Hebrew into the Greek Septuagint.

The New Testament Agrees

We will also see shortly how these times agree with the New Testament regarding the keeping of the Passover. It is only when we come to the *English translations* that

---

352 Yonge, *The Works of Philo Judaeus*, "Special Laws II," 27:145, http://www.earlyjewishwritings.com/text/philo/book28.html.

353 Philo's two Greek words above are πρὸς ("toward") and ἑσπέραν ("evening"), hence "toward evening."

354 Marcus, *Philo Supplement II*, p. 20.

355 Babylonian Talmud, Book 3, Tract Pesachim, ch. 5, p. 113, http://sacred-texts.com/jud/t03/psc09.htm.

the idea of *after sunset* appears for the time to slay the Passovers. All of the Jewish histories and the scriptures (when correctly translated) contradict such an idea. Remember that the English translations were written by people who came from a centuries-old *tradition* of Jesus eating the Passover at the Last Supper. So they wanted Jesus to both eat the Passover one night and be slain as the Passover the following day, and have both events somehow happen on the legal 14th day.

Part of the confusion over the proper time of "between the evenings" stems from the fact that the Jews *added* a late evening prayer called "Ma'ariv." *Gateway to Judaism* describes the time for this late "evening" service as "twenty-five minutes after sundown, when three stars are visible."[356] Many Bible commentators incorrectly refer to this time of evening "when three stars are visible" as the time to sacrifice the Passovers. However, *Gateway to Judaism* also makes it clear that "actually, there were only two services in the Temple—morning and afternoon. The late evening prayer was added ***after*** the destruction of the Second Temple."[357]

So those who take the Hebrew phrase "between the evenings" to mean the time "when three stars are visible" are incorrect, because this "late evening" prayer *did not exist in Jesus's day*. In fact, this late evening (non-Temple) service did not even come into being until many years after Christ was crucified, and therefore it has no bearing whatsoever.

All of this brings us to the New Testament evidence, which tells us the *exact time* of the day when the evening incense offering would follow the daily continual evening sacrificial offering and therefore also shows the proper time to slay the Passovers:

> YLT Acts 3:1 And Peter and John were going up at the same time **to the temple**, at the hour of **the** prayer, **the ninth *hour***,

> GNT Acts 3:1 Πέτρος δὲ καὶ Ἰωάννης ἀνέβαινον εἰς τὸ ἱερὸν ἐπὶ τὴν ὥραν τῆς προσευχῆς τὴν ἐνάτην.

In the Greek scriptures, the definite article "the" (τῆς) is in front of the word "prayer" (προσευχῆς), so the exact wording is the hour of *the* prayer (at the ninth hour). This was not just any random prayer; it was the time when many of the Jewish faithful would be gathered together for the prayer that accompanied the daily "even-ing" sacrifice and the Temple incense offering. They would come together in the Temple each day for these morning and evening sacrificial offerings and for *the prayer* at the time of this incense offering. The timing was highly symbolic, as it represented their prayers being acceptable to God (after the sacrifices were offered) and symbolically rising up to Him as the *evening incense offering*. We have an excellent picture of this in Luke:

---

356 Shulman, *Gateway to Judaism*, vol. 1, p. 331.
357 Shulman, *Gateway to Judaism*, vol. 2, pp. 607–608.

> ^{NAS} Luke 1:5 In the days of Herod, king of Judea, there was a certain priest named Zacharias, of the division of Abijah; and he had a wife from the daughters of Aaron, and her name was Elizabeth.
>
> ^{NAS} Luke 1:8 Now it came about, while he was performing his priestly service before God in the *appointed* order of his division,
>
> ^{NAS} Luke 1:9 according to the custom of the priestly office, he was chosen by lot to **enter the temple** of the Lord and **burn incense**.
>
> ^{NAS} Luke 1:10 And the whole multitude of the people were **in prayer** outside **at the hour of the incense offering**.
>
> ^{NAS} Luke 1:11 And an angel of the Lord appeared to him, standing to the right of the altar of incense.

This was the Temple service that Peter and John were going up to, because this was when all the people would be gathered in the Temple. As mentioned, Acts 3:1 gives us this exact time for the even-ing offering of incense in the New Testament (i.e., the ninth hour, about 3 PM, which was of course "between the evenings"):

> ^{YLT} Acts 3:1 And Peter and John were going up at the same time to the temple, at the hour of **the** prayer, the **ninth** *hour*.

Josephus agreed with this exact same time specified in scripture, stating that the service of the evening sacrifice was at the **ninth hour** and that even during the siege of the Temple by Roman troops, while soldiers were throwing stones down upon them, the priests were still careful to do everything as God had commanded:

> And anyone may thus learn how very great piety we exercise towards God, and the observance of his laws, since the priests were not at all hindered from their sacred ministrations, by their fear during this siege, but did still twice a day, in the morning and **about the ninth hour**, offer their sacrifices on the altar; nor did they omit those sacrifices, if any melancholy accident happened by the stones that were thrown among them;[358]

---

358 Whiston, *The New Complete Works of Josephus*, "Jewish Antiquities," 14.4.3, p. 459.

Now we'll turn to the book of Revelation for more New Testament proof that in the time of Jesus, the Temple authorities kept the Passover, the evening offering, the incense offering (the prayer) at this same time—"between the evenings"—as commanded by God. In John's vision, it was after the lamb had been slain (picturing Christ) that the bowls of incense (representing the prayers of the people) were seen as ready to be offered:

> NAS Revelation 5:6   And I saw between the throne (with the four living creatures) and the elders **a Lamb standing, as if slain**, having seven horns and seven eyes, which are the seven Spirits of God, sent out into all the earth.

> NAS Revelation 5:8   And when He had taken the book, the four living creatures and the twenty-four elders fell down before the Lamb, having each one a harp, and golden **bowls full of incense, which are the prayers of the saints**.

Notice that the bowls of incense represent the prayers of the saints. These reverent Jews were obviously not ignorant of these pictures.

> NAS Revelation 8:3   And another angel came and stood at the altar, holding a golden censer; and much incense was given to him, that he might add it to **the prayers of all the saints** upon the golden altar which was before the throne.

> NAS Revelation 8:4   And the smoke of the incense, with the prayers of the saints, went up before God out of the angel's hand.

This picturing of the slain lamb and then the bowls of incense ready to be offered aligns with the timing mentioned in the Talmud:

> The rabbis taught: "The daily (evening) offering precedes the Passover-sacrifice, and the Passover-sacrifice precedes the burning of the incense, and the incense precedes the lighting of the candles."[359]

---

359   Babylonian Talmud, Book 3, Tract Pesachim, ch. 5, p. 108, http://sacred-texts.com/jud/t03/psc09.htm.

The Jews were acutely aware that the incense offering, which came after the daily evening sacrifice,[360] represented the prayers of the believers being accepted by God as the smoke floated heavenward. This is why they would be gathered in the Temple for the incense offering, at the time of the prayer (Luke 1:10).

King David was also well aware of these meanings:

> [NAS] Psalm 141:2   May **my prayer** be counted **as incense** before Thee; The lifting up of my hands as the **evening offering**.

The scholars who translated the Septuagint show (in the Greek below) that both the evening offering and the incense offering were made every morning and every **afternoon** (δείλης), contrary to how the English reads (every "evening"):

> [NIV] 2 Chronicles 13:11   Every morning and **evening** they present burnt offerings and fragrant incense to the LORD.

> [LXT] 2 Chronicles 13:11   θυμιῶσιν τῷ κυρίῳ ὁλοκαυτώματα πρωὶ καὶ δείλης[361]

Above, you can see that the Greek word in the Septuagint is "after-noon," not "evening" (which can imply "night-time" in English). So when we connect all this together, we see that what Acts 3:1 gives is within this same time frame (the ninth hour, around 3 PM) that these three Temple services (Passover, even-ing offering, and incense offering) were performed. And this is the exact same time given in all the Jewish histories—the after-noon period of the day, centering around ***the ninth hour***. It was also, of course, the ninth hour of the 14th day when the Jewish Messiah, "Christ our Passover"—the true Passover—fulfilled the sacrifice at God's appointed time of "between the evenings":

> [NAS] Mark 15:34   And at the ninth hour Jesus cried out with a loud voice, "Eloi, Eloi, lama sabachthani?" which is translated, "My God, My God, why hast Thou forsaken Me?"

> [NAS] Mark 15:37   And Jesus uttered a loud cry, and breathed His last.

---

360 Or after the Passover on the 14th day of Nisan each year.
361 Liddell and Scott's *A Greek-English Lexicon* defines δείλης as "**afternoon**" (p. 373).

468 | THE MESSIANIC FEAST

We saw in "Setting the Table 1" that the Jewish Quartodecimans (Fourteenthers) were derided for their keeping of the 14th day special and for fasting until the ninth hour on this day to honor the Lord's sacrifice, but the better history shows that their timing was correct.

What Does John Mean by the Sixth Hour?

There is a controversial verse in John that commentators have debated; John pictures the Messiah before Pilate at the sixth hour, with a band of chief priests demanding his crucifixion:

> YLT John 19:14 and it was the preparation of the passover, and **as it were the sixth hour**, and he saith to the Jews, 'Lo, your king!'

> YLT John 19:15 and they cried out, 'Take away, take away, crucify him;' Pilate saith to them, 'Your king shall I crucify?' the chief priests answered, 'We have no king except Caesar.'

> YLT John 19:16 Then, therefore, he delivered him up to them, that he may be crucified, and they took Jesus and led *him* away,

Some have thought verse 14 was a scribal error, for how could Jesus be here with Pilate about noon (the sixth hour) when the other Gospels say he was on the cross at the third hour (9 AM)? Commentators have pointed to a manuscript error since a few weaker manuscripts have "third hour" in the Greek. However, in his *Textual Commentary of the Greek New Testament*, Bruce Metzger points out that the manuscripts that change "sixth hour" to "third hour" are "an obvious attempt to harmonize the chronology with that of Mark 15:25."[362] He goes on to say that while some believe the disagreement arose when copyists confused the Greek numerals 3 and 6, the manuscript evidence is "***overwhelmingly in support of*** the Greek word for "***sixth***."

Some may jump to the conclusion that the scriptures contradict each other and that we should therefore throw our Bibles away and go home.

I believe, however, that the truth lies in the *Jewish idiom* for the sixth hour and what this hour meant to John and the other Jews as it relates to the Passover. From the Talmud, the importance of the sixth hour to Jews becomes clear, for the Passover *had to be selected* by the sixth hour, and from the sixth hour on was the *legal* time to kill the Passover. The other Greek word John used (ὡς), which Young's properly translates into "as it were" (John 19:14 above), shows its subtle meaning. John used

---

362 Metzger, *A Textual Commentary on the Greek New Testament*, p. 252.

the Jewish natural-to-spiritual idiom[363] to say the "sixth hour" in the natural sense, but he *means* the sixth hour in the spiritual sense by saying "as it were the sixth hour."

John subtly referred to Christ as the Passover in other ways also, one of them below:

> NAS John 19:32 The soldiers therefore came, and broke the legs of the first man, and of the other man who was crucified with Him;

> NAS John 19:33 but coming to Jesus, when they saw that He was already dead, they did not break His legs;

> NAS John 19:36 For these things came to pass, that the Scripture might be fulfilled, "**Not a bone of Him shall be broken.**"

John connects this truth from the scripture (concerning the command for the Passover sacrifice) with something that the Jews would understand from their history and in their idiom:

> NAS Exodus 12:46 "It is to be eaten in a single house; you are not to bring forth any of the flesh outside of the house, **nor are you to break any bone of it.**

Many have also wondered why there was darkness over the land from the sixth hour (noon) until the ninth hour (3 PM) on the day of the Crucifixion:

> NAS Matthew 27:45 Now from the sixth hour darkness fell upon all the land until the ninth hour.

Some commentators believed it was a solar eclipse, but Edersheim points out that there can be no eclipse at the time of the full moon, when Passover always occurs.[364] Some say it was because God could not bear to look upon His son as he suffered, but if this were the true reason, then why did God not cause the darkness right at the third hour (around 9 AM) when Jesus was nailed to the cross, instead of waiting until the sixth hour?

I believe the truth is found in the fact that the sixth hour was the final time for the Passovers to be designated, and the lawful time after which the Passover sacrifice could be killed (as we saw in the earlier quotes from Philo and the Talmud). God's

---

363 As explained in the chapter "Setting the Table 4."
364 Edersheim, *Life and Times*, Book 5, ch. 15, p. 604.

causing the darkness over the land at *noon* was His way of saying He would no longer look upon or accept the animal sacrificial system. This darkness at noon also fulfilled the scripture given by the prophet Amos:

> JPS Amos 8:9   And it shall come to pass in that day, saith the Lord GOD, that I will cause the sun to go down at noon, and I will darken the earth in the clear day.

> JPS Amos 8:10   And I will turn your feasts into mourning, and all your songs into lamentation; and I will bring up sackcloth upon all loins, and baldness upon every head; and I will make it as the mourning for an only son, and the end thereof as a bitter day.

God had now sent His son as a fulfillment of the sacrificial system, and He would no longer accept the sacrifices in the Temple. Thousands of the Jewish faithful would have been making ready (with their lambs already designated) at noon for the daily continual sacrifice to commence (remember Josephus said the doors for this afternoon Temple service open at noon). They would have had their spotless lambs picked out and ready to be sacrificed in the Temple, where their blood would be poured out at the altar before the great Holy of Holies. Some of these people would have had their Passover lambs in tow as they passed by the commotion where Christ was alongside the road on the cross, not far from the Temple. The Passover was the one time of year when the common Israelite could approach this great altar and sacrifice his Passover lamb; all other sacrifices were commanded by God to be performed by the priests.

Jesus said Peter would deny him three times before the cock crows. In fact that early morning "cock crow" ("cock summons" in Greek) was not a rooster, as many suppose, but the calling out to the priests to make ready for the morning sacrifice. There were three callings (summons) that went forth: early, middle, and late. The Talmud shows that there were twelve cocks (similar to faucets) at the laver in the Temple where the priests would first wash their hands and feet to prepare for the sacrifices.[365] *The Jewish Encyclopedia* (under Gebini) says this Temple crier's voice (cock crow) could be heard for miles as he called the priests to prepare for the sacrifice.

So while the priests were being summoned to the Temple to make ready for the morning sacrifice, Christ was being led toward the Crucifixion. The reason the chief priests are pictured at the cross at the time of the Crucifixion but not seen at the time of

---

[365] The mention of the cock crow appears in the Babylonian Talmud, Book 3, Tract Yomah, ch. 1, pp. 27–28, http://sacred-texts.com/jud/t03/yom06.htm; the reference to the twelve cocks at the laver where the priests would wash appears in Book 3, Tract Yomah, ch 3, pp. 51–53, http://sacred-texts.com/jud/t03/yom08.htm.

death is that by then were already back readying for the Passover sacrifice in the Temple (Mark 15:29–33). Those "passing by" (some even reviling the Messiah) were most likely on their way to the Temple, bringing their lamb sacrifice alongside them, all set for the day's proceedings. They thought they were going to offer their Passover sacrifice, all the while missing the fact that Christ—the true Passover—was fulfilling God's plan.

However, starting later this day, these lamb sacrifices in the Temple would no longer be accepted by God for atonement. Only by accepting the sacrifice of His son, Christ our Passover, is there forgiveness of sin. When Christ our Passover loudly cried out, "It is finished," around 3 PM, the darkness fled away. The lamb of God had paid the penalty for our sins, the sacrifice was complete, and the price for our atonement was paid.

God was now going to allow each person to make their own decision as to whether they would accept God's provision for sin, His own beloved son, the true Passover sacrifice. As the light of the sun again showed forth and the events of the day became widely known, many hearts had to wrestle with a decision. Once the sunlight came back out, there must have been pandemonium in the Temple among the priests and the multitudes who were waiting with their lambs as the darkness went away. The people beheld that the veil before the Holy of Holies was now torn in half and that the venerated place of God's presence and glory now lay bare and open before them. Not far away at Golgotha, at the foot of the cross, the Roman centurion spoke out, declaring, "truly this was the son of God" (Matthew 27:54).

So when we think back to John's words about the sixth hour (John 19:14), we must consider that there may be another truth being shown, before we take the position that the scriptures contradict themselves.

God's plan of redemption for humanity was fulfilled. Just as Joseph had comforted his brethren and told them that his being sold into Egypt was all part of God's plan from the beginning **to preserve many people alive**, so would the Lord speak similar words of comfort to all today.

> NAS Genesis 50:20 "And as for you, you meant evil against me, *but* **God meant it for good** in order to bring about this present result, **to preserve many people alive**.

The Nation of Israel, too, will see these things, as given in the following prophecy by Zechariah:

> NAS Zechariah 12:10 "And I will pour out on the house of David and on the inhabitants of Jerusalem, the Spirit of grace and of supplication, so that they will look on Me whom they have pierced; and they will mourn for Him, as one mourns for an only son, and they will weep bitterly over Him, like the bitter weeping over a first-born.

PART 2

The Ritual—
Why Didn't the Jewish Disciples Teach It?

*All truth passes through three stages: First, it is ridiculed;
Second, it is violently opposed. Third, it is accepted as self-evident.*
—Arthur Schopenhauer (1788–1860)

If the Messiah had wanted his followers to keep an ongoing ritual of Communion in which we eat bread and drink wine in his remembrance, surely he would have provided clear instruction for this. Also, surely his Jewish disciples would have gone out teaching this ritual. In this chapter, we will carefully consider any possible scriptural evidence of this supposedly important ritual. But first, a few historical dots need to be connected for us to see where our present-day Protestant ritual originated.

Setting the Stage

In "Setting the Table 1," we saw that the early Messianic Jews firmly adhered to the understanding that Jesus was crucified on the 14th day of Nisan as the true Passover, and therefore he could not have eaten the Passover at the Last Supper on the previous night. Their adherence to this day caused them to be mocked as Quartodecimans (Fourteenthers) by the Romans and subjected to persecution.

Course 1 presented proof from the scriptures that Jesus, in his parable at the Last Supper, held and broke one leavened bread—which makes sense since this meal was the night *before* the Passover, when leavened bread was perfectly legal. Of course this raises the question that if Jesus was teaching a ritual with *leavened* bread, then why do Roman Catholics and Protestants use *unleavened* bread in their rituals? Course 2 showed that the followers of the Messiah understood that his instruction was given in figurative language (in parables), meaning that we, the believers, represent the pieces of the one bread and are the members of one body—the spiritual body of Christ.

We saw no fewer than 50 reasons why the Last Supper was not the Passover (in the chapter of the same name). The only way to fit the New Testament events into the Passover template is with the Last Supper *not* being the Passover but instead with Jesus being slain on the 14th day as the fulfillment of the Passover (covered in the

"Template Challenge"). These proofs support the scriptures that present Jesus and the disciples eating regular bread at the Last Supper, and this opens the door to question the unleavened bread ritual that has been handed down through the centuries. Now we will examine the scriptures to see if the ritual of Communion was indeed what the Messiah taught and wanted.

The "Great Commission"

In what commentators call the "Great Commission," Jesus specifically told his disciples to go out to "all the nations" and to teach them "**all that I commanded you**":

> NAS Matthew 28:19a "**Go therefore** and make disciples of **all the nations**....
>
> NAS Matthew 28:20 **teaching them to observe all that I commanded you**; and lo, I am with you always, even to the end of the age."

With such clear instruction from the Messiah, surely these Jewish apostles and various scripture writers would not have neglected to teach this supposedly important ritual of Communion to the nations (if in fact it was a holy ritual commanded by the Lord). Although Jesus commissioned his disciples to teach "all that I commanded," this still would have implied that they teach what he *meant* and not just what he said, for on the night of the Last Supper, he also told them the following:

> NAS John 16:25 "These things I have spoken to you **in figurative language**; an hour is coming when I will speak no more to you **in figurative language**, but will tell you plainly of the Father.

Right after the Last Supper, when Jesus finally spoke plainly to his disciples, they specifically commented on this, exclaiming to him:

> NIV John 16:29b "**Now** you are speaking clearly and **without figures of speech**.

At the Last Supper the Messiah had given many statements in parables, for he knew his disciples could not bear to hear the new truths at that time while they were still locked into their Old Covenant traditions and methodology. But as he said after supper, he knew that when they received the outpouring of God's spirit at Pentecost, the meaning of his statements would be revealed to them:

> ^{NAS} John 16:12 "I have many more things to say to you, but **you cannot bear** *them* **now**.
>
> ^{NAS} John 16:13 "But when He, the Spirit of truth, comes, **He will guide you into all the truth**; for He will not speak on His own initiative, but whatever He hears, He will speak; and He will disclose to you what is to come.
>
> ^{NAS} John 14:26 "But the Helper, the Holy Spirit, whom the Father will send in My name, **He will teach you all things**, and **bring to your remembrance all that I said** to you.

The spirit of God would take the Messiah's statements at the Last Supper and reveal the fullness of what he meant in his parables:

> ^{NIV} John 16:14 He will bring glory to me by taking from what is mine and **making it known to you**.

So we have to determine—from what the apostles would later go out and teach—which of the things Jesus taught at the Last Supper were to be understood *figuratively* and which (if any) were to be taken literally.

When we see what the Jewish apostles went out and taught—that now *we* are the body of Christ (see Course 2)—it quickly becomes evident that they understood the Last Supper teachings concerning the bread to contain *figurative language*. Roman theologians, however, would later interpret the teachings literally, resulting in the creation of their ritual of Communion.

As we've seen, the Messiah's teachings were filled with figurative language and parables. For instance, right after the Last Supper, Jesus said he was the grapevine and that his disciples were the branches that needed to stay connected to the vine or they would dry up. Nowhere does Jesus say, "This is a parable," and nowhere does the Bible qualify that Jesus did not actually become a grapevine (John 15:1–14). In the same way, Jesus mentioning the bread and fruit of the grapevine at the Last Supper does not mean that these words were to be taken literally to become a new ritual. We do not conduct a ritual of holding hands and pretending to be branches connected to a grapevine based on what Jesus said, yet we have been told to eat a wafer of bread and drink a little cup of grape juice in the belief that this is what the Jewish Messiah wanted for "communion" with God.

Since we are taught in the scriptures to prove all things (Titus 5:21), we will now go through the books of the New Testament to see if the scriptures prove a ritual of Communion, or if this ritual was in fact passed down from Rome as a tradition of man.

The Apostles: Did They Teach or Even Mention a Ritual?

Did John the Beloved Teach This Doctrine?

We will begin with John, who (along with Peter and James) was one of the inner three closest to Jesus. John was "he whom Jesus loved" and the one who leaned on his chest at the Last Supper (John 21:20). Despite being so close to Jesus, John completely omits this Last Supper account of the supposed ritual where the Lord shares the bread and the fruit of the vine. Nothing whatsoever is mentioned in the Gospel of John that would cause anyone to think they should keep this ritual.

Although Rome misunderstood the Messiah's words concerning his flesh and blood in John 6:53–63 to apply literally in their ritual, these scriptures were meant as spiritual truth (as we saw in Course 11). John mentions nothing about a ritual with bread and fruit of the vine, and nothing at all about a recurring Blessed Eucharist or Communion service. Nor is this supposedly important ritual mentioned in 1, 2, or 3 John. When John writes to the seven churches in Asia in the book of Revelation, he has a great opportunity to teach these churches all about this ritual and how to perform it correctly, yet he writes nothing of it. John never even touches on this continual ritual that the Messiah supposedly commanded and thus fails terribly (if we are to believe that the Messiah commanded this ritual).

Surely Peter the Apostle Taught This Ritual?

If this ritual were something the Lord really wanted, surely it would have been taught by Peter (another of the Lord's inner circle). The Jewish Peter wrote two letters (1 and 2 Peter) to the scattered Jews, providing another excellent opportunity to teach this important new ritual to those Jews. He begins his first letter as follows:

> NAS 1 Peter 1:1   Peter, an apostle of Jesus Christ, to those who reside as aliens, **scattered**[366] throughout Pontus, Galatia, Cappadocia, Asia, and Bithynia, who are chosen

So this is Peter's big chance to obey the Lord, teach the nations all that Jesus commanded, and use his letters to teach this supposed ritual to the scattered Jews in the Diaspora. However, Peter completely drops the ball, for if we search 1 and 2 Peter for any teaching on this supposed ritual, we see that he never mentions bread, wine, grape juice, or the importance of keeping any ritual of Communion. Nor does Peter mention the Blessed Eucharist. So are we to believe that all these people whom Peter addressed missed out on this important ritual that Jesus commanded? Or is the truth rather that Peter knew exactly what Jesus meant at the Last Supper, and that he was not teaching a new ritual?

---

[366] The Greek word translated as "scattered" is *diaspora*.

Twice Peter speaks of Jesus's blood, yet never in connection with the ritual. In fact, in one of the references Peter tells the Jews of the Diaspora to be "sprinkled" with Jesus's blood, something Jesus never said to do in any scripture. Yet Peter says to do this to **obey** the Lord:

> ^{NAS} 1 Peter 1:2 according to the foreknowledge of God the Father, by the sanctifying work of the Spirit, that you may **obey Jesus Christ and be sprinkled with His blood**: May grace and peace be yours in fullest measure.

Was this scripture really something Jesus commanded? Or was this instead what Jesus *meant* at the Last Supper, aligning with the existing Jewish natural-to-spiritual idiom in which the blood sprinkled on the people under Moses pointed spiritually to applying Christ's blood for sanctification under the New Covenant?

The Jews of the Diaspora would have understood that Peter was not speaking of a new ritual of literally sprinkling blood, but rather making a connection to the way in which Moses sealed the first covenant. So Peter does not even qualify his statement to them. The concept of Moses inaugurating the first covenant by the sprinkling of blood was very familiar to these first-century Jews:

> ^{NAS} Exodus 24:8 So Moses took the blood and **sprinkled *it* on the people**, and said, "**Behold the blood of the covenant**, which the LORD has made with you in accordance with all these words."

If the Roman Catholics are right and we are to keep this ritual, then the only time we would ever have Jesus's blood available to sprinkle on one another would be during the ritual of Communion. So why do we not obey Jesus and do this? No church—Catholic or Protestant—follows this command literally by having the members sprinkle one another with wine at their ritual of Communion, because they understand that Peter is speaking spiritually in this scripture. Yet when they then turn around and consider the words Jesus spoke at the Last Supper, they accidentally take his words literally, as if this were a new ritual that the Jewish Messiah wanted. This begs the question—why would Peter completely omit this supposed commandment from the Lord to carry out a ritual when he writes to these scattered Jews?

The answer, of course, is that Peter never thought the Lord wanted such a ritual, so he never even mentioned it.

Let's Check James—Surely He Will Follow the Lord's Commandment, as He Also Writes to the Scattered Jews

> NAS James 1:1 James, a bond-servant of God and of the Lord Jesus Christ, to the twelve tribes who are dispersed[367] abroad, greetings.

Okay, this is a good start. James is writing to those in the nations as Christ asked; surely he will tell them of this most holy and important ritual. However, we quickly see that James "fails" to teach this ritual, just as Peter and John "failed" to do. James does not once mention bread, wine, grape juice, the Blessed Eucharist, or anything about a ritual of Communion.

So we know that the Lord's inner circle (Peter, James, and John) wrote absolutely nothing in the scriptures about going out and keeping the Last Supper teachings as a ritual of Communion. You would certainly think that those three men who were closest to Jesus would teach this important ritual if the Jewish Messiah had commanded it. Why didn't they obey the Lord, who, according to the scripture, told them to teach the nations "to observe **all** that I commanded you" (Matthew 28:19)?

What about the Other Gospels?

We have already seen that the Gospel of John mentions nothing about the ritual, but some may say, "What about the three other Gospels, don't they teach it?" It is true that the synoptic Gospels—Matthew, Mark, and Luke—explain what Jesus said and what the disciples ate at the Last Supper. But throughout his life Jesus spoke of many things in the form of parables that were meant to be understood *spiritually* instead of literally. Let's look at the Gospel accounts of Matthew and Mark (we'll get to Luke later) to see if either of them says that we are to keep this Last Supper teaching as a new and perpetual ritual.

Surely Matthew Obeyed the Lord's Injunction and Taught This Ritual?

No. Matthew also says nothing about the Lord wanting everyone to eat bread and drink grape juice in a continuing ritual. He does recount the events of the Last Supper—that Jesus broke a bread, poured a cup of grape juice (fruit of the vine), and gave these to the twelve to eat and drink—but not once does he say that Jesus wanted everyone in the future to act this out in a ritual of Communion. He never even ekes out a "do this." If the Lord wanted this ritual to be taught and performed by all believers throughout history, Matthew completely failed to communicate this. If Matthew (and the other Gospel writers) wanted to inform us that this was a ritual

---

367 The Greek word translated into English as "dispersed" is again *diaspora*, so the verse reads "to the twelve tribes, those in the Diaspora …."

to be followed from then on, he simply had to say something like, "This holy ritual of the Blessed Eucharist shall be performed by all believers forever, using unleavened bread, amen." But he says *nothing* about continually performing any such ritual.

How about Mark—Will He Teach It?

Surely Mark will come through for us? No. Upon reading Mark's account, we see the exact same failure to teach the ritual as in John, Peter, James, and Matthew. In Mark, we see the same basic account of the Last Supper as in Matthew, whereby the Lord gives the twelve apostles the pieces of the bread and the grape juice (fruit of the vine) *without a word* about a ritual of Communion. Mark's account simply says that the disciples ate bread and drank fruit of the vine, *but nothing more about all the nations keeping it in the future as some kind of ritual with unleavened bread.*

Why do these Gospel writers fail so miserably to teach this as a recurring ritual? The truth is that they are not failing, because they never thought that the Lord wanted such a ritual, because the Lord himself never desired it. Some have tried to see this ritual in the book of Acts, when the apostles were supposedly having a ritual of Communion—either in the Temple or going from house to house in Jewish Jerusalem. However, we saw the impossibility of that in Courses 3 and 4, where we viewed "breaking bread" through the spiritual idioms of the first-century Messianic believers.

What about Paul's Letter to the Romans and Others?

The Roman Catholics are very big on this ritual, so surely the former Pharisee Paul taught them all about it in his letter to the Romans?

No. Even Paul did *not mention a Last Supper ritual* in his letter to the Romans, nor grape juice, fruit of the vine, the ritual of Communion, or the Blessed Eucharist. He didn't even mention bread to them. So the Roman Catholics must have received their teaching from some other source.

Paul also wrote to the Galatians, Ephesians, Philippians, and Colossians, and again failed to teach the ritual to the believers in these cities by saying nothing about the Last Supper or keeping this supposed ritual with grape juice and unleavened bread. If Paul wrote the Epistle to the Hebrews, as most believe, once again he failed by saying *nothing* about a ritual or how to conduct it.

Paul also wrote two letters to the Thessalonians, and nowhere did he mention that they should be eating unleavened bread or drinking the fruit of the vine in a ritual.

What about Paul's letters to his student, Timothy? Paul warned Timothy to not teach any of the strange doctrines that were floating around at the time:

> NAS 1 Timothy 1:3 As I urged you upon my departure for Macedonia, remain on at Ephesus, in order that you may instruct certain men not to teach strange doctrines,

Was Paul warning against those who might question the ritual? How could he be, since no one taught the ritual. Sadly for those wanting it, we do not see any instruction from Paul to Timothy—or to any of these several cities that Paul wrote to—on how to celebrate this supposedly important ritual. There is a complete lack of direction as to whether regular bread is fine or if *matzah* (unleavened) should be used, or how often the ritual should be kept. In short, nothing is mentioned about eating bread or drinking fruit of the vine in a ritual. Nor is there anything in Paul's letter to Titus about performing this Blessed Eucharist or how to do it properly, and nothing about bread or wine. Nor is there any mention about a ritual of Communion in Paul's letter to Philemon.

Have We Missed Anyone?

What about Jude—did he mention the ritual? No, in fact, Jude also completely failed to teach it.

Of the 27 books of the New Testament, we have now covered 24, and not a word or hint suggests that we are to keep this ritual of Communion, or how often, or with what type of bread (regular leavened bread such as at the Last Supper, or unleavened bread as most churches teach today). If Jesus had truly wanted this ritual to be taught to all nations and he had commanded his disciples to teach it, then the Jewish apostles have turned the Great Commission into the "Great Omission."

In his second letter to the Corinthians, Paul mentioned nothing about a ritual of Communion or about eating bread and drinking from a cup in a Blessed Eucharist.

So now only two books are left in the whole Bible that could possibly tell us to keep this important ritual: Paul's first letter to the Corinthians and the Gospel of Luke. We have already seen in Courses 5, 6, and 11 what Paul meant in 1 Corinthians chapters 10–12, so here it suffices to remind the believer that Paul was speaking *spiritually* throughout those chapters. He said that *we* are the body of Christ (not that the ritual bread was his body), and individually we are members of Christ's spiritual body (Course 2). Paul said we all partake from the one bread, and that the one bread (which Jesus broke and shared) showed that *we* are all members in one body (1 Corinthians 10:17). He said nothing to the effect that the bread in a ritual was Christ's human body. All of this shows that Paul understood Jesus was speaking in parables at the Last Supper.

"Do This," but Do What?

Those who are hoping for proof of this ongoing ritual are down to one book in the New Testament: the Gospel of Luke. Happily for those who want this ritual, we have a tiny shred of evidence. The totality of proof for a continued ritual of Communion from the Gospels is found in these two words—"do this"—from Luke 22:19 (in boldface below). However, even here we are given no instruction, such as to "do this

480 | THE MESSIANIC FEAST

in a new ritual with unleavened bread"; the Lord just tells his disciples to drink from the cup and to eat from the bread:

> NAS Luke 22:17   And when He had taken a cup *and* given thanks, He said, "Take this and share it among yourselves;

> NAS Luke 22:18   for I say to you, I will not drink of the fruit of the vine from now on until the kingdom of God comes."

> NAS Luke 22:19   And when He had taken *some* bread *and* given thanks, He broke *it*, and gave *it* to them, saying, "This is My body which is given for you; **do this** in remembrance of Me."

> NAS Luke 22:20   And in the same way *He took* the cup after they had eaten, saying, "This cup which is poured out for you is the new covenant in My blood.

The question is whether Jesus meant "do this" literally, or was he yet again speaking spiritual truth in figurative language?

Remember from Course 2 that the Greek word for "This" (as in "This is my body" from verse 19 above) does not align grammatically with the Greek word for "bread," which shows that Jesus was speaking spiritually. He was *not* saying "this bread is my body, and I want you to eat my body (only symbolically for Protestants) in a new ritual."

Remember, too, the multitude of examples where Jesus or the apostles said something in the natural that was to be taken spiritually, as seen in "Setting the Table 4." There we listed many examples, such as Paul telling the Hebrews that "we have an altar" that was understood spiritually by the churches; we do not literally go out looking for the lost altar of Paul to offer sacrifices on. The same is true when Jesus spoke of himself as the bread of life; he was speaking of something in the natural but intended spiritual truth with his use of figurative language.

So now we would have to consider whether "this do" or "do this" (depending on the translation in Luke 22:19) is meant to be taken spiritually or naturally. In 26 of the 27 New Testament books, no evidence exists whatsoever that the followers of the Messiah taught a ritual of Communion. So against this overwhelming lack of evidence, are we now to interpret these two words in Luke as a natural ritual that is important to keep? Or instead should we see that Jesus wanted the disciples to "do this" *spiritually*,[368] fulfilling the meaning behind the figurative language he used in his Last Supper parables?

---

368   As covered in Course 2 in the section " 'This Do,' But Do What—a New Ritual?"

^{NAS} John 16:25 "These things I have spoken to you in figurative language; an hour is coming when I will speak no more to you in figurative language, but will tell you plainly of the Father.

It's important that we see Jesus not as a Roman Catholic priest teaching a new ritual at the Last Supper, but as the first-century Jewish Messiah teaching spiritual truth using figurative language. If Jesus intended to teach a new Roman or Protestant ritual, then Luke (like the other three Gospel writers) failed to get the full information across to us. The two Greek words translated as "do this" say nothing about the disciples keeping this as a new ritual, nor do they say anything about all people on earth throughout all time keeping this as a *ritual*. Neither do they give any specifics, such as how often the ritual should be kept or with what kind of bread.

It is true that "do this" is also found in 1 Corinthians 11:23–25, but the same rules of Bible interpretation apply there as well. As mentioned earlier, Course 5 made it clear that Paul was teaching spiritual truth based on what he received from the Lord, and was not teaching a ritual. Jesus was also not teaching a ritual. He was teaching *spiritual* truth in parables. Jesus wanted the disciples to understand—and then go out teaching—that the bread he broke into pieces showed that we are members of his spiritual body. He wanted them to understand that we are to partake of God's love in and through one another; this is how he will provide spiritual sustenance in the New Covenant.

The fruit of the vine that he poured out represented his shed blood that would provide the New Covenant. This blood would flow spiritually in the spiritual body, providing cleansing from sin (1 John 1:7), and it would symbolize the spiritual life provided in the New Covenant, of God's love and His spirit. We "do this" and remember the Messiah as we fulfill what he *meant* in his Last Supper parables, by sharing and fellowshipping among the members of the spiritual body with Christ and God's presence in the midst. These are the kinds of things the followers of the Messiah taught. This is what they knew the Lord wanted, which is why we did not see any of them teaching the ritual.

One could ask—when Jesus says in Luke "***do this*** in remembrance of me"—how these disciples could "remember" Jesus if they did not keep doing this as a Communion ritual? However, many Protestant churches keep this ritual just twice a year, so do they therefore only "remember" Jesus twice a year? Most Catholic churches and some Lutherans have a Communion ritual at every service; shouldn't the Protestants also "remember" Jesus *at every service* if this ritual is how Jesus wanted us to remember him?

The Protestants would argue and say "No, we remember Jesus every day and at every service; it is the ritual we only do twice a year." So, by their own admission, one can remember Jesus *without* performing rituals of eating unleavened bread and drinking grape juice. Jesus wanted us to remember him as we fulfill what he *meant*, which was the true spiritual communion in God's love.

The Azymites Shed Light on the Protestant Ritual

There is a very important part of history, although often ignored or untold, that sheds light on the true origins of the Protestant ritual with unleavened bread. In Course 1 we saw that Jesus held one regular leavened bread at the Last Supper, so why do the Catholics and Protestants both keep a ritual today using *unleavened* bread?

History is clear that the Roman Catholic Church made a change in their ritual from regular leavened bread to unleavened bread sometime around the 9th to 11th century. Prior to this time Rome, along with the Greek and Eastern Churches (those of them that actually kept this ritual), used regular leavened bread. In fact the Greek and Eastern Churches derided the Romans for making this change, calling them "Azymites" (meaning "unleavened ones" in Greek). So the resistance to Roman decrees that had begun with the Asiatic Fourteenthers in the east (see "Setting the Table 1") took a new turn when the Greek and Eastern Churches ridiculed Rome's change to unleavened. Rome's new focus on certain aspects of their ritual came to the forefront, which contributed to the ultimate separation between the Eastern Churches and the Western Roman Church in what came to be known as the Great Schism.

Those Greek and Eastern Churches that kept this as a ritual had always used regular leavened bread. To the Greeks, the "risen" bread (from the leaven that expanded the dough in the heat, aerating it when baked) was symbolic of the risen Christ. At the time of this controversy and name-calling, the Greeks wrote to Rome stating that their word for bread (*arton*) was derived from their Greek word αἴρω (pronounced *"airo"*) meaning "elevated" or "raised up" (from which we get our English word "air"). *The Catholic Encyclopedia* preserves part of this letter that was written to Rome:

> You call bread *panis;* we call it artos (ἄρτος). This from airoel (αἴρω), to raise, signifies a something elevated, lifted up, being raised and warmed by the ferment and salt; the azym, on the other hand, is as lifeless as a stone or baked clay, fit only to symbolize affliction and suffering.[369]

Most Protestant Bible encyclopedias mention nothing about this Roman change to unleavened bread in their ritual, and nothing about the Azymites. The following quote from McClintock and Strong, however, does mention them. Furthermore, it states that there was no history of using **unleavened** bread in the Latin Church before this late change took place:

---

[369] Herbermann et al, *The Catholic Encyclopedia*, vol. 2, p. 172, s.v. "Azymites."

> Azymites: (from ἀ *negative* and ζύμη, *leaven*), a title applied by the Greeks to the Western Church, because it uses unleavened bread in the Eucharist. The **Greek Church has always maintained the use of leavened bread** (*Conf. Ecc. Orient.* c. 9). The practice in the Latin Church of consecrating with unleavened bread was one of the charges brought against that Church by the Greeks in the middle of the eleventh century, and there does not appear to have been any dispute on the subject between the two churches much before that period. Indeed Sirmondus maintains that **the use of unleavened bread in the holy Eucharist was unknown to the Latin Church before the tenth century**, and his opinion has the support of Cardinal Bona (*Per. Litur.* i, 23), Schelstrat, and Pagi. — Bingham, *Orig. Eccles.* bk. xv, ch. ii, § 5.[370]

After the Protestants left the Catholic Church, they took along this same unleavened bread ritual that originated in Rome, but left off certain aspects of it in stages. Luther dropped transubstantiation (the belief that the bread and wine are turned into Christ's flesh and blood), but he could not let go of a literal understanding of John 6:53 and thus taught consubstantiation, the sad belief that the flesh and blood must still somehow be contained in the bread and wine. Obviously, neither Rome's nor Luther's interpretation would have aligned with the first-century Jewish concept of what Jesus meant in these parables.

Zwingli, a leader of the Reformation in Switzerland in the early 1500s, also continued to keep the unleavened bread ritual, believing it was what the Lord wanted, but he taught that it was just symbolic and that the bread and wine did not change. For this "outrageous" belief, Luther said Zwingli was of the devil. Most Protestants today who follow Zwingli's lead in the ritual (believing that bread and wine are symbolic and do not change substance) would therefore be of the devil, according to Luther.

It must be remembered that most of the earliest Protestants were men (some were priests or monks) who had grown up in the Roman Catholic Church. When they protested and departed from the Catholic Church, they accidentally brought along this unleavened bread ritual while dropping the disturbing belief in transubstantiation. Although the Protestant cry was "back to the Bible," it is clear that this unleavened bread ritual did not come from the Bible, for Jesus held one regular leavened bread at the Last Supper (as Course 1 proved). Prior to Rome's change, there was no history of a ritual with unleavened bread or any such instruction given in the scriptures from which these Protestants could draw.

---

[370] McClintock and Strong, *Cyclopedia*, vol. 1, pp. 577–578, s.v. "Azymites."

This information is not meant to denigrate those original Protestants, for we owe a great debt of gratitude to those brave men, many of whom gave their lives so that we could have the freedom to choose our own beliefs. It is only to point out that the Protestant ritual grew out of the Roman ritual, and did not come from the scriptures. Thus we should distance ourselves from it as we move forward to the true scriptural communion, a spiritual communion that God desires with His people.

The Catholic Encyclopedia claims that the Roman use of unleavened bread in their ritual became obligatory in the ninth century, and it also provides more information on the Azymites:

> Azymites (α, privative and $\zeta\acute{\upsilon}\mu\eta$, leaven), a term of reproach used by the schismatic Greeks since the eleventh century against the Latins, who, together with the Armenians and the Maronites, celebrate the Holy Eucharist with unleavened bread. Since reviling is apt to beget reviling, some few Latin controversialists have retorted by assailing the Greeks as "Fermentarians" and "Prozymites." There was, however, but little cause for bitterness on the Latin side, as the Western Church has always maintained the validity of consecration with either leavened or unleavened bread. Whether the bread which Our Lord took and blessed at the Last Supper was leavened or unleavened is another question. Regarding the usage in the primitive Church our knowledge is so scant, and the testimonies so apparently contradictory, that many theologians have pronounced the problem incapable of solution. **Certain it is that in the ninth century the use of unleavened bread had become universal** and obligatory in the west....[371]

Whether *The Catholic Encyclopedia* is correct and their change to unleavened bread occurred in the ninth century, or if the McClintock and Strong quote is correct and the use of unleavened bread in their ritual was unknown before the 10th century, the same point is true. Prior to this period, the Church in Rome (along with Greek and Eastern Churches) kept the ritual with regular leavened bread.

As an aside, these same facts expose the unleavened bread Communion ritual of the Jehovah's Witnesses as well as the Mormon Communion ritual and that of other sects, revealing that they were all offshoots of the Roman Catholic ritual. It shows they all misunderstood the Messiah's teaching when he used regular bread in his parables, for neither he nor the early disciples ever taught this ritual, nor did they want it.

---

[371] Herbermann et al, *The Catholic Encyclopedia*, vol. 2, p. 172, s.v. "Azymites."

Why Make This Late Change to Unleavened Bread?

After having conducted their ritual with regular leavened bread for several hundred years, why would Rome make such a dramatic change to unleavened bread?

History shows that sometime around the ninth century new words began to be applied to the Roman ritual, beginning with *transitio*, then later *transubstantiatio*, and eventually *transubstantiation*. The *New Catholic Encyclopedia* writes of a "new epoch" in the Catholic Eucharist during this period, when these Latin words for transubstantiation were starting to be used in connection with their ritual:

> **Medieval Period.** A **new epoch** of reflection on the Eucharist opened up in the 9th century. The outstanding figure in this period was PASCHASIUS RADBERTUS (d. *c.* 859), who clearly set forth **the Catholic teaching on transubstantiation**.[372]

McClintock and Strong attribute the first probable usage of the Latin term *transubstantiatio* in connection with their ritual to Peter Damili around the beginning of the 11th century, although *transitio* had been in use some time before that:

> Probably the first to make use of the word *transubstantiatio* was Peter Damin (*Expositio Can. Miss.* cap. vii; Mai, *Script. Vet. Nov. Coll.* VI, ii, 215), A.D. 988–1072; though similar expressions, such as *transitio*, had previously been employed.[373]

Although these new Latin words first came into use around the time of their "new epoch" of teaching on transubstantiation, the first official Roman Church document that declared their bread and wine "changed" was written in the 11th century:

> The most important of these was the Roman Council of 1079, which for the first time in an official document declared that the bread and wine were "substantially changed" into the body and blood of Jesus (*Enchirdion symbolorum*, 700).[374]

The first written appearance of the actual term in an official Roman Church document was in 1215 at their fourth Lateran Council, where bread and wine are spoken of as being "transubstantiated" into the body and blood of Christ.

---

372 *New Catholic Encyclopedia*, vol. 14, p. 158, s.v. "Transubstantiation/Medieval Period."
373 McClintock and Strong, *Cyclopedia*, vol. 10, p. 526, s.v. "Transubstantiation."
374 *New Catholic Encyclopedia*, vol. 14, p. 158, s.v. "Transubstantiation/Medieval Period."

With this new epoch and new focus on transubstantiation, Rome also decided to switch its ritual bread to unleavened at this time. The most likely explanation for this late and drastic change is that with their focus on the bread being *transubstantiated* into Christ's sinless flesh, it should be unleavened. They certainly did not get this new teaching from the Bible, for we saw Jesus held one regular leavened bread in his parable at the Last Supper (since it was not the Passover).

The only other possible reason for such a major change in their doctrine is that, coming to the realization that (since they believed) the Last Supper was the Passover (where unleavened was required), Jesus would have taught the ritual using unleavened bread. But this isn't much of an explanation since, from about 350 AD onward, most churches believed the Last Supper was the Passover, yet this did not hinder them from using regular bread in their ritual all those years.

Regardless of the true reason for Rome's change to unleavened bread, we can see from history that this was where the Protestant ritual originated, for prior to Rome's late change in the ritual, no other foundation existed for a ritual using unleavened bread. All the apostolic writings refer to regular leavened bread at the Last Supper (as Course 1 made clear), and the early, mostly Jewish writers of scripture did not teach this ritual.

So the last question to consider is this: If the apostles and all the early Messianic believers had taught the importance of such a ritual using unleavened bread (and the Last Supper had been the Passover, as we have been told), how could all the churches from Rome to Greece and farther east have got it completely wrong by using regular leavened bread for some 1,000 years? And furthermore, why was there not a single remark by any teacher, church writer, or historian about the error of this? Why was it only when Rome switched its ritual from using regular bread to unleavened bread that this controversy occurred? The reason is that neither the Messiah nor his early followers taught that we were to keep this as a ritual—with unleavened bread or otherwise—and that's why there was no controversy prior to the 9th century.

A Few More Points from the First-Century Jewish Idioms

Rome interpreted the "breaking bread" that the disciples wrote about in Acts 2 and 20 as early evidence for its ritual, as we saw in Courses 3 and 4. But the proofs listed in those Courses showed the impossibility of the first-century Jewish disciples in Jerusalem going around from house to house conducting a ritual of Communion—or doing so in the Temple. God had told Moses that anyone who ingested blood would be cut off from the nation, and the Talmud stated that even the high priest would be whipped should he ever ingest blood. Remember that the Temple authorities were going to kill Paul when they wrongly believed he had brought an uncircumcised Gentile into the Temple.

Yet despite all this, those who teach this ritual would want us to believe that Acts 2 showed the followers of Jesus meeting in groups to conduct a blood-drinking ritual—whether literally (Roman Catholic) or figuratively (Protestant). And furthermore, that the Temple authorities, Pharisees, and others were absolutely fine with the new ritual and that they allowed those who partook in it to freely enter the Temple. The reality is that this simply would not have happened. The Jewish idioms of the day would never have allowed for such a ritual in Jerusalem to go on completely uncontested, with no word from anyone.

The Jewish disciples even warned the Gentiles who were coming to God that they should **abstain from blood** (Acts 15:20, 29; 21:25). There's no point in warning people against something they would never do, so obviously the Gentiles were sometimes ingesting blood (possibly while eating meat or for other reasons). And when the Jews wrote to the Gentiles, they did not say, "Abstain from blood except during the ritual, because then it is fine to ingest it." No—a new ritual of Communion that involved eating bread (as the Messiah's body) and drinking grape juice (as his blood) would never have gone over in first-century Jerusalem.

The Jewish idiom of the natural to spiritual makes it clear that first-century believers were breaking bread *spiritually* by fellowshipping among the believers, sharing the word of God, and partaking of Christ the bread of life in and through one another. The "breaking bread" of the first-century Jewish believers was not a ritual.

Since the Ritual Was Not Taught, How Then Did It Begin and Gain Its Foothold?

Some may question how the longstanding Jewish concept of a coming Messianic Banquet (or Feast) could be turned into a ritual with a small morsel of unleavened bread and a Dixie cup of grape juice.

The above scenario is not what the Lord's Supper pointed to, for in Course 6 we saw that the Lord's supper pointed to the same Messianic Banquet/Feast that had been a continual part of Israelite history. It pointed to a *spiritual* Feast—a wedding Feast (Revelation 19:7, 9) with the sharing of God's love and partaking of the fruit of the spirit. God has far more in His storehouse for His people than a thin wafer of unleavened bread and a sip of grape juice. His spiritual Feast will fulfill the third annual Jewish Festival (the Ingathering), where we partake of the fruit of the spirit and God's *agape* love as we make ourselves ready as the promised spiritual bride.

Personally I am not that interested in how the ritual developed, but I would like to touch on a few considerations for others who may want to delve more deeply into this. It's fairly easy to see how it probably began. All the Roman theologians had to do was fail to understand the Jewish idioms of speaking the natural and *meaning the spiritual* (as covered in "Setting the Table 4") and then apply the *natural* interpretation to John 6, the Last Supper, and 1 Corinthians chapters 10 and 11, and presto, you have the ritual of Communion and the Roman Catholic "breaking bread." However, all of those sections of scripture were to be taken spiritually, just as when Peter wrote we should be sprinkled with Christ's blood or when Jesus said the apostles were branches of the grapevine. They were meant as spiritual truth and not to be interpreted naturally as future Roman rituals.

The *agapais* (Greek for feasts of God's love) among the early believers began as *spiritual* partaking of the one *spiritual* bread that fulfilled the meaning of the Messiah's figurative language at the Last Supper. But over time the Church lost its initial spiritual love—as well as its understanding of the Jewish idioms and the scriptures—and the Church reverted into ceremonialism:

> NAB Revelation 2:4 Yet I hold this against you: you have lost the love you had at first.

We know that when the Church began losing its light and the moving of God's spirit, it descended into darkness and ritualistic observances—such as the introduction of prayers to Mary, Mary becoming the Mother of God, etc.—that were not from the original Jewish believers. Paul had warned that, after his departure, grievous wolves would enter in. He saw that no one was coming behind him to carry the torch, and it did not take the churches long to lose the spiritual life and fall back into church liturgy and ceremonialism. The following Alfred Edersheim quote seems to say it all:

> Ceremonialism rapidly develops, too often in proportion to the absence of spiritual life.[375]

Many new doctrines and rituals entered in after the Fourteenthers—those mostly Jewish believers who wanted to continue to keep the 14th day special—were persecuted and rejected.[376] Emperor Constantine saw Christianity as "our religion," so it's not surprising that Rome would have its own communion as well, one that was completely different from any Jewish concept of communion with God.

We must become better at understanding the first-century Jewish idioms, otherwise we run the risk of putting scriptures together and coming up with doctrines that Jesus did not teach and did not want. As one minister suggested when warning people about this very possibility, taking the verse where Judas went out and "hung himself" (Matthew 27:5) and joining that to the scripture where Jesus says "go and do the same" (Luke 10:37) would create a bad outcome by misconstruing the scriptures.

---

375 Edersheim, *Life and Times*, Book 5, ch. 10, p. 492.
376 See "Setting the Table 1."

It must also be remembered that whenever an early church writer mentions the Greek word "communion," this does not mean or prove that this Roman ritual (or any other ritual) was being celebrated. The Jews who translated the Old Testament into the Greek Septuagint used this same Greek word, and it continued to be used by Jews for all those years before the time of Christ; certainly to them it did not mean a Roman ritual. The same is true for the Greek word "eucharist," which simply means "thanksgiving"; the Jews used this word eucharist for hundreds of years before the New Testament was written, and it never referred to a Roman ritual. So when Paul and the other Jewish scripture writers use these Greek words, we must not assume a later meaning that originated in Rome when such a meaning did not exist in Paul's day.

Early Picture of the Roman Ritual Coming In

Tertullian, the son of a Roman centurion, was often called the founder of *Latin* Christianity. It was from this form of Christianity that the Latin term *Quartodeciman* (Fourteenther) originated. Historians tell us that it was Tertullian who coined the term "Trinity" or *trinitas* in Latin (as we saw in "Setting the Table 2").

Below, Tertullian provides one of the earliest writings (around AD 200–225) for what looks like an actual *ritual* of Communion, giving a picture of the ritual that does not exist in the Gospels or in any writings of Paul. In this passage he refers to the people no longer being allowed to handle the bread and wine in their ritual, lest some of the Lord's body fall to the ground:

> It was heretofore tolerated in some places that **communicants** should take each one his portion, with his own hand, but now we suffer none to receive this sacrament except at the hand of the minister.... **We are concerned if even a particle of the wine or bread, made ours, in the Lord's Supper, falls to the ground, by our carelessness.** In all the ordinary occasions of life we furrow our foreheads with the sign of the Cross, in which we glory none the less because it is regarded as our shame by the heathen in presence of whom it is a profession of our faith.[377]

Does this text have a first-century Jewish ring to it, or does it sound more Roman Catholic in origin? *The Catholic Encyclopedia* quotes Tertullian to substantiate the Catholic ritual of Communion, while admitting that certain aspects of it are not found in scripture:

---

377   Roberts and Donaldson, *Ante-Nicene Fathers*, vol. 3, p. 103.

Tertullian explains: "When you have received and reserved the Body of the Lord, you will have assisted at the Sacrifice and have accomplished the duty of fasting as well" (De oratione, xix). Tertullian's list of customs observed by Apostolic tradition **though not in Scripture** (De cor., iii) is famous: the baptismal renunciations and feeding with milk and honey, fasting Communion, offerings for the dead (Masses) on their anniversaries, no fasting or kneeling on the Lord's Day and between Easter and Pentecost, **anxiety as to the falling to the ground of any crumb or drop of the Holy Eucharist**, the Sign of the Cross made continually during the day.[378]

We can see that the Roman ritual takes Paul's teachings in 1 Corinthians chapter 11 literally—as a natural ritual—as does the Protestant ritual. Yet the Catholic ritual is carried to such an extreme degree so that *one must fast from the previous night* (thus the body of Jesus is kept separate from common food in your stomach):

> That Holy Communion may be received not only validly, but also fruitfully, certain disposition both of body and of soul are required. For the former, a person must be **fasting from the previous midnight from everything in the nature of food or drink**.[379]

Not All Quotes Are What They Appear on the Surface

We will not go into a lot of quotes from those called "Church Fathers," because Jesus specifically said that the men who were the foundation stones of the assembly were *not* to be called "fathers." Instead, we must build our doctrine on the "foundation of the apostles and prophets" and on Christ the chief cornerstone (Ephesians 2:20).

However, I do want to consider one famous quote because it portrays the early Messianic Fourteenther Polycarp—said to be a disciple of John the Apostle—administering a Blessed Eucharist. I believe this to be a false picture handed down to us through an inaccurate translation of what was actually meant. Here is the quote, which comes from a Greek letter written by Irenaeus (a student of Polycarp) to the Roman bishop Victor, defending the Messianic custom of keeping the 14th day special:

> These things being so, they **communed together**; and in the church Anicetus yielded to Polycarp, out of respect no doubt, the **celebration of the eucharist** (τὴν εὐχαριστίαν), and they separated

---

378 Herbermann et al, *The Catholic Encyclopedia*, vol. 14, p. 525, s.v. "Tertullian."
379 Herbermann et al, *The Catholic Encyclopedia*, vol. 7, p. 402, s.v. "Holy Communion."

from each other in peace, all the church being at peace, both those that observed and those that did not observe [the fourteenth of Nisan], maintaining peace."[380]

The original Greek words that have been translated as "communed together" are ἐκοινώνησαν ἑαυτοῖς. The Greek words translated as "celebration of the eucharist" above simply say "the eucharist" (τὴν εὐχαριστίαν) and refer to the giving of thanks.

The meaning of this letter from Irenaeus has been disputed, with some scholars (such as Valesius) translating these Greek words as "administer the Eucharist," indicating that the Roman bishop Anicetus allowed Polycarp to administer the Eucharist ritual on his visit to Rome. Others, such as Heinichen, say it only means that Anicetus allowed Polycarp to partake in the "celebration of the Eucharist" ritual in his church. I do not believe either view is correct here, for Polycarp was a leading Fourteenther, almost certainly Jewish (his relatives always kept the 14th day before him), and the early Messianic followers of Christ did not keep this as a ritual since they understood that Jesus spoke spiritual truth in his Last Supper parables.

We must be careful here because commentators often see these Greek words for "eucharist" (εὐχαριστίαν) and "commune/communion" (ἐκοινώνησαν) through Roman Catholic glasses. If we wear those glasses, then we too might picture two men in Roman sacramental vestments sharing a Blessed Eucharist. However, if we understand that Polycarp was a Messianic Fourteenther who was later martyred for continuing to keep the 14th day special and for refusing to go along with Rome's new commands, quite a different picture might emerge. We might then see that he and Anicetus "fellowshipped together" or partook in the praise and thanksgiving to God together (ἐκοινώνησαν ἑαυτοῖς), and that Polycarp was probably allowed to share some scriptures as they "gave thanks" (εὐχαριστίαν) in the assembly together.

※※※

The Catholic Encyclopedia defines "Holy Communion" in the following manner:

> By Communion is meant the actual reception of the Sacrament of the Eucharist.[381]

Obviously, this definition is different from how the Jews used this word. "Communion" among the early Messianic believers did not mean sharing actual bread and wine in a sacrament, but sharing God's love, partaking of Christ the bread of life

---

380 Schaff, *History of the Christian Church*, vol. 2, p. 213.
381 Herbermann et al, *The Catholic Encyclopedia*, vol. 7, p. 402, s.v. "Holy Communion."

and the word of God in and among the members in the spiritual body and in their *agapais* (feasts of God's *agape* love).

Remember the Jews used these same words in the Septuagint hundreds of years *before* the New Testament was written, and they certainly did not refer to a Roman ritual in their usage but rather to sharing, partaking, and fellowshipping. In the Septuagint (the Greek scripture below), the Jewish translators used this same Greek word ἐκοινώνησεν (meaning "sharing, partaking") that Irenaeus used above concerning Polycarp. Here in English it means that Jehoshaphat and Ahaziah, the king of Israel, were "allied" together:

> NAS 2 Chronicles 20:35a   And after this Jehoshaphat king of Judah **allied himself** with Ahaziah king of Israel.

> LXT 2 Chronicles 20:35   καὶ μετὰ ταῦτα **ἐκοινώνησεν** Ιωσαφατ βασιλεὺς Ιουδα πρὸς Οχοζιαν βασιλέα Ισραηλ καὶ οὗτος ἠνόμησεν

Clearly these two Israelite kings were not celebrating a Roman ritual of Communion. Yet when Irenaeus wrote that Anicetus and Polycarp "communed" together, many read into the text a Roman ritual. Similarly, the Greek word often translated into English as "communion" is used in the Septuagint below, where it means "fellowship":

> LXE Leviticus 6:2   The soul which shall have sinned, and willfully overlooked the commandments of the Lord, and shall have dealt falsely in the affairs of his neighbour in the matter of a deposit, or concerning **fellowship**, or concerning plunder, or has in anything wronged his neighbour,

> LXT Leviticus 5:21[382]   ψυχὴ ἐὰν ἁμάρτῃ καὶ παριδὼν παρίδῃ τὰς ἐντολὰς κυρίου καὶ ψεύσηται τὰ πρὸς τὸν πλησίον ἐν παραθήκῃ ἢ περὶ **κοινωνίας** ἢ περὶ ἁρπαγῆς ἢ ἠδίκησέν τι τὸν πλησίον

Just as we would not assume that the translators of Leviticus meant a ritual of Communion when they wrote concerning the Israelites in their "fellowship," we should not leap to a Roman ritual when we see Irenaeus, Polycarp, Paul, other New Testament writers, or Jewish people in general use these same Greek words. In 1 Corin-

---

382   The Septuagint often has different verse numbering; the above Leviticus 5:21 is the Greek for Leviticus 6:2.

thians 10:16 Paul uses this same Greek word,[383] and he was not speaking of a Roman ritual there either. More than 150 years before Christ or Paul lived, the Jewish Maccabees used the Greek word "eucharist," as preserved in the Septuagint below and translated as "gratitude":

> [NAB] 2 Maccabees 2:27 just as the preparation of a festive banquet is no light matter for one who thus seeks to give enjoyment to others. Similarly, to win the **gratitude** of many we will gladly endure these inconveniences,

> [LXT] 2 Maccabees 2:27 καθάπερ τῷ παρασκευάζοντι συμπόσιον καὶ ζητοῦντι τὴν ἑτέρων λυσιτέλειαν οὐκ εὐχερές ὅμως διὰ τὴν τῶν πολλῶν **εὐχαριστίαν** ἡδέως τὴν κακοπάθειαν ὑποίσομεν

And the Maccabees use this Greek word "eucharist" again, translated here with the meaning of giving thanks to God:

> [NAB] 2 Maccabees 1:11 Since we have been saved by God from grave dangers, **we give him great thanks** for having fought on our side against the king;

> [LXT] 2 Maccabees 1:11 ἐκ μεγάλων κινδύνων ὑπὸ τοῦ θεοῦ σεσωσμένοι μεγάλως **εὐχαριστοῦμεν** αὐτῷ ὡς ἂν πρὸς βασιλέα παρατασσόμενοι

These translations shed light on the quote from Irenaeus, who wrote that Polycarp and Anicetus "communed together" in a good spirit and shared in the "eucharist." The only possible way to see a ritual of Communion or a Blessed Eucharist happening among the Maccabees, Paul, or Polycarp is to look at these Greek words through Roman Catholic glasses. Irenaeus used this exact same Greek word "eucharist" that the Jewish Paul also used below when speaking of the "giving of thanks," and without a doubt, Paul is not speaking of a ritual:

> [NAS] 2 Corinthians 4:15 For all things *are* for your sakes, that the grace which is spreading to more and more people may cause **the giving of thanks** to abound to the glory of God.

---

383 Covered in more detail in Course 6.

GNT 2 Corinthians 4:15   τὰ γὰρ πάντα δι' ὑμᾶς, ἵνα ἡ χάρις πλεονάσασα διὰ τῶν πλειόνων **τὴν εὐχαριστίαν**[384] περισσεύσῃ εἰς τὴν δόξαν τοῦ θεοῦ.

If we were to translate Paul's words as historians have translated Irenaeus's words concerning Polycarp, we would write the above scripture to say "that the grace that is spreading to more and more people may cause **the administration of the Eucharist** to abound," when all Paul really spoke about was the giving of thanks.

Similarly the following scripture that uses the Greek word *koinonias*, often translated as "communion" or "fellowship," does not mean that the Jewish leaders in Jerusalem (James, Cephas, and John) gave the right hand of the "ritual of Communion" to Paul and Barnabas:

> NAS Galatians 2:9   and recognizing the grace that had been given to me, James and Cephas and John, who were reputed to be pillars, gave to me and Barnabas **the right hand of fellowship**, that we *might go* to the Gentiles, and they to the circumcised.

> GNT Galatians 2:9   καὶ γνόντες τὴν χάριν τὴν δοθεῖσάν μοι, Ἰάκωβος καὶ Κηφᾶς καὶ Ἰωάννης, οἱ δοκοῦντες στῦλοι εἶναι, δεξιὰς ἔδωκαν ἐμοὶ καὶ Βαρναβᾷ **κοινωνίας**, ἵνα ἡμεῖς εἰς τὰ ἔθνη, αὐτοὶ δὲ εἰς τὴν περιτομήν·

The actual Greek words ("communed" and "eucharist") that Irenaeus used to describe what Polycarp did with Anicetus in Rome could just as easily be interpreted "they fellowshipped together, and in the church Anicetus gave way in the thanksgiving, to Polycarp." This would make for a much better translation of the original Greek.

Regardless of how some might translate this or other quotes, we should not look to ritualistic ceremonies handed down from the "Church Fathers" in Rome for our spiritual direction. Whether a pope (called Holy Father), Tertullian, or others (called Church Fathers) taught a Blessed Eucharist, this does not mean it was taught by the apostles and the early followers of the Messiah.

The True Communion Is Spiritual

Instead, we should follow the Messiah, who said to call no man father (meaning father in a spiritually exalted sense). There is no better example of neglecting one of

---

384   The *UBS Greek-English Dictionary* defines this Greek word εὐχαριστία as thanksgiving, thanks, gratitude, thankfulness (p. 77).

the Lord's commandments by turning it into a "tradition of men" than the ritual of Communion:

> NAS Mark 7:8 "Neglecting the commandment of God, **you hold to the tradition of men.**"

> NAS Mark 7:9 He was also saying to them, "**You nicely set aside the commandment** of God in order to **keep your tradition**.

Now that we have seen that neither the Messiah, Paul, nor the early disciples taught this ritual, let's turn our attention back to what Jesus meant in his Last Supper parables and what Paul meant his spiritual teachings in 1 Corinthians chapters 10, 11, and 12. On the same night in which Jesus broke the one bread, giving pieces of it for the disciples to partake of, he also gave them the new commandment (John 13:34) to love one another (see Courses 5 and 6). The ritual of Communion has taken that commandment to love and share and turned it into a bread ritual that was a tradition of men that nicely sets aside what the Lord *meant* at the Last Supper.

The assembly must shake off the ceremonial religious spirit that has portrayed the Messiah in this false ritualistic sense. The Lord's commandment to love one another was wrongly interpreted as a ritual with bread (with condemnation attached for not being holy enough when you partake of it). God's love is eternal (Jeremiah 31:3) and His mercy endures forever (Psalm 136). He does not condemn people for failing to eat a piece of Communion bread just right—this has been a false portrayal of God's heart and His will for His people. It is not what the Messiah wanted, nor what Paul taught. And the ritual of Communion has contributed to the Church becoming somewhat of a Leah bride (focused on a dry ritual), but the greater Jacob desires a Rachel bride who seeks the true spiritual communion that God wants for His people (see Genesis 29 and 30 for the story of Rachel and Leah).

In this book's introduction, I mentioned that when I came to realize that the Last Supper was not the Passover (by seeing the weakness of the English translations and how the four Gospels harmonize), and that Jesus indeed held and broke one regular *leavened* bread, I felt in my spirit that the unleavened bread ritual had, in a way, tricked us. Christians have always been bewildered at how first-century Jewish authorities—because of their traditions—could not accept the Messiah's teachings. Now that we have seen that the Last Supper was not the Passover and what this means for the ritual of Communion, it may be our turn in the box. And hopefully we Christians will do as well, or even better, at releasing those man-made traditions and rituals that God does not want.

The time to move beyond this Roman ritual is now. God desires an intimate love relationship and true communion with every individual and with the collective body as well. We must unite as one body and enter into true spiritual communion with God, sharing His *agape* love in and among the members in the one body, with Christ in the midst. This is what the Lord *meant* in his life-giving parables at the Last Supper and what Paul *intended* in 1 Corinthians 11, and this is what will spiritually fulfill the third Israelite Feast, the Ingathering. We must move into this true spiritual communion to become the spiritual bride the Lord is seeking.

Appendix A:
Proper Authority

This appendix is particularly geared toward those who may believe the truths in this book (or any other truths for that matter) against the prevailing beliefs of the leaders of their church, assembly, or synagogue. In some forums today, a false teaching says that you can be submissive to God only if you believe in whatever doctrine your leaders may bring. This is not the kind of doctrine the Israelites in the Old Covenant followed, nor is it what the New Covenant apostles or the early Messianic believers taught.

We will first consider a few scriptures to get a true picture of the authority of each person to believe what their own conscience tells them is true. In one instance, Peter and John tell those sent from the high priest in Jerusalem that it is more important to obey God than to follow any rules from man (even from the high priest) if they are contrary to God:

> NAS Acts 4:19 But Peter and John answered and said to them, "Whether it is right in the sight of God to give heed to you rather than to God, you be the judge;

Jesus held back certain truths when he knew that a better opportunity to reveal them would come later (John 16:12). Yet, we see that when a truth was important to understand at the time and the disciples knew it was from God, they did not shrink back from teaching it, even if the high priest forbade it.

When Peter was going astray by refusing to eat with the Gentiles in Antioch (when the prominent Jewish entourage arrived from Jerusalem), Paul confronted Peter. Paul understood that those Gentiles who had received the Messiah were not to be treated as unclean or as second-class citizens. He also knew that Peter had already been given a vision to this effect (Acts 10), so he made it very clear to Peter that his conduct was not right according to the Gospel:

> NIV Galatians 2:11 When Peter came to Antioch, I opposed him to his face, because he was clearly in the wrong.

Paul did not say, "Well, Peter is one of the inner circle of the Messiah and an original apostle, so even when he's wrong we must submit, knowing that God will bring correction." No, seeing that others were also being drawn into this dissimulation (verse 13), Paul stood up to something that was blatantly wrong.

One church I formerly attended taught the concept that even if a leader went astray, the believers should be like David, who was called to rule Israel when God was deposing King Saul, yet who still remained submitted to the king while Saul still held office. David felt it best to let God remove Saul, saying that he would not touch God's anointed. However, *we* are now in the New Covenant, and we do not have a king who rules over us. Instead, we have the Messiah who rules from heaven and who has given us his word and teaching. This does not mean that no true authority exists among those in charge of each assembly, because clearly there is. It only means that all authority must act as an extension from God and His truth and not promote its own agenda or doctrines that do not line up with scripture. When such authority goes sideways of God, we are not required to follow it. The Messiah is the head of the assembly under God, and all other authority must serve as an extension of the teaching he has brought or of the understandings he brings by the spirit. Any new understandings would not contradict the word of God.

Even in the days of King Saul, Israel did not blindly follow the king's every command. When Saul's legalism concerning an oath required him to put his own son Jonathan to death for eating some honey, the Israelites rose up against this. They argued that Jonathan, who had not heard the oath, had fought valiantly for the Lord (1 Samuel 14). Thus by standing up to King Saul when he was clearly wrong, they were able to save the son's life. Jonathan would later go on to be a huge support to David.

> NAS 1 Samuel 14:45 But the people said to Saul, "Must Jonathan die, who has brought about this great deliverance in Israel? **Far from it!** As the LORD lives, there shall not one hair of his head fall to the ground, for he has worked with God this day." **So the people rescued Jonathan and he did not die**.

The Jews living in the first century were similarly minded. They did not blindly follow their religious leaders when the leaders were mistreating a prophet, as they held Jesus to be:

> NAS Matthew 21:45 And when the chief priests and the Pharisees heard His parables, they understood that He was speaking about them.

> ^{NAS} Matthew 21:46   And when they sought to seize Him, **they feared the multitudes, because they held Him to be a prophet**.

The same thing held true with John the Baptist when Herod wanted to put him to death:

> ^{NAS} Matthew 14:3   For when Herod had John arrested, he bound him, and put him in prison on account of Herodias, the wife of his brother Philip.

> ^{NAS} Matthew 14:4   For John had been saying to him, "It is not lawful for you to have her."

> ^{NAS} Matthew 14:5   And although he wanted to put him to death, **he feared the multitude, because they regarded him as a prophet**.

Even members of the powerful Jewish Sanhedrin knew the people would follow God above their own commands, for when the Sanhedrin commanded that Jesus be arrested, they said for him ***not*** to be arrested during the Festival, ***lest there be a riot among the people*** (Matthew 26:3–5).

The Sanhedrin did not say "go ahead and arrest him right in the Festival, for these Israelites will submit to *our* authority even above what God commands." They knew the people would never allow their leaders to disregard God's Sabbath laws and would likely riot if such an arrest took place.

It is possible that standing up for truth is what Paul alludes to after telling the Corinthians that the head of every man is Christ (1 Corinthians 11:3), for he then says that nature itself shows it's a shame for a man to have long hair (verses 14, 15). Remember the Jewish idiom of the natural to spiritual here; there is *natural* long hair, which God gives to the woman in part to show submission, and there is *spiritual* long hair whereby man removes God (and the authority extended to Christ) from the head and instead places a man on earth as his ultimate head. In other words, Paul is quite possibly saying that the Corinthians should hold to truth and not submissively yield (essentially having long hair) to any tradition, ordinance, or doctrine *of men* that does not come down from God through Christ (verses 2, 14). Earlier, Paul had admonished them for saying they were of Paul or Apollos (1 Corinthians 3:4–11), for Christ was to be their head.

Some may not agree with this specific point and that's fine, but the rest of the scripture in this section stands on its own. The biblical history of the Jews does not portray a people who remain in perfect submission to their leaders when those leaders have gone astray or are contrary to God. Proper biblical submission does not replace the legitimate line of command—from God through the Messiah—with an earthly leader. Rather, the earthly shepherd is to be an *extension* of the teaching that comes from God's spirit or is revealed by the Messiah. Believers should not feel forced to yield to popular traditions, rituals, or teachings that do not align with the scriptures. Proper authority does not require the leaders to be perfect, for there are no perfect earthly leaders. It only requires them to be extensions of the Messiah—by seeking to be honest before God and open to truth.

❦

Returning now to King Saul's day, when the Israelites wanted a king to rule over them and Saul was about to be appointed, God saw this as ***their rejection of Him, in not allowing God to lead***:

> NAS 1 Samuel 8:4   Then **all the elders of Israel gathered together** and came to Samuel at Ramah;

> NAS 1 Samuel 8:5   and they said to him, "Behold, you have grown old, and your sons do not walk in your ways. Now appoint a king for us to judge us like all the nations."

> NAS 1 Samuel 8:6   But the thing was displeasing in the sight of Samuel when they said, "Give us a king to judge us." And Samuel prayed to the LORD.

> NAS 1 Samuel 8:7   And the LORD said to Samuel, "Listen to the voice of the people in regard to all that they say to you, for **they have not rejected you**, but **they have rejected Me from being king over them**.

So we see that all the elders of Israel were united in belief, yet they still completely missed God's will. This was not the only time Israel's leaders were united but wrong, for at one point they were united in Ahithophel's plan to put King David to death (2 Samuel 17:1–3). David was the king whom God said was a man after His own heart, yet the leaders were deceived into thinking he should die, and they agreed on a plan to accomplish this:

> NAS 2 Samuel 17:4   So the plan pleased Absalom **and all the elders of Israel**.

Later, God promised Israel that He would raise up shepherds who would properly guide them:

> ᴺᴬˢ Jeremiah 3:15   "Then I will give you shepherds after My own heart, who will feed you on knowledge and understanding.

However, these shepherds needed to be willing to yield to any new truths that God brings forth, for He is always the highest authority. God warns of some who assume the position of shepherds yet who do not feed the proper truths and doctrine that God desires for the people:

> ᴺᴬˢ Jeremiah 23:2   Therefore thus says the LORD God of Israel concerning the shepherds who are tending My people: "You have scattered My flock and driven them away, and have not attended to them; behold, I am about to attend to you for the evil of your deeds," declares the LORD.

> ᴺᴬˢ Ezekiel 34:2   "Son of man, prophesy against the shepherds of Israel. Prophesy and say to those shepherds, 'Thus says the Lord God, "Woe, shepherds of Israel who have been feeding themselves! Should not the shepherds feed the flock?

> ᴺᴬˢ Jeremiah 50:6   "My people have become lost sheep; Their shepherds have led them astray. They have made them turn aside *on* the mountains; They have gone along from mountain to hill And have forgotten their resting place.

People should not be regarded as rebellious for holding to a doctrine they believe is from the Messiah, even though their assembly leader may not believe in it. For when it comes to the New Covenant authority structure, Jesus is the head of every man (1 Corinthians 11:3) and of the assembly:

> ʸᴸᵀ Ephesians 5:23   because the husband is head of the wife, as also the **Christ *is* head of the assembly**, and he is saviour of the body,

Thus, for a leader or teacher in the assembly to expect others to submit to a certain doctrine, this person would have to be an extension of Christ's authority, teaching pure doctrine that properly aligns with the scriptures. Knowing human nature, Jesus deliberately warned the apostles to not see themselves as great, powerful leaders or as "Fathers" (in the sense of being a spiritual father over other believers):

> ^{NAS} Matthew 23:8 "But do not be called Rabbi; for One is your Teacher, and **you are all brothers.**
>
> ^{NAS} Matthew 23:9 "And do not call *anyone* on earth your father; for One is your Father, He who is in heaven.
>
> ^{NAS} Matthew 23:10 "And do not be called leaders; for One is your Leader, *that is*, Christ.

Of course Jesus did not mean all of this literally, because it is not wrong to call your dad "father" or to be called a "leader" in an assembly. Paul uses the same Greek word translated as "teacher" (above) for a position in the church in Ephesians 4:11. What the Lord meant was that he did not want them to become exalted authorities who saw themselves as great rulers, the source of all truth, or as spiritual fathers who could lord it over others. Rather, he wanted them to remain humble and regard one another as "brothers." He wanted us to always remember that the true source of proper teaching comes from God through Christ, "for one is your teacher."

A few scriptures have been taken out of context to imply a powerful ruling by church leaders, such as the following verse:

> ^{KJV} Hebrews 13:17 **Obey them that have the rule over you**, and submit yourselves: for they watch for your souls, as they that must give account, that they may do it with joy, and not with grief: for that *is* unprofitable for you.

However, when we examine the original Greek while also considering established church history, the true meaning of this scripture becomes clearer. The King James Bible was translated during a time when a growing number of Protestants were withdrawing from Roman Catholic authority as they realized that many doctrines and rituals taught by the Catholic Church were not contained in the Bible. If the above verse is true as translated—without any qualifications—then the Protestants should have returned to Roman Catholic authority, saying to themselves that God would work it all out and that they must "obey them that have the rule over you." Thankfully, for all who enjoy freedom of thought and choice, they did not follow through with this reasoning.

Since God is always the highest authority, a scriptural doctrine that comes from a church authority has to line up with His word; otherwise it does not have to be followed. In the same sense, obviously a church leader could not command another person to rob a bank and expect submission based on the above scripture. Since other scripture teaches us to not steal, that would be the higher authority we would follow instead of such an earthly command from a wayward or corrupt leader.

There are a few aspects of the Greek that provide a better picture of what this scripture truly means, particularly the words translated, "Obey them that have the rule over you." The Greek verb for "obey" (Πείθεσθε) is passive here, meaning to "be persuadable." It does not mean to empty your mind and insert whatever any church leader tells you. Instead, it means to be willing to move out of a doctrinal position (such as a church tradition) and into a new truth when a teacher convinces you with sound logic of its veracity.

The Greek word ἡγουμένοις, translated as those who "*rule over*" you, simply means those who "lead, guide, or are regarded among you as leaders and teachers." The original Greek does not picture a Roman Church or other church leaders **ruling over you** with unquestioned power from God, but rather it portrays that we be *persuadable* when solid scriptural truth is brought forth by God's anointed teachers or leaders.

Paul commended those in Berea, saying they were "more noble-minded" than others he had taught, because they sought the word of God and checked if Paul's teaching really aligned with the scriptures:

> NAS Acts 17:10 And the brethren immediately sent Paul and Silas away by night to Berea; and when they arrived, they went into the synagogue of the Jews.

> NAS Acts 17:11 Now **these were more noble-minded** than those in Thessalonica, for they received the word with great eagerness, examining the Scriptures daily, *to see* **whether these things were so**.

Paul did not rise up with insecurity and say, "How dare you question my teaching for I am an apostle of God." On the contrary, Paul was glad to see them searching out the scriptures to verify that his teaching aligned with them. Some leaders may demand unquestioned submission to every word they teach, even to the point of forbidding others to seek out or discuss certain doctrines. Peter, however, warned that leaders should not behave as overlords but rather serve as good examples:

> NAS 1 Peter 5:2 shepherd the flock of God among you, exercising oversight not under compulsion, but voluntarily, according to *the will of* God; and not for sordid gain, but with eagerness;

> NAS 1 Peter 5:3 **nor yet as lording it over those allotted to your charge**, but proving to be examples to the flock.

Romans chapter 13 is another portion of scripture that is often taken out of context concerning authority. Some have interpreted it as meaning that believers should submit to any and all rulers at all times. Some items Paul writes of in chapter 13 do apply to secular as well as religious rulers and state that we should obey the rules of the governments that we live under (by paying tribute, etc.), so we can enjoy a peaceable life. Yet the commands of secular rulers should always be secondary to God's commands; otherwise everyone would be obligated to obey the Antichrist and take the mark of the beast, in opposition to God.

Paul does not mean for us to submit unquestioningly to any and all rulers, or any and all teaching, because he understands that God's authority always comes first. If the God-anointed scriptures tell us to prove all things (1 Thessalonians 5:21), then we are to follow God's will and prove each doctrine, regardless of whether any church leader forbids or commands a particular belief. If we believe that a doctrine is true and from God, then we are commanded to hold to it, yet be open if God reveals new light on any truth. Remember, Paul rebuked Peter to his face when he knew Peter was in the wrong by treating the Gentiles as second-class citizens. Paul therefore *did not follow* what some people claim he is teaching in Romans 13 by submitting to Peter (who was one of the Lord's inner circle and an original apostle) when he knew Peter was wrong, but instead he pointed out the error.

God established authority for the family: the children were subject unto their parents until they came of age and the husband was given authority (concerning the home) over the wife. These positions were set up as a type that pointed forward to the Messiah as the head of the spiritual bride. So God always had established authority, and this was also true in the first-century assemblies. At the same time, Jesus said that his sheep will hear *his* voice (John 10:27). So even new believers who are not well versed in the scriptures can ask the Lord for discernment and leading when a teaching from a leader does not feel right in their spirit.

In Old Covenant days, when God gave Israel the Promised Land, the Israelites did not come into the land and say "Oh, these evil authorities in the land don't want to yield to us, so we must obey these kings of Canaan." To the contrary, they knew that God was the higher authority, and He had clearly said to drive out those ungodly nations (even though He had also previously said "Thou shalt not kill"). Israel understood that the commandment to drive out those nations superseded His commandment to not kill. In the Old Covenant they were fighting for an earthly kingdom, because God had plans to bring forth a Messiah and wanted Israel as a nation separated unto Himself to fulfill this plan.

But in the New Covenant we are not fighting for an earthly kingdom but for a spiritual one, where the weapons and the armor are spiritual (2 Corinthians 10:3–5,

Ephesians 6:10–18). Jesus was not against fighting per se; he said that *if* his kingdom were of this earth, his servants would fight. But his kingdom is a spiritual kingdom (John 18:36), so we do not war with earthly means.

If history teaches us anything about those who have authority over others, it is that sometimes they take this authority unto themselves to set up their own kingdoms, as it were. This is why Jesus told the apostles not to see themselves as great leaders and teachers over the people but rather to see themselves as brothers. We have seen in other scriptures that leaders are warned not to lord it over the flock. Yes, there is authority in the assembly that comes from God, but it must always properly represent His heart and mind. There is also a sense in which all people are to be subject to one another, and that goes for rulers like Peter, should any ever stray from God's heart:

> KJV 1 Peter 5:5   Likewise, ye younger, submit yourselves unto the elder. **Yea, all *of you* be subject one to another**, and be clothed with humility: for God resisteth the proud, and giveth grace to the humble.

Throughout history God has shown that some in the position of shepherds will lead the people astray, instead of leading them to follow the Lord:

> NAS Jeremiah 10:21   For the shepherds have become stupid And have not sought the LORD; Therefore they have not prospered, And all their flock is scattered.

> NAS Jeremiah 23:2   Therefore thus says the LORD God of Israel concerning the shepherds who are tending My people: "You have scattered My flock and driven them away, and have not attended to them; behold, I am about to attend to you for the evil of your deeds," declares the LORD.

> NAS Jeremiah 50:6   "My people have become lost sheep; **Their shepherds have led them astray**. They have made them turn aside *on* the mountains; They have gone along from mountain to hill And have forgotten their resting place.

> NAS Ezekiel 34:8   "As I live," declares the Lord God, "surely because My flock has become a prey, My flock has even become food for all the beasts of the field for lack of a shepherd, and My shepherds did not search for My flock, but *rather* the shepherds fed themselves and did not feed My flock;

However, God also promises to raise up shepherds who have His heart and provide spiritual food:

> ^{NAS}Jeremiah 3:15 "Then I will give you shepherds after My own heart, who will feed you on knowledge and understanding.

God's called leader Gideon did not want to be a ruler over the people. He wanted the Lord to rule:

> ^{NAS}Judges 8:23 But Gideon said to them, "I will not rule over you, nor shall my son rule over you; the LORD shall rule over you."

The goal of this appendix is not to attempt a full explanation of proper church authority. It is to focus on the authority of each believer—before God—to use his or her own reasoning and come to a conclusion, without fear of being labeled rebellious. Not agreeing with every doctrine a particular leader might insist to be the word of God does not make one a heretic or a dissident.

If the way some interpret Paul's teachings in Romans 13 is true, then we should all repent and go back under the Roman Catholic Church, from which the Protestants rebelled. However, this would necessitate replacing Christ as the head and teacher of doctrine, and instead setting up human authority.

We must use the example of the spiritual leaders in Acts 15, where Paul, Peter, James, some elders, and even some of the Pharisees came together and yielded to what the spirit of God was bringing. Paul showed that the true sons of God are those who are led by His spirit:

> ^{YLT}Romans 8:14 for as many as are led by the Spirit of God, **these** are the sons of God;

This scripture does not say "as many as are led only by a pastor, priest, or rabbi," but "these" who are led by the spirit of God. This does not contradict the fact that God provides and anoints His called leaders and teachers, and that we need those provisions from God and should be very thankful for them, but ultimately it is His spirit that will be leading us to perfection. Those who are ultimately led by His spirit are the ones He considers true sons and daughters.

The Lord, in fact, warns that those who do not receive a love for the truth are vulnerable to further delusion:

> ᴷᔾⱽ 2 Thessalonians 2:10   And with all deceivableness of unrighteousness in them that perish; **because they received not the love of the truth**, that they might be saved.

> ʸᴸᵀ 2 Thessalonians 2:11   and because of this shall God send to them a working of delusion, for their believing the lie,

The Lord is not seeking a bride that will resist Him over what is truth and what is proper doctrine. She will not say, "But my people always saw it this way, and I refuse to consider new truth with an open heart, because I stick with what my pastor, my denomination, or my rabbi says." The Lord looks for those who will yield to His word:

> ᴺᴬˢ Isaiah 66:2   "For My hand made all these things, Thus all these things came into being," declares the LORD. "But to this one I will look, To him who is humble and contrite of spirit, and who trembles **at My word**.

The spiritual bride will be those who are teachable and yield to God's truth. The people who seek this relationship with the Lord will be willing to accept any truth that is anointed from God and will seek to verify that it aligns with the scriptures that He has given:

> ʸᴸᵀ 2 Timothy 2:15   be diligent to present thyself approved to God—a workman irreproachable, rightly dividing the word of the truth;

Appendix B:
Recommended Bible Study Tools

I have found many of the following resources to be especially helpful:

BibleWorks
www.bibleworks.com
Although other excellent computer Bible study programs may exist, the BibleWorks program is the most powerful that I know of. One especially useful feature is that you can hover the mouse over any word in the Greek or Hebrew text and see the English words that define it. It has Greek lexicons like *Louw-Nida* and *BDAG*, and excellent Hebrew lexicons like *BDB* and *HALOT*. Double-clicking on any English, Hebrew, or Greek word reveals all the other places where that word is used in the scriptures, as well as different ways each Hebrew or Greek word is translated into English. The Greek Septuagint and its English translation are just two of the many add-ons that come with the BibleWorks program. It can sometimes be very helpful to search on a New Testament Greek word and see how it was used among the Israelites long before Jesus lived. How a Greek word was used in the Septuagint can also help clarify what that word meant in the first-century idiom. Among the program's many other features are the writings of the Maccabees, the Apocrypha, and numerous Bible translations. If a person can make only one purchase, they might really consider this.

PC Study Bible
www.biblesoft.com
This is a very good Bible program for beginners and scholars alike, with many excellent resources, including Josephus, the early church writers, and Keil and Delitzsch. It also contains the excellent religious encyclopedia that I have found to be the best, *McClintock and Strong Cyclopedia*.

A Textual Commentary on the Greek New Testament:
A Companion Volume to the United Bible Societies' Greek New Testament
Bruce M. Metzger. 1975. Third edition. United Bible Societies, London.
There is nothing worse than building proof for a doctrine from a portion of verse that was not actually in the original Greek. Although, as Westcott and Hort stated,

only about one in a thousand Greek variants actually bring a word in the scriptures into question, this book can be a helpful tool for checking those rare variants that affect doctrine. Most variants (between the manuscripts) consist of changes in word order, the insertion or omission of an article with proper names, and other such comparative trivialities. Only one-fifth of one percent of the New Testament variants affect a major doctrine or teaching, and none of those affect any teaching that is not substantiated elsewhere by parallel texts and the tenor of scripture. Still, it is always a good idea to check the better manuscripts and consider all evidence for any variant.

Bible Commentaries

Many Bible commentaries exist with lots of good research and helpful information. Of course, one must always consider their limitations, such as the time period in which they were written, the prevailing beliefs of their day, etc. In my Bible college, we were taught that it is often best to seek the Lord and be led by God's spirit first, then go to the commentaries. That way one does not become fixed in an idea without first seeking God for direction and truth.

That being true, a few commentaries I have found that are especially good or might add insight from another perspective are as follows:

Commentary on the New Testament from the Talmud and Hebraica
John Lightfoot. 1979. Baker Book House, Grand Rapids, MI.

Commentary on the Old Testament
C. F. Keil and Franz Delitzsch. 1985. William B. Eerdmans Publishing, Grand Rapids, MI.
(Keil and Delitzsch is very good on the Old Testament Hebrew.)

The Jewish Study Bible
Jewish Publication Society. Adele Berlin and Marc Zvi Brettler, eds. 2004. Oxford University Press, New York.

A Commentary on the Holy Scriptures: Critical, Doctrinal and Homiletical, with Special References to Ministers and Students: The New Testament.
John Peter Lange. Philip Schaff, translator. 1867. Charles Scribner, New York, NY.

Lenski's Commentary on the New Testament
R. C. H. Lenski. 1964. Augsburg Publishing House, Minneapolis, MN.
(Lenski's commentary is excellent on going into the New Testament Greek.)

Greek Language Books

The Basics of New Testament Syntax: An Intermediate Greek Grammar
Daniel B. Wallace. 2000. Zondervan, Grand Rapids, MI.

Greek Grammar Beyond the Basics: An Exegetical Syntax of the New Testament
Daniel B. Wallace. 1996. Zondervan, Grand Rapids, MI.

Greek-English Lexicon of the New Testament Based on Semantic Domains
Johannes P. Louw and Eugene A. Nida, eds. 1989. Second edition, two volumes. United Bible Societies, New York, NY.
(Comes with the BibleWorks software program.)

A Greek-English Lexicon of the New Testament and Other Early Christian Literature (also sometimes known informally as *BDAG*)
Walter Bauer. 2000. Third edition, revised and edited by Frederick William Danker. University of Chicago Press, Chicago and London.
(Comes with the BibleWorks software program.)

Verbal Aspect in New Testament Greek
Buist M. Fanning. 1990. Clarendon Press, Oxford, England.

(Note: Some of these lexicons, commentaries, and encyclopedias are included in various software Bible programs)

Encyclopedias

Cyclopedia of Biblical, Theological, and Ecclesiastical Literature
John McClintock and James Strong. 1981. Baker Book House, Grand Rapids, MI.
(This is one of my favorite encyclopedic resources, and it comes with *PC Study Bible* software program mentioned above.)

Jewish Encyclopedias
The Jewish Encyclopedia
www.JewishEncylopedia.com

Encyclopedia Judaica
Encyclopedia Judaica Research Foundation, 1972. Keter Publishing House Ltd., Jerusalem, Israel.

Other Online Resources

BibleGateway.com
http://www.biblegateway.com
(For those without a New Testament Bible yet have online access, this is a great place to look up various translations of any scripture.)

Christian Classics Ethereal Library
www.ccel.org
(This lists early church writers and other historians online.)

Early Christian Writings
www.earlychristianwritings.com

Early Jewish Writings
www.earlyjewishwritings.com

Sacredtexts.com
www.sacred-texts.com
(This useful, comprehensive site contains many ancient writings as well as Josephus, the Talmud, Maimonides, and many other works.)

The Catholic Encyclopedia
www.newadvent.org/cathen

Perseus Digital Library Project
www.perseus.tufts.edu/hopper
(Perseus has many ancient writings that can be searched.)

Other

The Feast of Tabernacles: The Hope of the Church
George H. Warnock. 1951. The Church in Action, George Warnock Publications, Cranbrook BC, Canada.
(For a good entry-level study of the three annual Israelite festivals.)

Glossary

Note: These entries are not intended to serve as comprehensive resources on these subjects, but rather as brief definitions or notes in relation to the content presented within this book.

Aaron
The brother of Moses from the tribe of Levi. He was the first high priest in the Tabernacle, and subsequent high priests were to come from his lineage.

Abib
A Hebrew word that pertains to a certain stage in the ripening of barley that occurs in spring. The first month (Nisan) was determined by when the barley ripened. If the barley was not maturing by the new moon, Nisan would be put off until the next new moon (by adding a second month of Adar), so that the grain would be ready for the first-fruits offering that followed the Sabbath after Passover.

agape
This English transliteration of the Greek word (*agape*) is often used to refer to the highest form of love—God's love.

agapais/*agape* **feasts**
Translated as "love feasts" (NAS) in Jude 1:12. This was an early spiritual fulfillment of the third annual Jewish festival, the Feast of Ingathering, where believers experienced and shared the powerful love of God and the fruit of the spirit (i.e., love, joy, peace, etc.). *See also* spot.

altar
A structure on which sacrifices are offered to God and roasted.

Antichrist
That which is against God's anointed (anti-Messiah). It can refer to either a general spirit of wickedness or directly to the man of sin or man of lawlessness (2 Thessalonians 2:3) that heads up the seventh head of the beast, the final evil empire.

antitype
A person, thing, or event that was prefigured or foreshadowed by a type that previously existed. The Passover lamb was a type of the Messiah (who was called the lamb of God). Therefore, the Messiah would be the antitype in this example.

aorist tense
According to Buist M. Fanning in his book *Verbal Aspect in New Testament Greek*, the aorist tense in Greek "presents an occurrence in summary, viewed as a whole from the outside, without regard for the internal make-up of the occurrence." Refer to the chapter "The Three Major Greek Keys That Unlock the Gospels" for more information.

apostle
From the Greek word *apostollos*, meaning "sent forth," which was also used to depict a root or vine shooting forth.

Archaic Triad
The early version of the Roman Triad of deities that included Jupiter, Mars, and Quirinus. *See also* Capitoline Triad and Trinity.

arton
The Greek word for "bread," commonly used to refer to daily leavened bread.

Ascension
The ascension of Christ refers to his visible ascension from earth into heaven as witnessed by his disciples. This occurred on the Mount of Olives 40 days after his resurrection (Mark 16:19; Luke 24:50, 51; Acts 1:1–11).

Asiatics
Those living in the region called Asia Minor, where the seven churches in Asia (Revelation 1:4, 11) were located. During the early disputes with Rome, the term was used for those (mostly Messianic Jewish) believers wanting to keep their longstanding custom of observing Passover while at the same time seeing it as being fulfilled by the Messiah. They were also called "Quartodecimans," a Latin word meaning "fourteenthers." *See also* Jewish assemblies.

assemblies
A term used in the English New Testament for gatherings of believers.

atonement
From the Hebrew word *kaphar*, meaning "to cover." By extension this referred to the covering and forgiveness of sins.

azumos
The Greek word meaning "without leaven." *See also* unleavened (bread).

Azymites
A Greek term meaning "unleavened ones." The Eastern Churches used it as a derisive term when the Roman Church changed their ritual of Communion from using regular leavened bread to unleavened bread around the 9th to 11th century. The Eastern Churches did not follow Rome's new edicts and continued their ritual with regular leavened bread as they had for many centuries.

baptize
From the Greek word *bapto*, meaning to "dip, plunge, immerse." This referred to Jewish ritual immersions (see also *mikveh/mikvah*) that were later practiced by the Christians.

Beast
The book of Daniel and the book of Revelation (of John) both portray a figurative beast rising up in the last days to war upon God's people. Refer to Course 12 for details of this beast.

Bible
The book of writings containing both the Old Testament and New Testament, all directly inspired by God.

blood sacrifices
Animal sacrifices that were offered to God, whereby the blood would provide provisional atonement and also point forward to the Messiah's sacrifice.

body of Christ
Used figuratively to refer to all the members of the spiritual body, the believers in the Messiah (Yeshua/Jesus Christ).

Booths
See Tabernacles, Feast of

bread of affliction
A figurative term used for matzah (unleavened bread) because it was less flavorful than regular leavened bread. When the Israelites fled Egypt, they left in haste and did not have time to bake regular leavened bread. God commanded for the bread at Passover to be unleavened in remembrance of that first Passover.

bread of God
Refers to offerings to God (usually of grain) that were symbolically considered as His food.

breaking bread
A phrase used by Jews for many years before Christ that originated with the weekly breaking of the twelve breads (later called Showbread) in the Temple. In New Testament usage in the Jewish natural-to-spiritual idiom, it mainly refers to sharing God's word and the words of Christ (the bread of life) as well as the spiritual sharing among believers.

bride (of Christ)
Used figuratively in the scriptures for the spiritual bride and the perfected assembly (church), where the Messiah is pictured spiritually as the bridegroom.

bridegroom
Used figuratively to refer to Christ, where the bride is the church (John 3:29; Revelation 21:9).

calendar theory (two-calendar theory)
This is a theory that on the night of the Last Supper, two calendars were in effect, so Jesus supposedly ate the legal Passover on the 14th day of the Pharisaic calendar but was then crucified the following day on the legal 14th day of the supposed Sadducee calendar.

Capitoline Triad
The later version of the Roman Triad of deities that came after the Archaic Triad. In the Capitoline Triad, the deities were Jupiter, Juno, and Minerva. *See also* Trinity.

Catholic
From the Greek word *katholikos* meaning "universal," commonly applied to the Roman Catholic Church.

Catholic Council of Nicaea (AD 325)
See Nicaea, Catholic Council of

Christ
From the Greek word *kristos*, meaning "anointed" or "anointed one." *See also* Messiah.

church
The English word for "church" is most likely a derivation of the Greek word *kuriakos*, which means "pertaining to the Lord" or "belonging to the Lord." It is translated as "Lord's" in "Lord's Supper" (which should properly read "The supper (or feast) pertaining to the Lord," 1 Corinthians 11:20; refer to Course 6). Some say the term came down to us as a joining of the two Greek words *Kurios* (Lord), and *oikos* (house), hence *Kuri-ok* for the "Lord's house." The current word transitioned through a series of terms used over time as the English language evolved, such as "kirk," "kyrke," "kirche," "chyrch," "churche," and today, "church."

circumcise
The cutting off of the foreskin on the penis, a command by God that was to occur on the eighth day after birth for all males under the law of Moses in the first covenant.

cock crow
Twelve "cocks" or faucets were present at the laver in the Temple where the priests washed in preparation before the sacrifices were brought. The cock crow, or cock summons, was a calling out to the priests, either by a loud calling with a man's voice (as described in the Babylonian Talmud, Book 3, Tract Yomah, ch. 1, pp. 27–28, and also *The Jewish Encyclopedia* under "Gebeni") or with a trumpet. There were early, middle, and late summonses. The cock crow is what Jesus referred to when, shortly before he was led out to the crucifixion, he told Peter that he would deny him three times before the second cock crow (Mark 14:30). Thus, he was not referring to a rooster as many have supposed, but to the second calling of the priests for the sacrifice.

communal meal
This often refers to the meals centered on the Temple, such as the Showbread, or those connected to the three annual Jewish feasts, where ritual purification was required.

communal sacrifice
Sacrifices brought on behalf of the whole nation, as opposed to individual sacrificial offerings.

communion
From a root word in Greek meaning "common," i.e., a common bond of fellowship among people or between the people and God.

Constantine
The emperor of Rome from AD 306 to AD 337, and the first supposedly to be converted to Christianity. During his reign, Constantine sought to have all Roman-controlled territories fully submitted to Roman beliefs. He convened the Council of Nicea in AD 325 in an attempt to bring Messianic Jews (ridiculed as "Quartodecimans," meaning "Fourteenthers" in English) into doctrinal obedience to Rome, including belief in the triune nature of God and celebrating Easter as Rome decreed. In his famous letter to the churches, he raged against the Jews who would not yield, calling them parricides, and declared that the Roman Church should have nothing in common with them.

consubstantiation
This was Martin Luther's concept that Christ's flesh and blood were contained "with" (*con*) the bread and wine at the Communion ritual. Luther developed this belief as he moved away from the Catholic doctrine of transubstantiation, wherein it is believed that bread and wine are completely changed into Christ's flesh and blood during their ritual. Once Luther left the Roman Church, he was excluded from Communion, which meant he needed a belief other than that of the Roman priest transubstantiating the bread and wine.

Council of Laodicea (AD 364)
See Laodicea, Council of

crucifixion
A brutal form of punishment whereby the offender is nailed to a stake or a cross.

dative case
A case for Greek words that often has "to" as being primary to the meaning when the indirect object is in the dative case. Refer to the chapter "The Three Major Greek Keys That Unlock the Gospels" for more information.

dative of reference
According to Greek scholar Daniel Wallace in his book *Greek Grammar Beyond the Basics*, to correctly interpret the dative of reference, you should do the following: "Instead of the word *to*, supply the words *with reference to* before the dative. (Other glosses are *concerning, about, in regard to*, etc.)." Refer to the chapter "The Three Major Greek Keys That Unlock the Gospels" for more information.

David
King of Israel, whom God called "a man after my own heart" (Acts 13:22; 1 Samuel 13:14). Future kings were often compared with David as to whether or not they measured up.

day, the Jewish
The 24-hour period that began and ended with each new sunset (Genesis 1:5). The word "day" was also used to denote the daylight period, basically from 6 AM to 6 PM ("Are there not 12 hours in the day?" John 11:9). The hours were counted from 6 AM, so the third hour was from 8 AM to 9 AM, and the ninth hour was from 2 PM to 3 PM. Refer to Figure 9 in the chapter "Between the Evenings."

Dead Sea Sect
A sect of Jews living at the Dead Sea who had withdrawn from offering Temple sacrifices and obeying Pharisaic authority. Many believe the sect was started by the Sadducees, those derived from the lineage of Zadok, the faithful high priest under King David. The Dead Sea Sect also held a sacred service and partook of bread and wine together, similar to the Showbread service but apart from the Temple.

demon
Any fallen spirit, being one of the angels who rebelled against God by following Satan (Jude 1:6). Contrary to some beliefs, they are not able to cohabit or impregnate women, but they have deceived many as they work against God and do various evil things (1 Timothy 4:1; Revelation 16:14). Some people have even been tricked into believing that these demon spirits are really alien beings from other planets. Casting demons out of people was a common aspect of Jesus's ministry (Mark 1:34, 39), and Jesus gave believers the authority to cast them out in his name (Mark 16:17; Luke 9:1).

devil
From the Greek word *diabolos*, a combination of two Greek words, *dia* ("through") and *bolos* ("to throw"), hence "to throw through" with accusations. It can refer to Satan as the chief of the devils (demons) or to individual fallen spirits.

Diaspora
From the Greek word meaning "scattered" or "dispersed," usually referring to Jews living outside of Israel.

discernment
Speaking biblically, this refers to having the spiritual discernment to sense whether something is right or wrong, true or false.

disciple
One who engages in learning or instruction from another. It was often applied in the New Testament to those who followed Christ. The similar Greek term was also used prior to Christ for those who attended rabbinic schools (John 7:15).

doctrine
In the New Testament, this is usually translated into English from the Greek *didache*, meaning "teaching" or "instruction." It is that which is taught (whether true or false), coming from a certain set of beliefs or understandings.

Easter/Astarte celebration
From the old English *Eostre* or *Ostara*, a goddess that morphed throughout history as Ashteroth (the Greek is *Astaroth*), Astarte, and Ishtar. Acts 7:42–43 says there was a time when God gave the people up to worship the host of heaven, as they deified the sun, planets, and stars. The word "star" is often seen in the name of this goddess: Astaroth, Astarte, Ishtar (Ish-star), and Eostar. Usually it is connected to a spring goddess of sexuality and fertility, hence Eostar eggs. Astarte is often connected to Venus, the Roman goddess of fertility, hence the egg at Easter.

epistle
From the Greek word *epistole*, meaning "letter."

Essenes
A sect of Jews that existed from the second century BC until about the end of the first century AD. Some scholars believe they were an offshoot of the Zadokite priests. The Essenes held a service outside of the Temple in which, after a ritual bath, they would partake of bread.

Eucharist
Originally from the Greek word *eucharistia*, which meant "thanksgiving." Later it was used to refer to the Roman ritual of Communion.

feast or festival
In Bible usage, when from the Hebrew *chag* and then from the Greek *eorty*, a term referring to one of the three annual festivals in which Israelites would come together as commanded by God. They consisted of Passover, Pentecost, and the Feast of Tabernacles (Sukkot, Ingathering). (For more information, refer to the end of Course 5 and the early part of Course 6.)

Festival of Booths (Ingathering, Sukkot, or Tabernacles)
See Tabernacles, Feast of

Feast of Unleavened Bread
The seven-day Jewish festival wherein leaven was forbidden, but its Hebrew and Greek names never included the word "bread." The feast followed the slaying of the Passover and began at sunset as the 14th day ended, when the people were ready to eat the Passover lamb.

Festival of Weeks (Shavout, Pentecost)
See Pentecost, Feast/Festival of

first-fruits offering
The word "fruits" here can be misleading, as these were primarily grain offerings. Various first-fruits offerings gave thanks to God by giving Him the first portion harvested. One of these took place at the Passover that was to be on the morrow of the Sabbath, and first-century Jewish historian Josephus stated that it offered the first ripe barley. After 50 days were counted to Pentecost (the morrow of the seventh Sabbath), another first-fruits offering took place, whereby two loaves of regular leavened wheat bread were "waved" before God.

fruit of the vine
The juice from the grapes of the grapevine, or grape juice.

Fourteenthers
See Quartodecimans

Gemara/Gemarah
From the Aramaic word meaning "learn," which came to refer to that which has been learned and passed down to scholars by tradition. It was often used in place of the word "Talmud."

Gentile
In the scriptures it is translated into English from the Latin word *gentilis*. It originally comes from the Hebrew word *goy*, and then from the Greek word *ethnos*, meaning one from another nation. Some translations also use the word "Gentile" for the Greek word *Hellen* (Hellenism), meaning "person of Greek descent, language, or culture," which could also refer in the broader sense to all people (including Israelites) who came under the influence of Greek (as distinguished from Israeli) culture.

great Sabbath
See Sabbath, high or great

Golden Table
Refers to the Showbread table, which God commanded to be overlaid with gold.

Gospel/s
From the Greek word *euaggelion*, meaning "good news" or "glad tidings." It has come to refer to the first four books of the Bible (Matthew, Mark, Luke, and John) as accounts of the Messiah's life and redemptive death.

grain offering
Sometimes translated as "meal" or badly as "meat" offering (see KJV). This was a fine-flour offering to God from the harvest grains. Sometimes it was ground and baked in the oven, and sometimes it was prepared in a pan (Leviticus 2:4, 5).

Great Commission
The common term for the Messiah's directives just before his ascension to heaven (Matthew 28:18–20).

hermeneutics
The interpretation of scripture using the proper guidelines for exegesis. This includes the accurate definition of words, the context in which they were spoken, any idioms of the day, and other factors. When there is clear agreement among the scriptures, yet one verse seems to oppose that which is obvious, it is best to seek another explanation of that one verse in light of the majority of truth.

Herod's Temple
Often called the "second Temple." Herod the Great was appointed king of Judah in 40 BC at the advice of Antony with the consent of Octavion; he began constructing this massive temple about 20 years later. He was the father of Herod (Antipas), who lived when Jesus ministered.

high priest
The highest-ranking priest whose ministry included entering the Holy of Holies once a year on the Day of Atonement. According to the law of Moses, he was to be from the lineage of Levi through Aaron.

high Sabbath
See Sabbath, high or great

Hippolytus
An early Fourteenther who was considered a church father. Some say he was a disciple of Clement of Alexandria, others say of Irenaeus.

Holy of Holies
The innermost sanctuary in the Tabernacle and the Temple that contained the Ark of the Covenant, considered the dwelling place of God.

Holy Place
The first room and entry into the two-room structure containing the Holy Place and the Holy of Holies. It contained the altar of incense, the seven-branch oil lamp stand (the Menorah), and the table of Showbread that held the twelve breads, wine offerings, and frankincense.

Holy Spirit
This usually refers to God's spirit in action. God is holy and an infinite eternal spirit; thus He was called *Ruach HaKodesh* (the Holy Spirit) in Hebrew.

Immanuel
A name given figuratively to the Messiah by God in the book of Isaiah, saying he would be born of a virgin and be called by this Hebrew name, which means "God with us" (Isaiah 7:14; Matthew 1:22, 23).

Ingathering (Tabernacles, or Booths [Sukkot])
See Tabernacles, Feast of

Irenaeus
An early Fourteenther and disciple of Polycarp; both were considered church fathers. Some say Hippolytus was his disciple.

Jacob
Son of Isaac. He wrestled with the Angel of the Lord and his name changed to "Israel," meaning "prince with God" or "prevailed with God." He fathered the twelve sons who would later become the twelve tribes of Israel.

James
Or rather "Jacobus" (*Iakwbos*), from the Greek word for "Jacob." Apostle and brother of John, writer of the book of James.

Jerusalem
Originally the Canaanite city of Jebus, which was captured by David (2 Samuel 5:8) and later renamed "Jerusalem." This was where Solomon's Temple was built.

Jew/Jewish
From the son of Jacob/Israel named "Judah." Judah was the leading tribe when the Israelites were encamping in the wilderness and going into battle. The first-century Jewish historian Josephus relates that Judah also led when the Israelites entered Babylonian captivity. The land given to this tribe was called "Judea," and thus the descendants dwelling there were known as Judeans; the English term "Jew" is a shortened form of this. With many people from the 10 original northern tribes having scattered into captivity, it came to refer to anyone of Israeli lineage.

Jewish assemblies
Assemblies of believers in the Messiah living in the Asiatic region and elsewhere who were more Jewish-leaning in their customs, worship, and religious traditions (as opposed to those leaning toward Roman customs). *See also* Asiatics.

John
Apostle and close friend to Jesus, who leaned on Jesus's chest at the Last Supper and was "he whom Jesus loved" (John 13:23). He wrote the book of John and the book of Revelation as well as the books of 1 John, 2 John, and 3 John.

John the Baptist
Born in the priestly lineage under miraculous circumstances (Luke 1:5–80), he was a Jewish prophet who was accepted by almost everyone in Israel (per *The Jewish Encyclopedia*), such that even the Pharisees came out to be baptized by him. The first-century Jewish historian Josephus writes that he exhorted the Jews to live virtuously and with justice toward one another and reverence toward God (Antiquities 18.5.2). He was the voice in the wilderness that would pave the way for the Messiah, as Isaiah had prophesied (Matthew 3:1–3; Luke 3:3–6; Isaiah 40:3–5), and the messenger the Lord would send before appearing in His Temple (Malachi 3:1; Matthew 11:10, 11).

Josephus
A Jewish historian of royal ancestry born around 37 AD and raised in Israel. He recorded much of the Jewish history to his day.

Judah
One of the twelve sons of Israel; the land of Judah bears his name.

Judaism
The term originally applied to the law of Moses and the writings of the prophets as followed in the Mosaic covenant by the descendants of Israel, to whom these laws were given (Galatians 1:13, 14 NAS). After the Talmud was written and later in history, Judaism shifted away from the belief in their scriptures and more toward following the oral traditions of the Talmudic rabbis.

Judaizer
A term used for any Jews who were trying to entice New Covenant believers in the Messiah to return under the law of Moses, the previous covenant. The term was often misapplied to refer to Jews in the New Covenant who wanted to continue their age-old customs, such as commemorating the Passover.

klasmata
A Greek word referring to a fragment or piece resulting from the breaking of bread.

koinonia
The Greek word referring to fellowship, sharing, or communion.

kosher
Comes from the Hebrew word meaning "right" or "proper." It often refers to that which was proper to eat based on the dietary laws in the first covenant under Moses (Leviticus 11).

Laodicea, Council of (AD 364)
A form of Christianity with its own doctrines and observances more aligned with Roman beliefs, as opposed to Eastern Christianity, where the Asiatic Fourteenthers held to certain Jewish customs and beliefs. Latin was the native language of Rome, although most Romans also spoke Greek in Jesus's day. Tertullian (born in Carthage to a Roman centurion) was considered the father of Latin Christianity. The Eastern Christians did not follow Rome's ninth-century change to using unleavened bread in the Communion ritual, and derided those making this change, calling them "Azymites" (Greek for "unleavened ones"—*see* Azymites). This helped lead to the ultimate separation between the Eastern Churches and the Western Roman Church in what came to be known as the Great Schism.

Last Supper
The last meal the Messiah ate with his disciples before his Crucifixion.

Latin Christianity
A form of Christianity with its own doctrines and observances more aligned with Roman beliefs, as opposed to Eastern Christianity, where the Asiatic Fourteenthers held to certain Jewish customs and beliefs. Latin was the native language of Rome, although most Romans also spoke Greek in Jesus's day. Tertullian (born in Carthage to a Roman centurion) was considered the father of Latin Christianity. The Eastern Christians did not follow Rome's ninth-century change to using unleavened bread in the Communion ritual, and derided those making this change, calling them "Azymites" (Greek for "unleavened ones"—*see* Azymites). This helped lead to the ultimate separation between the Eastern Churches and the Western Roman Church in what came to be known as the Great Schism.

laver
A large basin containing water that was commanded by God to be placed between the altar and the tent of meeting (Exodus 30:18) for the priests to wash at.

leaven
Any leavening agent like yeast that causes dough to rise when cooked. When flour becomes leavened, a portion puffs up with air (aerates), from which we get the word "heresy," from the Greek word *airo*, meaning "to rise up." "Leaven" thus came to symbolically refer to a type of sin and false doctrine (the Israelites' first meal coming out of Egypt contained *matzah*, the Hebrew word for unleavened bread). This symbolism was not taken to legalistic extremes, however, for it was understood that regular leavened bread was a desirable food, except when commemorating Passover.

leavened bread
Flour with leaven that is baked into bread.

lechem
The Hebrew word used for regular leavened bread, as opposed to *matzah*, which is unleavened.

Levitical priesthood
The priesthood given in the law of Moses for descendants of Levi, one of Israel's twelve sons.

literal/natural
See natural-to-spiritual idiom

living water
In Jewish history, a moving body of water such as a river (hence "living," as opposed to a stagnant pond) used for ritual cleansings (baptisms). Jesus applied this cleansing spiritually by referring to the word of God that he spoke (John 15:3). This living water also refers to God's spirit (John 4:10–11) as the spiritual living water that would flow out from the believer after Pentecost (John 7:37–39).

logos
The Greek word meaning an inward thought with outward expression, often translated as "word." Refer to Course 8 for a full explanation of how it was used.

Lord
In the Old Testament, capitalizing the first letter shows that the Hebrew word is *Adonai*, which, along with the Greek word *kurios*, can refer to either God or a man in a high position of authority, such as a master, ruler, or Lord. Most translations use the all-capitalized "LORD" to show that the name "YAHWEH" is in the Hebrew.

Lord's Supper
Usually mistakenly applied to the Communion ritual. In reality this term was from two Greek words: *kuriakon*, meaning "pertaining to the Lord," and *deipnon*, meaning "supper, feast, or banquet" (1 Corinthians 11:20). These words could just as easily be translated as "Lord's feast" or "Messianic feast/banquet." Paul used them to refer to the spiritual feast that was a longstanding part of Jewish history, and to what Jesus was pointing to in his Last Supper parables (refer to Course 6 for more details).

love feasts
See *agapais/agape* feasts

Lucifer
This word comes from the King James translation, which used this Latin name (from the Latin Vulgate) for the morning star (in Isaiah 14:12). The Latin was a translation of the original Hebrew word in this scripture, meaning "light bearer" or "morning star," which in Isaiah appears to refer to Satan before he rebelled. Lucifer therefore is not really the pre-fallen name of Satan as has been supposed but was the Latin word for the morning star.

Luke
Evangelist and writer of the gospel of Luke and the Book of Acts. He was not an apostle, nor was he a witness to Christ's ministry, but he did convert at some point. A close friend and associate of Paul, he was probably a physician and either a Gentile or a Hellenistic Jew (Colossians 4:11 and 4:14 show he was not counted among the circumcision).

Luther, Martin
Considered by some to be the greatest religious reformer, he was a powerful force for Protestantism, boldly standing against the abuses of the Roman Catholic Church in his day. Yet, growing up Roman Catholic he could not get fully away from certain Catholic beliefs, such as a literal understanding of John 6:53, and therefore he taught the belief of consubstantiation (where the Communion bread and wine contain Christ's actual flesh and blood).

man child
A scriptural picture of the group of people who are figuratively birthed from the visible church (the woman in Revelation 12) and fulfill the plan of God by coming into His image and likeness and who are later caught up to God in the rapture. Refer to Course 8 and Course 12 for more details.

manna
A substance ("bread of heaven," Psalm 105:40) that God caused to come down from heaven to feed the Israelites in the wilderness. The Hebrew word "manna" meant "What is it?" Jesus showed that he was the spiritual fulfillment of this bread of God that came down from heaven (John 6:31–63).

Mark
One of the original twelve apostles called by the Lord. Wrote the Book of Mark.

Matthew
One of the original twelve apostles called by the Lord. Wrote the Book of Matthew.

matzah
A Hebrew word meaning "unleavened." Often in the form of a cracker or cake without leaven, used especially during Passover. *See also* unleavened (bread).

Melchizedek
The priest of the most high God (Genesis 14:18) who brought out bread and wine to Abraham. He was the king of Salem (later named "Jerusalem"), and his name meant "king of righteousness."

memorial
The name given to a number of remembrances and offerings, such as the frankincense that was upon the Showbread (Leviticus 24:7).

Messiah
From the Hebrew word *mashiach*, meaning "anointed." Specifically applied to the anointed one, the Messiah. The Greek word used was *Christos*, or "Christ" in English.

Messianic
Pertaining to the Messiah.

Messianic feast/Messianic banquet
A longstanding Jewish belief of a coming feast or banquet among God's righteous people with the Messiah present and God's spirit in the midst.

Messianic Jew
A popular term referring to an Israelite who has accepted Jesus (Yeshua) as the promised Messiah sent from God, as foretold by the scriptures that he would both suffer and die to pay the penalty for sins.

mikveh/mikvah
A bath used in Judaism for ritual cleansing by immersion in water. Many have been found throughout Jerusalem in archaeological digs.

mishnah
Hebrew word meaning "oral instruction." It is the compilation of oral law and rabbinic commentary that is the foundation for much of the Talmud.

Moses
The prophet and lawgiver from the tribe of Levi. His Hebrew name Moshe means "drawn out," signifying that he was drawn out of the water in Egypt by the daughter of Pharaoh. Moses said that another prophet would rise up like unto him to whom the people must listen (Deuteronomy 18:15, referring to the Messiah).

move of God
A true moving of God's spirit among the people, one that often includes various outward signs and miracles.

natural-to-spiritual idiom
This refers to the often-used idiom of the Jews, especially among those in the New Covenant, who drew spiritual truth and application from natural or literal things, such as the Temple and its sacrifices. They understood the Old Covenant types that God intended to be spiritually fulfilled in the New Covenant.

New Covenant
This refers to the long-promised New Covenant (more details in Course 10), which the Messiah was prophesied to bring.

New Testament
This usually refers to the God-anointed scriptures from Matthew to Revelation, written by the followers of the Messiah.

new wine
In the natural or literal sense, new wine came from newly harvested grapes from the vine and was often shared during the annual festivals. Spiritually it pointed to the love of God and His spirit being partaken of and shared among believers.

Nicaea, Catholic Council of (AD 325)
A council convened by the Roman emperor Constantine to clarify their Trinity doctrine and to enforce a uniform ritual celebration of Easter throughout the Roman Empire by removing Jewish Messianic observances of the Passover and all things Jewish.

Nicene Creed
A written explanation of the Roman doctrine of the Trinity, whereby Christ was a God who pre-existed. Anyone who said there was ever a time when Christ did not exist would be cast out of the church. Later creeds on this belief would revise and add to this first creed.

Nisan
The first month in the Hebrew calendar of the ecclesiastical year (seventh month in the civil year), occurring in spring. A few times in Exodus and Deuteronomy (Exodus 13:4; 23:15; 34:18; Deuteronomy 16:1), this period of time is called "Abib," which refers to when the barley ripens; this usually corresponds to our March and April months.

Noah
Second father of the human family. He was directed by God to build an ark wherein the faithful would be lifted up and saved from the coming flood.

Old Covenant
This refers to the law as given by God to Moses.

Old Testament

This refers to the God-anointed scriptures written by various Israelites in books ranging from Genesis to Malachi.

omer

A sheaf or measure of grain. In Leviticus 23, God commanded Moses to offer this sheaf or omer on the morrow of the Sabbath (Sunday), and the people were not to eat any bread or grain from the Promised Land until this offering was made to God. This would then begin the 50-day count to the second festival, Pentecost (Shavout).

parable

The word "parable" comes from the Greek word παραβολή (parabolē), a combination of *para* (meaning "alongside") and *bolē* (meaning "to throw"). Hence, its true meaning is found in understanding the symbolic or figurative words that were "thrown alongside" the intended meaning.

Passover

Initially "Passover" referred to the lamb sacrifice, and then it was used for the 14th day of Nisan in which the lamb was to be sacrificed, and eventually for the whole festival. The 15th-day Sabbath also came to be called "Passover," because it was the main Sabbath and entry point into the seven-day Feast of Unleavened Bread, which sometimes itself was called "Passover" (the proximity of these two events caused them to be lumped together, Luke 22:1). The Messiah fulfilled this 14th-day original Passover type when he was crucified on the 14th day of Nisan.

paraskeuy

The Greek word for the day before the Sabbath, which included the Saturday Sabbath or any of the seven Festival Sabbaths. This *paraskeuy* in later times came to denote "Friday," the day before the Sabbath. But for the Jews, it referred to the day before any Sabbath. For more details on this, see the subsection "The 13th-Day Question" in the chapter "The Template Challenge," "The Gospels All Agree" in the chapter "50 Reasons the Last Supper Was Not the Passover," and "The Gospels Do Not Contradict Each Other" in the chapter "Three Major Keys that Unlock the Gospels."

Paschal meal

The eating of the Passover.

Paul

This Jewish apostle was originally named saoul, the Greek name from the Hebrew *Shaul*, which reads "Saul" in English. Upon his conversion he came to be called Paul, which was the Greek form of the Latin name, and he went by this in his letters. He was considered as the apostle to the uncircumcised nations, whereas Peter was considered the apostle to the circumcised (Galatians 2:8).

Pentateuch
The name given to the first five books of the Bible.

Pentecost, Feast/Festival of
Also called Shavout, or Festival of Weeks. The second of the three annual Jewish festivals commanded by God. It was the day in the book of Acts in which the New Covenant believers were filled with God's spirit, which ushered in the new phase—the spirit-filled assembly of believers in the Messiah (Acts 2 and Joel 2:28, 29).

Peter
From the Greek word *petros* (meaning "rock"). Considered the apostle to the Jews, he was a fisherman in Galilee and wrote the books 1 Peter and 2 Peter. Early on in the New Covenant, he was given the vision by God that uncircumcised Gentile believers were to no longer be considered unclean (Acts 10).

Pharisees
A powerful and strict sect of Jews who, according to the first-century Jewish historian Josephus, gained considerable control among the people to install their own traditions, which were not written in the law of Moses. The Pharisees were opposed to the affluent Sadducees, whose lineage came from Zadok and thus still had control of the high priesthood, but who had lost some respect and authority among the people. The Pharisees believed that the Showbread should be made and eaten unleavened (as the less appetizing matzah); during Jesus's time the Sadducee priests had to eat this "bread" as such.

Philo
A Jewish biblical philosopher and writer born in Alexandria, Egypt, around 20 BC.

phylacteries
Small leather boxes containing a few Bible verses. Many Jews wore a phylactery, believing that the words of Moses (i.e., in Deuteronomy 6:8; 11:18; Exodus 13:9, 16) were to be taken literally. Jesus wore tassels on his garments, as did many Jews (Numbers 15:38, 39), and "tassel" is usually translated into English as "hem" or "fringe" (Matthew 9:20; 14:36). Because of the Council of Laodicea's commandment, anyone who wore phylacteries could be thrown out of the Roman Church.

prefiguring
This word often denotes an Old Covenant type that "prefigures" the New Covenant fulfillment of the type, such as the Passover lambs prefiguring Christ as the true lamb of God.

Polycarp
An early Fourteenther who was considered a church father, and one of the rare ones who lived alongside some of the apostles.

preparation day
Speaks of the day of preparation (*see also paraskeuy*), which occurs before the Jewish Sabbath (Saturday), but also occurs before the other seven Sabbaths that are connected to the three annual Jewish festivals. The day the Passover was slain (14th of Nisan, the day of Christ's death) was a preparation day, as it was the day before the 15th-day Sabbath. For more details on this, see the subsection "The 13th-Day Question" in the chapter "The Template Challenge," "The Gospels All Agree" in the chapter "50 Reasons the Last Supper Was Not the Passover," and "The Gospels Do Not Contradict Each Other" in the chapter "Three Major Keys that Unlock the Gospels.""

presence bread
Refers to the twelve breads placed upon the golden table of Showbread in the Holy Place of the Tabernacle and Temple.

priest
In the Mosaic covenant, a male descendant from the tribe of Levi who ministered before God in the sacrifices and other Temple functions, often on behalf of the people.

priesthood
A grouping of priests who minister before God.

preenactments
Currently portraying an event that has a future fulfillment.

Promised Land
The natural promised land is Israel, promised by God to Abraham and his descendants. This points forward to the true Promised Land, which is the spiritual inheritance of being filled with God's spirit and experiencing His love and indescribable joy forever.

prophet
From the Hebrew word meaning "to bubble forth," it referred to a man who spoke forth under God's inspiration, often predicting future events.

Protestant
According to McClintock and Strong, "Protestants" "is a collective name for all genuine believers in evangelical Christianity—those who protest against the errors and renounce the communion of the Romish Church."

psomion
A Greek word for a small morsel of bread.

Quartodecimans
From the Latin word meaning "Fourteenth," this term applied to Messianic Jews who believed in Jesus as the Messiah and were keeping the 14th day as a special commemoration day. The Quartodecimans knew that Jesus was crucified on this day and fulfilled the prophecies by bringing redemption to mankind, and they did not want to be forced to drop their custom and keep Rome's celebration of Easter (from Astarte) as was commanded. They have been falsely portrayed as a heretic fringe group ever since, rejected by both Roman Catholics and Pharisaic-leaning rabbis. I use the term "Fourteenther" in this book for all those early believers who believe the Messiah was crucified on the 14th day.

rabbi
A Hebrew word meaning "master," "great," or "lord." Often used for Jewish leaders schooled in the Torah and later the Talmud.

Rapture
Used to describe the biblical promise of a catching away of God's people. Refer to 1 Thessalonians 4:17, where the remaining believers are "caught up" in clouds to meet the Lord in the air. Refer also to Revelation 12:5; Matthew 24:37–43; etc.

repent
Translated into English from two Hebrew words: *shub*, meaning "to turn back" (to God), and *nacham*, meaning "to be sorry" or "regret." Usually *metanoeo* in Greek, which in scripture means to have a change of heart and a change of way in behavior and attitude (with assistance by God's spirit).

resurrection
The rising back to life of a person who has been dead.

revelation
The disclosure of something that had previously been hidden or unknown.

ritual
An external system of words and actions. Certain Old Covenant ritualistic observances were done away by the Messiah's sacrifice, for he said, "But an hour is coming, and now is, when the true worshipers shall worship the Father in spirit and truth; for such people the Father seeks to be His worshipers" (John 4:23). Another ritual, called "Communion" or the "Blessed Eucharist," was created many years after the Messiah's death by some who misapplied the scriptures and then required it for salvation.

ritual purification
In the Old Covenant, God required certain outward purifications, such as washing or dipping in water (such as a *mikveh*) to prepare oneself for entering His presence, or for cleansing and acceptance back into the camp of Israel.

sanctified
To be set apart or be consecrated to God.

Sabbath
From the Hebrew word meaning "to rest from labor," which was used on the seventh day of creation when God "rested" (the Hebrew word is *Shabath*) and was later given as a command for the Israelites under Moses to cease from labor on the seventh day (our Saturday). It was first written as a command when the manna fell (Exodus 16:23) and Israelites were not to gather on the seventh day. This Sabbath day would begin at sundown on our Friday.

Sabbath, high or great
From the Greek word *megaly* (which means "high" or "great"), it referred to any seven of the high holy Festival Sabbath days, which were closely connected to the three annual Jewish festivals.

sacrament
McClintock and Strong's *Cyclopedia* states the following:
"SACRAMENT (from the Lat. *sacramentum*, a military oath of enlistment), a word adopted by the writers of the Latin Church to denote those ordinances of religion by which Christians come under an obligation of obedience to God, and which obligation, they supposed, was equally sacred with that of an oath" (vol. 9, p. 212).

Sadducees

The Sadducees were a Jewish sect of high priestly lineage, descended from Levi through Aaron and then through Zadok. Thus they had the right to the high priesthood and to partake of the Showbread. The Greek word for "Zadok" is **Saddouk**, and for "Sadducee" is **Saddoukaios**.

According to Jewish-studies scholar Lawrence Schiffman, the Dead Sea Sect was probably started by the Sadducees, who had withdrawn from the Pharisaic-controlled Temple services. They rejected the Pharisaic claim of an oral law, and said that only what was written in the law of Moses was binding. They had somewhat backslidden by Jesus's day, and the Pharisees despised them (as seen the Talmud and the New Testament), were probably jealous of them, and were able to strip away some of their control (as seen in Josephus).

Satan

From the Hebrew word meaning "adversary" or "accuser," the scripture name for the chief of the fallen angels, the demon spirits.

Schiffman, Lawrence

A prominent American professor of Jewish studies who specializes in the Dead Sea Scrolls, Judaism in late antiquity, Jewish law, and Talmudic literature.

scripture

In the Bible, "scripture" is an English word translated from the Hebrew *kethab* (meaning "writing") and from the Greek *graphy* (also meaning "writing" and usually referring to one of the Old Testament books, or to a certain verse). In common usage among believers, it refers to the Old and New Testament books that are directly inspired by God's spirit.

seed of the woman

In Revelation 12, it refers to the remaining believers who refused to become part of the man child (also pictured as the bride), were not caught up to God at the rapture, and later fled into the wilderness for protection.

Septuagint

A translation of the Hebrew bible by Jewish scholars into Greek. Jewish historian Josephus relates that Ptolemy wrote to the high priest Eleazar requesting this translation, and six properly skilled elders from each tribe of Israel began to undertake this work (Antiquities 12.2.1–6). The exact date is uncertain, but the task was completed around 200 years before Jesus ministered. This translation was highly esteemed among Jews even before Jesus lived and was widely used in Greek-speaking nations of the Diaspora. It was common when Jesus lived and was used by the mostly Jewish writers of the New Testament, where the majority of scripture quotes used from the Old Testament are from this Greek translation. Although Jesus and some Jews also spoke Aramaic, the most common language used among them was Greek.

shadow/substance
In the scriptures, these terms denote something that points forward and is considered a shadow of the true substance that it points to.

Showbread/Shewbread
The twelve breads that were instructed by God to remain in His presence in the Holy Place (in the Tabernacle and then the Temple) all week long, then to be shared among the higher order of priests from Aaron's lineage on the Sabbath. (Refer to Courses 7 and 9 for more information.) These twelve breads were not called "Showbread" in biblical times, for this English word was not used until after William Tyndale coined the term "Shewbread" in the 1500s. Course 9 details that the Greek words used in the Septuagint and also by Jesus and Paul in the New Testament are better translated as "breads of the plan (or purpose)" or "plan (or purpose) of the breads."

Solomon's Porch
Also called "Portico." This is the outer eastern area of the Temple where believers in the Messiah would often gather both before and after his death (John 10:23; Acts 3:11; 5:12).

Solomon's Temple
See Temple

spiritual
Biblically refers to things inspired by or pertaining to God's spirit, as well as the heavenly spirit realm.

spot
Translated from the Greek word *spilos*, this term refers to the stains that would sometimes appear on the priests' garments when they were roasting sacrifices or preparing offerings. Among New Covenant believers (using the natural-to-spiritual idiom), a spot referred in a spiritual sense to those who did not show the proper spirit before God and were rather seeking sensual pleasure during the time of spiritual fellowshipping in the agape feasts (KJV Jude 1:12, 23; 2 Peter 2:13; Ephesians 5:27). *See also agapais/agape* feasts.

Stephen
A disciple of Christ who was stoned to death. He was one of the seven who were chosen in Acts 6 who did great wonders and signs (Acts 6:8).

subjunctive mood
A mood in Greek that sometimes expresses possibility, doubt, or even unreality. Refer to the chapter "The Three Major Greek Keys That Unlock the Gospels" for more information.

Sukkot/Succoth
See Tabernacles, Feast of

Tabernacle
The habitation of God built by Moses in the wilderness, where God would meet His people (Exodus 29:42). In the new covenant in the book of Revelation, the term referred to the people who assembled together, specifically to those who would be caught up to God (Revelation 13:6).

Tabernacles, Feast of
Also called "Ingathering," "Booths," or "Sukkot." It was the third of the three great annual Jewish festivals (the other two were the Feasts of the Passover and Pentecost) on which the entire male population was required to appear before the Lord in the Temple at Jerusalem. It was a celebration of the harvests.

Talmud
The name of two works, primarily referring to the Babylonian Talmud, but also to the Jerusalem Talmud, both of which detail and often debate the traditions and laws of the Jews, mostly written from the standpoint of the Pharisees. Although as believers in the God-anointed scriptures we do not get doctrine from the Talmud, it does contain a wealth of accurate information concerning the festivals that the Jewish scholars wanted to preserve and pass down to future generations. One often has to weed out certain concepts where there was an ax to grind (since the Talmud was written by the descendants of the Pharisees, who despised the Sadducees as well as the followers of the Messiah). But there is still much historical value and insight regarding Temple services and the festivals.

tamid offering
The continual daily lamb sacrifice, also called the "morning and evening offering" ("evening" from the first-century Jewish standpoint meant the late after-noon period), as one lamb was offered in the morning and one in the afternoon each day.

Tammuz
Name of the Babylonian idol god.

Temple
The stone Temple planned by King David and finished by his son Solomon. It was considered a permanent dwelling place (or house) of God after years of the Tabernacle of Moses, which was transitory in location.

theology
From two Greek words meaning "God" and "study of." Hence, it is the study of God, usually as it relates to the interpretation and study of the scriptures, and of Christ, who was the exact representation of God's nature (Hebrews 1:3, NAS).

Therapeutae
A Jewish sect in Alexandria that Jewish biblical philosopher Philo wrote about, who continued a Showbread-type service with bread in which those who partake must ritually bathe before eating the bread.

Tishri
The first month of the Jewish civil year and the seventh month in the ecclesiastical year, corresponding to our September and October. The Hebrew word means "to begin," and it was in this month that the shouting (probably of joy, Deuteronomy 16:15) went forth on the first day of this month (Leviticus 23:24, called "trumpets" in English but "shouting" in Hebrew). The Day of Atonement would occur shortly thereafter on the 10th day, and the seven-day Feast of Tabernacles would begin on the 15th of this month.

Torah
From the Hebrew word meaning "law," "teaching," or "instruction." Often referring to the first five books of the Pentateuch (Genesis, Exodus, Leviticus, Numbers, and Deuteronomy), it is also called the "books of Moses." The Septuagint translation from the Hebrew into Greek used the word nomos, and among the New Covenant believers this often referred to the Old Covenant (especially the ceremonial) laws given to Moses that were fulfilled in Christ.

tradition
From a scriptural standpoint, a tradition usually refers to a human-made commandment forced upon people that does not have God's authority behind it.

transliteration
A translation from one language into another that often replicates the sound of the original word.

transubstantiation
The Roman Catholic doctrine that in their Communion ritual, the bread and wine actually transform into the flesh and blood of Christ.

Trinity
A belief that originated in Rome, in part from the tradition of the previous Roman Triads (the Archaic Triad and the Capitoline Triad that succeeded it). In the Trinity, God is seen as three entities who are each God (the Father, the Holy Spirit, and Jesus), and yet these three together are believed to make up the one God. The word "Trinity" was not used in the New Testament; it was a concept and word that came from the Latin word *trinitas*, which is a Latinization of the Greek words *he trias*, which meant "the Triad" and eventually became the word "Trinity." (Refer to the section "What about the Word "Trinity"? in "Setting the Table 2" and the discussion about logos in Course 8 for more information.)

Tertullian
Born in Carthage in about 160 AD to a Roman centurion, Tertullian converted to Christianity and was later considered the father of Latin Christianity. He coined the word *trinitas*, which was a Latinization of the Greek *he trias* ("the Triad"), which came down in English as the word "Trinity." He provides one of the earliest writings on what appears to be the Catholic ritual of Communion, when he writes. "We are concerned if even a particle of the wine or bread, made ours, in the Lord's Supper, fails to the ground, by our carelessness" (Roberts and Donaldson, *Ante-Nicene Fathers*, vol. 3, p. 103).

twelve breads
See Showbread/Shewbread

type
A form, example, pattern, or figure. From the Greek word *tupos* (refer to the Greek in Romans 5:14 and 1 Corinthians 10:6, where it is often translated as "examples"). Certain events, sacrifices, items in the Temple, etc., from the Old Covenant are seen to prefigure Christ or other New Covenant truths or events.

typology
A belief in the study of types from the Old Covenant and correctly applying them to the antitype in the New Covenant. For instance, the Passover lamb that was sacrificed to bring the Israelites out of Egypt is a type, and Christ's sacrifice for forgiveness of sins and ritual cleansing and deliverance from spiritual Egypt is the corresponding antitype.

unleavened (bread)
The Hebrew word for "unleavened" was matzah, and in Greek it was *azumos*. These single Hebrew and Greek words are often translated in the Bible as two words by adding the word "bread," such as in the Feast of "Unleavened Bread." The Hebrew and Greek words refer to that which is without leaven.

Victor
This bishop of Rome (around AD 190) was responsible for a change in attitude toward the Messianic Jews who kept the fourteenth day of Nisan as a special commemoration day of Passover and for the Messiah's sacrificial death on that day. Victor branded these Asiatic "fourteenthers" as heretics and openly threatened them.

winnowing
In the Bible, this term comes from the Hebrew word meaning "scattered." It was used for the chaff that was blown away after the grains were threshed and thrown into the air.

Yeshua
The English transliteration of the Hebrew name given by Moses to Joshua (i.e., "Oshea" was changed to "Yah-Oshea" by Moses) because of God's calling on his life (Numbers 13:16). The Greek translation was *Iesous*, and this was the same name given to Jesus by the angel (Matthew 1:21), meaning "Yahweh is savior," or "Yahweh saves."

Yahweh
Commonly considered the proper name of God. In Exodus 3:14 God answered the question by Moses as to what His name was, saying, "I Am that I Am." Scholars say the exact meaning in Hebrew is uncertain, and the Jewish Study Bible writes that it is "… probably best translated as 'I Will Be What I Will Be,' meaning 'My nature will become evident from My actions.' " (Jewish Study Bible, Exodus 3:14).

Zadok

A Hebrew name meaning "Righteous." Primarily refers to the faithful high priest in the time of King David. Ezekiel bears witness to the faithful priests ("sons of Zadok") who came from his lineage, and Ezekiel relates the special position they are given of drawing close to God (Ezekiel 40:46; 43:19; 44:15; 48:11). The Sadducees (Zadokites) were descendants of Zadok and derived their name from him. The Greek word for "Zadok" is **Saddouk** and for "Sadducee" is **Saddouk**aios.

Zwingli, Ulrich

The main leader of the Reformation in Switzerland, just as Martin Luther was in Germany. He was accused of being of the devil by Luther for not believing that the bread and wine in the Communion ritual contained Christ's flesh and blood. He was the forerunner of the Protestant ritual of today, which believes Christ wanted it kept as a ritual, but that it is only symbolic, with no actual change in the bread or wine.

Bibliography and Resources

Barnes, Albert. *Barnes' Notes on the New Testament*. Edited by Ingram Cobbin. Grand Rapids, MI: Kregel Publications, 1962.

Bauer, Walter. *A Greek-English Lexicon of the New Testament and Other Early Christian Literature* (also known informally as *BDAG*). 3rd ed. Revised and edited by Frederick William Danker. Chicago: University of Chicago Press, 2000.

The Catholic University of America. *New Catholic Encyclopedia*. 2nd ed. Farmington Hills, MI: Thomson Gale, 2003.

Clarke, Adam. *Clarke's Commentary*. Vol. 1, *Genesis–Esther*. Nashville, TN: Abingdon Press, 1977.

Clarke, Adam. *Clarke's Commentary*. Vol. 3, *Matthew–Revelation*. Nashville, TN: Abingdon Press, 1977.

Dana, H. E., and Julius R. Mantey. *A Manual Grammar of the Greek New Testament*. New York: Macmillan Publishing, 1955.

Disraeli, Benjamin. *Coningsby*. 2nd ed. Vol. 2. London: Henry Colburn, 1844.

Edersheim, Alfred. *The Life and Times of Jesus the Messiah*. Grand Rapids, MI: Wm. B. Eerdmans Publishing, 1986.

Edersheim, Alfred. *The Temple: Its Ministry and Services*. Peabody, MA: Hendrickson Publishers, 1994.

Encyclopedia Judaica Research Foundation. *Encyclopedia Judaica*. Jerusalem: Keter Publishing House, 1972.

Fanning, Buist M. *Verbal Aspect in New Testament Greek*. Oxford: Clarendon Press, 1990.

Henry, Matthew. *Matthew Henry's Commentary on the Whole Bible*. Vol. 6, *Acts to Revelation*. McLean, VA: MacDonald Publishing, 1994.

Herbermann, Charles G., Edward A. Pace, Condé B. Pallen, Thomas J. Shahan, and John J. Wynne. *The Catholic Encyclopedia*. New York: Robert Appleton Company, 1907–1912.

Hyslop, Alexander. *The Two Babylons*. 2nd ed. Neptune, NJ: Loizeaux Brothers, 1959.

Jackson, Andrew. *Farewell Address, March 4, 1837*. The American Presidency Project. Online by Gerhard Peters and John T. Woolley. Accessed July 4, 2012, http://www.presidency.ucsb.edu/ws/?pid=67087.

Jamieson, Robert, A. R. Fausset, and David Brown. *A Commentary, Critical, Experimental, and Practical, on the Old and New Testaments*. Grand Rapids, MI: Wm. B. Eerdmans Publishing, 1978.

The Jewish Encyclopedia. 12 vols. New York: Funk & Wagnalls Company, 1901.

Keil, C. F., and Franz Delitzsch. *Biblical Commentary on the Old Testament*. Vol. 1, *The Pentateuch*. Grand Rapids, MI: Wm. B. Eerdmans Publishing, 1985.

Keil, C. F., and Franz Delitzsch. *Biblical Commentary on the Old Testament*. Vol. 5, *The Pentateuch*. Grand Rapids, MI: Wm. B. Eerdmans Publishing, 1985.

Lange, John Peter. *A Commentary on the Holy Scriptures: Critical, Doctrinal and Homiletical, with Special References to Ministers and Students. The Acts of the Apostles*, Vol. 4, *The New Testament*. Translated by Philip Schaff. New York: Charles Scribner, 1867.

Lange, John Peter. *A Commentary on the Holy Scriptures: Critical, Doctrinal and Homiletical, with Special References to Ministers and Students. John, The New Testament*. Translated by Philip Schaff. Grand Rapids MI: Zondervan Publishing, 1960.

Lenski, R. C. H. *Commentary on the New Testament: The Interpretation of St. Paul's First and Second Epistles to the Corinthians*. Minneapolis, MN: Augsburg Publishing House, 1963.

Lenski, R. C. H. *Commentary on the New Testament: The Interpretation of St. Luke's Gospel 12–24*. Minneapolis, MN: Augsburg Publishing House, 1961.

Lenski, R. C. H. *Commentary on the New Testament: The Interpretation of St. Matthew's Gospel 15–28*. Minneapolis, MN: Augsburg Publishing House, 1964.

Liddell, Henry George, and Robert Scott. *A Greek-English Lexicon*. London: Oxford University Press, 1968.

Lightfoot, John. *Commentary on the New Testament from the Talmud and Hebraica*. Vol. 2. Grand Rapids, MI: Baker Book House, 1979.

Lightfoot, John. *Commentary on the New Testament from the Talmud and Hebraica*. Vol. 3. Grand Rapids, MI: Baker Book House, 1979.

Louw, Johannes P., and Eugene A. Nida, eds. *Greek-English Lexicon of the New Testament Based on Semantic Domains* (also known informally as *Louw-Nida Lexicon*). 2nd ed. Vol. 1. New York: United Bible Societies, 1999.

Makow, Henry. *Illuminati, The Cult that Hijacked the World*. Winnipeg, MB: Silas Green, 2011.

Maimonides, Moses. *The Guide for the Perplexed*. Translated by M. Friedländer. 2nd ed. London: Routledge & Kegan Paul, 1904. http://sacred-texts.com/jud/gfp/index.htm.

Marcus, Ralph. *Philo Supplement II: Questions on Exodus*. Cambridge, MA: Harvard University Press, 1953.

Mauriello, Matthew R. *Mercies Remembered*. Maitland, FL: Xulon Press, 2011.

McClintock, John, and James Strong. *Cyclopedia of Biblical, Theological, and Ecclesiastical Literature*. 12 vols. Grand Rapids, MI: Baker Book House, 1981.

Metzger, Bruce M. *A Textual Commentary on the Greek New Testament: A Companion Volume to the United Bible Societies' Greek New Testament*. 3rd ed. London: United Bible Societies, 1975.

Mounce, William D. *Basics of Biblical Greek Grammar*. 2nd ed. Grand Rapids, MI: Zondervan, 2003.

New World Bible Translation Committee. *The Kingdom Interlinear Translation of the Greek Scriptures* (also incorporates *The New Testament in the Original Greek* by

Brooke Foss Westcott and Fenton John Anthony Hort). Brooklyn, NY: Watch Tower Bible and Tract Society of Pennsylvania, 1969.

Perschbacker, Wesley J., ed. *The New Analytical Greek Lexicon*. Peabody, MA: Hendrickson Publishers, 1990.

Roberts, Alexander, and James Donaldson, eds. *Ante-Nicene Fathers*. Vol. 2, *The Writings of the Fathers down to A.D. 325., Fathers of the Second Century: Hermas, Tatian, Athenagoras, Theophilus, and Clement of Alexandria (Entire)*. With revisions by A. Cleveland Coxe. Peabody, MA: Hendrickson Publishers, 1994.

Roberts, Alexander, and James Donaldson, eds. *Ante-Nicene Fathers*. Vol. 3, *Latin Christianity: Its Founder: Tertullian; The Writings of the Fathers down to A.D. 325*. With revisions by A. Cleveland Coxe. Grand Rapids, MI: Wm. B. Eerdmans Publishing, 1993.

Roberts, Alexander, and James Donaldson, eds. *Ante-Nicene Fathers*. Vol. 5, *Fathers of the Third Century: Hippolytus, Cyprian, Caius, Novatian, Appendix, The Writings of the Fathers down to A.D. 325.*, With revisions by A. Cleveland Coxe. Grand Rapids, MI: Wm. B. Eerdmans Publishing, 1995.

Robertson, A. T. *A Grammar of the Greek New Testament in the Light of Historical Research*, Nashville, TN: Broadman Press, 1934.

Robertson, A. T., and W. Hershey Davis. *A New Short Grammar of the Greek Testament*. New York: Harper and Brothers, 1931.

Schaff, Philip. *History of the Christian Church*. Vol. 2, *Ante-Nicene Christianity (A.D. 100–325)*. 5th ed. Grand Rapids, MI: Wm. B. Eerdmans Publishing, 1995.

Schaff, Philip. *History of the Christian Church*. Vol. 3, *Ante-Nicene Christianity (A.D. 100–325)*, 5th edition. Grand Rapids, MI: Wm. B. Eerdmans Publishing, 1981.

Schaff, Philip, and Henry Wace, eds. *Nicene and Post-Nicene Fathers*. Second Series, Vol. 3, *Theodoret, Jerome, Gennadius, Rufinus: Historical Writings, Etc*. Peabody, MA: Hendrickson Publishers, 1995.

Schaff, Philip, and Henry Wace, eds. *Nicene and Post-Nicene Fathers*. Second Series, Vol. 14, *The Seven Ecumenical Councils*. Peabody, MA: Hendrickson Publishers, 1995.

Scherman, Nosson. *The Chumash, the Stone Edition*. Brooklyn: Torah Educational Software, 1993. CD-ROM.

Schiffman, Lawrence H. *Reclaiming the Dead Sea Scrolls*. New York: Doubleday, 1995.

Shulman, Albert M. *Gateway to Judaism: Encyclopedia Home Reference*. 2 vols. New Jersey: Thomas Yoseloff, 1971.

Stendahl, Krister, ed. *The Scrolls and the New Testament*. London: SCM Press, 1957.

Strong, James. *Strong's Exhaustive Concordance of the Bible*. Iowa Falls, IA: Riverside Book and Bible House, 1980.

Sutton, Antony C. *Wall Street and the Rise of Hitler*. Cutchogue, NY: Buccaneer Books, 1976.

Theopedia.com, s.v. "Biblical typology," accessed May 20, 2013, http://www.theopedia.com/Biblical_typology.

New World Bible Translation Committee. *The Kingdom Interlinear Translation of the Greek Scriptures* (also incorporates *The New Testament in the Original Greek* by Brooke Foss Westcott and Fenton John Anthony Hort). Brooklyn, NY: Watch Tower Bible and Tract Society of Pennsylvania, 1969.

United Bible Societies. *A Concise Greek-English Dictionary of the New Testament* (known widely as *UBS Greek-English Dictionary*), incorporated inside *The Greek New Testament*, 3rd corrected ed. United Bible Societies: Stuttgart, 1983.

Wallace, Daniel B. *The Basics of New Testament Syntax: An Intermediate Greek Grammar*. Grand Rapids, MI: Zondervan, 2000.

Wallace, Daniel B. *Greek Grammar Beyond the Basics: An Exegetical Syntax of the New Testament*. Grand Rapids, MI: Zondervan, 1996.

Walvoord, John F., and Roy B. Zuck, eds. *The Bible Knowledge Commentary (New Testament)*. Colorado Springs, CO: David C. Cook, 1983.

Westcott, Brooke Foss. *Introduction to the Study of the Gospels*. 6th ed. Cambridge: MacMillan, 1881.

Whiston, William, translator. *The New Complete Works of Josephus*. Revised ed. Grand Rapids, MI: Kregel Publications, 1999.

Josephus, Flavius. *Antiquities of the Jews—Book 3*. Accessed May 23, 2013. http://earlyjewishwritings.com/text/josephus/ant3.html.

Wikipedia, s.v. "Therapeutae," last modified May 8, 2013, http://en.wikipedia.org/wiki/Therapeutae.

Wise, Michael, Martin Abegg, Jr., and Edward Cook. *The Dead Sea Scrolls: A New Translation*. San Francisco: Harper, 1996.

Yonge, Charles Duke. *The Works of Philo Judaeus*. Vol. 1. (London: H. G. Bohn, 1854–1890.) http://earlyjewishwritings.com/text/philo/book13.html http://earlyjewishwritings.com/text/philo/book34.html

Permissions

Page 31, from left to right, Jesus images: © Depositphotos.com (Jozef Sedmak), Jesus Christ from Slovakia by painter Zabateri; © Depositphotos.com (Andreus); © Depositphotos.com (Jozef Sedmak).

Page 128: image of the Arch of Titus at Rome, from *Cyclopedia of Biblical, Theological, and Ecclesiastical Literature* by John McClintock and James Strong, Baker Books, 1981.

Page 324: Picture courtesy of Calgary Coin Gallery, Calgary, Alberta, Canada.

BWHEBB, BWHEBL, BWTRANSH [Hebrew]; BWGRKL, BWGRKN, and BWGRKI [Greek] PostScript® Type 1 and TrueType fonts Copyright © 1994–2013 BibleWorks, LLC. All rights reserved. These Biblical Greek and Hebrew fonts are used with permission and are from BibleWorks (www.bibleworks.com).

Excerpts from the Babylonian Talmud are from www.Sacred-Texts.com. Excerpts from the Soncino Babylonian Talmud are from www.Come-and-Hear.com.

Scripture taken from the New American Standard Bible®, © Copyright 1960, 1962, 1963, 1968, 1971, 1972, 1973, 1975, 1977, 1995 by The Lockman Foundation. Used by permission.

Many Bible and scripture translations (DBY, GNT, LXE, LXT, JPS, NAB, NAS, NIV, NJB, KJV, YLT) come from BibleWorks™ Copyright © 1992–2001 BibleWorks LLC. All rights reserved.

Greek Bible text from: The Greek New Testament, Fourth revised edition, Edited by Barbara Aland and others, © 1993 Deutsche Bibelgesellschaft, Stuttgart.

Index

This index is not meant to be comprehensive but is only to aid in the study of the subjects in this book.

Symbols

1 Corinthians. *See also* spots and Course 5
    and Paul and the Last Supper 153–182
    bad conduct of Corinthians 155, 499
    teaching or mentioning the supposed ritual of Communion 479
13th day
    13th-day question 12–13
    13th-day question template section 377–381
    timing for Passover 429–451
14th day
    14th-day true Passover template section 383–388
    controversy of observing 3–21, 20
    Jesus crucified on 11
    Jesus eating the Passover 10, 12
    timing for Passover 429
15th-day Sabbath
    15th-day high Sabbath template section 389–393
    as the day after the Crucifixion 441–443
    no illegal activity during 433–440
    timing contradictions 13
40, significance as a number 308
50-day counting to Pentecost 231, 234
50 reasons the Last Supper was not the Passover 428–450

A

Aaron, lineage order and sons of 106, 184, 190, 196, 205, 221, 245, 292, 335, 512
Abib 512
abiding in the spiritual grapevine 338–341
Abihu 211
Abraham
    God's promises to 315
    God summoning him 222
    name of 35
Adam 249
agapais/agape feasts
    allusion to communal meal in heaven 183, 197, 198, 207–208, 357
    beginning of fulfilling Tabernacles 181, 182, 197
    definition of 512

Paul's teaching of 198. *See also* Course 5
  role in communion 492
  spots coming to 173–175
agape love. *See also* agapais/agape feasts
  and new wine 207
  definition of 94, 261, 512
  feast 170
  fulfilling the law 314
  kiss of 176
  New Covenant, and Christ's commandment 94–95, 177–178, 179, 180–182
  reciprocal nature of spiritual love 167–173, 180–182, 188
  relationship to word "charity" 9
  spiritual bride receiving and perfecting 208, 273, 355
  spiritual life flow 337
  timing of fasting during 14th-day Passover 6
Ahab, King 356
Ahaziah, king of Israel 492
Alexander the Great 263
altar
  bread that we break 112, 191
  communion with 192
  definition of 512
  dining table symbolic for altar of God 107, 193
  golden 59, 466
  grain fire, bread, or burnt offering at 241, 242, 244, 287
  incense or frankincense at 218, 230, 235, 243, 245, 257, 465, 466, 522
  leaven at 241
  natural-to-spiritual examples 63, 65–66
  sacrificial blood or sacrifices at 126, 191, 316, 327, 332, 334, 462, 465, 470
  Showbread on 224
  spiritual 51, 112, 193, 197, 223, 480
  spiritual eating at 171
Anicetus 492
Antichrist
  as world leader 349, 351
  identity, role of, and reason for his anger 352–355, 512
  in Revelation 13:6 253
antitype 513
aorist tense (Greek) 397, 417–418, 419, 421–427, 513
Apollinaris, Claudius (bishop of Hierapolis) 13, 14
apostles. *See also* Peter, apostle; *See also* Paul; *See also* John; *See also* Philip; *See also* Mark; *See also* Matthew
  abiding in the spiritual grapevine 338
  allusion of Jesus reaching out to the Diaspora 146
  and bread at Last Supper 74–78, 85, 86–88
  and breaking bread 97, 113, 114–115, 117, 117–118, 119, 121, 134, 136, 283. *See also* Courses 3 and 4
  and Eucharist 494
  and keeping a ritual 81
  and Polycarp 6

    as branches of the grapevine 37–39, 488
    being anointed with God's spirit 117–118, 122, 124, 137
    definition of 37–39, 222–223, 513
    evolution of term 37–39
    gathering the lost sheep 19, 132
    growing in New Covenant understandings 27, 322–323
    not to see themselves as ultimate authorities 501–502, 505
    seeing the resurrected Messiah 132, 141
    symbolism of the number twelve 147–148, 223
    teaching or mentioning a supposed ritual of Communion 473, 475–483, 486
    teaching the Trinity? 33–37
    understanding of Last Supper parables 298, 474
    use of term "Christians" 28
    what the apostles taught about the spiritual body 86, 90–96, 132
apostolos 37
Archaic Triad 36–37, 513, 539
Ark (Noah's)
    as a type 250–252
ark of God's presence 355
Ark of the Covenant 181
arton
    definition of 513
    use of term 73, 75, 77, 83, 230, 372, 482
Ascension 277, 513, 521
Asiatics. *See also* Jewish assemblies
    Asiatic Jewish assemblies keeping the more Jewish customs 3–4, 14, 18, 513
    definition of 513
    keeping the 14th day special 6, 18
    of the Diaspora 4
    refusal to convert to Roman decrees 5
    violation against by Victor 7, 9
assemblies. *See also* sacred assemblies
    building up in love 180
    definition of 26, 513, 523
    God sending teaching rain to 282
    makeup 4
    rejoicing in the Feast 14
    religious authority among 497–507, 504
    seven assemblies 4
Astarte
    association with Easter 6, 15, 79
    definition of 519
atonement
    and Old and New Covenant 307, 334
    definition of 514
    sacrifices for 188, 190, 297, 327, 329, 471
    through natural-to-spiritual Jewish idioms 61
authority, proper 497–507
Autolycus 37

azumos
    definition of 514
    use of term 74, 75, 78, 244, 372, 429, 540
Azymites
    definition of 514
    naming of 81, 525
    what they reveal on Communion rituals 482–486

B

Bahr, Carl 299–300
banquet. *See* Messianic feast
    translation of 201–202
baptize 514
Bar Kochba 305, 324
Barnes, Albert
    in reference to breaking bread 113
Basics of New Testament Syntax, The 510
BDAG: A Greek-English Lexicon of the New Testament and Other Early Christian Literature 510
beast
    definition of 514
    seven-headed dragon (or beast) 346–355
Belshazzar, King 358
Bethlehem
    meaning "house of bread" 285
between the evenings and legal time to slay the Passover 451–471
Bible 514
bible commentaries 509
BibleGateway.com 511
bible study tools 508–511
BibleWorks 508
blood
    ingesting as taboo 126–127, 327–328
    inheriting lifeblood from Christ 341–343
    in parables 45, 325–331
    Messiah's and sacrificial relating to symbolic cup 302–304
    Messiah's shed blood, meaning of 190, 333–337, 336–337
    of the Covenant 164, 316–318
    of the grape 327
    of the two Covenants compared 329–333
    sacrifices, definition of 514
    sacrificial providing communion 190
Boaz 285
body as tabernacle and tent 100–103
body of Christ
    definition of 514
    what it means 87–100
Book of Acts
    and breaking bread. *See* Courses 3 and 4
    timing in history 134

Booths
    as one of the three annual Jewish festivals 181, 185
    definition of 537
"Branch," the 38, 101, 257–258
bread. *See also* twelve Temple breads
    as instruction from God 293–296
    bread and wine related to scripture reading and prayer 214–215
    bread from heaven 53, 155, 168
    bread of affliction 239–241
    bread of deceit 239
    bread of God 241–242
    bread of life 53, 91, 95
    bread of sorrows 239
    bread of the face 299–300
    bread of the Presence 105, 112, 276, 278–279
    definition of 532
    significance of name 105
    bread of the row 276
    bread of wickedness 239
    breads of the plan 277, 278
    breads of the purpose 277, 278
    breaking of. *See* breaking bread
    among early believers 104–129
    at Sabbath 109–110
    confusion with common meals 119–125
    confusion with Communion ritual 113–119, 125–129
    connection to reading of the law 116–117
    definition of 515
    on different occasions 108–110
    spiritually, natural to spiritual 110–112
    the spiritual progression 130–152
    called "cakes" or "challah" 233, 276
    change from leavened to unleavened in Communion 485–486
    children's 239
    commandment that some contain leaven 231–233
    connection to lost tribes of the Diaspora 145–149
    continual bread 276
    English translations that cause confusion 78–80
    figurative uses of 237–247
    Last Supper prophecy betrayed with 81–85
    leavened and Essenes 227
    leavened bread at the Last Supper 71–85
    leavened bread, definition of 525
    lechem, definition of 525
    names used reveal spiritual truths 276–277
    natural-to-spiritual idiom 52–54, 134
    not good during Passover 428–431
    of high priest Melchizedek 203–207
    Pharisaic tradition of twelve breads being unleavened 225–232
    plan of the twelve breads 277–280

    purpose of the twelve breads 277–280
    regular bread at the Festival of Unleavened Bread? 71–85, 141–142
    representing spiritual believers 77–78
    role in three Jewish festival communal meals 185
    row bread 276
    spiritual and Corinthians 155–156
    that we break 112, 133–136
    the one bread 155–156, 164
    true, and Jesus 53, 111
    unleavened. *See* unleavened (bread)
    washing hands before eating 106–108
breaking bread. *See also* Jewish history of breaking bread in Courses 3 and 4; breaking bread in Acts chapter 20 in Course 4
    among early believers 104–129
    at Sabbath 109–110
    confusion with common meals 119–125
    confusion with Communion ritual 113–119, 125–129
    connection to reading of the law 116–117
    definition of 515
    in the Talmud 109–110, 116–117
    on different occasions 108–110
    Showbread "broken" each Sabbath 104
    spiritually, natural to spiritual 110–112
    the spiritual progression 130–152
bridegroom 515
bride (of Christ) 515
bride (spiritual). *See also* man child
    and the Messianic feast and the beast 344–362
    growing into the perfected bride 177–182
    keeping focus on God's leading 355–358

C

Caleb 325
calendar theory (two-calendar theory) 432–433, 515
Capitoline Triad 36–37, 515
catching away 251–252. *See also* Rapture
Catholic. *See also* Christianity, Christians, Catholic Council of Nicaea, Rome
    definition of 515
Catholic Council of Nicaea
    definition of 529
Catholic Encyclopedia, The 10, 20, 127, 482, 484–485, 489–490, 511
chaff 285–286
Chagigah 439
Christ. *See* Jesus Christ
Christian Classics Ethereal Library 511
Christianity
    evolution of the term 28
    imposition of practices on 3–21
    Latin, definition of 525

Christians
    early Jews becoming 27–28
    nickname 28
church
    definition of 516
    in Darby Bible 26
    in Young's Literal Translation 26
    use of term and controversy over 23–27
circumcise 516
Clarke, Adam
    double Passover option 369–370
    reference to breaking bread 113
Clement of Alexandria
    crucifixion timing on the 14th day 12, 374
cock crow 470, 516
commandment
    Jesus giving that we love one another 95–96, 179–182
    that certain breads contain leaven 230–232
Commentary on the Holy Scriptures, A 509
Commentary on the New Testament from the Talmud and Hebraica 509
Commentary on the Old Testament 509
commentators shoehorning the Passover into the Last Supper 431–433
commentator views on breaking bread in Acts 2 113–115
common bond
    for the communal meals 189–190
communal meal
    and communal sacrifices 187–189
    common bonds for 189–190
    definition of 516
    first bread and wine 183–185
    Last Supper as 199–202
    Sectarian 197–198
    three annual Jewish festivals as 185–187
communal sacrifices
    and communal meals 187–189
    definition of 516
communion
    further definition of 23, 156, 189–192, 492–494, 517
    natural to spiritual 190–193
    true communion is spiritual 494–495
    true Jewish and the Messianic Feast 183–216
Communion, ritual of. *See also* transubstantiation and consubstantiation
    and 1 Corinthians 10:16, 156, 190–192, 492–494
    and how it got started 88–89, 487–490
    and Jehovah's Witnesses 484
    and Mormons 484
    and Protestants 481–484
    and reciprocal giving and accepting 171
    Azymites, what they expose concerning it 482–487
    changed from leavened to unleavened bread 485–486

556 | THE MESSIANIC FEAST

    definition of 534
    Greek word often mistaken for ritual 23, 134, 191–195, 491–496
    in a spiritual sense, not as a ritual 153–182
    not taught by early Jewish believers 472–482
    not taught in Acts 2 113–127
    not taught in Acts 20 137–139
    not what is meant by breaking bread 125–129
    supposed scriptural evidence for 473–482
    why Jewish disciples didn't teach it 472–495
concepts
    changing from early Jewish idiom 22–39
congregation
    definition of 26
Constantine, Emperor
    definition of 517
    imposing Roman Christian practices on Jews 3, 16, 17
consubstantiation
    definition of 517
    formation of 86
    Luther's doctrine of 89, 483
continual bread 276
Corinthians. *See* 1 Corinthians
Council of Laodicea
    definition of 524
    impacts on Jewish people 18
Council of Nicaea
    and Easter Sunday 11, 20
    and Nicene Creed 16
Crucifixion
    15th day as the day after the Crucifixion 441–443
    definition of 517
    timing on the 14th day 10, 12, 374
cup, symbolic and the promised New Covenant 300–323
Cyclopedia of Biblical, Theological, and Ecclesiastical Literature 510
Cyrus, King 249

D

Dana and Mantey, Greek scholars 167, 398, 404
Daniel
    foretelling of New Covenant 305
    God speaking to 307
    warning of final beast empires 345, 349–351, 356
Darby Bible
    in reference to breaking bread 115
    use of word "church" 26
dative case 517
dative of reference, Greek
    definition of 397, 517
    unlocking Gospels 405–413

David, King
   and King Saul 498
   and meaning of incense offering 467
   and Showbread 184–185
   definition of 518
   given God's pattern to build Temple 256–260
   Messiah born of lineage 285
Day of Atonement 74, 134, 181, 234, 390, 415, 433, 521, 538
day, the Jewish
   chart of the 12-hour day 452
   definition of 518
Dead Sea Scrolls
   bathing and eating bread 107
   festival calendar 433
   picturing battle 357
   service with bread and wine 196–197
Dead Sea sect
   and connection to Sadducees 227
   beliefs about great battle 357
   bread and wine service 199, 227
   definition of 518
   final Messianic banquet 196–197
   started by Zadokites who withdrew from Temple sacrifices 198, 227
demon
   definition of 518
Deuteronomy 16:3
   bread of affliction used figuratively in 239–241
devil
   alienating Israelites away from their New Covenant 311
   definition of 518
   temptations of 351
Diaspora
   and symbolic bread 144–146
   apostle Peter talking about 4
   definition of 518
   God's promises to draw them into New Covenant 144–149, 305–315
discernment 518
disciple 519
Disraeli, Benjamin 351
doctrine
   definition of 519
   from men versus God 76
   importance of 282–283
double negative 403–405
dragon
   seven-headed 345–354
drinking figuratively
   figurative use of in 1 Corinthians 154–156, 159–161, 173–177
   spiritual 53–56
drink offering or wine offering 60, 190, 213, 214

E

Early Christian Writings 511
Early Jewish Writings 511
Easter
    as opposed to 14th-day Passover remembrance 5, 16, 20, 21
    Easter/Astarte celebration 519
    evolution of 15, 79
eating figuratively
    eating unworthily 173–176
    figurative use of in 1 Corinthians 154–156, 159–161, 173–177
    spiritual 53–56
Edersheim, Alfred 370, 385, 386, 488
eight days unleavened bread during the festival 379–381, 384, 388, 406–408
ekklesia 24
Elijah 356
Emperor Constantine. *See* Constantine, Emperor
empire, last-days world or beast 345–362
Encyclopedia Judaica 108, 109, 115, 116, 510
encyclopedias (religious) 510
English translations
    confusion concerning "bread" 78–80
Epiphanes, Antiochus (king) 219
epistle 519
Essenes
    and regular bread 227
    definition of 519
    hallowed bread service 106
etoimazo 416
eucharist
    definition of 6, 23, 493–495, 519
    Greek word often mistaken for ritual 23, 191–195, 489–494
    interpretation of in letter from Irenaeus 491
    wrong connection with meal at Qumran 198–199
Eusebius, Roman historian 8
evening, definition of 452–454
Ezekiel
    and the New Covenant 305
    foretelling last days' attack on Israel 355
    God speaking through 306
    parable 77–78

F

fasting
    Roman Easter 15
feast
    definition of 519
    of God's love 186, 207–208
    translation of 200–201

Feast of Tabernacles, The: The Hope of the Church 511
Feast of Unleavened Bread
    translation of 78–79
fellowship 340
Festival of Ingathering *See also* Ingathering
    joy at 186–187
    spiritual latter rain during 281–283
Festival of Unleavened Bread
    "bread" was not in the original name 78–80
    definition of 520
    name 232, 239
    no regular bread at 141–142
Festival of Weeks. *See* Pentecost
festivals
    definition of 519
    festival Sabbaths, all seven enumerated 390
    three annual Jewish festivals as communal meals 185–187
fifteenth day. *See* 15th-day High Sabbath
figurative uses of bread 237–247
first-fruits offering
    argument between Pharisees and Sadducees concerning 231–232, 442
    definition of 520
    fulfilled by the Messiah 143–144
    timing with Resurrection 374
flesh and blood
    in John chapter 6. *See* Course 11
    referring to humanity 341–342
food
    used symbolically by the Messiah, Paul, and all Jews 51, 159–162, 168
food and bread
    natural-to-spiritual idiom 51–53
    spiritual eating and drinking 53–56, 154–161
fourteenth day. *See* 14th day
Fourteenthers. *See also* Setting the Table 1
    Asiatic assemblies keeping the more Jewish customs 4, 14, 18, 513. *See also* Quartodecimans
    general persecution against by Rome 3–21
    were correct that the Last Supper was not the Passover 13, 75, 85
frankincense 218–219
fruit of the vine
    and Jacob and Moses 324–343
    definition of 520
    partaken with Showbread 209–215
    representing the New Covenant 316

G

Gamaliel, Rabbi 313
Gemara/Gemarah 520
Genesis 249

Gentiles
    abstaining from blood 487
    definition of 520
    no longer to be considered unclean 222
    Peter and Paul 497–498
    status of cleanliness 222
    status of uncircumcised 235
gladness 187
God
    as highest authority 502
    commanded when unleavened bread was required 232–233
    commandment that certain breads contain leaven 230–232
    directing Moses to build tabernacle 253–256
    drawing the Israelites back into relationship with Him 311–315
    feast of His love 186, 208–209. *See also* Course 5
    fellowship with God, Christ, and one another 340
    instruction from as bread 293–296
    love and wine 215–217
    part in the process 281–283
    plan as seen in the Showbread 275–299
    plan for mankind 248–274
    plan from the beginning 248–249
    plan given to Stephen 260–261
    portrayed as a Trinity 33–37
    providing an open door 358–362
    rain from and natural rain 281–282
    reciprocal giving and receiving in the house of 169–175, 179–180, 184, 281–290, 296–298
    speaking through the logos 270–271
    spirit to indwell the believer 333–336
    sunlight from and natural sunlight 283
    truths in His words 180–181
God's Law 56
Golden Table 521
Gospel of Luke
    teaching or mentioning the supposed ritual of Communion 96–100, 479–483
Gospels
    agreement that the Last Supper was not the Passover 413–417, 421–427, 443–445
    definition of 521
    harmonizing timing of Passover 13
grain offering 521
grapes and grapevines, and Israel's connection to it 324–326
grapevine, Christ as 336–337
grapevine, spiritual and abiding in 338–341
Great Commission 473–474, 479, 521
Greek
    aorist tense 397, 417–418, 419, 421–427, 513
    dative of reference 397
    Greek double negative 403–405
    imperfect tense 118

indicative mood 402–403
Jesus and disciples spoke in Greek 263
language books 510
subjunctive mood 167, 397–402
the three keys 397–426
Greek-English Lexicon of the New Testament and Other Early Christian Literature, A (BDAG) 510
Greek-English Lexicon of the New Testament Based on Semantic Domains 510
Greek Grammar Beyond the Basics 510

H

Hadrian, Roman emperor
    persecution against Jews 37, 305
Hagigah 439
Henry, Matthew
    reference to breaking bread 113
hermeneutics
    as applied to Luke 22:7 424–426
    definition of 521
Herod 219, 499
Herod's Temple 521
high priest
    and Showbread 145, 206
    and twelve stones on his garment 221
    definition of 521
    entering the Holy of Holies 234, 292, 329, 330, 332, 462
    Messiah gathering those scattered "into one" 151
    natural high priest and Jewish idiom 62, 126
    punishment for eating leaven at Passover 74–75, 372, 486
    questioning authority of 497
Hippolytus 522
    Last Supper and Passover 11
Holy of Holies 522
Holy Place 522
Holy Spirit 522
horns of the unicorn 13
hour
    12 hours in the Jewish day 452
House of David 258
Hyslop, Alexander 15

I

idiom
    and the Communion ritual 486–487
    natural to spiritual 50–69
    of breaking bread among early believers 104–129
Iesus
    Greek name of Jesus 29

Illuminati, the Cult that Hijacked the World 351
Immanuel
    definition of 522
    Messiah being called 35
incense offering
    natural-to-spiritual Jewish idiom 59, 115–116, 118–119
    procedure of and meaning 461–467
indicative mood (Greek) 400, 401, 402–403
Ingathering
    as one of three annual Jewish festivals 185
    definition of 537
    early believers partially fulfill 181–182, 185–187
    spiritual rain during Festival of 281–283
    when to celebrate 186
Irenaeus
    appeal for peace among Fourteenthers 9
    definition of 522
    letter to Victor 490
Isaac 313, 315
Isaiah
    foretelling of fulfillment of God's plan 348
    Messiah as the lamb sacrifice 309–310
    speaking of New Covenant 295, 305
    talking about coming son of David 257–258
Ishtar 15
Israel
    natural-to-spiritual examples 67–68
Israelites
    God drawing back into relationship with Him 311–315

J

Jackson, Andrew 351
Jacob
    definition of 522
    spiritual fulfillment of washing of robes in wine 326–327
    with Moses and fruit of the vine 324–343
James
    definition of 522
    no mention of the ritual of Communion 477
Jamieson, Fausset, and Brown
    in reference to breaking bread 114
Jaubert, Anne 432
Jehoshaphat 492
Jehovah's Witnesses 484
Jeremiah 257, 258, 305, 355
Jerusalem
    definition of 523
    natural-to-spiritual examples 67–68

Jesus Christ. *See also* Messiah
    as covenant to family/nation 150–151, 308
    as the fulfillment of God's plan and pattern 271–274
    as the grapevine 336–337
    as the logos 265–274
    body of and supposed ritual of Communion 86–103
    body of as anointed tabernacle 100–103
    body of, definition of 514
    bread of God pointing to 242
    breaking bread 131–133
    bridegroom 515
    bride of 515
    bringing in the promised New Covenant 305
    commandment that we love one another 179–180
    crucifixion on 14th day 10
    definition of 516
    direction to John 4
    Father speaking through him 270–271
    fellowship with the Father and one another 340
    God speaking to prophetically 249
    his blood and the New Covenant 316–319
    his flesh as bread 294
    inheriting the lifeblood from and growing into likeness 341–343
    "in remembrance of me" and sacrifice 97–100
    in terms of Trinity 34–36. *See also* logos
    leavened bread at the Last Supper 71–85
    long hair 31
    name of 29–31, 101
    not to be arrested during Passover 437–441
    promise of recovering the Diaspora 150–153
    spiritual body 90–97
    and 1 Corinthians 157–159
    spiritual fellowship 156–157
    use of natural-to-spiritual idioms 51–53, 55
    use of parables at the Last Supper 43–44, 46
    using Greek subjunctive mood 400–402
    what Jesus said versus what he meant 46–49
Jewish
    annual festivals as communal meals 185–187
    assemblies, definition of 523
    communal meals 183–216
    definition of 523
    first-century idioms and supposed Communion ritual 486–487
    groups emulating the Showbread service 193–199
    idiom of breaking bread among early believers 104–129
    natural-to-spiritual idiom 50–69
    persecution of by Romans 3–21, 27
    tradition of speaking in parables 40–48
    true communion and the Messianic Feast 183–216
    words and concepts changing from early idioms 22–39

564 | THE MESSIANIC FEAST

Jewish disconnect 3–21
Jewish Encyclopedia, The 7, 106, 170–171, 387, 413–414, 444, 451, 459, 470, 510
Jewish Study Bible, The 509
Jews
    becoming Christians 27–28
    forbidden to enter Jerusalem by Roman Emperor Hadrian 37
    God's promises to 144–149, 305–315
    many thousands came to believe in the Messiah 132
    meaning of logos to 263–271
    name of 30–31
    natural-to-spiritual examples 67–68
    rejected by Roman Emperor Constantine 16–18
John
    about Christ's arrest 438
    and the 14th day 388, 439
    and the sixth-hour controversy solved 468–471
    definition of 523
    his ministry to decrease as the Messiah comes forth 100
    in letter of protest from Polycrates 8
    John chapter 6 flesh and blood explained. *See* Course 11
    no teaching or mentioning the ritual of Communion 475
    showing day of crucifixion was not the Sabbath 442
    spiritual fulfillment of Jacob's washing of robes in wine 326–327
    telling of disciples eating bread 430
    ten horns 350
    use of logos 263–265
    with Asiatics 4
    writing about Messiah's shed blood 303
John the Baptist 499
    definition of 523
Jordan 355
Joseph of Arimathea 436–437
Josephus, Jewish historian
    and seven-day Festival 379
    and timing of Passover 460–462, 465
    at time of Pharisees 225–226
    bread ritual of Essenes 106, 195
    definition of 523
    explaining how people were walled up 307, 465
    explaining the Showbread table history 219
Joshua
    relationship to the name of Jesus 29, 101, 325
Judah 523
Judaism 524
Judaizers 3, 312, 524
Judas 424–425, 430, 434, 435
Jude
    no teaching or mentioning the ritual of Communion 479

K

kat (Greek word) 115, 120–121
katharoi 319
klasmata 524
koinonia
    definition of 524
    true meaning of 23, 134, 156, 189
kosher 524

L

Lange, John P.
    in reference to breaking bread 114
    in reference to flesh and blood 342
Laodicea, Council of 524
Last Supper
    50 reasons it was not the Passover 428–450
    and Paul and 1 Corinthians 153–182
    as a Messianic feast and communal meal 199–203
    commentators shoehorning Passover into 432–434
    controversy of Jesus eating Passover on 10, 11
    definition of 524
    Gospels in agreement that the Last Supper was not the Passover 413–427, 443–445
    hypothetical Last-Supper-Passover story 440–441
    leavened bread at 71–85
    parables at the time of 43–44, 46, 317–318
    pointing to Messianic feast 201–205
    proofs that it was not the Passover 363–494
    prophecy betrayed with bread 81–85
    term in the scriptures 200
Latin Christianity 525
laver 525
law of Moses
    about 312–315
    certain aspects endure 314
    changing over to New Covenant 141–142
    fulfill the law by loving with God's *agape* love 314
    fulfill the law by walking in the spirit 314
leaven
    at Last Supper 71–85
    change from leavened to unleavened in Communion 485–486
    commanded when unleavened was required 232–233
    commandment that certain breads contain 230–232
    definition of 525
    forbidden to eat at Passover 71–74
    in a figurative sense 236
    leaven removed by sixth hour on 14th day Passover 380–385, 455–461
    not always symbolic of bad things 231
    punishment for eating at Passover 74
    typological significance of leavened showbread 236–237

leavened bread 525
lechem 525
Lenski, R. C. H.
    and word for "this" 89
    and "wretched conduct" 168
    discussion of New Covenant and blood 302–303
    understanding of parables 41
Lenski's Commentary on the New Testament 509
Lent 15
Levitical priesthood 525
Lightfoot, John 371
living water
    definition of 526
    from the Messiah 54–55
    to be reciprocal 96, 172, 338–339
logos
    definition of 526
    God speaking through 270–271
    meaning in Rome 262–263
    meaning to first-century Messianic Jews 263–271
    of God 262–274
    the fulfillment of God's plan and pattern 271–274
Lord 526
Lord's Supper
    definition of 526
    pointing to Messianic Feast or Banquet 201–205
Louw and Nida 425
love. *See also* agape love
    God's and wine 215–217
love-feasts 207. *See also* agape/agapais feasts
Lucifer
    definition of 526
Luke. *See also* Luke 22: 7
    day of crucifixion was not the 15th-day Sabbath 443
    definition of 526
    telling of Jesus eating bread 429
Luke 22:7
    deciphering intended meaning 417–426
Luther, Martin
    and consubstantiation 89, 483
    biography 527

M

Maccabees 219
Magdalene, Mary 323, 375
Maimonides, Moses
    and meaning of Showbread 230
    use of words "eating" and "drinking" 160–161
Makow, Henry 351

Malachi 305, 308
man child
    and the beast 348–356
    definition of 527
    what it represents 254–258
mankind
    God's overall plan for 248–274
    part in the process 284–287
manna
    as a type 293–294
    definition of 527
    figuratively called bread 237–238
Manoah 245–246
Mark
    definition of 527
    Mark 14:12 intended meaning 379–381, 407–415. *See also* template
    no teaching or mentioning the ritual of Communion 478
    showing Jesus was on the cross 442
    telling of Jesus eating bread 429
Mark 14:12 intended meaning. *See also*
Martin Luther. *See* Luther, Martin
Mass
    as a piece of bread 127
Matthew
    definition of 527
    Matthew 26:17 intended meaning 378–382, 407–415. *See also* template
    Matthew 26:18 402
    Matthew misinterpreted concerning Passover 13–14
    teaching or mentioning the ritual of Communion 477–478
    telling of Jesus eating bread 429
matzah 527
McClintock and Strong's *Cyclopedia of Biblical, Theological, and Ecclesiastical Literature* 5–6, 9, 13–14, 18–19, 36, 218, 220, 225, 299, 482–485, 510
meals
    first bread-and-wine communal 183–185
    reciprocal communal 167–173
    spiritual 139–140
    three annual festivals as communal meals 185–187
Melchizedek, high priest
    and the Dead Sea Sect 205
    and the future Messianic feast 184–186, 195, 199, 203–210
    as a future messiah 204–205
    bread and wine of 203–207, 210
    definition of 527
    identity 183–185
    written highly of in most all Jewish sources 204–205
memorial 527
Messiah. *See also* Jesus Christ
    and ritual purification 318–321
    and supposed Trinity 34–36

as "lion of the tribe of Judah" 31
definition of 528
in the Talmud 7, 102, 308, 387
making a firm covenant 307–310
name of 29–31
shed blood, meaning of 190, 332–337
speaking in parables 40–49
spiritual lifeblood of the New Covenant 328–329
the fulfillment of God's plan and pattern 271–274
Messianic 528. *See also* Messianic Feast/Messianic Banquet and Messianic Jew
Messianic Feast/Messianic Banquet
and the bride and the beast 344–362
and the communal meal xx, 199–203
and the Last Supper 199–203, 201–205
and the true Jewish communion 183–216
definition of 528
future overtones of 196–197
in the Dead Sea Scrolls 196–197
Schiffman quotes concerning 197, 357
Messianic Jew 528
mikvah/mikveh 528
milk
used symbolically by Paul 168
Mishnah 229, 528
Mormon 484
Moses. *See also* law of Moses
definition of 528
God directs to build Tabernacle 253–256
with Jacob and fruit of the vine 324–343
Mounce, William D. 404, 410
move of God 528

N

Nadab 211
natural communion to spiritual communion 190–193
natural-to-spiritual idiom
definition of 528
examples 57–69
general discussion 50–69
New Covenant
and the symbolic cup 300–323
apostles growing in understandings 322–323
as prophesied by Jewish prophets 306–310
blood of compared to Old Covenant 329–333
comparison of communion to the Old Covenant 192–193
definition of 305, 529
not like the Old Covenant 315–318
promised 141–144

the Messiah and the spiritual lifeblood of 330–331
   transition of laws from Old Covenant 27–28, 322–323
New Testament
   and timing of Passover 463–467
   definition of 529
new wine 529
Nicaea, Catholic Council of 529
Nicene Creed
   definition of 529
   origins of 16
Nicodemus 425, 437
ninth hour
   significance of 5
Nisan 3, 529
Noah
   definition of 529
   pattern given to in type 250–252
numbers five and seven
   significance of 145–149
numbers twelve and seven
   significance of 147–148
number forty
   significance of 308

O

Old Covenant
   blood of compared to New Covenant 329–333
   comparison of communion to the New Covenant 192–193
   definition of 529
   transition of laws to New Covenant 28, 316, 322–323
Old Testament 530
omer/Omer (the sheaf)
   counting of 186, 393, 442
   definition of 530
   Messiah fulfills first fruits 143–144
online biblical resources 511

P

parables
   at the time of the Last Supper 43–44, 46, 71–85, 317–318
   bizarre statements pointing to 44–45
   definition of 530
   in the Jewish tradition 41–43
   Messiah speaking in 40–49
   Messiah speaking of eating his flesh and drinking his blood 328–329, 332–337
   spoken by Jacob and Moses 325–327
   what Jesus said versus what he meant 46–49

paraskeuy. See also preparation day
    before each Festival Sabbath 413–417, 443–446
    definition of 413, 530
parousia 251–252
Paschal meal 530
Passover
    14th-day controversy 7, 8, 10
    14th day or 15th day? 386, 448–449
    50 reasons it was not eaten at the Last Supper 428–450
    as one of three annual Jewish festivals 185
    between the evenings and legal time to slay the Passover 451–471
    body and blood at 334–337
    commentators shoehorning into Last Supper 431–433
    definition of 530
    Gospels in agreement that the Last Supper was not the Passover 413–427, 443–446
    Greek indicative mood used to perform 402–403
    hypothetical Last-Supper-Passover story 440–441
    Jesus eating of 11, 12
    Jesus not to be arrested during 437–439
    Jesus using Greek subjunctive mood in reference to eating 400–402
    leaven removed before noon 455–456
    not valid if slaughtered before noon 456, 458–459
    proofs that the Last Supper was not the Passover 363–494
    ritual preparations for 412–414
    when celebrated 3, 5, 10, 186
pastor
    definition of and early Jewish believers 32–33
pattern
    given to David to build the Temple 256–260
    God's pattern for mankind 248–274
    God's pattern given to Stephen 261–262
    God's pattern shown to Moses to build the tabernacle 253–256
    Messiah fulfills God's plan and pattern 271–274
    seen in the logos 262–271
    shown to Noah 250–252
Paul
    and admonishing Corinthians 499
    and I Corinthians and the Last Supper 153–182
    and submitting to rulers and teaching 504
    and the law of Moses 142–143, 312–313
    and the "one bread" 92–93, 96–97, 133–134, 430
    calling Jesus "first fruits" 374
    comparing the blood of the two Covenants 329–332
    definition of 530
    depicting bread as spiritual truth 77, 430
    discussion of unleavened versus leavened bread 72–73
    explaining the seed of Abraham 306
    intended meaning in 1 Corinthians 162–167
    letter to the Romans 152–153
    no teaching or mentioning the ritual of Communion 478–479

    Peter's going astray with Gentiles and Paul's correction 497–498
    praise of Bereans for studying the scriptures 503
    reference to true altar 112
    sacrificial purification 27
    showing giving and receiving 361
    speaking of bread as food meant spiritually 295. *See also* Course 5
    speaking of coming priest after order of Melchizedek 205
    speaking of Melchizedek 183
    speaking of symbolic cup 301
    spiritual and natural provision 288–289
    teaching of *agapais/agape feasts* 197. *See also* Course 5
    use of natural-to-spiritual idiom 51, 54–55
    with Asiatics 4
    writing about Messiah's shed blood 303
PC Study Bible 508
Pentateuch 531
Pentecost
    as one of three annual Jewish festivals 185
    definition of 531
    when to celebrate 186, 231
Perseus Digital Library Project 511
Peter, apostle
    and applying the sacrificial blood spiritually 318
    and the yoke of the law of Moses 313
    coming into truth 27
    definition of 531
    going astray with Gentiles and Paul's correction 497–498
    Lord's parable of unclean animals 321
    no teaching or mentioning the ritual of Communion 475–476
    picturing Messiah as cornerstone of spiritual temple 258–259
    referring to spiritual living stones 361
    refusing to eat with Gentiles 222
    speaking of Lord's presence 252
    spirit of God filling the people 235
    writing to Jews of dispersion 4
Pharisees
    argument with Sadducees regarding countdown to Pentecost 231–233, 442
    definition of 531
Philadelphus, Ptolemy 219
Philip
    in the letter of protest by Polycrates 8
Philo
    and the wine of God's love 195
    at time of Pharisees 225
    identity of 531
    Passover timing 463
    writing of Therapeutae 194–195, 228
phylacteries 19, 531
piggul 372

plan
    given to David to build the Temple 256–260
    God's pattern shown to Moses to build the tabernacle 253–256
    God's plan as seen in the Showbread 275–299
    God's plan for mankind 248–274
    Messiah as the fulfillment of God's plan and pattern 271–274

planting the seed 284

Polycarp
    identity of 6, 532
    portrayal of 490–491

Polycrates, bishop of Ephesus
    letter of protest to Victor 7, 8

preenactments 183, 197–198, 532

prefiguring 532

preparation day. *See also* paraskeuy
    before each Festival Sabbath 392, 413–417, 443–446
    definition of 532
    Jewish preparation for Passover 413–415

presence bread 104–105, 278–280, 532. *See also* Showbread

priest
    adding water and flour for the Showbread 289–290
    definition of 532
    overseeing baking of the Showbread 291
    part in fulfilling God's plan 287–293
    placing Showbread on golden table 292

priesthood 532. *See also* Zadok

priests
    natural-to-spiritual examples 62–65

Promised Land
    definition of 532

proofs that the Last Supper was not the Passover 363–494

proper authority 497–507

prophet 533

Protestants. *See also* Luther, Martin
    and Communion ritual 481–484
    considered heretics by Roman Church 26
    definition of 533

psomion 430, 533

purification, ritual
    and the Messiah 318–321
    as requirement to partake of the Passover 412–414
    definition of 534

Q

Quartodecimans. *See also* Fourteenthers
    Asiatic Jewish assemblies keeping the more Jewish customs 3–4, 14, 18, 523
    called heretics by Rome 20
    definition of 3, 312–313, 449, 533

Qumran
    meal at and wrong connection with Eucharist 198–199

R

rabbi 533
Rabbi Akiva 305
rain
    from God and natural rain 281–283
    spiritual teaching rain 281–283
Rapture
    definition of 251–256, 533
    God's open door to fulfill this 358–362
    Noah's Ark a type of 250–252
reciprocal
    commandment by Jesus to love with reciprocal love 95–96, 179–182
    giving and receiving in the house of God 296–298
    meaning of with communal meals 170–171, 188
    Showbread showing reciprocal giving and receiving 280–297
remembrance
    Messiah's sacrifice and "in remembrance of me" 97–100
repent 533
resurrection 533
    the Resurrection was not on Saturday 373–376
revelation 534
Ritual
    and body of Christ 86–105
    change from leavened bread to unleavened 482–486
    Communion ritual and how it got started 88–89, 487–490
    definition of 534
    eating leavened versus unleavened bread at the Last Supper 71–85
    of Communion, and Jewish disciples didn't teach it 472–495
ritual purification 412–414, 534
    and the Messiah 318–321
Robertson, A. T. 398, 410
Rome
    imposing traditions on Messianic Jews 5–21
row bread 276
Ruth 285

S

Sabbath
    breaking bread at 104, 109
    definition of 534
    no illegal activity during 15th-day 434–441
    Sabbath, high or great 534
    seven Festival Sabbaths 390
sacrament 534
sacred assemblies 391
Sacredtexts.com 511
sacrifices. *See also* altar, sacrificial blood or sacrifices at; *See also* communal sacrifices
    blood, definition of 514

574 | THE MESSIANIC FEAST

Sadducees
    and Dead Sea sect 210
    conflict with Pharisees 226, 231–233
    definition of 535
    had authority to eat the Showbread 226
    name derived from Zadokites 227
saint
    definition of and early Jewish believers 32
sanctified 534
Sanhedrin 384, 438, 499
Satan 349, 351, 352, 535
Saul, king 498, 500
Schaff, Philip
    14th-day dispute 6
    Roman custom ritualistic tendencies 14, 18
    writing about Victor 7
Schiffman, Lawrence 197–199, 227, 357, 535
scriptures
    bread and wine related to scripture reading and prayer 214–215
    definition of 535
    misunderstandings as Roman rituals 53
    no use of term Last Supper in 200
    praise of Bereans for studying the scriptures 503
Sectarian Communal Meal 197–198
seed of the woman 535
Septuagint 535
seven-headed dragon (or beast) 345–358
seventh empire 345–358
shadow/substance 536
Shavout (Pentecost)
    as one of three annual Jewish festivals 185
shepherds
    definition of and early Jewish believers 32–33
Shewbread. *See* Showbread
Showbread. *See also* twelve Temple breads
    actual meaning of words used 276–281
    and ten tables with ten bowls 213–214
    breads of the plan 277, 278–281
    breads of the purpose 277, 278–281
    broken and shared on the Sabbath 104
    confusion with twelve breads 105
    definition of 536
    fruit of the vine partaken with 209–215
    God's plan in 275–299
    identity and significance 217–247
    importance of table 107
    in the natural sense 218–220
    into His image and likeness 280–281
    Jewish groups emulating the service 193–199
    location of in Temple 233–234

    name of from "bread" 105
    offering vessels 209
    priest's part in making 287–293
    table being carried off 128
    table in Temple 194
    twelve breads now one spiritual bread 298–299
    typology of whether leavened or unleavened 223–225, 233–237
    whether leavened or not 223–246
Shulamite 211
sixth hour
    importance of in the Jewish idiom 380–381, 455, 468–470
    scripture controversy solved 468–471
Solomon 257
Solomon's Porch 137, 149
    definition of 536
Solomon's Temple 213, 257
Song of Solomon
    and the bride 355–356
    comparing wine with love 215
    prefiguring with Messiah 344–345
spiritual
    body growing 178–179
    body of Christ 86–105
    in 1 Corinthians 157–159
    bride and the Messianic feast and the beast 344–362
    communion 153–182, 167–173
    definition of 536
    drink/drink offering 53–55, 60, 95–96, 154, 206, 304
    eating and drinking in 1 Corinthians 154–156
    grapevine and the spiritual flow 338–341
    meals 139–140
    natural-to-spiritual idioms 50–69
    supper 169
    tasting 138–139
    "this do" as a remembrance 96–97
    what the apostles taught about the spiritual body 90–96
spiritual flow
    of God's spirit from the believers 172
spots
    and love feasts 207–208
    in the natural-to-spiritual idiom 63
    meaning of 173–176, 536
Stephen
    definition of 537
    given progression of God's Plan 260–261
subjunctive mood
    definition of 537
    general discussion of 397–402
    in relation to ritual of Communion 167–169
    in relation to whether Last Supper was the Passover 400–402

Sukkot. *See also* Tabernacles and Ingathering
    as one of three annual Jewish festivals 185
        definition of 537
sunlight
    spiritual sunlight and natural sunlight 283
supper pertaining to the Lord 162–163, 169, 199–203
Sutton, Antony C. 351
symbolic cup and the New Covenant 300–323
Synoptic Gospels 443

T

Tabernacle and Temple
    as spiritual house of God 254–255
    definition of 537
    God directing David to build 256–260
    God directing Moses to build 253–256
    natural-to-spiritual examples 57–62
    role of believers in 101–103
Tabernacles, Feast of. *See also* Ingathering
    as one of three annual Jewish festivals 185
    definition of 537
    early believers partially fulfill 180–182, 186–188
    spiritual latter rain during this festival 281–283
table
    role in Jewish bread customs 107
    role in Jewish culture 193–194
table of Showbread 128, 218–220
    ten at Solomon's Temple 213–214
table of the Lord 112–113
Talmud
    concerning breaking bread 109–110, 116–117
    concerning no large loaves at Passover 228–229
    concerning penalty for leaven at Passover 74
    concerning the Messiah 7, 102, 308, 387
    concerning the time to remove leaven 380–381, 455–456
    definition of 537
    on the subject of between the evenings 454–460
    Passover slaughtered before noon not valid 456, 458–459
tamid offering
    definition of 188, 537
    procedure 115–116, 136
Tammuz 15, 538
tasting, spiritual 138–139
template
    13th-day question 377–382
    14th-day true Passover 383–388
    15th-day high Sabbath template section 389–393
    challenge 365–396
    double Passover option 369–372

Early Roman Catholic option 367–368
of the Passover as commanded by God 366
Saturday resurrection option 373–376
true scriptural position 376–393
Temple
as "the house" 118
definition of 538
Temple service 115–116
tenses (Greek). *See* Greek tenses
tent
human body functioning as 102–103
tent of meeting 101
Tertullian
and Latin Christianity 525
and term Triad/trinitas/Trinity 37, 489
definition of 539
Textual Commentary on the Greek New Testament, A 508
theology 538
Theophilus, bishop of Antioch
and term "triad" 36
Therapeutae
definition of 538
holy meal emulating Showbread 194, 228
third day since 446–447
thirteenth day. *See* 13th day
"this do" as a remembrance 96–97
three days and three nights in the tomb 395, 446–448
and Sunday being the third day since 394–396
three major Greek keys 397–426
tilling the ground 284
Tishri 181, 538
Titus, Roman emperor 128
Torah 538
tradition 538
translations
of "bread" causing confusion 78–80, 232–233, 244–245
transliteration 539
transubstantiation 81, 485–486, 539
triad. *See also* Trinity
Archaic 36–37, 513
Capitoline 36, 36–37, 515
definition and use of 36–37
Roman 36
Trinity
definition of 539
definition of and teaching of doctrine 33–37
did the apostles teach it 33–37
logos 264–276
origin 36–37, 489
standardizing the Roman doctrine of 16

truths in His words 182–183
twelve stones (sons of Israel) 221
twelve Temple breads. *See also* Showbread
    as a communal meal 108–109
    as the one spiritual bread 298–299
    broken and shared on the Sabbath 104
    definition of 536
    God's plan in 275–299
    identity and significance 217–247
    into His image and likeness 280–281
    leavened versus unleavened 194
    now one bread 298–299
    Pharisaic tradition of being unleavened 225–232
    relation to Showbread and confusion with 105
    ritual of washing hands before eating 107–108
    showing forth God's plan 233–236
    symbolic of twelve tribes 92–94, 220–223, 233
    typology of whether leavened or unleavened 223–225, 233–237
    whether leavened or not 223–246
twelve tribes
    twelve breads symbolizing 112–113, 131, 144, 147, 220–223, 233
Tyndale, William 26, 105
type
    definition of 144, 539
    example of 54, 224
    pattern given to Noah 250–252
typology 144, 223–224, 280
    definition of 540

U

unleavened (bread)
    change from leavened to unleavened in Communion 485–486
    commanded when unleavened was required 232–233
    definition of 540
    eight days unleavened during Festival 379–381, 384, 388, 406–408
    typological significance if the twelve breads were 236–237
    misconception about at the Last Supper 71–85

V

Verbal Aspect in New Testament Greek 510
Vespasian, emperor 219
Victor, bishop of Rome
    definition of 540
    demands on Asiatics 7
    imposition of Catholic rule 9
    letter of protest from Polycrates 7
    letter written to by Irenaeus 490

W

"wait for one another" explained 167–170
Wallace, Daniel B. 137, 398, 410–418
Wall Street and the Rise of Hitler 351
washing hands
    before eating bread 106–108
Weeks
    as one of three annual Jewish festivals 185
Westcott, Brooke Foss
    14th-day crucifixion 10
    and the 14th day 450
    Gospel agreement 413
William Tyndale. *See* Tyndale, William
wine
    and God's love 215–217
    forbidden to drink strong 211–212
    mixed 209–212
    new 209–213
    of high priest Melchizedek 203–207
    partaken of with Showbread 209–215
    pure wine of God's love 195–196
    role in three Jewish festival communal meals 185
winnowing
    definition of 540
    winnowing the grain (natural and spiritual) 285–287

Y

Yahweh 540
Yeshua
    definition of 540
    name of 29, 450
Young's Literal Translation
    Last Supper prophecy betrayed with bread 82
    translation and use of word "bread" 79
    use of word "church" 26

Z

Zadok 541
    Zadokite priests 198, 227–228
        had authority before God to eat the Showbread 226
        had authority over the high priesthood 226
        Sadducees' name derived from 227
Zechariah 257, 355
Zwingli, Ulrich 483, 541

About the Author

After graduating from Bible college in Seattle in 1983, Mr. Tennent then entered the graduate-degree theology program. Motivated by a love for God's word, he continued studying the Greek language to better interpret and understand the original scriptures. This journey led to harmonizing the Greek scriptures relating to the Last Supper controversy, in turn opening the door to even greater understandings.